THE ECOLOGY OF OIL

This book explores the social and environmental consequences of oil extraction in the tropical rainforest. Using northern Veracruz as a case study, the author argues that oil production generated major historical and environmental transformations in land tenure systems and uses, and social organization. Such changes, furthermore, entailed effects, including the marginalization of indigenes, environmental destruction, and tense labor relations. In the context of the Mexican Revolution (1910–1920), however, the results of oil development did not go unchallenged. Mexican oil workers responded to their experience by forging a politicized culture and a radical left militancy that turned "oil country" into one of the most significant sites of class conflict in revolutionary Mexico. Ultimately, the book argues, Mexican oil workers deserve their share of credit for the 1938 decree nationalizing the foreign oil industry – heretofore reserved for President Lazaro Cárdenas – and thus changing the course of Mexican history.

Myrna I. Santiago is Associate Professor of History at St. Mary's College of California. Before earning her Ph.D. in history from the University of California at Berkeley, she traveled to Mexico on a Fulbright Fellowship and later worked in Nicaragua as a Human Rights investigator. Her work has appeared in *Environmental History*.

Studies in Environment and History

Editors
Donald Worster, University of Kansas
J. R. McNeill, Georgetown University

THE ECOLOGY OF OIL

ENVIRONMENT, LABOR, AND THE MEXICAN REVOLUTION, 1900–1938

Myrna I. Santiago

St. Mary's College of California

CAMBRIDGE
UNIVERSITY PRESS

CAMBRIDGE UNIVERSITY PRESS
Cambridge, New York, Melbourne, Madrid, Cape Town, Singapore, São Paulo, Delhi

Cambridge University Press
32 Avenue of the Americas, New York, NY 10013-2473, USA

www.cambridge.org
Information on this title: www.cambridge.org/9780521115377

First published 2006
This digitally printed version 2009

A catalog record for this publication is available from the British Library

Library of Congress Cataloging in Publication data

Santiago, Myrna I., 1960–
The ecology of oil : environment, labor, and the Mexican Revolution,
1900–1938 / Myrna I. Santiago.
    p.   cm. – (Studies in environment and history)
Includes bibliographical references (p.) and index.
ISBN-13: 978-0-521-86324-7
ISBN-10: 0-521-86324-4
1. Petroleum industry and trade – Environmental aspects – Mexico – Huasteca
Region – History – 20th century.   2. Mexico – History – Revolution,
1910–1920 – Economic aspects.   3. Industrial relations – Mexico – Huasteca
Region – History – 20th century.   I. Title.   II. Series.
HD9574.M615H837   2006
338.2′7282097262 – dc22   2006006970

ISBN 978-0-521-86324-7 hardback
ISBN 978-0-521-11537-7 paperback

to Josefa De Alba Martínez,
for giving to me the education she never had

CONTENTS

LIST OF MAPS, FIGURES, TABLES, AND APPENDICES

ix

Appendices

ACKNOWLEDGMENTS

A dissertation turned into a book such as this one accumulates more debts than can ever be acknowledged. However, a few are an absolute must. The intellectual debts reach back in history. When she was at Princeton, Linda Lewin never could have imagined that I would return to haunt her as a graduate student at Berkeley nearly a decade later. She has traveled the road from undergraduate professor to dissertation chair to colleague and friend with patience, grace, and a large supply of red ink that I have come to depend on. I am in her debt forever. David Abalos and Manuel del Valle share the blame for steering me into academia after a prolonged hiatus from the ivory tower: I owe them for pointing me in the right direction. Unbeknown to them, a group of scholars nourished this work: William Cronon, Donald Worster, Candace Slater, and Richard White. I owe them thanks for exploring the world with new eyes. Carolyn Merchant pushed me to go where no Chicana had gone before and thus influenced my formation as an environmental historian; for that I am truly grateful. John R. McNeill and Linda Lewin read and reread versions of the manuscript and provided the critiques it begged for, although I alone am responsible for the final product and its shortcomings.

I have many institutional debts as well. In Mexico, the staff at the Archivo General de la Nación, the Instituto Nacional de Antropología e Historia, the Archivo General del Estado de Veracruz, the Archivo Histórico del Ayuntamiento de Tampico, the Biblioteca del Instituto de Antropología at the Universidad Veracruzana, the librarians at the Instituto Nacional de Antropología e Historia at Chapultepec Castle, and Dr. Lief Adleson were good-natured beyond the call of duty. In the United States, the archivists at Occidental College, the American Heritage Center at the University of Wyoming at Laramie, Southern Methodist University, the University of Texas at Austin, the University of Southern California, and the Bancroft Library at the University of California at Berkeley retrieved, photocopied, and even mailed to me rare gems as well as the pedestrian lode that historians mine on a daily basis; I thank them very, very much. In Europe, the staff at the Institute for Social Research in Amsterdam and at the International Center for Research on Anarchism in Lausanne were not only helpful, but also extraordinarily welcoming and friendly. Graciela Jolidon introduced me to the archive at the International Labor Organization in Geneva and to its accommodating staff, and I thank them all. Joshua Borkowski produced the two wonderful maps under the expert guidance of Darin Jensen at the University of California, Berkeley, and I thank them both for their good cheer and assistance with all matters technical. Jan Williams did a wonderful index under a lot of time pressure and I thank her for that. Katie Greczylo and the team at Cambridge University Press were methodical, accommodating, and superb with questions and editing. My gratitude to them for all their hard work.

The financial support for this project came from many sources. St. Mary's College provided me two summer travel grants for research in the United States and Europe. Southern Methodist University allowed me a visit through the Clemens-DeGoyler Research Travel Grant, and the American Heritage Center honored me with the Bernard L. Majewski Fellowship to complete my research. I owe my graduate education and the completion of the manuscript in large part to the Ford Foundation Fellowships for Minorities. Between 1990 and 2001, the Foundation granted me predoctoral, doctoral, and postdoctoral fellowships. Without that support, I would not have been able to join that infamous dozen, the Chicana historians. I can only hope that seeing the finished product born of their collective efforts can begin to repay the debt of trust I incurred with all these institutions and individuals.

Finally, I thank the men of my life, René G. Santiago, René Víctor Macleay-Santiago, and Garrett D. Brown, for sharing archival and other adventures in this lengthy but fun decade.

Map 1. Major Oil Fields in the Huasteca, Veracruz, ca. 1921.
Sources: Boletín del Petróleo, Map section, Vol. 3, No. 1 (January, 1917);
Boletín del Petróleo, Map section, Vol. 3, No. 5 (May, 1917); John M. Muir,
"Figure 12, Map Showing Surface Geology of Tampico Embayment,"
Geology of the Tampico Region, Mexico. Tulsa, Oklahoma: The American
Association of Petroleum Geologists, 1936.

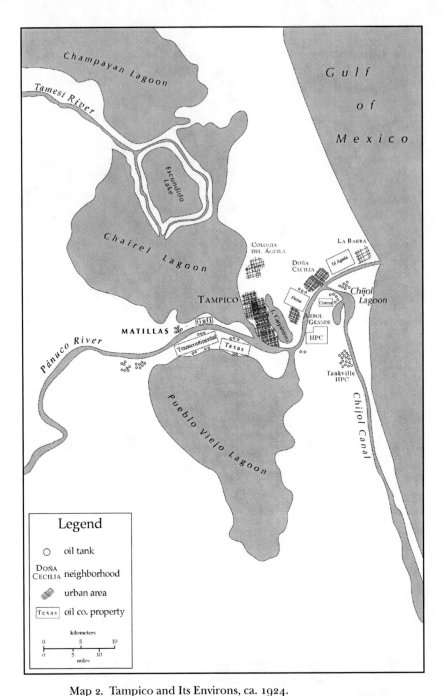

Map 2. Tampico and Its Environs, ca. 1924.
Sources: Boletín del Petróleo, Map section, Vol. 4, No. 4 (October 1917);
Boletín del Petróleo, Map section, Vol. 22, No. 4 (October 1926); Secretaría
de Industria, Comercio y Trabajo, Departamento de Petróleo, Comisión
Técnica, *Carta de la Zona Petrolífera del Norte de Veracruz y de las regiones coli-
dantes.* Mexico City: Secretaría de Industria, Comercio y Trabajo, Marzo
1925.

INTRODUCTION

The casual traveler on tour through northern Veracruz today might never guess that in 1921 oil spurted from the area in such prodigious quantities that Mexico became the third largest petroleum producer in the world. The main economic activities along the 120 miles from Tuxpan to Tampico, part of the territory known as the Huasteca, are cattle ranching and citrus production. With the exception of the town of Cerro Azul, which welcomes visitors with a gigantic commemorative oil derrick, the fields that produced millions of barrels of crude in the first three decades of the twentieth century are nowhere in evidence. Potrero del Llano, a legendary and once immensely rich oil field, has a main street that is one block long and unpaved. Slow-moving cows ruminate in the grasslands, seeking relief from the heat and the humidity underneath scattered palms or short trees. Zacamixtle, Juan Felipe, and others are likewise small cattle ranching communities where oil ghosts roam undetected.

The observant tourist, nonetheless, can find the imprint of the oil industry in the landscape. The most obvious signs are the bright mustard-yellow *Petróleos Mexicanos* (PEMEX) posts painted with black skull-and-crossbones alerting passersby to the presence of underground pipelines. The signs admonish *PELIGRO* and prohibit "banging" and "excavating." When they are at water's edge, the signs also ban "anchoring." In former refinery towns, such as El Ebano and Mata Redonda, the oil relics are the wooden bungalows the companies built to house Mexican workers. Scattered among new concrete homes, some bungalows are crumbling. Their wooden doors are falling off the hinges and the stilts to prevent flooding are eroded and gnawed. But many more are painted in brilliant pinks, greens, yellows, and blues, surrounded by potted plants and trees recently planted, still inhabited nearly ninety years after they were built. More difficult to find is San Diego de la Mar, the location of the most notorious oil well explosion in the history of the industry, "Dos Bocas." The road begins at Ozuluama, once exclusively populated by Huastec

1

aboriginals but now a *mestizo* town, but it is not marked. The crater made by the blowout is about thirty miles southeast from town, but the journey takes more than three hours because the road is only fit for four-wheel-drive vehicles. There are no signs pointing the way. Eventually, green pasture gives way to tall grass that is dry in great patches despite the rain. A white sign saying "Caution. Private Property. Authorized Personnel Only" appears along low cattle fencing enclosing the yellow grass. Something is unusual about the fence: one of the wires is electrified. Turning from the main road to follow the branch around the fence, the stench announces the enclosure is Dos Bocas. Hydrogen sulfide strikes the nostrils and the lungs hard, just as the grasses shorten to display the lake that formed in the aftermath of the 1908 explosion. No explanation is offered – no identification, no mention of whose private property the stinking lake is and who the authorized personnel might be. The "lake" is without history.

Similarly, not even the most attentive trekker could surmise that the Huasteca once was a tropical rainforest. Only the heat, the humidity, and the sweat hint of a time when the land was so thick with imposing trees and vines that the sky was obscured and the fastest route between the ports of Tampico and Tuxpan was the Gulf of Mexico. That was one hundred years ago, before oil. Today, in the aftermath of petroleum extraction, the predominant flora of the Huasteca consists of cultivated grasses and citrus – both heavily fertilized by processed hydrocarbons. The most important element of the fauna is cattle. In the twenty-first century, the Huasteca produces the primary ingredients for hamburger meat and orange juice. Oil is but a faded memory and the tropical rainforest that preceded it not even that.

This is the story of both. It is a story of oil and the tropical rainforest, fossil fuel extraction and the environment, industrial production and ecology – and revolution. It focuses on one geographical location, the Huasteca veracruzana, the first site of oil extraction in Mexico, the first site of oil production in the tropical areas of the world, and one of the most important sites of global oil production in the early twentieth century. The story takes place during the period of foreign ownership of the oil companies, 1900 to 1938, from the date when British and American oilmen decided to invest in Mexico until the year that President Lázaro Cárdenas decreed the nationalization of the industry. The period straddles, or rather, bridges two eras generally considered quite different in Mexican history, the end of the *Porfiriato*, the thiry-five years that Porfirio Díaz ruled Mexico (1876–1911), and the Mexican Revolution, both in its violent phase (1910–1920) and reconstruction (1920–1940).[1] The era of foreign ownership of the oil industry extended over both periods, highlighting the differences and continuities between the two.

The importance of oil to Mexican history, politics, and economics has generated a rich scholarship.[2] However, it lacks an environmental history approach. That is the singular difference between this book and its predecessors. The fundamental aim of environmental history is to locate human actions not only within their social, political, and economic spheres, but also within a network of ecological relationships.[3] That is, just as human beings interact with one another, they interact with the environment and the entire gamut of organisms and phenomena within it, what we typically call "nature." An environmental history of the Mexican oil industry, therefore, takes into account human relations as well as the interactions between human beings and the environment. To do that, it is necessary to examine the local effects of oil extraction in their social and environmental dimensions. In the case of the Huasteca, it means writing a history that centers on actors typically peripheral or neglected in the historiography of Mexican oil: indigenous people, nature, and oil workers.[4]

[1] The notion that the *Porfiriato* and the Mexican Revolution represent two completely distinct eras in Mexican history is undergoing revision in the historiography, as suggested in, for example, Eric Van Young, *Mexico's Regions: Comparative History and Development* (San Diego: Center for U.S.-Mexican Studies, UCSD, 1992); Gilbert M. Joseph and Daniel Nugent, eds., *Everyday Forms of State Formation: Revolution and the Negotiation of Rule in Modern Mexico* (Durham: Duke University Press, 1994); and Mauricio Tenorio-Trillo, *Mexico at the World's Fairs: Crafting a Modern Nation* (Berkeley: University of California Press, 1996).

[2] The classic is Lorenzo Meyer, *México y los Estados Unidos en el conflicto petrolero* (Mexico City: El Colegio de México, 1972). Other examples include Jonathan Brown and Alan Knight, eds., *The Mexican Petroleum Industry in the Twentieth Century* (Austin: University of Texas Press, 1992); Jonathan Brown, *Oil and Revolution in Mexico* (Austin: University of Texas Press, 1993); Linda B. Hall, *Oil, Banks, and Politics: The United States and Postrevolutionary Mexico, 1917–1924* (Austin: University of Texas Press, 1995); Lourdes Celis Salgado, *La industria petrolera en México: Una crónica, I: de los inicios a la expropiación* (Mexico City: PEMEX, 1988).

[3] William Cronon, "A Place for Stories: Nature, History, and Narrative," *Journal of American History*, Vol. 78, No. 4 (March 1992), p. 1352.

[4] There are few published articles about the history of the union movement among Mexican oil workers. Most appeared in the journal of the Universidad Veracruzana, *Anuario*, the defunct journal *Historia Obrera*, and four collections: *Memoria del primer coloquio regional de historia obrera* (Mexico City: Centro de Estudios Históricos del Movimiento Obrero Mexicano, 1977); *Memoria del segundo coloquio regional de historia obrera* (Mexico City: Centro de Estudios Históricos del Movimiento Obrero, 1979); *Veracruz, un tiempo para contar . . . Memoria del primer seminario de historia regional* (Veracruz: Universidad Veracruzana and

The main argument this book makes is that fossil fuel extraction entailed the creation of an entirely new ecology, what I call the ecology of oil. By that I mean that the oil industry generated a specific set of changes. These were rapid and radical, roughly sequential but also overlapping, summarized under three categories: shifts in local land tenure patterns, changes in local land use, and transformations in local social structures and composition. Ensconced in these three overarching processes were a series of other changes and effects: the displacement and marginalization of aboriginal populations; unprecedented and often destructive alterations in the landscape; the formation of new social groups, cultures, and economic regimes; and the creation of pronounced differences in the human experience of nature based on newly manufactured social distinctions. All relationships in this ecological network were hierarchical by design: humans lorded over nature on principle, but distinctions among men depended on economic regimes and ideological constructs. At the dawn of the twentieth century in Mexico, the economic regime under construction was capitalism, which, coupled with American and European racism, determined the development of the oil industry. Class, nationality, ethnicity, or "race," therefore, shaped both the relationships among humans and those between humans and other living organisms and natural phenomena. The ecology of oil, therefore, denotes an integrated package of human interactions, interactions between humans and/in nature, and historical processes.

The triad of changes and their concomitant transformations and effects was no accident. The changes in land tenure systems, land use, and social formations were the product of human agency. The designers and implementers of this network of relationships were the British and American capitalists who inaugurated the oil industry in Mexico. They received support from the men of the Porfiriato, the Mexican ruling elite whose goals since the nineteenth century had been to transform Mexico into a capitalist country. The oilmen and the Porfirians thus shared the objective of controlling nature and men to generate wealth. Success in that dual enterprise was called progress. And it was good.

Within those parameters, the oilmen were immensely successful in the Huasteca. Between 1900 and 1910, they forged an extremely fruitful

Instituto Nacional de Antropología e Historia, 1989); and *El trabajo y los trabajadores en la historia de México*, edited by Elsa Cecilia Frost, Michael C. Meyer, and Josefina Zoraida Vázquez (Mexico City: El Colegio de México, 1979). The scholars who produced most of the work are Lief S. Adleson, Rebeca Nadia de Gortari, Mirna Alicia Benítez Juárez, Manuel Uribe Cruz, Alberto J. Olvera Rivera, and Leopoldo Alafita Méndez.

partnership with the men of the Porfiriato. Both operated from an
"Edenic narrative" in their interpretation of the rainforest: that is, they
saw it as a "paradise," devoid of human intervention and ripe for capitalist development.[5] Thus, with the legal blessings of President Díaz and
more, the oilmen turned the Huasteca into a capitalist microcosm, with
a booming market economy, commodification of nature and labor, and
rigid social divisions. Moreover, as segregation-era Americans and imperial Englishmen saw it, their handiwork was enlightening: they brought
civilization to people and places where nothing but wilderness had existed
before. They were proud "pioneers." Certainly, in constructing the ecology of oil, they were the single most important catalyst for social and
environmental transformation in the Huasteca since Cortes' arrival in
Veracruz in 1519.

The first change in the new ecology was the transformation of local
land tenure patterns. In the Huasteca two systems coexisted uneasily until
1900: communal land ownership and private ownership. The first was
most common among aboriginal people, principally the Huastecos, or
Teenek as they call themselves, whereas the second was more pronounced
among the local *hacendado* elite of Spanish extraction. In little more than
a decade, however, the oilmen gained control over extensive expanses of
tropical forest, either through outright purchase or by introducing the
new concepts of leasing and royalties. In both cases, the oil companies
set the stage for the displacement and marginalization of the indigenous
population as the rainforest became an "oil field."

That transformation is the second component of the ecology of oil.
The new owners and leasers overturned the previous ecological regimes
and replaced them with industrial landscapes. Such work entailed
unprecedented changes in land use, or "changes in the land" in the
words of one historian.[6] As indigenous agriculture and hacendado cattle ranching made way for oil extraction and processing plants, deep

---

[5] Candance Slater developed the concept to analyze current discourse on the Brazilian
rainforest. I borrow it because it applies to the Huasteca as well. Candace Slater, "Amazonia as Edenic Narrative," in *Uncommon Ground: Toward Reinventing Nature*, edited by
William Cronon (New York: W.W. Norton & Co., 1995), pp. 114–159. The idea of Eden
is a recurring theme in Western culture in general, specifically as a "recovery narrative"
that longs for the idealized, mythical garden that existed before civilization, as Carolyn
Merchant shows in "Reinventing Eden: Western Culture as a Recovery Narrative," in the
same volume, pp. 132–159.

[6] William Cronon, *Changes in the Land: Indians, Colonists, and the Ecology of New England* (New
York: Hill and Wang, 1983) was the original inspiration for the dissertation phase of this
book.

ecological change in the Huasteca became inevitable. Early technology, cyclical or unpredictable natural phenomena, and unbridled exploitation, moreover, meant those changes led to the wholesale destruction of many of the ecosystems of northern Veracruz, from sand dunes to mangrove forests, from marshes to the tropical forest, with all the implications for wildlife inscribed therein.

The extremely arduous physical task of replacing a forest with derricks and refineries involved the third process that comprised the ecology of oil: changing the social composition of the Huasteca. The companies imported labor in great quantities, spurring unprecedented population growth in northern Veracruz and the port of Tampico in Tamaulipas. The flood of immigrants rapidly overwhelmed local populations and thus completed the task of displacing native groups in number and social importance. The convergence of capitalist labor organization and European and American racism, moreover, meant that the social hierarchies the oilmen built were based on class and "race." That is, the social order in the oil industry had a specific look: European and American executives and professionals rested at the top; foreign "white" skilled working-class men were next; and Mexican menial laborers stood at the bottom. The companies distributed the rewards of oil work accordingly, with pay, benefits, and general working and living conditions improving significantly from one level to the next.

The labor hierarchy, moreover, also influenced the experience of each group in nature. The top echelons reshaped the environment to fit not only production needs, but also their own sense of aesthetics and pleasure. The oilmen, in other words, played with and in the environment. Foreign white working-class men and Mexicans by contrast knew nature through work.[7] Their experience of the environment was tied to the labor they performed outdoors every day. However, that interaction was mediated by color/nationality: foreign workers were exposed to the dangers of explosions and fires, but they were spared from other occupational hazards and from disease. Those at the bottom of the labor ladder, Mexican workers, felt the full impact of the inhospitability of the tropical forest toward humans, the occupational dangers of working with highly flammable and noxious natural substances, and the whole gamut of diseases that thrived in those environmental and social conditions. The pattern of strict "racial" segregation in housing the companies enforced

---

[7] Richard White introduces the concept of "knowing nature through labor" I borrow here in *The Organic Machine: The Remaking of the Columbia River* (New York: Hill and Wang, 1995), Chapter 1.

also meant that Mexican workers and their families lived in toxic neighborhoods, exposed not only to fire but also to dangerous emissions and effluents from the petroleum plants next door. Thus, although Mexicans did the physical labor of altering the environment, they were hardly in control of nature. In their experience, the opposite was true.

However, just as relationships and historical processes are never static, neither was the ecology of oil. There were tensions inherent in the network of relationships the oilmen built and in the processes of change they set in motion. Neither men nor nature acted in accordance with the plan. Control proved difficult to achieve and maintain in both cases. Nature played its role through unpredictable oil yields, dangerous chemicals, cyclical but inclement weather, a difficult terrain, and endemic disease. Indigenous peoples resisted the loss of their lands. The local hacendado elite fought back against the oilmen to protect their interests. Workers organized militant leftist unions to demand better working conditions. And, finally, Mexico caught fire.

The outbreak of the Mexican Revolution in late 1910 magnified the tensions in the industry. In the Huasteca, aboriginals, workers, and Mexican revolutionaries of all stripes pulled in different directions, sometimes in coordination, oftentimes at odds, continuously challenging the edifice the companies were constructing. Indeed, the tug of war over oil that the Mexican Revolution started was nothing less than a struggle for the ownership and control of nature itself. The organization and conduct of the petroleum business, as well as the purpose of oil production overall, became contentious issues at the local, national, and international levels. They remained so through the decade of armed conflict and after the peace came in 1920.

In the course of the reconstruction of the country and the state apparatus that followed 1920, the Mexican revolutionary leadership brought new pressures to bear on the oil companies. They sought to wrestle control over nature from the oilmen as part of a nationalist development program based on a platform of conservation of natural resources. The result was the intensification of the conflict between the revolutionary government and the companies. Combined with the hyperexploitation of the Huasteca oil reserves, the clash between the state and the companies led to the abrupt oil "bust" of 1921 after a decade of "boom." The punishing crisis of unemployment and economic depression that ensued shook the Huasteca and awoke the entire nation to the full implications of rapid capitalist development under foreign control. Moreover, for the first time Mexico became aware of the devastating environmental effects of petroleum extraction and refining. The idea that the oil industry represented progress and civilization was unmasked as a cruel hoax. In the aftermath, what I call a narrative of wasteland emerged. Journalists, novelists, writers, and policy makers thereafter highlighted the destructive qualities of the oil industry above all others. Ideologically, the oil companies were on the defensive. Politically, however, they remained as strong as ever, extracting concession after concession from the revolutionary leadership over the next decade.

There was one group that resisted the oil companies, however: the Mexican oil workers. Consistently nationalist and to the left of the revolutionary leadership, the oil workers challenged the social and environmental order the industry created from the mid-1910s. Time and again they paid dearly for their defiance, punished not only by the companies but also by revolutionary leaders; yet they never stopped fighting back. In fact, confrontation became a hallmark of oil workers' culture until they made their most daring bid to unravel the ecology of oil altogether. In the mid-1930s, Mexican men sought worker control of the oil industry as an alternative to the arrangement in place. The confrontation that followed lasted four years. It ended in 1938 with arguably the single most important moment for the forging of modern Mexico: the nationalization of the oil companies. The March 19 decree immediately catapulted President Lázaro Cárdenas to the summit of the pantheon of Mexican revolutionary heroes, a place he holds to this day.

In the process, the workers' role was overshadowed. They deserve credit for the nationalization of the industry, however. In challenging the oilmen for decades, the workers embodied a process of revolution "from below" that changed the course of Mexican history. Their unflinching defiance of the logic of early twentieth-century capitalism, foreign ownership of natural resources, and the joint exploitation of nature and labor, moreover, had truly global implications. Mexican oil workers had precipitated a crisis whose resolution set a dangerous precedent the oil companies understood fully: the expropriation of foreign property in general and the total loss of a key energy sector in particular. In the aftermath of the March 19 decree, preventing other Mexicos became mantra among transnational oil conglomerates – a notion that resonates down to our own day.[8] Investigating the ecology of oil in the Huasteca, therefore, also means understanding processes that marked the history of the twentieth century and beyond.

[8] Although the Bolsheviks had nationalized the Russian oil industry earlier than Mexico, in April 1920, their inability to manage it on their own led them to make arrangements with Standard Oil to exploit their fields in 1921. See Daniel Yergin, *The Prize: The Epic Quest for Oil, Money and Power* (New York: Simon and Schuster, 1992), pp. 237–240, 276–279.

This book is divided into seven chapters distributed in three parts. Part I focuses on the natural and political history of the Huasteca in the nineteenth century. Chapter 1 shows that the oil industry did not operate in a historical vacuum. On the contrary, the chapter reviews the discourses surrounding the tropical forest and the century-old history of social conflict in the Huasteca to argue that those struggles arose from a competition between two distinct views of the rainforest and the two ecologies implied therein. That is, the small indigenous farmers and the aspiring hacendado elite who inhabited the region clashed throughout the nineteenth century over the uses and shape of the local environment. By and large, native peoples owned the land communally and focused on production for family consumption first, whereas the hacendados subscribed to notions of individual ownership and organized their production for the market first and foremost. The friction between a regime of communal and subsistence agriculture in a tropical rainforest and a capitalist agricultural project that entailed razing the forest explains much of the violence over land tenure that wracked the Huasteca in the nineteenth century.

Part II lays out the ecology of oil in three chapters. Chapter 2 analyzes the transformation of land tenure patterns. Commanding vast amounts of capital and armies of lawyers, the oil companies succeeded where the Mexican elites had failed. They transformed the tropical forest into a commodity. In less than two decades, the oilmen acquired the forest and supplanted communal and private ownership with corporate control. The chapter examines the reasons government officials, the hacendados, and indigenous family farmers alike had for negotiating with the oilmen, as well as the strategies the companies used to gain access to the land when they met peaceful and armed resistance.

Once the companies secured land titles, the process of transforming the rainforest into an oil "field" began. That is the subject of Chapter 3. It documents how the oil barons exerted control over nature in the process of extracting and processing oil, and thus changed the landscape. I describe the replacement of the forest with the infrastructure of oil production (camps, terminals, ports, and refineries) in addition to analyzing its environmental effects (fire, pollution, and habitat loss). The chapter highlights the ways in which nature emerged as an actor and belied the oilmen's hubris. The runaway wells, "gushers," and the spectacular spills and fires that became the trademark of Mexican oil extraction demonstrated the illusion of control.

Chapter 4, the last in Part II, zooms in from the landscape and the industry to humans in nature and humans and nature. The chapter examines the labor recruitment processes the oil companies used, the

techniques they used to instill discipline in the labor force, the ways in
which they institutionalized discrimination in Mexico and thus injected
class and nationality (understood as race by Europeans and Americans)
into the human experience of nature. I document how executives and
professionals mastered and tamed nature through recreation, sport, and
home landscaping, while foreign and Mexican workers encountered
nature at its most dangerous, through work-related explosions, fires,
and poisonous gases. I also examine the effects of intraclass distinctions
between foreign and Mexican workers in terms of exposures to occupational and health hazards, including malaria and other endemic diseases.

The challenges to the network of relations and the historical processes
the oil industry set in motion in the Huasteca is the subject of Part III. The
overarching argument of this last section is that the Mexican Revolution
offered unexpected and excellent opportunities to challenge the ecology
of oil. The first to take advantage of the historical moment was the first
generation of Mexican oil workers. They are the subjects of Chapter 5,
which traces their cultural and political formation, arguing that their
location in the ecology of oil resulted in a militant labor force with strong
anarcho-syndicalist leanings. The coincidence of revolution at home and
a world war abroad fueled by petroleum distillates meant that the first
generation of Mexican oil workers quickly realized they had the power
to disrupt production through strikes. They exercised their leverage with
varying degrees of success until 1921, when the oil companies decimated
their ranks just as the industry reached its peak of production in Mexico.

Chapter 6 traces the efforts of the revolutionary leadership to regulate the industry beginning in 1915. It shows that the revolutionaries
were well aware of the environmental costs of oil production and advocated conservation as an alternative. They inscribed those concerns in
the 1917 Constitution, in fact, in Article 27. I argue that what was at stake
in the long and well-documented battle between the government and
the companies over Article 27 was the question of whether the nation
or the private sector should own nature. Article 27, referring to nature
as "natural resources," established the principle that the nation did; yet
the weakness of revolutionary institutions eventually doomed exercises of
state authority to failure. Nevertheless, the change in discourse after 1921
allowed the Huastec to reemerge as local actors and reclaim ownership
of the land, with mixed results. The chapter ends with the government's
joint venture with Royal Dutch Shell in 1937. The failure of the proposed
joint venture reveals that into the late 1930s, the Mexican revolutionary
state-in-formation remained too weak to rein in the oil companies.

The last chapter follows the revolution brewing among the second generation of oil workers in the late 1920s and early 1930s. Its themes include the battles for unionization, as well as the clash of visions between the oil workers and the revolutionary leadership over the shape of revolutionary Mexico. The period unfolded as a three-way struggle among the oil companies, the government, and the oil workers, but implicit in these confrontations was the lingering question of who should "manage" nature in a revolutionary country: the working class, the private sector, or the state. Nevertheless, the 1934 election of Lázaro Cárdenas as president opened up political opportunities that the oil workers did not miss. They took the presidential agenda of economic nationalism laced with socialist rhetoric at face value to press for workers' control over the industry and the nationalization of the most productive oil fields. I argue that although Cárdenas tried his best, he could not find a negotiated solution to the crisis. His last option became the resolution: expropriating the foreign oil companies and, thus, changing the trajectory of the revolution and Mexican history in the twentieth century.

What was the aftermath of the 1938 nationalization in environmental and labor terms? The epilogue addresses these and other questions still with us today regarding the ownership and control of nature under changing social and political circumstances.

PART ONE

THE HUASTECA BEFORE OIL

1

"PARADISE" AND "PROGRESS"

THE HUASTECA IN THE NINETEENTH CENTURY

> A great variety of other trees are met with here, of magnificent
> size and splendid foliage, waving their brilliant branches in
> the breeze, and presenting strong inducements to the traveler
> continually to pause in wonder and admiration. In good sooth,
> it may be said that "man is the only thing that dwindles here."
>
> B. M. Norman, 1845

In 1921 the California oil magnate Edward L. Doheny delivered a speech
before his colleagues at the American Petroleum Institute. In addition to
reporting that his Mexican Petroleum Company made over 100 million
dollars in profits, he recalled his first visit to northern Veracruz in 1900. As
the train descended from the mountains of the *Sierra Madre Oriental*, even
an unsentimental businessman like him could not help but be moved by
the landscape. Before his eyes lay

> beautiful and awe-inspiring scenery...down past rivers of clear blue-
> green water; past the [water]falls...where the leap of the water to where
> it falls in a mass of white foam is over 270 feet;...and for a short space
> one sees only the skies before plunging into a forest so dense that it
> is hidden almost completely as it winds its way through the jungle to
> the Pánuco [River], thence to the sea; jungle-covered country which
> extends clear to the harbor of Tampico.[1]

The "jungle" Doheny remembered was the northernmost end of the Mexican tropics, an area known as the Huasteca. Besides hiding the forest and,
indeed, because of the forest itself, the place "hid" a complex natural history and a turbulent political past the oilman could hardly imagine. As
soon as Mexico had won its independence from Spain in the early nineteenth century, different actors – indigenous peoples, Mexican elites,

---

[1] PanAmerican Petroleum & Transport Company, *Mexican Petroleum* (New York: 1922),
pp. 16–17.

foreigners, and nature itself – had become entangled in fierce struggles over the ecology of the area. Although the forest still stood outside Doheny's private railroad car in 1900, the conflict over its future was far from resolved. Unknowingly, Doheny was also entering into a history of ecological war.

The Huasteca

The state of Veracruz rests like a half moon on the shores of the Gulf of Mexico. Scholars divide the state into three geographical slices: north, center, and south.[2] The northern part is further cut in two: Totonacapan on the south and the Huasteca in the north. Whereas the first geographic demarcation is recent, the division of the north is ancient. The notion that two distinct regions existed in northern Veracruz dates from before the fifteenth century, from the Aztec empire via the Spanish.[3] According to the sixteenth-century friar Bernardino de Sahagún, the Nahua told him that the name of the landmass from the eastern steppes of the Sierra Madre (modern-day states of San Luis Potosí, Hidalgo, and Puebla) to the Gulf coast was Cuextlan, itself the name of a local royal authority. But the north-south boundary was not easily defined. Colonial officials placed the northern boundary of Cuextlan's dominions at the banks of either the Soto la Marina River or the Tamesí, and the southern border at the edge of either the Tuxpan River or the Cazones. The Nahua called all who lived in Cuextlan, "cuextecatl." The Europeans hispanicized the sound they heard into "huaxteca" or Huasteca.[4]

---

[2] See: William T. Sanders, "The Anthropogeography of Central Veracruz," *Huastecos, Totonacos y sus vecinos,* Special issue, *Revista Mexicana de Estudios Antropológicos,* vol. 13, nos. 2–3 (1952–1953), pp. 28–29, 52; Rebeca de Gortari, "Petróleo y clase obrera en Veracruz: 1920–1935," in *Memoria del Primer Coloquio* (Mexico City: Centro de Estudios del Movimiento Obrero Mexicano, 1977), pp. 286–288.

[3] The concept and definition of "region" has been a topic of much debate in Mexican history and geography recently, particularly around the question of how "regions" are produced and reproduced and who does the construction. See, for example, Magnus Mörner, *Region and State in Latin American's Past* (Baltimore: John Hopkins University Press, 1993), and the discussion in the Introduction to Glen David Kuecker's "A Desert in a Tropical Wilderness: Limits to the Porfirian Project in Northern Veracruz, 1876–1910," Ph.D. Dissertation, Rutgers, The State University of New Jersey, 1998.

[4] Bernardino de Sahagún, "¿Quiénes eran los huaxtecos?" in *Huaxtecos y Totonacos: Una antología histórico-cultural,* edited by Lorenzo Ochoa (Mexico City: Consejo Nacional para la Cultura y las Artes, 1990), p. 133; Janis B. Alcorn, *Huastec Mayan Ethnobotany* (Austin: University of Texas Press, 1984), p. 38; "Ladrón de Guevara's Report Concerning the Kingdom of Nuevo León (1739)," in *The Presidio and Militia on the Northern Frontier of*

Despite its uncertain geographical boundaries, the idea of a Huasteca region remained current throughout the colonial period. The same notion held true after independence (1821), but the territory was divided differently. The state of Puebla now jutted eastward to the Gulf, encompassing Totonacapan, Tuxpan, and Tamiahua as it cut a wedge through northern Veracruz.[5] Then, in 1853, Puebla lost access to the Gulf and Veracruz sealed the rupture in its body politic to acquire its crescent shape. Most of the Huasteca zone then became enclosed within Veracruz borders, but parts spilled over into the neighboring states of San Luis Potosí, Hidalgo, and Tamaulipas.[6] The northern boundary of the Huasteca became the border between Tamaulipas and Veracruz, the Tamesí River. The southern border most commonly accepted was the Cazones River. Until the foreign geologists arrived and began exploring for oil, however, the area remained unmapped.[7] Through mapping, the Huasteca acquired some dimensions. From north to south, the Huasteca measured roughly 195 kilometers (117 miles). Its width was approximately 120 kilometers (72 miles) from the Gulf to the Sierra Madre. Thus demarcated, the Huasteca *veracruzana* covered 23,400 km² (8,424 sq. miles) or 2,340,000 hectares (5,018,400 acres), slightly larger than the state of New Jersey.[8] Yet though the territorial boundaries of the Huasteca evolved over time, the descriptions of its landscape achieved a

New Spain, The Central Corridor and the Texas Corridor, 1700–1765, vol. II, part II, edited by Diana Hadley, Thomas H. Naylor, and Mardith K. Schuetz-Miller (Tucson: University of Arizona Press, 1997), p. 93.

[5] A map of Puebla and Veracruz during this time is in Antonio Escobar Ohmstede, *Ciento Cincuenta Años de Historia de la Huasteca* (Veracruz: Instituto Veracruzano de Cultura, 1998), p. 134.

[6] Scholars today prefer to use the plural Huastecas, depending on their area of study: *huasteca veracruzana, huasteca tamaulipeca, huasteca potosina,* or *huasteca hidalguense.* See, for example, the articles in *Huaxtecos y Totonacos;* and Jesús Ruvalcaba and Graciela Alcalá, eds., *Huasteca I. Espacio y tiempo. Mujer y trabajo, Huasteca II. Prácticas agrícolas y medicina tradicional. Arte y sociedad,* and *Huasteca III. Movilizaciones campesinas* (Mexico City: Centro de Investigaciones y Estudios Superiores en Antropología Social, 1993); Joaquín Meade, *La Huasteca tamaulipeca,* vols. 1–2 (Ciudad Victoria, Tamaulipas: Editorial Jus, 1978). There are scholars, moreover, who argue that Totonacapan (Papantla), home of the Totonac people, should be included as part of the Huasteca. See Jesús Manuel Macías, "L.M. Gatti: una vision antropológica del espacio-región," in *Huasteca I,* pp. 119–129.

[7] In fact, the art and science of mapping did not become systematic in Mexico until the last two decades of the nineteenth century. Tenorio-Trillo, *Mexico at the World's Fairs,* p. 131.

[8] The calculations are based on the 1995 Map of Veracruz produced by the Gobierno del Estado de Veracruz, Dirección General de Turismo. The size of New Jersey is 20,175 km² (7,790 sq. mi.) according to *The World Book Encyclopedia,* vol. 14 (Chicago: World Book Inc., 1999), p. 232.

peculiar uniformity in the nineteenth century. All who described it shared Doheny's wonder.

The Eye of the Writer

No one who laid eyes on the Huasteca and wrote about it was indifferent to it. Most surviving impressions date from the mid-nineteenth century through the 1920s and all affirm the same vision. The Huasteca was "paradise." Both Mexicans and foreigners expressed themselves in those terms, forging an "Edenic narrative" around the Huasteca before the advent of oil extraction.[9] The narrative could be more or less complex, drawing on different components of the biblical Eden depending on the beholder. Colonel Albert S. Evans and travel-guide writer Philip Terry associated it with plenty. On account of that abundance, wrote Evans in 1880, "the day will come – I trust it may not be far distant – when she [Mexico] will be regarded, with reason, as the Paradise of the world."[10] In 1909, Terry echoed the sentiment. He highly recommended adding the Huasteca to the tourist itinerary because "the entire district recalls the primitive biblical region flowing with milk and honey." The Pánuco River alone was "a Tamaulipecan Eden," Terry argued.[11] Generalizing less, other Americans focused on aspects of the Huasteca that evoked a garden of delights for them. Naturalist Frank M. Chapman was so elated by the avian life he encountered that he flatly declared he had found "an ornithologist's paradise."[12]

Delving deeper into the allegory was Mexican Dr. Pehr Olsson-Seffer and American writer Marian Storm. They commented on the human element of the Garden and on the relationship between plenty and work. Writing as a "former Commissioner of Tropical Agriculture" for *The National Geographic* in 1910, Dr. Pehr asserted that in tropical Mexico "people are able to live easily" because "the land is capable of producing everything necessary for life." Upon visiting the Huasteca in 1924, Storm likewise concluded that "the . . . peon lives in a Paradise . . . Has he

---

[9] Slater, "Amazonia as Edenic Narrative," p. 114.

[10] Evans is quoted in Herman W. Konrad, "Tropical Forest Policy and Practice During the Mexican Porfiriato, 1876–1910," in *Changing Tropical Forests: Historical Perspectives on Today's Challenges in Central and South America*, edited by Harold K. Steen and Richard D. Tucker (Forest History Society, 1992), p. 136.

[11] Philip T. Terry, *Terry's Guide to Mexico* (Boston: Houghton Mifflin Company, 1923), p. 49, 50h.

[12] Frank Chapman, "A Naturalist's Journey around Veracruz and Tampico," *The National Geographic Magazine*, vol. 25, no. 5 (May 1914), p. 541.

not always superabundant sunlight and clean air to breathe? Is there a better-ventilated home in the world than his? Does not a tender Providence fairly thrust upon him building materials and the fruits of the earth?"[13] In other words, both Pehr and Storm looked at the men of the Huasteca and saw Adam before the fall from paradise: without the need for toil because the bounty of Eden allowed him to live without working. But did that image of the Huasteca illuminate or obscure the environment and the people? What kind of an ecosystem was this heaven?

Communities of Life

The task of unveiling the environment of the Huasteca in the nineteenth century with the precision of twenty-first-century biological standards is not simple. The sources are vague and the terminology imprecise.[14] Nonetheless, the evidence shows that the hot and humid Huasteca was the northernmost tropical region in the Americas, the northern ecological boundary of what biologists call the "neotropics."[15] As such, the Huasteca hosted a rich and diverse ecology composed of different yet intimately linked ecosystems in constant flux.

[13] Pehr Olsson-Seffer, "Agricultural Possibilities in Tropical Mexico," *The National Geographic Magazine*, vol. 25, no. 5 (May 1914), p. 1024; Marian Storm, "Wells at the World's End: Life in the Pánuco Oil Region of Mexico," *The Atlantic Monthly* (April 1924), pp. 516–517.

[14] The scarcity of sources is a common lament among historians of the Huasteca. One reason was the periodic burning down of archives during nineteenth- and twentieth-century rebellions, according to Manuel B. Trens, *Historia de Veracruz*, Tomo V, Primer Volumen (Mexico City: n/p, 1950), p. 470, and Leticia Reina, *Las rebeliones campesinas en México (1819–1906)* (Mexico City: Siglo XXI Editores, 1988), p. 346. Fires also destroyed regional archives, including the one belonging to the Tuxpan Petroleum Agency in 1920: Telegram from Agencia Tuxpan, September 30, 1920, Archivo General de la Nación (AGN), Departamento del Petróleo (DP), Caja 16, Exp. 10. See also Antonio Escobar Ohmstede, *Historia de los pueblos indígenas de México. De la costa a la sierra: Las huastecas, 1750–1900* (Mexico City: Centro de Investigaciones y Estudios Superiores en Antropología Social and Instituto Nacional Indigenista, 1998), p. 16.

[15] "Neotropical" refers to the Western Hemisphere. Susan E. Place, "Introduction," in *Tropical Rainforests: Latin American Nature and Society in Transition*, revised and updated edition, edited by Susan E. Place (Wilmington, DE: Scholarly Resources, 2001), p. xiv. The Tamesí River seems to have been the transition zone for different ecosystems. The rainforest did not extend north of it. Instead, the transition followed a pattern of rainforest below the Tamesí, swamps and marshes to its immediate north, then low, scrub forests. See "Ladrón de Guevara's Report," p. 93; Dirección General de Geografía del Territorio Nacional, Secretaría de Programación y Presupuesto, "Carta del uso del suelo y vegetación," (1981). In 1924, for example, one geologist remarked that the land north of the Pánuco River was more like "desert and semi-desert," whereas the land south of the river was "jungles and swamps." Project for Geologic Explorations in Southern Tamaulipas, Tampico, June 17, 1924, International Archive of Economic Geology (IAEG), Charles L. Baker Collection (CB), Acct. no. 3328, Box 3: Correspondence Folder.

Approaching from the east, the Gulf coast itself was a mosaic of environments. From Tampico to Tuxpan, the coastline was punctuated with lakes and lagoons. The largest was the Tamiahua Lagoon, a shallow body measuring 100 kilometers (62.5 miles) in length and 18 kilometers (11 miles) in width. But there were many smaller ones. Tampico, the major city of the Huasteca, though across the state boundary in Tamaulipas, was itself surrounded by water. The port city was located at the intersection of one of the largest drainage systems in Mexico, framed by the Tamesí and Pánuco Rivers like "half a Venice," as novelist Jack London described it.[16] On the east, Tampico bordered on the spout of the funnel-shaped Chairel Lagoon, which stretched north into the much larger and elongated Champayal Lagoon. Between the two was the rounder, smaller Escondida Lake. All three drew their water from the Tamesí River running northeast. The Carpintero Lagoon bordered the city on the northwest. The southern boundary was the Pánuco, and across from it glistened the Pueblo Viejo Lagoon. Southeast from Pueblo Viejo began the Tamiahua Lagoon. Eleven miles east from Tampico along the sinuous and slow moving Pánuco was the Gulf of Mexico.[17] The shallow lakes and lagoons provided a rich habitat for migratory birds and ducks. At times, Muscovy ducks were so numerous that they "blackened" the horizon, according to *Saturday Evening Post* journalist Carl W. Ackerman writing in 1918. The abundance of such wildlife, in fact, elicited Ackerman's own peculiar contribution to the Edenic narrative. Upon reflection, he concluded that "there is so much game and there are so few hunters that this is undreamed of paradise."[18]

Instead of sandy beaches, the shores of the lakes and lagoons, in addition to the streams, rivers, and estuaries that led to the Gulf, were covered with red and black mangrove forests. These tree communities extended inland anywhere from ten to twenty miles. The characteristic features of the mangroves, the odorous soft mud and the gangly root system that sinks

---

[16] Jack London, "Our Adventurers in Tampico," *Collier's*, vol. 53, no. 15 (June 27, 1914), p. 6.

[17] Carta de la Zona Petrolífera, *Boletín del Petróleo* (BP) vol. 20, no. 3 (September 1925); BP, vol. 5, no. 4 (April 1918), p. 354; William T. Sanders, *The Lowland Huasteca Archeological Survey and Excavation*, 1957 Field Season, University of Missouri Monographs in Anthropology, no. 4 (1978), pp. 2–3; Robert R. Lankford, "Coastal Lagoons of Mexico: Their Origin and Classification," in *Estuarine Processes*, vol. 2, edited by Martin Wiley (New York: Academic Press, 1976), pp. 197–203.

[18] Chapman identified the ducks as Muscovy, "A Naturalist's Journey," p. 541; Carl W. Ackerman, *Mexico's Dilemma* (New York: George H. Doran Company, 1918), p. 83. See also Frederick Starr, *In Indian Mexico: A Narrative of Travel and Labor* (Chicago: Forbes & Company, 1908), p. 278.

into it like mangled forks into chocolate mousse, were also the source of its great ecological richness. Decomposing leaves and gnarled roots that aerated the soil and made it fertile also housed seahorses, shrimp, crabs, worms, snails, clams, anemones, oysters, and other small creatures. These, in turn, sustained numerous fish. Together they supported animals higher up the food chain, including the birds that convinced Chapman he had reached nirvana: parrots, parakeets, grackles, trogons, flamingoes, flycatchers, orioles, macaws, woodpeckers, toucans, pelicans, "delicately colored" pink spoonbills, owls, and dozens of other species. Less appealing were the malaria-carrying mosquitoes and their predators, the dragonflies that buzzed and fluttered on the surface of sluggish mangrove waters. The mangrove forests also served another function. They protected the coastline from storm waves and the seasonal hurricane winds common to the Gulf.[19]

The entire Cabo Rojo Peninsula, the Gulf-side sand barrier that enclosed the Tamiahua Lagoon, contained its own extensive sand dune habitat. Sand dunes, forever shifting with the winds, waves, and storms of the Gulf, grew up to eighty feet high in places. They were not bare sand hills, however. At intervals the dunes were "thickly grown with trees," or covered with grasses or shrubs. That vegetation helped prevent erosion, protected the coastline from severe weather, and created attractive nesting grounds for birds.[20]

[19] Leon Tinkle, *Mr. De: A Biography of Everette Lee DeGolyer* (Boston: Little, Brown, and Company, 1970), p. 54; Rick Gore, "The Tree Nobody Liked," *The National Geographic*, vol. 151, no. 5 (May 1977), pp. 668–686; María Elena Sánchez R., "Datos relativos a los manglares de México," *Anales de la Escuela Nacional de Ciencias Biológicas*, vol. 12, n/d, pp. 61–72; "Survey of Tannin Resources in Mexico," *Journal of Forestry*, vol. 43 (1945), pp. 56–57; Manuel Fernando Soto, *El Nuevo Estado* (Mexico City: Imprenta de Ignacio Cumplido, 1856), p. 15. Chapman gives the Latin names for the birds listed in "A Naturalist's Journey," pp. 540–544; the Latin names for the mangrove species are in Lorenzo Bozada and Zeferino Chávez, *La fauna acuática de la Laguna del Ostión*, Serie Medio Ambiente en Coatzacoalcos, vol. 9 (Mexico City: Centro de Ecodesarrollo, Universidad Veracruzana, 1986), p. 30. On malaria, see Sergio Florescano Mayet, "Las epidemias y la sociedad veracruzana en el siglo XIX," *Anuario*, VII (July 1992), pp. 68, 89; Informe del Consejo de Salubridad, December 31, 1915, Archivo General del Estado de Veracruz (AGEV), Fondo: Gobernación, Serie: Salubridad, Códigos sanitarios, Caja 1; Enrique Beltrán and Eduardo Aguirre Pequeño, *Lecciones de Paludogía* (Monterrey: Ediciones del Instituto de Investigaciones Científicas de la Universidad de Nuevo León, 1948), p. 44. Malaria did not have its origins in the Americas; rather, it was among the diseases the Europeans introduced in the sixteenth century. See William H. McNeill, *Plagues and Peoples* (New York: Anchor Books, 1998), pp. 65, 221–223.

[20] Sanders, *The Lowland Huasteca*, pp. 4–5, 77; John J. Poggie, Jr., *Coastal Pioneer Plants and Habitat in the Tampico Region, Mexico*, Coastal Studies Series, no 6 (Baton Rouge: Louisiana State University, 1963), p. 6; Ignacio Ochoa Villagómez, *Vegetación espontánea y repoblación de los médanos de la zona litoral de Veracruz* (Mexico City: Secretaría de Fomento, 1885),

Inland from the mangroves were the estuaries. These waters created yet another type of ecosystem, the swamps. Containing a mixture of fresh and salt water, the swamps fostered the growth of tiny aquatic organisms such as plankton and algae as well as a panoply of insects. These became food for birds and saltwater fish like mackerel, perch, sea bass, sardines, red snapper, haddock, and the heavyweights of the Huasteca estuaries: one-hundred-pound tarpon and trout. In the swamps other types of vegetation grew in addition to mangroves: ferns, dwarf palms, "royal" palms rising seventy to eighty feet, bamboo twenty feet tall and six inches in diameter, and tall grasses reaching a height of seven feet. Among all these plants, moreover, a great variety of animals found ample grounds for nesting and feeding in the estuaries. Birds, frogs, and turtles were ubiquitous.[21] So was the tropical cousin of the crocodile, the "horrid" caiman, as the wife of a diplomat, Fanny Calderón de la Barca, described the creature she saw basking in the Huasteca sunshine in 1842. And could there be a Garden of Eden without serpents? The swamps of the Huasteca were a "paradise for ophidia," according to the daughter of an oil worker, Martha Chávez Padrón. As a child, she encountered snakes with common names like *chirrionera, negra, mano-de-metate, coralillo, nauyaca,* and *mazacoata.* American geologists crossed paths with some of these in their exploration work in the early 1900s, too. They recognized them as rattlesnakes, water moccasins, and "twenty-foot long" boa constrictors.[22]

p. 9; Starr, *In Indian Mexico,* p. 290; T. N. Vaughn, "Report on Laying Sea Line No 1A at Tuxpam Bar," November 1912, S. Pearson & Son Ltd. (P&S), Historical Records (HR), File C 43/1.

[21] Francisco Contreras, *La riqueza del pantano,* Series El Medio Ambiente en Coatzacoalcos, vol. 5 (Mexico City: Centro de Ecodesarrollo, 1986), pp. 18–19, 25; Lorenzo Bozada y Margarito Páez, *La fauna acuática del litoral,* Series El Medio Ambiente en Coatzacoalcos, vol. 14 (Mexico City: Centro de Ecodesarrollo and Universidad Veracruzana, 1987), p. 27; *Protección a la Naturaleza,* vol. 2, no. 5 (January 1938), pp. 19–20; Terry, *Terry's Guide,* pp. 50i, j, l; Roberto Williams, *Introducción a las culturas del Golfo* (Mexico City: Instituto Nacional de Antropología e Historia and Secretaría de Educación Pública, 1961), pp. 1, 7; José Ramírez, *La Vegetación,* pp. 17, 46, 63; Charles W. Hamilton, *Early Day Oil Tales of Mexico* (Houston: Gulf Publishing Company, 1966), pp. 47, 130; B. M. Norman, *Rambles by Land and Water, or Notes of Travel in Cuba and Mexico* (New York: Paine & Burgess, 1845), p. 169.

[22] Howard T. Fisher and Marion Hall Fisher, eds., *Life in Mexico: The Letters of Fanny Calderón de la Barca* (Garden City, NY: Anchor Books, Doubleday & Co., 1970), p. 620; Martha Chávez Padrón, *Testimonio de una familia petrolera* (Mexico City: PEMEX, 1988), pp. 66–68; Tinkle, *Mr. De,* p. 54; Hamilton, *Early Day,* p. 48. See also, Starr, *In Indian Mexico,* p. 277. Traveling through Tuxpan, Henry H. Harper reported having seen a local man bitten by a "four-nosed" snake measuring 4 to 6 feet in length, with "sixteen great fangs, eight above and eight below" and "the ferocity of a bulldog" in *A Journey in Southeastern*

Stretching west toward the Sierra Madre was the mythical land of "milk and honey," the tropical rainforest.[23] The "jungle-covered country" that surprised Doheny was a complex habitat that contained a rich biodiversity. The trees were the most obvious components. They grew "luxuriant" and close together, like "forest giants . . . in close ranks," wrote one American.[24] So "completely covered with trees of the largest growth" was the forest, noted another American, "that even the sun, or daylight itself, can scarcely find its way among them."[25] What sorts of tree species made the Huasteca forest "so very dense and dark" is not easy to determine, however. British Captain George Francis Lyon, passing through in 1826, recognized that identification was problematic: the forest had "a vast number of trees whose names we didn't know" because they did not exist

Mexico: Narrative of Experiences, and Observations on Agricultural and Industrial Conditions (Boston: The DeVinne Press, 1910), pp. 94–96. Notions about fantastic snakes have a long history in the Huasteca: some scholars speculate that the region might have been the original source for the king-god of Mesoamerica, Quetzalcoatl, the "Plumed Serpent." See Lorenzo Ochoa, "El origen de los huaxtecos según las fuentes históricas," in *Huaxtecos y Totonacos*, pp. 144–153.

[23] There are scholars who consider the Huasteca something other than a rainforest. According to late twentieth-century science, tropical forests were either "dry," "moist," or "wet/rain." The difference lies in the amount of annual rainfall. Whereas the rain is seasonal in most tropical forests, the longer the rainy season, the moister the forest. Based on those classifications, Jenzen, Murphy, and Lugo, for example, assert that late twentieth-century northern Veracruz fit into the dry forest category. Others, like Jerzy Rzedowski, believe that the Huasteca was a tropical rainforest until around 1900. What accounts for the difference in evaluation is the date of the sources the authors use and the changing definitions and classifications of "jungles," the catchall term most nonscientists used for tropical forests throughout the nineteenth and most of the twentieth century. See Daniel H. Janzen, "Tropical Dry Forests: The Most Endangered Major Tropical Ecosystem," in *Biodiversity*, edited by E. O. Wilson (Washington, DC: National Academy Press, 1988), p. 130; Peter G. Murphy and Ariel E. Lugo, "Ecology of a Tropical Dry Forest," *Annual Review of Ecology and Systematics*, vol. 17 (1986), pp. 67–69, 71–72, 76; Jerzy Rzedowski, *Vegetación de México* (Mexico City: Editorial Limusa, 1986), pp. 160, 162; Arturo Gómez-Pompa, *Ecología de la vegetación del estado de Veracruz* (Mexico City: Editorial Continental, 1977), p. 45. See also Gerardo Bustos Trejo, "El Paisaje," *Guía México Desconocido: El Mundo Huasteco y Totonaco*, no. 19 (1994), p. 20; Janis B. Alcorn, "Development Policy, Forests, and Peasant Farms: Reflections on Huastec-managed Forests' Contributions to Commercial Production and Resource Conservation," *Economic Botany*, vol. 38, no. 4 (October-December 1984), p. 393; Robert L. Sanford, Jr., Pia Paaby, Jeffrey C. Luvall, and Eugenie Phillips, "Climate, Geomorphology, and Aquatic Systems," in *La Selva: Ecology and Natural History of a Neotropical Rain Forest*, edited by Lucinda A. McDade, Kamaljit S. Bawa, Henry A. Hespendheide, and Gary S. Hartshorn (Chicago: University of Chicago Press, 1994), pp. 19, 21.

[24] Reau Campbell, *Mexico: Tours through the Egypt of the New World* (New York: C.G. Crawford, 1890), p. 46.

[25] Norman, *Rambles*, pp. 127–128.

in Europe. Yet there were some that Europeans knew well: rubber and ebony.[26] Another visitor similarly described "trees of curious and rare growth" in 1845. He identified only one, a tropical species of *Ficus* (fig), which "grows here to a vast extent and beauty, having, from its wide-spreading branches, suckers, which hang down and touch the ground, where they take root and grow in size equal to the original trunk."[27] From the local inhabitants of the Huasteca, a list with some common names of trees emerges. In 1852 they saw *chijol* (*Piscidia erythrina*) and *chintel,* whereas in the 1890s, Tuxpan merchants listed mahogany (*cedro*), chicle (*zapote*), ebony (*ébano*), and rosewood (*palo de rosa*) among the trees they bought locally.[28]

[26] Quoted in Carlos González Salas, *Tampico es lo azul* (Mexico City: Miguel Angel Porrúa, 1990), p. 513. The first list of scientific names of species for the Huasteca Veracruzana was compiled in 1940 by Carlos Basauri, *La población indígena de México: Etnografía,* Tomo II (Mexico City: Secretaría de Educación Pública, 1940), pp. 57–59. Nonetheless, in 1984 Alcorn compiled a list of trees found in an area not touched by oil production, the Huasteca Potosina. A comparison of her list with those compiled at other late twentieth-century tropical rainforest sites (Los Tuxtlas and Coatzacoalcos, Veracruz; and La Selva, Costa Rica) yields several common species: *Ficus, Pithecellobium, Protium, Manilkara, Tabebuia rosa, Spondias mombin, Brosimum alicastrum, Dendropanax arboreus, Zuelania guidonia, Ceiba,* and *Pouleria.* See Alcorn, "Development Policy," p. 393; Miguel Cházaro, *La vegetación,* Serie Medio Ambiente en Coatzacoalcos, vol. 6 (Mexico City: Centro de Ecodesarrollo and Universidad Veracruzana, 1986), p. 34; Gary S. Hartshorn and Barry E. Hammel, "Vegetation Types and Floristic Patterns," in *La Selva,* pp. 74–77; Sally P. Horn, "Microfossils and Forest History in Costa Rica," in *Changing Tropical Forests,* p. 19; Gómez Pompa, *Ecología,* pp. 46–47, 49; Beatriz Córdova Casillas, "Demografía de árboles tropicales," in *Investigaciones sobre la regeneración de selvas altas en Veracruz, Mexico,* vol. II, edited by Arturo Gómez-Pompa and Silvia Del Amo R. (Xalapa: Instituto Nacional de Investigaciones sobre Recursos Bióticos, 1985), p. 121.

[27] Norman, *Rambles,* p. 142. There is a photograph of a ficus tree, labeled "Igurron tree, Tampico Oil Fields," which accompanies an article entitled "Mexico's Petroleum Industry" in *The Mexican Review* (n/d), p. 3, Southern Methodist University (SMU), The Papers of Everette Lee DeGolyer, Sr. (ED) Mss 60, Box 107, Folder 5220.

[28] The first group is listed in the *Noticias Estadísticas,* as quoted by Ana María Graciela Gutiérrez Rivas, "La familia Herrera, miembro del grupo de poder del norte de Veracruz, 1743–1890," M.A. Thesis, Centro de Investigaciones y Estudios Superiores en Antropología Social, 1998, p. 80. Gutiérrez Rivas also documents the use of Tuxpan forests for mohagany and chicle on pages 108, 127. On logging in Tuxpan, see also Frederick A. Ober, *Mexican Resources and Guide to Mexico* (Boston: Estes and Lauriat, 1884), p. 29 and Norman, *Rambles,* p. 114. By 1932, only one tree type from the mid-nineteenth century remained in the area, chijol (*piscidia erythrina*). The 1932 list is as follows: *chijol, huanacaste, chilab, sabino, jobo, palo azul, palo de arco, guayacan, amate, palo de leche,* and *ceiba.* See Censo, AGEV, Comisión Agraria Mixta (CAM), Exp. 1113, Tierra Blanca, Tepetzintla. Many photographs in the S. Pearson & Son, Ltd., Photographic Albums (PA) give a glimpse of the tropical forest before oil production. See, for example, the 1914 photographs in P4/2/150. Similarly, the Photographs File in IAEG/CB

Just as unusual and fascinating to foreign observers were the denizens of the canopy: the vines and epiphytes. Doheny described them as "a vast network of creeping plants and vines, which range from threadlike fila-ments to hawser-like arms of great strength, mounting serpent-wise amid the tree trunks or searching downwards in weird loops and threaten-ing free-swinging ends."[29] The most striking were the epiphytic orchids, which grew in "great variety" and brilliant colors, giving "indescribable richness and beauty" to the Huasteca.[30]

The rain made it all possible. In the Huasteca, the rainy season lasted seven months, from June through December.[31] Heavy afternoon rains drenched the mangroves, swamps, and forests. Thunderstorms were com-mon at the beginning of the season. So were the Caribbean Sea storms the Maya named *hurakanes.* Hurricane "season," in late summer from August through October, was (and is) part of the overall rainy season in the Gulf. Between 1831 and 1938, for example, at least eighty-one hurricanes struck the Huasteca.[32] Dozens more came close and flung rain on the region at about five cm (two in.) of rain per hour during peak hurricane activity, often lasting from three to fourteen days.[33] Each hurricane resulted in the swelling of rivers, lakes, and lagoons. The swelling was so predictable,

show the forest in the Huasteca, on the San Luis Potosí side of the border. Although Baker labeled the photographs "tropical rain forest," he did not date them. See Box 11; also Box 39, Group T, Packet #2, i18T, Packet #4, i51T; Packet #6, i65T, i70T; Packet #7, i126Ta, i86T; and Packet #8 il99T, i200T.

[29] PanAmerican, *Mexican Petroleum,* p. 69.

[30] Norman, *Rambles,* p. 142; Storm, "Wells," p. 514.

[31] Unfortunately, only two measurements of the amount of rain that fell in northern Veracruz exist in the historical record. In the late 1890s, the prominent coffee planter and government official, Matías Romero, reported "an average" of 1,654 mm of rain in Tuxpan. Geologist Charles Baker, similarly, wrote in 1921 that Tampico received 36 inches (914.5 mm) of rain, while Sanders put the figure at "slightly over" 1,000 mm. These figures are significantly smaller than the 2,000 mm typical of forests classified as tropical at the end of the twentieth century. Matías Romero, *Coffee and India-Rubber Culture in Mexico* (New York: G. P. Putnam's Sons, 1898), p. 38; Charles Laurence Baker, "Geologic Studies in Northeastern Mexico," March 1921, IAEG/CLB, Acc. 3328, Box 11, Manuscripts Folder; Sanders, "The Anthropogeography," p. 41.

[32] Compiled from the National Climatic Center in cooperation with the National Hur-ricane Center and National Hurricane Research Laboratory, *Tropical Cyclones of the North Atlantic Ocean, 1871–1980* (North Carolina: Asheville, July 1981), *passim*; Ivan Ray Tannehill, *Hurricanes, Their Nature and History* (Princeton: Princeton University Press, 1956), pp. 153, 155, 252, 253–254.

[33] Gordon E. Dunn and Bauner I. Miller, *Atlantic Hurricanes* (Baton Rouge: Louisiana State University Press, 1964), p. 76; Louis A. Pérez Jr., *Winds of Change: Hurricanes & the Transformation of Nineteenth-Century Cuba* (Chapel Hill: University of North Carolina Press, 2001), pp. 17, 28.

in fact, that a local writer in 1856 compared it to "the flooding of the Nile."[34]

Less powerful than hurricanes but just as important in supplying water to the Huasteca were the rains of the dry season. Beginning in October and lasting into March, strong Gulf winds loaded with moisture known as *los nortes* blew in almost weekly. The *nortes* typically dropped their cargo in a manner that was "uniform and gentle," as a drizzle or mist.[35] Often, however, the *nortes* brought rain "in torrents" or "cascades."[36] A Mexican botanist described one 1885 episode thus:

> At first there is gentle land wind; [then] one experiences suffocating heat; immediately [after] a breeze blows;... the humidity precipitates like dew on cobblestone streets, balcony railings, and wooden and metal objects... The storm breaks out. The sea raises its crisp waves, furiously striking the piers.[37]

Any given *norte*, moreover, could blow anywhere from twenty-four hours to a week, soaking northern Veracruz. It is no wonder that novelist Jack London complained in 1914 that in Tampico "rain falls every month of the year, the 'rainy' season merely connoting the period of excessive rain."[38] The annual weather cycles of the Gulf of Mexico shaped the evolution and maintained the ecology of the Huasteca rainforest, estuaries, and lagoons.

Beneath and among the trees unimaginable numbers of mammals, reptiles, arachnids, and insects made their homes. The Huasteca forest was habitat for peccary, deer, tapir, wild boars (*jabalí*), otters (*perro de agua*), spider monkeys, iguana, bats, armadillos, and monkeys. Elusive

---

34 Soto, *El Nuevo Estado*, p. 17.
35 P. C. A. Stewart, "The Petroleum Industry of Mexico," reprinted from *The Journal of the Institution of Petroleum Technologists*, vol. 2 (December 1915), p. 1, P&S/HR, Box C 43, File C 43/1; Esteban Maqueo Castellanos, "Breves apuntes sobre geología y climatología del Istmo de Tehuantepec," *Boletín* of the Sociedad Mexicana de Geografía y Estadística, Quinta época, vol. 4 (1909), pp. 174–175. Writing in 1890, Campbell described the *nortes* as "the stream of moist air ever pouring from the Gulf," Campbell, *Mexico*, p. 46.
36 H. R. H. Prince William of Sweden, *Between Two Continents: Notes from a Journey in Central America, 1920* (London: Eveleigh Nash and Grayson, Ltd., 1922), pp. 73–74.
37 Ochoa Villagómez, *Vegetación espontánea*, pp. 9–10; *La Opinión* (Los Angeles) noted in January 14, 1931 that the *nortes* could have the strength of hurricane winds sometimes. In 1932 an Agrarian Commission inspector noted that the rainy season in Tepetzintla lasted from June to September, "with storms in May, and tropical storms [*temporales*] the rest of the year because of the *nortes*," Census, AGEV/CAM, Exp. 1113, Tierra Blanca, Tepetzintla. All translations from the Spanish are mine.
38 London, "Our Adventurers," p. 5.

jaguars, pumas, and ocelots – which the locals called "tigers" and "lions" – were the "graceful" cats of the Huasteca, feared and worshipped in the region since pre-Columbian times.[39] More forthcoming were the millions of "infinitesimal monsters" that annoyed and frightened human beings and elicited detailed descriptions from visitors. There were hairy tarantulas, ferocious army ants, blood-sucking burrowing ticks (*garrapatas, pinolillas,* and *niguas*), poisonous scorpions, stinging wasps, a fly that laid eggs under animal or human skin, and centipedes "potent with venom in every one of their fang-like legs," in "all sizes, from one inch to over a foot long" and "in all colors from dull brown to brilliant mottled blacks, red, and yellow."[40] There were also highly specialized organisms that escaped all observers, such as a unique parasitic wasp that pollinated fig trees.[41] More beautiful and noticeable were the "clouds of exquisite butterflies – white, yellow, and pale green" that fluttered among milkweeds bursting with "half gold, half vermilion" flowers.[42] Lastly, the Huasteca rainforest was also home to humans.

The Human Population

The rainforest the Aztec called Cuextlan was home to several ethnic groups since pre-Hispanic times. The Huastec, distant cousins of the Maya who called themselves Teenek, occupied the overwhelming majority of the territory. But they shared it with Otomí and Tepehua and, uncomfortably, with conquering Nahua. In the colonial period, people of mixed Spanish and indigenous descent, *mestizos*, began to appear, but accurate population counts are nonexistent. In the late nineteenth century, when statistics became a discipline and practice in Mexico, ethnicity was not a category; all were simply "Mexicans." The revolution of the first two decades of the twentieth century, of course, made numbers little

---

[39] Román Piña Chán, "El desarrollo de la tradición huasteca," in *Huaxtecos y Totonacos,* pp. 166, 171; Manuel Toussaint, "Conquista de la Huasteca por los mexicanos," in *Huaxtecos y Totonacos,* p. 160; Norman, *Rambles,* pp. 138–139; Harper, *A Journey,* pp. 35, 87; Storm, "Wells," p. 521. Starr saw a captured jaguar in 1901, describing it as "a beautiful little creature, graceful in form and elegantly spotted. But it snarled and strove to get at everyone who came near it." Starr, *In Indian Mexico,* p. 279.

[40] Storm, "Wells," p. 526; Harper, *A Journey,* pp. 18, 22, 70, 94, 96; Hamilton, *Early Day,* pp. 143–149; PanAmerican, *Mexican Petroleum,* p. 17; Tinkle, *Mr. De,* p. 57; Prince William, *Between Two Continents,* p. 99.

[41] W. Wayt Gibbs, "On the Termination of Species," *Scientific American* (November 2001), p. 47.

[42] Storm, "Wells," p. 521.

Table 1.1. *Population Census for the Huasteca, State of Veracruz,*
1868–1882

Year	1868	1878	1882
Population	102,768	126,255	134,625

Source: Ana María Graciela Gutiérrez Rivas, "La familia Herrera,
miembro del grupo de poder del norte de Veracruz, 1743–1890,"
M.A. Thesis, Centro de Investigaciones y Estudios Superiores en
Antropología Social, 1998, p. 64.

more than crude estimates.[43] However, even flawed figures are a useful
guide to population trends. The census figures available for the nineteenth century (Table 1.1) counted slightly over 100,000 children and
adults in the Huasteca. A general idea about the distribution of ethnici-
ties in the late nineteenth century and early twentieth may be drawn from
the respondents who reported speaking indigenous languages. Table 1.2
shows Spanish-speakers as the majority group in northern Veracruz by
1885. Those numbers, however, included bilingual individuals in the
Spanish-speaking category, so the totals may not necessarily reflect net
growth in the nonindigenous population. The 1910 and 1921 language
census, although incomplete, reflected the growth in the mestizo population brought by oil production.

What is clear from municipal rolls is that in the nineteenth century most Spanish-speakers lived in coastal towns (Tamiahua, Tuxpan,
and river-edge Pánuco), a typical pattern for mestizos and families of
Spanish descent throughout Spanish America. In the twentieth century,
Spanish-speakers were also dominant in oil installations. Nahuátl speakers were the largest indigenous group. They too were highly concentrated, largely in the west, on the border with Hidalgo and San Luis
Potosí. The case of the Otomí and Tepehua was similar. They occupied
the southwest corner of the Huasteca, overlapping Hidalgo and Puebla.
At a time when Mexico's total inhabitants oscillated around ten million,
nineteenth-century northern Veracruz was not an important population

[43] Tenorio-Trillo, *Mexico at the World's Fairs*, p. 129; Escobar Ohmstede, *Historia de los pueblos*,
p. 135.

Table 1.2. *Speakers of Various Languages in Northern Veracruz, 1885–1921*

Language	1885	1895	1910	1921*
Otomí	7,897	4,737	9,322	1,685
Nahuátl	52,760	48,334	24,209	23,921
Tepehua	1,423	1,163	2,903	–
Huastec	15,696	23,385	27,138	18,843
Spanish	59,612	101,101	112,702	84,229

* The 1921 census missed several municipalities altogether.
Sources: México, Dirección General de Estadística, *Censo General de la República Mexicana,* verificado el 28 de octubre de 1900; *Tercer Censo de Población,* verificado el 27 de octubre de 1910; Departamento de Estadística Nacional, *Censo de Veracruz, 1921*; Antonio Escobar Ohmstede, *Historia de los pueblos indígenas de México. De la costa a la sierra: Las huastecas, 1750–1900* (Mexico City: CIESAS, 1998), p. 141.

center. Its population density ranged between five and ten people per square kilometer. Children, moreover, made up a high proportion of the inhabitants.[44] That low population was a key factor in the dominance of tropical forest in the Huasteca until 1900, but it was not the only one.[45]

[44] Escobar Ohmstede, *Historia de los pueblos,* p. 48; Roberto Williams García, "Los tepehuas, otomíes, y nahuas," in *Huaxtecos y Totonacos,* pp. 64–80; Starr, *In Indian Mexico,* pp. 277–279; Ministerio de Fomento, Dirección General de Estadística, *Censo General de la República Mexicana,* Hidalgo, vol. 25 (Mexico City: Oficina Tipográfica de la Secretaría de Fomento, 1897), pp. 61–62; Jacques Galinier, *N'yũhũ les indiens otomìs: hiérarchie sociale et tradition dans le Sud de la Huasteca* (Mexico City: Mission Archeologique et Ethnologique Française au Mexique, 1979), p. 238; Escobar Ohmstede, *Ciento Cincuenta Años,* pp. 32–33, 36–37, 49. Cosío Villegas noted that in 1878 children made up almost 50% of the population of Veracruz. Daniel Cosío Villegas, *Historia Moderna de México,* vol. 5 (Mexico City: Editorial Hermes, 1957), pp. 19, 31, insert.
[45] In the case of the Huasteca, population numbers and forest ecology were surely affected by conquest, but the sources are too skimpy for details. First, the Aztec conquest of the Huastec in the fifteenth century entailed several waves of attacks and much loss of life, with its ensuing disruption in farming activities that disturb the forest. More significant was the Spanish conquest because it meant not only the loss of life through war and enslavement, but also wholesale depopulation on account of epidemics. It is likely that the native populations of the Huasteca did not recover for centuries, as it happened elsewhere in Mexico. One of the results of depopulation was the expansion of the rainforest. By the late nineteenth century, according to a German writer, the ruins

The People and Their Ecology

Over the centuries, the indigenous peoples of the Huasteca elaborated knowledge and ways of life that allowed them to reproduce their cultures without destroying their habitat. That is not to say that they did not alter the rainforest. On the contrary, like all tropical forest dwellers, they had a significant impact on their environment.[46] The necessities of life required that they make use of the forest and, in the process, change it. The systems of production and science they developed, however, did not result in a wholesale ecological metamorphosis. Despite outsiders' images, life in tropical Mexico was not easy, but human culture and forest ecology adapted to each other.

The same abundant rainfall that made the Huasteca a land of lagoons and forests provided humans with an adequate subsistence. The Huastec, the Nahua, and the Tepehua took advantage of that habitat to engage in fishing, hunting, and farming. Of the three, agriculture was the most important. The native people of the Huasteca developed and practiced a particular type of farming: slash-and-burn, or swidden, agriculture. As long as the population size remained small and stable, the method was sustainable in a tropical ecology. It was, in fact, the only one that made the rainforest capable of producing annual crops. Rainforest soils are typically fragile, thin, and poor for agriculture; nutrients are stored not in the ground, but in the trees and plants that have adapted to those conditions. Swidden agriculture transferred nutrients to the soil for human crops. The method entailed chopping down trees, setting them ablaze, and planting seeds amidst the ashes and charred tree stumps. The fire and ashes were crucial in the process. The flames not only opened up the canopy and allowed sun to reach the forest floor, but also killed fungi, bacteria, parasites, and other organisms that might eat or hurt seeds. The

of pre-Conquest architecture had been swallowed up by the forest entirely. "Ancient Settlements in the Land of the Huaxteca," by E. Seler, a translation from *Zeitschrift für Ethnologie*, vol. 20, (1888) in SMU/ED, Box 110, Folder 5295. Ordoñez, in fact, noted that when he explored the Huasteca for oil he found a "variety of pre-hispanic artifacts throughout." Ezequiel Ordoñez, *El Petróleo en México: Bosquejo Histórico* (Mexico City: Empresa Editorial de Ingeniería y Arquitectura, 1932), pp. 33–36. On disease and conquest, see Toussaint, "Conquista de la Huasteca," pp. 158–163; S. Jeffrey K. Wilkerson, "Presencia huasteca y cronología cultural en el norte de Veracruz Central, México," in *Huaxtecos y Totonacos*, pp. 275–276; Alcorn, *Huastec Mayan Ethnobotany*, pp. 41–43; and Elinor G. K. Melville, *A Plague of Sheep: Environmental Consequences of the Conquest of Mexico* (Cambridge: Cambridge University Press, 1994).
[46] The best study of the ways in which indigenous peoples affected the tropical forest is Warren Dean, *With Broadax and Firebrand: The Destruction of the Brazilian Atlantic Forest* (Berkeley: University of California Press, 1995), Chapters 1–2.

ashes, in turn, served as organic fertilizer for the seedlings that appeared with the first rains. Using that method, a family plot in the Huasteca, typically 1.8 hectares (3.6 acres), produced food crops for some twelve years before the soil's acquired fertility was sapped and weeds intruded. After those dozen years, another slice of forest was cut down while the previous one lay fallow for at least another dozen years to regenerate.[47] This swidden cycle meant that over the centuries, wherever human settlement had taken place, parts of the forest had been felled and burned. With low population density, however, the tropical forest had sufficient time to regenerate and recolonize abandoned plots.

Other types of ecological knowledge served the people and the Huasteca forest well. The Teenek, specifically, learned to identify which forest trees, grasses, and palms were appropriate for building roofs, carving out canoes, and designing fishing implements such as harpoons, nets, and hooks. They also discovered which tree had a waxy bark that was good for making candles. Teenek women, similarly, knew soils: which were suitable for wattle-and-daub walls; which made good pots, dishes, and other kitchen implements; and which were appropriate for vegetable gardens and fruit orchards. Teenek shamans, as well, were expert botanists. They collected and cataloged to memory the curative or preventative properties of leaves, barks, stalks, roots, flowers, seeds, and animal products like honey. They also kept track of poisonous plants and insects.[48] The Teenek also knew oil. They collected the *chapopote* (tar) from its natural springs in the forest and used it as a sealant for canoes, decorative paint for pottery, or fragrant incense in ceremonies.[49] As a whole, such knowledge and practices translated into selective rather than indiscriminate use of the environment for human use. In the long run, Teenek praxis resulted in a coevolutionary approach to life in the rainforest, where they adapted themselves to environmental conditions and lived within their limitations.

[47] William T. Sanders, "Cultural Ecology and Settlement Patterns of the Gulf Coast," *Handbook of Middle American Indians: Archeology of Northern Mesoamerica*, part 2, vol. 11, edited by Gordon F. Ekholm and Ignacio Bernal (Austin: University of Texas Press, 1971), pp. 546–547; H. R. Harvey and Isabel Kelly, "The Totonac," *Handbook of Middle American Indians: Ethnology*, part 2, vol. 8, edited by Evon Z. Vogt (Austin: University of Texas Press, 1969), pp. 643–645; Michael Thomas Ducey, "From Village Riot to Regional Rebellion: Social Protest in the Huasteca, Mexico 1760–1870," Ph.D. Dissertation, University of Chicago, 1992, p. 37.

[48] Starr, *In Indian Mexico*, p. 284; Piña Chán, "El desarrollo," pp. 170–174; Luis Antonio González Bonilla, "Los Huastecos," *Revista Mexicana de Sociología*, año 1, vol. 1, no. 2 (May–June 1939), p. 42; Soto, *El Nuevo Estado*, p. 21. An extensive treatment of twentieth-century Teenek science can be found in Chapters 4–5 of Alcorn, *Huastec Mayan Ethnobotany*.

[49] Piña Chán, "El desarrollo," p. 172.

Even with knowledge, however, life in the tropical forest was competitive and labor intensive, far from Eden. Humans were not assured a place at the top of the hierarchy. On the contrary, they survived only through sustained work and creativity. Growing the staple crop of the Huasteca, corn, is a perfect example. Although not physically exhausting, the *milpa* ruled the rhythms of life in every household and demanded the energies of men, women, and children for most of the year, particularly because the weather patterns of the Huasteca allowed for two annual crops. In the spring of every year, the male head of a household, along with his male relatives, friends, and neighbors, convened to cut down the forest giants. Then the trees, vines, ferns, and orchids went up in flames. Insects and other animals scattered in all directions, while men planted the seeds among smolders and prayed for the rains to arrive. Once the rainy season started, males and females, "old and young," provided the "constant attention" the milpa demanded, as a would-be American plantation owner noted in the late 1890s.[50]

Competition for the corn was fierce. First, a myriad of red ants emerged from the shade to eat the germ of the seed-kernels "as soon as they [were] planted." Then birds with "insatiable appetites" pecked at the sprouts. Next, when the stalks were just over a foot tall, "army worms" gnawed on them if humans did not pick the worms off first. After that, another type of worm ate the cornsilk, while a small bird with a "needlelike" bill pecked at the growing husks "of almost every ear." Finally, parrots, parakeets, raccoons, and deer kept humans busy day and night, chasing them away into the trees, or hunting them as they tried to eat the corn on its cob. Hurricane season then threatened to rot the ripened corn if the family failed to harvest it on time. When hurricanes struck land, the entire crop could be lost. Yet even after the corn had been gathered and husked, a job the entire family shared, it had to be guarded against "the worst of all evils, the black weevil." If the family faltered in caring for the harvested corn, the weevil feasted, destroying the ears in only six weeks.[51] Thus, the life cycle of corn, the weather, and the survival needs of other forest dwellers imposed a particular discipline to indigenous life and reminded them constantly that they were simply one of many beings struggling to reproduce themselves in the tropical rainforest.

Although most daily work and activity in the indigenous communities was dedicated to family subsistence, their system of production

[50] Harper, *A Journey*, p. 73.
[51] Ibid., pp. 74–76, 81; Alcorn, *Huastec Mayan Ethnobotany*, p. 91.

included the world beyond the forest. In the precolonial period, the con-
quered Huastec had been forced to pay tribute to their Nahua overlords
from products they cultivated or animals they captured. Thus, the Aztec
received cotton cloth, macaws, pigments, *chiles*, colorful feathers, and
animal skins from their Teenek subjects. In the Spanish colonial era, all
indigenous peoples were obligated to pay tribute from their products and
perform personal service for a host of Spanish personalities, from Crown
representatives to priests. As the nineteenth century progressed and the
market economy evolved in independent Mexico, Huastecs began to participate in it, too. They dedicated a piece of cleared land for small quantities of coffee or sugar cane and fruit orchards to exchange for cash. They
also extracted sap from the *zapote* tree and sold it as *chicle* (chewing gum
paste). With the proceeds from their sales, Huastec men and women purchased goods brought from the cities by itinerant salesmen on market
days: soap, salt, needles, scissors, and newly indispensable tools such as
machetes.[52]

Thus, the demands indigenous peoples made on the tropical forest
were not sufficient to transform its ecology radically. Their technology
was limited to hand tools powered by human muscle, which meant their
impact was highly localized, mainly to those parts of the forest to which
they periodically returned, their *milpas*. The number of adults was small,
so the tribute per adult was not so taxing of the environment, even if it was
vexing for those who had to pay it. The Teenek, moreover, did not build
towns that entailed clearing larger areas of terrain. Their houses and
milpas were scattered, keeping deforestation to a minimum. There were
few homes and boats, and minimal government offices and churches, the
largest source of demand for local building materials.[53] As a whole, then,
the combined factors of low population numbers, light technologies,
low levels of consumption, and knowledge of ecology accounted for the
maintenance of the tropical forest in the Huasteca.

---

[52] Toussaint, "Conquista," p. 161; González Bonilla, "Los Huastecos," p. 88; Lina Odena,
Totonacos y Huastecos (Mexico City: Museo Nacional de Antropología, 1968), p. 16;
Rosendo Martínez Hernández, "La explotación petrolera en la Huasteca veracruzana. El
caso de Cerro Azul, Ver., 1884–1922," B.A. Thesis, Universidad Nacional Autónoma de
México, 1990, p. 114; Alcorn, *Huastec Mayan Ethnobotany*, pp. 101–102; Escobar Ohmst-
ede, *Ciento Cincuenta Años*, pp. 94, 98–99; Sociedad Mexicana de Geografía y Estadística,
Boletín, vol. 4, no. 2 (ca. 1852), p. 260.

[53] From the colonial period into the nineteenth century, the Huasteca had less than a
dozen towns, spread out over the three modern states of Veracruz, Hidalgo, and San
Luis Potosí. Escobar Ohmstede, *Historia de los pueblos*, p. 38; Ducey, "From Village Riot
to Regional Rebellion," pp. 36–37.

But how did the Teenek see the forest? Did they share a narrative of paradise with other nineteenth-century contemporaries? The question is extremely difficult to answer because very little is known about the Huastec worldview before the second half of the twentieth century. Nevertheless, twentieth-century Huastec indigenous religious beliefs and sentiments reflected vulnerabilities both natural and human that, at the very least, echoed an earlier time. Although the Teenek gradually became Catholic after the Spanish conquest, their cosmology included its own special features into the late twentieth century. They considered the earth female, a "great mother" with power over animals and humans alike. She had a male companion, Time, which was also the wind. The sun was both male and female and governed the world as Jesus, whereas the moon was female, the Virgin, and in charge of plants, animals, and humans. Alongside those omnipotent beings there were many lesser divine figures who influenced rain, wind, plants, and animals. The Teenek also believed there were other deities, sometimes addressed as "saints," that controlled human cultural realms like dance, medicine, health, agriculture, pottery, weaving, construction, and more. The forest, from the Huastec point of view, was not an idyllic paradise. Rather, it was a living entity teeming with not just the creatures that men and women fished, hunted, or harvested, but also with good and evil beings and forces humans could neither see nor control. From pre-Columbian times, in fact, the Teenek were notorious among their neighbors and Nahua conquerors for believing in evil spirits that could become human as male and female witches. Teenek cosmology was nearly as diverse as Huasteca ecology. In this vastly complicated universe, the Teenek concluded that human beings were not the favored children of creation, nor the pinnacle of evolution. Instead, they saw humans as "weak suffering powerless creatures living in the midst of dangers both natural and human."[54]

Human dangers indeed pursued Teenek and forest alike with persistency in the nineteenth century and no doubt reinforced their sense of vulnerability.[55] Both caught the attention of the governing elite in faraway Mexico City as well as the local descendants of Spanish colonists eager to bring capitalist progress to the Huasteca. The Huastec faced

---

[54] Alcorn, *Huastec Mayan Ethnobotany*, Chapter 3.

[55] I do not wish to suggest that other centuries were free of conflict, simply that the ecological dangers that subsided after the devastation of the Spanish Conquest accelerated substantially again in the nineteenth century. For a political history of the Huasteca in the colonial period, see Escobar Ohmstede, *Ciento Cincuenta Años*, and Ducey, "From Village Riot."

intense competition from fellow human beings. At stake was the future of the forest and all its inhabitants.

"Paradise" and "Progress"

Upon gaining independence in 1821, the Mexican founding fathers believed that the nation was an agrarian "backwater" desperate for change. When they sought the cause of such misfortune, they found the culprits in the indigenous population and their communal system of land tenure. The solution they proposed was to shift land ownership to individuals to increase the number of economic actors and propel Mexico into modernity. The impulse toward individualization of land ownership, moreover, became an imperative after Mexico lost close to half of its national territory to the United States in the 1846–1848 War, a defeat the elites blamed partly on Mexico's own weakness. Thus, in the second half of the nineteenth century, the governing elite decided to accelerate the "natural law of progress" and throw open the doors to capitalism, a pattern that held true for all of Latin America at the time.[56] What that meant for the ecology of the Huasteca was determined by the plans powerful Mexicans had for "paradise."

Whenever the Mexican elites saw verdant forests, they felt awed but uneasy. The very existence of "heavenly" landscapes seemed anomalous in a world of railroads, factories, and cities – and a powerful northern neighbor. Under such pressures, the elites soon missed the forest and the trees. They saw "limitless fertility" instead, capable of supporting "40,000,000 people."[57] Engineer Ezequiel Ordoñez, the most important Mexican in the oil industry until 1938, for example, having explored the Huasteca extensively, mused that "it would be difficult to overestimate the production possibilities of this area if it were properly cultivated and attended."[58] Clearly all was not well in "paradise." But, precisely what was wrong? Regarding northern Veracruz, foreigners had offered the answer

[56] Michael T. Ducey, "Liberal Theory and Peasant Practice: Land and Power in Northern Veracruz, Mexico, 1826–1900," in *Liberals, the Church, and Indian Peasants: Corporate Lands and the Challenge of Reform in Nineteenth-Century Spanish America*, edited by Robert H. Jackson (Albuquerque: University of New Mexico Press, 1997), p. 73; Donathon C. Olliff, *Reforma Mexico and the United States: A Search for Alternatives to Annexation, 1854–1861* (Alabama: University of Alabama Press, 1981), pp. 1–22.

[57] Olsson-Seffer, "Agricultural Possibilities," p. 1024.

[58] Ezequiel Ordoñez, "Principal Physiographic Provinces of Mexico," *Bulletin* of the American Association of Petroleum Geologists, vol. 20, no. 10 (October, 1936), p. 1286.

since 1845: the Huastecs. They were "a listless, idle race of Mexicans, retrograding as the year rolls on . . . rapidly," wrote an American. Whereas the *ficus* the same writer described epitomized nature at its most exquisite, "a temple" in fact, the Teenek represented human retrocession rather than progress.[59] Indeed, Chapman the ornithologist concluded that "man himself was here [in the Huasteca] sufficiently primitive to be a part of the fauna."[60] Much less delicate in his language, but more revealing of contemporary elite Mexican attitudes, a Huasteca landowner described his aboriginal neighbors as "wild animals."[61]

The idea that indigenous peoples in the Americas were wild animals rather than humans was not new, of course, harking back to the sixteenth century and the European conquest. In the nineteenth century, however, the notion resurfaced to explain why a landscape remained "Edenic" so late in human history.[62] If the land was completely swathed in green, the elites reasoned, then it was "obviously" fertile. If it was fertile, then it had great agricultural "potential." If its "potential" was not realized, the reason was that there were no people on location to fulfill it. Indeed, the paradise allegory predominated precisely because those who propagated it conceived of the Huasteca as devoid of "real men" – men who worked, sweated, raised crops, and produced culture. Understanding modern capitalist economy as a world where human beings were defined through labor, where daily toil replaced nature with roads, railroads, factories, and cities, the Mexican elites interpreted the rainforest as a place filled entirely with "wild" plants and animals to the exclusion of human beings. That was why the "jungle" was truly Edenic, "only waiting for the hand of man to make it extremely productive."[63]

What these interpretations reveal, ironically, is that the ecology that the Teenek participated in and helped maintain obscured their very presence. The forest hid their crops and labor to the point where outsiders simply erased them from view, to the point where they became faunal specimens, "picturesque" fixtures in the landscape at best, ferocious beasts at

59 Norman, *Rambles*, pp. 116, 118, 143, 169–170.
60 Chapman, "A Naturalist's Journey," p. 539.
61 Quoted in Ducey, "From Village Riot," p. 163.
62 The notion subsisted well into the twentieth century, moreover. As late as the 1990s, a Huasteca mestizo official told his interviewer that the aboriginals were "dumb . . . they don't talk, just like little animals." See Juan Briseño G., "Paz, orden, progreso y solidaridad. Notas sobre la represión en la Huasteca (Hidalgo y San Luis Potosí)," in *Huasteca III*, p. 39.
63 Terry, *Terry's Guide*, p. 49.

worst, but never historical and ecological actors.[64] To outsiders, therefore, agriculture was merely a future possibility, not an ongoing daily
process with centuries of history. Likewise, nature itself was completely
inanimate.[65] The hurricanes, swamps, dunes, mangroves, and forest had
no life of their own as indigenous inhabitants thought. They were objects,
simplified and reduced to passive matter, "land," sometimes imagined as
a female waiting for a male to arrive and make it "extremely productive." Dreams of progress, then, rendered the rainforest and its indigenous ecology as uninteresting, almost invisible, and profoundly disappointing to those tantalized by visions of progress. A new vista was in
order.

Challenging the Indigenous Ecology

Nineteenth-century Mexican elites did not think in ecological terms.
They were economic men, political men, military men forged in the heat
of battles against the Spanish (1810–1821), the Americans (1835–1836;
1845–1848), the French (1861–1867), and each other. Most were men
enamored of the law. So when they decided that communal property was
the greatest structural obstacle to Mexican progress, they changed the
law. Their actions, however, had ecological consequences.

In Veracruz land reform began early in the independence period. On
December 22, 1826, the government issued a decree ordering that "all
the land of indigenous communities, forested or not, will be reduced
to private property, divided with equality to each person...who belongs
to the community."[66] Espousing Liberal notions that accompanied the
nineteenth-century model of capitalist development throughout Latin
America and Europe, the legislature sought to destroy communal land
ownership and replace it with the basis for capitalism, individual private
property. The intent of the law was to transform the aboriginal population into the Mexican equivalent of the yeoman farmer. Instead of patchy

---

[64] The "picturesque" is from Chapman, "A Naturalist's Journey," p. 539.

[65] Merchant calls this "the death of nature," a process of objectification of nonhuman
nature that began in the Western world with the Scientific Revolution of the fifteenth
century. See Carolyn Merchant, *The Death of Nature: Women, Ecology and the Scientific Revolution* (New York: HarperCollins Publishers, 1990).

[66] Ley número 39 sobre división de terrenos de comunidades indígenas y disposiciones
relativas, quoted in José Velasco Toro, "La política desamortizadora y sus efectos en la
región de Papantla, Veracruz," *La Palabra y el Hombre*, no. 72 (October–December 1989),
p. 141.

cornfields hidden amidst solid green, the governing elite wanted recognizable farms open to the sky, aligned along roads, divided by fences, producing crops in neat rows for a market economy, land "properly cultivated and attended," as Ordoñez wrote. The Mexican elite thus imagined a different ecology altogether in the tropical rainforest, the ecology of the cultivated garden. The cultivated garden implied a different relationship between humans and nature from the one that the indigenous population practiced. Instead of humans adapting to their environment so they coevolved, the elite proposed an alternative relationship where man controlled nature and worked to reshape all its elements for his own purposes.

In the Huasteca, mestizo and Spanish elites shared the belief in individual ownership of land, but had no interest in yeoman farmers or gardens: they preferred cattle ranches. Within months of the 1826 decree, they rushed to appropriate indigenous land.[67] They did so by trying to change the ecology themselves: they let loose cattle herds in indigenous communities to trample the milpas and occupy the land. Teenek families found themselves unable to scare away cows as easily as raccoons. Then they found themselves unable to prove to complicit local authorities that the cattle had not always been there: the cattlemen claimed the land belonged to them.

The struggle against cattle was not new. There were Teenek communities, such as the two hundred inhabitants of Amatlán, where old Spanish families from Tuxpan had accumulated land at their expense and pushed them into tenancy agreements by the end of the eighteenth century.[68] These landowners had taken advantage of the natural grasses around Tuxpan and Tampico to introduce cattle and horses and expand their range wherever possible. For most of the colonial period, that expansion had been limited. Weather patterns affected the size of cattle herds. Floods drowned them and droughts starved them, forcing cattlemen to retreat and let the forest reverse the incursion of grass.[69] The wars of independence, likewise, hurt cattle ranching. Hacendados were forced to sell their cattle for slaughter to finance the rebellion against the Spanish Crown. The shortage of coinage on account of the fighting, moreover, momentarily turned cattle into acceptable legal tender and took them off pastures. Hungry troops, furthermore, procured their meals by hunting

[67] Ibid.
[68] Escobar Ohmstede, *Ciento Cincuenta Años*, p. 44; Ducey, "From Village Riot," p. 37.
[69] Escobar Ohmstede, *Historia de los pueblos*, p. 115.

cows.[70] As a result, individual hacendados, no doubt bankrupt from the war, sold out to their tenants. The widow of former Marquis of Uluapa, María Josefa Rodríguez de Uluapa, for example, sold her large 15,380-hectare Buenavista hacienda in Temapache to her 187 indigenous tenants in 1826. The price tag was 3,120 silver pesos "in two payments."[71]

The 1826 law tilted the scales in the hacendados' favor. Eager to recover their losses, the hacendados read the law as an opportunity to let the cattle do the job of appropriating native land. The process was uneven, however. By 1831 a government census found five constituted haciendas in the municipality of Ozuluama, six in Tantima, and thirteen in Tantoyuca. The total number of cows counted was relatively small, however, only 85,613, including 8,397 from neighboring Tampico. The land holdings, moreover, were perceived as "small" or "medium" in size, with the largest around ten thousand hectares (twenty-four thousand acres).[72]

The haciendas, furthermore, were not deforested. Transforming forest into pasture required extensive human muscle: the "forest giants" had to be chopped down by hand with unsophisticated tools, the remains burned and removed to the roots before the land could be seeded for grass. New grass, moreover, required continuous tending to prevent opportunistic weeds from choking it. Cattle herds, in addition, required the carving out of roads to reach their markets. All those activities required labor and capital, neither of which existed in sufficient quantities in the Huasteca in the nineteenth century. The indigenous ecology, thus, had effectively kept the herds, grasses, and hacendados at bay.

Intending to keep that situation intact, indigenous people throughout the Huasteca protested the cattle incursions that followed the 1826 law. They did so peacefully at first, suing in court to expel bovines from their land. As their petitions explained, the Teenek considered cattle herds to be "against the natural order" and wanted them removed.[73] However, the authorities, representatives of the hacendado class, proved unresponsive

---

[70] Ducey, "From Village Riot," pp. 135, 164, 181, 259–260.

[71] Ibid., pp. 207–208; Escobar Ohmstede, *Ciento Cincuenta Años*, p. 197.

[72] By the late nineteenth century, "large" haciendas tended to be around forty or fifty thousand hectares (96,000 to 120,000 acres), with several in the northern states running into the millions of hectares. In Veracruz, the large haciendas were in the southern tropical rainforests, where logging and rubber were the main economic activities. Those haciendas measured over 100,000 hectares (240,000 acres), according to Daniel Cosío Villegas, *Historia Moderna de México* (Mexico City: Editorial Hermes, 1965), vol. 7, part 1, pp. 212–215.

[73] Proposiciones de Olarte al Gobierno General, Tomadas en Junta de Guerra, December 6, 1836, reprinted in Reina, *Las rebeliones*, p. 337. That did not mean that indigenous communities had a peculiar hatred of cows. On the contrary, they kept and raised them

to their concerns or even "abusive."[74] Convinced they had exhausted the legal process, indigenous men opted for violence in 1832. That rebellion would be the first in a series of ecological wars that would last a half-century.

Defending the Native Ecology

Between 1832 and 1874, indigenous communities took up arms in northern Veracruz six times. The rebellions varied in length: 1832–1839; 1847–1848; 1857–1861; 1862–1867 sporadically; 1868–1869; and the last, brief one, in 1872. The immediate causes differed. Some were direct responses to dispossession; others were opportunistic insertions into intra-elite conflicts that promised political advantages to the communities. All armed struggle, however, had the same motivations and objectives: to protect the rainforest and maintain the indigenous ecology. In that endeavor the Huastec were remarkably successful. Many of their communities managed to retain collective control of their lands into the last quarter of the nineteenth century.

The 1832 uprising began in Totonacapan and spread north through the Huasteca. Little documentation remains from this rebellion, but the record shows that mestizos and whites of Spanish descent led the fighting. Indigenous men joined in, however, because the leadership promised what they wanted: the removal of abusive officials and local autonomy.[75] The fighting was intermittent, but it lasted six long years, until government troops finally crushed the leadership in late 1838 and early 1839. Although the rebels lost, the clashes disrupted economic activity in the region, forcing the hacendados to halt their encroachment on indigenous lands and to postpone any attempt at dividing communal lands into individual property.

In the aftermath, elite political perceptions began to change. The state government abandoned the idea that the indigenous men could evolve into yeoman farmers, concluding instead that "*el indio*" was opposed to progress "by nature." By 1844 state authorities decided that only the division of native lands could jumpstart agriculture and raise "the Indian" from his "prostrate" position – an ironic image for men that only five years previously had fought for six years, but in line with the elite's inability to

whenever they could, according to Escobar Ohmstede, *Ciento Cincuenta Años*, pp. 155–156. What they objected to was the replacement of the rainforest ecology with what the hacendados announced with the onslaught of herds.

[74] Velasco Toro, "La política," p. 141.

[75] Ducey, "From Village Riot," pp. 234–240.

see *el indio* as a historical agent. Officials recommended enforcing the 1826 law more vigorously.[76] The movement to break up the forest into grids slowed to a crawl one more time, however, because of war.

One year after the United States and Mexico went to war in 1846, the Huasteca burned again. Contemporaries dubbed the 1847 uprising a "caste" war because "people of color" were in the leadership and "whites" were the target of their rage. Judges were killed, "well-known persons" were jailed, and towns where "Spaniards" congregated were torched like the forest in spring.[77] "Many haciendas and *rancherías* were burned down and sacked; murder and destruction appeared everywhere. Blood ran in torrents, and for ten months the Huasteca was the stage for the most horrible scenes," wrote the hacendado Manuel Soto.[78]

The rebellion had its origins in the same lack of redress the indigenous communities had experienced in the court system in 1827. In 1845 indigenous families had organized to raise funds to obtain copies of the titles to the land invaded by hacendados and thus establish them as the legal owners of disputed land.[79] But their efforts had failed. In Tepezintla, Tantima, Tancoco, San Antonio, and Ozuluama local authorities had handed the land titles over to the hacendados, insisting native families had to rent (their own) land to farm.[80] In protest "several hundred" Teenek from Amatlán peacefully occupied the municipal capital, Ozuluama, in March 1846. Within a week, a federal force from Tampico violently expelled them. By November 1847, the Huasteca was in revolt again. Anywhere between five hundred and fifteen hundred indigenous men armed themselves and waged the form of war most suited to the terrain: guerrilla warfare.[81]

Thus, the rainforest ecology itself played an important role in the war. From their forest fortress, rebels dashed out to destroy "beautiful towns" and "many haciendas," and to hang a judge who "refused to show them the original land titles stored in the municipal archives" that established them as owners.[82] The fact that the forest hid them from elite view now became

---

[76] Velasco Toro, "La política," p. 142.

[77] Manuel B. Trens, *Historia de Veracruz*, Tomo IV, Primer Volumen (Mexico City: 1950), pp. 558–559, 581.

[78] Soto, *El Nuevo Estado*, p. 59.

[79] Ducey, "From Village Riot," pp. 292–294.

[80] General Cos a la Secretaría de Guerra, Programa Rebelde, and Peticiones, reprinted in Trens, *Historia*, Tomo IV, Primer Volumen, pp. 560–564.

[81] Ducey, "From Village Riot," p. 295.

[82] Trens, *Historia*, Tomo IV, Primer Volumen, pp. 581–582; José Velasco Toro, "Desamortización civil y resistencia india en México y Veracruz: de la Independencia a la Reforma," *Anuario* VIII [1992], p. 23; Reina, *Las rebeliones*, p. 343.

an advantage. Time and again, government authorities complained that the rebels were difficult to rout because they disappeared into the forest they knew intimately. From the darkness, rebels could control the only transport routes of the region, narrow foot and horse trails, and ambush troops at will. No one knew where the rebels would strike next, which "disconcerted military and civilian authorities and frightened the landowners of the region."[83] The weather, similarly, favored the rebels and demoralized government troops. Constant rain turned trails into mud troughs. Poorly equipped troops refused to risk their lives trudging through ankle-deep mud and deserted at every opportunity.[84] Undoubtedly the presence of numerous ferocious cats, poisonous plants, and venomous snakes in rebel territory were incentives for desertion, too.

Although indigenous war tactics eventually paid off, the Teenek paid an extremely high price in the short term. A few notorious state commanders met guerrilla tactics with a "war of extermination." They "made war without quarter on [the indigenous population] and carri[ed] off their families; burning the small huts they had built in the hills to avoid death." They used terror against "defenseless Indians," murdering them, stealing their meager possessions, and "treating them badly" when they surrendered.[85] Then federal troops arrived. The retreat of United States troops from Mexican territory in June and July 1848 ended the war in the Huasteca, although not in predictable ways. Freshly defeated by the Americans, the federal troops were supposed to "pacify" the indigenous population, but the terror they encountered affected their decisions. Perhaps federal commanders also took note of the fact that indigenous guerrillas had clashed with U.S. forces occupying Tampico, and hence changed their course of action. In either case, the federal army captured the rebel leadership in July 1848 after bitter fighting near Tamihua. To obtain the surrender of the rest, federal commanders offered a surprisingly attractive amnesty: communal lands could stay.[86] The rebels accepted the offer. The military defeat thus became a political and ecological victory.

A survey of the state of the hacienda in the Huasteca in 1850 confirms that violence had worked as a means of protecting the native ecology. In the aftermath of the rebellion, for instance, some of the 4,839 Teenek of Amatlán recovered parts of their lands. The courts forced landowner Juan N. Llorente to sell them "a good portion" of the Hacienda San Benito. A

---

[83] Reina, *Las rebeliones*, pp. 328, 330, 354.

[84] Ducey, "From Village Riot," p. 315.

[85] *El Noticioso*, August 9, 1848, quoted in Ducey, "From Village Riot," pp. 307–308.

[86] Ibid., pp. 309–310, 321–324.

similar process took place around Tuxpan, where various communities bought out ruined hacendados.[87] The native population then resumed their agricultural and cultural practices, protecting the forests of Amatlán from wholesale bovine assault.

The rebellions, likewise, had protected the forest from cattle in another way: through the consumption of the animals themselves. Insurgents and soldiers alike stole cattle, butchered it, and ate it on the run, depleting the herds once again.[88] As the local elite admitted, the hacienda was in undeniable decline at mid-century. The herds tended "to degenerate" and the owners "abandoned everything to nature."[89] The few figures available illustrate the point. Around 1852, the municipalities of Tuxpan and Tamiahua had three haciendas each.[90] Property values plummeted. An hacendado lamented that land costing 100,000 pesos in Mexico City did not even fetch 500 in the Huasteca.[91] Such low prices, no doubt, helped native communities purchase (their own) land. Indigenous victory was undeniable, if not acknowledged.

The next armed conflicts the Huasteca engaged in left very little documentation behind but suggest an opportunistic intent. The context was the War of the Reform (1857–1861) and the French occupation (1862–1867). The first conflict was triggered by the Liberal reforms of 1856, which deprived the Catholic Church of its extensive landholdings, separated it from the state, introduced freedom of thought, speech, and religion and other civil liberties as part of the overall plan to modernize Mexico along capitalist lines. Mexican Conservatives, however, rose up in arms against the Reform in 1857.[92] Although the *Ley Lerdo* (named after its author, Miguel Lerdo de Tejada) also dismantled communal indigenous land tenure systems, there is no evidence that native men took the Conservative side when the hacendados of the Huasteca split and fought each other. In all likelihood, indigenous men fought against particular hacendados based on their own local grievances. What the record does

[87] Sociedad Mexicana de Geografía y Estadística, *Boletín*, vol. 4, no. 2 (ca. 1852), pp. 263–265; Ducey, "Liberal Theory and Peasant Practice," p. 69; Ducey, "From Village Riot," p. 312; Escobar Ohmstede, *Ciento Cincuenta Años*, pp. 127, 197.

[88] Cosío Villegas, *Historia Moderna*, vol. 7, part 1, p. 136.

[89] Francisco López Cámara, *La estructura económica y social de México en la época de la reforma*, cited in Ducey, "From Village Riot," p. 210.

[90] Sociedad Mexicana de Geografía y Estadística, *Boletín*, vol. 4, no. 2 (ca. 1852), pp. 241, 257.

[91] Soto, *El Nuevo Estado*, p. 53.

[92] The Conservatives also objected to the new 1857 Constitution's Liberal principles in general. See Michael C. Meyer, William L. Sherman, and Susan M. Deeds, *The Course of Mexican History* (Oxford: Oxford University Press, 1999), pp. 359–369.

show is that the intra-elite war in northern Veracruz hurt the hacienda system overall, thus serving the cause of indigenous communities in the short term.[93] Embattled haciendas meant native forest left alone.

There is no question that Teenek men entered the fray in 1862, however. In January the French invaded Mexico, with Conservative support, and toppled the victor of the War of the Reform, the Liberal President Benito Juárez. In the Huasteca, the Liberal hacendado faction raised a one-thousand-man army to fight the thirteen hundred French troops that occupied Tampico. Many volunteers were seasoned indigenous guerrillas.[94]

Although their ostensible enemies were the French, the Teenek must have had recent Veracruz legislative maneuvers in mind as well. In 1862 the state government decreed that undivided communal land would be considered "vacant" (*terrenos baldíos*) from then on. That meant that anyone could file a formal claim (*denuncio*) to such land and obtain title on a first-come, first-served basis.[95] Thus, the state of Veracruz finally made legal the metaphorical disappearance of the indigenous population and the forest ecology implied in the Edenic narrative. As of 1862, "paradise" was legally empty land. The missing "hand of man" that would make it "productive," moreover, would be preferably foreign, the war against the French notwithstanding. The legislature decided that land declared vacant would be made available to colonists from abroad. In this program the Veracruz elite shared the view, then widespread in Latin America, that European immigration was the perfect cure for all that ailed them.[96] Those who refused to comply with the law would face "severe penalties."[97] The fighting, however, prevented the enforcement of the law for another six years, until the French-anointed monarch, Emperor Maximilian, was captured, tried, and executed in 1867.

The war against the French, like the War of the Reform, had hurt the hacienda system in the Huasteca, with a little help from nature, too. Flooding during the war in the 1863–1864 rainy season damaged

---

[93] Ducey, "From Village Riot," p. 343; Trens, *Historia*, Tomo V, Primer Volumen, p. 455.

[94] Ducey, "From Village Riot," pp. 392–393, 340–341, 402.

[95] The 1869 Veracruz law had a precedent. The Ley Lerdo included a provision for turning *terrenos baldíos* into private property through *denuncias*, but its application had been limited by political turmoil, according to Konrad, "Tropical Forest Policy," p. 126.

[96] José Velasco Toro, "Indigenismo y rebelión totonaca de Papantla, 1885–1896," *América Indígena*, vol 39, no. 1 (1979), p. 86; Soto, *El Nuevo Estado*, pp. 23–24.

[97] Memoria presentada por el ciudadano gobernador Francisco Hernández, del estado libre y soberano de Veracruz-Llave, a la H. Legislatura del mismo, en noviembre 30 de 1870, reprinted in Escobar Ohmstede, *Historia de los pueblos*, p. 224.

haciendas in Ozuluama and beyond. Cattle epidemics followed. Then clashes with the French in 1864 resulted in the burning of the town of Ozuluama itself. The same year, Liberals sacked the town of Tantoyuca while the French and their Conservative allies burned down Amatlán and Tamiahua. The Liberals burned Pánuco in 1866. As was customary, all armies attacked cattle directly. Countless cows ended up on soldiers' dinner plates instead of indigenous land.[98]

Native men used their arms against the haciendas directly, too. An hacendado lawyer wrote that in Temapache, for instance, indigenous guerrillas "accustomed to being in the vanguard of all the political revolutions" flexed their military muscle to secure land titles. In 1868 they "influence[d] the decision of the courts" in their favor and "confiscated" cattle to boot.[99] Likewise, a group of Nahuas forced the pro-French Llorente clan to sell them the Hacienda El Nopal in 1867.[100] In the mid-century national wars, therefore, a number of factors conspired against the hacienda in the Huasteca, giving indigenous men the opportunity to exercise the leverage of arms not only against foreign invaders but also to reclaim land that was historically theirs.[101] The departure of the French, however, did not mean the end of armed conflict over land and ecology in the Huasteca.

The restoration of the Republic brought traditional enemies back to center stage in the Huasteca. The peace allowed state officials to fan out across northern Veracruz and implement land division with a vengeance. The forest was cut up into small pieces and assigned to heads of household. In enough cases the hacendados, more often than not members of local officialdom themselves, increased their own holdings enough to elicit indigenous response.[102] Nahuas, Otomíes, and Teenek staged armed protests in 1868 and again in 1869 against such abuses. None of these clashes, however, became full-scale insurrections.[103]

---

[98] Trens, *Historia*, Tomo V, Primer Volumen, pp. 455, 470, 546; Cosío Villegas, *Historia Moderna*, vol. 7, part 1, p. 150.

[99] Quoted in Ducey, "Liberal Theory," p. 80.

[100] In this case the property encompassed 18,695 hectares (44,868 acres) and was sold for seventy-five hundred pesos. Escobar Ohmstede, *Ciento Cincuenta Años*, p. 183; Trens, *Historia*, Tomo V, Primer Volumen, p. 457.

[101] The proof is in the fact that in areas remote from the fighting communal lands were divided. See Escobar Ohmstede, *Historia de los pueblos*, pp. 157–159. Ducey also notes that "four or six towns" had carried out the law before 1880 in "From Village Riot," pp. 367–368.

[102] Gutiérrez Rivas, "La familia Herrera," pp. 34–41; Escobar Ohmstede, *Ciento Cincuenta Años*, pp. 108–109.

[103] Escobar Ohmstede, *Historia de los pueblos*, p. 182.

In 1870, Governor Francisco Hernández summarized the advances and failures in land reform to date. He began by expressing his frank exasperation with native resistance to the privatization of land ownership. He deplored that "the Indian professes a fanatical adoration for the land and he does not understand its utility," even after a half-century of elite efforts to do the contrary. Elite ideas about the slothfulness of the indigenous population, their degenerate nature, and the Edenic quality of the tropical rainforest remained obviously unchanged, as the governor reiterated that the reason for the "negative communion" between indigenes and land was because *el indio* was "rich" because of fertile soil. The native "lives easily," Hernández lamented, needing only to "reach out his hand" to obtain his daily bread like Adam in the Garden. Thus, the Indian responded to land reform with "inflexible apathy," argued Hernández, an inaccurate characterization in light of fifty years of indigenous armed resistance, but in keeping with a narrative of paradise where effort of any kind is unnecessary. The solution the governor proposed, predictably, was more of the same: enforcement of the law, application of penalties for noncompliance, and, when necessary, "the use of force" and "the spilling of blood" until all vestiges of communal land were but a distasteful memory and indigenous men were "useful members of society," "producers . . . consumers . . . taxpayers."[104]

Despite his frustration, the governor had good news for Liberal modernizers. His report on individual Huasteca municipalities showed that indeed most communal land had been carved into individual lots. At the time, the Huasteca was divided into four large *cantones*, themselves divided further into municipalities. The *cantones* were, from north to south, Tampico de Veracruz (or Ozuluama), Tantoyuca, Tuxpan, and Chicontepec. According to the report, Tampico de Veracruz had no communal land left. Tantoyuca was almost all divided, with the exception of the Teenek municipality by the same name. In Tuxpan the recalcitrants were the indigenous communities in Temapache and Amatlán, the same who had bought land from the hacendados over the last half-century. Chicontepec, the Nahua *cantón* on the southwest Sierra Madre piedmont, was the least divided of them all. There none of the municipalities reported successful privatization of land.[105] Thus, the relative peace and stability the region enjoyed during the restoration of the Republic had

---

[104] Memoria, pp. 225–226.
[105] Ibid., pp. 226–227.

yielded results. Most of the tropical forest in the Huasteca had individual owners. Individual ownership, however, did not mean automatic ecological change. A shift in land use patterns was necessary, and given the history of the Huasteca, those were not guaranteed. Political turmoil, however, was.

In 1872 President Benito Juárez suffered a heart attack and died in office. Although Lerdo became president without major incidents, the hacendados in the Huasteca clashed over local political control. The fighting lasted two years. Although the evidence is sketchy, it is likely that indigenous men participated in the conflict, given that the factions hurt the haciendas directly. Armed men sacked individual haciendas and set others aflame. Records, land titles, and other evidence of land reform turned to cinders as rebels torched towns. Finally, hungry guerrillas feasted on quadrupeds again in the last armed combat of the century.[106] Thus elite violence unwittingly benefited the native ecology. The fighting halted hacendado economic pursuits, removed the environment threat that cattle represented in the areas of active conflict, and forced the state to respond to indigenous concerns at long last. At the end of the war, a new Veracruz land reform was in place. This one was a political victory for indigenous communities and the ecology they continued to defend so fiercely.

The 1874 Compromise

The December 7, 1874 law begrudgingly recognized the legitimacy of indigenous communal landownership at last. It stipulated that in those municipalities where the division of land into individual property was impossible "owing to the conflicts it could generate," local authorities could proceed to divide communal land into large lots with multiple owners each, a land tenure pattern known as a *condueñazgo* (collective ownership or joint tenure). The condueñazgo was a modified version of communal property that had existed in the Huasteca in practice, if not in legal theory, since colonial times. It was the system that Teenek and other groups that obtained land in Temapache, Amatlán, and elsewhere used to establish ownership over the haciendas they had bought over the course of the nineteenth century.[107]

---

[106] Trens, *Historia*, Tomo VI, pp. 132–137; Escobar Ohmstede, *De la costa a la sierra*, p. 182.
[107] Velasco Toro, "Indigenismo," p. 87.

The system was not complicated. A group of male or female heads of household (anywhere from ten to two hundred individuals) owned the land collectively. In theory, each *condueño* owned a clearly delineated lot within the condueñazgo. In practice, however, none did. The ninety-six Teenek of the future oil town of Zacamixtle who bought 41,150 hectares (98,800 acres) in 1884, for example, neglected to subdivide it into ninety-six individual lots.[108] The co-owners, as well, were banned from selling any part of the condueñazgo, a prohibition that was easy to enforce so long as the owners did not delineate individual lots. Furthermore, the owners added regulations to condueñazgos not contemplated in state law. They required forest conservation measures on their land and prohibited felling trees for commercial use, a clear recognition of the fact that their forest was under pressure.[109]

After 1874, the condueñazgo became as important a land tenure system as the hacienda. The historical record is silent on how it compared to the hacienda in total acreage because many condueñazgos did not register their titles, but it is clear that most indigenous communities with access to land preferred it to other arrangements.[110] It is likely, furthermore, that the success of the condueñazgo explains why indigenous men ceased violent activity in the Huasteca after 1874. That is not to say, however, that the hacendados followed their example or the Mexican elite gave up their assault on native land in the name of "progress."[111] On the contrary, the winds were gathering for the last, brief political hurricane of the nineteenth century.

"Order and Progress"

In 1876 the Huasteca hacendados put on their final belligerent performance of the century. This time the clash involved partisans of the

---

[108] Escritura, AGN/DP, Caja 9, Exp. 39, 040/60.

[109] Escobar Ohmstede, *Ciento Cincuenta Años*, pp. 143–144, 180–181, 190–191.

[110] There is substantial debate about the dominance of the hacienda at the end of the Porfiriato in general, as the older historiography that cast it as hegemonic comes under question. Even those old estimates, however, argued that Veracruz was among the states with the lowest percentage of families living in haciendas: less than 25% in 1910, which suggests that the condueñazgo had strength. See Jean Meyer, "Haciendas y ranchos, peones y campesinos en el porfiriato. Algunas falacias estadísticas," *Historia Mexicana*, vol. XXXV, no. 3 (January–March 1986), pp. 477–509.

[111] Scholars continue documenting cases of violent repression of native communities in Hidalgo and San Luis Potosí in the second half of the twentieth century in *Huasteca III*, for example.

incumbent presidential candidate, Lerdo, and the armed challenger, Porfirio Díaz, both old Liberals. Before Díaz emerged as the victor, the whole of the Huasteca witnessed combat. Guerrillas set the town of Temapache on fire as a few more cattle met their demise.[112] The merry-go-round of nineteenth-century political violence in the Huasteca was on its last spin, however. The new strongman who occupied the presidential chair soon put an end to regional conflicts and unveiled a novel plan for national progress. Indigenous land ownership systems and ecology were the main targets – again. In contrast to his predecessors, Díaz made rapid impact on the former, setting the stage for others to tackle the latter later.

Díaz took possession of a country wracked by three-quarters of a century of political turmoil. His priorities, therefore, were explicit in his motto: "order and progress," in that exact sequence. Order was entrusted to a special rural police force known as the *rurales*. Their efficiency would keep Díaz in power for the next thirty years.[113] Progress was the task assigned to a group of highly educated men who called themselves *los científicos*. They studied, espoused, and put in practice the most fashionable American and European ideas, which made them economic liberals and social conservatives.[114] As such, none entertained the idea of equality for indigenous peoples, much less the acknowledgment of their ecological knowledge and practices. The transformation of the tropical rainforest, that blank screen for the projection of the Científicos' development fantasies, became more urgent than ever.

The Porfirians developed the most comprehensive plan ever to change indigenous land tenure patterns and thus eliminate the indigenous ecology. It took into consideration both the people and the forest in different but complementary ways. The idea of making yeoman farmers out of indigenous men was abandoned. The relative optimism of earlier Liberals gave way to a profound disillusionment with Mexico's native population. A Mexico City newspaper summarized that despair succinctly when it editorialized in 1895 that "nothing, absolutely nothing could be expected" from indigenous men who "could not even imagine the possibility of cultivating" something other than "corn and beans."[115] Their tropical location, however, was valuable insofar as it "represented an untapped

---

[112] Trens, *Historia*, Tomo VI, pp. 156, 169, 171.

[113] On the rurales, see Paul J. Vanderwood, *Disorder and Progress: Bandits, Police, and Mexican Development* (Wilmington, DE: Scholarly Resources, 1992).

[114] On the Científicos, see Charles A. Hale, *The Transformation of Liberalism in Late Nineteenth Century Mexico* (Princeton, NJ: Princeton University Press, 1989).

[115] Quoted in Cosío Villegas, *Historia Moderna*, vol. 4, p. 150.

economic potential."[116] To fulfill it, the Científicos decided to tear apart "the negative communion" between aboriginals and land the Veracruz governor deplored by means of a simple yet ecologically radical scheme. They would sell Eden to foreign investors.[117]

Foreigners, in turn, would simplify the tropical ecology by mutating it into a mosaic of monocrop plantations producing for an international market. "Vacant land" would be filled with a cornucopia of exotica destined for foreign consumers: "coffee, tea, cacao, sugar, spices, fruits, fibers, rubber, camphor, vegetable oils, condiments, drugs, tobacco,... rice ... arrowroot and cassava."[118] If the investor was not partial to plantations, the Mexican government could oblige. The "magnificent arboreal vegetation," announced the Mexican Ambassador to the United States, could just as easily become "cabinet woods."[119] Few other economic activities were (and are) as destructive of life in a forest than logging, as systematic removal of the "giants" affects the habitat of every other creature and the contours of the land in general. But the Mexican elite dismissed such changes as "side-effects."[120] In either case, indigenous men had a role to play. They would become the hands that picked the fruit of the plantations. If farm work did not suit them, they could become loggers instead.[121] However, before the forest could attract investors from abroad to transform it into a capitalist paradise, the prickly question of indigenous property had to be revisited and resolved once and for all.

As in the early days of the Liberal Republic, state and federal governments teamed up to implement land reform. This time around, however,

---

[116] Konrad, "Tropical Forest Policy," p. 127.

[117] Tenorio-Trillo, *Mexico at the World's Fairs*, pp. 114–115.

[118] Olsson-Seffler, "Agricultural Possibilities," pp. 1025–1026.

[119] Quoted in Konrad, "Tropical Forest Policy," p. 127.

[120] Dean demonstrates the effects of logging in Brazil, whereas Cronon illustrates the New England case. Dean, *With Broadax*, Chapter 12; Cronon, *Changes*, Chapter 6. Konrad does note that the Díaz government was concerned about forest conservation because they knew that deforestation affected climate, flood control, and rainfall. However, those concerns focused only on the Mexican highlands and coniferous forests. Konrad, "Tropical Forest Policy," pp. 128–131.

[121] Many indigenous men did indeed become loggers in the *monterías* of Tabasco and Chiapas, but the topic has not been researched. The most vivid descriptions of logging camps in southern Mexico come from the six "jungle novels" that B. Traven wrote in the 1930s. Traven traveled extensively through southern Mexico and derived his fiction from that experience. See B. Traven, *Government; La Carreta; March to the montería; Trozas; The Rebellion of the Hanged;* and *The General from the Jungle;* also, Friedrich Katz, *La servidumbre agraria en México en la época porfiriana* (Mexico City: Ediciones Era, SepSetentas, 1976), p. 27.

the objective was more ambitious: wrestling land out of the hands of indigenous proprietors altogether. To move in that direction, the national Congress passed the *Ley de Colonización* in 1883. The new law authorized private land companies to survey "public" lands "for the purpose of subdivision and settlement." In payment, the companies could retain up to one-third of the land they mapped out and could be the first in line to buy the remaining two-thirds "at bargain prices." For the purposes of the law, "public land" was defined as any plot whose occupiers could not produce a legal title on demand.[122] Following suit, the Veracruz legislature passed a law in 1889 (*Ley sobre subdivisión de la propiedad territorial*) that forced the condueñazgos to assign individual lots to each owner for the purposes of receiving individual land titles. Those persons who did not comply with the law thus risked having their land declared public. Five years later, Congress passed additional legislation allowing the exploitation of "public" lots all over the country. As a result, over 134 million acres of Mexico's territory ended up concentrated in the hands of survey companies and hacendados.[123] Included among the first was the English engineer and surveyor, Weetman Pearson, whose Mexican properties would transform him into one of the world's richest oilmen.

In Veracruz, the new laws had profound consequences for indigenous landowners. The condueñazgos were subdivided among their multiple owners, despite much peaceful and legal resistance. The Teenek who had purchased the San Benito hacienda in 1859, for example, divided their condueñazgo into individual lots in 1895. So did the inhabitants of San Jerónimo, a condueñazgo near the coast of the Tamiahua Lagoon, who partitioned their land into individual plots in 1906. Similarly, the Teenek of Zacamixtle broke up their land into ninety-six individual plots in November 1896, fourteen years after its initial acquisition.[124] By the early twentieth century, the reapportionment was complete. Table 1.3 lays out a sample of the partitioning as recorded by various oil companies. Although the total number of lots is unknown and their ownership disputed, it is clear that for the first time in history, hundreds of indigenous

[122] Meyer et al., *The Course*, p. 433. The Colonization Law was meant to attract foreigners, too. See *La Gaceta Oficial* (LGO), State of Veracruz, no. 60 (May 2, 1893).

[123] Velasco Toro, "La desamortización," p. 148; Konrad, "Tropical Forest Policy," p. 128; Meyer et al., *The Course*, p. 444.

[124] On San Benito, see Ducey, "Liberal Theory," p. 69; on San Jerónimo, see Escritura, AGN/DP, Caja 7, Exp. 18, 032(2)/14; and on Zacamixtle, see Escritura, AGN/DP, Caja 9, Exp. 39, 040/60.

Table 1.3. *Land Divided into Individual Lots in the Huasteca*

Municipality	Number of Individual Lots
Tantima	421
Tancoco	174
Chinampa	316
Amatlán	393
Tamalín	290
Zacamixtle	130
Tamiahua	200
San Diego de la Mar	87
Cerro Azul	4
Toteco	5

Sources: List of Applications for Confirmatory Concessions Pending, Enclosure No. 1-B to dispatch No. 1550 of June 28, 1934, from the Embassy at Mexico City, Record Group 59, General Records of the Department of State, Records of the Department of State Relating to Internal Affairs of Mexico, 1930–1939, Roll 125, 812.6363.2779; Map by J. Corry, Tampico, June 1915, American Heritage Center, International Archive of Economic Geology, Edward D. Lynton Collection, Acct. 4553, Box 14.

households became private owners of individual lots. What experiments would they carry out under the new status? Would private ownership affect their ecological practices?

Private Property and Ecology in the Late Porfiriato

The privatization of the condueñazgos during the late Porfiriato introduced new dynamics to the social and ecological struggle in the Huasteca. The hacendados' agenda advanced in some areas, but in others indigenous communities emerged stronger. In some places indigenous private ownership did not last. Before long, the plots became the property of hacendados. By 1895, for instance, Ozuluama boasted a total of twenty-five haciendas; Tantoyuca counted thirty-one. The majority of these belonged to the influential Herrera family, but the Saínz Trápaga clan was not far behind. The patriarch, Spanish-born Angel, acquired all the land between the Tamesí and Pánuco rivers, about seven miles in length, and called the family's new haciendas El Tulillo and Chapacao. Other minor haciendas were sold to American colonizers, who began felling nameless trees along the Pánuco River and replacing them with orange and banana seedlings.[125] As the hacienda grew, predictably, some indigenous communities disappeared as such. By 1900, for example, census takers in Ozuluama and Pánuco reported that neither municipality had any individuals who spoke a native language.[126]

Further south the transfer of property can be outlined in more detail. In Temapache, for instance, the Gorrochótegui clan raised to dominance in the process. Manuel Gorrochótegui, an old Liberal, had held the post of *jefe político* (chief political officer) of Tuxpan since 1872, while another member, Gabriel, became the "administrator" for the Buenavista condueñazgo (in native hands since they bought out the Marquis de Uluapan in 1826). Gabriel held that post for five years and, as a result, became Tuxpan's *jefe político*, while Manuel took the same post in Tantoyuca. By the early twentieth century, those political appointments helped the family accumulate 13,040 hectares (31,296 acres) of prime Huasteca forest at the expense of Teenek and Nahuas. Included among those landholdings were 6,343 acres (2,537 hectares) off the Buenavista hacienda itself.[127] The Herrera family, similarly, successfully combined political and economic ambitions to acquire 65% of the haciendas in Tantoyuca by the last decade of the nineteenth century.[128] The realignment of property

[125] Gutiérrez Rivas documented that the Herrera family owned a total of sixty-two different pieces of land in northern Veracruz. They ranged from four hundred to five thousand hectares in size (nine hundred sixty to twelve thousand acres), but there is no information on the total acreage they controlled. Gutiérrez Rivas, "La familia Herrera," pp. 57, 67–77; 79, 93–95. By 1910, Angel Saínz Trápaga was the Spanish Consul in Tampico and a loyal Porfirian, according to Marcial Ocasio Meléndez, *Capitalism and Development: Tampico, Mexico 1876–1924* (New York: Peter Lang, 1998), pp. 121, 136. The information on Americans comes from Testimony of Herbert S. Gilkey, in U.S. 66th Congress, Senate, Committee on Foreign Relations, *Investigation of Mexican Affairs*, vol. 2 (Washington, DC: Government Printing Office, 1920), pp. 980–989; Testimony of Herbert S. Gilkey, ibid., p. 1710; Testimony of J. G. Ward, ibid., p. 1163.

[126] Mexico, Dirección General de Estadística, *Censo General de la República Mexicana*, verificado el 28 de octubre de 1900 (Mexico City: Oficina Tipográfica de la Secretaría de Fomento, 1904).

[127] Trens, *Historia*, Tomo VI, p. 127; Alma Yolanda Guerrero Miller, *Cuesta Abajo: Declinación de tres caciques huastecos revolucionarios: Cedillo, Santos y Peláez* (Mexico City: Editorial Miguel Angel Porrúa, 1991), pp. 74–76; Informe, AGEV/CAM, Exp. 1759.

[128] Gutiérrez Rivas, "La familia Herrera," p. 67.

relations brought about social changes as well, even if the forest itself endured.

As hacendados increased the size of their properties, the indigenous households affected found themselves unable to provide for their families as before, or, if they were made landless, not at all. Those realities pushed males to work for wages or to become tenants, or some combination thereof, soon after becoming private owners – often in their own former landholdings. Although the evidence is extremely thin, it seems that men preferred to perform temporary labor until they earned enough cash to rent land for family farming.[129] As one American in Tuxpan complained, indigenous men "collect[ed] their earnings and return[ed] to their homes, no matter how urgent the demand for their continued service may be."[130] Because population size remained low, however, social and economic developments did not threaten the forest as seriously as they did the well-being of individual families. The haciendas still lacked sufficient labor and capital to spread ranching rapidly.

The Huasteca hacendados were caught in a bind during the late Porfiriato. They needed capital and labor to change the ecology, but the ecology made both scarce. Even though the expansion of the hacienda forced indigenous men into a labor market, the low population density forced the hacendados to pay higher wages than their brethren elsewhere in Veracruz.[131] An American shopping for an hacienda in Tuxpan in 1896 noted, for instance, that "the price of labor here has increased greatly of late years."[132] In Ozuluama that meant that day laborers earned 37¢ for agricultural work and up to 50¢ for tending cattle in 1887.[133]

Better wages in northern Veracruz, nonetheless, did not support a landless family. In 1896 an American reported that "a pound of coffee" in Tuxpan cost 50¢, "the equivalent in value to the labor of an able-bodied man for twelve hours."[134] Similarly, in February 1910, before the

---

[129] That may explain why temporary labor was much more common in Veracruz than in any other Gulf state, according to Francisco G. Hermosillo Adams, "Estructura y movimientos sociales," in *México en el siglo XIX (1821–1910): Historia económica y de la estructura social,* edited by Ciro Cardoso (Mexico City: Nueva Imagen, 1994), p. 481.

[130] Harper, *A Journey,* p. 67.

[131] Doheny Mexican Collection (DMC), Labor File I, Item #1101; Katz, *La servidumbre,* pp. 29–30; and Alan Knight, "Mexican Peonage: What Was It and Why Was It?" *Journal of Latin American Studies,* vol. 18, part 1 (May 1986).

[132] Harper, *A Journey,* p. 57.

[133] Cosío Villegas, *Historia,* vol. 7, part 1, p. 137.

[134] Harper, *A Journey,* p. 68.

Revolution broke out and overthrew Díaz, the U.S. Consul in Veracruz reported the following prices:

  1 kilo of beans, 36¢
  1 kilo of beef, 46¢
  1 kilo of corn meal, 46¢
  1 kilo of potatoes, 20¢
  1 dozen eggs, 3¢
  1 dozen sugar cubes, 11.5¢

Given that the Huasteca had no transportation links to large cities and their commercial facilities, it is safe to assume that prices would have been higher.[135] For an indigenous family, therefore, as long as there was land available, using relatively high wages to rent relatively cheap land made economic sense. One result of the privatization of indigenous land, then, was an increase in land rental agreements.

One arrangement in particular reveals the complex interplay between ecology, capital, labor, and the hacendados' determination to transform the forest into a profit-making enterprise. In Cerro Azul the hacendados developed a tenancy system that did not require monetary transactions. Instead, they contracted tenants to change the ecology themselves. The arrangement was called *a cuenta zacate* (in exchange for grass). It entailed the following: The hacendado who did not have sufficient capital to underwrite the transformation of the rainforest allowed the tenant to use a plot of land for a specific number of harvests without paying rent. At the end of the last harvest, however, the tenant paid the hacendado by leaving the land seeded with grass.[136] Under this system, the tenant who had no money to lease could nonetheless farm and feed his family. It was his responsibility, however, to find the means to obtain grass seed on the last year of the lease. It is quite likely, therefore, that the tenant and his family performed some wage labor for the hacendado, or that the family made the extra effort to raise a small cash crop alongside the milpa for the money needed for seed. Thus, indigenous families adapted flexible strategies to manage the vagaries resulting from their introduction into the world of private ownership. It is likely that similar arrangements existed beyond Cerro Azul, accounting for the *potreros* (pastures) that Doheny found in neighboring haciendas, such as "Potrero

[135] Monthly Trade and Consular Reports, no. 353, February 1910, DMC, Labor File I, Item #1149.
[136] Martínez Hernández, "La explotación petrolera," p. 108.

del Llano" in Temapache.[137] Slowly, but not surely given the prolonged history of ecological struggle in the region, the grass and cattle that the native population fought throughout the nineteenth century began to spread under the Porfiriato.[138]

Nevertheless, there is evidence that private ownership had been beneficial to indigenous families and the forest alike. Anthropologist Frederick Starr, for example, found the Teenek of Tancoco meeting their needs well into 1901. The candid photographs he took of the community show almost all inhabitants wearing shoes. In addition, he reported that the community had a schoolhouse and the homes were lighted with kerosene lamps. A sure sign that Tancoco had crossed the threshold of survival was the fact that the families bought labor saving machinery for the women. "Many, if not all, of the women had sewing-machines," reported Starr. To greet him, in fact, the women dressed in their "best calico, muslin, silk and satin." Moreover, the women of Tancoco fixed their hair with "laces and artificial flowers," neither of which they produced themselves. In addition, Starr noted that the women wore what must have been their most expensive personal luxuries: high heels.[139] The fact that they had such possessions reveals that their families had confidence in their ability to pay for them and that whoever sold them the goods shared the same optimism.[140] So did Starr, in fact, who praised the Teenek as "the cleanest, most industrious, best dressed and most progressive Indians whom we had seen in any part of Mexico."[141]

The Teenek of Tancoco were clearly not living in abject misery in 1901, but neither were they experimenting extensively with the ecology. Although Starr did not mention farming practices, other observers described "Indians" farming in the familiar pattern of corn for family consumption and sugarcane "growing in little patches spread out like handkerchiefs" for the market.[142] In other areas where indigenous

---

[137] PanAmerican, *Mexican Petroleum*, p. 95.

[138] Indeed, in neighboring Totonacapan comparable changes led to renewed violence through the 1890s and early 1900s, but in the Huasteca, apparently, tensions did not reach crisis proportions in those years. Reina, *Las rebeliones*, p. 359.

[139] Starr, *In Indian Mexico*, p. 285.

[140] Traveling salesmen made their way to the Huasteca by 1896, according to Serapio Lorenzana, who produced a small Huasteco-Spanish dictionary just for that purpose. He failed to report what was sold and what sorts of payment arrangements were made, however. Serapio D. Lorenzana, *Un intérprete huasteco* (Mexico City: Oficina Tipográfica de la Secretaría de Fomento, 1896).

[141] Starr, *In Indian Mexico*, p. 285.

[142] Campbell, *Mexico*, p. 46.

communities maintained their access to land, cotton was the preferred cash crop of the late Porfiriato.[143] In Tancoco, moreover, cash income derived also from selling palm hats, "the single industry" Starr noticed. Thus, the Teenek of Tancoco showed that through legal and extralegal means, on both communal and privately held land, indigenous communities of the Huasteca had accomplished something that was becoming increasingly rare not only in Mexico but also in the world: they managed to protect the rainforest, to coexist and evolve with it, its flora, and its fauna, not in harmony, but at least reciprocally. With Doheny's arrival in 1900, all would change rapidly, radically, and permanently.

Throughout the nineteenth century, indigenous Mexicans checked the advance of the hacienda in northern Veracruz and maintained the complexity of the region's ecosystems. Confronted with an elite eager to transform the tropical rainforest from an "Edenic" site into a thriving capitalist enterprise, the native population of the Huasteca successfully resisted repeated attempts to eliminate their communal land tenure patterns. Using peaceful and violent means as necessary, the Teenek of northern Veracruz rejected fashionable notions of progress and individualism that dispossessed them of their land and threatened to destroy the ecology. In contrast to local and national elites, indigenous farmers did not see the rainforest as unproductive and rejected every nineteenth-century law that transferred land to the hacienda system. Thus they spent a half-century waging ecological warfare until they succeeded in gaining recognition of their land tenure practices in 1874. And even though a new group of policy makers compelled native owners to become private owners and accelerated the expansion of the hacienda in the last quarter of the century, many aboriginal communities managed to make private ownership work for them or to negotiate relatively flexible tenancy and labor agreements with hacendados. As a result, when the nineteenth century closed, the indigenous ecology prevailed over all others in the Huasteca. But just ahead, in 1900, the oil hurricane was beginning to form.

[143] Kuecker, "A Desert," p. 262.

PART TWO

THE ECOLOGY OF OIL

2

CONTROLLING THE TROPICAL FOREST

THE SHIFT IN LAND TENURE PATTERNS

> Mientras trabajaba en Zacamixtle, una vez llegó un norteamericano, empleado del departamento de terrenos de una de tantas compañías petroleras, se alojó en mi campamento unos cuantos días y después desapareció sin decir a dónde iba, ni qué hacía, para regresar pasadas varias semanas, con la barba crecida, mugroso y enlodado...se trataba de un agente de la compañía que andaba en busca de un campesino, para lograr que le vendiera las regalías correspondientes a su propiedad...de los tantos que con engaños...obtenía los derechos correpondientes a los propietarios cuando el petróleo brotara, disfrutando de una ganancia que los convertía en rentistas, sin haber hecho otra inversión, que la pérdida de varios días o semanas.
>
> Manuel Mesa Andraca, 1981

Although the hacendados did manage to increase their landholdings during the Porfiriato, they did not succeed in breaking the Indians' "negative communion" with the tropical rainforest of the Huasteca. The oilmen from the United States and Britain did. They took two decades, from 1900 to 1920. Dispensing pesos as readily as the hacendados had dispensed bullets, the oilmen achieved what had eluded Mexican elites for at least a century: the wholesale alienation of indigenous land and conversion of the lush forest into a revenue stream. But the native population was not the only one who lost control of the rainforest. The hacendados did, too. Eagerly entering into deals with the oil companies, they found themselves shortchanged when the wells started producing oil like sprinklers on a lawn. Both groups reacted to the changes. In all cases, the protesters extracted small and large sums of money from the companies, but there was no stopping the oil entrepreneurs. They created a true real estate market out of the rainforest, commodifying it thoroughly for the first time in its history.[1] Thus, the foreign oilmen achieved in two decades what Mexican elites had failed to do in a century: a radical shift in land tenure patterns. That was the first major transformation in the ecology of oil.

Law and Nature

The foundation for the transfer of the rainforest from indigenous peoples and hacendados to the oilmen was the legislation that President Díaz passed to promote capitalism in Mexico. Facilitating capitalism had been the intent of land laws in the nineteenth century, but they had not been sufficient to encourage private enterprise and attract foreign investment in the extractive industries, mining and petroleum. Until the Porfiriato, the mining laws derived from colonial Spanish law, which maintained that "the juices of the earth" (*los jugos de la tierra*) belonged to the Crown. Upon independence in 1821, the Mexican governing elites kept the concept of national ownership of the subsoil spelled out in the 1783 Royal Ordinances for Mining in New Spain.[2] The Liberal Constitutions of 1824 and 1857 retained that principle, and President Juárez reiterated that the nation had "direct dominion" over carbon deposits and similar products once again in 1863.[3] The assumption the Spanish had made since the fifteenth century was that the Crown owned nature within its dominions, including whatever rested deep within the earth. The Crown had obtained that privilege from the Pope as the official protector of the Catholic faith, and, hence, as God's designated steward of "all the world" and its creatures.[4] The Mexican Liberals had dropped the religious justification but they had maintained the assumption that the state, as the steward of the nation, owned nature as well.

[1] The process is comparable to the one Brian Black describes for Pennsylvania in the nineteenth century in *Petrolia: The Landscape of America's First Oil Boom* (Baltimore: John Hopkins University Press, 2000).

[2] *Reales Ordenanzas para la Minería de la Nueva España*, quoted in Petróleos Mexicanos, *El Petróleo* (Mexico City: PEMEX, 1980), pp. 14–15. The idea that the earth produced "juices" that became metals and minerals had a long history in European thought, beginning with Aristotle. See Merchant, *The Death of Nature*, p. 26.

[3] Ocasio Meléndez, *Capitalism*, p. 99; José Vázquez Schiaffino, Joaquín Santaella, and Aquiles Elorduy, *Informes sobre la Cuestión Petrolera* (Mexico City: Imprenta de la Cámara de Diputados, 1919), pp. 17–18.

[4] The quote is from the *Requerimiento* as reproduced in Patricia Seed, *Ceremonies of Possession in Europe's Conquest of the New World, 1492–1640* (Cambridge: Cambridge University Press, 1995), p. 7.

The Porfirians of the late nineteenth century, however, abandoned the concept of state control. They privatized nature. Just as they privatized communal land based on the assumption that nature was not productive on its own or under indigenous land tenure systems, they abandoned the idea that gave the state ownership of the subsoil. Five times between 1884 and 1909, the Mexican government passed laws asserting the principle that whoever owned the surface of the earth owned whatever existed below it. Moreover, the owner was free to exploit both at leisure and without government permits. The first two laws, passed in 1884 and 1892, made no particular reference to oil, limiting their terms to mining. Both established, however, that all mineral products were the "exclusive property" of the surface owners. The first law specific to petroleum appeared in December 1901. It authorized oil exploration on "vacant" lands, defined as areas controlled by the federal government. The law also allowed oil exploitation on riverbeds and coastal lands up to fifty miles from shores, both officially under federal jurisdiction. In addition, the law "granted the right of way through private lands" as needed. The question of ownership of the subsoil, however, was missing from the 1901 law. The oversight was corrected in the second petroleum law of November 1909, which declared outright that oil was the "exclusive property" of the surface owner, following the principle established in the mining law of 1884.[5]

Several writers have argued that it was President Díaz's personal friendship with the oilmen that motivated the 1901 and 1909 legislation.[6] Although that was probably the case, it was also true that oil did not figure prominently in the Científico agenda. Díaz's Minister of Hacienda (Treasury) for two decades (1893–1911), José Ives Limantour, organized a two-man commission to investigate "the country's oil prospects" in 1901, but did not give it high priority. When the two researchers presented contradictory reports, the Díaz cabinet believed engineer Juan D. Villarello, who concluded that "the countless oil seepages of [northern Veracruz] indicated that any substantial oil deposits which might have existed had been dissipated through leakage." Engineer Ezequiel Ordoñez, who argued exactly the opposite, found himself unemployed. Never one to let a good opportunity pass him by, Doheny promptly hired Ordoñez as a consultant. That settled the issue for the Científicos: if the foreigners

---

[5] Meyer, *México y los Estados Unidos*, pp. 49–50; Petróleos Mexicanos, *El Petróleo*, pp. 17–19; Ocasio Meléndez, *Capitalism*, p. 113.

[6] See, for example, José López Portillo y Weber, *El petróleo de Veracruz* (Mexico City: Comisión Nacional Editorial, 1976), p. 18; Javier Santos Llorente, *Episodios petroleros* (Mexico City: PEMEX, 1988), pp. 26–30; Ocasio Meléndez, *Capitalism*, p. 113.

wanted friendly legislation to invest in a losing proposition, they were happy to oblige.[7] The oilmen, of course, knew a winning proposition when they saw one.

"Men of Greed and Grandeur"

Twentieth-century foreign oilmen understood crude. They did not see it either as the Spanish "juices of the earth" or as the mid-nineteenth-century American "Nature's secret spring" that healed aches and pains.[8] They saw oil as "black gold." In similar fashion, they saw the forest as real estate, as a commodity that could be leased, bought, or sold for the purpose of making a profit. In that sense, the oilmen were truly pioneers in the Huasteca: harbingers of the new age of capitalism. Although many foreigners invested in the Mexican oil industry, only two "men of greed and grandeur" mattered to the early history of oil in northern Veracruz: Doheny the American and Weetman Pearson, the English engineer.[9]

When Edward L. Doheny descended on the Huasteca in 1900, he had just struck "liquid gold" in Los Angeles, California and was determined to reproduce his success in Mexico.[10] Beneath the stunning foliage, Doheny found what he was really looking for, "a bubbl[ing] spring of oil," one of hundreds scattered throughout the rainforest. The "joy of the discovery" led him straight to the bank. He secured a loan and immediately purchased two enormous haciendas five miles west of Tampico from the Saínz Trápaga family, El Tulillo and its neighbor, Chapacao. Together they covered 448,000 acres (181,496 hectares).[11] The total purchase price for

[7] E. DeGoyler, "Memorial," *Bulletin* of the American Association of Petroleum Geologists, vol. 34, no. 5 (May 1950), pp. 985–987; Ordoñez, *El petróleo*, pp. 52–53.

[8] The quote is from a poem that Seneca Oil used to advertise the supposed "curative powers" of oil, reproduced in Yergin, *The Prize*, p. 20.

[9] The description of the oilmen comes from Richard O'Connor, *The Oil Barons: Men of Greed and Grandeur* (Boston: Little, Brown and Company, 1971). For a more laudatory view, see Ruth Sheldon Knowles, *The Greatest Gamblers: The Epic of American Oil Exploration* (New York: McGraw-Hill Book Company, 1959). For a brief history of other early foreign oilmen in Mexico, see Jonathan Brown, *British Petroleum Pioneers in Mexico and South America*, Texas Papers on Latin America, Paper no. 89–17, Institute of Latin American Studies and Department of History (Austin: University of Texas, 1989).

[10] He had made his first million only a few years before. Caspar Whitney, *Charles Adelbert Canfield* (New York: D.B. Updike, 1930), p. 149; Margaret Leslie Davis, *Dark Side of Fortune: Triumph and Scandal in the Life of Oil Tycoon Edward L. Doheny* (Berkeley: University of California Press, 1998), pp. 20–33.

[11] Robert Glass Cleland, *The Mexican Year Book, 1920–1921* (Los Angeles: Mexican Year Book Publishing Co., 1922), p. 293; PanAmerican Petroleum, *Mexican Petroleum*, p. 85.

both haciendas was the princely sum of 925,000 pesos ($479,500).[12] Doheny, nonetheless, was confident. His investment was sound. "We felt that we knew," he told his audience in 1921, "and we did know, that we were in an oil region which would produce in unlimited quantities that for which the world had the greatest need – oil fuel."[13] The fact that Mexico itself had no market for petroleum in 1900 was not a deterrent. Based on his California experience, Doheny knew he could create a national market and export oil, too. Thus, he incorporated the Mexican Petroleum Company and built an experimental plant in his new properties as he enticed another U.S. concern, the Mexican Central Railroad, to convert its locomotives from coal to fuel oil. While contract negotiations with the railroad proceeded, Doheny convinced the cities of Guadalajara, Morelia, Durango, Puebla, Chihuahua, Tampico, and Mexico City to pave their streets with a novelty item derived from petroleum, asphalt. As an incentive to city officials, Doheny made the terms easy: the cities could pay *en abonos* (installments) for the pavement.[14] In 1905 Doheny signed with the Railroad and in 1907 he organized a second company, the one that made Cuextlan famous worldwide, the Huasteca Petroleum Company. To grease the political wheels, moreover, he made available 508 shares of preferred stock in Mexican Petroleum to President Díaz, who accepted them no doubt graciously. Thus, Doheny began to acquire the "jungle kingdom" that would make him a multimillionaire many times over before he sold out to Standard Oil in 1925.[15]

Weetman Pearson enjoyed a longer acquaintance with Mexico and its president. In 1889, President Díaz contracted Pearson to engineer the first of several major environment-altering projects.[16] These included the drainage of Mexico City, the dredging of Veracruz harbor, and the

---

[12] Javier Santos Llorente, "Los gobernadores," in *El Petróleo en Veracruz*, by Javier Santos Llorente, Manuel Uribe Cruz, Mirna Alicia Benítez Juárez, Rodolfo Zavala, and Alberto J. Olvera Rivera (Mexico City: PEMEX, 1988), pp. 35–37; Fritz L. Hoffman, "Edward L. Doheny and the Beginnings of Petroleum Development in Mexico," *Mid-America*, vol. 24, New Series vol. 13, no. 2 (April 1942), p. 100.

[13] PanAmerican, *Mexican Petroleum*, p. 17.

[14] *El Mundo*, March 13, 1938; BP, vol. 11, no. 2 (February 1921), p. 103; "Sketch of the Career of a Famous Oil Pioneer," *The Petroleum Review*, vol. 34, no. 718, New Series (April 22, 1916), p. 341.

[15] Davis, *Dark Side*, pp. 104–105; Kevin Starr, *Material Dreams: Southern California through the 1920s* (Oxford: Oxford University Press, 1990), p. 125.

[16] Pearson had extensive experience in such projects. Yergin notes "he was responsible for several of the engineering marvels of the nineteenth century," which included tunnels under the River Thames in London and the East River in New York. Yergin, *The Prize*, p. 230.

building of the southern Veracruz Tehuantepec Isthmus railroad line, among others.[17] The most ecologically sensitive project, oil exploitation, Pearson undertook on his own. In April 1901, he was in Laredo, Texas, waiting for a train connection. The town was "wild with excitement" over the "Lucas Gusher well" drilled at Spindletop in February. As he reflected on the news, a brilliant idea occurred to him. He cabled his agent in southern Veracruz, ordering him "to secure an option on oil land with all land for miles around." He explained further "that oil deposits frequently extend over big areas, so the oil rights must extend over a large district to be really valuable. 10, 20, or 40,000 acres appears to be no uncommon size – so in getting the option, get it over as big a country as possible."[18] Thus, Pearson and Doheny transformed the rainforest into a prized commodity almost overnight.

Doheny and Pearson became the principal beneficiaries of Porfirian legislation, but not equally. The 1901 petroleum law allowed them to explore far and wide, and helped them erect the duopoly they would hold over the industry until they both sold out in the 1920s. Pearson, however, took the lead in gaining concessions in 1903 when he bought out a British company called the Oil Fields of Mexico, which owned 390 square miles in Totonacapan, immediately south of the Huasteca. In January 1906, moreover, the Mexican government accepted Pearson's bid to survey the "vacant" rainforest throughout Veracruz. He received one-third of the land surveyed in payment as the 1883 Colonization Law permitted. He won similar bids for the states of San Luis Potosí, Tamaulipas, Tabasco, Chiapas, Campeche, and Puebla, much to Doheny's chagrin. The terms of the concessions were for fifty years and included "valuable exemptions from taxation."[19] By March, Pearson reported that he owned "about 600,000 acres" (240,000 hectares) and had leases for up to 300,000 more (120,000 hectares).[20] In recognition of the special relationship between the Englishman and the president, Díaz posed with Pearson at one of the early wells, holding a *jícara* (gourd) full of the "first Mexican petroleum"

[17] Brown, "British Petroleum Pioneers," p. 7; J. A. Spender, *Weetman Pearson First Viscount Cowdray, 1856–1927* (London: Cassell and Company, Ltd., 1930), p. 188.
[18] W. D. Pearson to Body, San Antonio, Texas, April 19, 1901, P&S/HR, Box C 43, File C 43/1.
[19] Agreement with Oil Fields of Mexico Company, June 15, 1911, P&S/HR, Box C 45, File C 45/1; C. Reed, "History of S. P. & Son's Oil Interests in Mexico," P&S/HR, Box C 43, File C 43/1; Ocasio Meléndez, *Capitalism*, pp. 114–115; Petróleos Mexicanos, *El Petróleo*, p. 23.
[20] Quoted in Spender, *Weetman*, p. 152.

extracted from the earth.[21] When Pearson incorporated the *Compañía de Petróleo "El Aguila," S.A.* in 1908, furthermore, he included Díaz's son on its Board of Directors. That same year in July, El Aguila drilled one of the world's richest wells at San Diego de la Mar. Legislation clarifying the ownership of the substances residing deep within the earth became understandably urgent. Hence the 1909 law reaffirming that the owner of the surface of the earth also had "exclusive" ownership of nature below it. With the earth's depths legally established as private property, nearly five hundred different oil companies opened offices in Mexico. Pearson himself, described by contemporaries as "physically and morally a bulldog," became Lord Cowdray in 1910 and so closely identified with his Mexican interests that his British Parliamentary peers dubbed him the "member for Mexico."[22]

The Land Grab

Details regarding the oil companies' control of land are neither exact nor orderly. The evidence is too fragmentary to establish which company controlled how much, where, and when. Nonetheless, there is no doubt that the Doheny (Huasteca Petroleum) and Pearson (El Aguila) interests dominated the landscape, competing favorably with Mexico's greatest hacendados.[23] Two tables make the case. Table 2.1 shows the acreage that Doheny and Pearson controlled throughout Mexico, in comparison to that held by all other oil companies together as well as by a third large American company that operated in the Huasteca, PennMex, and the smaller Royal Dutch Shell subsidiary, La Corona. Table 2.2 shows how much those four companies controlled in northern Veracruz alone.

A comparison of the tables shows that the entire one million acres (489,512 hectares) that Doheny controlled by 1922 was in the Huasteca. Similarly, the three hundred thousand acres (120,000 hectares) that PennMex accumulated by 1916 was all in the region, specifically around Alamo, on the northern banks of the Tuxpan River, whereas La Corona's

[21] Igancio Muñoz, *La tragedia del petróleo* (Mexico City: Ediciones Cicerón, 1938), p. 40.

[22] The characterization of Pearson comes from the article "Lord Cowdray: The British Oil-King Behind the Mexican Crisis," *Current Opinion* (February 1914), in SMU/ED, Box 139, Folder 5823, Scrapbook, Clippings, Vol. 1; Ocasio Meléndez, *Capitalism*, p. 116.

[23] The Terrazas family of Chihuahua was Latin America's largest landholder, controlling some seven million acres during the same period, but they were exceptional. The richest landowners after the Terrazas owned three hundred thousand acres, less than the oil companies. Meyer et al., *The Course*, p. 444.

Table 2.1. *Acres of Land Owned or Leased Throughout Mexico, Selected Oil Companies*

Company	1900	1906	1917	1919	1922
Huasteca	448,295		514,051		1,223,780
El Aguila		900,000	1,410,237	1,604,212	1,890,286
PennMex			300,000		
La Corona			20,000		
Total			5,892,665	6,720,392	

Sources: Robert Glass Cleland, *The Mexican Year Book, 1922–1924* (Los Angeles: Times-Mirror Press, 1924), p. 293; PanAmerican Petroleum & Transport Company, *Mexican Petroleum* (New York: 1922), p. 85; J. A. Spender, *Weetman Pearson First Viscount Cowdray, 1856–1927* (London: Cassell and Company, Ltd., 1930), p. 152; *The Petroleum Review,* vol. 34, New Series, no. 706 (January 29, 1916), p. 87; *Boletín del Petróleo,* vol. 12, no. 2–3 (August–September, 1921), p. 153; Informe de la Comisión Técnica, Departamento del Petróleo, Caja 7, Exp. 3.011/3; *Boletín del Petróleo,* vol. 3, no. 3 (March 1917), p. 215; Draft of Letter proposed for Report, 1922, The Papers of Everette Lee DeGoyler, Sr. Mss 60, Box 101, File Folder 5106; Summary of El Aguila Company's Holdings in Mexico, March 1, 1919, The Papers of Everette Lee DeGoyler, Sr., Box 104, File Folder 5157; José Vázquez Schiaffino, Joaquín Santaella, and Aquiles Elorduy, *Informes* (Mexico City: Imprenta de la Cámara de Diputados, 1919), p. 37.

Table 2.2. *Acres of Land Owned or Leased in Northern Veracruz, Selected Oil Companies*

Company	1900	1916	1919	1922
Huasteca	448,295			1,223,780
El Aguila			550,542	770,321
PennMex		300,000		
La Corona		20,000		
Total				2,314,101

Sources: Robert Glass Cleland, *The Mexican Year Book, 1922–1924* (Los Angeles: Times-Mirror Press, 1924), p. 293; PanAmerican Petroleum & Transport Company, *Mexican Petroleum* (New York: 1922), p. 85; *The Petroleum Review,* vol. 34, New Series, no. 706 (January 29, 1916), p. 87; Summary of El Aguila Company's Holdings in Mexico, March 1, 1919, The Papers of Everette Lee DeGoyler, Sr., Box 104, File Folder 5157; PanAmerican Petroleum & Transport Company, *Mexican Petroleum* (New York: 1922), p. 85.

Table 2.3. *Acres of Land Owned and Leased Throughout Mexico, All Companies*

Land Status	1917	1919
Owned	1,755,332.5	1,693,882
Leased	4,137,332.5	5,026,510
Total	5,892,665	6,720,392

Sources: Boletín del Petróleo, vol. 12, no. 2–3 (August–September, 1921), p. 153; José Vázquez Schiaffino, Joaquín Santaella, and Aquiles Elorduy, *Informes* (Mexico City: Imprenta de la Cámara de Diputados, 1919), p. 37.

acreage was concentrated around the Pánuco River in Ozuluama. El Aguila, by contrast, divided its nearly two million acres (756,114 hectares) roughly in half between northern Veracruz and the Isthmus of Tehuantepec, which included land within the borders of Veracruz, Tabasco, and Chiapas. In the 1930s when Huasteca Petroleum was already part of Standard Oil and El Aguila was a subsidiary of Royal Dutch Shell, the companies would expand beyond the Gulf and control at least twenty-four million acres (ten million hectares) before expropriation. According to the Mexican government, more than half of the land the companies held throughout Mexico until the 1920s was leased, rather than owned. The breakdown between them for the two years recorded is as follows (Table 2.3): in 1917 the companies leased 70% of the nearly six million acres (2,357,066 hectares) under their control. Two years later, that number had grown to 74%.[24]

Although similar breakdowns for the two million acres of Huasteca land the companies held are not available in the record, it is possible

[24] The Department of Petroleum reported the companies controlled 10,859,300 hectares (26,833,330 acres) by 1927. In 1931, the Los Angeles daily *La Opinión* put the acreage at 30,854,403, but the government recorded "between 15–24 million acres" by 1938. "Revista de las actividades petroleras en México, durante el año 1926," *Boletín del Archivo General de la Nación*, La legislación petrolera en México, 1887–1927, Tercera Serie, Tomo VII, vols. 3–4 (July–December 1983), p. 79; *La Opinión*, March 1, 1931; Government of Mexico, *Mexico's Oil: A Compilation of Official Documents in the Conflict of Economic Order in the Petroleum Industry, with an Introduction Summarizing Its Causes and Consequences* (Mexico City, 1940), p. 90.

to approximate the percentage of the Huasteca rainforest leased and owned by the companies. Taking the rough estimate of five million acres as the size of the Huasteca, the fact that the companies held the rights to 2,314,101 acres meant that by 1922 they had legal control of approximately 46% of the territory. That shift in land tenure had no precedent in the history of the Huasteca. Neither the Aztec nor the Spanish empires had affected local land ownership patterns to such a degree. When the Mexican governing elite and the local hacendados had tried in the nineteenth century, they had failed. How were the oil moguls able to carry out such a dramatic transformation in two decades without inciting armed rebellion as the hacendados had done before them? The answer lies in the convergence of legal, political, and economic factors, not the least of which was the role of the hacendados themselves.

The Hacendados Do Business

The oil barons appeared in the Huasteca at a time of intense local maneuvering around land issues. As the state government forced indigenous communities to divide their condueñazgos into individual lots, the local hacendados had siphoned off some of those lots and increased their own holdings. The base they had accumulated thus put them in a good position to negotiate with oilmen eager to acquire as much land as possible as rapidly as possible. And negotiate they did. Some hacendados with properties in Tuxpan began selling exploitation rights to foreigners as early as 1881.[25] Others followed the example of the Sainz Trápaga clan who sold El Tulillo and Chapacao to Doheny in 1900 and became handsomely rich in the process. As Mexican Petroleum reported in 1913, "every landowner who sold to us during the early days of our operation was the envy of his neighbors, and was convinced that he had made a good bargain."[26] Appendix I lists forty-five of those "enviable" deals that influential hacendado families made with oil companies. A quick glance shows that some families became regular clients: the Cárdenas family leased or sold five properties; the Sánchez, four; the Nuñez and the Gorrochótegui-Peláez clans seven each. The Herrera clan closed the most deals, at eleven.

The hacendados were highly motivated businessmen. The reason most gave for leasing or selling land to the oil companies was, ironically, that the

---

[25] Cleland, *The Mexican Year Book, 1920–1921*, pp. 290–291.
[26] Quoted in Wendell C. Gordon, *The Expropriation of Foreign-Owned Property in Mexico* (Washington, DC: American Council on Public Affairs, 1941), p. 49.

terrain was unsuitable for cattle ranching. The *chapopote* puddles in the rainforest floor, they said, were cow traps. Temapache hacendado Manuel Peláez Gorrochótegui, for example, was seventy-five years old when he explained that his family had leased its lands to the oil companies because the "damned *chapopoteras*" in their properties mired the animals and "with ropes and tree trunks we had to make every effort to rescue" them before the crude oil vapors poisoned and killed them.[27] Such occurrences were so routine that, according to American geologist Everett Lee DeGolyer, the hacendados were happy to part with their "worthless jungle" when oilmen came calling.[28] The notion that bovine asphyxiation accounted for hacendado dealings with oil companies was repeated so often that it became legendary, reproduced in Mexican popular literature from 1928 to 1986 to the exclusion of all other reasons.[29] The imagined Eden, on closer inspection, had turned out to be a living hell for the ranchers, who saw oil companies' cash as their only salvation.

Although cattle poisonings were not rare in forests with oil pools and no fences, there were more weighty environmental reasons for the hacendados to traffic in Huasteca land. The ecology of the region overwhelmed their capacity to transform it. El Tulillo and Chapacao, for example, were huge swamps and rainforests, packed with "thousands of precious woods," particularly ebony, the tree that gave its name to the town where Doheny set up his experimental refinery – El Ebano, over the San Luis Potosí border. Despite their size, neither had produced much by way of agriculture or meat.[30] As an adventurous American hacendado named Henry Harper discovered, the precondition for any large-scale agricultural economic activity in the region, the felling of the forest, was an impossible proposition in the absence of abundant supply of both labor and capital. Nature

---

[27] Quoted in Gabriel Antonio Menéndez, *Doheny el cruel: valoración histórica de la sangrienta lucha por el petróleo mexicano* (Mexico City: Ediciones Bolsa Mexicana del Libro, 1958), p. 76.

[28] Tinkle, *Mr. De*, p. 27.

[29] For example, Gregorio López y Fuentes wrote in his 1939 novel that "all the lands that had *chapopoteras* were considered of the worst quality, to the extent that the owners wanted nothing more than to sell them or exchange them. This is due to the fact that the cows, when their waterholes dried up, went to those places looking for water and died stuck in them." *Huasteca* (Mexico City: Ediciones Botas, 1939), p. 15. See also Francisco Martín Moreno, *México negro, una novela política* (Mexico City: Joaquín Mortiz, 1986), p. 13; Xavier Icaza, *Panchito Chapopote* (Xalapa: Universidad Veracruzana, 1986), reprinted from the 1928 original, p. 18; Indiana Nájera, *Poza negra (la tragedia de Poza Rica)* (Mexico City: Ediciones Océano, 1985), p. 102; and Carlton Beals, *Black River* (London: Victor Gollancz, Ltd., 1935), p. 69.

[30] Menéndez, *Doheny*, p. 21.

began to regenerate as soon as men put down axes and machetes. Harper described the tribulations shared by his neighboring hacendados thus:

> Mr. A. was delayed in getting his foreman and had the customary diffi-
> culty in hiring help. Three hundred men were all he could muster at
> first, and they were secured only by paying a liberal advance of twenty-
> five per cent over the usual wages. They began cutting timber about the
> 28th of April – the season when this work should have been finished,
> and continued until the rainy season commenced, when scarcely any of
> the clearing had been burned; and after the rains came it was impossi-
> ble to start a fire, so the whole work of felling upwards of four hundred
> acres of forest was abandoned. Every stub and stump seemed to shoot
> up a dozen sprouts, and growing up through the thick layer of brush,
> branches and logs, they formed a network that challenged invasion by
> man or beast. The labor was therefore all lost and the tobacco project
> abandoned in disgust.[31]

Even men of capital felt the pressures of the rainforest when they first approached it. Pearson was a good example. He incorporated the Veracruz Land and Cattle Company in 1907 to produce meat for his pro-jected oil camps and its anticipated hungry workers. But the Englishman found out what the hacendados already knew, that cows were alien to the rainforest and did not thrive in it without major ecological transforma-tions. Pearson's heifers were easy targets for snakes and tarantulas. They also fell victim to illness-bearing ticks. Because they had to be imported from outside the rainforest, the "cattle have not learnt what to eat and what not to," so they ingested poisonous plants that made them "stop eating and wont [sic] touch anything until they die," wrote a despondent employee. Felling the forest to make it comfortable for cows, moreover, was costly and often futile: as soon as the rainy season started, the forest began growing back and the fences nailed in to protect the cattle rot-ted and rusted. As Pearson's manager reported, the "artificial pastures" burned in May by November had *monte* (bush) "grown up so thick it was impossible for a man on horseback to ride through it...One can never get a job finished, for by the time it is done it is nearly time to do it again."[32] The Veracruz Land and Cattle Company, therefore, regretted to inform its owner that it was losing money.[33] Harper himself, "after a

---

[31] Harper, *A Journey*, p. 61.

[32] A. Primrose to Harold Pearson, Minatitán, December 6, 1909, March 30 and Novem-ber 16, 1910, P&S/HR, Box E6, File E6/3.

[33] Brief Report of Work Carried on by the Vera Cruz Land & Cattle Company, S.A. from April 1 to December 18, 1909, P&S/HR, Box E6, File E6/3.

few months' experience in contending with the multiplicity of pests and perversities" he found in Tuxpan in 1896, gave up on his sugar plantation dreams. Instead, like other Huasteca hacendados, Harper found a way out of his "injudicious investment": leasing his land to an oil company. He made a contract with an unnamed company in 1908 for "a sum nearly as large as I expected ever to realize" in tropical agriculture.[34]

The difficult and uncooperative environment, therefore, gave plenty of economic reasons for hacendados to make transactions with oil companies. Selling rendered them infinitely more cash than they could hope to earn from agriculture or ranching, as the case of El Tulillo and Chapacao shows. The Romero Rubio family, President Díaz's in-laws, likewise, sold their recently acquired 346,562 acres in the Isthmus of Tehuantepec to Pearson for five hundred thousand pesos in cash.[35] In northern Veracruz, the situation was no different. The hacendados remained as indebted as they had been since independence. Although the Porfiriato had given them the opportunity to encroach on indigenous lands legally, it had not protected them from the expenses associated with their new possessions.[36] Furthermore, if selling seemed too drastic a proposition, leasing was a very attractive way to ensure a steady income. Pearson, for example, had advised his manager in 1901 to pay "a nominal sum down say 500 to 1000 [pesos] a month for the option for [a] period of not less than two years nor more than three years," rendered in cash. In addition, he recommended offering "a sum for oil – say 10, 20, 50, or 100,000 as you may be able to arrange." Although he was confident the terms would be more than acceptable to local hacendados, he reminded his manager that "if you are not careful they will jump up their terms." Hence he recommended to act "peremptorily and promptly" to "get the thing very cheaply."[37] And cheap he managed, acquiring the Romero Rubio rainforest for 1.44 pesos per acre, compared to the two pesos an acre that Doheny paid for El Tulillo and Chapacao. Before it became clear that underground rivers of oil crossed the Huasteca, in fact, hacendados in

---

[34] Harper, *A Journey*, p. 62.

[35] Main Points Re: Purchase of Land from the Romero Rubio Estate, P&S/HR, Box E 3, File E3/3.

[36] Velasco Toro argues that was the case for the hacendados that appropriated Totonaca land in neighboring Papantla. He does not specify what the money was spent on, however, but he implies that some indigenous families were paid cash for their individual lots. Velasco Toro, "La política desamortizadora," p. 162.

[37] W. D. Pearson to Body, San Antonio, Texas, April 19, 1901, P&S/HR, Box C 43, File C 43/1.

Tuxpan sold their lands to Pearson at rock-bottom prices: as little as 60 Mexican cents per acre.[38] The hacendados, however, were elated. Given their difficulties with the Huasteca rainforest, the offers that oilmen made looked like their financial salvation.

Nevertheless, there were also political reasons for the hacendados to participate in the process of transforming the rainforest into a commodity. Although the historical record is silent in this regard, it is safe to assume that indigenous insurrection was not far from the hacendados' minds when they signed on the dotted line. After all, they had acquired their holdings at the expense of indigenous inhabitants whose violent resistance to loss of land was etched in recent memory. If the hacendados feared that uprisings taking place in neighboring Totonacapan in 1906 might spread to the Huasteca, it would make perfect sense to extract whatever possible and immediate economic gain the oil companies offered.[39] Some hacendados, moreover, might have sold out calculating that if the indigenous population rose up in rebellion over the land taken, they would have pulled a double coup: their money would be in the bank and it would be the companies who would have to contend with angry guerrillas.[40] Surely, then, both environmental reality and historical memory encouraged the hacendados to sell off the rainforest quickly and cheaply.

Indians and Geologists

Unlike the hacendados, indigenous owners had no political or ecological reasons to make deals with the oil companies. Yet hundreds of them did. Why? Why would the indigenes whose guerrilla forefathers fought to retain control over the rainforest give it all up when it was still largely theirs? The answer is both easy and complex. The bait that attracted indigenous owners was simple: money. The process that led to the wholesale alienation of the rainforest, however, was mystifying to most indigenous households. By the time they understood fully the implications and the meaning of the transactions, it was too late. The oilmen controlled the forest.

---

[38] Tinkle, *Mr. De*, p. 27.

[39] Reina, *Las rebeliones*, p. 359.

[40] Also in 1906 the indigenes who claimed the land the Romero Rubio family sold to Pearson, the Popoluca, rebelled in protest against their dispossession. Richard Bradley, "Processes of Sociocultural Change and Ethnicity in Southern Veracruz, Mexico," Ph.D. Dissertation, University of Oklahoma, 1988, p. 118–119. The conflict between the Popoluca and El Aguila was still simmering in 1936, as reported in Mexican Estates, February 25, 1936, P&S/HR, Box E3, Cia. Mexicana de Bienes Inmuebles, S.A.

Most indigenous owners never met Pearson or Doheny. Their encounters with oilmen occurred piecemeal, as discrete groups of company men, each with its own agenda and task in the master plan for changing local land tenure patterns, appeared in individual communities. Indigenous owners did not know how these men were related to each other or what sorts of blueprints they carried in their heads. They had to find out in the process, and this time around they were woefully ill-equipped to respond to the new challenges.

The first oilmen indigenous people met were young geologists desperately seeking *chapopoteras*. As speculation that Mexico might possess as much oil as Texas circulated in 1900, the oilmen sent neophyte professionals to the Huasteca to confirm the rumors. The local ecology, however, was uncooperative. The "dense vegetation" of the rainforest covered the hillsides that might identify rock formations potentially rich in oil.[41] The heat, the humidity, and the "crawling and cutting our way through the jungle," confessed El Aguila's chief geologist, DeGolyer, made survey work extremely difficult, uncomfortable, and time consuming.[42] But since "there was not a moment to lose" in the incipient oil rush, the professionals had little choice but to rely on local knowledge and labor to find oil. They paid local folk to find the black puddles. In 1900, in fact, Doheny "discovered" his much-anticipated dark spring because he hired "Indian guides" to lead him to it.[43] DeGolyer himself paid five pesos to whoever could point out "tar spots" to him. Thus, when word spread that foreigners paid ten times hacienda wages to swing machetes and be escorted to oil pools, local men took the opportunity to earn easy cash. Before long, DeGolyer found that men "of Indian stock" were "eager" to lead him to tar pits.[44]

Guiding lone geologists through the rainforest was not only good wages, but also must have seemed like a harmless activity to Indian men. Despite their new social position as subordinates to a foreign employer, they retained the upper hand in the journeys, anywhere from four days to three weeks.[45] They set the pace of exploration because the

[41] Ordoñez, *El petróleo*, p. 56. See also K. D. White, "Report on the Properties Held by the International Petroleum Corporation in Tuxpan County, State of Vera Cruz," 1919, IAEG, Edward D. Lynton Collection (EL), Acct. 4553, Box 14.

[42] Tinkle, *Mr. De*, p. 28.

[43] William E. McMahon, *Two Strikes and Out* (Garden City, NY: Country Life Press Corporation, 1939), p. 28.

[44] Tinkle, *Mr. De*, pp. 47, 54.

[45] "Reconnoissance [sic] Geological Report of the Perez-Cruz-Rosas Leases and Juan Casiano," June 15, 1914, and "Report on the Hacienda de Acontitlan (also Tuxpan Oil Co.)," October 1912, SMU/ED, Box 112, Folder 5316.

geologist-boss was totally dependent on their knowledge to locate seepages. Not yet versed in the capitalist concept that time is money, neither
indigenous nor mestizo guides were in a rush to reach the coveted black
bubbles. Unlike a milpa, tar pits were not ruled by seasons and weather,
so the guides did not feel obligated to be single-minded in their pursuit –
a practice that irritated the foreign professionals. In language tinged with
the "lazy native" corollary to the paradise narrative, DeGolyer's biographer described the frustrations thus:

> Up at the crack of dawn and ready to work before the heat of the day set
> in, he [the geologist] was frustrated by his missing *mozo* [male servant].
> The *mozo* had probably waked at dawn too, but in the land of *poco tiempo*,
> he found it good, as in the Mexican saying, that God had given us the
> night to sleep in and the day to rest in.[46]

The social dynamics then favored the local inhabitants. At every turn, the
guides subverted the servant-master relationship the foreign professionals assumed. As geologist Charles Baker complained, Mexico was a place
"where *mozos* do your urgent tasks when they feel inclined."[47]

Similarly, the unusual experience of working closely with outsiders
gave the guides great liberties for mischief at their bosses' expense.
Charles Hamilton recalled with amusement, for example, the time he
and his guide were "geologizing" and came on a Teenek procession with
plenty of *papier-mâché* masks and homemade liquor. When a passing gourd
found its way to Hamilton, he made a contribution and received in return
a rattle and a wooden dagger from "the head man of the funsters." In
no time his guide disappeared and men in brightly colored headdresses
surrounded the young geologist. They danced and chanted around him
without explanation. Hamilton began to panic, turning pale with fright,
whereupon the dancers guffawed and the geologist realized his life was
not in danger.[48]

Likewise, local men had ample opportunity to demonstrate their superior ecological knowledge to protect the oilmen's lives or, at least, to spare
them unpleasant experiences. In 1903, for example, Totonac men res-
cued English oil investor Percy Norman Furber from the "many wild
cats and some mountain lions" that he was certain would have devoured

[46] Tinkle, *Mr. De*, p. 56.
[47] "Adios to Mexico, More Truth than Poetry With Apologies to Whatever Element of
Decency May Yet Remain in Mexico," IAEG/CB, Acct 3328, Box 29, Poems.
[48] Hamilton, *Early Day*, pp. 51–52.

him when he ventured into the rainforest alone and lost his way.[49] Similarly, indigenous and mestizo guides saved one of the half-dozen Mexican professionals working for the oil companies from army ants. In 1919, engineer Manuel Mesa Andraca was busy surveying Zacamixtle when, he wrote,

> I heard very strange noises, something like the movement of dry leaves dragged by the wind, noises that increased their buzzing, like an army of invisible beings on the march. Lizards, small vipers, grasshoppers, crickets, and the long-tailed birds with a sharp beak called "road-runners" began to cross the path in a mad race. "Get out of the way, engineer – the [men] yelled at me, the *tlatentellotas* are coming." A true army of large red ants, . . . were encircling all insects and vermin to devour them, spreading out like army battalions do to their enemies.

Had the guides not warned Mesa Andraca, the ants would have tried to nibble him to oblivion as they did "cockroaches, scorpions, and mosquitoes."[50]

When the Mexican Revolution reached the Huasteca in 1914 and the horse trails became violent highways, moreover, foreign professionals had more to fear and often owed their lives to their indigenous guides. Hamilton, for instance, recalled riding through Chicontepec with a guide who spoke no Spanish. Somewhere along the trail, the two heard bird-songs, birdcalls, and the rustle of animals. The calls turned out to be signals from indigenous revolutionaries that the guide recognized. He replied, waited for an answer, and when it came back positive, the two passed through the ambush without incident.[51] On an individual level, therefore, indigenous men had nothing to fear from single professionals sniffing around for tar pits.

The first encounters between indigenous women and men from the oil industry, rare in the historical record, were more limited but similarly benign. They tended to involve payment for traditional unpaid female labor, such as cooking or sewing. Hamilton, for instance, paid a woman and her daughter to wash his laundry and mend his clothes when he was out in the rainforest. On another occasion, he fell in love with a skirt that a teenage Teenek girl was embroidering "for an upcoming *fiesta*." She spoke sufficient Spanish to negotiate a price that satisfied her. She sold

[49] Percy Norman Furber, *I Took Chances: from Windjammer to Jets* (Leicester: Edgar Backus, 1954), pp. 124–125.

[50] Manuel Mesa Andraca, *Relatos autobiográficos: con las compañías petroleras; mi vinculación con la reforma agraria* (Mexico City: Editorial Nuestro Tiempo, 1981), pp. 42–43.

[51] Hamilton, *Early Day*, p. 95.

the skirt for fifteen pesos – a trifle for Hamilton, but the equivalent of several months worth of chores in any hacienda for her.[52] Thus, the initial meetings between indigenous men and women and representatives of the oil companies proceeded smoothly, apparently mutually beneficial. The geologists mapped the boundaries of oil country without loss of life or limb or much time, while aboriginal men and women earned unheard of wages for traditional work. The apparent harmlessness of those encounters must have surely influenced the dealings of indigenous families with the second group of oilmen who found their way to the Huasteca: the land agents.

Alienating the Rainforest

Once the geologists finished mapping any given community, they returned to their company offices with a list of potential oil sites. It was the land agents' job to acquire rights to the lands pinpointed by the geologists. In the Huasteca the rainforest the geologists branded as "oil country" through 1920 coincided with the cultural areas occupied by the Teenek.[53] The most oil-rich portion was further restricted to an arc that began about the middle of the Tamiahua Lagoon, curved inland through Tantoyuca, and ended on the banks of the Tuxpan River: "the Golden Lane." Eighty-five kilometers long (53 miles) and forty-five kilometers wide (28 miles), the aptly named archway would be the center of Mexican oil production until 1921.[54] Although a number of haciendas were located within the Golden Lane proper, primarily those of the

[52] Hamilton wrote that the skirt ended up hanging on the wall of his U.S. home as an attractive and inexpensive art piece. Ibid., pp. 28, 49–50.

[53] Hamilton, for example, explored Chicontepec and recommended "No Lease." Ibid., p. 94. There was another area of production identified in this period in northern Veracruz: Papantla, the land of the Totonacos. El Aguila bought the land from the Englishman Percy Norman Furber. Even though the company sank about a dozen wells, the area did not achieve full production until the 1930s. Then it became known as "Poza Rica," or "rich well." Most scholarly research on Poza Rica is the work of Alberto J. Olvera Rivera. See "Acción obrera y nacionalización del petróleo: Poza Rica (1938–1939)," *Historias* 16 (January–March, 1987); "La evolución de la conciencia obrera en Poza Rica, 1932–1959," in *Veracruz, un tiempo;* "Origen social, condiciones de vida y organización sindical de los trabajadores petroleros de Poza Rica, 1932–1935," *Anuario* IV (1986); "Los trabajadores ante la nacionalización petrolera: el caso de Poza Rica," *Anuario* V (1988); and "The Rise and Fall of Union Democracy at Poza Rica, 1932–1940," in *The Mexican Petroleum Industry.*

[54] J. M. Muir, "Geology of the Tampico-Tuxpan Oilfield Region," *The Science of Petroleum,* vol. 1 (Oxford: Oxford University Press, 1938), p. 100; Hisakichi Hisazumi, "Informe preliminar acerca de la geología petrolera de la zona comprendida entre los ríos de

Gorrochótegui-Peláez clan, most of the forest belonged to the Teenek. For that reason, the Teenek experienced the guile of the company land agents in full measure.[55]

Dubbed *coyotes* because of their scurrilous operational methods, the land agents trailing the geologists seemed just as innocuous at first glance. They did not offer to buy indigenous land. The division of the con- dueñazgos in the late Porfiriato fragmented indigenous property into plots too small to make purchases worthwhile for the companies. Leas- ing the subsoil rights was preferable, particularly before 1908, when it was not yet proven that northern Veracruz had petroleum in commercial quantities. The land agents, therefore, told individual owners that they were only interested in renting the land to look for oil. The offers they made were unbelievably attractive to indigenous families more familiar with subsistence economies than capitalist markets. As the agents put it, the deal was appealing: the family received a large amount of money, but they did not have to move away, they did not have to perform any labor, and they could continue farming as usual. To receive the money, the only task required of the head of household was his or her signature on a piece of paper. The fact that most Teenek could neither read nor write was not an obstacle. Penning an "X" or affixing a thumbprint was just as good. Starting in 1901, land agents deployed throughout the Golden Lane repeated that simple story dozens of times. By 1908, they had acquired the subsoil rights to most of the rainforest within the Golden Lane proper. The rest would come under oil company control by late 1919. In re- turn, the land agents received excellent monthly wages and, most impor- tant, royalties for whatever oil was found in the properties they obtained.[56]

From the indigenes' point of view, the offer was appealing not only because it meant economic gain, but also because it promised ecological stability. Land agents were totally different from the hacendados, the indigenous household's point of reference. They did not bring cows into the forest to trample cornfields, they did not ask that the land be turned to pasture, they did not live nearby to threaten or harass them, they

Tuxpan y Misantla, en los estados de Puebla y Veracruz," *Anales* of the Instituto Geológico de México, vol. 3 (1929), pp. 3–48.

[55] The Nahua stronghold of Chicontepec on the border with Hidalgo, for instance, did not undergo extensive geological study until 2001. *La Jornada*, January 12, 2002, www.jornada.unam.mx/0181eco.html.

[56] H. H. Hallat, El Aguila Lands Department to T. J. Ryder, Tampico, November 20, 1920, SMU/ED, Box 103, Folder 5148; [Eduardo L. Castillo], *Ramón Díaz vs. International Petroleum Co* (Mexico City: Talleres Tipográficos de El Día Español, 1925), p. 7.

promised the family could keep the milpa unmolested, and they paid immediately. Such offers were simply unheard of in those parts of the world. They were also too good to be entirely true.

The case of Cerro Azul illustrates the process well. Cerro Azul is in the heart of the Golden Lane, in Tancoco, the community where the anthropologist Starr saw Teenek women with sewing machines in 1901. Cerro Azul would become world-famous in 1916 when Huasteca Petroleum captured on film the spurt of oil rising from well #4, a well so extraordinarily productive that Doheny called it "the world's greatest oil well."[57] In the mid-nineteenth century Cerro Azul had become a condueñazgo. Antonio Pulido, Antonio Maranto, Ignacio Flores, Apolonio Jácome, and Antonio Hernández pooled their resources and purchased 9,558 hectares (22,940 acres) in April 9, 1861, at the end of the War of the Reform and before the French invaded Mexico. In keeping with the relatively low price of local rainforest, they paid 120 pesos for the property.[58] Sometime during the Porfiriato, the forest they owned was divided into four lots and assigned to the heirs of the original owners. By 1901, lot #3 belonged to Laureano Pulido; lot #2 to Ignacio Flores; and the other two to the heirs of Jácome and Maranto. For whatever reason, Hernández disappeared from the record. Flores owned approximately 2,279 hectares (5,470 acres), whereas Pulido owned 955 hectares (2,292 acres).[59]

The subsoil rights of both Pulido and Flores ended up in the hands of a land agent on July 30, 1902. How that happened, however, is not entirely clear. Neither Flores nor Pulido signed the contract. Because they were both illiterate, it is probable that a mestizo neighbor offered to negotiate on their behalf for what might have seemed like a reasonable fee, as often happened in other transactions. Thus, a man by the name of Genaro F. Avendaño appeared in the lease as acting on behalf of the condueños, who thereby yielded their rights to another intermediary by the name of Ulises Benistant, who, in turn, represented one Enrique Juan María Coucier de Julvecourt. In the contract, Avendaño agreed to lease the

---

[57] Mexican Petroleum Company of Delaware, *Cerro Azul No. 4: World's Greatest Oil Well* (New York: The DeVinne Press, n/d).

[58] AGN/DP, Caja 7, Exp. 20, 032(02)/55. The Cárdenas family also acquired lots in Cerro Azul in 1895, which they later leased to an oil company. Gutiérrez Rivas, "La familia Herrera," p. 110. It is unknown who the seller was in both cases.

[59] List of Applications for Confirmatory Concessions Pending, Enclosure No. 1-B to dispatch No. 1550 of June 28, 1934, from the Embassy at Mexico City, General Records of the Department of State, Records of the Department of State Relating to Internal Affairs of Mexico, 1930–1939, Record Group 59 (RG 59), Roll 125, 812.6363.2779.

Flores and Pulido rights for a total of five hundred pesos per year, for ten years. To sweeten the deal, no doubt, Benistant promised to pay the rent all at once, in cash, a total of five thousand pesos each. That was certainly more money than either Flores or Pulido had seen in their entire lives and there is no doubt that they received it all.[60] As was the case with other indigenous contracts, the Flores and Pulido lease did not include production royalties. The reason was, an American agent confessed, that just as aborigines had no idea what "subsoil rights" meant, "they didn't understand what royalties were."[61]

It is also not altogether clear that Flores and Pulido realized what else they had given up. Because they could not read the lease, they did not know that they had granted all the trees necessary to build houses and barracks for oil workers, in addition to those that needed to be cleared to reach the tar pits easily. They were obligated as well to allow the felling of trees for road construction. Furthermore, they had granted the right to transform fourteen hectares (thirty-three acres) of forest into pasture in exchange for twenty pesos per year. Finally, Avendaño agreed on their behalf that when the contract expired in 1912, whoever held it could take with him "the machinery, tools, utensils, animals and other objects used in the exploitation of *chapopote*." Pulido and Flores, however, stood to inherit any barracks built.[62]

Julvecourt and his men followed the same script in other communities. In 1902 alone, they signed leases with private owners in Amatlán, Chinampa, Palo Blanco, San Jerónimo, and La Merced. In a pattern that would be repeated by other agents, Julvecourt transferred the rights he acquired from indigenous households to Doheny in 1906. In payment he received 87,800 Mexican gold ($43,900) and then disappeared like

---

[60] The lease contract is reprinted by Santos Llorente, "Los gobernadores," pp. 30–32. Pulido renewed his lease in 1921. The new payment increased to forty thousand pesos per year, for a period of sixteen years, that is, until 1937. Sometime after 1921, however, Huasteca Petroleum unilaterally changed the terms to pay only five thousand pesos per year. Pulido protested, but the company did not budge, putting the family under surveillance instead. One day Pulido was shot by two men pretending to be interested in his two younger sisters. He survived. He told his interviewer he was convinced the would-be assassins worked for Doheny. His testimony appears in Antonio Rodríguez, *El rescate del petróleo: Epopeya de un pueblo* (Mexico City: Ediciones El Caballito, 1975), pp. 33–35.
[61] Testimony of Michael E. Spellacy in *Investigation*, pp. 939–942. See also Mesa Andraca, *Relatos*, pp. 35–36.
[62] Santos Llorente, "Los gobernadores," p. 29.

a stealthy coyote.[63] Julvecourt, of course, did not consult or advise the landowners of his dealings before he retired from the business. Thus, if they had any complaints or questions, they would have to address themselves to entirely new company representatives.

For a decade or more in some cases, however, there were no questions. Daily life did not change for the indigenous communities of northern Veracruz. Neither did the ecology. In fact, most communities probably enjoyed a greater sense of security than they had in a long time. The rush to secure land leases worked to their advantage in the short term. It kept their historical enemies, the hacendados, at arm's length. Furthermore, it is possible that indigenous owners felt that contracting with obviously rich and powerful outsiders gave them some protection from hacendados as well; certainly the company men presented themselves as allies and promised stability and minimum change in addition to extraordinary income.

Flores herself was an excellent, if atypically lucrative, example. The same year that Julvercourt transferred her lease in Cerro Azul, 1906, she married Hilario Jacinto. To secure the property with the new condueño, another land agent appeared. He made an unusual and unprecedented offer. If Flores and Jacinto extended the lease for thirty years, they would receive twenty-five thousand pesos in cash for the first fourteen years, and one thousand per year for the rest. Totally unaccustomed to such sums of money, the newlyweds could not resist the proposal. What made it even more attractive was that the lease stipulated that if Doheny's company did not begin exploiting the land in five years, the lease would expire and the couple did not have to return the money. It was possible, then, that the ecology would remain the same until 1911. And, since no great oil wells had sprouted in the Huasteca by 1906, who knew what "exploitation" meant?[64] Measuring around and poking the earth as the geologists did seemed innocent enough. Maybe nothing would change even after 1911 and they would still have a fortune to raise a family. Jacinto and Flores agreed to the offer and became immensely rich by local standards. Others did the same.[65] But change did come, with a big bang in 1908.

[63] Ibid., p. 32.
[64] The only commercial well at the time was La Pez #1, brought in on April 3, 1904 in El Tulillo, far enough north for most people not to know what an "oil camp" looked like yet. Ordoñez, *El petróleo*, p. 55.
[65] Storm writes that a geologist giving her a tour of the Pánuco fields in 1924 gave two examples of Mexican subsistence farmers who earned thousands of pesos in royalties and rentals. Storm, "Wells," p. 522.

The Earth Trembles

In July 1908, Pearson struck oil. The location was San Diego de la Mar, the condueñazgo that had been divided into at least eighty-seven lots, on the swampy shores of the Tamiahua Lagoon. The well was proof positive that northern Veracruz was indeed sitting atop "oceans of oil."[66] It was also an unprecedented ecological disaster, which I examine in the next chapter. The entire Huasteca felt the shockwaves, and as a result the continuing shift in land ownership patterns became difficult and costly in more ways than one.

When the well at San Diego de la Mar shot petroleum into the air, some of the oil landed on glowing ashes, igniting in a gigantic explosion. Gonzalo Bada Ramírez, a mestizo whose mother was Teenek, was six years old when the incident took place. "The earth trembled," he recalled, as the oil the earth vomited caught fire. Within seconds, boiling crude began falling down "like, like a light rain," blistering and burning the skin of animals and humans caught under it. People became terrified. With his mother and grandmother, Bada Ramírez ran out of the house. His uncle, a worker at the well, rushed home and picked the child up on his horse. As they galloped away, the boy saw that "people were leaving, some on foot, others running, some without shoes even, others didn't even have time to put on a shirt."[67] As the communities in the immediate vicinity were evacuated, people could see an oil fountain rising high into the sky, burning like "a monster with a dark mane crowned by a wide and shiny headdress of fire," wrote a Mexican engineer. The flaming torch soon reached twelve hundred feet, so that ships two hundred miles out to sea spotted it.[68]

Panic spread in all directions. In Ozuluama, to the north, the inhabitants watched in horror as their houses mysteriously turned black, a result of chemical reactions between the sulphuric acid from the well and house paint. In nearby Tantima, the local treasury official saw the gold-plated rims of his glasses turn dark red, while seventy miles to the south, in Totonacapan, similar reactions turned elegant English silverware black.[69]

---

[66] Davis, *Dark Side*, p. 71.

[67] Interview with Mr. Gonzalo Bada Ramírez, conducted by Lief Adleson in Tampico, Tamaulipas, on September 30, 1978, Proyecto de Historia Oral (PHO), 4/91.

[68] Juan Palacios, "Memoria sobre el incendio del pozo de petróleo de Dos Bocas," *Boletín* of the Sociedad Mexicana de Geografía y Estadística, Quinta Epoca, vol. 3, no. 1 (1908), pp. 10, 17.

[69] Juan D. Villarello, "El pozo de petróleo de Dos Bocas," *Parergones* of the Instituto Geológico de México, vol. 3, no. 1 (1909), pp. 21–22; Furber, *I Took Chances*, p. 185.

Over the next several weeks, as the well continued burning, people began to fall ill. In Tamiahua 297 adults and "even more" children out of a population of one thousand found themselves with burning eyes and swollen eyelids. Eighty more sulphur-drenched people within a twenty-one-mile radius of the fire sought medical assistance because their eyes burned and turned red and watery. The symptoms, the doctor discovered, worsened according to the wind currents. "When the wind blows from the direction [of the well] the nauseating smell of rotting eggs is almost unbearable," reported the doctor. "I felt my eyes, my nose, and my throat burning."[70]

As the fire raged unabated for the next fifty-seven days, rumors fanning the worst fears of the communities flew throughout the Huasteca. Some "superstitious natives," wrote the American Vice-Consul at Tampico, believed "that the world had come to an end."[71] Others worried the fire would spread and burn down their thatch-roof houses and the entire forest. Many swore that all the fish in the Tamiahua Lagoon had died, while others were convinced that a volcano was rising at San Diego de la Mar.[72] Speculation about human deaths was rampant. Some heard that "many died gassed," whereas others were convinced that those who tried to put out the fire "all died there, not even one was left alive."[73] Furthermore, many heard that the Mexican government had sent federal troops to force indigenous men to fight the fire at bayonet point.[74] Although some of the rumors were true and others were false, local inhabitants had no reliable sources of information to help sift through them. Suddenly, oil meant terror and oilmen of all types were not to be trusted. Yet, simultaneously, everyone understood that the burning well meant something else: the Huasteca was indeed exceedingly rich. The Teenek, moreover, also realized that getting at those riches implied vast environmental risks that they might not want to take. A change of attitude began to appear among both indigenous landowners and hacendados.

---

[70] Informe del médico cantonal, October 12, 1908, AGEV, Gobernación, Salubridad: Enfermedades y Medicinas, Caja 2, No. 77, Letra C, Conjuntivitis. I visited Dos Bocas with my husband in August 2004 and we both felt the ill effects of the hydrogen sulfide that impregnated the air. Having spent less than thirty minutes taking photographs of the crater, we both had pounding headaches for hours afterwards. The difference in our body weight and mass made a difference: whereas my husband was back to normal in about three hours, my headache lasted eight hours and I felt such fatigue I was unable to go for an evening walk.

[71] Russell Hastings Millward, "The Oil Treasure of Mexico," *The National Geographic Magazine*, vol. 19, no. 11 (November 1908), p. 805.

[72] Villarello, "El pozo," pp. 22–23; Santos Llorente, *Episodios*, p. 24.

[73] Bada Ramírez, PHO/4/91; Rodríguez, *El rescate*, p. 23.

[74] Santos Llorente, *Episodios*, p. 49.

Indigenous Resistance

In contrast to the nineteenth century, indigenous resistance to the oil companies entailed no violence on their part. The reasons were overwhelmingly but not exclusively economic. Wherever opposition arose, the oil companies wielded their most effective weapon: cash. When immediate tender failed to persuade a head of household, however, the companies were not above resorting to violence until an agreeable family member, typically a woman, came to the fore and accepted their offers. Thus from 1908 until 1920, independently of national and state politics, the Huasteca witnessed dozens of hard-fought individual battles in the war for control of the tropical rainforest. But in the end, the companies always won.

Indigenous lines of defense against the oil companies took different forms and elicited new company responses. One tactic was simply to refuse to work with geologists. Sometime after 1909, DeGolyer noticed that "the natives" became "secretive" about the location of oil pools. Another American, Michael Spellacy, likewise noticed that the indigenes resisted making land deals with him. "When I would come along the little youngsters would run and hide and the old fellows would gaze at me as if I was a horse thief," he admitted. Overcoming that distrust now took time and more money. Spellacy developed a strategy involving the distribution of coins and crackers among the children until "in a few months" he had gained the adults' confidence. DeGolyer similarly won local cooperation by increasing the five peso rate to undisclosed higher amounts.[75]

In other cases, resistance to geologists became so pronounced that rumors of indigenous violence against unauthorized entry into the area began to circulate. Duke K. White, for example, reported that before he traveled to Cerro Azul he had to "await a sort of passport to enter Indian country" because he had been told that "these Indians...had the unpleasant habit, unless one was properly identified and accepted for admittance, to cut off the soles of the feet and to start the intruders walking back from whence he came."[76]

Rumors of indigenous ferocity notwithstanding, the more common tactic was to sever ties with the oil companies altogether. That was what Flores and Jacinto, the couple that had received twenty-five thousand pesos for their Cerro Azul lot in 1906, tried to do. Four years passed and

---

[75] Tinkle, *Mr. De*, pp. 57–58; Testimony of Michael E. Spellacy in *Investigation*, pp. 939–942.
[76] Diary, 1914, p. 5, IEAG, Duke Kessack White (DW), Acct. 2116, Box 9.

Doheny had not touched their lot. The lease was close to expiring, but to keep competitors' coyotes away, Doheny decided to purchase the lot outright. His land agent offered "hundreds of thousands," then "one million, two," but the pair refused to sell. To protect their lot, moreover, Jacinto, who had learned what leasing meant by this time, transferred the subsoil rights to his sister, María Luisa. The third clause of the contract stated explicitly that Jacinto had taken that course of action because Huasteca Petroleum employees had "threatened" his life.[77] Failing to convince the family to give up their land even for two million pesos, the company men left Cerro Azul and the Flores-Jacinto family thought they had won. But then they encountered another legendary company figure: the thug.

In difficult cases the oil companies resorted to violence to keep or acquire Huasteca rainforest. The Jacinto-Flores household is a case in point. Thirty-three days after Jacinto turned over the subsoil rights to his sister, in June 1911, a man by the name of Otilio López stabbed him to death. Although López eluded capture and was never tried, the community knew the murderer worked for Huasteca Petroleum, a fact confirmed decades later.[78] Within days of Jacinto's assassination, another company employee implicated in the murder plot, Jacobo Valdéz, arrived in Cerro Azul to impart his condolences to the widow, now the sole owner of the lot. Testifying in another case, Valdéz admitted that he had used charm and subtle intimidation to convince Flores that she should emigrate from Cerro Azul with her two boys, lest they suffer the same fate as her husband. On December 11, 1911, Eufrosina Flores agreed to sell her piece of Cerro Azul forest for a veritable fortune: five hundred thousand pesos. The company was not altogether satisfied, however. To make sure none of the Jacinto-Flores heirs challenged their mother's decision, Doheny invited the widow and her children to his hometown of Los Angeles, California. Presented with a house and a "pension" of $500 per month, Flores never returned.[79]

Other Teenek women told similar stories, but few became wealthy like Flores. When the Chinampa condueñazgo was divided into individual plots in January 1895, Encarnación Cruz took possession of lot #165,

---

[77] A reproduction of the contract appears in Santos Llorente, *Episodios*, pp. 50–51.

[78] The company's complicity was confirmed in a fraud case tried in 1938 and reported in *El Dictamen*, April 11, 1938. See also García Granados, *Los veneros*, p. 78.

[79] Inviting indigenes to Tampico and Los Angeles was not atypical, according to Mesa Andraca, *Relatos*, p. 72. As of 1932, the Jacinto children were still receiving a monthly stipend from Huasteca Petroleum, according to García Granados, *Los veneros*, pp. 84–88, 93–94, 96. See also Santos Llorente, *Episodios*, pp. 51–52, 76.

which measured 95.46 acres. Because Cruz was blind, her son Adolfo
Merinos was in charge of negotiations when Doheny's land agent came
knocking in 1901. Merinos, illiterate himself, signed a lease for an undisclosed amount. In 1906 the rights to the subsoil were transferred to Tamiahua Petroleum, a subsidiary of Huasteca Petroleum. That contract stated
that the Cruz-Merino family agreed to rent their rights for fifteen hundred pesos per year until 1916. It is safe to assume that the family received
the rent in one payment: fifteen thousand pesos (Doheny reported the
property was worth $10,674,000 in 1911).[80] Cash in hand, life for the
Cruz-Merino family improved while the ecology remained the same for
another eight years. In 1909 Tamiahua Petroleum arrived and began to
build a camp in Cruz's backyard. The following year, two of Cruz's adult
grandchildren died accidentally from the inhalation of poisonous gas
emanating from one of the wells. The widows and brothers demanded
compensation. A grief-sticken Adolfo Merinos even confronted company
employees in the camp. The company called on Jacobo Valdéz once again
to resolve the problem. In the next five years, four of Cruz's male children and grandchildren were murdered under suspicious circumstances.
In contrast to Flores, however, Cruz only received twelve thousand pesos
from Huasteca Petroleum for all her losses. One of her daughters-in-
law received three hundred pesos in compensation for her widowhood.
Furthermore, a male heir, a grandchild, was invited to headquarters in
Tampico in 1921 to renew the expiring lease. He received forty thousand
pesos for his thumbprint and was invited to tour Huasteca Petroleum's
refinery before returning home so that he may know what happened to
the crude flowing from his family's land. Once inside refinery grounds,
the guides locked the gates behind him. He was not permitted to leave.
He was still there, shriveled and alcoholic, when Huasteca Petroleum was
expropriated in 1938.[81]

In other cases, the violence took the form of burning down the property of uncooperative landowners. Jacobo Valdéz admitted setting fire
to the homes of reluctant indigenes as a Huasteca Petroleum employee.
The task, he testified, was "easy because the roof was made out of grass."[82]

[80] PanAmerican, *Mexican Petroleum*, p. 36.
[81] Francisco Viesca and Martín C. Cruz, *Juicio Reivindicatorio vs. Tamiahua Petroleum Company*
(Mexico City: Imprenta Franco-Americana, 1921). See also García Granados, *Los veneros*,
pp. 31–67.
[82] Quoted in García Granados, *Los veneros*, p. 101. In another court case, Valdéz confessed
that he had set fire to sugarcane fields belonging to the American-owned Tampico Sugar
Company on orders from Huasteca Petroleum Company, which coveted the land. Ibid.,

The tactic became common enough to catch the eye of novelist Carleton Beals, who memorialized it in his 1935 novel, *Black River*. In a long passage, Beals described the arrival of armed men in the fictional indigenous village of "María Guerrero":

> The streets were patrolled. House after house was entered. The occupants were disarmed and herded out. Men, women and children were driven down the street like so many cattle, without a chance to take a single personal possession...Kerosene was poured about. The village was set on fire. The flames leapt up from thatched roof to thatched roof. The hot air from the blaze stirred the near-by leaves of the jungle. The sparks shot upwards into the clear sky – fireflies darting through wreaths of dense black smoke. Frightened birds chattered overhead, circling frantically about the burning roofs where they had suspended their nests. Some, scorched by the flames, fell with piercing cries...The villagers were scattered into destitution. A small strip of property of no petroleum value was granted to them to reconstruct their homes if they so desired.[83]

Thus the Teenek lost the rainforest. Company maps show the Golden Lane carved up like "a checker-board" by 1919 (see Figure 2.1).[84] The companies succeeded where the hacendados had failed because they moved the arena of struggle from the forest to the business office, from native terrain to company turf. The division of property Liberals and Científicos imposed on aboriginals succeeded beyond their expectations. Private property allowed the companies to isolate owners, engaging them one at a time in byzantine contractual negotiations that disconnected each from the community. The paper alienation of one private plot became the affair of a lone head of household with no apparent immediate threat to the group as a whole. The sums of money the companies offered to individual owners further atomized communities. Although there had never been equality in access to land among the Teenek in

p. 102. Another company employee accused of similarly destroying a home in Alamo was Carlos Veloz, although he denied the allegations. LGO, vol. 13, no. 86 (October 18, 1924).

[83] Beals, *Black River*, pp. 203–205. Huasteca Petroleum used those tactics against rival oil companies, too. See Linda Hall, *Oil, Banks, and Politics: The United States and Postrevolutionary Mexico, 1917–1924* (Austin: University of Texas Press, 1995), pp. 111–112. On February 12, 1934, Andrés Herrera wrote to President Abelardo L. Rodríguez that Huasteca Petroleum had "invaded" his lot with "armed people" to force him to let the company drill. AGN, Presidentes: Abelardo L. Rodríguez (P/ALR), Exp. 526.22/75.

[84] Report on the Properties Held by the International Petroleum Corporation in Tuxpan County, pp. 22, 28, IAEG/EL, Acct. 4553, Box 14.

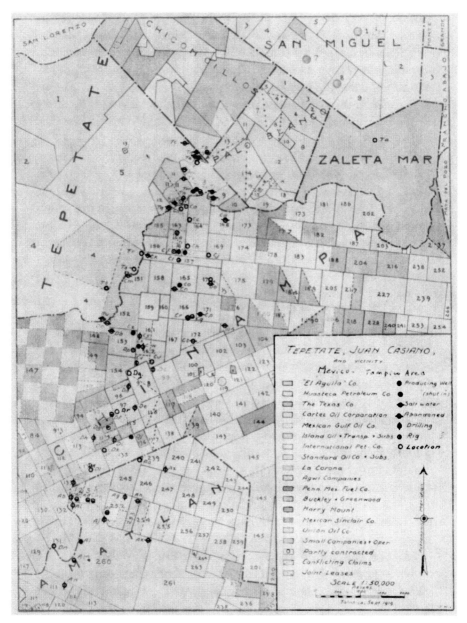

Figure 2.1. Illustration showing property lots in Tepetate, 1919. Negative #30875, courtesy Edward D. Lynton Collection, American Heritage Center, University of Wyoming.

recorded history, the sudden and capricious introduction of massive capital must have created enormous tensions within communities, a process
unfortunately lost to historians. By the same token, individual dissatisfaction with any given transaction became merely one individual's plight,
probably one that did not elicit much sympathy from neighbors who did
not partake of the companies' largesse to the same degree.[85] Similarly,
when heads of household realized what oil exploitation meant, they had
to fight back individually, each relying exclusively on the power of his
or her own negotiating skills to tackle the companies. As the aforemen-
tioned cases demonstrate, however, indigenous men and women were
simply not equipped to confront powerful foreigners. Time and again,
the oilmen proved stronger than individual Indians, having more money
and more information. But how did the indigenes' erstwhile nemesis, the
hacendados, fare? Were they better negotiators than the Teenek? Did they
lose as much?

The Hacendados Fight Back

Those hacendados who did not become rich upon their first deals with
the oilmen fought back after 1908. Oblivious to the local ecology, they
focused their energies on extracting more money from the companies.
After the explosion at San Diego de la Mar, the hacendados often tried
to renegotiate their leases, asking for higher payments for the rights to
the subsoil and, more importantly, demanding royalties on future oil
production. Their demands, in fact, in addition to fierce competition for
rainforest acquisition among the oil companies themselves, increased the
price of land in the Huasteca. In 1914, moreover, the hacendados went
one step further to protect their economic interests: they staged an armed
rebellion. The revolt led by Manuel Peláez Gorrochótegui between 1914
and 1920, in fact, became the most successful military adventure the
hacendados ever undertook.

The first Huasteca hacendado rumblings began in 1906. As noted
earlier, in January of 1906 Pearson gained a major concession from the
Díaz government to explore vast lands in Veracruz, including the subsoil of lakes and rivers. The hacendados were not amused with the federal government's generosity. They complained bitterly, but they did not
have political clout in Mexico City to match Pearson's. Their pleas were

---

[85] Although the changes in land tenure patterns alone must have led to important social
changes in the Huasteca, the sources I consulted do not give any hints of what those
changes were and how they played out.

ignored.[86] The hacendados then concentrated their efforts on extracting wealth from nature vicariously. Two cases demonstrate the trend. The first involved one of the influential Tuxpan clans: the Gorrochótegui-Peláez, a family that had increased their land holdings during the Porfiriato. They also sold or leased seven of their properties in Tuxpan to various oil companies starting in the late 1890s. By 1906, Cerro Viejo, Cuchilla de Cal, Tierra Amarilla, Cuchillo del Pulque, Buenavista, Llano Grande, and Potrero del Llano were sold or leased to El Aguila.[87]

Although details are sketchy, it is clear that Manuel Peláez Gorrochótegui in particular was deeply involved in a variety of business arrangements with Pearson's company by 1909. He was acting as an intermediary between El Aguila and his neighbor to lease the Horcones hacienda. El Aguila reported he was also helping them outmaneuver Huasteca Petroleum in another lease in Cerro Viejo, although it seems more likely that Peláez was more interested in increasing the value of his own properties by helping one of his landowner neighbors make the best deal possible. In addition, the versatile hacendado took on the role of labor contractor for the El Aguila in 1914. Furthermore, one of his sons joined El Aguila's legal department.[88] All those ties must have emboldened Peláez to make demands that exasperated El Aguila. Without giving details, Pearson simply wrote to his administrator in 1909: "If we are going to settle with Peláez let us settle forthwith."[89] But the squabbles between El Aguila and the Gorrochotégui-Peláez clan continued. At some point, El Aguila discovered that the family had sold the rights to Cerro Viejo and Cuchilla del Pulque not only to El Aguila, but also to two other companies: Huasteca Petroleum and Tuxpan Petroleum.[90] The final economic settlement El Aguila reached with the clan sometime before 1915 was nothing to scoff at: ten thousand pesos, per year, per property, for a total of seventy thousand pesos in annual rent.[91] Adding that to labor contract fees, salaries, and assorted commissions for services rendered, there can

[86] Ocasio Meléndez, *Capitalism*, p. 115.

[87] Minutes of the Special General Meeting of Shareholders, May 22, 1909, P&S/HR, File C 43/2/1.

[88] Pearson to Body, March 9, 1909, and Body to Cowdray, August 30, 1911, P&S/HR, Box A4: Mexico, Miscellaneous Private Correspondence; Guerrero Miller, *Cuesta Abajo*, p. 74; Tinkle, *Mr. De*, p. 14.

[89] Pearson to Body, March 9, 1909, P&S/HR, Box A4.

[90] Memorandum of Agreement between El Aguila and HPC and Tuxpan Petroleum Company, December 16, 1918, P&S/HR, File C 43/3.

[91] The source does not specify the number of years the lease held, but it seems to have been an annual lease. Subsoil Contract No. 16, due March 24, 1915, 1916, 1917, Tierra Amarilla, Etc., SMU/ED, Box 104, Folder 5166.

be no doubt that the Peláez-Gorrochóteguis were reaping the economic benefits of oil production in the Huasteca.

Another hacendado clan that clashed with the oil companies over leases was the Sánchez. The Sánchez family leased three properties of unknown size to El Aguila: Tamemas, Tanhuijo, and Tematoco, all in Tantoyuca.[92] Reports of trouble with the Tanhuijo lease first appeared in a letter dated August 3, 1912. Armando Sánchez alerted the company he wanted to renegotiate the lease because El Aguila had failed to pay royalties to his father "on time." In response the company raised the offer to $5 per hectare, per year. Even though Pearson considered the amount "outrageous," Sánchez turned down the offer, arguing that an American company offered him a much more attractive offer for the Tamatoco property: $6 per hectare, plus $10 per barrel. The negotiation lasted for another month, when Sánchez settled for $4 per year, plus 6% royalty, for ninety-nine years.[93] The case settled, Tanhuijo became a training camp for American drillers working for the company, an "oily quagmire," according to a geologist.[94] There is no indication that the Sánchez family was concerned about what happened to the environment in their hacienda, however. Although by 1916 El Aguila realized that Tanhuijo was "disappointing" in terms of production, the negotiating capacity of the family guaranteed them a handsome income for decades beyond that.[95]

Thus, having failed to replace the Huasteca ecology with grasses and cattle, the hacendados found a godsend in the oil companies. For these landowners, petroleum meant total success in putting the "worthless jungle" to work for them. For once they did not have to invest much effort, time, money – or many bullets – to derive an income. They were laying the foundation for a modern, progressive, and capitalist Mexico right in their backyard. Nonetheless, the hacendados were not blind to the fact that the companies were making millions of dollars while they were only pocketing thousands of pesos. Their wrestling with the oilmen was precisely about obtaining a fairer distribution of the riches buried in the belly of their private piece of earth. Just as the good times started rolling, however, the clouds of political turmoil appeared in Mexico City again.

[92] Minutes of the Special General Meeting of Shareholders, May 22, 1909, P&S/HR, File C 43/2/1.
[93] Body to Cowdray, Mexico, August 3, 17, 23, and 30, 1912 and September 21, 1912, P&S/HR, Box A4; Notebook 3, 1912, P&S/HR, Box A2: "Chief's notebooks, 1910–1915."
[94] Hamilton, *Early Day*, pp. 23–24, 31.
[95] Body to Cowdray, Tampico, May 29, 1916, P&S/HR, Box A4.

In 1910 as the Golden Lane hemorrhaged oil, the Mexican Revolution broke out. The idea of ousting Porfirio Díaz did not find favor among the Huasteca hacendados. Porfirian legislation had been good to them. Expert political animals that they were, however, the hacendados gauged the situation before they committed themselves to their benefactor. They needed to choose correctly. At stake was not just a dream of what could be, as in the nineteenth century, but their tangible prosperity in the twentieth. The man who decided to plunge into the treacherous political waters was none other than Manuel Peláez Gorrochótegui.

The Peláez rebellion is well documented and hotly debated. Placing the revolt in the context of the Revolution and its clash with the oil companies, revolutionary Mexicans and postrevolutionary writers painted him as a mercenary for the companies, a counterrevolutionary, and a traitor to his country. Using that same framework, historians portrayed him as a quintessential *cacique*, the regional military strongman whose vision did not extend beyond his circumscribed fiefdom.[96] Most recently, an American historian has argued that Peláez was an opportunist who ran a successful extortion racket against the oilmen.[97] Put in the context of the century-old local battle to control the rainforest, however, Peláez emerges as a true champion of the hacendados intent on making the tropics profitable. His rebellion was the most successful hacendado revolt in Huasteca history since Independence.

Peláez made all the right political choices. In late 1910, when Díaz was under political siege, he abandoned the president and declared himself a supporter of the revolutionary forces led by presidential candidate Francisco I. Madero. Having selected a winner, Peláez was rewarded upon Díaz's exile in May 1911. In 1912, fellow hacendados voted Peláez municipal president of Temapache, continuing in the illustrious tradition of the Gorrochótegui-Peláez *políticos* who had presided over the expansion of hacendado landholdings during the Porfiriato.[98] Within a year, however, as the hacendados witnessed the crumbling of the Madero presidency, they did not hesitate to switch sides. Peláez and his brother Ignacio publicly supported the counterrevolutionary rebellion led by Porfirio Díaz's nephew, Felix Díaz. Upon Madero's assassination in 1913, moreover, the hacendados and Peláez changed sides once more and supported the new

---

[96] Guerrero Miller summarizes the historiography in *Cuesta Abajo*, pp. 72–93.
[97] See Brown, *Oil and Revolution*, pp. 253–306. Brown has the most detailed account of the rebellion to date.
[98] Brown, *Oil and Revolution*, p. 257; Guerrero Miller, *Cuesta Abajo*, pp. 75–76; Menéndez, *Doheny*, p. 80.

president, the former head of the Díaz's presidential guard and accomplice in Madero's death, General Victoriano Huerta. Because the situation was becoming more complicated than expected and Huerta was considered a "usurper" by multiplying revolutionary groups, the hacendados decided to go beyond pronouncements and raise their own army in support of Huerta. As Peláez explained it, his fellow hacendados chose him to organize "a small force with trustworthy people" with a limited purpose: to "enjoy some tranquility for myself and impart it among the inhabitants of the region."[99] Those trusted allies included eleven sub-lieutenants, all of them descendants of colonial Spanish families from Tuxpan and Tantoyuca. One of them was Alfredo Peláez; another one was a member of the Sánchez family from Tanhuijo, Alfonso Sánchez; and a third was from the Herrera clan, Daniel Martínez Herrera.[100]

In 1914 the political situation became even more unstable and unpredictable. The United States invaded the port of Veracruz in April, just as the various revolutionary factions fighting against Huerta reached El Ebano, Tuxpan, and Tampico. The Revolution was in the hacendados' backyard. They were now at risk of losing what they had been accumulating. The outsider guerrillas posed a real threat to their political hegemony in the Huasteca, a fact the revolutionaries amply demonstrated by sacking Tancoco, Amatlán, San Antonio, and Chinampa, and by occupying Tuxpan, Tamiahua, and Tampico.[101] Peláez and his men shifted allegiances again. They abandoned Huerta and declared themselves *villistas*, supporters of the rebel leader from Chihuahua, Francisco Villa. They were Villistas until early 1916; then they decided to become autonomous.[102] The hacendados created their own movement. Although they flirted with Díaz in 1918–1919, they ultimately chose to be *pelaecistas*.[103] In the leadership role, Peláez was totally successful. As the hacendado standard-bearer, he drove the revolutionaries out of the Golden Lane and remained its de facto military leader until 1920. During that time,

---

99 Quoted in Guerrero Miller, *Cuesta Abajo*, p. 77.

100 Diary Entry, February 18, 1916, SMU/ED, Box 105, Folder 7; Brown, *Oil and Revolution*, p. 254, 263; Menéndez, *Doheny*, p. 88.

101 J. B. Body to Lord Cowdray, New York, January 24, 1917, P&S/HR, Box A3, "Mexican political, 1911–1927;" DeGoyler to Nell Goodrich DeGolyer, Havana, Cuba, June 17, 1915, SMU, Nell Goodrich DeGolyer Collection (ND), Mss 56, Box 1, Folder 15; Brown, *Oil and Revolution*, p. 259.

102 Bennet to John B. Body, Tampico, February 9, 1916, P&S/HR, Box A3.

103 John Womack, Jr. *Zapata and the Mexican Revolution* (New York: Vintage Books, 1968), pp. 301, 310, 313, 318.

he acquired a reputation among his peers as "a gentleman, distinguished and arrogant in his demeanor, so just, very honest, fair."[104]

Early on in the turmoil, Peláez decided to deepen the relationship between the hacendados and the oil companies. If the business of oil production were to continue during wartime, the oil companies had to do their part. Peacekeeping was not cheap. Thus, as soon as the revolutionary factions reached the Huasteca in 1914, Peláez requested "loans" from the companies to shape and sustain the hacendado army. The companies acquiesced to the rebel leader's petitions, a routine practice for extractive industries in areas of the world where political leverage was insufficient to protect their investments. They provided monthly "contributions" for six years, until the violent phase of the Revolution ended in 1920. Although the "donations," as Peláez called them, started at ten thousand pesos per company, per month in late 1914, by 1915 the "standard payment" had become thirty thousand pesos per month from each producer. The Pelaecistas thus became the best paid, best fed, best armed, and best outfitted men in arms in the entire country.[105] Peláez himself became a very wealthy man, a proud sponsor of weekend *fiestas*, featuring full orchestras and a "tenor and baritone" to perform the "classic *huapango*" music of the Huasteca while the Revolution raged on around him.[106]

In shielding the Huasteca from the chaos of revolution, the hacendados were protecting their own stake in the business of controlling the environment for financial gain. Because they lacked the resources to become capitalists themselves and exploit nature on their own, they had to leverage the power that Porifirian legislation had granted them. Some had proven to be tough negotiators, but as a group they knew the companies were tougher and they often felt cheated. As the caudillo confessed decades later, he "realized" that the oil companies "were a soulless organism, ready to crush whomever let them, as it had happened to those of us who naively had signed contracts with them; and I decided that in every transaction I had with the companies, I would try to get the juiciest deal possible."[107] The Revolution provided the best opportunity to make the best deals possible. It gave the hacendados the perfect reason to use the force of arms to extract better terms from the companies, to remind them who owned nature in this corner of Mexico. Firearms gave them a

[104] Brown, *Oil and Revolution*, pp. 254–255; Guerrero Miller, *Cuesta Abajo*, p. 73.
[105] Brown, *Oil and Revolution*, pp. 266–270.
[106] Mesa Andraca, *Relatos*, pp. 48–49.
[107] Quoted in Menéndez, *Doheny*, p. 83.

source of power. The same weapons that kept the revolutionaries away could be used against the companies if the occasion arose – as it did when El Aguila hesitated to pay Peláez, and his men responded by tampering with its pipeline.[108]

Thus the hacendados and the companies navigated the violence of the Revolution in an uneasy symbiotic relationship. The relative tranquility that Peláez's rule imposed on the Golden Lane allowed the oil to flow and the hacendados to fatten their bank accounts with rent receipts. The companies, according to *The New York Times*, meanwhile posted "a record of earnings unsurpassed in history" as they took the Golden Lane to third place in world oil production, behind the United States and Russia, revolution notwithstanding.[109] But what about the indigenous population? Did they join Peláez as their parents or grandparents had joined liberal hacendados a half-century earlier?

In theory, the revolt was a potential opportunity for those Teenek discontent with the oil companies. They could participate to strike back at the coyotes and those responsible for the deaths of loved ones. They could negotiate with Peláez so that he might take their concerns into account. Yet that does not appear to have happened. There is a record of one individual following Peláez: José Merinos, grandchild of Encarnación Cruz from Chinampa. He "enlisted" for a few months, but not on account of oil grievances. He joined the Pelaecistas to escape from a crime he committed during a barroom brawl.[110] Beyond that, there is little solid evidence of Teenek volunteers amongst Peláez's troops. His first men came from among the workers he provided to El Aguila as a labor contractor. Others, part-time fighters who balanced rebellion with farming, came from the region's "independent small-holders," mestizo *rancheros* resentful of outsider revolutionaries. Yet others were the "ranch workers" in his properties, his family's lands, and his friends'

---

[108] Doheny accused Peláez of breaking the pipeline to Cerro Azul three times during the period he was in charge, but Peláez admits only to "disconnecting" the pipeline. Doheny's comment is in the Testimony of Edward L. Doheny in *Investigation*, p. 280; Peláez's version is in Menéndez, *Doheny*, p. 84.

[109] The Mexican Petroleum Company, a Doheny company, reported $22,449,425 in profits in 1921, "for a gain of $5,979,693 over 1920, when profits were $15,469,733." *The New York Times*, June 22, 1922, in SMU/ED, Box 115, Folder 5352.

[110] García Granados, *Los veneros*, pp. 50–51. According to García Granados, Merinos soon became homesick and went home to Chapopote. He found a company man by the name of Mitchell visiting his wife. An argument ensued, and Mitchell shot Merinos and killed him.

haciendas.[111] Insofar as the increase of hacendado landholdings meant that indigenous households were thrown into the incipient hacendado labor force, it could well be that indigenous men working in the haciendas were drafted into the Peláez force, at least in the early months of the uprising.[112] But after 1914, Peláez's solvency allowed him to attract fighters without having to make promises of a political nature. He simply paid men well. After 1917, moreover, Peláez's programmatic pronouncements (Chapter 6) became patently Porfirian and, hence, hardly appealing to indigenous men, particularly those most affected by the shifting land tenure systems, the Teenek. Therefore, if some were incorporated into the force by virtue of their labor ties to the haciendas, it is also likely that they did not last long, but were supplanted by mestizo recruits. What seems clear, however, is that either inadvertently or purposely, Peláez's rebellion had the added effect of increasing the price of jungle real estate.

The continuing commodification of the rainforest aided and abetted by Peláez and his men brought further economic benefits to the hacendados and indigenous owners after 1914. According to Mexican officials, contracts concluded roughly between 1911 and 1916 showed that rents ranged from 8.50 to 2,000 pesos annually per lot, in addition to approximately 1,000 pesos as a bonus on production. Rare was the leaser who obtained a maximum of 5% in royalties, mostly hacendados and land agents.[113] By 1916, records show that the hacendados had doubled the rents they charged, although the inflationary pressures the revolution created probably affected those rental prices. However, most hacendados were now receiving 10% in royalties or more, a trend that continued

---

[111] Interview with Mr. Francisco Solís Cabrera conducted by Lief Adleson on September 7 and 18, 1976 in Tampico, Tamaulipas, PHO/4/56; Santos Llorente, *Episodios*, pp. 64, 136; Menéndez, *Doheny*, p. 84; Linda Hall and Don M. Coerver, "Oil and the Mexican Revolution: The Southwestern Connection," *Americas*, vol. 41, no. 2 (1984), p. 239; Guerrero Miller, *Cuesta abajo*, p. 79; Brown, *Oil and Revolution*, pp. 260, 263–264; Alan Knight, *The Mexican Revolution*, Vol. 2, *Counter-revolution and Reconstruction* (Lincoln: University of Nebraska Press, 1990), p. 388. The existence of rancheros as a particular group of producers is mentioned in passing in the literature, but it has not been studied systematically.

[112] Heather Fowler Salamini, *Agrarian Radicalism in Veracruz, 1920–1938* (Lincoln: University of Nebraska Press, 1978), pp. 162–163; Lourdes Alvarez Fragoso, "Alamo Temapache: formación de una región" in *Huasteca I*, pp. 110–111; Report from the Topographer, July 30, 1933, AGEV, Comisión Agraria Local (CAL), Exp. 887, Ranchería Tierra Amarilla, Municipio Temapache.

[113] BP, vol. 1, no. 4 (April 1916), p. 379.

into 1922 and was not caused by inflation.[114] By comparison, indigenous owners did not do as well, although their prices also increased.
Instead of lump sums, owners now received annual rents ranging from
seventeen to one thousand pesos.[115] Others, however, continued being
cheated. The heirs of Tomás Anacleto, one of the original ninety-six condueños of Zacamixtle, for example, lost their lot altogether to Huasteca
Petroleum's henchman, Ventura Calderón, around 1920. Calderón mus-
cled Anacleto into signing a piece of paper that allegedly leased the subsoil rights to the company. Anacleto was illiterate, however, so he did
not realize that what he had signed was not a lease, but a sales receipt.
In exchange for his "X" on the dotted line, Anacleto received a total of
5,670 pesos.[116]

According to local legend, moreover, Zacamixtle experienced one of
the worst episodes of company-inspired violence during Peláez's watch.
Apparently the Teenek tried to repel the Huasteca Petroleum crews
that arrived to begin drilling in Zacamixtle sometime around 1919. In
response, Doheny's men removed the population altogether. The village, wrote a Mexican engineer, "was transported in is entirety, with all its
inhabitants, in one night, by force, to another place to be able to explore

[114] The Peláez clan rented two Buenavista lots for 1,860 and 1,397 pesos, for instance.
LGO, vol. 4, no. 267, September 23, 1916. In 1917, likewise, the Pérez hacendados of
Tampuche, Pánuco, rented two lots (nine and seven has.) for three hundred pesos
plus 10% in royalties. Another renter, Domingo Lacorte, contracted part of lot #4 in
Tepetate for 12,450 pesos annually. Lands Department to T. J. Ryder, August 31, 1917,
Folder 5173, and Subsoil Contract No. 138, due April 11, 1917, Folder 5166, SMU/ED,
Box 104. In 1918 Doheny reported that prices had increased from one to ten pesos
per hectare to "a maximum of $1000 dollars" per hectare, Testimony of Edward L.
Doheny in *Investigation*, p. 353. In 1922, the Sánchez clan reported leasing 170 hectares
at seventy-five pesos per hectare annually, in addition to 14% royalties, for fifty years,
whereas a dozen other landwoners reported rents ranging from fifteen to fifty pesos
per hectare, per year, and royalties from 5% to 24%. At least three of these deals were
made by land agents, since the "contracting party" lists names such as "J. R. Chapman,"
"Martin F. Head," and "Wm. H. Fortine and Alex Smith." BP, May 1926, inserts.

[115] The Teenek owners of lot #145 in Amatlán, the Hernández-Zumaya household, for
instance, received 75.90 pesos in annual rent in 1918. Subsoil Contract No. 96, due
March 18, 1917, SMU/ED, Box 104, Folder 5166. Pedro Pascual, owner of lot #39 in
Tancoco, similarly leased the subsoil for a flat 91.80 pesos per year. Subsoil Contract
No. 2-I, due April 12, 1917, SMU/ED, Box 104, Folder 5166. The "hottest" piece of
Teenek real estate to enter the market during the Peláez rebellion, Zacamixtle paid
less than hacendado land: 45.36 pesos annually for lot #36; 17.42 pesos annually for
lot #68. Notificación, LGO, vol. 27, no. 37 (March 26, 1932). The Méndez family, by
contrast, leased two lots in Zacamixtle for a total of one thousand pesos, according to
García Granados, *Los veneros*, pp. 161–165.

[116] Santos Llorente, *Episodios*, p. 86.

the terrain where it stood."[117] In any case, thirteen different leases had been signed in Zacamixtle by 1920. As a result, by 1936 locals remembered the whole episode as the "burning down" of Zacamixtle.[118]

Thus, the hacendado rebellion facilitated the continued conversion of the Huasteca rainforest into a prized commodity. For all their frictions, there were no fundamental differences between the oilmen and the hacendados. They shared the same vision and ideology promoted by the overthrown Científicos and worked toward the same goals in spite of Díaz's demise: transforming nature for profit. The Peláez revolt, in fact, helped guarantee that the Golden Lane remained a Porfirian oasis amidst revolutionary chaos: a site of "remarkably rapid progress," according to the companies.[119] It was also a site of the equally fast disintegration of indigenous land control and land tenure systems – the first step on the way to changing land use patterns and remaking the landscape.

The twentieth century dawned in the Huasteca with radical new laws allowing landowners to claim what lay below the surface of the earth. The unprecedented removal of the state from direct control over nature favored American and British investors eager and able to exploit Mexico's subsoil. Already accustomed to treating land and nature as commodities, the foreign entrepreneurs spared no effort to acquire as much of the Huasteca as possible. They bought out hacendados and indigenous owners alike, rapidly supplanting local land tenure systems with monopolistic landholding. They quelled the indigenous resistance they generated with

[117] José Domingo Lavín, *Petróleo: Pasado, presente y futuro de una industria mexicana* (Mexico City: EDIAPASA, 1950), p. 125. Something similar took place in Juan Felipe, the condueñazgo contiguous to Cerro Azul. Huasteca Petroleum's General Manager, William Green, "had the town torn down" to gain possession of nineteen thousand acres there. Hall, *Oil, Banks, and Politics*, p. 122.

[118] Apolo García Herrera, *Memorias de un trabajador petrolero* (Mexico City: n/p, 1965), p. 46. Mesa Andraca noted that by the time he arrived in Zacamixtle to map its topography for Mexican Gulf Oil Company in 1918, the area had been "abandoned by the aboriginal Huastecs," but he does not mention a forced removal or a burning. Mesa Andraca, *Relatos*, p. 31. Similarly, correspondence from El Aguila employees shows that a number of Zacamixtle lots were leased illegally, but there is no mention of violence against the population. See C. P. Peralta to T. J. Ryder, New York, December 20, 1918; H. H. Hallahn, Land Department to E. DeGolyer, Tampico, July 27, 1918; A. Jacobsen to T. J. Ryder, Tampico, February 20, 1920; and H. H. Halland, Lands Department, to E. DeGolyer, Tampico, August 10, 1920, SMU/ED, Box 101, Folder 5102. The thirteen leases are recorded in the pamphlet published by the Mexican Senate, *El Petróleo: La más grande riqueza nacional* (Mexico City: Mexican Senate, 1923), pp. 255, 260–261, 264.

[119] Huasteca Petroleum Company and Standard Oil Company of California, *Expropriation: A Factual Study of the Causes, Methods, and Effects of Political Domination of Industry in Mexico* (New York: Macben Press, Inc., 1938), p. 1.

money or selective violence. When revolution broke out in 1910 and the hacendados created their own army to protect their interests, the oilmen did not hesitate to supply the financial backing necessary to shelter the Huasteca from political violence. In relative stability, thus, the oil companies proceeded to extract the "juices of the earth" from the Huasteca. That meant, first and foremost, changing the face of the tropical rainforest radically and profoundly.

3

THE ANATOMY OF PROGRESS

CHANGING LAND USE PATTERNS

The landscape is too vast, too glorious, to be defaced by these slight tokens of human handiwork, and their presence brings up, besides the idea of the sublimity of nature, another great thought, for they speak eloquently of the power of the mind of man and the strength of his hand when united to the performance of a great work.

Reau Campbell, 1890

The beauty of nature vanishes, in the oil fields, once her wealth appears.

Marian Storm, 1924

It took nature millions of years to evolve into rainforest, mangroves, swamps, and sand dunes in northern Veracruz. It took indigenous peoples of the Huasteca millennia to adapt to and coevolve with the environment nature created. It took American and British petroleum companies less than four decades to uproot the ecosystems of northern Veracruz and replace them with an industrial landscape. Huasteca Petroleum summarized the process thus:

> Discovery and development of the known oil fields in Mexico were the achievement of British and American pioneers, who came into this region at a time when it was a little-known, pest-infested, tropical wilderness . . . In the face of almost insuperable obstacles, they made remarkably rapid progress. In less than 10 years Mexico had begun to attract world-wide attention as an oil producer. Development of the famous "Golden Lane," one of the world's greatest known oil fields, discovered in 1910, placed Mexico in the first rank among oil-producing countries. The transformation was profound. Tampico, a sleepy little fishing port, became almost overnight a thriving city . . . In the oil fields, where formerly the tropical jungle supported only a few Indians, 50,000 oil field workers, largely Mexicans, found immediate, continuous employment.[1]

---

[1] Huasteca, *Expropriation*, pp. 1–2.

Indeed, upon gaining control over nature through land and other deals, the foreign oil companies proceeded to reshape the anatomy of the Huasteca beyond recognition. Like plastic surgeons gone mad, the oil pioneers eliminated the mangroves, scarred the sand dunes, razed the rainforest, filled in the swamps, and degraded the rest of the environment as never before in the history of the Huasteca. Such was the result and definition of progress in the early twentieth century: a landscape of drastic man-induced metamorphosis, where men replaced ecosystems with industry and urbanization, where metal substituted for trees and grays and blacks replaced shades of green. In the package of changes that I call the ecology of oil, those transformations were the results of the shift in land use patterns that followed the shift in land tenure systems in the Huasteca. Environmental destruction and degradation were the unavoidable consequences of the process. Although the terms did not exist then, their presence was imprinted on the land. They were not hidden, lurking behind the changes. On the contrary, environmental destruction and degradation were omnipresent, clasping hands with everything that oil represented – progress, modernity, and capitalism – in a seamless continuum from change to ecosystem annihilation. The difference was that the oilmen boasted about the landscape they created, as Huasteca Petroleum made abundantly clear, but ignored the one they degraded or destroyed. It is that continuous spectrum of change to destruction that this chapter documents.

How Large a Transformation?

Oil extraction, transport, and use inevitably alter the landscape. How else can men retrieve crude from the underground, transport and use it, if not by tampering with what lies aboveground? In the early twentieth century going from the surface to the subterranean required an apparatus that was not particularly sophisticated, but did mandate extensive land use. Some sites also experienced intensive use, including those hosting camps, refineries, storage depots, terminals, and ports. Others required the vacating land for pipelines, railroads, airplane landing strips, and telephone and telegraph lines. In unison they reconfigured the land beyond recognition. But exactly how much terrain was involved?

If by 1922 the British and American oilmen controlled about 46% of the Huasteca, one might assume that that was the fraction of territory subjected to ecological change. Moreover, since not all the land went into production, the transformation in the landscape might have covered a smaller portion. But the matter was not so straightforward. Between 1900 and 1938 production fluctuated as the companies exhausted some oil mantles and discovered new ones. In 1921 American geologists, for example, argued that the Huasteca acreage ripe for drilling was a mere 6,540 acres.[2] Yet already by late 1920, the official *Boletín del Petróleo* had reported that 14,525 hectares (35,877 acres) were under exploitation in northern Veracruz. By March 1921, that figure had increased to 58,020 acres.[3] By 1930 engineer Ordoñez reported 37,500 hectares (93,375 acres) under production throughout the country; in 1937, another engineer wrote that production in the Huasteca alone covered a total of 45,500 hectares (109,200 acres).[4] According to the highest figures, then, a hundred thousand acres out of more than two million the companies controlled in the Huasteca experienced changes in land use and ecology before expropriation.

Although no one will ever know how much land underwent changes because of oil production in the Huasteca, one hundred thousand acres is an extremely conservative estimate. The changes in land use affected a significantly larger land mass. Geologist DeGolyer wrote that the area within which "exploratory drilling" was taking place in 1912 measured some 105 miles from Tampico south and 65 miles from east to west, a minimum of 6,825 square miles.[5] Out of some 8,424 square miles from the border with Tamaulipas to the Cazones River, the territory subject to oil work therefore extended over 81% of the entire Huasteca – even if it did not actually produce oil. The industry, furthermore, changed vast areas not only through drilling, but also by installing infrastructure for communications, transport, and refining. Moreover, the spills, explosions, and fires the oil companies produced affected areas beyond the acreage stipulated in their land contracts. Thus, the oilmen pockmarked

[2] L. G. Huntley and Stirling Huntley, "Mexican Oil Fields," *Mining and Metallurgy* of The American Institute of Mining and Metallurgical Engineers, no. 177 (September 1921), pp. 27–28. The figures are: 1,500 acres in Tepetate-Chinampa; 1,800 in Amatlán-Naranjos-Zacamixtle; and 3,240 in Cerro Azul-Toteco.

[3] The 36,000 acres of 1920 were not necessarily included in the total. BP, vol. 10, no. 3 (September 1920), p. 269; BP, vol. 11, no. 3 (March 1921), p. 211.

[4] Ezequiel Ordoñez, "¿Por qué ha disminuído la producción de petróleo en México?" August 1930, AGN, Archivo Histórico de Hacienda (AHH), Legajo 1856–116; M. Méndez, Report to the governor of Veracruz, February 1, 1937, IAEG, Chester Cassel Collection (CC), Acct. 4403, Box 9, Folder on Mexico.

[5] DeGolyer wrote that drilling extended nintey-five miles north of Tampico as well. E. DeGolyer, "The Mexican Petroleum Industry during 1912," *The Petroleum Review*, November 22, 1913, p. 559, P&S/HR, Box C 43, File C 43/1.

a region stretching over some seven thousand square miles, ultimately transforming the Huasteca as a whole.

From Milpa to Oil Camp

To observe the metamorphosis of the Huasteca from "wilderness" to "oil country," it is best to follow the map of the typical petroleum route, from forest to port. The initial search for oil itself gave hints of the changes in store. The geologists' guides chopped down vegetation to reach the *chapopoteras*, to explore geological formations, and to make camp at night. With teams of two or three, the men carved out tiny, but numerous spaces.[6] Strenuous as exploration work was in 90°F (32°C) temperatures and high humidity, it was nonetheless impermanent. When the rainy season arrived, the forest reclaimed its space. Once the geologists decided on a drilling site and the land agents secured the necessary subsoil rights, however, it was only a matter of time before the systematic transformation of rainforest into an oil camp began.

No one knows how many camps the oil companies built in the Huasteca. What the record shows is that, by 1921, at least fifty-one separate fields were under production, each with a minimum of one camp each (see Appendix II). Although numerous leases were signed by 1906, the companies faced severe labor shortages that forced them to postpone extraction. The majority of the camps in the Huasteca were built in one decade, between 1910 and 1921.[7]

An oil camp made intensive use of the land. First, it overturned the previous ecology through deforestation. Work crews chopped down and burned as much vegetation as necessary to accommodate a camp. Once the first group of men created a charred bald spot, another crew built the accommodations: cafeterias, dormitories, and offices. Carpenters, electricians, boilermakers, tank builders, and mechanics assembled derricks, built workshops, and set up the infrastructure to drill. The only wood the men brought along was that destined for derricks. For all other construction, they used the precious woods on location. When the camp was set up, the drillers arrived. Later, sometimes months later when the wells were already flowing, additional laborers appeared. Their task was to dig

---

[6] Mesa Andraca, *Relatos*, p. 28.

[7] The lot belonging to Eufrosina Flores in Cerro Azul, for instance, was leased to El Aguila in 1906, but Huasteca Petroleum did not have enough workers to fell and build until 1909. Zacamixtle, likewise, became company land in 1910, but with production flush elsewhere, the company did not begin drilling until 1919.

enormous pits in the ground to catch the oil gushing from the wells, while *tuberos* rushed to sew together pipeline and lay it along paths they cut out of the forest floor to take the oil to port.[8]

The dimensions of the clearings for camps are unknown, but they varied substantially. A number of factors determined the size of the space: the acreage a company controlled; the number of workers, oil dams, and storage tanks; the decision to build a pumping station or power plant on location; and the measures the companies might take to keep flammables at safe distances from the wells. The hacienda El Alamo, which began production in 1913, has no record of the acreage Josefa Nuñez de Llorente leased to PennMex. However, by 1923 the camp on her property had a total of 959 worker houses, at least 25 wells, one gasoline refining plant, three fifty-five-thousand-barrel storage tanks, a pumping station, and two pipelines to Tuxpan.[9] The gasoline plant alone occupied at least 225 hectares (556 acres), while the wells occupied at least 132 hectares (325 acres), which means that no less than 357 hectares (882 acres) were deforested for the camp. In comparison, El Aguila clear-cut 984 acres alone for a gas-burning plant in neighboring Los Naranjos.[10]

A major factor that influenced the expanse of deforestation for camps was the number of wells drilled. According to geologist DeGolyer, 252 wells had been drilled in the Huasteca by December 31, 1912.[11] The number had grown to 637 by 1915, and to no less than 6,029 throughout Mexico by June 1936.[12] According to the 1901 law, each well was

---

[8] Contrato entre Obreros y Patrones del Centro de Labor, "El Maguey" y La Corona, en Tantoyuca, Article 3, June 1923, AGEV, Junta Central de Conciliación y Arbitraje (JCCA), Caja 34, Exp. 8; Bada Ramírez, PHO/4/91; *Asunto Nuñez y Rocha vs. Pen.Mex. Fuel Company* [sic] (Mexico City: n/p, 1925), pp. 11, 27. A photograph dated May 23, 1916 shows an area prepared for building with a caption that reads "cleared, burned, and grubbed," P&S/PA, P15: Minatitlán, Tuxpam, Puerto México, Etc., 1916–1922, P15/149.

[9] Censo, 1923, AGEV/CAM, Exp. 344, Alamo Temapache; *Asunto Nuñez*, pp. 19, 46; The Oil Fields of Mexico. Memorandum re: Accessibility and Transportation, prepared by Everett Lee DeGolyer for the War College, April 1917, SMU/ED, Box 50, Folder 3401, Correspondence with the War Department.

[10] Ubicación de la Planta de Gasolina en "Alamo" Tux. Ver., BP, vol. 14, no. 3 (September 1922); Carlos Iglesias, "Extensión aproximada de los terrenos petrolíferos de México, en explotación actualmente," BP, vol. 27, no. 1 (January 1929), p. 10. Photos of Los Naranjos can be found in BP, vol. 22, no. 1 (May 1926), photographic section.

[11] Everett L. DeGolyer, "The Mexican Petroleum Industry during 1912," *The Petroleum Review*, November 22, 1913, p. 560, and P. C. A. Stewart, "The Petroleum Industry of Mexico," reprinted from *Journal* of the Institution of Petroleum Technologists, vol. 2, (December 1915), p. 18, P&S/HR, Box C 43, File C 43/1.

[12] Méndez, Report to the governor, IAEG/CC, Acct. 4403, Box 9. Méndez actually reported a total of 5,671 wells, but he missed 358 wells that Pearson's men reported. He wrote that prior to 1917, the companies had drilled 279 wells, but DeGolyer and Stewart reported

supposed to be surrounded by a three-kilometer protection zone where no other wells could be drilled.[13] Had the companies obeyed the law, the six thousand wells would have required an area several times the size of the Huasteca. Instead, the distribution of the wells across the landscape was arbitrary (and thus unlawful). By 1921, for example, Cerro Azul had nine wells within five kilometers; Toteco had eleven in 330 acres; one of the Peláez properties, Tierra Amarilla, had sixteen wells in 2,056.5 hectares (5,059 acres).[14] The Pánuco haciendas – El Tulillo, Chapacao, Cacalilao, Topila, and others – had the most wells: 3,330 in 1929.[15]

How much land the companies cleared around each well, however, is guesswork. Although lawyer Luis Cabrera argued in court that the companies typically cordoned off fourteen acres per derrick in the mid-1920s, the *Boletín del Petróleo* noted in 1929 that many of the wells in the Pánuco haciendas occupied seven acres each. In Toteco, by contrast, the average was thirty acres per well, while in Tierra Amarilla the average was 128.5 acres per well. No standard was followed. Depending on the number of companies competing in any given area, the wells could be relatively close to each other or not, requiring more or less deforestation.[16] Oil reservoirs occupied added space in the camps and totally subverted the rainforest ecology. Through the 1930s, the companies dug "earth dams" at least seven feet deep to store oil.[17] In July 1918 there were sixty-six reported pits in the Huasteca, holding a total of 3,065,143m³ of crude oil, down from 6,200,291 in 1915.[18] Six were at Potrero del

---

637 wells drilled up to 1915 (footnote 11 above). Adding the missing 358 wells to Méndez's total gives us 6,029 wells. The Mexican government documented a slightly larger number than Méndez in 1936: 5,698 wells. Government, *Mexico's Oil*, p. 108.

[13] Ocasio Meléndez, *Capitalism*, p. 113.

[14] San Jerónimo – unknown acreage – had forty-three wells; Zacamixtle at least sixty-one; Chinampa, seventy; and Amatlán, 224. Index of Zacamixtle Wells, List of Chinampa Wells, Index of Amatlán Wells, SMU/ED, Box 103, Folder 5148; A. Jacobsen to T.J. Ryder, Tampico, September 14, 1921 and Paul Weaver to E. DeGolyer, New York, August 32, 1921, SMU/ED, Box 103, Folder 5149; *Asunto Nuñez*, p. 14.

[15] BP, vol. 27, no. 1 (January 1929), pp. 8–10; Hamilton, *Early Day*, p. 214.

[16] Although DeGolyer argued correctly in 1917 that in the Huasteca "a very small number of wells had been drilled" compared to the United States or the Caspian Sea, their impact was no less critical, given the sensitive nature of the tropical rainforest. DeGolyer, "The Mexican Petroleum Industry during 1912," p. 560. For the United States, see Frank J. Taylor and Earl M. Welty, *Black Bonanza: How an Oil Hunt Grew into the Union Company of California* (New York: McGraw-Hill Book Company, Inc., 1950), *passim*; and for Russia, see Yergin, *The Prize*, pp. 57–72.

[17] The Mexican government insisted on steel tanks since the early 1910s and prohibited open pits altogether in 1921. *California Oil World*, August 25, 1921.

[18] BP, vol. 2, no. 2 (August 1916), p. 101; BP, vol. 6, no. 1 (July 1918), pp. 84–92.

Figure 3.1. One of six earthen dams belonging to El Aguila Petroleum Company at Potrero del Llano. From the DeGolyer Library, Southern Methodist University, Dallas, Texas, the Everette Lee DeGolyer Papers.

Llano, a property of 5,412 acres. One of the dams, moreover, was truly extraordinary in its dimension: it stretched over forty-five acres and measured thirty feet at its deepest point (see Figure 3.1).[19] Most others were dwarfed by comparison.[20]

Besides requiring reforestation, the earth dams yielded enormous volumes of loose dirt that had to be disposed of somehow. Some of the soil was molded like putty into low firewalls to surround the pits themselves,

---

[19] R.P. Brousson, "The Oil Industry of Mexico," Lecture given at the World's Oil Exhibition, London, March 24, 1914, P&S/HR, Box C, File C 43/1. For photos of the Potrero del Llano dam, see P&S/PA, P/41: Potrero 1910–1915.

[20] Labor inspector Joaquín Bustamante, for instance, saw one in the 1930s that measured 280m². The Consolidated Oil Company dug up two dams for one camp in 1928; one was 2,420m² and the other one 280m². Acta no. 58, February 14, 1938, AGN, Departamento Autónomo del Trabajo (DAT), Caja 358, Exp. 10; Receipt from the Consolidated Oil Company, May 14, 1928, AGN, Junta Federal de Conciliación y Arbitraje (JFCA), Caja 156, Exp. 930/336.

but much ended up simply piled up like giant molehills, choking and burying vegetation underneath and disrupting life there.[21]

Like the pits, steel storage tanks eliminated plant life. In 1918 there were approximately 562 tanks across the Huasteca, each typically holding fifty-five thousand barrels of crude (at forty-two gallons per barrel).[22] By 1936 the number of tanks had reached 3,109, with a capacity to store 7,709,771m³ of crude oil.[23] A camp had as many tanks as the company judged necessary to store the oil from its local wells. In addition to the six open pits, for example, Potrero del Llano had nine tanks. Further north, within miles of Tampico, two communities disappeared altogether to give way to oil tanks. El Zapote, located between the Pueblo Viejo Lagoon and the Gulf, changed its name to "Tankville" when sixty-one oil tanks replaced swamps and humans. Neighboring Buena Vista, four miles from the banks of the Pánuco, disappeared under seventy-five tanks.[24] Along the Pánuco River itself, wrote Jack London, "the landscape on either side sprouted into the enormous, mushroom growths of the tank farms" that displaced swamps altogether.[25]

Given infrastructure requirements, it is easy to see how the camps eliminated the previous ecology. The four Cruz-Merino lots in Chinampa are a good example. There Huasteca Petroleum sank nine "Juan Casiano" wells, dug one earth dam, set up three storage tanks, built one pumping station, and erected a small plant to extract gasoline and burn off natural gas, in addition to housing and dining facilities.[26] As company photos show, those lots had no vegetation by 1909. In addition, the wells

[21] See photo of the dam at the Juan Casiano wells, SMU/ED, Box 139, Folder 5823, Scrapbook, "Clippings, Vol. 1."

[22] The standard measure for a barrel of oil was forty-two gallons during this period, not the fifty-five-gallon standard of today. Ocasio Melénez, *Capitalism*, p. 121, ft. 16.

[23] Government, *Mexico's Oil*, p. 160.

[24] The number of tanks increased to 1,142 in 1919; 1,259 in 1920; and 1,698 in 1924; while the pits dropped to sixteen by 1919. By 1919 the pits were used largely to capture the first oil that spilled from a well, not for long-term storage. BP, vol. 10, no. 3 (September 1920), pp. 296–297; Cleland, *The Mexican Yearbook 1922–1924*, p. 261; The Oil Fields of Mexico. Memorandum, p. 11, SMU/ED, Box 50, Folder 3401; *The Petroleum Review*, vol. 34, new series, no. 707 (February 5, 1916), pp. 116–117. Photographs of the Buena Vista tanks are in BP, vol. 23, no. 5 (May 1927), photographic section. Tankville photographs are in BP, vol. 23, no. 4 (April 1927), photographic section.

[25] London, "Our Adventurers," p. 5.

[26] The Oil Fields of Mexico. Memorandum, p. 8, SMU/ED, Box 50, Folder 3401; BP, vol. 6, no. 1 (July 1918), p. 88; L.G. Huntley, "The Mexican Oil Fields," *Bulletin*, Transactions of the American Institute of Mining Engineers, no. 105 (September 1915), p. 49. Photographs of the gas plant and the pumping station at Cerro Azul are in BP, vol. 22, no. 1 (May 1926), photographic section.

saw three major spills between 1910 and 1918. One spilled 220,000 to 280,000 barrels.[27] As Mexican officials reported, the well "flooded with *chapopote* great extensions of terrain."[28] Moreover, when Juan Casiano No. 7 became exhausted in 1919 (after ten productive years), the well spewed boiling salt water onto the ground.[29]

The impact of the shift in land usage could not be more profound. German novelist B. Traven captured it in fiction after touring the Huasteca in the 1920s. The forest that had "flourished during hundreds of years," Traven wrote, became akin to paradise lost, "a black hole, noisy, ugly, and smelly." Machines like

> caterpillars dug with their merciless claws, torturing the earth that whimpered in pain. A labyrinth of steel pipes covered the ground and on top of them could be seen an intricate weaving of cables and wires that chased away thousands of birds... [where] there used to be celestial quietude, there were now shouts, orders, crashing metals, whistling vapor.[30]

Yet the camps were only the nucleus of environmental change. Extending from each camp, tentacles of razed forest led to Tuxpan, Tampico, and Puerto Lobos. Here, too, work crews knocked down trees for railroads, roads, pipelines, and telegraph, telephone, and water lines. The rail lines were cut out first because they were necessary to transport workers and building materials. By 1915, at least 170 miles of railways had been built.[31] Although the cars and locomotives were imported, railroad ties were made from locally cut trees.

The shift in land use patterns was fraught with natural difficulties, nevertheless. The tropics eroded infrastructure systematically. To "prevent the tree shade from keeping the ground humid," for instance, the companies were forced to build veritable highways. The roads workers chopped out of the forest were twenty to thirty meters wide, like two-lane city streets.[32] Still, every rainy season, the roads were "covered by a few

---

[27] PanAmerican, *Mexican Petroleum*, pp. 31–33, 55–56; Memorandum Re: Cerro Azul Well Number 4 of the Huasteca Petroleum Company, P&S/HR, Box C 45, File C45/5: Mr. Body's Visit to Mexico, January–April 1916; Body to Cowdray, Tampico, February 12, 1916, P&S/HR, Box A4. There is a photograph of the Juan Casiano camp in Chinampa in SMU/ED, Box 139, Folder 5823, Scrapbook, "Clippings, Vol. 1."

[28] BP, vol. 19, no. 1 (January 1925), p. 29.

[29] Ordoñez, *El Petróleo*, p. 70.

[30] B. Traven, *La Rosa Blanca* (Mexico City: Selector, 1994), pp. 56–57, 300, 437.

[31] Stewart, "The Petroleum Industry of Mexico," SMU/ED, Box C43, File 43/1.

[32] Ordoñez, *El Petróleo*, p. 42.

inches to a few feet of water."[33] Similarly, the rain turned the earth under railroad tracks into quicksand under the heavy tonnage, causing delays in construction and accidents. Even the asphalt the companies laid out in the mid-1920s succumbed to the weather. Until nationalization, the companies never ceased to bemoan the fact that the roads were "in an impassable condition" for the months of the rainy season, costing them time and, therefore, money.[34] The rains also rusted metals: pipelines, storage tanks, tools, and the like wore down quickly, creating conditions for spills and accidents, as discussed below.

To contend with a hostile natural environment, each company tried to use a single route for all its needs. Water and oil pipelines and telephone and telegraph lines often followed the same highway.[35] That practice helped contain the razing through the 1910s, when men still clear-cut the forest with hand tools. In 1923 the companies introduced tractors, excavators, and heavy equipment driven by internal combustion engines.[36] The introduction of machinery meant faster and more expansive deforestation since the pace of environmental change no longer depended on human energy alone. How many miles of forest were cut down for pipeline and communications is difficult to estimate, however. Only the extension of pipeline was recorded, but the fact that the other lines tended to be parallel means that pipeline figures represent a reasonable minimum estimate of the mileage involved. By late 1924, 2,589 miles of pipeline crossed the Huasteca, an increase from 600 miles in 1920 made possible by the new machinery.[37] Recalling that the distance between the Tamesí and the Cazones Rivers was roughly 117 miles, the 2,000 miles of pipeline represent twenty-two times the length of the region that oil created. By any measure, that meant extensive clearing of land.

---

[33] Quoted in Kuecker, "A Desert," p. 241. See also D. W. Reid to E. M. Johnson, Tampico, June 18, 1925, IAEG/CB, Acct. 3328, Box 11, Correspondence File.

[34] E. M. Johnson to C. L. Baker, Tucson, June 27, 1925, IAEG/CB, Acct. 3328, Box 11, Correspondence File.

[35] London, "Our Adventurers," p. 24.

[36] Gustavo Ortega, *Los recursos petrolíferos de México y su actual explotación* (Mexico City: Talleres Gráficos de la Nación, 1925) shows photos of tractors and machines, on pp. 9–11. Additional photos of new machinery are in BP, vol. 15, no. 6 (July 1923) and BP, vol. 19, no. 1 (January 1925), photographic section. There is a picture of "Clearing the Jungle in Oil Fields," showing laborers using machetes in "Mexico's Petroleum Industry," *The Mexican Review*, ca. 1920, in SMU/ED, Box 107, Folder 5220.

[37] Desarrollo e importancia de la industria petrolera mexicana, June 20, 1923, AGN/DP, Caja 7, Exp. 4, 029(02)/35; Cleland, *The Mexican Yearbook 1920–1921*, p. 314; Cleland, *The Mexican Yearbook 1922–1924*, p. 256; "Métodos de obtener, conducir, transportar y almacenar petróleo," BP, vol. 5, no. 2 (August 1917), pp. 126–129.

Along the pipeline at different intervals, the companies used more land for pumping stations. These kept the heavy crude oil moving, but because they did not require a large retinue of workers on site to keep them functioning, their size was much smaller than the drilling camps. By 1917, there were at least twenty-nine different pumping stations between Tuxpan and Tampico. The oil flowing from Cerro Azul No. 4, on the lot that belonged to the Flores widow who migrated to Los Angeles, for example, passed through nine pumping stations. Similarly, the crude from the Peláez clan well, Potrero del Llano No. 4, traveled 155 kilometers (93 miles) through eight pumping stations before reaching El Aguila's refinery in Tampico.[38] Typically built on the banks of streams, the pumping stations were about as large as a city block. Once they were running, they did not need permanent employee quarters. Less than two dozen men operated the stations on a rotating basis. El Aguila, for example, had a crew of eighteen men in charge of five stations between Potrero del Llano and Tuxpan, a distance of fifty-two kilometers (thirty-one miles).[39]

The pumping stations changed land use patterns in other ways as well. In addition to land, they required fresh water. As the leases stipulated, the stations could use as much water as necessary from any available source, often at rates ranging from 100 to 800 liters per second. The water went into boilers to heat the crude and keep it flowing inside the pipeline. The amounts of water used over time were considerable: the oil from Cerro Azul No. 4, for example, used sixteen boilers at each station. Therefore, this trunk of pipeline alone required daily rations of water for a total of 144 boilers.[40] Even though not all pumping stations had that many boilers, clearly the twenty-nine stations throughout the Huasteca increased fresh water consumption to unprecedented levels.

In addition to the rainforest, ecosystems like swamplands, mangroves, and sand dunes experienced fundamental environmental upheaval as the companies built terminals and refineries on them. By 1921, the oil barons

---

[38] The Oil Fields of Mexico. Memorandum, pp. 8–9, SMU/ED, Box 50, Folder 3401. The Cerro Azul pumping stations were spaced at an average of fourteen miles apart and located, from south to north, at Cerro Azul (two within five km), Juan Casiano (Chinampa de Amatlán), San Jerónimo, La Laja, Horconcitos, Garrapata, Tankville, and Mata Redonda. The Potrero del Llano crude went through stations located at Potrero del Llano, Tierra Amarilla, Tanhuijo, San Diego de la Mar, San Gregorio, Bustos, Santo Tomás, and Chijol.

[39] Chief's Estimates and Schedules, 1916, P&S/HR, Box C 45, File C45/6.

[40] BP, vol. 12, no. 5 (November 1921), p. 286; LGO, vol. 11, no. 14 (February 10, 1923); BP, vol. 5, no. 3 (March 1918), pp. 325–326, 331. There are photographs of pumping stations in Ortega, *Los recursos*, photographic section.

Table 3.1. *Refineries Located in the Huasteca and Tampico, 1887–1924*

Date, ca.	Company	Location
1897	Waters Pierce	Arbol Grande, Tampico, Tamaulipas
1914	El Aguila	Doña Cecilia, Tampico, Tamaulipas
1914	Transcontinental	Las Matillas, (Tampico) Veracruz
1915	Huasteca	Mata Redonda, (Tampico) Veracruz
1916	Huasteca	Juan Casiano, Chinampa, Veracruz
1916	El Aguila	Los Naranjos, Amatlán, Veracruz
1916	PennMex	Alamo, Temapache, Veracruz
1917	El Aguila	Port of Tuxpan, Veracruz
1919	PennMex	Port of Tuxpan, Veracruz
1920	Texas Co.	Puerto Lobos, Cabo Rojo, Veracruz
1920	El Agwi	Puerto Lobos, Cabo Rojo, Veracruz
1920	La Atlántica	Puerto Lobos, Cabo Rojo, Veracruz
1920	Island Refining	Puerto Lobos, Cabo Rojo, Veracruz
1921	La Corona	Pueblo Viejo, (Tampico) Veracruz
1921	Continental	Pueblo Viejo, (Tampico) Veracruz

Sources: *Boletín del Petróleo*, vol 8, no 3 (September 1919), p. 227; vol. 10, no. 3 (September 1920), pp. 306–307; vol. 14, no. 1 (January 1922), pp. 83–84; vol. 14, no. 3 (September 1922), pp. 191–195; Robert Glass Cleland, *The Mexican Yearbook, 1920–1921* (Los Angeles: Mexican Yearbook Publishing Co., 1922), p. 315; E. DeGolyer, "The Petroleum Industry of Mexico," The Papers of Everette Lee DeGoyler, Sr. Mss 60, Box 107, Folder 5220; *Weekly News Summary*, New York, June 11, 1917, Pearson & Son, Historical Records, Box A4: Mexico – Miscellaneous Private Correspondence.

inaugurated fifteen plants in northern Veracruz and Tamaulipas (listed in Table 3.1). There was one more in San Luis Potosí (Doheny's El Ebano) and two more in southern Veracruz (Minatitlán and Veracruz). Two more would be built before 1938, at Poza Rica and Atzcapotzalco. Of the 1921 plants, seven were concentrated along the Pánuco River near Tampico (including El Ebano). Three smaller plants to extract gasoline and burn natural gas were located in Los Naranjos, Chinampa de Amatlán, and Alamo. Two more refineries were built at the mouth of the Tuxpan River in the port of Tuxpan itself.[41] In addition, there were other installations,

[41] LGO, vol. 10, no. 823 (November 11, 1922); BP, vol. 12, nos 2 and 3 (August–September, 1921), p. 92; BP, vol. 19, no. 1 (January 1925), p. 34; BP, vol. 14, no. 4 (October 1922), map section; Cleland, *The Mexican Yearbook 1920–1921*, p. 315; Cleland, *The Mexican Yearbook 1922–1924*, pp. 262–263.

like terminals, used for loading the crude onto tankers to be refined later in places like Texas. For illustration purposes, I will examine only two sites of transformation: Puerto Lobos and Tampico.

Oil on the Sand Dunes: Puerto Lobos

Puerto Lobos was the name given to the complex of terminals and refineries erected on the southern end of the Cabo Rojo Peninsula that encloses the Tamiahua Lagoon. Ruthless competition among the companies led to the establishment of an industrial belt amidst the sand dunes of the Cabo. By the mid-1910s, several outfits extracting oil in Chinampa, Amatlán, Toteco, Tepetate, and Zacamixtle realized that the closest port, Tuxpan, was closed off to them. The British El Aguila and the American PennMex controlled the land at the mouth of the Tuxpan River, foreclosing the possibility to build there. The only other alternative, Tampico, was at least sixty-five miles of pipeline away. Cabo Rojo, however, was only eighteen to twenty-four miles away and had the added benefit of lacking custom officials to collect petroleum taxes.[42]

There were, moreover, environmental reasons for building at Cabo Rojo. The companies had found that "regretfully" the natural patterns of the Gulf interfered with the plans of their best engineers.[43] The combination of *nortes*, hurricanes, and Gulf currents made the laying of submarine pipeline for loading tankers at sea extremely difficult. Because of the winds and waves, "the pipe continually got washed around and broken," wrote an El Aguila employee.[44] The *nortes*, moreover, made docking and loading oil tankers a risky proposition throughout the five or more months of the windy season. Hurricane season, of course, halted loading altogether. The coastal sand dunes of Cabo Rojo, however, promised to shelter the pipeline from the wind and the waves while the coves did the same for the tankers.[45]

---

[42] BP, vol. 6, no. 1 (July 1918), pp. 84–89; Antonio L. Luna, "Procedimiento empleado por diversas compañías petroleras en la zona de Tuxpan, Ver., para el tendido de líneas submarinas para la carga de petróleo," BP, vol. 9, no. 2 (February 1920), pp. 94–95 and map; BP, vol. 14, no. 4 (October 1922), map section; Summary of Mexican Oil News, August 31, 1918, SMU/ED, Box 108, Folder 5246.

[43] As an employee put it, "I should regret seeing this topping plant placed right at the bar." Body to Cowdray, New York City, May 4, 1916, P&S/HR, Box A4.

[44] P. C. Stewart, "History of the Laying of Submarine Pipelines," November 28, 1918, SMU/ED, Box 107, Folder 5220.

[45] James H. Hall, "How the Sea Lines Are Laid," *The Petroleum Age*, vol. 7, no. 3 (March 1920), p. 43, SMU/ED, Box 107, Folder 5220.

Thus, construction of Puerto Lobos began in earnest in 1916. Four companies erected terminals and refineries there, while two more laid out pipeline across Cabo Rojo and into the Gulf. The first shipping terminal was inaugurated in 1918.[46] Five docks stretched over white sands and blue waters to welcome ships packed with equipment, supplies, and workers. A narrow gauge railroad used to facilitate the transportation of pipes also made its debut across the sand. To keep incoming oil warm and flowing, workers built several pumping stations on the beaches as well. Four refineries rose over the sands by 1921. By 1922, pipelines running through the bottom of the Tamiahua Lagoon climbed over and across the sand dunes, injecting crude into twenty-four big storage tanks at the refineries. A total of twenty-seven separate tendrils of pipeline undulated over the sand dunes until they submerged underwater for three more kilometers to load tankers waiting in the open Gulf. Within one year of the opening of the first terminal, the pipelines were pouring crude into several tankers "every hour, night and day," at the rate of "over 1,200 barrels of oil, or . . . 20 barrels a minute," for a total of two million barrels per month.[47]

Conscious of the threat of *nortes* and hurricanes, moreover, the companies built an observation bridge to watch the pipelines as well as a signal tower to communicate with tankers at sea. Offices, roads, dormitories, houses, and cafeterias complemented the picture of industrial progress, completed by a pair of derricks in 1925. Two wells were drilled in Cabo Rojo, but it is not clear that they produced any oil. The whole complex occupied approximately eighteen of the seventy-seven miles that made up Cabo Rojo, at a minimum of one hundred hectares (247 acres) per terminal.[48]

---

[46] The six companies involved were the Texas Co. of Mexico, Cortés Oil Corp., La Atlántica, Compañía Metropolitana de Oleoductos, Transcontinental Petroleum (Doheny subsidiary until 1921), and El Agwi. Luna, "Procedimiento," BP, vol. 9, no. 2 (February 1920), pp. 95, 101.

[47] Hall, "How the Sea Lines Are Laid," p. 42, SMU/ED, Box 107, Folder 5220.

[48] Chief Inspector to Department of Labor, August 21, 1921, AGN/DT, Caja 329, Exp. 30; Chief of Department of Petroleum to Chief of Department of Labor, January 12, 1920 AGN/DT, Caja 224, Exp. 27; Javier Santos Llorente, "Nuestras raíces," *Nosotros los petroleros*, year 2, no. 12 (1980), pp. 6–9; Gonzalo Morales vs. El Agwi, AGN/JFCA, Caja 6, 1927, Exp. 15/927/135c; Luna, "Procedimiento," pp. 91–101; BP, vol. 20, no. 3 (September 1925), p. 201. Photographs of submarine pipelines under construction in Puerto Lobos can be found in Leopoldo Alafita Méndez, Mirna Benítez Juárez, and Alberto Olvera Rivera, *Historia gráfica de la industria petrolera y sus trabajadores (1900–1928)* (Xalapa: Universidad Veracruzana, 1988), p. 39.

The transformation of the southern Cabo was startling. Imagined in 1910 as "an ornithologist's paradise," by 1919 Cabo Rojo was "Puerto Lobos,"

> the center of that bleak stretch of wind-blown tropic shore . . . Only now wireless stations occupy the eye where pelicans and aigrettes did formerly. Native towns, housing hundreds of employees, have replaced the shrub growth of the coastal vegetation . . . The scene that yesterday thrilled the philosophical soul of the dreamer with broad reaches of turquoise sky flecked with feathery clouds, and the limitless expanse of a crystal sea that give to the languor of the tropics its most charming setting, today has given place to a new picture – the picture of busy effort . . . Powerful pumping stations dot the coast and bring oil from the wells far inland to store it in great tank farms from where they pump it through submarine feeding lines to tankers flying the flags of all nations.[49]

Oil replaced avian life. It also flattened miles of sand dunes. Furthermore, pipelines and submarine lines ruptured with regularity, dumping oil on the sand, the beaches, and the Gulf. Repairs, moreover, took days because only foreign divers knew how to fix underwater pipeline.[50] In addition, just as there was "no littoral current to speak of" to batter ships, there was not sufficient wave action to wash away spilled oil before the tropical sun and heat cooked it into a "brittle crust" over the sand.[51]

Ultimately, the "picture of busy effort" did not last much beyond a decade in Puerto Lobos. When the companies shut down the Golden Lane in 1921, business at Puerto Lobos was doomed. The companies dismantled the refineries within four years of building them, in 1925. By 1929 the oil cycle had ran its course in Cabo Rojo. Terminals and pipelines disappeared. The only remnants left were the thirty-foot walls of the pumping stations and foundations of structures.[52] Nearly sixty years after the closure of Puerto Lobos, the archaeological ruins of the oil industry remained "buried and semi-covered" by "coastal pioneer plants" attempting to reclaim the sand dunes that the winds and storms had

---

[49] Hall, "How the Sea Lines Are Laid," p. 42, SMU/ED, Box 107, Folder 5220.

[50] Luna, "Procedimiento," pp. 93, 95.

[51] Stewart, "History of the Laying of Submarine Pipelines," p. 4, SMU/ED, Box 107, Folder 5220. The "brittle crust" effect was observed in the 1991 Persian Gulf war spills by Thomas Y. Canby, "After the Storm," *The National Geographic*, vol. 180, no. 2 (August 1991), p. 10.

[52] BP, vol. 20, no. 2 (August 1925), pp. 99–101; José Luis Melgarejo Vivanco, *Tamiahua: Una historia huasteca* (Xalapa: Ediciones Punto y Aparte, 1981), p. 208; Santos Llorente, *Episodios*, p. 125.

rebuilt.[53] Over the course of a half-century, nature was making progress in restoring the sand dunes of Cabo Rojo. Nothing of the sort happened at the quintessential oil town of the early twentieth century: Tampico.[54]

From Swamp to Refinery: The Transformation of Tampico

Until 1905 Tampico was "a desolate region in a tropical zone." Despite its "promise," the port was disconnected from "its hinterland," the Huasteca, and languished in fifth or sixth place in customs house receipts in the late Porfiriato.[55] As the oil companies realized early on, Tampico "necessitated extensive and expensive work" before it could become the world-class port they envisioned.[56] That meant environmental changes in land use of unprecedented scale, the kind only men of greed and grandeur could afford.

Despite its location, Tampico's environment posed serious challenges for modernizers. The seasonal hurricanes, the *nortes*, and the currents of the Gulf worked against development. The weather and ocean currents erected a sand bar at the mouth of the Pánuco River that limited navigation. In 1895 the sand bar was 25.5 feet high and ships with a draft deeper than 8 feet could not enter the river and reach Tampico except twice daily at high tide, and high tide was "slight – only about 18 inches."[57] The *nortes*, furthermore, made maneuvering into port quite difficult. As Fanny Calderón de la Barca found out in 1842, the fierce winds could make the Pánuco flow in reverse and turn ships into "floating prisons" for days at a time.[58]

Furthermore, even when a calendar year passed without hurricanes, the city was prone to flooding. With every rainy season, rising waters fused

53 John J. Poggie, Jr., *Coastal Pioneer Plants and Habitat in the Tampico Region, Mexico*, Coastal Studies Series Number Six (Baton Rouge: Louisiana State University Studies, 1963); Santos Llorente, *Episodios*, p. 126.
54 Tampico was not the only city that oil built, only the most important. In the Huasteca, several camps became real towns, including places like Zacamixtle, Cerro Azul, Tancoco, and Alamo. Tuxpan also grew substantially as a result of oil production. Not all survived past the boom years, however, but little has been written about them in general. The urban history of the oil towns of the Huasteca is a fertile area for research.
55 Quotes are from Kuecker, "A Desert," pp. 1, 234. The information on custom house receipts is from Table 3, Ocasio Meléndez, *Capitalism*, p. 250.
56 T. N. Vaughn, "Report on Laying Sea Line no. 1A at Tuxpam Bar," November 1912, p. 1, P&S/HR, Box C 43, File C 43/1.
57 Campbell, *Mexico*, p. 50; Ocasio Meléndez, *Capitalism*, p. 71; Thomas L. Rogers, *Mexico: Si Señor* (Boston: Mexican Central Railway Co., Ltd., 1893), pp. 273–274.
58 Fisher and Fisher, eds., *Life in Mexico*, p. 622.

rivers and lagoons into one gigantic lake.[59] By the same token, as the waters receded, old swamps were replenished and new ones were created. Such natural cycles offended Tampico's city fathers. The stagnant waters and "foul odors" moved them to clamor for environmental engineering as early as the mid-nineteenth century.[60] In 1849, for example, the daily *El Noticioso* noted drainage works to tackle the flooding problem were long overdue.[61] But all drainage plans came to naught.

Other environmental transformations of Tampico did ensue, nonetheless. Communications links opened up commercial opportunities for the city after the telegraph arrived in 1883 and the railroad joined the port to the rest of the nation in 1885. Despite severe flooding during the 1889–1890 rainy season, local authorities and the railroad company undertook the construction of new piers and jetties to widen and deepen the mouth of the Pánuco River to accommodate larger ships. Major dredging works also began to remove the sand blocking the ships' entry. Public works of this sort were a hallmark of the Porfiriato across the country, and thus in 1895 the port welcomed its first large merchant ships, although three tropical storms between August and October began rebuilding the sand bar again. The following year, the hacendado Angel Sáinz Trápaga of El Tulillo offered land he owned in the port to the Waters Pierce Corporation (a subsidiary of Standard Oil of New Jersey) for a refinery. In 1897 Waters Pierce began producing kerosene from imported American crude oil and shipping it to the rest of Mexico via the new railroad. By 1899 large commercial houses had become the predominant architectural feature flanking Tampico's downtown plaza.[62]

Unwittingly, the modernizers of Tampico created conditions beneficial for another natural nemesis: the mosquito. The increase in communications, development, and population in the port allowed the vector of yellow fever, *Aedes aegypti*, to travel and settle there. The railroad and the merchant ships brought the dreaded insect to Tampico, while construction projects built prime mosquito habitat, such as "cisterns, gutters, and standing water."[63] The growing number of people working to upgrade the port's infrastructure and transform its environment likewise augmented

[59] BP, vol. 5, no. 4 (April 1918), p. 354; Alejandro Prieto, *Historia, Geografía y Estadística del Estado de Tamaulipas* (Mexico City: Tipografía Escalerillas, 1873), p. 292.
[60] Ocasio Meléndez, *Capitalism*, p. 202.
[61] Quoted in Carlos González Salas, *Del reloj en vela (Crónicas históricas de Tampico, Ciudad Altamirano y Ciudad Madero)* (Tampico: Grupo Unido de Alijadores de Tampico, 1983), p. 53.
[62] González Salas, *Del reloj*, p. 71; González Salas, *Tampico es lo azul*, p. 77; National Climatic Center, *Tropical Cyclones*, p. 57; Ocasio Meléndez, *Capitalism*, pp. 103–104.
[63] Kuecker, "A Desert," p. 160.

the mosquito's food supply. The immediate result was the 1898 yellow fever epidemic, the worst recorded in Tampico history. Between 290 and 300 people died in the city over the course of the rainy season. Although cases of yellow fever were reported the following year, forceful city efforts to "sanitize" the port and quarantine travelers shifted the pattern of the disease from epidemic to endemic.[64] The lesson was not lost on the recent arrivals, the oil companies, who would invest significant capital and labor to protect foreign employees from the unintentional consequences of environmental engineering, efforts the following chapter discusses.

In the twentieth century *el auge* (the oil boom) began and Tampico became the oil city it remains in the twenty-first. From 17,569 inhabitants in 1900, Tampico grew to 23,452 by 1910 and jumped to 94,736 by 1921, when it became the country's fifth largest city. The 432 acres the port occupied in 1910 expanded eightfold to 3,461 by the late 1920s.[65] The quiet city with "not much to see" that Calderón de la Barca toured at mid-nineteenth century was by 1916 a thriving cosmopolitan city boasting of twenty-four law firms, four casinos, seventy-seven liquor stores, thirty-four bars, seven professional photographers, nine watchmakers, six mineral water bottlers, two ice factories, nine Chinese laundries, twelve tailors, six bakeries, four fancy food shops, but no church.[66] More than fifty-eight oil companies made the port their official headquarters, expanding the city's core with new multistoried buildings. Downtown avenues were paved with Doheny asphalt and the square was lit with kerosene lamps. Tampico became an international city, according to a journalist,

> a gigantic stage set; neat, precise streets, towering office buildings; hotels with Simmons beds and filtered water; soda fountains with menus in English; cut-rate French perfumes; orchid-colored beauty shops; shops

[64] Ocasio Meléndez, *Capitalism*, pp. 163, 167; Telegrams regarding yellow fever in Ozuluama, August–September, 1903, AGEV, Ramo: Gobernación, Sub-Ramo: Salubridad, Fiebre Amarilla, Caja 1, Exp. No. 21, Letra F.

[65] Ocasio Meléndez, *Capitalism*, pp. 81, 173; Censo de 1921, Archivo Histórico del Ayuntamiento de Tampico (AHAT), Exp. 43–1921, no. 48; *Tampico/Madero: Plan Directorio de Desarrollo Metropolitano* (Mexico City: Secretaría del Patrimonio Nacional, 1975), p. 100.

[66] Fisher and Fisher, eds., *Life in Mexico*, p. 620; *Directorio de Tampico*, pp. 35, 37, 39–65. The church house in Tampico was in ruins through the 1920s: "no pews, a dirt floor, poorly made altars," according to W. L. Connelly (WC), A trip to Tampico, IAEG, Account 1722, Box 1, Diaries. In 1921, Mrs. Doheny, the General Manager of HPC (William Green), and "several American families" formed a committee to rebuild it. See R. Jordán to José Vasquez Schaffino, January 29, 1921, AGN/DT, Caja 326, Exp. 7. Today there is a plaque in the atrium of the cathedral recognizing Mrs. Estelle Doheny's contribution to its construction.

with American dresses, American shoes, American bathing suits, and American prices.[67]

The landscape alterations that engulfed Tampico as it mutated into a major oil port were without precedent. The first task was to connect the Huasteca to Tampico, a trip that had taken anthropologist Starr over sixty hours in canoes and horseback in 1901. The companies could not squander so much time, so they formed a partnership with the city to gouge out a canal ten feet deep, thirty feet wide, and eight miles long between the Pánuco River and the Tamiahua Lagoon for "fast gasoline launches" to race through. Excavation began in 1901 to scoop out the oil waterway that became the Chijol Canal.[68] In 1906 the companies built the oil deposit lot known as Tankville alongside the Pueblo Viejo Lagoon. The refineries followed: El Aguila began construction in 1912 and opened in 1914; so did Transcontinental. Huasteca opened in 1915; La Corona and Continental were finished in 1921. In addition, smaller companies bought the swamplands and mangroves on the banks of the Pánuco to build loading terminals, canneries, warehouses, pumping stations, storage tanks, and the like.[69] In 1919, likewise, one of the islands formed by the rivers and the lakes, Moralillo, bid farewell to its birds to welcome airplanes. Moralillo was Mexico's first airport (the fourth in the world), used to transport oil payrolls to the Huasteca, thus bypassing bandits and revolutionaries.[70]

The Pánuco River became an oil highway. Equipment and workers going between Tampico and the Huasteca moved up and down the river like schools of fish. As *The Gulf Coast Oil News* reported in May 1917, "Tampico's tugs, launches and barges [were] working as they never worked before. Everything that can carry freight or tow a barge is working almost day and night" plowing the Pánuco's waters.[71] Oil from El Tulillo

---

[67] Verna Carleton Millan, *Mexico Reborn* (Cambridge, MA: The Riverside Press, 1939), p. 216.

[68] González Salas, *Tampico es lo azul*, pp. 135; Hamilton, *Early Day*, p. 140.

[69] Some smaller companies were Mexican Gulf, Texas Co., El Agwi, East Coast Oil, International, and Magnolia Oil. BP, vol. 5, no. 3 (March 1918), pp. 236–237, 326; BP, vol. 5, no. 5 (May 1918), pp. 456, 554–555; BP, vol. 19, no. 1 (January 1925), p. 34; Ocasio Meléndez, *Capitalism*, p. 148; London, "Our Adventurers," p. 5. El Aguila's refinery in Doña Cecilia alone occupied approximately 600 hectares (1,476 acres). See General Layout of the Tampico Refinery, 1922, P&S/HR, Box C46, File C46/6. There are over sixty photographs of the construction of El Aguila's refinery in P&S/PA, P1: Tampico Refinery, 1913–1917.

[70] Ocasio Meléndez, *Capitalism*, pp. 218–219.

[71] Quoted in LaBotz, *Edward L. Doheny*, p. 72.

and Chapacao, too, "was taken down the Pánuco River in wooden barges pushed by stern-wheel steamers," at the rate of seventy-five thousand barrels per day until pipelines bypassed the "turns and twists" in the early 1920s. In 1918, alone, 105 tankers loaded oil daily in the river.[72]

That bustling activity required incessant modification of the Pánuco to keep nature at bay. The sand bar grew seasonally, so dredging became a serious concern. By 1912, the *nortes*, the hurricanes, and the Gulf currents had piled enough sand to require a scraping of ten meters in depth.[73] In 1916 a major hurricane filled the trench in the riverbed again, and sandblasted and damaged the jetties.[74] A planning fever ensued. Dredging began amidst delirious talk of digging east toward El Tulillo and El Ebano and of broadening the Chijol Canal to "giv[e] access to tankers all the way to the production centers themselves."[75] By 1918, however, those plans had been abandoned, as the companies focused on the "urgent" need to rebuild the jetties before nature refilled the sandbox at the bottom of the river. To rush construction, they offered to finance the project at the rate of a tax of six Mexican cents per barrel the city could reimburse later.[76] The projects were completed in 1920, and the Pánuco proceeded to transport "unlimited quantities" of oil.[77] There would be no great dredging again until 1927.[78]

The sand and mud scooped from the riverbed proved useful in the service of further environmental engineering. The city used the dredging to fill in swampland and reshape the contours of Tampico. The city gained at least 270 hectares (675 acres) of "real estate" in such a fashion. One result of the literal growth of city land was the sealing off of the Tamesí altogether, making the Pánuco the only river whose shores touched the city.[79] Another result was the expansion of working-class

[72] William W. L. Connelly, *The Oil Business as I Saw It: Half a Century with Sinclair* (Norman: University of Oklahoma Press, 1954), p. 73; Stewart, "The Petroleum Industry of Mexico," p. 17, P&S/HR, Box C 43, File C 43/1.

[73] Body to Cowdray, September 27, 1912; Body to Cowdray, October 9, 1912, P&S/HR, Box A4.

[74] Ackerman, *Mexico's Dilemma*, p. 88; National Climatic Center, *Tropical Cyclones*, p. 78.

[75] *El Universal*, November 16, 1917.

[76] BP, vol. 5, no. 5 (May, 1918), p. 456; Ackerman, *Mexico's Dilemma*, p. 88; Joaquín Santeaella, *El Petróleo en México: Factor Económico* (Mexico City: Lubrija y Aguilar, Impresores, 1943), p. 42.

[77] PanAmerican, *Mexican Petroleum*, p. 17.

[78] *El Mundo*, January 20, 1927.

[79] Some of the landfill became the basis for the fortune of William F. Buckley, who had also acquired land in the Huasteca from small landowners. Ocasio Meléndez, *Capitalism*, pp. 204–205.

neighborhoods at the expense of mangroves and swamps along the eleven miles of riverbanks leading to the Gulf. Relatively established neighborhoods like Arbol Grande, La Barra, and Doña Cecilia grew through landfill, while others like Llanos del Golfo, Talleres, Mata Redonda, Refinería, and Miramar arose from it.[80]

In contrast to the downtown area, working-class neighborhoods lacked the infrastructure necessary to repress natural patterns and cycles. Asphalt, potable water, or sewage systems were nonexistent in workers' neighborhoods.[81] Communal outhouses were the rule, discharging waste into the Pánuco – the water source many working-class families used for bathing and household chores. Housing consisted of "row after row of rickety unscreened shacks" on stilts "to prevent the damp swamp water beneath from seeping through the floors."[82] But sandy landfill over swampland made the neighborhoods extremely vulnerable to floods. Despite the stilts, the houses were submerged by no fewer than eight hurricanes between 1921 and 1928. The 1927 flood was so severe it lasted three months.[83] Among working-class families, then, it was abundantly clear that nature could not be held at bay altogether. Water, seeping from below and pelting from above, would remain the main characteristic of Tampico, trying in vain to wash away landfill and recreate the swamps every season.

Nonetheless, Tampico became famous for its other liquid, oil. Popular *corridos* called it "The Port of Black Gold," a "great port, famous the world over."[84] Foreigners and Mexicans boasted the city was "the New York of Mexico," "the Sultana of the South," and "the Queen City of the Mexican Gulf." Americans fancied that Tampico was "destined to be

---

[80] Housing construction in the swamplands had begun in 1897 for railroad and Waters Pierce workers, but it accelerated as soon as El Aguila announced plans to build its refinery in 1912. Manuel González to Municipal President, May 8, 1913, AHAT, Exp. 17, no. 31; Interview with Mr. David Robles Saldaña, conducted by Lief Adleson on March 12, 1975 in Ciudad Madero, Tamaulipas, PHO/4/39; Kuecker, "A Desert," pp. 90–91; Ocasio Meléndez, *Capitalism*, pp. 109, 279–280, 288.

[81] R. Jordán to José Vasquez Schaffino, January 29, 1921, AGN/DT, Caja 326, Exp. 7.

[82] Millan, *Mexico Reborn*, p. 220. There are photos of working-class housing in Doña Cecilia, ca. 1924, in the AGN, Archivo Personal de Emilio Portes Gil, Gráfica, Caja 17, 982/1873.

[83] National Climatic Center, *Tropical Cyclones*, pp. 83–90; Interrogatorio, March 1930, AGN/JFCA, Caja 156, Exp. 930/336; BP, vol. 24, no. 5 (November 1927), p. 239, plus photographic section.

[84] *Corridos* are popular songs written by amateurs about historical events or personalities. "El Puerto del Oro Negro" was written by Samuel Lozano, but the date is unknown. Samuel Lozano, *El Puerto del oro negro; o Tampico en un sueño* (Mexico City: Imprenta Guerrero, n/d).

one of the premier cities of Spanish America." Their reason was straightforward: "Tampico strikingly illustrates what dynamic American energy coupled with brains and purpose can accomplish in the warm and languid South."[85] The British shared the same opinion, but claimed the credit for themselves.[86] The changes in land use were more than worth it for them. Before oil, wrote an American, Tampico was "a small and poverty stricken city tributary to a few unimproved wooden wharves . . . a remote, sleepy little port which existed to ship the scanty production of the back country," but within "a decade," the city was a "metropolis" where "money flowed like water, the air seemed to quiver with optimism."[87] Tampico was the jewel in the crown of the Golden Lane, the pinnacle of environmental transformation in the new ecology of oil.

Destruction and Degradation

The shift in land use that the infrastructure for oil extraction required was not the sole trigger for environmental change in the Huasteca. Ensconced in the remaking of the landscape was a process of wanton environmental destruction and degradation that affected all life in northern Veracruz. By the time of expropriation in 1938, the cumulative effects of oil development meant that the northernmost tropical rainforest of the Americas existed no more. Four specific and related environmental effects of oil exploitation illustrate the process: fire, pollution, habitat loss, and runaway wells.

Fire

If oil meant liquid gold, it also meant blazing fires. Whereas *hot, rainy,* and *humid* were the hallmark descriptions of the tropical rainforest, *flammable* was the operative adjective for the Huasteca in the oil era. Fire permeated hydrocarbon extraction from start to finish, to the point where the oil companies introduced a new season in the Huasteca, one that lasted all year: fire season.

[85] Terry, *Terry's Guide*, p. 50b.
[86] See Percy Norman Furber to Prime Minister Neville Chamberlain, New York, June 9, 1938, P&S/HR, File C44/8; "Mexican Eagle Oil Company, Ltd.," Supplement to the *Stock Exchange Gazette,* January 22, 1914, P&S/HR, Box C 43, File C 43/1; and Brousson, "The Oil Industry of Mexico," p. 8, P&S/HR, Box C 43, File C 43/1.
[87] McMahon, *Two Strikes*, pp. 27, 40–41.

Fire, first of all, was deliberately used to deforest the Huasteca. After cutting the trees, the companies used "controlled" fires to dispose of the remains, the same way that slash-and-burn farmers had done, but with a difference: the number, size, and intensity of the fires were exponentially larger. Continuous burning followed by construction of structures diminished the forest's capacity to recover. Over time, as more forest burned and more infrastructure went up, the industry prevented the rainforest from reclaiming the land as it formerly had done with fallow milpas. Thus, the oil companies created the conditions that eradicated the rainforest.

Second, the companies used fire as a cleaning agent for spilled oil, a practice called "burning dead oil."[88] Petroleum spills, which were numerous and voluminous, were collected in pits workers dug solely for that purpose and subsequently torched. In the case of Cerro Azul No. 4, for example, the well heaved oil for nine days, causing a gargantuan spill. The flow was caught in a number of dams three to six kilometers from the well and then set ablaze.[89] In cases where the wells were so close that the *chapopote* bleeds merged and burning risked exploding entire oil fields, the oil could remain on the ground "some years" before a match was lit to it. By then the heat and the sun had baked the crude into soft asphalt that took long hours to burn.[90]

Third, fire also increased in the Huasteca because the companies dotted the landscape with numerous petroleum storage tanks. During the "lightning season" of the spring and summer rain and storms, tanks burned down with systematic regularity. As geologist Hamilton wrote, "seldom was there a severe electric storm in the oil fields or around the terminals where the oil tankers were loaded, that one or more crude storage tanks was not struck and burned."[91] In 1920, for instance, during the month of September alone, lightning struck tanks 103, 114, and 120 in El Aguila's refinery. The fire spread to two more tanks, 115 and 125. It took over sixty men to put it out several days later (see Appendix III).[92]

---

[88] Thus labeled in the photographs. P&S/PA, P4/2: Potrero 1913–1919, P4/2/66.
[89] Memorandum Re: Cerro Azul Well Number 4 of the Huasteca Petroleum Company, P&S/HR, Box C 45, File C45/5: Mr. Body's Visit to Mexico January–April 1916.
[90] Report from V. González, August 6, 1918, AGN/DP, Caja 7, Exp. 10, 031(02)/3.
[91] Hamilton, *Early Day*, pp. 202–203; Body to Cowdray, Tampico, March 3, 1916, P&S/HR, Box A4; Stewart, "The Petroleum Industry of Mexico," p. 2, P&S/HR, Box C 43, File C 43/1.
[92] Unión Pro-Defensa Obrera Nacional to President Alvaro Obregón, September 30, 1924, AGN/DT, Caja 725, Exp. 2; BP, vol. 10, no. 3 (September 1920), p. 242 and photographic section.

Fourth, oil company negligence in the face of abundant and highly flammable chemicals in a tropical forest environment meant that fire hazards were omnipresent. Although lightning was clearly a natural element beyond the oilmen's control, the quality of the tanks was not. Short of not storing flammable chemicals in areas prone to thunderstorms, the safer alternative was using hermetically sealed steel tanks instead of the wood-and-metal or concrete-and-wood tanks the companies built. Saving time and money, however, was more important for the oilmen, who did not switch to steel tanks until the 1930s.[93] Likewise, lax maintenance of infrastructure eroded by rain increased fire danger. Cerro Azul was a case in point. In 1923 or 1924, a rusty pipe leaking natural gas caused an explosion that destroyed "a good number of houses and commercial establishments."[94] Careless waste disposal similarly courted fire. The oil companies used open trenches as dumpsters to flush out flammable waste to the nearest body of water. Thus, in 1927 a fire that started in an oily toilet in the Huasteca refinery inadvertently spread to the waste canal. Within seconds, the fire reached a pumping station and exploded it. The ensuing conflagration swallowed an unreported number of working-class homes, killed three children, and burned several firefighters severely.[95]

Lastly, what the fires did not destroy, they degraded. The "excessive heat" they caused shriveled vegetation, as government officials noticed since 1918.[96] More recently, Mexican researchers have found that plant life in the immediate perimeter of oil fires dies, while plants and trees further away bake slowly or lose their foliage, depending on their distance from the blaze. Even vegetation further away suffers because burning oil releases toxic metals that leaves absorb and carry throughout the plant. In time the toxins act like poison, killing the plant.[97] Four decades of oil fires in the Huasteca, then, must have released enough toxins not only to destroy vegetation all around but also to contaminate the bare soil left behind. Any landscape as splattered with oil as the Huasteca was needed only the occasional spark, cigarette, or lightning strike to ignite great fires, introducing greater stresses on the local ecology in general.

[93] Hamilton, *Early Day*, pp. 202–203.

[94] *El Universal*, December 12, 1924, reprinted in "Para evitar accidents en los campamentos petroleros," AGN/DP, vol. 705, Exp. 2.

[95] *El Mundo*, July 3, 1927; Receipt from the Consolidated Oil Company, November 15, 1928, AGN/JFCA, Caja 156, Exp. 930/336.

[96] Telegram from the Municipal President of Pánuco to the Secretary of Industry, Commerce, and Labor, July 18, 1918 and July 26, 1928, AGN/DP, Caja 7, Exp. 10, 032(02)/3.

[97] Rodolfo Reyes, "Otro 'flamazo' en los ductos de Tabasco deja tres heridos," *El Financiero*, February 24, 1995.

Pollution

If the oil industry was one of the worst global polluters of the twentieth century, the Huasteca was certainly the first tropical site of contamination.[98] Water and land were subject to the fallout from oil exploitation. Although it is impossible to reconstruct the full extent of the pollution across all ecosystems, the historical record is sufficiently rich to show that the impact was deep and widespread indeed. The waters of the Huasteca experienced the pollution component of the ecology of oil directly.[99] Rivers were among the most seriously contaminated. Through the 1920s, the refineries dumped "a good quantity of oil" directly into the Pánuco in daily clean-up operations, according to a worker.[100] Tankers and barges also dumped their oily rubbish into the Pánuco, while rivulets of petroleum escaping from leaky pipelines found their way there. In a 1918 study Mexican engineers found out just how much oil could be involved. The refineries alone incurred the following "losses" of petroleum in one year:

El Aguila	21,163,745 m^3
Pierce	4,779,625 m^3
Huasteca	21,874,701 m^3
Standard of New Jersey	6,016,955 m^3

Although the engineers did not say where the "lost" oil went, logic and location point to the Pánuco.[101] In the Huasteca the waterways near

98 On pollution in early sites in the United States, see Nancy Quam-Wickham, "'Cities Sacrificed on the Altar of Oil': Popular Opposition to Oil Development in 1920s Los Angeles," *Environmental History*, vol. 3, no. 2 (April 1998), pp. 189–209; and Brian Black, "Oil Creek as Industrial Apparatus: Re-creating the Industrial Process Through the Landscape of Pennsylvania's Oil Boom," ibid., pp. 210–229. On more recent rainforests, see Paul Sabin, "Searching for Middle Ground: Native Communities and Oil Extraction in the Northern and Central Ecuadorian Amazon, 1967–1993," ibid., pp. 144–168; and Judith Kimerling, *Amazon Crude* (Washington, DC: Natural Resources Defense Council, 1991).

99 The industry also increased water demands for its camps, pumping stations, and refineries. Despite the abundance of rain in the forest, the fluctuation in water levels during the dry season meant that water removed from streams and rivers during low flows affected all other uses in the immediate vicinity and further downstream: subsistence agriculture, mammal watering holes, and amphibian, reptile, and fish spawning grounds, not to mention the countless species of thirsty plants inhabiting swamps, mangroves, and estuaries. The historical record, however, is silent on all these issues.

100 Quoted in Ariel Martínez Gallegos, Alfonso Díaz Rey, Manuel de la Torre Rivera, and Gabino González Aguilar, *Testimonios de la expropiación* (Mexico City: Editorial Nuestro Tiempo, 1990), p. 58; *El Universal*, March 18, 1918.

101 BP, vol. 9, no. 1 (January 1920), p. 79.

Potrero del Llano were flooded when well No. 4 flowed uncontrollably for thirty days between December 27, 1910 and January 25, 1911. Geologist DeGolyer estimated that six million barrels of crude went into the Buenavista and Tuxpan Rivers. Through 1915 that meant the Buenavista carried "an average" of eight inches of oil.[102]

That pollution often turned into deadly river fires. In January 1923, for example, a gasoline slick on the Pánuco caught fire and spread to a tanker loading fuel. The *San Leonardo* exploded in mid-river and burned for over twenty-four hours. Five men died and five more were seriously burned. Several more disappeared, presumed dead.[103] A similar case exploded the *Essex* in 1927, killing thirty-eight workers.[104] The American consul in Tampico, Claude Dawson, described a 1917 incident thus:

> The burning barges afforded a spectacular and awe-inspiring sight, said to be unique to the Pánuco River, and which threatened for a while to involve surrounding property and shipping on the river. The fire started about 11:30 a.m. from an explosion, and burned 20 hours. The element of greatest danger occurred after midnight, when the upper works of the barges were consumed to the water's edge and flaming oil boiled over and was carried downstream with the swiftly flowing current. Fortunately the flaming sheet was obstructed in its progress by the current deflector which juts into the river about midway between the burning barges and the interned German passenger liner "Antonina," and was thus broken into small patches which burned out before reaching that vessel.[105]

River fires were not unique to the Pánuco, however. The six million barrels dumped into the Buenavista and Tuxpan Rivers between December 1910 and January 1911 burned both rivers when El Aguila torched the spill to clean it up.[106] The fire ran for twenty kilometers in the Buenavista, then burned in the Tuxpan River until it entered the Tampamachoco Lagoon on the Gulf. According to engineer Ordoñez, the flaming liquid seared the riverbanks. "Until a few years ago," he wrote in 1932, "one

---

[102] DeGolyer, "The Oil Industry of Mexico," p. 469, P&S/HR, Box C 43, File C 43/1; T.H.V. to J.B.B., 7.4.1915, P&S/PA, P4/2/26, P4/2: Potrero 1913–1919; P&S/PA, P4/1/66, P4/1: Potrero 1910–1915.

[103] *El Mundo*, January 20, 1927. Photographs showing "Damage done by the fire to the S.S. San Leonardo on January 25th, 1923," are located in P&S/PA, P18 n/t, P/6/94, 95, 96, 97.

[104] *El Mundo*, January 20, 28, 30, 1927; *Sagitario*, March 26, 1927.

[105] Consul Dawson to Secretary of State, Tampico, September 7, 1917, RG 59, File 863.

[106] A. E. Chambers, "Potrero No. 4. A History of One of Mexico's Earliest and Largest Wells," *Journal* of the Institution of Petroleum Technologists, vol. 9, no. 37 (1923), p. 143.

could still see imprinted on the walls that box in the Buenavista River the fire's track... like a fire snake."[107]

The pollution harmed life in rivers and related ecosystems. Hamilton witnessed the punishment the Buenavista suffered: "the gravel beds all along the stream were saturated with oil, which solidified in the heat and air and became a natural wide-spread bed of impervious asphaltic gravel."[108] As recent scientific research has shown, mangroves and swamps like those of the Huasteca are extremely sensitive and "susceptible to long-term impacts" from just one oil spill.[109] Crude spilled from tankers in Puerto Rico and Panama, for example, was trapped in mangrove roots, defoliating and killing the trees. Even where the trees survived, the organisms dependent on their roots for reproduction died. Most affected were the eggs, larvae, and juveniles of fish, crabs, shrimp, shellfish, urchins, and small creatures. Furthermore, spill clean-up crews have found that in sluggish swamp waters the oil takes longer to degrade, evaporate, or be washed away. Instead, it sinks to the bottom, especially when it is heavy crude like that of the Huasteca. Oysters, mussels, and bivalves living below the surface ingest the sinking petroleum, often dying within twelve to twenty-four hours. Numerous species of clams, snails, and worms also die soon after exposure.[110] In the Potrero spill, for example, one writer noted that "fishing was destroyed in the Tuxpam River; the oyster beds were ruined by the thick asphalt which sank from the surface."[111] Mexican officials recognized in 1926 that fishing villages had been hurt by oil production. By 1937 they acknowledged as well that

---

[107] Ordoñez, *El petróleo*, p. 72.

[108] Hamilton, *Early Day*, p. 79.

[109] Miles O. Hayes, *Black Tides* (Austin: University of Texas Press, 1999), pp. 147, 170.

[110] José M. López, "Ecological Consequences of Petroleum Spillage in Puerto Rico," *The Proceedings of the Conference on Assessment of Ecological Impacts of Oil Spills* (Keystone, Colorado: American Institute of Biological Sciences, 1979), p. 897; Irma Rosas, Armando Báez, and Raul Belmont, "Oyster (*crassostrea virginica*) as Indicator of Heavy Metal Pollution in Some Lagoons of the Gulf of Mexico," *Water, Air, and Soil Pollution*, vol. 20, no. 2 (August 1983), pp. 127–135; Keith R. Cooper and Angela Cristini, "The Effects of Oil Spills on Bivalve Mollusks and Blue Crabs," in *Before and After an Oil Spill*, edited by Joanna Burger (New Brunswick, NJ: Rutgers University Press, 1994), pp. 142–145, 154; J. W. Anderson, J. M. Neff, B. A. Cox, H. E. Tatem, and G. M. Hightower, "The Effects of Oil on Estuarine Animals: Toxicity, Uptake and Depuration, Respiration," in *Pollution and Physiology of Marine Organisms*, edited by F. John Vernberg and Winona B. Vernberg (New York: Academic Press, 1974), pp. 304, 306; Hayes, *Black Tides*, pp. 30, 103, 154.

[111] Cleland, *The Mexican Yearbook, 1920–1921*, p. 296.

fishing had become "difficult" in the Pánuco on account of the industry.[112] The effects pollution had on sharks, alligators, and swordfish that
swam upriver were not recorded; neither was the effect on mammals that
drank from Huasteca streams, rivers, and lakes. An observant traveler,
nonetheless, left a crumb of evidence. While visiting a Pearson camp,
Bess Adams Garner captured an infant crocodile from a river "with teeth
all black from oil."[113]

Chronic pollution was detrimental for beaches, too. Sluggishly the
Pánuco flushed crude and oily wastes into the Gulf. Along the way, these
"sewage fingers" formed "slimes and scums," bacteria colonies that fed
on the waste, belching foul gases in the process and making the ocean
breezes offensively odorous.[114] Gulf waves, in turn, deposited the thick
mixtures back onto the beaches. The "beautiful sand dunes almost as
white as sugar" that *tampiqueños* enjoyed in 1900 were rapidly disfigured,
as oily "scabs" covered them. The "very pretty shells" found on the beach
disappeared.[115] By 1920 Tampico's Chamber of Commerce complained
to the municipal president about

> the absolute loss of both the best promenade in this city and the most
> acclaimed beaches ... [because] they are totally covered with *chapopote*
> and one can neither walk one step without one's shoes getting soaked
> by such bothersome and sticky object nor take a bath without one's body
> being totally tarred.[116]

Daring bathers, in fact, discovered that soap was a useless cleanser after
a dip in the water. To peel off the tar broth the waves slapped on them,
they scrubbed their bodies, ironically enough, with kerosene. Not even
the seaside dressing rooms were spared, moreover, as the waves crashing
against the buildings left petrol residues on the floor.[117]

In open waters, pollution hurts marine life. Oil slicks in the ocean
prevent oxygen from reaching organisms living below, threatening fish
with asphyxia and killing photosynthesizing life forms that feed larger

[112] Enrique Krauze, *Lázaro Cárdenas: General Misionero* (Mexico City: Fondo de Cultura
Económica, 1987), p. 28; BP, vol. 22, no. 6 (December 1926), p. 459; Departamento
Forestal de Caza y Pesca, *Boletín*, year 3, no. 9 (December 1937–February 1938), p. 54.
[113] Bess Adams Garner, *Mexico: Notes on the Margin* (Boston: Houghton Mifflin Company,
1937), p. 118.
[114] A. Nelson-Smith, *Oil Pollution and Marine Ecology* (New York: Plenum Press, 1973), p. 18.
[115] Chávez Padrón, *Testimonio*, p. 34; Ordoñez, *El petróleo*, p. 8; Notes, n/d, SMU/ED, Box
24, Folder 2437; Robles Saldaña, PHO/4/39.
[116] Chamber of Commerce to Municipal President, 1920, AHAT, Exp. 38, no. 32.
[117] Mesa Andraca, *Relatos*, p. 19; *El Universal*, March 18, 1918; *El Mundo*, May 15, 1929.

animals. Eggs and larvae fare the worst when the oil that does not evaporate sinks into crevices and rocks, forming "oil-cakes" that stick to the shells of mussels and other immobile sea creatures. Crude at the bottom of the ocean hardens over time, in essence paving the seafloor. In cases of chronic oil pollution of ocean waters, as was (and is) the case of the Gulf off Tampico, the carcinogenic oil compound benzene sinks and is ingested by bottom dwellers such as lobsters, sea stars, crabs, and others. Those species weaken or perish. When that happens, aquatic pests free of predators thrive. Fast swimmers migrate if possible, diminishing biodiversity in the process.[118]

Although there are only three instances of oil pollution in the Gulf on record before 1940, they are important. The first was the 1910 cascade from Potrero del Llano No. 4, which created an oil slick one hundred miles in length in the Gulf of Mexico. The second was the chronic spillage from Puerto Lobos over the decade the port was open. The third was the sinking of the fully loaded tanker *San Dunstano* in October 1929. Upon hitting "a submerged object" off Tampico, the captain jettisoned the crude into the Gulf, causing an enormous spill.[119] Thus, the marine life within the semi-circumferences of Tampico, Puerto Lobos, and the mouths of the Huasteca Rivers was deluged with spilled oil for decades, suffering untold but certainly negative consequences.

Chronic pollution affected not only water, but also inland territories. Earth dams, pipelines, and even abandoned wells caused pollution in the Huasteca. Although most occurred because of human error, environmental conditions in the tropics also played a role. Hastily built infrastructure succumbed to the weather. The rains chiseled cracks on the earth dams and floods broke them altogether, as the first successful Doheny well, La Pez No. 1 in El Tulillo, showed. As was customary, the company drilled

---

[118] Nelson-Smith, *Oil Pollution*, pp. 84, 86, 95, 98, 105, 111, 118, 124–125; Rebecca Arenas, *Museo vivo o naturaleza muerta* (Xalapa: Editorial de la Universidad Veracruzana, 1989), p. 16, 41. To the degree that oil pollution off the coast of Tampico remains constant to this day, it could well be the case that the composition of local marine life forms has changed. In 1996, for instance, the *National Geographic* photographed the organisms "living on the edge" in the deep, oil-drenched Mexican Gulf waters off the neighboring Texas and Louisiana shores: only mussels, crabs, eels, and sea worms thrived. Other marine animals exposed to chronic petroleum pollution exhibited "extremely abnormal and grotesque behavior," possibly on account of the carcinogens that saturate the waters. "Life Without Light," *National Geographic*, vol. 190, no. 4 (October 1996), pp. 86–97.

[119] Cable from Tampico to London, October 14, 1929, P&S/HR, Box C48, File C48/2 and C48/10.

before laying out pipeline, so when the well surged in 1904, it caused a giant spill. Laborers hastily dug up a pit to trap the cataract. The pool filled up and then the rainy season began. Torrential rains elevated the water level in the nearby La Pez Lagoon, ruptured the walls of the oil dam, and joined the two. As Ordoñez wrote, "the oil covered an immense extension of the lagoon with a black, thick and iridescent blanket where thousands of aquatic birds died, stuck in the viscous liquid."[120]

The rain also rusted, gnawed, and unearthed pipelines, increasing spillage. After the rainy season, in February 1938, a Mexican official reported finding "eighteen *chapopote* spills of larger or smaller extension" within two kilometers of pipeline on the Corcovado drillings in Pánuco. Near the boilers, the inspector found another leaky pipeline that had filled a hole "approximately 70 meters long by 4 meters deep."[121] In October 1930, a flood completely destroyed the pipeline heading north from PennMex's camp in Alamo. Dead cattle and crude oil floated down the swollen Tuxpan River to the Gulf, contaminating both bodies of water.[122] Likewise, a flood destroyed the pipeline built in 1932 from Poza Rica to Mexico City in September 1937. In every case the repairs remained on hold until floodwaters receded. Workers waited days, weeks, or even months before the ground reappeared and allowed them to find the source of the spill to plug it.[123] The 1927 rainy season, for instance, kept the Huasteca underwater anywhere from four to twelve weeks. As the water level dropped, however, roads and riverbanks eroded. Mud slides ensued, cracking pipeline, dragging down pumping stations, and burying installations under several feet of earth.[124] Fixed infrastructure of the sort the oil companies needed fared poorly in the dynamic and unstable landscape of the Huasteca, to the detriment of both the industry and the land.

The end of oil production, furthermore, did not necessarily spell the end of pollution. Abandoned or exhausted wells often continued polluting. Exhausted wells were covered with dirt and cement only. Over the course of a few seasons, the rain eroded the cement and the dirt, exposing the cavity, filling it up with water, and oozing remnant oil to

[120] Ordoñez, *El petróleo*, pp. 55, 58.
[121] Acta Num. 58, February 14, 1938, AGN/DAT, Caja 358, Exp. 10, p. 3.
[122] *El Mundo*, October 24, 1930. See also *El Mundo*, May 15, 1932.
[123] Josephus Daniels to Secretary of State, Mexico City, September 26, 1937, RG 59, File 812.5045/563.
[124] Interrogatorio, AGN/JFCA, Caja 156, Exp. 930/336; BP, vol. 24, no. 5 (November 1927), photographic section.

the surface.[125] In the training camp of Tanhuijo, for instance, none of the twenty-five wells was capped at all. They continued percolating oil and salt water into 1935. The meandering rivulets cascaded into an open trench, which, in turn, emptied into an estuary. Eventually the rainbow-hued cocktail drained into the Tamiahua Lagoon and thence to the Gulf, polluting every inch of land and water along the way.[126]

Tanhuijo was not exceptional. As early as October 1923, a Mexican engineer reported that there were 315 abandoned wells in Chinampa, Amatlán, Zacamixtle, Cerro Azul, and Potrero del Llano that had not been covered and were polluting the land.[127] In 1927 *El Mundo* photographed an abandoned well near the town of Pánuco and reported that "the pressure from the salt water has destroyed the cap and is spilling onto the surface forcefully... [and] has inundated a large zone." "The salt water," added the reporter, "is extremely high in temperature, and because it is sulfurous has completely killed all the vegetation around it."[128] The twelve Puerto Lobos wells must have affected the Tamiahua Lagoon directly as well. Even though none seem to have been successful producers, the boring of holes at the bottom of the lagoon must have caused serious disruption to the life forms that survived the contamination and asphalting of their environment.[129]

In the Pánuco fields, furthermore, abandoned wells created an unusual type of pollution. Upon exhausting their oil, some wells spewed out what is commonly known as dry ice. The wells expelled millions of cubic meters of carbon dioxide, whose sudden expansion caused "the condensation and solidification of water vapor in the atmosphere," that

---

[125] Cosmos Oil Company to Jerónimo Gómez, September 8, 1928, AGN/JFCA, Caja 108, Exp. 929/781.

[126] Hamilton, *Early Day*, pp. 24, 31; telegram from Tanhuijo neighbors to President Lázaro Cárdenas, December 28, 1935, AGN/Presidentes: Lázaro Cárdenas (P/LC), Exp. 432.3/167; BP, vol. 28, no. 1 (July 1929), pp. 81–82, photographic section.

[127] Chief of Tuxpan inspectors to Chief of Departament of Petroleum, March 28, 1923, and Lista de pozos con permiso pero sin haber sido taponeados, October 5, 1923, AGN/DP, Caja 40, Exp. 9 310/11.

[128] *El Mundo*, May 15 and July 17, 1927.

[129] Ibid., January 10 and April 15, 1928; E. DeGolyer to T.J. Ryder, New York, June 8, 1923, and Paul Weaver to R. D. Hutchinson, Tampico, May 13, 1922, SMU/ED, Box 117, Folder 5374. There are photographs of three of the wells in the lagoon in BP, vol. 25, no. 6 (June 1928), photographic section. El Aguila reported in 1925 that its first "test" well in the lagoon itself "proved a failure," but there was another test underway. Report of the Directors and Accounts, to 31st December, 1925, to be submitted to the Annual General Meeting to be held in Mexico City on 5th July, 1926, P&S/HR, Box C 43, File C43/3.

is, ice. A well Marian Storm saw in Loma del Pozo in 1924, for instance, had been blanketing the land with "white flecks" of "pure carbon dioxide snow" for at least a year. Quebrache No. 1 produced the same "strange" phenomenon, shooting out "gleaming fragments of snow." Its neighbor, Quebrache No. 2, meanwhile, produced "frozen oil" the consistency of "very good fudge just before it hardens." The result was the same: the wells "had laid waste the land around."[130]

Habitat Loss

In addition to degrading the environment through fire and pollution, the oil companies also reduced habitat for species other than humans. The deforestation required for infrastructure plus urbanization around refineries, gasoline plants, and ports fragmented ecosystems or eliminated them altogether. From there the effects rippled further. The record in the Huasteca is meager in regard to flora. The only information extant shows that by 1932 and 1940, only two types of trees observed in the mid-nineteenth century still existed, the *chijol* (*Piscidia erythrina*) and the mangrove (*Rhizophora mangle*). The other trees spotted in the 1930s and 1940s were not mentioned in 1852, suggesting not only that the lists were incomplete, but also that as the rainforest disappeared, introduced or opportunistic species replaced it.[131]

The effects of ecosystem fragmentation and habitat loss were more noticeable on the fauna. Some species were forced to migrate further away or closer to humans. Newspaper accounts show that as Tampico expanded, jaguars and leopards found themselves perilously close to human settlement. That proximity led to occasional big cat attacks on humans, which, in turn, made the felines subject to vigorous hunting campaigns.[132] Martha Chávez Padrón, born and raised in Tampico, was observant enough to notice that during her lifetime the butterflies that had swarmed to the port in springtime had disappeared entirely.[133] By 1932 engineer Ordoñez similarly noticed the absence of yesteryear's "herds" of deer and wild ducks, writing that only "corners" of the Huasteca still

---

[130] Storm, "Wells," pp. 522–525; *El Mundo*, August 9, 1923. For a photograph of the Quebrache ice well, see BP, vol. 26, no. 2 (August 1928), photographic section.

[131] For 1932, see Censo, AGEV/CAM, Exp. 1113, Tierra Blanca, Tepetzintla. For 1940, see Basauri, *La población*, pp. 57–62. For 1852, see Gutiérrez Rivas, "La familia Herrera," p. 80.

[132] Ordoñez, *El petróleo*, p. 90.

[133] Chávez Padrón, *Testimonio*, p. 17.

housed wildlife.[134] Two years later, the dearth of animal life sounded enough alarm for authorities to limit the hunting of crocodiles and caimans to certain months of the year. To protect the reptiles, the Mexican government thus created a new official season, hunting season.[135] Elsewhere in the Huasteca where urbanization was insignificant, the fragmentation of ecosystems resulting from roads, railroads, pipelines, and communication links also had an adverse impact on both the flora and the fauna, especially the larger predators that roam large territories. Infrastructure disrupted feeding and nesting grounds, restricted migration and disturbed reproduction patterns, causing a general decline in biodiversity. Despite the absence of firm figures on the populations of flora and fauna in the early twentieth-century Huasteca, it is safe to assume that loss of habitat for multiple species was an integral component of the changes in land use imbedded in the ecology of oil.

Runaway Wells

The most remarkable source of wealth and environmental destruction in the Huasteca was one and the same: the "gusher" wells. Although gushers were known in the United States, they were dwarfed in comparison to Mexico's. As one oilman remarked to Doheny, "those we drilled in Illinois and Caddo were just little creeks of oil. I tell you those Mexican wells are oceans."[136] The Mexican gusher became a "phenomenon" because of the peculiar natural composition of northern Veracruz oil. It contained atypically high quantities of hydrogen sulfides and had unusually high temperatures: 140°–150°F (in contrast, Texas and Louisiana oil measured 90°F). That combination meant that the oil in the entrails of the Huasteca was under extreme natural pressure – hence the seepages throughout the rainforest. When a driller broke the rock roof above the liquid, therefore, the oil literally exploded out of the earth.[137] The mixture of highly toxic and flammable gases and extremely high temperatures gave the wells extraordinary destructive capacity. Forty are documented in the literature (listed in Appendix IV), twelve of which caught fire,

[134] Ordoñez, *El petróleo*, p. 42.
[135] *El Mundo,* June 24, 1934.
[136] Quoted in Davis, *Dark Side*, p. 74. Taylor and Welty wrote in 1950 that in the United States "hitting a gusher, of course, is a rare experience," *Black Bonanza*, p. 136.
[137] E. DeGolyer, "The Significance of Certain Mexican Oil Field Temperatures," reprinted from *Economic Geology*, vol. 13, no. 4 (June 1918), pp. 275, 296, 300, IAEG, Kessack D. White Collection (KW), Acct 2116, Box 3, File 1919.

several of them on more than one occasion. The gusher wells, although only a tiny fraction of the total, thus epitomized the environmental consequences of oil production in Mexico in the early twentieth century. The most spectacular was San Diego de la Mar No. 3, better known as "Dos Bocas."

Dos Bocas put Mexican oil production on the map in more ways than one. It trumpeted to the world that Mexico's subsoil was soaked in fossil fuels. It also left an indelible imprint on the landscape that remains to this day. San Diego de la Mar was located approximately sixty-five miles (108 kilometers) south of Tampico, in the San Jerónimo condueñazgo. The terrain was swamp alternating with sand dunes and mangroves, a few kilometers from the Tamiahua Lagoon to the east. On the west, San Jerónimo was flanked by the rainforest. In 1900, the municipality to which San Jerónimo belonged, Tantima, had a total of 6,774 inhabitants. Of these, 27% were Teenek, 3% Nahua, and the rest were mestizos. All worked in agriculture, but the mestizos included fishermen.[138] In 1901 the Barber Asphalt Company of California acquired the subsoil rights to the condueñazgo and transferred them to El Aguila by 1906.[139]

In 1908 El Aguila men were drilling their third well in San Diego de la Mar when the "marvelous and ill-fated fountain of oil" that became Dos Bocas burst through the earth's crust.[140] It was the 4th of July. The Texan Charley Radford and his American and Australian crew had stopped drilling early to celebrate U.S. independence with "a few beers." As they enjoyed some relief from the 99°F temperature and the humidity, sulfuric gas began to crack the ground around the drilling hole, rising to the surface through the fissures.[141] A "thick smoke just like fog" quickly engulfed the derrick.[142] The chief geologist, Charles Hamilton, described how "the hole began to crater – drilling rig, derrick, pumps and boilers, all disappeared" into a concave forming in the earth.[143] To avoid the "head of

[138] Mexico, Dirección General de Estadística, *Censo general de la República Mexicana*, verificado el 28 de octubre de 1900 (Mexico City: Oficina Tipográfica de la Secretaría de Fomento, 1904).

[139] Charles W. Hamilton, "Geology of the Hacienda San Geronimo," December 25, 1913, SMU/ED, Box 112, Folder 5316.

[140] E. DeGolyer, "Mexican Petroleum Industry – Historical," May 25, 1920, p. 19, SMU/ED, Box 107, Folder 5220.

[141] W. M. Hudson, Pioneers in Texas Oil (PTO), Tape 79, p. 29; Kuecker, "A Desert," p. 311.

[142] Bada Ramírez, PHO/4/91.

[143] Hamilton, *Early Day*, p. 74.

poisonous gases" blowing out, the workers ran from the scene.[144] Mexican worker Pablo Guzmán rushed to put out the fires of the steam boilers that powered the drilling rigs, but then the earth "rumbled" below him and crude shot out like a projectile. It began raining oil. Droplets landed on the smoldering cinders, igniting the well in a tremendous explosion that shook the earth for miles around (see Figure 3.2).[145]

Less than a half hour had passed since the sulfur had cracked the earth. The fire now "roared," the "sun was completely dark," and the bright glow from the burning oil jet colored the skies red.[146] Within hours, people in Tampico could look to the southeast and see "over there, very far, a huge smoke column that rose gigantically until it blended into the clouds."[147] At nighttime, the urbanites saw "a brightness" coming from the "pillar of fire." From the Gulf, mariners sailing to Tampico saw the fire's "ruddy glow like a mammoth beacon."[148] By morning, neighbors noticed that, "over all of Tampico an extremely fine rain of intangible cinders fell." When it rained, "it seemed as though it rained ink."[149] The black cumulus cloud from the fire spread down the Gulf for no less than two hundred kilometers as the heat on site rose to unbearable temperatures.[150]

Despite all efforts, the first significant Mexican oil discovery literally went up in smoke. Lacking effective technology to put out oil fires despite a half-century of world oil exploitation, El Aguila could not suffocate the fire. It burned for fifty-seven days, until the fuel spent itself. In its wake, two enormous holes pockmarked the earth like twin gaping mouths open to the sky; hence "Dos Bocas." The amount of oil spilled and burned was astronomical. Mexican engineer Juan Palacios and American geologist Charles Hamilton estimated that 100,000 to 129,000 barrels spilled on a daily basis for the duration of the fire alone.[151] The owner of the well, Pearson, estimated the loss at ten million barrels, the equivalent of 420 million gallons of crude – by far the greatest oil spill in history, roughly

---

[144] Hamilton, "Geology of the Hacienda San Geronimo," SMU/ED, Box 112, Folder 5316.

[145] Kuecker, "A Desert," p. 310.

[146] Bada Ramírez, PHO/4/91; Palacios, "Memoria," p. 14.

[147] Juan Manuel Torrea and Ignacio Fuentes, *Tampico: Apuntes para su historia* (Mexico City: Editorial Nuestra Patria, 1942), p. 285.

[148] DeGolyer, "Mexican Petroleum Industry," p. 20, SMU/ED, Box 107, Folder 5220

[149] Torrea and Fuentes, *Tampico*, p. 285.

[150] Ordóñez, *El petróleo*, p. 65.

[151] Palacios, "Memoria," p. 21; Hamilton, "Geology of the Hacienda San Geronimo," SMU/ED, Box 112, Folder 5316.

Figure 3.2. Well on fire at San Diego de la Mar, better known as "Dos Bocas," caught on film by Russell Hastings Millward for *The National Geographic Magazine,* vol. 19, no. 11 (November 1908).

twice the amount burned in all the fires of the 1991 Gulf War.[152] The ecological impact of the first Mexican gusher was presumably catastrophic. Despite their richness, the sources lack the detail necessary to establish the depth and breath of the environmental legacy of Dos Bocas. An examination of the historical record in the light of more recent scientific scholarship, however, provides clues to uncover what geologist Everett Lee DeGolyer meant when he said the blowout and fire "devastated the surrounding region for many kilometers."[153]

Perhaps the most obvious question that Dos Bocas poses is whether the well killed human beings. It did, but it is unclear how many and under what circumstances. A local doctor reported that over 150 firefighters were hospitalized because sulfur dioxide emissions poisoned their eyes and swelled their eyelids shut, but he did not report any deaths.[154] Engineer Palacios by contrast reported that "several men" died poisoned, while the official *Boletín del Petróleo* noted that the dead were "many," mainly firefighters.[155] More recently, a scholar found that only two workers died, of asphyxia.[156]

The opportunities for human death were certainly ample, particularly in the futile firefighting efforts that followed the explosion and extended the reach of Dos Bocas to populations far beyond the local. At Pearson's request, President Díaz dispatched the Mexican army to battle the burning well. The soldiers labored feverishly, dumping dirt, gravel, and water on the flames, digging trenches, and erecting a dike "200 meters long by 15 meters wide and 8 meters tall" to contain the rushing oil. The dam was useless: it lasted "a few hours," melted by boiling oil like butter in a pan.[157] For weeks the soldiers were exposed to noxious gases and temperatures above 120°F without any protective equipment whatsoever.[158] In such

[152] "Mexican Eagle Oil Company, Ltd.," P&S/HR, Box C 43, File C 43/1. The 1989 Exxon Valdez spill in Alaska was 10.8 million gallons; the 1979 Ixtoc I spill in the Gulf of Mexico was 140 million gallons; and the 1991 Gulf War spills lost 240 million gallons. Of these, only the Gulf War spills went up in flames like Dos Bocas. See Hayes, *Black Tides*, p. 29.

[153] DeGolyer, "Mexican Petroleum Industry," p. 20, SMU/ED, Box 107, Folder 5220.

[154] Report from the Doctor Cantonal, October 12, 1908, AGEV, Gobernación, Salubridad, Enfermedades y Medicinas, Caja 2, No. 77, Letra C.

[155] Palacios, "Memoria," p. 29; BP, vol. 19, no. 1 (January 1925), p. 29.

[156] Kuecker, "A Desert," p. 317.

[157] Villarello, "El pozo," pp. 24–27.

[158] Arthur B. Clifford, "Extinguishing an Oil Well Fire in Mexico," *Transactions* of The Institution of Mining Engineers, vol. 63, no. 3 (1921–1922), p. 7. The figure refers to the 1910 fire at Potrero del Llano, not at Dos Bocas. No one recorded the temperature at Dos Bocas, but it must have topped the 120 degrees at Potrero del Llano because the fire was far greater. There are photographs of the troops working without protective equipment in P&S/PA, P6/1 and P6/2, P6: Northern Oil Fields Mexico, 1913–1916.

conditions, the absence of human deaths would have been miraculous indeed.

Although they failed to end the fire, the soldiers limited the burning of the rainforest nearby. El Aguila realized the danger of a firestorm and acted quickly, ordering the army to clear-cut all vegetation in a broad perimeter around the blaze. According to Palacios, the measure was successful. Ordóñez nevertheless observed that "the jungle burned in the surrounding area." Similarly, Bada Ramírez, the oil worker who was six when the well exploded, argued that the "tremendous forest" around the well "collapsed," but did not specify how.[159] One of Pearson's employees also noted that the firm incurred "heavy costs... in compensating local land owners for damages to property," but offered no explanation.[160] What seems to have happened was that the forest on the western flank of the well became "carbonized jungle," but the soldiers' efforts and the prevailing winds blowing southeast prevented the fire from spreading west.[161] Had the well been drilled during the *nortes* in the fall, the rainforest might not have escaped the fire as unscathed as it did.

The devastation was undeniable, nonetheless. As the oil fountain burned, a mixture of oil and salt water inundated San Diego de la Mar. Reaching temperatures of 158°–160°F (70°C), the scalding liquid became a river carving its way out to sea.[162] As it ran, it seared all life in its path. Two kilometers east the fiery current of oily water met the Carbajal River, merged into it, and set it alight. "Inches deep" in oil, the burning current reached the Tamiahua Lagoon within hours. For weeks afterwards, "floating islands of fire cross[ed] the lagoon waters like phantom ships."[163] The spill floated down the lagoon, scorching its sand dunes, beaches, and mangrove swamps and clogging the narrow channel that separated the mainland from Cabo Rojo. In late fall burning crude entered the Gulf at Tanhuijo – fifty kilometers (thirty-one miles) south of the explosion.[164]

San Diego de la Mar and its environs changed forever. By year's end, the camp was a "lake of oil." The twin holes measured three hectares

[159] Palacios, "Memoria," p. 3; Ordóñez, *El petróleo*, p. 65; Bada Ramírez, PHO/4/91.
[160] Reed, "History of S.P. Son's," P&S/HR, Box C 43, File C 43/1.
[161] Palacios, "Memoria," pp. 13, 24.
[162] I. C. White, "Petroleum Fields of Northeastern Mexico Between the Tamesi and Tuxpan Rivers," 1913, IAEG/KW, File 1919.
[163] Palacios, "Memoria," p. 16.
[164] Sindicato de Trabajadores Petroleros de la República Mexicana (STPRM), *Petróleo* (Mexico City: STPRM, 1939), p. 29.

(7.2 acres). More than thirty square kilometers of forest, swamp, and mangrove were covered with a thick black blanket of petroleum. Fires ignited on land and in the lagoon intermittently. Palacios described the scene thus:

> the ground, blackened, is covered by consumed asphalt, where not one life germ nests; in the distance the trees arise their spectral arms, contorted by fright, charred by the fire; not one leaf, not one speck of green brightens this landscape...Pacific ocean waves crash against coastal rocks crowned by flames.[165]

More than six months after July 4, engineer Juan Villarello reported that whereas the Carbajal River had flushed out all petroleum, the lagoon had not. Instead, "the chapopote had curdled, forming small platforms that float[ed] in the Tamiahua Lagoon."[166] In 1913, geologist Charles Hamilton reported that the hole that had started at eight inches had grown into a forty-acre cauldron. He estimated that three thousand barrels of salt water and oil continued to "boil out" every hour at temperatures above 170°F.[167] Much of the black broth ended up "cooked into balls of asphaltum," wrote another geologist, but hundreds of barrels reached a creek that fed the lagoon.[168] Hamilton wrote,

> the potent hydrogen sulphide [sic] gas had killed everything. What had been lush monte was now a gaunt specter of dead trees. The air stunk with the smell of rotten eggs. There was no sign or sound of animal, bird or insect life. Nothing stirred in the breeze. The silence was appalling. It was eerie and frightening. The great bowl had a high side flanked by a forest of dead trees and a low swampy side. Through this swamp poured the overflow of hot salt water, forming an oily stream without any vestige of either plant or fish life...The entire surface of the dark fluid in the crater was in constant motion of currents and eddies, whirlpools and blows of oily mush, hot salt water and evil smelling gas. It was evident that the high banks were undercut and could slough away into the heaving, seething, liquid cauldron. It was an awesome sight. It smelled and looked like I imagined hell might look and smell.[169]

"Paradise" had become "hell."

[165] Palacios, "Memoria," p. 30.

[166] Villarello, "El pozo," p. 34.

[167] Hamilton, "Geology of the Hacienda San Geronimo," SMU/ED, Box 112, Folder 5316; Hamilton, *Early Day*, p. 76. There are multiple photographs of Dos Bocas between 1913 and 1915 on file at P&S/PA, P6: Northern Oil Fields, Mexico 1913–1916, P6/7, P6/9, P6/119.

[168] White, "Petroleum Fields," p. 4, IAEG/KW, File 1919.

[169] Hamilton, *Early Day*, p. 76.

Time passed, but Dos Bocas remained the same bleak landscape. In 1917, foul-smelling gas shimmered over the surface of the lake, occasionally catching fire. In 1920, a Mexican writer likened Dos Bocas to "a forest of the dead." In 1921 hot salt water continued pouring out of Dos Bocas on a daily basis. In 1925, engineer Gustavo Ortega took photographs of the vat. His camera showed no life, only scorched mangroves. One year later, the *Boletín del Petróleo* published two more photos with a caption that read, in part, "in the photos taken in December 1926, one can appreciate the remnants of the exuberant vegetation that existed in this place before the well caught fire in July 1908." In 1929, the same journal published a photograph showing carbon dioxide crystallizing at the edge of the crater into a jagged three-foot mound of dry ice.[170] In the same year, twenty-one years after the explosion, a Tampico journalist visited the former condueñazgo. Upon approaching Dos Bocas, the reporter wrote,

> a horrific show … awaits … : in a broad extension, everything is charred, ashen in color, shuddering the soul. The light itself has livid reflections and there are no vestiges of life. No foliage on the trees, no birds in the sky, no living being in the solitude of the place … There is nothing left but an awful lagoon … But the grayish waters seem to boil like lead, emanating gases that close up, for an enormous radius, fill the air. All the trees have been robbed of their greenery, burned, and seem to raise up to the heavens, with anguishing contortions, their bare and gray branches.[171]

As late as the 1940s, Texan worker W. M. Hudson saw salt water and gas belching from the "crater."[172] As research in the Caribbean has demonstrated recently, grasses are among the sturdiest seaside organisms and tend to recover within months of most spills. At Dos Bocas, however, grasses took fifty years to colonize the vicinity. In 1988 Javier Santos Llorente, a descendant of the family that sold El Tulillo, published a photograph of "the great crater" showing thin blades of grass growing in tiny clumps at the base of dead mangroves.[173] In 2004, the remains

[170] Eduardo Cisneros to the Departamento del Petróleo, February 28, 1917, AGN/DP, Caja 42, Exp. 11, 321(02)/1; Francisco Espinosa y Rondero, "Breve historia del petróleo en México," BP, vol. 19, no. 1 (January 1925), p. 29; Secretaría de Industria, Comercio y Trabajo, *La industria del petróleo en México* (Mexico City: Talleres Gráficos de la Nación, 1927), photograph #10; BP, vol. 23, no. 2 (February 1927), photographic section; BP, vol. 27, no. 1 (January 1929), photographic section.
[171] *El Mundo*, June 2, 1929.
[172] W. M. Hudson, PTO, Tape 79, p. 30.
[173] López, "Ecological Consequences," p. 897; Joanna Burger, "Effects of Oil on Vegetation," in *Before and After an Oil Spill*, pp. 130–132; Santos Llorente, *Episodios*, p. 24.

Figure 3.3. The Dos Bocas site in July 2004. Oil slicks swirl over the water and coagulate at the base of the remains of mangrove trees. Brush and short trees populate the north side of the lake, but the prevailing winds, heavy with sulfur, keep the grasses short on the south side. The east end of the lake, not visible in the photo, is a vast field of dead mangrove tree trunks. Photo by the author.

of scorched mangroves like dry matchsticks still flanked one side of the crater next to a bare sandbank blackened with oil. Dry grasses swaying in the sulfurous air surrounded most of the crater, where a viscous black mixture lapped sluggishly at the edge (see Figure 3.3).

The effects of the blowout were far more widespread than photographs could capture or casual observers could document, however. The herbicide effects of crude oil raining on foliage killed flora within days of exposure.[174] That process probably explains why so many Huasteca farmers lost their crops in 1908, as a letter to President Díaz complained, and why El Aguila had to pay compensation for damages.[175]

The fauna suffered extensively as well. The documentation is thin but significant. Several mules working in the oil camp died from asphyxia within days of the accident, and the cited letter to Díaz argued that

[174] Villarello, "El pozo," pp. 19–20.
[175] The letter is cited in Kuecker, "A Desert," p. 316.

"cattlemen had lost their herds." Engineer Palacios was more specific, reporting in 1908 that "the estuaries and the [Tamiahua] lagoon [were] clogged with thousands of fish, crocodiles, and marine animal cadavers."[176] For the next decade, locals argued that cows fainted and died if they meandered near enough to catch a whiff of sulfur. Even after a half-century, "there were neither birds nor insects" at Dos Bocas.[177] Given that the well pumped hot oil and salt water into the river and the Tamiahua Lagoon as late as the mid-1940s, it is also likely that aquatic life disappeared not only from the craters, but also from parts of the lagoon. In the estuaries, like those at the mouth of the Carbajal River and Tanhuijo, plankton and aquatic animals must have cooked in the 160°F water. Survivors in cooler waters would have ingested large quantities of oil. Zooplankton consume hydrocarbons, which then move up the food chain to mollusks and fish. Clams, crabs, plankton, flatfish, starfish, shrimp, barnacles, and others also absorb oil directly and suffer metabolic damage as a result, particularly when the contamination persists as it did at Dos Bocas.[178] Over the long term, the sulfur compounds that leached into the Tamiahua Lagoon must have lowered the acidity of the water along the shores closest to the craters, continuing the deleterious effects on the remaining aquatic life.[179]

Birds, the poster children of twentieth-century oil spills, appear to have recovered fast. As noted in Chapter 1, ornithologist Chapman

---

[176] Palacios, "Memoria," p. 28.

[177] Santos Llorente, *Episodios*, p. 24.

[178] S. R. Carlberg, "Oil Pollution of the Marine Environment – With an Emphasis on Estuarine Studies," in *Chemistry and Biogeochemistry of Estuaries*, edited by Eric Olausson and Ingemar Cato (New York: John Wiley & Sons, 1980), pp. 395–397; I. Cato, I. Olsson, and R. Rosenberg, "Recovery and Decontamination of Estuaries," ibid., p. 410; Richard F. Lee, "Fate of Oil in the Sea," *Proceedings of the 1997 Oil Spill Response Workshop*, edited by Paul L. Fore and U.S. Fish and Wildlife Service (New Orleans: U.S. Fish and Wildlife Service, 1977), pp. 43–49.

[179] Villarello, "El pozo," p. 91. Even though the Tamiahua Lagoon acted as a buffer between Dos Bocas and the Gulf, the spill must have hurt Gulf waters too. An investigation of the 1979 Ixtoc-I explosion in the Gulf, for example, found that fishing off the Tamiahua Lagoon was seriously affected. Catches of mackerel and pike, particularly, "were minimal." Fishermen along the entire Gulf coast reported small catches of shrimp, octopus, snapper, and shark. Some told the Mexican weekly *Proceso* stories of catching "semi-cooked" fish. Yet Ixtoc I dumped 140 million gallons of oil into the water, a little more than half the quantity Dos Bocas expelled. See Arenas, *Museo vivo*, p. 16; Hayes, *Black Tides*, pp. 29, 172; Richard S. Golob and Daniel W. McShea, "Implications of the Ixtoc-I Blow-Out and Oil Spill," in *Petroleum and the Marine Environment* (London: Graham and Trotman Ltd., 1981), pp. 743, 752–753; "El petróleo sí daña la vida marina," *Proceso*, no. 143 (July 30, 1979), pp. 12–13; Isabel Morales, "Desprecia PEMEX los daños que causa su contaminación," *Proceso*, no. 139 (July 2, 1979), pp. 12–15.

documented a wealth of avian life in the Tamihua Lagoon in April 1910, less than two years after the explosion, a time when boiling water and oil continued spurting into the lagoon. His explorations into "paradise," however, did not extend far enough south to examine bird life carefully. Chapman traveled only a short distance from Tampico, watching birds as he passed through the eight miles of the recently excavated Chijol Canal and stopping only at a tiny island in the far north of the lagoon, Pájaro (Bird) Island.[180] Had Chapman proceeded further south into Tamiahua's waters, he might have witnessed something entirely different. In the two months of the fire, the locals reported watching birds fall from the sky, gassed by the chemical compounds wafting skyward from the burning well.[181] The *nortes*, moreover, carried the gas as far as Tampico and Tuxpan. Although concentrations over those urban areas were diffused, they were sufficiently powerful to cause nausea and headaches among humans, whose tolerance for the compound is almost twice that of birds. The effects on birds, therefore, must have been debilitating.[182] In addition, even if no one took photographs of oil-drenched birds in the Tamihaua Lagoon, there is no doubt that thousands suffered that fate. They probably dove in to drink and their feathers matted. Chances are that even the northernmost rookeries that Chapman saw in 1910 had experienced the effects of Dos Bocas earlier. Birds tend to carry the spilled oil they come into contact with back to their nests, killing their eggs in the process.[183] The fact that Chapman did not mention the spill nonetheless suggests that there were areas north of Dos Bocas sufficiently clean to allow many varieties of birds to flourish within two years of the explosion or that birds had immigrated from elsewhere. In San Diego de la Mar itself, however, the effects lasted longer: the only birds observed in August 2004 were vultures circling overhead.

Lastly, reptiles and amphibians probably did not fare as well as the more mobile species. Besides the crocodilian deaths Palacios mentioned, there is no other mention of their fate. Frogs, toads, snakes, iguanas, lizards, turtles, and similar wildlife must have perished. Survivors must have migrated. A pattern of sudden and slow death and migration of species, in fact, must have taken place in the aftermath of the fire. Alhough Dos Bocas was truly calamitous in scope and extraordinary in its

---

[180] Chapman, "A Naturalist's Journey," p. 543.
[181] Palacios, "Memoria," p. 28.
[182] Villarello, "El pozo," pp. 48–49, 57–58.
[183] Hayes, *Black Tides*, p. 187.

incessant emissions, variations on the theme were commonplace enough to conclude that other gushers wreaked similar sorts of ecological damage, albeit on a smaller scale.

Unlike fires and pollution, gushers were extremely difficult to prevent. The oil mantles of the Huasteca were heavy with gases that the oilmen could not control. Despite the weather and other natural cycles, the men could transform the landscape practically at will. But they could not predict which wells might explode. Even though the global industry had a fifty-year history, some technology was still elementary. The oil barons invested little in research and development. Instead they reacted to nature's obstacles as these showed up.[184] Technological innovation, as the next chapter discusses, was left to those directly affected by nature and accidents: the workers. Because gushers on the Mexican scale were new to the companies, the oilmen had no technologies to tackle them. The best they could do was to invest in measures to prevent spills and fires – the road not taken despite the fact that Pearson lost no less than one million pounds sterling in the Dos Bocas debacle alone.[185] Therefore, the age of gushers did not end until the Great Depression, when economic activity, drilling included, ground to a halt.

Of Gushers and Oilmen

Although the oil magnates despaired of the monetary losses the runaway wells represented, their testimony reveals more than concern about profit margins.[186] Their language betrays profound ideological notions about

---

[184] Yergin, *The Prize*, pp. 59, 66. Yergin also notes that the companies developed technology as a way to crush organized labor, just like pipeline was invented to defeat the teamsters, p. 33.

[185] "Mexican Eagle Oil Company, Ltd.," P&S/HR, Box C 43, File C 43/1. In the case of Dos Bocas, in fact, the Mexican government launched an investigation to see if negligence accounted for the disaster. Both Mexican and foreign workers denied that was the case, perhaps because they feared losing their jobs or perhaps because they were correct. Kuecker, "A Desert," p. 311. Oil workers interviewed in the 1930s, however, argued that two preventable errors accounted for Dos Bocas. First, the drilling hole had been improperly cased, which allowed the gas to escape; second, the boilers with their open flames were too close to the well, courting ignition as Hamilton confirmed in his memoirs. The workers' critique is in Rodríguez, *El rescate*, p. 21; Hamilton, *Early Day*, p. 74.

[186] Before Dos Bocas, for example, Pearson had written to his wife that he was "despondent," fearing his oil venture would "fizzle out" and not leave him enough money "to live quietly." The letter is quoted in Yergin, *The Prize*, p. 231. Doheny, too, was continually preoccupied with capital, as detailed in Davis, *Dark Side*, Chapters 3, 5.

the relationship between men and nature. Rather than understanding such events as cautionary tales about oil exploitation – the lesson motivating indigenous resistance, for instance – the oilmen typically interpreted the episodes as challenges to and assertions of their masculinity. The words they selected to describe the gusher phenomenon convey a universe of feminized nature and male sexual prowess.[187] El Aguila's chief geologist and administrator, Everett Lee DeGolyer, for instance, echoed sixteenth-century European scientists' perceptions of the earth's core as a womb cooking up metals, in depicting Dos Bocas as a female tease. The well, he wrote, was "a real publicity card played by Dame Nature to serve notice upon all and sundry that it was worth their while to give heed to the wares and quality of the wares at last she stood ready to dispense from her underworld chemical and mineralogical laboratories in Mexico."[188] The oilmen, reacting as their masculinity dictated, took up the challenge. Male creativity, not nature or the absence of technology, the men suggested, deserved the credit for runaway wells. In defining the term "gusher," for example, Doheny explained that "it implies that the flow of the oil is due to the pressure of imprisoned forces of Nature released by the drill."[189] That is, masculine technology – the drill – released "the flow" "imprisoned" by nature. Uncontrolled wells, then, were not nature exploding in men's faces, but rather male technology coaxing the flirtatious Dame to dispense her wares. Doheny pursued the allusion to male creativity further into procreative masculinity, describing the runaway well Cerro Azul No. 4 as "a birth." The inseminator was the oilman.[190]

Not surprisingly, then, the offspring born from "the riotous abandon and disorder of Nature" and man – the gusher – was a superhuman male being, dangerous and threatening but nonetheless befitting its paternal descent.[191] Palacios thus referred to Dos Bocas as "a furious Cyclops" and a "monster," descriptions that DeGolyer reiterated when Potrero del Llano No. 4 burst in 1910. In that case, the American geologist likened the well to "a raging monster" and a "wild animal" that "resist[ed] capture."[192] Frederic R. Kellogg's prose was even more explicitly masculine. The Standard Oil man wrote, "these wells are born into the full virility of

[187] The oilmen did not invent the idea of nature as female, of course. Merchant analyzes the idea in the West from its roots in the prescientific revolution in *The Death of Nature*.
[188] E. DeGolyer, "Mexican Petroleum Industry," p. 20, SMU/ED, Box 107, Folder 5220.
[189] PanAmerican, *Mexican Petroleum*, p. 87.
[190] Ibid., p. 98.
[191] Ibid., p. 69.
[192] Palacios, "Memoria," p. 10; Tinkle, *Mr. De*, p. 45.

their gigantic powers. They live like giants, straining the chains that bind them, and they die as giants should, stricken as by a thunderbolt."[193] It was the oilman, the twentieth-century Zeus, who wielded the thunderbolt that struck and killed the "giants" who dared him. Thus the men of greed and grandeur presumed to achieve ultimate control over both "Dame Nature" and her male offspring, the gusher wells.

Therein lay the oilmen's power as industrial creators indeed – in their aggressive and even hostile stance toward nature and their willingness and capacity to "subdue nature's power" enough to "wrest" from "her bosom" the wealth within.[194] Although the language the oilmen used contained more than a small dose of bravado to disguise the fact that they were helpless to prevent oil from exploding out of the ground, it dovetailed seamlessly with the paradise narrative and the ideal of progress. In building an oil industry where only jungle and Indians used to be, the oil barons fulfilled the dream of the nineteenth-century Mexican elite: they made the Huasteca produce. As Doheny exulted in 1922, "a more vivid contrast than the pathway bustling with automobiles, tractors, trucks, mule wagons, and the riotous motionless growth and decay of the jungle to the depths of which the fierce rays of the tropical sun never reach, can scarcely be imagined."[195] The companies swept away disorder and stasis, the feminine, replacing it with movement and technology, the masculine. If the landscape became, as Hamilton wrote, "Dante's inferno" in the process, the price and the prize were worth it.[196] Hence the pioneers forged ahead with the third element in the ecology of oil: changing the social composition of the Huasteca. They did so proudly and unapologetically, for, as Doheny declared, their handiwork was "testimony to the ability of man."[197]

[193] Frederic R. Kellogg, *The World Petroleum Problem: Mexico* (New York: Association of Petroleum Producers in Mexico, 1921), p. 7.
[194] Davis describes the efforts to cap Cerro Azul No. 4 as subduing nature's power in *Dark Side*, p. 107. The other quotes are from an editorial that eulogized Doheny's partner, Charles Canfield, as a man who "believed that Mother Earth had hidden in her bosom great stores of mineral wealth, and he dared much and endured much that he might wrest these secrets from the archives of Nature." *Los Angeles Herald*, August 18, 1913, reprinted in Whitney, *Charles Adelbert Canfield*, p. 209.
[195] PanAmerican, *Mexican Petroleum*, p. 70.
[196] Hamilton, *Early Day*, p. 203.
[197] Doheny was referring to the fact that when Cerro Azul No. 4 exploded, the well vomited the heavy drilling tools with such force that they flew 120 feet from the derrick and then dug a sixteen-foot hole upon landing. And, Doheny said, "there they stand today, at once a monument to the relentless forces of Nature and an inspiring testimony to the ability of man to overcome great obstacles." PanAmerican, *Mexican Petroleum*, p. 98.

Concomitant with changing of land tenure systems, the oil industry inaugurated new land use patterns in the Huasteca. These, in turn, meant radical transformations in the landscape. Despite the difficulties the tropical environment posed, no ecosystem escaped alteration as the industry built the infrastructure necessary to take Mexican crude to the world market. The fires and pollution the companies unleashed on the land, air, and water, moreover, meant that humans, animals, vegetation, and soils were adversely affected in the process. Although evidence supports the notion that certain locations and individual species eventually recovered, the widespread deforestation and urbanization that accompanied oil production degraded or eliminated swamps, mangroves, and forests across northern Veracruz. Despite the fact that the oilmen were never in total control of nature, their capacity to reshape the landscape fed that illusion and permitted them to turn the idea into a self-fulfilling prophecy. The oilmen thus understood changes in the land and environmental destruction and degradation as progress. They took pride in their agency and did not hesitate to reconfigure the social fabric of the Huasteca as well.

4

"MASTERS OF MEN, MASTERS OF NATURE"

SOCIAL CHANGE IN THE HUASTECA

> The foreigner, having increased the worker's wage so that bet-
> ter living became a possibility, went on to teach him how, and
> surrounded his attempts with kindly thought and guidance.
> There is not another field of labour in the world the lowly
> have had the considerate and intelligent treatment as is given
> in Mexico to this great helpless labouring class by the English
> and Americans. Schools for their children, hospitals for their
> sick, baths, recreation centers for their entertainment, sanitary
> homes for their families; water and gardens furnished.
>
> Caspar Whitney, 1916

> All petroleum companies in Mexico have been a blessing to
> the communities in which they have operated.
>
> Edward L. Doheny, 1922

The oil tycoons could not change the landscape alone. They needed
numerous men working for them to do so. Yet one of the problems that
had bedeviled the Huasteca elite for a half-century was precisely the low
population density and, therefore, the lack of labor available for modernization. The oilmen had to solve that conundrum. To exploit oil they
needed not only to change land tenure patterns and uses, but also to find
men to do the physical work. They needed, in other words, to change the
social composition of the Huasteca. As they did so, the oilmen also introduced new social relations to the area: early twentieth-century capitalist
industrial relations, with the added peculiarities of English and American
racism. The hierarchies implied therein, moreover, encompassed the
environmental realm. Even though bosses and workers changed the landscape together, their experience of and in the neotropics differed substantially depending on their position in the occupational ladder. That is, class
and color deeply influenced the relationship between men and nature
in the production process. The ecology of oil thus entailed changes in
the social composition and structure of the Huasteca.

The Recruitment of the Labor Force

The tycoons had to confront the reality that the object of their desire was buried in what they considered inaccessible areas with no workers. To extract the oil, the companies had to import labor. Migration, then, became essential to the enterprise.[1] Both English and American companies followed a pattern of multinational labor recruitment typical of other foreign-owned industrial enterprises in Mexico: supervisory positions were reserved for men from abroad, whereas the menial labor was procured locally.[2] The creation of the oil industry's labor force went through two periods, depending on the nationality of the workers. The first stage was roughly from 1900 until 1914 and the second from 1914 until 1921. After 1921, Mexican oil workers were abundant and redundant, whereas foreigners, particularly drillers, shifted from being directly employed by the companies to working as contractors.

By design, the work force was divided occupationally along nationality lines. Scientists, administrators, master craftsmen, and drillers and their assistants were foreigners and remained so, with exceptions, until expropriation in 1938. Their numbers hovered between twenty-five hundred and four thousand.[3] Household employees were likewise foreign-born, exclusively Chinese. Craftsmen assistants and *"machete* men" were Mexican, including indigenous men until around 1914.[4] The demand for both foreign and domestic labor began as soon as the oilmen started closing land deals with hacendados and indigenous condueños. Let us begin with the scientists, the geologists.

Cutting Their Teeth

Expediency accounted for the importation of experienced men for professional positions. Given that the oil industry had fifty years of history in the United States, there were plenty of knowledgeable men available for work in Mexico north of the border, whereas there were none in Mexico itself. With the exception of engineers Ezequiel Ordoñez and Manuel Mesa Andraca, the geologists, who were the top executives as well, were

[1] S. Lief Adleson, "The Cultural Roots of the Oil Workers' Unions in Tampico, 1910–1925," in *The Mexican Petroleum Industry*, p. 37.
[2] See, for example, Michael J. Gonzáles, "United States Copper Companies, the State, and Labour Conflict in Mexico, 1900–1910," *Journal of Latin American Studies*, vol. 26, part 3 (October 1994), pp. 659–660.
[3] Brown, *Oil and Revolution*, p. 319.
[4] Testimony of Edward L. Doheny in *Investigation*, p. 220.

recruited in the United States. Not all of them were as experienced as the companies would argue in defense of discriminatory policies, however. Geology as a profession was altogether new. In the early twentieth century geologists were not widely used in the United States, where they had yet to prove their mettle to "old-time . . . oil hunters" who derided them as "rock hounds," "mud slingers," or "ridge runners."[5] The Huasteca thus became a geology lab where "dozens of American geologists cut their teeth," undergraduate geology majors spent their summer vacations acquiring field experience, and geology professors found well-paid consulting jobs.[6] Everett Lee DeGolyer, El Aguila's chief geologist, for example, had not finished his degree when he began working for the company in the early days of the new century. Pearson sent DeGolyer back to university in 1911, paying his fees and providing him a stipend that made him "the richest student on campus."[7] The terms of employment for budding scientists were excellent: one geologist DeGolyer hired in 1919 received a salary of $350 a month, in addition to "field and transportation expenses."[8] DeGolyer himself was well remunerated beyond his college tuition. Although there is no record of his salary, letters from Pearson confirm that he received a total of 850 shares in El Aguila between 1912 and 1913 as "a bonus." Other top geologists enjoyed comparable packages at salaries ranging from $9,000 to $15,000 a year.[9] An American oil worker, in comparison, earned an average of $1,000 a year in 1917.[10]

The American "Fraternity"

The drillers were the second most important group of foreign men the companies introduced to Mexico. They were the key men in the oil industry in the United States, and they enjoyed a remarkable level of authority in the camps of the Huasteca long after they had lost it in their home

---

5 Taylor and Welty, *Black Bonanza*, p. 198; Ellen Sue Blakey, *Oil on Their Shoes, Petroleum Geology to 1918* (Tulsa: The American Association of Petroleum Geologists, 1985), pp. 16–22.

6 Tinkle, *Mr. De*, p. 78; E. H. Sellards to Baker, Victoria, Tamaulipas, March 5, 1925, IAEG/CB, Box 3, Correspondence Folder; Hall and Coerver, "Oil and the Mexican Revolution," p. 231.

7 Cowdray to DeGolyer, Mexico City, March 13, 1911, SMU/ED, Box 24, Folder 2437; Hall and Coerver, "Oil and the Mexican Revolution," p. 230.

8 DeGolyer to J. S. Smith, New York, July 28, 1919, SMU/ED, Box 117, Flder 5384.

9 Secretary of S. Pearson & Son, Limited to E. DeGolyer, Westminster, September 19, 1912 and Cowdray to DeGolyer, Westminster, June 13, 1913, SMU/ED, Box 24, Folder 2437; E. DeGolyer to T. J. Ryder, November, 4, 1920, SMU/ED, Box 102, Folder 5138.

10 At a rate of $3–4 per twelve-hour day, seven days a week. Nancy and Jeff Quam-Wickham, "The petroleocrat's nightmare: when oil workers organize," *OCAW Reporter* (July–August, 1991), p. 12.

country. They knew which kinds of drill bits to use for what kind of geo-logical formations and when to switch from one tool to the next. In fact, the drillers themselves had invented and named most of the technol-ogy used in the industry. In an era when locating oil was still educated guesswork, drillers shared with the professionals a degree of knowledge and authority that they were very proud of and would protect at the expense of Mexican workers. Because they hired their own assistants, they controlled the composition of their crews and decided who learned the secrets of the trade. It was not unusual, in fact, for drillers to go to Mexico as teams.[11] American drillers, moreover, earned higher wages in Mexico than in the United States. Whereas they could earn as much as $10 per day in U.S. fields in 1921, American drillers in Mexico earned a minimum of $10.25 and up to $20 a day after 1917, plus food and lodg-ing.[12] The Mexican Revolution, moreover, worked to their advantage. As the uncertainty increased over the 1910s, the men refused to work for the same price. In 1918, for instance, the drillers threatened to abandon one company unless they received combat pay. The company raised wages from $375 to $425 per month, and others followed suit.[13] Furthermore, if drillers wanted to keep their independence by becoming contractors or obtaining a percentage of oil production, the companies acquiesced to both as early as 1908. After 1921, such arrangements became more the rule than the exception.[14] Prizes for gusher wells were also common, either expensive watches with the drillers' names engraved on the back or bonuses worth 50% of their total wages.[15]

[11] Mody C. Boatright and William A. Owens, *Tales from the Derrick Floor: A People's History of the Oil Industry* (Garden City, NY: Doubleday & Co., Inc., 1970), pp. 152–170, 197–223; Mody C. Boatright, *Folklore of the Oil Industry* (Dallas: Southern Methodist University Press, 1963), pp. 120–121, 124, 129–131; Leopoldo Alafita Méndez, "Perforación y per-foradores: 1906–1938," *Anuario* VII (February 1990), pp. 151–152; Testimony of J. W. Gray in J. V. Ferguson vs. El Aguila, May 4, 1919, AGN/JFCA, Caja 99, Exp. 15/929/553.

[12] U.S. wages are from *The Oil Age* (August 1921), as reprinted in BP, vol. 14, no. 6 (Decem-ber 1922), p. 576. Wages paid in Mexico appeared in Aime-Marin, "Informe del consul francés en México," BP, vol. 3, no. 1 (July 1917), p. 7. See also Alafita Méndez, "Per-foración," pp. 147–159.

[13] Summary of Mexican Oil News, July 26, 1918, P&S/HR, Box 108, Folder 5246.

[14] A. Jacobsen to J. B. Body, Tampico, October 7, 1922, SMU/ED, Box 101, Folder 5108; B. F. McDawell to Junta, November 13, 1928, AGN/JFCA, Caja 62, Exp. 15/928/1117; PTO, Tape 104, p. 29; Cuestionario de salarios, Continental Mexican Petroleum Com-pany, May 1921, AGN/DT, Caja 279, Exp. 9; Félix Flores and Antolín López vs. Cosmos, AGEV/JCCA, Caja 30, Exp. 46, 1922; Julio Carranza vs. El Aguila, AGEV/JCCA, Caja 71, Exp. 29, 1928; *El Mundo,* January 26, 1927.

[15] Fields Superintendent to A. Jacobsen, Tampico, October 29, 1920, SMU/ED, Box 101, Folder 5102; A. Jacobsen to E. DeGolyer, Tampico, 22, 1920 and E. DeGolyer to A. Jacobsen, New York, December 12, 1919, SMU/ED, Box 117, Folder 5378; Nancy

Another group of foreign men was European. Information about them is scarce, but they were important for their mechanical skills and their politics. They were divided into two subgroups. The first comprised Germans, French, South Africans, and Englishmen imported by El Aguila.[16] The second group arrived in Tampico sometime after 1915, but not because the companies recruited them. Rather, they were single men fleeing from World War I: Catalans, Irish, Russians, and Spaniards. Most were literate and craftsmen, assets the oil companies recognized at once. They were hired as master mechanics, carpenters, machinists, boilermakers, and the like.[17] What the companies did not know at first was that many of these men were also political radicals, a fact that would cause them endless headaches, as the next chapter will show.

As was the case with the geologists, moreover, not all the foreign workers were highly experienced. El Aguila, in fact, used the Tanhuijo lease from the Sánchez family as a training camp for drilling crews. The men spent "weeks or even months" practicing and teaching each other techniques in Tanhuijo before going to the camps.[18] Similar training programs for European workers were put in place in El Aguila's refinery in Tampico.[19] Thus, the oil companies made the Huasteca into an important geological and technical school for foreigners, leaving physical labor for Mexicans.

Chinese Men

The last group of foreign workers the oil companies imported was the Chinese. They remained a largely invisible subgroup of workers in the forty-year history of foreign oil in Mexico. What little information survives about them does not explain where or how they were recruited.

Lynn Quam-Wickham, "Petroleocrats and Proletarians: Work, Class, and Politics in the California Oil Industry, 1917–1925," Ph.D. Dissertation, University of California Berkeley, 1994, p. 26.

[16] Interview with Mr. Cecil Knight Montiel, conducted by Lief Adleson on April 18, 1974, in Ciudad Madero, Tamaulipas, PHO/4/35.

[17] Interview with Mr. Francisco Vega Soria, conducted by Lief Adleson on May 31, April 2 and 7, 1976, in Naucalpan de Juárez, Estado de México, PHO/4/49; Interview with Mr. Pedro Rabishkin Masloff, conducted by Lief Adleson on March 21, 1978, in Ciudad Madero, Tamaulipas, PHO/4/87; Lief Adleson, "Historia social de los obreros industriales de Tampico, 1906–1919," Ph.D. Dissertation, El Colegio de México, 1982, p. 352.

[18] Hamilton, *Early Day*, pp. 31, 34; Sullivan Machinery Company, "Diamond Drilling for Oil," p. 15, IAEG/EL, Acct. 4553, Box 4. See also Paul Weaver to Mr. Chambers, Tampico 15, 1918, P&S/HR, Box 103, Folder 5146.

[19] Rabishkin Masloff, PHO/4/87.

In the American records they lacked names. They were only "Jumbo, the cook," or "John," or more often "Chinamen" and "Chinese boys."[20] The Mexican records show little more: the men were Cantonese and never worked in production. Instead the companies recruited them for the kitchens, cafeterias, clubs, hotels, and houses reserved for foreigners. Their range of occupations was limited to service work, as cooks, waiters, house servants, and laundrymen, typical tasks for Chinese men in the Americas at the time. Their salaries, however, were higher than Mexican laborers and on a par with Mexican craftsmen assistants, $3 to $4 daily through the 1910s, and sometimes increasing to $5 and $6 in the late 1920s.[21] In recruiting Chinese men for the type of service work traditionally performed by women, the companies kept the industry overwhelmingly, although not thoroughly, male.

Machete Men

The last group of workers the companies recruited was the largest: Mexican nationals. Their place in the architecture of the industry was restricted by design. The companies wanted the majority for hard physical labor deemed unskilled: deforestation, construction, clean-up, and work that required "only strength and some *maña* (cunning)."[22] The best jobs were as assistants, regardless of experience and expertise. Mexican master craftsmen were thus demoted to "helpers," even if their wages in the oil industry were higher than elsewhere.[23]

The industry also reserved a few jobs for Mexican women and children. Literate young women in Tampico and Tuxpan found employment as secretaries in company offices and, as the companies built infirmaries in the late 1910s and early 1920s, others were hired as nurses.[24] Some Mexican boys joined the labor force as soon as they turned ten years

---

[20] Storm, "Wells," p. 515; Testimony of Amos L. Bearty in *Investigation*, p. 529.
[21] Manuel Su vs. El Agwi, AGN/JFCA, Caja 159, Exp. 15/930/340; Juan Fong vs. Huasteca Petroleum Company, AGN/JFCA, Caja 188, Exp. 15/930/1093; Juan Fong vs. Mexican Petroleum Company, AGN/JFCA, Caja 136, Exp. 15/919/1562; Employee List no. 34, Departamento de Exploración, Campo Tecuanapa, El Aguila, August 25, 1928, AGN/JFCA, Caja 63, Exp. 928/1153.
[22] Quoted in Olvera Rivera, "Origen social," p. 22.
[23] According to the companies, Mexican craftsmen made twice as much money working as assistants than they did working as masters elsewhere in Mexico. Méndez, Report to the governor, IAEG/CC, Folder on Mexico.
[24] Chávez Padrón, *Testimonio*, p. 59; Report from Labor Inspector, Tampico, January 1922, AGEV/JCCA, Caja 29, Exp. 31.

old.[25] In the camps, they carried bucketfuls of drinking water for Mexican workers, hauled sacks full of dirt on their backs, banged on pipeline to remove rust, maneuvered small boats, or became "lonch boys" [sic]. The lunch boys assisted the Chinese cooks and were responsible for keeping the drillers' food warm. They also enjoyed the privilege of eating the foreigners' leftovers.[26] In Tampico, children did assembly line work in El Aguila's case and can factory; in Pierce's warehouse they moved, packed, stored, and loaded products. Fair-skinned Mexican boys qualified to join the few Mexican-born sons of foreign administrators as interoffice mail carriers.[27]

The incorporation of Mexican men into the labor force occurred in stages, although they overlapped. The first stage was the use of local indigenous and mestizo men to open up the camps. Although the dates for this are difficult to pin down, the process repeated itself every time a new camp opened until around 1914. The second stage ran concurrently with the first, from shortly after 1910 until its peak in 1914 and final decline in 1921. In this period the companies systematically recruited men from outside the state and took them to the Huasteca. The last stage was independent of the oilmen, but they reaped the benefits. It began with the outbreak of the Mexican Revolution near the Huasteca after 1914, which, like World War I, brought a flood of refugees to Tampico desperate for work. The Revolution, then, unwittingly ended the labor shortage that the would-be modernizers had endured for decades in northern Veracruz.

Indigenes and Oil Work

Although the historical record is thin, it shows that indigenous men were among the very first laborers the companies hired. Their participation in oil work, however, was temporary by choice and by design. As noted earlier, indigenous men first worked as *mozos* for geologists

[25] A 1920 report noted that several companies, including Huasteca Petroleum, Standard Oil (Transcontinental), and Texas Oil, provided education for workers' children at company schools but only until age ten. After that the male children became workers like their fathers. Cayetano Pérez Ruíz al C. Jefe del Departamento del Trabajo y Previsión Social, Mexico City, September 16, 1920, AGN/DT, Caja 220, Exp. 6.

[26] Bada Ramírez, PHO/4/91.

[27] Interview with Mr. Camilo Román Cota, conducted by Lief Adleson, on December 23, 1975, in Poza Rica, Veracruz," PHO/4/47; Knight Montiel, PHO/4/25; A. Araujo to Jefe Int. del Depto. del Trabajo, Tampico, January 12, 1923, AGN/DT, Caja 491, Exp. 1; P16/131, P16/132, n/d, P&S/PA, P16: Tampico, 1916–1920.

doing exploratory work. In the immediate aftermath of Dos Bocas in 1908, however, indigenes and mestizos alike balked at the idea of working in oil extraction, just as they did in relation to leasing their lands.[28] Nevertheless, their resistance to oil work sometimes became as futile as their attempts to maintain control of the tropical forest. As the events at the Juan Casiano and Potrero del Llano wells illustrate, many indigenous men found themselves toiling in the young oil industry against their will.

Three black geysers sprang in the Golden Lane at the end of 1910. Huasteca Petroleum found black gold in Juan Casiano No. 6 and No. 7 in September, whereas El Aguila struck oil with Potrero del Llano No. 4 in December. In both places, the companies were severely understaffed and lacked the necessary infrastructure. As a result, oil drowned the terrain. To manage, the companies sought government assistance, as El Aguila had done to fight the Dos Bocas blowout in 1908. The local hacendado officialdom responded quickly, obviating the need for troops. They scoured the surrounding communities, Amatlán and Temapache respectively, rounding up every able-bodied adult male and boy they found. Indigenous and mestizo men and boys alike were sent "to report to the company for work assignments," willingly or not.[29]

In the Juan Casiano case, local officials procured "close to one thousand Indians" and a great number of mestizos to contain the spill.[30] Convinced that "it is difficult to get the natives to work as long as they have a little corn for *tortillas* or a pound of beans in the house," the local authorities advised that the men not be paid until the work was completed.[31] At Potrero del Llano the only person paid on time was the woman hired to feed the workmen, at the rate of fifty Mexican cents a day for three meals per man. And in case good pay did not overcome the woman's fear for her life, Pearson instructed DeGolyer to "do the best possible threatening that you will ask the *rurales* [rural police] to see that she feeds the men," but "only if she be too unreasonable." Thus, for one week hundreds of local indigenous and mestizo men worked for "mostly bean-filled tacos" and coffee. The next week, the officials produced "gangs from the same villages" to relieve their compatriots until "thousands" had been "pressed-in-to-service."[32]

[28] Villarello, "El pozo," p. 23.
[29] Tinkle, *Mr. De*, p. 42.
[30] BP, vol. 19, no. 1 (January 1929), p. 29.
[31] Harper, *A Journey*, p. 67.
[32] Tinkle, *Mr. De*, pp. 42, 45–46; Spender, *Weetman*, pp. 160–161.

The task indigenous men were assigned at Juan Casiano was strenuous. They had to dig a deep earth dam-cum-moat to isolate well No. 7. The well was raining oil at a rate of twenty-five thousand barrels a day, and huge quantities had invaded a local tributary. To prevent a disaster comparable to Dos Bocas, Doheny's men decided to carry out a controlled burn and torched the stream. That meant, however, that the dam builders had to accelerate their excavation to make sure the flames did not travel back to the spurting well and ignite it. Working around the clock in shifts, the men achieved success in fourteen days. By the end of September 1910, American drillers had capped well No. 7 and prevented the dreaded blow-out.[33] Indigenes and mestizos returned home, exhausted. They apparently kept their opinions about their stint in oil work to themselves, but the fact that the companies had to increase their monetary offers and resort to violence to obtain more leases in the years following suggests that few were pleased with it.

At Potrero del Llano the work was similar, but lasted longer. There the drillers "cut an artery" that took hundreds of men one month to contain.[34] In this case, conscripted indigenous and mestizo men and boys performed a number of different tasks. They hammered "portable frame dwellings, which were really primitive shacks, fitted with numerous bunks" for off-duty crews to rest a few hours if they managed to shut out the roaring noise of the well. They also dug trenches for pipeline and excavated the first five of the six pits that became Potrero del Llano's earthen dams. For close to thirty days, the men worked literally day and night until the American drillers put in a first partial cap on the well in January 1911. After that, the men could slow the pace down until the second capping device closed the well altogether in March.[35]

That was not the end of forced labor for indigenes in the vicinity of Potrero del Llano, however. On August 14, 1914, lightning struck the well and set it aflame. The conflagration lasted six months, causing casualties and protest in the process. The fire was the result of the collusion between nature and rushed craftsmanship. Because the well had been drilled and capped poorly between 1910 and 1911, three years later there were 130 cracks in the ground around it. In February 1914, DeGolyer reported, some two thousand barrels of oil were leaking through the cracks daily. By June 6, the seepages had increased to nintey-six thousand barrels

[33] BP, vol. 27, no. 1 (January 1929), p. 34; Hoffman, "Edward L. Doheny," p. 107.
[34] Taylor and Welty, *Black Bonanza*, p. 140.
[35] Menéndez, *Doheny*, p. 78; Spender, *Weetman*, p. 161; Chambers, "Potrero," p. 143.

per day.[36] In addition, gases escaped through the pores intermittently throughout the day, forming a visible, flammable mist around the well.[37] At the beginning of the rainy season, the predictable happened: lightning ignited one of the cracks, set the gas on fire, and rolled out a carpet of flames that encompassed forty acres.[38]

The rounding up of all indigenous and mestizo men within a wide radius was replayed. This time, the hacendado Manuel Peláez joined the efforts to save his clan's investments. He obtained his first contract to excavate the sixth earth dam at Potrero del Llano. By his own account, Peláez brought in his own hacienda workers to dig two-to-three cubic meters of dirt per day. El Aguila paid him 1.50 pesos per cubic meter, but he did not say how much he paid the men.[39] Thus, "all the available workmen, to the number of about 3,000, were immediately mobilized and armed with shovels," wrote a fire expert, Arthur B. Clifford. Then, protected with nothing more than "wet sacs" [sic] around their heads and hands,

> they commenced the stupendous task of building fire-walls round the basin; and, when built, these walls were made to converge on the well itself, making the basin less and less each day, and bringing the seat of the fire nearer. Shovelful by shovelful the work was carried on without intermission, day and night shifts succeeding each other...The fire-walls were, in due course,...pushed sufficiently close for some attempt to be made to extinguish the fire.[40]

"Owing to the huge amount of oil burning and the intense heat," wrote a geologist, the men built firewalls eighteen feet in height far enough away to enclose approximately thirty-six thousand square yards and worked their way closer to the fire little by little.[41] Other men, "holding a flat shovel, were stationed at intervals of a few yards" to beat off, literally, any "burst of flame" that flew from the burning fuel fountain and landed on the oil that soaked the earth for acres around (see Figure 4.1).[42]

[36] E. DeGoyler, "The Petroleum Industry of Mexico," n/d, SMU, Box 107, Folder 5220.
[37] Hamilton, *Early Day*, p. 79; P4/2/18 to P4/2/22, March 9, 1915, P&S/PA, P4/2: Potrero 1913–1919.
[38] Chambers, "Potrero," p. 147; Arthur B. Clifford, "Extinguishing an Oil-Well Fire in Mexico, and the Part Played Therein by Self-Contained Breathing-Apparatus," *Transactions* of The Institution of Mining Engineers, vol. 63, no. 3 (1921), p. 3.
[39] Menéndez, *Doheny*, p. 78.
[40] Clifford, "Extinguishing," p. 3; P4/2/24, March 20, 1915, P&S/PA, P4/2: Potrero 1913–1919.
[41] Chambers, "Potrero," p. 148.
[42] Clifford, "Extinguishing," p. 3.

Figure 4.1. Well No. 4 at Potrero del Llano was struck by lightning on August 14, 1914. From the DeGolyer Library, Southern Methodist University, Dallas, Texas, the Everette Lee DeGolyer Papers.

Mexican indigenous men began to relive the experience the people and firefighters of San Diego de la Mar had endured in 1908. The oil dropped "in an almost blinding deluge" around them. The "roaring of the oil gushing out . . . induced partial deafness for a time, whilst the suffocating gases given off from the oil made working impossible for more than a few minutes at a time in the vicinity of the well."[43] The gas filtering through the fissures caused the men "agonizing pain" in the eyes, swelling their eyelids, and making them completely blind "for several days." Boric acid and cocaine applied directly to the eyes was the standard treatment, but it made the conscripts howl in such pain that Clifford wondered why "Mexicans seemed to suffer more than the white man in this respect."[44] Some indigenous men refused the painful company treatment altogether, relying on their own medicinal knowledge to relieve the searing eye pain. According to DeGolyer, they covered their swollen eyes with raw potato slices with effective results.[45]

Nevertheless, the worst was yet to come. Sometime in November, seventeen Mexicans "were badly burned" in a gas explosion. Eleven died. As a result, a massive "desertion" of hundreds of men took place. Francisco Solís Cabrera, who went to Potrero del Llano from Tampico hoping to make good money fast, was one of them. He found he could not cope with the stress and the 120°F temperatures and quit. As he departed, he left behind "nothing but little Indians" (*puros inditos*), for whom quitting was much more difficult because they would be recruited again (see Figure 4.2).[46]

The men who stayed proved they were not entirely powerless nonetheless. They organized an impromptu labor protest, a "picket" as Clifford described it. Because the only record of the walkout is Clifford's testimony and he was a monolingual English speaker, it is difficult to determine

---

[43] Chambers, "Potrero," pp. 144–145.

[44] Clifford added, "I had the task of assisting the doctor with his eye cases on odd occasions and . . . several times treated as many as two hundred natives at a 'sitting.' Anyone who has had to handle the average Mexican Indian will understand that it was not exactly a pleasant task." Clifford, "Extinguishing" p. 4; Chambers, "Potrero," p. 24.

[45] Tinkle, *Mr. De*, p. 46.

[46] Interview with Mr. Francisco Solís Cabrera, conducted by Lief Adleson on September 7 and 18, 1976 in Tampico, Tamaulipas, PHO/4/56. The photographic record confirms Solís Cabrera's words. Several photos of Potrero del Llano show men and boys in traditional indigenous garb, white cotton knee-high trousers and coarse white cotton tunics, digging the earth dams. The adults shoveled, while the barefoot children carried sacks of dirt on their backs. See Celis Salgado, *La industria*, p. 207 and P&S/PA, P4/1/9, P4/1/16, P4/1: Potrero, 1910–1915.

Figure 4.2. Mexican workers putting out the fire at Potrero del Llano No. 4, 1914. From the Pearson & Son Photographic Archive at the Science & Society Picture Library, Science Museum in London.

what exactly took place during the strike. As Clifford explained it, the work stoppage lasted eight days, leaving "about fifty white men" to "take the duties of 3,000 natives" while the fire raged on. From what he could determine, the men demanded a pay increase and "a commissariat" to take care of necessities because they could not go home. The negotiations deteriorated rapidly, however, leading one of the strikers to throw "a heavy stone" at the foreigners. The rock barely missed Clifford and hit a protester instead. The superintendent then "reduced his hearers to an abject state of submission," paused, cracked a few jokes in Spanish that Clifford did not understand, and, after "a tremendous burst of laughter," sent the men back to the firefighting. "The strike was over," wrote Clifford. The men received their raise. By April 1915, six months after lightning started the blaze, the well was put out and the conscripts were free to return home. They left behind them a blackened earth caked and cracked like overbaked brownies.[47]

---

[47] Clifford, "Extinguishing," pp. 7–8; Chambers, "Potrero," p. 152; BP, vol. 22, no. 3 (September 1926), p. 205. See also P&S/P4/2/86, P4/2/87, January 11, 1916, and P4/2: Potrero 1913–1919.

Given the realities of oil work, it was not surprising that indigenous men would not be seduced by high wages. Indeed, ignorant of the fact that the men performed forced labor, the president of the Institution of Petroleum Technologists found it "extraordinary" that "it was possible to get men to work under the terrible conditions."[48] Doheny's vice president and general manager, Herbert George Wylie, admitted as much, confessing that the first workers "were not altogether a success." He did not interpret their rejection of oil work as one more aspect of their resistance to the industry in general, however.[49] On the contrary, the oilmen reverted to the idea of the lazy native to explain indigenous resistance to oil work. The first draftees did not stay, Doheny said, because the "natives...[were] not accustomed to the continuous application which was necessary in the opening of an oil field."[50]

Nonetheless, some indigenous men did accommodate to changing circumstances and became selective of the types of work they would perform in an oil camp. They predominated in Cerro Azul, Amatlán, and Potrero del Llano, camps that according to Ciriaco Brigas "shone with breeched Indians and their enormous hats." But they did only *destajo* or *tarea* work, that is, single projects.[51] That specialization gave indigenous men safety, flexibility, and control over their labor absent in firefighting. As Doheny described it, under the *tarea* system, a man "can work at will, beginning his task before sunrise, resting during the midday heat, and completing as much as he desires to do during the cooler hours of the evening."[52] According to a Mexican oil worker, the favorite task of indigenous men was erecting barracks for incoming crews of Mexican immigrant laborers.[53] The structures were easy to build, simply larger versions of their own homes: long, rectangular buildings with thatched roofs, dirt floors, and mud walls. Thus, some indigenes participated in the building of oil camps and met their need for cash in that manner. Through their own choices and the decisions the companies made, nevertheless, indigenes became marginal as soon as large numbers of workmen could be had

[48] Quoted in Chambers, "Potrero," p. 156.
[49] Interview with Herbert Wylie, V. P., General Mananger, Doheny Mexican Collection (DMC), Labor File I, #959.
[50] Testimony of Edward L. Doheny in *Investigation*, p. 234.
[51] The exact quote is "¡*Todo esto blanqueaba de indios calzonudos con tamaños sombrerotes!*" Guerrero Miller, *Cuesta abajo*, p. 76.
[52] Testimony of Edward L. Doheny in *Investigation*, vol. 2, p. 234.
[53] Bada Ramírez, PHO/4/91.

elsewhere. They then became silent witnesses to the transformation of
the ecology they had known.

El Enganche

While they made do with the labor available, the companies set up the
machinery for contracting the thousands of Mexicans they needed. Until
around 1920, they relied on an old method of labor recruitment known
as *el enganche* (the hooking). Under this practice, the companies sent
agents to comb the Mexican countryside in search of males willing to sell
their labor for a specific period of time.[54] Wherever they landed, labor
recruiters made deals with friendly authorities to help them "organize a
party..., set up a table with money and strike up the music" to attract
the men. Those like Santiago Contreras whose curiosity was aroused by
the festivities were warmly received and encouraged to imbibe liberally
from the free spirits at hand.[55] Then the *enganchador* made his offer:
free transportation, lodging, and food to Tampico; a return ticket when
the *enganche* was over; and best of all, extremely high wages. The agents
promised three gold pesos per day, and, to sweeten the deal, they offered
to take the family along, too.[56] As a worker recalled, "they offered the
moon and the stars (*los bueyes y la carreta*). We would have houses, good
wages, payment in gold!"[57] The *fiestas* turned out to be immensely successful recruitment fairs. In one 1920 trip, for example, the agents recruited
5,000 men from rural Jalisco and Michoacán, to be delivered to Tampico
"in lots of 600 to 700 persons every 10 or 15 days." Those figures were
not exceptional. Through 1920, Tampico authorities reported that the
enganchadores were delivering men in groups of five or six hundred at a
time.[58]

As it happened, the promises the agents made were indeed too good
to be true. Single and married men alike found themselves in dire straits
upon their arrival in Tampico, as the companies refused to honor the

[54] Interview, DMC, Labor File I, #959.
[55] Quoted in Manuel Uribe Cruz, "El movimiento obrero-petrolero en Minatitlán, Veracruz,
1908–1924," B.A. Thesis, Universidad Veracruzana, 1980, p. 92.
[56] El Aguila to Department of Labor, Mexico City, December 16, 1920, AGN/DT, Caja 217,
Exp. 22.
[57] Quoted in Rodríguez, *El rescate*, p. 45.
[58] El Aguila to Department of Labor, Mexico City, December 16, 1920, AGN/DT, Caja 217,
Exp. 22; *El Universal*, April 15, 1920; J. S. Dickson to Municipal President, March 15,
1920, AHAT, Exp. 44, n/n; Telegram, September 13, 1919, AGN/DT, Caja 170, Exp. 26.

agents' words. Far from home and destitute, the men had no choice but to accept whatever conditions the companies offered if they wanted to work at all.[59] The promised three pesos dwindled to one. That amount, nonetheless, was still double or triple the daily rate in rural areas, so the deal seemed advantageous to the men, at least until they realized that the cost of living in Tampico eroded their pay below a living wage (Chapter 5).

The *enganchadores* experienced a heyday until the late 1910s, when labor became available through the unexpected channel of revolution. Despite their closeness to President Díaz, the companies weathered well his fall from power and exile in 1911.[60] Similarly, the companies continued drilling, recruiting workers, and building through Madero's presidency and his assassination in 1913. They were concluding construction in several Tampico installations when the revolt against Huerta engulfed neighboring Nuevo León and San Luis Potosí (including the El Ebano refinery). Hundreds of refugee families fled to the port.[61] In mid-1914, moreover, the *constitucionalistas* led by Venustiano Carranza wrestled Tampico from Huerta and turned the port into a haven for displaced families and anti-Huertistas of all stripes. Labor at last was becoming plentiful in northern Veracruz.

With refugees looking for work, some oil companies began to scale back their use of labor agents. Tales of employment for all in the oil fields became legendary, reflected in *corridos* with verses like "a dog told me one day/ with a big sandwich in his mouth/ if you want bread in loaves/ let's head for Tampico."[62] By the time peace finally descended on Mexico in 1920, furthermore, the adolescent sons of early *enganchados* were ready to join the labor force.[63] With the second generation of oil workers at hand, the *enganchadores* went into retirement. At the peak of employment in early 1921, the companies had some forty thousand Mexican men on the payroll.[64]

---

[59] Inspector Cayetano Pérez Ruíz to the Departament of Labor, Tampico, September 18, 1920, AGN/DT, Caja 220, Exp. 6; Statement by Luis Lagos, in Delfino Cruz vs. El Aguila, March 2, 1919, AGEV/JCCA, Caja 8, Exp. 11.

[60] Interview, DMC, Labor File I, #961.

[61] Interview with Mr. Cruz Briones Rodríguez, conducted by Lief Adleson on November 28, 1976, in Tampico, Tamaulipas, PHO/4/52.

[62] Lozano, *El Puerto*.

[63] Interview with Mr. Mario Ortega Infante, conducted by Lief Adleson on February 18, 1974, in Tampico, Tamaulipas, PHO/4/28; Rabishkin Masloff, PHO/4/87; José Barragán Camacho, *Memorias de un petrolero* (Mexico City: n/p, 1983), p. 73.

[64] Informe, November 18, 1921, AGN/DT, Caja 326, Exp 3; Cuestionario, March 1921, AGN/DT, Caja 274, Exp. 3.

Class, Nationality, and "Race" in the Oil Industry

The immigration of large numbers of oil company employees changed the social composition of the Huasteca and introduced new labor hierarchies and social divisions too. Just as Tampico grew, so did the Huasteca. The 1921 census in fact included a brand new category: the oil camp (*campamento petrolero*). And although the census takers failed to count several municipalities, they listed twenty-two new locations they categorized as oil camps.[65] The result was the numerical dilution of indigenous communities and their marginalization as social actors for the first time in the history of northern Veracruz.[66] Communities like Zacamixtle, moreover, were displaced altogether, while individual indigenous families emigrated to escape the dangers of oil production or company thugs.[67]

As the native population was swept aside, the companies organized the new population of the Huasteca along rigid class and "race" lines. In the Golden Lane and Tampico, the English and the Americans reproduced the system of segregation and discrimination that was then legal in the United States (but not in Mexico). A man's skin color, which the oil men interpreted as "race," determined his occupation; his occupation, in turn, determined not only what labor he could perform and who were his supervisors, but also where he ate, where he lived, and where he received health care. A deeply ingrained racism informed the oilmen's design for the industry's social hierarchy. Educated professionals like geologist Charles Baker believed, for example, that Mexicans were a "less-developed, perhaps weaker, tropical race."[68] Although they had their differences with the bosses, the white working-class men of the oil industry went to Mexico sharing their superiors' racism. They too believed that

---

65 Some of those locales listed as camps did not have a census count, however, so there is no record of the number of people living in them. Departamento de Estadística Nacional, *Censo de Veracruz, 1921*.

66 See, for example, Eva Grosser Lerner, *Los Teenek de San Luis Potosí: lengua y contexto* (Mexico City: Instituto Nacional de Antropología e Historia, 1991), p. 16.

67 Lavín, *Petróleo*, p. 125. The original Veracruz census sheets for the year 1930 suggest that some families from Zacamixtle emigrated, too. That year the village of Zaragoza, in Amatlán, reported having a population of 350. Of these, 237 were Teenek. Most of them seemed to have been born there, but at least thirteen were not. They had been born in Zacamixtle. The census did not record the birth dates; however, the ages of three children show that one was born in 1916, one 1920, and one in 1922, the years of intense oil company activity in Zacamixtle. The migrants, furthermore, were distributed among four families, three of them headed by women. That suggests to me that they had been displaced from Zacamixtle. See Departamento de Estadística Nacional, *Censo de Población*, Veracruz, 1930.

68 Baker, "To the Prize Contest Committee" p. 5, IAEG/CB, Acct. 3328, Box 8, Reports by Charles Baker.

Mexicans not only "didn't know a drill from a tamale shuck," but also that they were intellectually incapable of becoming drillers.[69] As a Texan explained at some length,

> Mexicans . . . course they never could learn the technical nature of the business. Hard to learn the technical nature of the business. And I thought so much of this I [sic] seems to me that no race of people ever accomplish anything that doesn't have curiosity or doesn't want to do anything better every time they do it. I notice so much Mexicans do it, or do his work, he just did it straight down the line, just what he was suppose [sic] to do, and he never varied in trying to improve his technique. He never seemed to be interested in why it was done, or why it was done that way.[70]

Mexicans, foreign workers and executives agreed, naturally, could never be "the executive type." Indeed, even Ordoñez, who consulted for the companies for three decades, never occupied an executive post like DeGolyer, Hamilton, or other American geologists.[71] By nature, the foreigners believed, Mexicans were "more effective for the rough labor."[72] Thus, the oil magnates also transformed northern Veracruz into a tropical version of the southern United States or an American echo of colonial India.[73]

In their four decades in Mexico, the companies built the camps along the same pattern of segregation and discrimination based on skin color they used for the occupational hierarchy. The Americans hired "experts" to help with the task of taking good care of foreign company employees; the English were just as meticulous.[74] Executives were housed in comfortable houses, nice hotels, wooden bungalows, or individual apartments at company expense (see Figure 4.3). One El Aguila executive apartment in Tampico, for example, sported elegant flowered-print sofas

---

[69] Quoted in Lambert and Franks, *Voices*, p. 46.

[70] PTO, Tape 31, p. 7.

[71] Ordoñez was a consultant for Doheny from 1906 to 1914. In 1914 he became the chief geologist for Huasteca Petroleum and remained in that position until 1927, whereupon he went back to consulting work until he retired in 1933. DeGolyer, "Memorial," pp. 987–988. The only other national mentioned in association with executives was a man named Muñoz, whom Brown called the "chief Mexican assistant" to an English manager, T. J. Ryder. Brown does not explain, however, what sort of assistant Muñoz was. Brown, *Oil and Revolution*, p. 201.

[72] PTO, Tape 183, pp. 15–16.

[73] The General Manager at the Huasteca Petroleum refinery in Mata Redonda, William Green, in fact, had been a military officer in the Philippines before Doheny hired him in 1910. As Hall wrote, "the colonial attitudes acquired there carried directly into his actions in Mexico." *Oil, Banks, and Politics*, p. 113.

[74] McMahon, *Two Strikes*, pp. 40, 109.

Figure 4.3. Housing for the foreign employees of El Aguila Petroleum Company in Tampico, ca. 1914. From the DeGolyer Library, Southern Methodist University, Dallas, Texas, the Papers of Nell Goodrich DeGolyer.

with cushions, hardwood tables, Persian rugs, a silver coffee set, porcelain table settings, fancy reading lamps, and an imported Chinese screen as a decorative touch.[75] Foreign facilities likewise were fitted with mosquito nets, screens, showers or baths, "pure water," and toilets that "revealed that attention to comfort, cleanliness and decency which are characteristic of English people wherever they go," wrote Pearson's biographer.[76] The same applied to Doheny camps, where potable water and electricity came with foreign housing. In the 1930s, foreign oilmen were the first Huasteca inhabitants to enjoy private radios and telephones, too.[77]

---

[75] Mr. Vaughan's apartment, P&S/PA, P5/40–43, March 25, 1916, P5: Tampico, 1913–1916.

[76] Spender, *Weetman*, p. 106; Storm, "Wells," p. 515.

[77] Testimony of Edward L. Doheny in *Investigation*, p. 214; Elvira Vargas, *Lo que ví en la tierra del petróleo* (Mexico City: n/p, 1938), p. 24.

Foreign craftsmen and drillers were one notch down in the social and labor hierarchy, but their skin color entitled them to privileges in Mexico they often did not enjoy in the United States. Men who paid their own way as they migrated from camp to camp in the United States, to begin with, traveled to Mexican fields with all expenses paid and using the best transportation available: motorboat, horseback, motor car, or airplanes.[78] Most foreign workers, as well, did not enter the forest until Mexicans led by foreign supervisors had carved out the roads and built the necessary housing facilities. Once at camp, foreign workers lived in whites-only hotels, where they were assigned "independent and separate" rooms equipped with "good electrical installations, English toilets and baths with cold and hot water," "white-enamel basins" for hand washing, imported mattresses, and laundry service.[79] Similarly, foreign workers ate in whites-only restaurants with mock fireplaces, Chinese waiters, white tablecloths, paper napkins, and other finery not typical of mess halls in the United States.[80] An American driller working for El Aguila, for instance, vividly recalled that in Mexico he partook of the riches of the empire:

> We didn't get slop like American companies used to put out in the boom days in this country [the United States]; no sir! We ate just as good as the limeys did back in London . . . All the food was shipped over from England, and if what I ate there was any sample, those Britishers eat damned good. Christmas dinner? Man, they fed us meals you couldn't buy for $5 anyplace in the world. They put out enough to sink a battle-ship for each man, candied fruits, from England and India and Persia and France . . . When I came back to the United States after working for those Britishers, my teeth was just about worn down to the gums, I'd eaten so much and so good![81]

A visitor to an American camp at Pánuco similarly reported that, "the menu seemed over elaborate." Even though it was "only Wednesday," she and the geologist feasted on:

Soup

Chicken à la Maryland, with string beans, sweet corn, roast potatoes and hors-d'œuvres

[78] Hamilton, *Early Day*, pp. 24–25, 34, 40; W. M. Hudston, PTO, Tape 79, pp. 9–10; PTO, Tape 130, pp. 5–6; J.A. Lander to J.V. Ferguson, Los Angeles, California, November 10, 1928, AGN/JFCA, Caja 99, Exp. 15/929/552.

[79] Report from Labor Inspector Juan Saldaña, Tampico, February 19, 1923, AGN/DT, Caja 492, Exp. 1; Lambert and Franks, *Voices*, p. 47; Storm, "Wells," p. 523.

[80] BP, vol. 22, no. 6 (December 1926), photographic section; BP, vol. 23, no. 6 (June 1927), photographic section.

[81] Quoted in Lambert and Franks, *Voices*, pp. 43–44.

Tomato and lettuce salad, self-made dressing
Limeade and coffee
Peaches and cake
Jelly pocketbooks.[82]

Imported craftsmen also received whatever health care the companies provided. Camp infirmaries were few and far between until the late 1920s, but in all of them ill or injured foreigners recovered in whites-only pavilions. Their attendants were American doctors. When the medical needs exceeded the rather basic first aid and emergency treatment available, the companies sent their foreign workers to the United States and covered expenses.[83] And although by World War I oil workers in the United States had accumulated enough grievances against the companies to form militant unions, those who ventured into Mexico until 1938 remained the "aristocrat[s] of the oil field."[84] In Mexico poorly educated drillers and other qualified white workers could taste amenities professionals took for granted. Those perks, their shared home experience, their wages, and small numbers turned foreign workers into "quite a fraternity," as one proudly recalled – a fraternity that fiercely protected its privileges and reinforced racism.[85] The "wages of whiteness" in the Mexican oil industry were not only psychological, but quite literal indeed.[86]

[82] Storm, "Wells," pp. 515, 524. There were exceptions, however. In 1922, the tool dresser Harry Boutwell and his three friends returned to the United States angry with PennMex over the mistreatment they received at La Pita. Poor food was one of the main reasons they gave for quitting before their three-month contract was up. Boutwell told a reporter that for two weeks he and his friends had nothing but "bacon, mush and coffee for breakfast; for dinner we had canned corn beef, salmon or sardines, and supper the same." The company argued the food was atypical on account of the weather. The rainy season had swelled the river and isolated that particular camp. As the worker admitted, other company camps had good food. "How Big Oil Companies Treat Men in Mexico," *The Labor News*, Long Beach, California, August 17, 1922.

[83] PTO, Tape 104, p. 22; Inspector Andrés Araujo to Chief of Department of Labor, Tampico, September 3, 1926, AGN/DT, Caja 990, Exp 5; *Revista Huasteca*, no. 2 (April 1925), p. 27, no. 19 (September, 1926), p. 1; Sindicato de Empresa de Obreros y Empleados de la HPC, Pliego de peticiones que presenta este sindicato a la Huasteca Petroleum Company en Ebano, SLP, Ebano, September 9, 1933, RG 59, 812.5045/244, Roll 59. For a photo of El Aguila's hospital at Tanhuijo, see, P&S/PA, P6/19, P6: Northern Oil Fields Mexico 1913–1916.

[84] Quam-Wickham, "Petroleocrats," p. 115; Lambert and Franks, *Voices*, p. 42; Boatright, *Folklore*, p. 120.

[85] Quoted in Lambert and Franks, *Voices*, p. 46; PTO, Tape 140, p. 29. As Quam-Wickham wrote, an intense camaraderie among oil workers was typical in the U.S. industry. That facilitated its transfer to Mexico. "Petroleocrats," pp. 42–50.

[86] David R. Roediger, *The Wages of Whiteness: Race and the Making of the American Working Class* (London: Verso, 1991).

Mexican workers, by contrast, enjoyed few privileges beyond wages higher than hacienda rates. The waves of *enganchados* and refugees who arrived in Tampico faced a severe housing shortage, which the companies resolved by providing some of their own. In the camps, the companies erected Mexican quarters as far as possible from the foreigners, both by design and because American workers demanded segregation.[87] Lucky Mexican arrivals lived in the barracks indigenous men had built. The men called them *galleras* because their shape reminded them of chicken coops. The *galleras* slept up to sixty-four men in rows of bunk beds. Potable water, showers, and toilets were nonexistent. Mexican crews transported to areas without indigenous men willing to work, however, were "free to rest under the trees or inside huts they made themselves from reeds and grass" until they built their own company barracks. Mexican tradesmen nevertheless did not have to endure the dormitories reserved for common laborers, especially if they brought family members along. The companies provided them instead with cottages, "wood blocks measuring $2\frac{1}{2}$ meters wide by 6 meters long, and 3 meters high," tightly packed and lacking water, toilets, or electricity.[88]

In Tampico, the companies met Mexicans' housing needs depending on their assigned occupational categories. The companies built and rented cottages inside refinery grounds to their full-time Mexican workers: the craftsmen and other assistants to foreign workers. The rest could rent company shacks in the swamplands adjacent to the refineries. Neither place had paved streets nor sidewalks. In both cases latrines overflowed after heavy rains, raw sewage ran freely, garbage accumulated in empty lots, while domestic animals, flies, roaches, rats, and other fauna wandered unobstructed through houses and alleyways.[89] As late as 1937,

---

[87] Adleson, "The Cultural Roots," pp. 41–42. In 1923 in Tecomate, for example, the entire Mexican housing section had to be moved further away because the American workers found the initial distance insufficient. Asunto: Que esta Secretaría ya ordena a la Agencia de Petróleo en Tuxpan señale a la Cía. Refinadora del "Agwi" las modificaciones que deben hacerse a las casas de obreros, sent to Secretary of Gobernación, January 18, 1923, AGN/DT, Caja 492, Exp. 1.

[88] Rebeca de Gortari, "Petróleo y clase obrera en Veracruz: 1920–1935," in *Memoria del primer coloquio*, p. 146; Al C. Jefe del Departamento del Trabajo y Previsión Social from Cayetano Pérez Ruíz, September 16, 1920, AGN/DT, Caja 220, Exp. 6; STPRM, *El Petróleo*, photographs, pp. 5, 7, 8.

[89] Neighbors from Doña Cecilia to Municipal President, April 12, 1921, AHAT, Exp. 96, bis-1921; Sanitary brigade to Municipal President, June 29, 1917, AHAT, Exp 145; Sanitary brigade to Municipal President, May 26, 1917, AHAT, Exp. 1, no. 374; Special Junta against the bubonic plague to Municipal President, August 18, 1920, AHAT, Exp. 130–1920; Interview, DMC, Labor File I, #2721.

Figure 4.4. Housing for Mexican craftsmen in Mata Redonda, still inhabited in 2004. The mango trees in the front did not exist prior to 1938; neither did the chain link fence. Photo by the author.

Mexican oil workers' houses in Tampico were "without baths or even toilets, save for a communal outhouse used by many families. One room within, a small alcove for the kitchen." Although the companies produced energy aplenty in Tampico and burned off natural gas, the houses they rented to Mexican workers were "without light and illuminated by candles," fitted with "a charcoal stove for cooking that fills the hot air with its stench." Furniture, similarly, was limited to whatever Mexican workers could afford, "small beds in a row... one rocker, one table, covered with newspapers; broken dishes" (see Figure 4.4).[90]

A third group of Mexican workers, however, was not eligible for company housing at all: the day laborers. Beginning around 1916, the companies hired literally hundreds of men on the spot to work in the Golden Lane or the refineries for the long twelve-to-fourteen-hour day.[91] Their status as "nonpermanent" workers meant they had to procure their own

---

[90] Millan, *Mexico Reborn*, p. 220.
[91] Ocasio Meléndez, *Capitalism*, p. 197.

lodging in Tampico from among the myriads of cheap hotels and board-
ing houses that mushroomed throughout the port.[92] By 1917 it was
common to find hundreds of oil industry day laborers living in hon-
eycomb residences of thirty rooms packed with more than two hundred
tenants.[93]

In theory, the companies provided Mexican workers with health services as they did foreigners. In practice, however, Mexicans bemoaned
their lack of access to extant medical care until the mid-1920s and,
after that, the segregation and discrimination they were subjected to in
the facilities.[94] More often than not, wives, sisters, or mothers nursed
sick or injured Mexican workers in their cottages or in company infirmaries. Single men had to fend for themselves.[95] As late as 1929 at least,
Mexican oil workers who consulted company doctors felt the attention
they received was so inadequate they subsequently sought treatment with
traditional *curanderos* (healers).[96] The enforcement of national, class,
and color difference as a matter of labor policy, moreover, was not limited to discrimination in occupational categories, housing, and services.
The practice extended to the types of discipline and social control the
companies implemented as part of the new hierarchies they constructed.

Forging a Disciplined Work Force

The introduction of industrial discipline in northern Veracruz was part
and parcel of the changes in social relations encompassed in the ecology
of oil. To transform nature into wealth, it was not enough to herd masses
of Mexicans into the rainforest and expect that they work for wages. The
oilmen had to impose the regimented life of the factory in a place where
it had never existed and among men whose work experience was in agricultural work and its seasonal rhythms, or, in the case of the small number
of Mexican craftsmen, among those used to small workshops and relative
independence. That is, the companies had to forge the first generation of

[92] The best descriptions of these decrepit facilities appeared in the novels that B. Traven
wrote, both in *The Treasure of the Sierra Madre* and *The Cottonpickers*. See Heidi Zogbaum,
B. Traven: A Vision of Mexico (Washington, DE: Scholarly Resources, 1992), pp. 17–19.

[93] Adleson, "The Cultural Roots," p. 42.

[94] Asunto – Ratificando demanda presentada en contra de la Pierce Oil Corporation, S.A.,
Tampico, December 10, 1927, AGN/JFCA, Caja 10, Exp. 15/927/237.

[95] Testimony of José I. Hernández, July 16, 1919, AGEV/JCCA, Caja 9, Exp. 35.

[96] Certificado Médico de Antonio Herrera, May 6, 1929, in José Valdez vs. La Corona,
AGN/JFCA, Caja 108, 15/929/780; Letter from Jesús María Chávez, in Petróleos Asuntos
Pendientes, AGEV/JCCA, Caja 50, Exp. 2.

Mexican oil workers. That meant that the supervisory corps had to make it plain to the worker that he must perform every task the boss demanded, when and how he wanted it, and for as long as he decided. The companies had to make sure the embryonic worker understood that the job included lines of authority that he must respect and submit to unquestioningly.[97] In other words, the industry had to ensure that the novice knew he was a subordinate and ought to behave like one at all times – a fact recognized and underscored in the description of Huasteca Petroleum's General Manager Wylie as the "Industrial General."[98] If the neophyte worker failed to grasp the new concepts, he should also comprehend that there were repercussions. In the early twentieth-century capitalist industrial relations of Mexican oil, the consequences surpassed reprimands and firings. Because the companies possessed inordinate power in the communities where they operated – more so in the camps than in Tampico – they exercised social control that reached beyond the work site proper. The companies thus molded the Huasteca into a hybrid of the colonial plantation and the company town.

The oil companies enforced labor discipline among Mexicans through a variety of means. The most common were the managerial ideas then in vogue in the United States and Europe. These included breaking down productive activities into separate tasks workers could do repetitively and rapidly; timing workers to make sure they finished their task in the least possible time; making sure the men asked for permission to leave their work station to drink water or use toilet facilities; controlling the work day by the clock; keeping time cards; and pacing the rhythms of life according to the "shrill" whistle.[99] El Aguila's *Book of Instructions* for the Tampico refinery, for instance, dictated the workmen's schedule thus:

> 6 a.m. to 8:30 a.m. work
> 8:30 a.m. to 9 a.m. breakfast
> 9 a.m. to 12 noon work
> 12 noon to 1 p.m. dinner
> 1 p.m. to 5:30 p.m. work

[97] Knight Montiel, PHO/4/35. The same battle over working-class formation and discipline took place wherever industrialization occurred, of course. For the U.S. case, see, for example, David Montgomery, *Workers' Control in America* (Cambridge: Cambridge University Press, 1979).

[98] Davis, *Dark Side*, p. 64.

[99] Adleson, "The Cultural Roots," pp. 47–48; Storm, "Wells," p. 516.

Saturday hours were shorter: from 6 a.m. to 1 p.m. Without overtime, the new worker could expect a workweek of 64$\frac{1}{2}$ hours minimum, although, as the *Book* explained, the company did not pay for mealtime.[100] Daily travel time to the Huasteca from Tampico, a trip shortened to several hours one way via narrow-gauge railroad after 1910, lengthened the total time a man could expect to spend at work.[101] The workweek did not shrink until the late-1920s, when the men won the eight-hour day and a forty-four-hour workweek in theory, if not in practice.[102]

There were also unacknowledged discipline methods. The most important was setting up color, or "race," boundaries around specific types of work. The companies not only excluded Mexican craftsmen from master positions, but they also excluded Mexicans from training that might encourage them to think they could achieve equality or replace foreign workers in the future. Although there was no formal prohibition against Mexican participation in training programs, only those whom the executives invited or recommended could enjoy educational opportunities. Mexicans were never invited.[103] Likewise, the idea of providing

[100] *Book of Instructions*, P&S/HR, Box A2: Chief's notebooks, 1910–1915. La Corona had a similar schedule, detailed in A los obreros de la refinería de la Cia. "La Corona," Chijol, May 8, 1922, AGN/DT, Caja 327, Exp. 1. In the United States the workweek was eighty-four hours until World War I, according to Quam-Wickam, "Petroleocrats," p. 121.

[101] Ocasio Meléndez, *Capitalism*, p. 197.

[102] The battle for the eight-hour day in the Mexican oil industry was bloody, as it was elsewhere in the world. Even though some tradesmen, like the mechanics, had the eight-hour workday by 1919 in theory, in practice "nobody here working 8 hour shifts" in October 1921, reported El Aguila. T. J. Ryder to J. B. Body, New York, October 30, 1921, SMU/ED, Box 104, Folder 5159; Informe de huelgas, DP, Caja 169, Exp 39, 1919; González Salas, *Del reloj*, pp. 196–199. Oil workers, moreover, reported working twelve-hour days still in 1925: Sindicato de Obreros y Empleados de la Sinclair, Demanda contra la Mexican Sinclair Petroleum Co., Jalapa, July 14, 1925, AGN/JFCA, Caja 199, Exp. 15/930/1419. Drillers in Mexico were still working twelve hours in 1922, as well. *The Labor News*, August 17, 1922.

[103] If the language barrier was an obstacle in the first decade of oil extraction, by the 1920s that difficulty could be overcome. As American drillers themselves admitted, much learning of the trade took place in silence, given the roar of the machinery, by watching and doing. If an American farm boy became a "top hand" in two years, a Mexican might have done the same in a couple of years more, while he learned enough English (or the driller learned some Spanish) and observed and tried out the driller's moves. See Gerald Lynch, *Roughnecks, Drillers, and Tool Pushers: Thirty-Three Years in the Oil Fields* (Austin: University of Texas Press, 1987), pp. 2, 20–21, 26, 28; Boatright, *Folklore*, pp. 124–125; PTO, Tape 103, pp. 6–7. In fact, by the late 1920s the English terms used in American oil fields were common currency among Mexicans, with enough variation in the pronunciation to create a "hybrid" vocabulary, according to BP, vol. 28, nos. 4–5 (October–November, 1929), pp. 550–551.

scholarships for formal education in geology or the applied sciences to Mexicans was unthinkable until the Mexican government legislated the matter in the mid-1930s.[104]

The men directly in charge of translating company labor policy into daily practice were not the oil barons themselves, but their foreign general managers, shop supervisors, camp superintendents, and master craftsmen. Most were part of the "fraternity" that prided itself in its whiteness, and they reinforced with gusto the racial and national hierarchy the magnates set up. They never let Mexicans forget that they were fit only for "low grade of labor," for work "not fit for a white man."[105] They often enforced industrial discipline harshly, through the use of ritual humiliation, verbal abuse, physical violence, incarceration, and, in extreme cases, death.

Ritual humiliation and verbal abuse were the most common methods the foreign supervisory corps used to instill labor discipline among Mexicans who did not meet managerial expectations. Although a few foreigners learned Spanish, most limited themselves to the acquisition of "bilingual" phrases and obscenities. As Juan Hernández recalled, his American supervisor showed exasperation with his work by saying "Yisoscrais, yu gare gel, Usté buro!" ("Jesus Christ, you go to hell, you ass!").[106] An English executive was more explicit, finding Mexicans so repugnant that he refused to look at them in the face when he was forced to address them. Whenever a Mexican entered his office, he turned his chair around, listening and responding with his back to him.[107] Derogatory language and gestures to "correct" Mexican workers were so routine, in fact, that they appeared matter-of-fact in arbitration records, inspection reports,

[104] Such scholarships, in fact, were among the demands the oil workers' unions began to make in the 1920s and were incorporated into the federal Labor Law passed in 1934. Once the law required that large enterprises like the oil companies provide scholarships for their workers or their sons and daughters, the oil companies began granting "one scholarship to a workman or the son of a workman, for every 400 men employed." [Huasteca Petroleum Company], *Mexico: Labor Controversy: 1936–1938; Memoranda on the Controversy Arising Out of Mexico's Impositions on Foreign Oil Companies in Mexico Leading up to the Expropriation Decree of March 18, 1938*, Reprinted by Huasteca Petroleum Company, n/d., p. 6. The only supervisory positions the companies made available to Mexicans throughout the 1910s were outside of production, including jobs such as foremen for construction crews, warehouse supervisors, and lead men in the collection and storage of work tools. Adleson, "Historia social," pp. 415–416.

[105] PTO, Tape 213, p. 22.

[106] Juan Hernández and Juan C. Hernández vs. International Petroleum Co., AGEV/JCCA, 1922, Caja 27, Exp. 17. See also Abelardo Muñoz to General Manager Hall, September 27, 1926, AGEV/JCCA, Caja 62, Exp 28; Mesa Andraca, *Relatos*, p. 41.

[107] Rodríguez, *El rescate*, p. 49.

and even company correspondence.[108] A 1935 internal review conducted by El Aguila's parent company, Royal Dutch Shell, for instance, acknowledged the problem as it recommended that from then on the company "should be very careful never to send to Mexico anyone, whatever his position, who...suffered from race-complex."[109]

Foreigners, moreover, were not above using more drastic measures to express displeasure with the performance of a Mexican worker. Through the 1930s, punching, slapping, or kicking Mexican workers were common, if not officially prescribed methods of reprimand.[110] The English magnate Percy Norman Furber himself recalled having "to discipline an Indian" whom he believed was drunk. Furber ordered the foreman put the man "in the stocks" for the night. In the morning, "I was told he had yelled blue murder all night and I found, to my dismay, they had put him on what was usually a quiescent ant hill whose occupants, black ants, had viciously resented his presence." Because Furber's house was sufficiently removed from Mexican quarters, he had been spared the worker's screams. Not so with the rest of the Mexican labor force, who most assuredly learned a lesson that night.[111]

The most unusual method of discipline in the oil industry was the establishment of company jails. Three companies appear on the record as making use of them. One was the Dutch company La Corona, which kept its private prison at Chijol at least until 1922.[112] PennMex, a Standard Oil subsidiary, saved itself the expenditure of a building and used an oil storage tank for the same purpose. Francisco Ariguznaga remembered being disciplined for trying to organize a union by landing in one of the tanks along with his coconspirators. He recalled how "they left us [in the tank] all night and all day, till the sun's heat really got us, and when the

---

[108] Letter from Tierra Blanca workers to Luis Morones, July 27, 1924, AGN/DT, Caja 725, Exp. 2; Salvador Romero vs. PennMex Fuel Co., July 28, 1928, AGN/DT, Caja 74, Exp. 72; Jesús Hernández vs. El Aguila, AGEV/JCCA 1921, Caja 17, Exp. 27; Inspector Andrés Araujo to Department of Labor, May 6, 1924, AGN/DT, Caja 813, Exp. 4.

[109] Mr. Murray to the Foreign Office, Mexico City, September 17, 1935, Foreign Office, Great Britain, File 18708.8565.

[110] Robles Saldaña, PHO/4/39; Interview with Mr. León Vargas Domínguez, conducted by Lief Adleson on February 7, 9, 11, 1974 in Ciudad Madero, Tamaulipas, PHO/4/27; Complaint, 1924, AGN/DT, Caja 725, Exp. 2; Sindicato de Empresa de Obreros y Empleados de la HPC, Pliego de Peticiones, September 9, 1935, RG 59, 812.5045/244, Roll 59.

[111] Furber, *I Took Chances*, p. 124.

[112] It was closed because of workers' protests. Inspectors Andrés Araujo and Juan Saldaña to Chief Inspector, February 27, 1922, AGN/DT, Caja 327, Exp. 1; Jesús Cabrera vs. La Corona, AGEV/JCCA 1922, Caja 30, Exp. 55.

tank was a true hell and the smell of gas had made us dizzy almost to the
point of losing consciousness. Mr. Rearden [the superintendent] arrived,
chastised us, and set us free."[113] Until the 1930s, Doheny's Huasteca
Petroleum had its own jail in El Ebano.[114]

In some cases, supervisors enforced discipline through extreme violence. Some incidents were unpredictable, the direct result of racism and
defense of white minority privilege in an industry divided along color lines
by design. Such was the case of a Mexican named Valentino murdered
by a driller in Tancoco in 1921. Enrique Barrera witnessed the incident:

> when going to the camps, [the foreigners] carried water along in rub-
> ber bags or little barrels. Us [Mexicans], even if we were dying of
> thirst, had to withstand it (*aguantarnos*). We could only drink water
> from muddy and dirty puddles...We were drilling...and there was
> no breeze...in the heat. The foreman Valentino had just arrived by
> car with a crew [of laborers] and was very thirsty. He saw the little
> wooden barrel sitting there and didn't think twice about taking a drink.
> The American, when he saw that one of us dark ones (*prietos*) had
> dared to drink his water, went bonkers, insulted him in English, calling
> him "son of a bitch."...Valentino who was very smart and understood
> English, answered in the same way. The American left without saying
> a word. He went to the camp, got his gun, returned to the well, and
> when he came face to face with Valentino, he shot him at point blank
> range.[115]

Other incidents of violence, however, were premeditated, used to
remove troublesome workers. In these cases, the violence did not involve
foreigners, but rather, one specific group of Mexican company employees: the "white guards." Formed as an armed corps in 1913 in response
to the risk the Revolution posed to oil property and employees, the
guards soon gained a reputation for doing the companies' most unsavory
work. They were widely suspected of eliminating indigenous landowners
who refused to deal with the oil companies, but they became infamous
for attacking workers, too. Ventura Calderón, who headed the Huasteca
Petroleum guards in the 1920s and 1930s, for example, killed Ramón
García in front of the Huasteca refinery in 1925 and Júan de León
in 1929, but was never detained or questioned. When León's nephew

[113] Quoted in Javier Santos Llorente, "La ley y los trabajadores," *Nosotros los petroleros*,
año 3, no. 19 (1981), p. 19.
[114] Robles Saldaña, PHO/4/39; Interview with Mr. León Vargas Domínguez, conducted
by Lief Adleson on February 7, 9, 11, 1974 in Ciudad Madero, Tamaulipas, PHO/4/27.
[115] Quoted in Rodríguez, *El rescate*, pp. 51–52.

demanded the authorities apprehend the known assassin, the Mayor of Pueblo Viejo admitted he was impotent in the case because "Mr. Calderón was under the wing of the flag of the bars and stars."[116] Accusations of guards shooting PennMex workers in El Alamo in 1928 met the same results.[117]

If on-the-job discipline could be that extreme, life outside work hours did not always escape management. In the camps of the Huasteca especially, the companies exercised a high degree of social control all the time. The industry controlled housing because they owned it. If a worker was fired, therefore, he was forced to evacuate himself and his family from company housing, too. Similarly, the companies owned the roads in and out of the camps until 1925 and kept a tight control over them. Only those with written permission from the camp superintendent could travel – on foot, animal, or vehicle – on the roads. Those stipulations applied to all Huasteca inhabitants, not only those on the company payroll. To enforce the rules, the companies built intermittent gates along the roads and posted armed guards. It was the guards' job to make sure the travelers carried permits and to deny access to whoever the companies considered undesirables, including fired workers, government inspectors, rival companies' employees, and blacklisted union organizers.[118]

Likewise, the companies exercised control over workers' lives through the company stores. The shops opened at the request of the workmen because there were no stores in the Huasteca and because the high cost of living greatly diminished their purchasing power.[119] They erroneously assumed the companies would sell the products at cost. Instead, El Aguila used the stores "as an alternative to doubling wages," whereas Huasteca Petroleum imposed surcharges for transportation, handling, and "a little advance upon the cost" of goods, increasing the prices to market value or above.[120] In some cases, moreover, the workers discovered that only

[116] *El Mundo*, August 31, 1925; Jesús de León to the president of the Republic, May 7, 1929, and Jesús de León to the Governor of Veracruz, AGN, Dirección General de Gobierno (DGG), Caja 4AA, Exp. 45, 2.331.1(24)2.

[117] Franciso Cobos vs. PennMex, 1928, AGEV/JCCA, Caja 79, Exp. 51.

[118] Hall, *Oil, Banks, and Politics*, p. 112; Lavín, *Petróleo*, p. 170; Menéndez, *Doheny*, p. 181; Federico Ladolph vs. Huasteca Petroleum Company, October 1927, AGN/JFCA, Caja 12, Exp. 15/927/285; Tampico Inspector to Chief of Department of Labor, March 5, 1921, AGN/DT, Caja 326, Exp. 7; Rodríguez, *El rescate*, pp. 38–39. A sample travel permission slip is reprinted in Santos Llorente, *Episodios*, p. 142.

[119] Anexo No. 3, Tampico, June 24, 1919, AGN/DT, Caja 169, Exp. 40.

[120] Cowdray to Body, London, December 29, 1916 and Body to Cowdray, New York, January 20, 1917, P&S/HR, Box A4; Interview, DMC, Labor File I, #2721.

the company store would cash the paychecks the company issued, forcing them to make purchases there. Through 1930, in fact, it was not uncommon for workers to become so indebted to the company store that they could not cancel their bills on payday.[121] Thus, in the Huasteca as elsewhere in North America, the company store became another vehicle for labor control, as the companies not only recovered some of the wages it paid, but also kept individual workers tied to their jobs, irrespective of the conditions, until they could clear their accounts.

Although the oil companies did not necessarily intend to cast such a long shadow in the lives of its Mexican workers, the social and environmental conditions they found in the Huasteca forced them into certain compromises. If they wanted to extract oil, they had to transform the landscape. To do that, they needed to increase population density. The population growth they created meant they also had to provide the minimum requirements for human survival, including shelter and food. The organization the companies selected to overcome environmental restraints, however, was their choice alone. The models and ideological constructs they used to organize the industry and its workers they imported wholesale from the home countries, where racism, segregation based on skin color, class exploitation, colonial haughtiness, and paternalistic attempts to control working-class life were the norm.[122] The extension of those schemes to the Huasteca was not surprising, therefore, even if one of its elements – formal segregation – was not legal in Mexico. If total control over the labor force was wholly undesirable in a post-slavery world, punishing methods to keep workers in line was a widespread practice across the industrialized world until well after World War I. In that sense, the changes in social relations and methods of organization of the Mexican oil industry were not unique at all. The foreign oilman behaved as he normally did, as both a "master of men and a master of nature."[123]

---

[121] Luis, Juan, and Antonio Jaramillo and Juan Pérez vs. Mexican Gulf, 1927, AGN/JCCA, Caja 64, Exp. 112; Inspector Cayetano Pérez Ruíz to Department of Labor, September 16, 1920, AGN/DT, Caja 220, Exp. 6; Letter from El Ebano workers to the president, September 7, 1923, AGN/DT, Caja 752, Exp. 9; Testimony of Jesús Calderón and Juan Muñíz, May 18, 1927, AGN/DT, Caja 1219, Exp. 23; Armando Kauffman to Labor Inspector, April 10, 1930, AGN/JFCA, Caja 164, Exp. 15/930/503.

[122] "In the Domain of Standard Oil," *The Industrial Pioneer*, vol. 1, no. 6 (October 1923), pp. 18–19. See also Roy Rosenzweig, *Eight Hours for What We Will: Workers and Leisure in an Industrial City, 1870–1920* (New York: Cambridge University Press, 1983). On the California oil industry and labor relations in particular, see Quam-Wickham, "Petroleocrats," Chapter 4.

[123] Quoted in Davis, *Dark Side*, p. 64.

Men and Nature

The social changes the oil companies generated in the Huasteca were as drastic as the changes they exercised on the landscape. Moreover, the two processes were intertwined in such a way that the social hierarchies deeply influenced and often determined the experiences between humans and nature as well. That is, as they lived and worked in the tropical forest, the social groups affiliated with the oil industry experienced and interacted with their surroundings in distinct ways. The class and race/nationality position of each group mediated that group's experience with nature at work and at home. For the bosses, the Huateca and Tampico were unpleasant but malleable locations that they did not hesitate to transform into something comfortable and even fun. For Mexican workers and their families, the opposite was true. The social divisions and labor hierarchies the companies implemented thus reached the environmental realm. The spheres where this divergence was most pronounced were in lifestyle, health, and safety.

The Masters and Nature

Segregated quarters and better quality housing was not the only difference between foreigners and nationals in the oil industry. To "make living bearable" in Mexico, the oilmen made the tropics as comfortable as possible by European and American standards. To attenuate temperatures of 90–98°F in the shade and sauna-like humidity, the companies imported fans and set up ice machines in the camps, Tuxpan, and Tampico. To counter the chilly *nortes*, offices and homes included wood-burning stoves and fireplaces.[124] To make employees feel at home in the tropics, the companies replaced the forest with reproductions of the landscapes left behind. El Aguila, for example, surrounded employee homes with "English gardens" planted with exotic flora like rosebushes ("Festival Collection" and "Killarny" varieties), chrysanthemums, begonias, and tanglefoot imported "by parcel post," which Mexican gardeners on the company payroll kept green and weeded.[125]

---

[124] A. E. Chambers to Body, Tampico, May 19, 1917, P&S/HR, Box A4; Storm, "Wells," p. 521; P5/12 n/d, P5/20, P5/26, March 24, 1916, P&S/PA, P5: Tampico 1913–1916.

[125] H. S. Wood to DeGolyer, Tampico, November 1, 1917; H. S. Wood to Peter Henderson & Co., Tampico, September 11, 1917; and H. S. Wood to DeGolyer, Tampico, September 11, 1917, SMU/ED, Box 117, Folder 5377; STPRM to Hacienda, June 29, 1937, AGN, Archivo Histórico de Hacienda (AHH), Legajo 1862–150; Luis Rodríguez vs. The Texas Co., AGEV/JCCA, 1928, Caja 74, Exp 79; Rabishkin Masloff, PHO/4/58; Mesa Andraca, *Relatos*, p. 39.

The Americans also reproduced their home environment in the tropical forest. In Huasteca Petroleum camps, employee bungalows were surrounded by white picket fences and gardens with a Southern California
flavor to them: palm trees uprooted and replanted in neat rows, citrus trees strategically planted to provide shade for the houses, green
front lawns, and grassy backyards.[126] In Tampico, the transformation of
the swamps prefigured Southern California suburbia by a few years, too.
The native vegetation was replaced by "rich green lawns and mosaic-like
flowerbeds" and tree-lined "boulevards." The neighborhoods – Altavista,
Americana, Campbell, Aurora, and El Aguila – were exclusive, built far
from downtown, beyond the reach of public transport, and landscaped
to please the eye of motorists roaring into "sweeping driveways" in their
brand-new company automobiles.[127] Perched on the northeastern slope
of the city furthest from the riverbanks, the "elegant residences" on the
hill enjoyed fresh air free of oily stenches, "a climate cooled by land or
seabreezes," and "beautiful views of the savannah extending to the west
of the Pánuco; of the city of Tampico and its great refineries; and at the
foot of the hill, of the very blue waters of the Chairel Lagoon and the
Tamesí River."[128]

As enormous oil spills drowned the vegetation and fires reduced forest
acreage to cinders, moreover, oil magnates exported threatened botani-
cal specimens to their home bases. The Dohenys became avid collectors
of Mexican tropical plants. In 1913, they hired an architect to build a
herbarium worth $150,000 behind their home in the Los Angeles desert.
"When the room was completed," wrote a biographer, Dohney "filled it
with over 10,000 orchids, cycads, palms, and tropical trees imported from
Mexico that would grow to reach the upper regions of the ninety-foot-high
conservatory."[129] The Englishman Furber also took orchids back to his

---

[126] The irony of the southern California landscape the oilmen tried to reproduce in northern Veracruz, of course, is that it was itself the product of men like Doheny who transformed it from a desert and semi-desert into their interpretation of a Mediterranean
landscape. Photographs of Cerro Azul in BP, vol. 25, no. 4 (April 1928), photographic
section; photographs in PanAmerican, *Mexican Petroleum*, p. 70; photographs of Mata
Redonda and Chopopote Nuñez in BP, vol. 23, no. 4 (April 1927), photographic section,
and Alafita Méndez et al., *Historia gráfica*, pp. 94, 108; Storm, "Wells," p. 515.

[127] Millan, *Mexico Reborn*, p. 216; Chávez Padrón, *Testimonio*, p. 41; Commentary by Rafael
Domínguez, *El Dictamen*, March 19, 1936; Tinkle, *Mr. De*, p. 79; *El Mundo*, June 2, 1930.
By 1919, the *calzada* (boulevard) that led to the oilmen's neighborhoods had to be
repaired, "deteriorated by so many vehicles," according to *Excélsior*, May 28, 1919.

[128] Ordoñez, *El petróleo*, p. 7.

[129] Davis, *Dark Side*, p. 88. Europeans had taken to uprooting and collecting American
rainforest orchids since the nineteenth century, according to Dean, *With Broadax*,
p. 163.

native England as gifts, while a Swiss professional who worked for El Aguila took advantage of his stay in Zacamixtle to collect butterflies "and other insects."[130]

The top brass also enjoyed taming wild animals as pets. Doheny once sent a monkey to his son in Los Angeles for his birthday. On another occasion, Doheny returned to Southern California with a deer that, having lost its habitat, "wandered" into company installations at El Ebano. The deer ended up in Doheny's private zoo.[131] Likewise, the Englishman Furber paid six indigenous men to trap a boa constrictor, "six feet or so in length and seven or eight inches in girth," to keep as a pet and a rat catcher. To show his appreciation for the snake's services, Furber "patted the snake fondly" and fired a storekeeper who objected to its presence. Furber's manager, Payne, and his daughter, Inez, went further. They kept a juvenile jaguar as a pet in their sprawling northern Veracruz home. Inez, in fact, posed for the camera under a veranda holding the young cat in her arms. Unlike the snake, which remained satiated by forest rats in the store, the feline became restless as he grew. Eventually he attacked both Inez and Payne, inflicting "sixteen serious bites" on the oilman before the jaguar was shot dead.[132]

In similar displays of mastery over the natural world, the upper echelons of the companies engaged in recreational contests that pitted them against animals. Hunting was the "chief" recreational activity of executives, superintendents, professionals, and their visitors from abroad. With Mexican guides to show the way, company men went on expeditions to hunt jaguars, pumas, ocelots, wild boars, wild turkeys, ducks, and other "game." Crocodiles, abundant upstream along the Pánuco, were harpooned.[133]

Second to hunting as a favorite activity of high company officials was prize fishing. Hamilton regularly organized outings to the upper waters of the Tamesí, where trout abounded and, presumably, were untainted by the oil pollution that saturated the lower Pánuco. By the late 1920s, the sport had metamorphosed into "brilliant" annual regattas that included the wealthiest of Tampico's society. The regattas, in turn, sponsored an annual international competition to catch the biggest shark or tarpon, a marine fish that swam upstream to spawn and could weigh up to

---

[130] Mesa Andraca, *Relatos*, p. 31; Furber, *I Took Chances*, p. 119.

[131] Davis, *Dark Side*, p. 47, photograph of Ned Doheny and the deer.

[132] Furber, *I Took Chances*, pp. 119, 124–125, 143. Payne's house also had a garden, P/10/56–58, P&S/PA, P10: Other Oil Companies in Mexico, 1914–1918.

[133] *Excélsior*, March 6, 1921; *El Mundo*, June 14, 1934; Chávez Padrón, *Testimonio*, p. 44; Davis, *Dark Side*, p. 49; A trip to Tampico, IAEG/WC, Box 1, Diaries.

100 pounds. Company wives excelled at the sport and their photographs with fish larger than themselves figured prominently in the society pages of *El Mundo*.[134]

Other diversions among oil bosses did not involve capturing fauna, but rather transforming their habitat. To satisfy avid golf players stationed in Tampico, company clubs replaced swamps and mangroves and their bird, amphibian, and aquatic life with "slick greens" with a tropical twist: tall palm trees dotting the courses and Mexican boys hauling golf clubs.[135] Similarly, swamps were drained and filled in for tennis courts and swimming pools where the Tampico staff and their few "pretty blond *gringuita* wives" sipped ice-cold drinks, read novels and magazines, or perused mail delivered by Mexican children.[136]

Thus, the top layers of the oil hierarchy forged a relationship with the natural world of the Huasteca based on their willingness and capacity to mold it into something familiar. From extraction to recreation, at work and at play, the oil barons' lifestyle demonstrated how thoroughly they commodified nature. Even as they found "paradise" in the tropical forest of the Huasteca, the oil men not only bought, sold, leased, and exploited it; they also treated the flora and fauna therein as objects subject to possession, to be collected, tamed, transferred as gifts, killed for sport, or dismantled for their recreation (and re-creation). Indeed, as unbridled industrialists, the oilmen gave almost literal meaning to the biblical injunction that men "have dominion over the fish of the sea, over the birds of the air, and over the cattle, and over all the earth, and over every creeping thing that creeps upon the earth . . . and over every living thing that moves upon the earth."[137]

---

[134] Hamilton, *Early Day*, p. 130; *El Mundo*, June 5, 1927, May 1, 1927, May 4, 1930; A trip to Tampico, IEAG/WC.

[135] Diary, February 27 and 29 1916, March 5, 1916, SMU/ED, Box 105, Folder 5; Terry, *Terry's Guide*, p. 50b; Millan, *Mexico Reborn*, p. 222; Interview with Mr. Maurilio Rocha Juárez, conducted by Lief Adleson in Tampico, Tamaulipas on October 2, 1978, PHO/4/92.

[136] Interview with Mr. Camilo Román Cota, conducted by Lief Adleson on December 23, 1975 in Poza Rica, Veracruz, PHO/4/47; Millan, *Mexico Reborn*, pp. 216, 221; *Revista Huasteca*, no. 8 (October 1925), pp. 20–21; *El Mundo*, May 20, 1935; Storm, "Wells," p. 515.

[137] Genesis 1:26, 28, *The Bible*, Revised Standard Version (New York: American Bible Society, 1971). The idea linking Christian belief to a mastery over nature comes from Lynn White, Jr., "The Historical Roots of Our Ecologic Crisis," *Science*, vol. 155, no. 3767 (March 10, 1967), pp. 1203–1207, but other scholars have developed the concept in more depth, including Carolyn Merchant, *Reinventing Eden: The Fate of Nature in Western Culture* (New York: Routledge, 2003).

Oil Field Aristocrats and Nature

Foreign workers, the middle rung in the occupational hierarchy of the Mexican oil industry, encountered nature in ways different from the professionals and the magnates. They experienced nature primarily through work.[138] That is to say, the drillers and master craftsmen did not assume an a priori position of mastery over their environment the moment they landed in the tropical forest. They came into contact with nature through their daily work routine and based on the conditions therein. In their case, the aspects of life and work in the tropical forest most revealing of their experience of and with nature were health, safety, and leisure.

When they first signed contracts with the oil companies, the foreign workers were not necessarily well informed about the health conditions they would encounter in the Huasteca. The oilmen, however, were, and went through great efforts to safeguard their incoming foreign employees from the ravages of microscopic life. Dysentery-causing microorganisms were the first to attack migrant labor populations and the main reason the oilmen were careful to provide potable water to their foreign employees.[139] They were not the most dangerous, however. That distinction belonged to the parasitic protozoa that caused malaria and the virus that caused yellow fever through mosquito bites. They inspired major public health programs among the oil companies. In that process, the industry also inadvertently protected its foreign workers from the other lethal scourges of northern Veracruz, smallpox and bubonic plague.

Herbert Wylie's public health measures were prototypical. Because he knew that there were "infinitesimal monsters" in the environment that threatened the success of the oil enterprise, he demanded total hygiene from his employees.[140] He introduced them to a "strict" sanitation program in the El Ebano refinery around 1901. The same project was later replicated in all Huasteca Petroleum installations. When yellow fever first appeared nearby, Wylie mobilized the camp like a true general: he quarantined the work force; disposed of standing water; scattered lime throughout the housing complexes to eliminate mosquito breeding grounds; and sprayed the vegetation with oil and burned it to remove

[138] White, *The Organic Machine*, Chapter 1.
[139] Russell B. Brown, Reply to Allegations as to "Cheap Peon Labor" in Foreign Oil Fields, June 22, 1937, RG 59, File 812.6363/2950. One American worker, for example, remembered that the doctor told him to drink wine instead of water to get rid of his "stomach trouble." PTO, Tape 103, p. 8.
[140] Storm, "Wells," p. 526.

insect habitat. To emphasize the severity of the crisis to the foreign workers, moreover, Wylie took possession of the men's clothing and blankets and burned them. Then he imposed a system of rules to preserve the foreigners' health. He decreed mandatory bathing, mandatory sleeping between two sheets, and mandatory weekly laundry service. In addition, he ordered the men to air their rooms during the day and submit them to regular inspections for cleanliness. If the methods seemed draconian to the men, they did not complain loudly enough to make it into the record. The reason could be that Wylie's sanitary and labor discipline worked. Until 1918, only two Americans had died at El Ebano from disease: one from peritonitis and one from smallpox.[141]

Safety was another issue. Oil became the second most dangerous industry in Mexico after mining.[142] In 1934 El Aguila alone reported 1,224 accidents, while Huasteca Petroleum reported 1,021, an average of three accidents per company per day.[143] As supervisor A. E. Jensen begrudgingly admitted in 1928, "it is true that most of our men at different times had suffered some very minor injury."[144] Accidents occurred both in the fields and the refineries, and many, if not most, were directly related to the natural chemical composition of Huasteca crude. Its gases could kill men in a flash, either through poisoning, burning, or blasting them into the air. When the most poisonous of them all, hydrogen sulfide, filtered through cracks around a well, off the top of a tank or an open pit, or through cracks in rusted or broken pipelines, workers knew death hung in the air.[145] Not even high-ranking employees like Hamilton were

[141] Interview, DMC, Labor File I, #958, #2724; Testimony of Edward L. Doheny in *Investigation*, pp. 235, 276.
[142] Santiago González Cordero, "El derecho de los trabajadores huelguistas y el derecho de la nación," AGN/AHH, Legajo 1857-117, Legajo #2.
[143] Summary of statistical data on accidents, 1937, AGN/AHH, Legajo 1857-119. In the United States the oil industry was equally dangerous. Oil workers suffered so many accidents that they transformed their exposure to danger into a source of pride, and their mutilated limbs into a mark of manhood and a symbol of working-class solidarity that distinguished them from the "pencil-pushers" in the administrative offices, according to Boatright, *Folklore*, p. 119.
[144] A. E. Jensen to A. R. Coleman, September 5, 1928, AGN/JFCA, Caja 55, Exp. 15/928/947.
[145] In 1923, for instance, *El Mundo* reported that four Mexicans had died from asphyxia from a well on the Topila-Ozuluama road that launched an "extraordinary quantity of gas." It also carried a story about Freeport Oil's well No. 2 in Cacalilao whose gas killed three Mexican workers, one soldier in a nearby barracks, one passerby and his donkeys, and "the wild animals around an extensive radius." *El Mundo*, April 16 and August 9, 1923. Three years later, the Labor Inspector at Tuxpan reported that eight Mexican workers died from "gas poisoning" in Tepetate and two in Amatlán in the month

exempt. While he was mapping the Huasteca in 1914, he inadvertently breathed a "good whiff" of the gas more than once. As a result, he experienced "severe headaches," fainted "once or twice," and before long he felt the glands all over his body getting "sore and swollen." Days into his assignment, he became "so blind that I had to be led around." His position in the corporate ladder, however, restored him: El Aguila evacuated him to Tampico, then sent him to the United States for treatment.[146] When the sulfur caught fire, the risks increased exponentially, as Potrero del Llano No. 4 amply demonstrated. Time and again, foreign workers recalled the deaths of coworkers under those circumstances as the worst of their Mexican experience.[147]

In contrast to the magnates, who found a gusher well exciting and saw it as an opportunity to prove their masculinity, drillers in particular understood they were putting their bodies at risk on a daily basis. The photographs of oilmen and foreign workers taken when Cerro Azul No. 4 gushed epitomized the class differences among foreigners in their relationship to nature in this context. The "officials at the well" were dapper in light-colored, spotless suits and hats, Doheny's mustache white as rabbit fur; the foreign oil workers, "all white American citizens," were drenched in oil from head to toe, their whiteness invisible beneath the black coat of crude.[148] Thus the foreign drillers' bodies literally stood between nature and wealth. Just as they were the agents that directly extracted the oil from the earth to transform it into material riches, theirs were the bodies liable to experience direct harm when nature released the sought-after chemicals. For that reason, it was the drillers and craftsmen who designed technologies to cap runaway wells and to prevent explosions. The daily threats to their safety and health motivated them to invent new devices and find novel applications for existing ones. Through their labor, then, foreign oil workers not only diminished the danger to their own lives, but also earned themselves a place in the club of men with the capacity to control nature.[149]

---

of September alone. Antonio L. Luna to the Chief of the Deparment of Petroleum, September 30, 1920, AGN/DP, Caja 41, Exp. 7 316(02)/4.

[146] Hamilton, *Early Day*, pp. 80–81.

[147] Texan driller W. M. Hudson described in detail the twin mangled bodies of a Mexican "boy" and an American driller killed in a "blow-out" at Pánuco, for example, in PTO, Tape 79, p. 35.

[148] Mexican Petroleum, *Cerro Azul*, last two photographs.

[149] Foreign master craftsmen and their Mexican assistants designed and built the "bell nipple" used at Potrero del Llano No. 4, a large, heavy iron valve. Likewise, foreign drillers in Mexico developed explosion-prevention devices such as mazes of pipes and

The relationship between working-class Americans of the oil industry and nature, therefore, was ambivalent at best. They did not find gushing wells a challenge to their masculinity, nor did they echo the Edenic narrative when they recalled their lives in the Mexican oil fields; yet they actively and consciously participated in devising ways to control nature as they encountered it at work. To foreign workers, nature was unpredictable and dangerous: that is what their work experience taught them. The men did not presume to be masters of nature; they only aspired to be so.

Leisure time illustrates the difference clearly. Foreign craftsmen and executives shared the privileges of whiteness in Mexico, but their class differences guaranteed they did not have much more in common. Even though the craftsmen were entitled to membership in the social clubs corporate executives and professionals sponsored in Mexico by virtue of their skin color and nationality, they abstained from golf, tennis, prize fishing, and collecting orchids, insects, or mammals. The reasons were perfectly illustrated in the experience of W. M. Hudson. Upon his arrival in the Huasteca, Hudson swam and fished in the Pánuco. Then two incidents made him give up both activities. One was his father's catch one afternoon: a shark's head with teeth marks revealing that the body was inside another shark. The second was an unexpected scene:

> a swordfish coming along that had his sword broken and laying back over his head; he'd been in a fight with a shark...About that time the water turned white. And this shark stuck his head out of the water, trying to get to this fish that was hugging the bank, but he was so big and the water was so shallow, all he could do was stick his head out, and his mouth open.

Hudson "poured a couple of 30-30's" into the shark and changed his behavior: "from then on I'd like, I'd rather take a bath in the bathtub, bathtub or washtub rather than to take it in the Pantico [sic] River."[150] In the encounters between foreign workers and tropical fauna, workers did not assume that they were always at the top of the food chain.

For foreign oil workers, therefore, seeking pleasure in the tropical forest became largely an indoor affair. By all accounts, the men spent their few off-duty hours inside or at the thresholds of the casinos, bars,

---

valves that could capture and channel the pressurized gas in the drilling hole before it cracked the surface. *Revista Huasteca*, no. 6 (August 1925); PanAmerican, *Mexican Petroleum*, pp. 102–107; Hudson, PTO, Tape 79, p. 34. The same process of innovation took place in the United States, of course, as described in Boatright and Owens, *Tales*, pp. 197–223.

[150] PTO, Tape 81, pp. 21–22.

brothels, and cabarets that sprung throughout the Huasteca to entertain them. In those ramshackle establishments the men passed the time telling stories; drinking imported whiskey; playing pool, poker, or dice; chewing or smoking imported tobacco; buying sex; engaging in drunken brawls; or simply "obstructing pedestrians."[151] Given the dangers and hazards nature exposed them to at work and at rest, it is perhaps not surprising that foreign workers found the idea of spending more time in the great outdoors than was necessary to earn a salary less than compelling. By their actions, foreign workers showed that nature in its tropical guise was not their site of choice to express their mastery or masculinity.

Mexican Oil Workers

If the foreign workers' occupational status, nationality, and color protected them from microorganisms and allowed them a measure of control over the natural environment of the Huasteca, Mexican workers enjoyed no such considerations and shared no such power. Even though they were also agents in the transformation of the landscape and like the foreign workers they knew nature through their work, their position in the labor hierarchy, woven into their nationality and skin color, meant their experience of nature was qualitatively different from Europeans and Americans. Mexicans were the most vulnerable human beings in the ecology of oil. If foreigners survived the grueling task of extracting oil from the tropical forest largely healthy and intact, hundreds of Mexicans did not. Life for national workers and their families in the Huasteca and Tampico became a daily struggle against the weather, disease, pollution, fire, and toxicity.

The location of segregated Mexican quarters in Tampico and the Huasteca guaranteed that the workers and their families would have an unpleasant experience of nature. Unlike foreign housing, Mexican cottages and barracks were built in the floodplains. That meant that heavy rainy seasons and hurricanes – simply inconvenient to those higher up in the labor hierarchy and the terrain – were disastrous for Mexicans. As the rains and storms swelled the region's rivers and lagoons, Mexican living quarters were the first to flood and be carried away in the currents. That happened in October 1930, for example, when ten consecutive days of rain swelled the Pantepec and Tuxpan Rivers to over four meters depth, destroying workers' housing at the PennMex camp and gasoline refinery

---

[151] Hamilton, *Early Day*, pp. 24–25, 34, 40; *El Luchador*, April 13, 1915; Miguel Lazcano vs. La Corona, LGO, vol. 13, no. 105 (December 2, 1924).

in Alamo. The Pánuco, more than 100 miles to the north, likewise rose enough to bury the neighborhoods on its banks under one-and-a-half meters of water. The following year, the Tamesí, the Pánuco, and the Tamuín Rivers reached flood stage again on August 1. The working-class neighborhoods along the Pánuco were completely underwater by the 5th and remained so until the waters and their cargo of dilapidated houses, animal carcasses, trees, and oil began to recede on the 14th.[152]

Mexican workers also faced the fallout from the rainy season: the population explosion among the *anopheles* mosquito that transmits malaria. Endemic in Veracruz since the nineteenth century, malaria was the second-leading cause of death in the state as late as 1940 and the plague of the oil workers until nationalization.[153] Deforestation and flooding created ample mosquito habitat. The lack of screens on windows and doors and the absence of mosquito netting over sleeping cots also provided plenty of flesh for mosquitoes to bite. Malaria devastated the immigrant Mexican labor force as a result. As Vice Consul Thomas H. Bevan informed an interested American pharmaceutical vendor in 1912, Tampico offered great business opportunities because "over 75%" of the population suffered from malaria "six months of the year."[154]

The Mexican workers who mustered enough strength managed to limp home to be cared for by wives and mothers for months on end.[155] Many simply collapsed by the side of the road and died. Oil worker Horacio Sierra recalled that on occasions so many men died in the camps that they were unceremoniously buried in shallow unmarked graves along the pipelines, in essence losing their lives to the environmental conditions of oil work in the tropical forest. In those cases, the families were rarely notified of the death of their loved ones. In Tampico, families fared slightly better: the bodies were hauled to a public hospital and left there, "on long tables, instead of beds, all covered, only their feet sticking out,"

[152] *El Mundo*, October 22–27, 1930; *El Mundo*, August 2, 5–7, 9, 11, 14, 1931.

[153] Beltrán and Aguirre Pequeño, *Lecciones*, p. 76; Interview with Dr. Ricardo Carrasco, *El Mundo*, August 1, 1937; Miguel A. Cruz Becomo, "El proceso salud-enfermedad en los petroleros 1938–1942 (Notas)," *Anuario* V, p. 205; *El Mundo*, October 30, 1923.

[154] Vice Consul Thomas H. Bevan to Harvey H. Watkins, Tampico, November 18, 1912, RG 59, File 1912.600. The medical report for El Aguila's infirmary in Tampico, for instance, reported eighty malaria cases in the month of July 1919 alone, while in 1921, Mexican officials estimated that thirty thousand oil workers had caught malaria over a period of six months. Medical report for Tampico District and Refinery Hospital, July 1919, AGN/DT, Caja 224, Exp. 24. *Excélsior*, June 12, 1921.

[155] Interview with Mr. Filogonio Olguín Rojo, conducted by María Isabel Souza and Lief Adleson on May 9, 1975 in Tampico, Tamaulipas, PHO/4/46.

until womenfolk appeared to claim them and take them away for burial at their own expense.[156]

Even more fatal was a particularly deadly strain known as *plasmodium falciparum*, commonly called hemorrhagic malaria. Without immediate and decent health care, it was nearly unstoppable, causing death within days of infection. That is what happened to Antonio Castillo, a worker in the Transcontinental ice factory in Las Matillas. In 1928 he became so feverish that he lost consciousness on the factory floor. He was taken to the company hospital, where he died a few days later.[157]

Although the malaria parasite was the most aggressive microorganism to afflict Mexican oil workers and their families in the Huasteca, it was not the only one. The smallpox virus, the scourge of indigenous peoples since the European conquest, made grim rounds through northern Veracruz until the late-1910s.[158] The virus responsible for the "black vomit," yellow fever, also took its toll on Mexican oil workers. Like malaria, yellow fever is transmitted by a mosquito (*Aedes aegypti*) whose breeding grounds expanded with urbanization and poor human living conditions. Headaches, nausea, "vomit the color of coffee grounds," a cyclical high fever, delirium, and deadly convulsions are the typical

---

[156] Interview with Mr. Horacio Sierra Aguilar, conducted by Lief Adleson in Tampico, Tamaulipas, n/d, PHO/4/94. Between 1919 and 1920, Tampico reported the following number of malaria victims: 1919: August, 48 victims; September, 78; November, 214; 1920: January, 86; October, 116; December, 99. Reports from the Médico Inspector to the Municipal President, AHAT, Exp. 119-bis-1919 and Exp. 20–1921.

[157] Medical Certificate, signed by Dr. Wallace Hubbard, in the case of Antonio Castillo vs. Transcontinental, AGN/JFCA, 1928, Caja 51, Exp. 15/928/861. Oil workers' children were equally vulnerable. Followed by clouds of mosquitoes cruising the swampy neighborhoods along the Pánuco, children succumbed to hemorrhagic malaria whenever the strain appeared. With mother's care as the only medical attention, those children infected with *plasmodium falciparum* could die within less than a day after the onset of symptoms. Interview with Mr. León F. Gual, conducted by Lief Adleson in Tampico, Tamaulipas, n/d, PHO/4/93.

[158] In 1908 state officials, alarmed by reports of squalid conditions among workers building the railway around Tuxpan at a time of a smallpox epidemic among the Totonaca in neighboring Papantla, ordered El Aguila to vaccinate all its workers. There is no record of the company's response. There is also precious little information on another burst of smallpox in the working-class neighborhoods and refineries of Tampico between late 1913 and early 1914. The county doctor only mentioned that the virus was sweeping through Arbol Grande, Doña Cecilia, and La Barra. Report from the Doctor Cantonal, February 14, 1908, and Letters from the Doctor Cantonal, September 25 and October 6, 1908, AGEV, Gobernación: Salubridad/Viruela-Linfa Vacunal, Caja 2, Exp. 1, Letra V, 1908; Report from Inspector Manuel Ortega Elorza, Tampico, March 25, 1914, AGN/DT, Caja 91, Exp. 18; Jefe de la Junta Local de Sanidad to the Municipal President, August 13, 1914, AHAT, Exp. n/n, 1914.

symptoms.[159] The first bout to affect the oil industry came in 1903, when 545 people in Tampico alone fell ill and 322 died.[160] Another outbreak took place in 1920. The fever began in Tuxpan and reached the Pánuco fields in 1921. In early 1922 it entered Tampico, only six months after the bubonic plague had swept through the city's working-class neighborhoods.[161] According to Doheny, the death toll was appalling, "men that we met one day we would see carried off to a cemetery the next, having died of yellow fever. We buried forty-five men from one of our own camps who died of *vómito*."[162]

At other times, however, neither menial worker nor high employee was safe, as disease-causing organisms thrived in the extraordinarily crowded and unsanitary conditions the oil boom and the Revolution produced in Tampico. The 1918 worldwide influenza epidemic arrived in October 1918 after floods had left the refineries submerged in water and hundreds of working-class Mexican families homeless. Between October and December, ten thousand *tampiqueños* caught the flu and over one thousand died.[163] According to Hamilton,

> the flood victims literally died like flies. Hundreds of bodies were carted to the cemetery each dawn. Mothers carried out their little dead babies in wooden wash trays on their heads. Men carried adults lashed to poles, carried on their shoulders. Some bodies were individually removed by relatives in a sort of stretcher over which temporary awning cover had been arranged. But the bulk were loaded like cordwood onto two wheeled carts over which a loose tarpaulin would be thrown. So many died in such a short time that the bodies could not be buried fast enough to avoid deterioration; therefore, the human bodies were thrown into great heaps and burned.[164]

[159] A. Matienzo, August 9, 1898, "Informe que rinde al Consejo Superior de Salubridad el Médico Sanitario en Tampico acerca de los primeros casos de fiebre amarilla observados en este Puerto en el año de 1898," *Boletín del Consejo Superior de Salubridad*, Tomo IV, No. 4 (October, 1898), quoted in Kuecker, "A Desert," p. 164.

[160] Health and Sanitation, DMC, Box 1, File H, #1596.

[161] How many Mexican oil workers fell ill from bubonic plague or yellow fever between 1920 and 1922 is unknown. The Tuxpan oil inspector was afraid to travel into the oil fields to investigate the effects of yellow fever. In Tuxpan proper, the inspector counted ten to twelve new cases per day in October. Those figures convinced him to close the office altogether for the duration and leave the Gulf coast. The Tampico health department reported that the worst of the bubonic plague took place between April and June, 1921 and that 114 people died. Telegrams from Tuxpan Agency, September 21, September 30, October 14, and October 16, 1920, AGN/DP, Caja 16, Exp. 10, 101 (04) 1920; Informe del Departamento de Salubridad, December 15, 1921, AHAT, Exp. 20-1921.

[162] Testimony of Edward L. Doheny, U.S. Senate in *Investigation*, p. 219.

[163] Informe del Presidente Municipal, December 1918, AHAT, Exp. 140-1918.

[164] Hamilton, *Early Day*, p. 152.

In the camps thousands of Mexican and foreign workers alike succumbed to the virus. So gravely concerned was the general manager of Huasteca Petroleum's refinery at Mata Redonda, former U.S. Marine constabulary in the Philippines William Green, that he paid Dr. León Gual a handsome sum to tour the camps and take care of the sick. According to the doctor, Green told him that "if you prescribe champagne for my men, champagne it is."[165] Green's laudable efforts notwithstanding, the refinery's carpentry shop stopped hammering derricks and instead produced "200 to 300 coffins per day" for Mexican workers and their families.[166]

By the late 1920s another disease had become of major concern for Mexican workers: tuberculosis. Not having enough information or adequate health education or medical advice, they did not know that tuberculosis was caused by yet another organism that thrived amidst social conditions of overcrowding and squalor. Instead, the men and their infected family members attributed their illness to the nature of oil work: they were convinced that the "irritating gases" they inhaled were the culprits.[167]

Therefore, Cruz Briones Rodríguez was not exaggerating when he said that for Mexican workers the joint experience of oil work and the natural environment of the Huasteca was first and foremost an encounter with "the devil's collection of plagues."[168] Work brought them to the tropical forest and exposed them to multiple disease-causing organisms. In their experience nature and work were inextricably linked; their daily working and living routines taught them there was no separation between oil work and disease. Disentangling mosquitoes or germs from oil production in the tropics was simply impossible. A popular *corrido* of the era illustrated the point clearly by saying "many of those who go to work in Tampico/ some find work/others hang their heads down/because they say they get sick/from vomit and fever/those end up without work/and go off to their tombs."[169] The workers' holistic approach to work and nature and

[165] Gual, PHO/4/39; Hall, *Oil, Banks, and Politics*, p. 113.

[166] Bada Ramírez, PHO/4/91.

[167] Alejo Salazar to Inspector del Departamento del Trabajo, Tampico, October 15, 1927, AGN/JFCA, Caja 10, Exp. 15/927/237; Cándido Zamorán to Inspector Federal de Trabajo, Tampico, February 12, 1931, AGN/JFCA, Caja 246, Exp. 15/931/1053; Unión de Empleados y Trabajadores de las Compañías Petroleras to Presidente de la Junta Regional de Conciliación y Arbitraje, AGN/JFCA, Caja 55, Exp. 15/928/952.

[168] Interview with Cruz Briones Rodríguez, conducted by Lief Adleson on November 28, 1976, in Tampico, Tamaulipas, PHO/4/52.

[169] In Spanish, the verses read: "Muchos de los que se van/a trabajar a Tampico/unos encuentran trabajo/otros agachan el pico./Porque dicen que se enferman/de vómito y calentura,/esos se quedan sin trabajo/y se van a la sepultura." Claro García, "Planchas de los que van a Tampico," in Lozano, *El Puerto.*

work in nature, in fact, led them to argue by 1918 that malaria was an occupational disease. By the same logic, in the late 1920s the men added tuberculosis to the list of occupational diseases of the oil industry.[170]

Needless to say, the workers never convinced the companies that their point of view was correct. As far as the oilmen were concerned, the workers did not compartmentalize their experience in the way they should, between what was work and what was nature. From their perspective, malaria, yellow fever, tuberculosis, and other diseases were the environment's fault, without connection to oil production at all. Indeed, the oil companies in Mexico went further, blaming workers for their frail health. When El Aguila fired tank builder N. M. Farrar after a bout of malaria in 1915, the company argued he had contracted the illness because he was "a drunk." PennMex gave the exact same explanation when it fired Pablo Chinetti in 1918, after three years of employment on the pipeline crew in Tuxpan. The supervisor, "Mr. Williams," attributed his illness to "disorderly living" and "alcohol abuse" and fired him for not returning to work within nine days of showing malaria symptoms.[171] Similar arguments appeared in a series of cases that involved a whole host of workers' maladies without obvious causes or reliable diagnoses. In these cases workers argued the companies had fired them because they had been disabled on the job. They complained of numb fingers, skin rashes, painful joints, arthritis, and other symptoms. The companies, however, held that the various ailments were not work-related at all; rather, they claimed the men had syphilis or something else. As La Corona argued, the men's health problems were of "moral character," the result of personal indiscipline rather than occupational risks.[172] Thus, the companies skirted responsibility for the health implications of oil exploitation in the tropical forest and burdened workers with individual responsibility for the ailments that befell them both in the production site and in the process of production.

---

[170] PEMEX recognized malaria, but not tuberculosis, as an occupational disease in the first collective contract it signed with the STPRM in 1940. Augusto Palma Alor, *Las Choapas, ayer, hoy y siempre* (Mexico City: Federación Editorial Mexicana, 1975), p. 48.

[171] N.M. Farrar vs. El Aguila, AGEV/JCCA, 1918, Caja 4, Exp. 39; Pablo Chinetti vs. PennMex Fuel Co., AGEV/JCCA, 1918, Caja 1, Exp. 2.

[172] In most of these cases there were contradictory medical diagnoses, with the workers' doctors attributing the symptoms to various maladies and the company doctors saying they suffered from venereal disease. Marino Goné, Miguel Robles, and Antonio Cabrera vs. East Coast Oil, AGN/JFCA, 1928, Caja 37, Exp. 15/1928/538; Guillermo Castillo vs. Mexican Sinclair, AGEV/JCCA, 1927, Caja 61, Exp. 55; Cesáreo Reyna vs. La Corona, AGEV/JCCA, 1927, Caja 60, Exp. 37.

Nonetheless, working-class families did find relief from endemic and epidemic illness beginning in the late 1920s. In 1928, Tampico joined the Rockefeller Latin American malaria eradication program. Although the intent was to make the region healthy for capitalism, it benefited working-class families as much as anyone.[173] The effort was spearheaded, however, by local government and labor unions. Squads of municipal workers sprinkled oil on stagnant waters, paved over muddy streets (in one case with oyster shells dredged from the bottom of the Chairel Lagoon, rather than asphalt), and sought to control raw sewage. In 1927 Tampico officials prohibited latrines within city limits and ordered homeowners to install English toilets like those that El Aguila had imported for foreign workers two decades earlier. In 1931 the oil and stevedore unions joined forces to build the first sewage system for the working-class neighborhoods along the Pánuco River. Although those benefits did not extend to segregated Mexican housing quarters within refinery grounds proper, they did make a difference in the overall health of oil workers and their families. As a result, "grave epidemics" in Tampico became history by 1934.[174] Problems stemming from oil pollution, however, did not.

Like endemic and epidemic illness, pollution was a class issue in the ecology of oil. Whereas the upper echelons of the industry avoided the unpleasant effluents of oil production by living on breezy hillsides, Mexican working-class families dwelt amidst pollution. The location of their houses did not let them escape "the stench of petroleum . . . and the acrid stagnant stench of backwater and rancid oil [that] lay heavily in the air." It also exposed them to fire and a host of other environmental dangers.[175] Mexicans lived in toxic neighborhoods.[176]

---

[173] Kuecker refers to previous American attempts to get rid of yellow fever in Mexico, Central America, Brazil, and the Caribbean between 1898–1899 as "sanitary imperialism." Rockefeller's efforts in the late 1920s were quite similar. Kuecker, "A Desert," p. 182.

[174] *El Mundo*, March 21, 1927; January 1, 30, 1929; March 12 and 23, 1930; April 16, November 18 and 20, 1931; September 16, 1932; August 27 and December 14, 1933; *El Mundo*, February 24, 1934.

[175] Millan, *Mexico Reborn*, p. 215.

[176] For a different approach to comparable issues, see the literature of the emergent field of environmental justice, such as, Lois Marie Gibbs, *Love Canal: My Story* (Albany: State University of New York Press, 1982); Laura Pulido, *Environmentalism and Economic Justice: Two Chicano Struggles in the Southwest* (Tucson: University of Arizona Press, 1998); Robert D. Bullard, *Dumping in Dixie: Race, Class, and Environmental Quality* (Boulder, CO: Westview Press, 2002); Joni Adamson, Mei Mei Evans, and Rachel Stein, editors, *The Environmental Justice Reader: Politics, Poetics, and Pedagogy* (Tucson: University of Arizona Press, 2002); and Thomas H. Fletcher, *From Love Canal to Environmental Justice: The Politics of Hazardous Waste on the Canada–U.S. Border* (Peterborough, Ontario: Broadview Press, 2003).

Worker housing was consumed by fire on more than one occasion. The first instance occurred before most of the refineries were built, in 1912, when lightning struck a tank at the Waters Pierce refinery in Arbol Grande. According to geologist Hamilton, the tank hurtled boiling oil "hundreds of feet into the air," but it only needed sixty meters (two hundred feet) to reach the houses.[177] Fire droplets rained on them, destroying at least thirty-five and "a great part of the neighborhood." No one knows how many people perished, but two witnesses remembered that "we had to lament many victims."[178] In August 1914, the neighborhood of Doña Cecilia lived the same experience, as lightning struck a tank located only twenty to thirty meters (65 to 100 feet) from the houses. "Many" were destroyed, "leaving the families out in the street," wrote the neighbors to the Mayor; yet despite protests, Pierce built additional tanks in Arbol Grande in 1916.[179] Not until steel tanks became the rule in the 1930s did the dangers of tank fires in working-class neighborhoods abate; but they did not end. In April 1938, for instance, a tank containing gasoline caught fire while a *norte* was blowing. The *norte* blew the flames into working-class housing, burning down three blocks with over fifty homes.[180]

In the camps, Mexican quarters were routinely exposed to chemical emissions. At Dos Bocas, for instance, workers' quarters were 2,230 feet from the well, so near that "noxious gases" circulated around the houses according to the wind currents. The rest of the Huasteca was no different. Referring to La Corona's Camp No. 3 at Tancoco, union leader Angel Z. Mendoza argued in 1924 that company housing for Mexicans was

> situated precisely next to some tanks filled with oil, which expel much gas, putting workers' health and even their lives in grave danger. Already they are continually sick in the eyes because of this and even domestic animals have died as a consequence of the poisoning gases.[181]

Early mornings were worst because the sulfurous chemicals exuded overnight hung low in the atmosphere, pushed down by the cooler

[177] Hamilton, *Early Day*, p. 203.
[178] Quoted in Adleson, "Historia social," p. 51. Brown wrote that one "little girl" died in the fire, *Oil and Revolution*, p. 325.
[179] Vecinos de Doña Cecilia to the Municipal President, November 24, 1917, AHAT, Exp. 216–1917; Adleson, "Historia Social," p. 283
[180] *El Dictamen*, April 7, 1938.
[181] Unión de Obreros Regionales to the Governor of Veracruz, August 1924, AGN/DT, Caja 813, Exp. 4.

night air and their own weight.[182] Into the 1930s, petroleum chemicals saturated the Huasteca. Arriving in the camps in May of 1932, journalist Vicente Garrido Alfaro wrote that he knew he had entered oil country because "the atmosphere was impregnated with an intense smell of tar" arising from large pools of "wasted liquid gold" and dozens of rusty tanks.[183]

In Tampico and Pánuco the situation was no better. Worker housing was showered with toxic chemicals routinely. In 1917 working-class families living in Arbol Grande complained that "smoke" from the Pierce refinery fell on their neighborhood and made them dizzy.[184] Three years later, a labor inspector reported that El Aguila's refinery had numerous escape pipes in every shop that expelled "explosive gases" into the air unfiltered.[185] In 1927 neighbors from Arbol Grande and Llanos del Golfo blamed the deaths of a worker and his wife on the emissions spewing out from the Pierce refinery, and in 1928 a worker severely burned in a Huasteca Petroleum fire reported that the complex regularly expelled "dense" emissions through its chimneys, putting at risk the lives of the three thousand workers and their families living on the grounds. "As it has happened at other times," testified Gonzalo Arvizo, the emissions "have forced all the people to get out of their homes and run desperately." Even if no human fatalities had taken place during those emergencies ("all the birds died," reported one witness), the men, women, and children exposed experienced "heavy vomiting."[186]

By 1929, nevertheless, knowledge about the toxicity involved in oil production was commonplace enough to provoke public opposition to further oil development in some quarters. In May, Pánuco neighbors protested against a Mexican contractor who proposed to drill more in an area already pockmarked with wells. They told a local newspaper that because they had "a solid experience" in the industry, they were worried about pollution and the dangers to their health. "They remembered," wrote the journalist, "that in 1912, when La Corona's great well

[182] Memorandum from the Engineer in Charge, November 10, 1929, AGN/DP, Caja 41, Exp. 7, 316(02)/4; Villarello, "El pozo," pp. 35, 48–49.

[183] *El Mundo*, May 15, 1932.

[184] Letter from the City Engineer to the Municipal President, July 7, 1917, AHAT, Exp. 225-1917.

[185] Report from Inspector Enrique S. Cerdán to the Secretario de Industria, Comercio y Trabajo, January 9, 1920, AGN/DT, Caja 224, Exp. 24.

[186] *El Mundo*, February 1, 1927; Gonzalo Arvizo to the president of the Junta Federal de Conciliación y Arbitraje, February 22, 1928, AGN/JFCA, Caja 13, Exp. 15/927/318.

No. 5 spouted and inundated more than six hectares, the [oil] remained dammed so for several months, threatening all Pánuco inhabitants." Furthermore, the people feared that "even without discovering a great well, there might be an abundant release of poisonous gases, as it happens with great frequency, cyanide-like even, . . . and dictate a violent death for every living creature within a perimeter of several kilometers."[187]

Although the most notorious health effects of oil production and pollution on Mexican working-class families left clear traces, the medium- or long-term health effects of chronic exposure to the chemical compounds in petroleum and its derivatives were never systematically investigated and cannot be adequately documented. Today we know a little more: that sustained exposure to petroleum products over a long period of time irritates the body's mucus membranes, adversely affects the nervous system and the liver, creates a susceptibility to asthma, and causes cancer.[188] No doubt Mexican workers experienced some or all of those, and like tuberculosis, they never really knew exactly what caused them but were pretty confident they knew where they acquired them.

Oil fields and refineries anywhere in the world were extraordinarily dangerous worksites. As much as company men prided themselves in

[187] *El Mundo*, May 5, 1929. In other quarters, however, the cycle of fire danger, pollution, and toxicity was just beginning. The foreign oil industry moved beyond the Huasteca in the 1930s, opening new fields and expanding the perimeter of environmental degradation and health risks to Poza Rica and the Tehuantepec Isthmus. The opening of the Atzcapotzalco refinery on the outskirts of Mexico City in the same years inaugurated the age of refinery pollution and fires in the capital city, a legacy neither Pearson nor Doheny lived long enough to witness. Pearson died in 1927 and Doheny died in 1935, but a stroke left him incapacitated since 1931. *El Mundo* May 1, 1933; Pierre de L. Boal, charge d'affairs to Secretary of State, Tampico, August 3, 1937, RG 59, Roll 60, 812.5945/588.

[188] In 1931, Tampico doctor Donato G. Alarcón noted that "it had been recognized" that benzine derivatives caused anemia, implying studies or observations of the chemical's effect on human health had taken place somewhere. More research into the matter is necessary to determine the source of the doctor's statements. Dr. Donato G. Alarcón, "La tuberculosis en la República Mexicana," AGN/DGG, Caja 71, Exp. 24, 2.017(24)10. Two works that summarize information about oil workers' health and occupational disease in the Mexican case are Monica Casalet, *Salud y bienestar de la fuerza de trabajo. Estudio de caso: automotriz y petroquímica* (Mexico City: Instituto Nacional de Estudios del Trabajo, Secretaría del Trabajo y Previsión Social, 1982), pp. 61–65; and Sylvia Vega Gleason, "Petróleo, medio ambiente y salud," *La industria petrolera ante la regulación jurídico-ecológica en México*, edited by Jorge Muñoz Barret, Sylvia Vega Gleason, and Maria del Carmen Carmona Lara (Mexico City: Universidad Nacional Autónoma de México and PEMEX, 1992), pp. 90–129. For the U.S. case, see Dorothy Nelkin and Michael S. Brown, *Workers at Risk: Voices from the Workplace* (Chicago: University of Chicago Press, 1984) and Daniel M. Berman, *Death on the Job: Occupational Health and Safety Struggles in the United States* (New York: Monthly Review Press, 1978).

controlling the natural world, the fact was that one of the most common causes of death in the oil industry, poisoning by hydrogen sulfide,
occurred because such control was so limited. The asphyxiating nature
of the Huasteca wells was common knowledge among industry men, yet
they could do nothing about it. The equipment that might have protected
men from exposures to toxic chemicals was either nonexistent or experimental in nature, and certainly not made available to Mexican workers.[189]
Because nature did not discriminate, when the hydrogen sulfide reached
the earth's surface, it could kill any human within reach, without distinction of class or nationality.[190] The discriminatory structure of the labor
hierarchy in Mexico, that is, the oilmen's more effective control over
men than nature, nevertheless meant that the foreign oil workers could
and did shield themselves from accidents by passing on the danger to
the Mexicans under their supervision (the exception being the drillers,
who did not admit Mexicans into their ranks and therefore shouldered
all the risks themselves). The social ecology of oil, therefore, mitigated
the occupational hazards for foreigners and accentuated them among
Mexicans, as the case of Arnulfo Sánchez and Richard Cross shows.

Arnulfo Sánchez was a forty-five-year-old oil worker who lost his life
to hydrogen sulfide in 1924. On November 19, Sánchez was helping the
Alabaman Richard Cross measure the amount of oil inside a storage tank
in the Tierritas Blancas pumping station, a routine operation. When the

[189] There was a certain "breathing apparatus" at El Aguila's refinery in Tampico since 1919.
The instructions for its use, however, were only in English, which leads me to believe that
if it was used at all, it was the foreign workers who used it. "Rules and Precautions to be
Observed When Using the Proto-Self-Contained Breathing Apparatus," 1919, AGN/DT,
Caja 224, Exp. 24. The masks that were available by the late 1920s, moreover, were "not
very efficient" and often proved more dangerous than none at all because they provided
a false sense of security to the workers using them, according to Jacobo Alvarado, "El
sulfuro de hidrógeno en la industria del petróleo," BP, vol. 27, no. 6 (June 1929),
p. 793.

[190] Although death by hydrogen sulfide was rapid, it was not inevitable if prompt rescue was
available. Upon first inhaling the gas, the worker became dizzy and disoriented. If no
one helped him leave the poisonous perimeter immediately, he lost consciousness. If no
one rushed to his side and dragged him out, the victim began to turn blue, his muscles
went limp, he trembled, and then convulsed until death. The whole process took up
to "several hours," giving crews enough time to remove the worker from the gas cloud
if they realized what was taking place and took whatever precautions were available
to protect themselves from the gas during the rescue operation. Indeed, many more
workers would have died had their companions been less attentive and brave. Alvarado,
"El sulfuro," pp. 792–793; W. A. Jacobs and C. W. Mitchell, "Métodos industrials usados
para la eliminación de los gases tóxicos, altamente sufurosos, desprendidos del petróleo
mexicano," translated from the *Bulletin* of the Department of the Interior, No. 231, BP,
vol. 21, no. 1 (January 1926), p. 2.

measuring tape did not reach the bottom, Cross testified that Sánchez climbed over the top of the tank and lowered himself several rungs down the metal ladder built onto the inside wall of the tank to stretch the tape. According to Cross, when he saw how far down the tank Sánchez had gone, he realized his assistant was risking asphyxia. He gestured and screamed at him to get out immediately – in English. But Sánchez did not come out. Cross lost sight of him somehow, even though he testified that he was at the top of the tank all the time. Cross then yelled for help to his driver, Frank Robert, saying he thought Sánchez had fallen into the tank. Robert, in turn, called out to Gabino Roque to come out of the pumping station and help. When the three peered into the tank, Sánchez was nowhere in sight. The tank contained approximately nine feet worth of oil. Two of the men left the tank to look for something to help them pull Sánchez out. They found "hooks" and "other utensils" and poked the bottom of the tank until they found the body. The autopsy report determined that "the esophagus, trachea, bronchi, bronchioles, and both lungs were filled with oil . . . the stomach was also found full of oil," so that the "direct, necessary, and immediate" cause of death was drowning by oil.[191]

Despite the efforts to save him, Sánchez died a victim of the labor hierarchy in an industry indifferent to worker health and safety. Cross's testimony notwithstanding, it is unlikely that Sánchez was ignorant of the danger implied in getting his whole body inside an oil tank. By 1924 there was not a single Mexican oil worker who did not know about the poisonous nature of Huasteca crude. It is more likely that, as a subordinate, Sánchez did what he was told to do, or what he understood Cross asked him to do. Perhaps he simply figured that since he had performed the same task many times before without breathing in enough hydrogen sulfide to lose consciousness, he could do so again safely. Perhaps he was concerned about the risks, but he could not explain them in a language Cross could understand. Perhaps he did refuse to enter the tank and Cross overruled the objections. Cross's testimony makes clear, nevertheless, that after seventy-five years of oil work, some companies lacked not only the proper tools to undertake the most basic routines (such as a measuring tape long enough to reach the bottom of a standard oil tank), but also the most rudimentary rescue equipment. Surely Sánchez was not the first man ever to fall into a tank or a dam or some other deep

[191] Acta de Inspección Judicial, November 19, 1924, AGN/JFCA 1928, Caja 22, Exp. 15/928/136.

oil container, but the men still had to use their creativity and improvise tools to reach his body.

Cross convinced Mexican officials that he was not responsible for risking Sánchez's life. If that was indeed the case, it was unusual. In most instances, it was men like Cross who ordered Mexican workers to enter tanks, boilers, and stills to take measurements and to clean them. Their supervisory positions gave them the power to pass the danger on to men lower in the hierarchy.

The case of six men working in Buenavista in 1922 illustrates the relationship between danger and location in the labor hierarchy. The men worked for La Corona under a foreign supervisor. Their last assignment was stapling cable to the interior of empty oil tanks, "extremely dangerous work because of the harmful gases that peel off the *chapopote* that used to be stored in there." At first they refused to go into the tanks, but when the supervisor threatened to fire them, they went into seven tanks and nailed the cable. When their superior told them to do the same in an eighth tank, they balked "because two of [us] were momentarily asphyxiated by the last job." Upon refusing to follow the order to climb into the eighth tank once more, they were all fired.[192] It was not surprising, therefore, that questions related to health and safety figured prominently in strikes and contract negotiations by the mid-1920s, as we will see below.

The Road Not Taken

Despite the fact that oilmen could not change the chemical composition of Mexican crude, they could prevent death by asphyxia through simple but vigilant precautions. In the United States oil workers had adopted such a safety program for Mexican petroleum products specifically. Since the late 1910s, men handling Huasteca crude oil in the docks and refineries of the Eastern seaboard and the Gulf coast of the United States had organized safety committees to protect themselves from sulfurous compounds. Oil worker committees "patrol[led] and observe[d]" all the areas where men transported and processed incoming Mexican petroleum. All Mexican petroleum products, moreover, were stamped with a skull-and-crossbones mark to make clear how dangerous they were. The effort, nevertheless, originated with the workers, not with the companies.[193]

---

[192] Six workers vs. La Corona, AGEV/JCCA, 1922, Caja 29, Exp. 39.
[193] Jacobs and Mitchell, "Métodos industriales," pp. 2–3.

The industry never seriously invested in prophylactic programs in Mexico either. The only related document extant in the archives, El Aguila's "Regulations Regarding Safety and Discipline that Must Exist in the Refinery," went into effect in 1927. Nonetheless, as its name explains, the rules emphasized the control of worker behavior rather than the prevention of accidents. The document listed prohibitions: no smoking, no gambling, no drinking, no guns. It also established a pattern of conduct in case of accidents: "no matter how insignificant, report them immediately to the Department Head"; "company will not be held liable for accidents not reported"; "upon returning to work, present a doctor's certificate." Yet the Regulations did not establish an occupational safety program to address toxins. To prevent asphyxia like Sánchez's, for instance, El Aguila did not prohibit men from entering tanks, nor did it require or provide the men with masks or other protective equipment. Instead, it instructed the men to "descend with a tight rope around them under the care of another operator, so that in case of danger or gassing, they can be pulled out immediately."[194] The organization of safety committees and accident-prevention programs, in fact, were still under negotiation on the eve of nationalization.[195]

The assumption behind documents such as El Aguila's Regulations in particular and the question of workers' health and safety in general was that accidents and injuries on the job were the workers' fault. The idea was in vogue among English and American firms in the 1920s. As the captains of industry reasoned, the bodily integrity of workers was unrelated to the social organization of labor or the organization of the labor process in a given environment. Ignoring factors such as the design of a work place or station, the design of tools and equipment, the maintenance of equipment and facilities, the rates of production demanded of workers, the environmental location of the workplace, or man's sheer inability to control nature to the extent imagined or desired, industrialists and their theorists decided that workers were at fault for their own injuries

---

[194] Reglamento relativo a las seguridades y disciplina que debe existir en la Refinería de Minatitlán con el fin de evitar accidents y enfermedades, February 8, 1927, AGEV/JCCA, Caja 65, n/n, "Asuntos pendientes diversos."

[195] Government, *Mexico's Oil*, pp. 204–205. In 1936 the Department of Labor began a nationwide campaign to prevent accidents on the job. "Sincerely wishing to cooperate in this campaign," reported the management of Huasteca Petroleum, the company donated five thousand posters with safety themes to the Department. One of them read "¡Esto es un suicidio!" and showed a man lighting a cigarette as he bent over a barrel marked "Gasolina." *Fanal* (March–April 1937), p. 23.

on the job. In 1926 the English actually introduced the concept of the "accident-prone" worker, arguing that the causes of injuries and death on the job were to be found "in the characteristics of individual workers." According to this industrial creed, worker "carelessness," "excitability," "lightheartedness," "deficiency in English," or "psychomotor retardation" were the roots of workplace accidents.[196]

Although there is no direct evidence to prove that this rationale also accounted for the idea that Mexican workers fell prey to disease owing to their individual behavior, the parallel is obvious. Both ideas were born of the same economic process subsumed in the ecology of oil, the development of twentieth-century industrial capitalism. The oil companies initiated and orchestrated social and environmental changes that carried enormous and often unprecedented implications for all living organisms in the places they explored and exploited. Yet, they defined their sphere of responsibility narrowly. They were happy to assume the role of pioneers, of torchbearers of progress to "hitherto primitive regions," and of civilizers "improv[ing] the minds, morals, and manners of these people," the Mexicans they inserted into their scheme.[197] They were also ready to respond to a specific group of people: the investors to whom they owed a profit and in whose name they engineered the changes in land tenure, land use, and social relations in the Huasteca. But there the responsibility stopped. Marginalization of native peoples, environmental destruction, and extreme social and environmental disparities were not responsibilities the companies were willing to acknowledge or accept. Similarly, loss of life or damage to workers' bodies were lamentable, but the companies reasoned the men knew there were dangers involved in the job when they accepted it.[198] The division of responsibility was as clear for them as the division of labor they designed. The companies paid wages and assumed the risks of doing business; the workers received their pay and assumed the risks of working. That was modernization and progress. That was the bundle of social and environmental changes that made up the ecology of oil.

That was also the edifice that Mexican workers were determined to subvert practically from the moment the companies built it. The Mexican oil

---

[196] Berman, *Death*, p. 22.
[197] The first quote is from the Testimony of Edward L. Doheny in *Investigation*, p. 235. The second belongs to U.S. Ambassador Henry Lane Wilson, who pronounced them in 1913 in reference to Doheny's work in Mexico, as quoted in LaBotz, *Edward L. Doheny*, p. 44.
[198] Response from the General Manager L. Smith in the case of Pablo Chinetti vs. PennMex Fuel Co., January 1918, AGEV/JCCA, Caja 1, Exp. 2.

workers would wage class warfare against the oil companies for over two decades, spanning both the armed phase of the Mexican Revolution and the period of reconstruction during peacetime after 1920. The twists and turns of the roller coaster that was the Revolution would unquestionably affect the workers' struggle against the companies, but would not determine its outcome. On the contrary, it would be the workers who would lead the challenge against the ecology of oil and in the process ultimately change the course of Mexican history itself.

The extraction of oil in the Huasteca was a complicated, multidimensional affair. It entailed a vast organizational project based on a well-defined architecture, a series of social changes with deep implications for the relationship between humans and nature. Working on the assumption that they possessed mastery over men and nature alike, the oil barons did not hesitate to arrange both to suit their purposes. They imported foreign labor, created a Mexican industrial work force, and engineered an occupational hierarchy along class, color, and nationality lines without much flexibility. Racism, segregation, and harsh disciplinary regimes became cardinal tenets in the social organization of labor as local communities were overwhelmed and marginalized. The rigid social divisions the companies devised also served as the matrix that defined the experience of each segment of the work force in the tropical environment of the Huasteca. Thus, a man's position in the labor hierarchy was inversely related to his access to the basic necessities of life and his exposure to the elements, the dangers of microbial life, and toxic chemicals. Whereas foreigners enjoyed comfortable accommodations, adequate health care, and even luxuries in the midst of the tropical forest, Mexican workers routinely confronted floodwaters, disease, and toxic emissions. At the same time, the companies ignored the vast and complex social and environmental consequences of their activities. Thus, if the set of changes the companies produced was profound enough to constitute an ecology of its own, the reaction to it was just as revolutionary in every way.

PART THREE

CHALLENGING THE ECOLOGY OF OIL

5

"COARSE IN MANNER"

MEXICAN OIL WORKERS, 1905–1921

The world is full of socialists and anarchists.

John D. Rockefeller, 1905

It is always the mixed breed who is unveracious, dishonest, and treacherous. It was the mixed breeds who composed the mobs in Tampico that cried death to the gringos. And many of these half-breeds, so crying, were the very employees of the gringos they wanted to kill and whose property they wanted to destroy.

Jack London, 1914

The conditions that Tampico workers are subjected to [are] terrible...entire families don't eat every day... Conditions...created by the unmeasured ambition of the oil barons; what do they care about the needs and the sufferings of an entire people? What do they care about the life of the poor, if in the end the slaves are in the millions and it doesn't matter if they kill them through starvation to increase profits or make political gains, or they kill them in war to conquer new markets or protect their interests?

Andrés Araujo, *Luz*, October 23, 1918

In 1941 Tina Sierra published a short novel about the oil industry in which she described the formation of a new segment of the Mexican working class. She wrote,

> On the first payday, a Saturday, a man leaves the pay-room with a hand-kerchief full of pesos, heads straight to a clothing store (rather, a clothing tent of the myriad that appear on Saturdays improvised in front of pay-windows), there he buys a silk shirt, blue jeans, heavy shoes and a Texan hat. There you have an oil worker.[1]

---

[1] Tina Sierra, *Oro Negro* (Mexico City: Ediciones Botas, 1941), p. 59. That was the typical attire of American oil workers in the United States, according to Boatright, *Folklore*, p. 120.

The cowboys who strutted out of improvised Huasteca stores on their first payday were indeed changed men. They belonged to a group of workers that experienced extraordinary growth numerically and politically in the first two decades of the twentieth century. By early 1921, the oil workers had grown to a peak of thirty-five thousand to fifty thousand men.[2] They were a minority within a minority, a miniscule fraction of the 750,000 men and women who made up the Mexican working class in 1910, out of a total population of fifteen million.[3] Nevertheless, what the oil workers lacked in size, they made up in bravado, as Sierra implied. They became one of the most militant labor groups in Mexico, precociously political in comparison to others with longer histories.[4] The Mexican oil workers were born political, in fact, imbibing from the clandestine waters of anti-Díaz propaganda and supporting his opponent, Francisco Madero, in the 1910 presidential race. Thereafter and until 1914, the first Mexican men recruited into the oil industry experienced a process of accelerated politicization. Although the historical record offers little detail, it suggests that three related developments account for the early awakening of political conscience among Mexican oil workers: working conditions in the industry, the course of the Mexican Revolution, and U.S. military intervention. By 1914, the workers were solidly in the revolutionary camp, nationalist in their sentiment, and deeply anti-interventionist.

By late 1914, as well, the violent phase of the Mexican Revolution had come to a close in the Huasteca, even as it engulfed the rest of the country. The end of the revolutionary war in the Huasteca created an oasis of military stability that brought a whole host of changes to the region. Refugees flowed into Tampico, not only from the war-scarred Mexican countryside, but also from the ravages of World War I in Europe.

[2] The total number of oil workers is difficult to establish because it fluctuated wildly. Although Huasteca Petroleum claimed in 1938 that the industry provided employment for fifty thousand Mexicans, that figure was exaggerated, even for the peak year, 1921. A report for the state of Veracruz estimated that before 1921 the figure was more like thirty-five thousand, which erred on the conservative side, since American Vice Consul Bevan estimated the companies had twenty thousand Mexican workers by 1915. The Department of Labor conducted a partial census in 1921, suggesting a figure of forty thousand. Huasteca Petroleum, *Expropriation*, p. 1; Méndez, Report to the governor, IAEG/CC, Acct. 4403, Box 9; Vice Consul Bevan to Secretary of State, January 14, 1915, in *Papers*, 1915, p. 872; Informe, November 18, 1921, AGN/DT, Caja 326, Exp 3; Cuestionario, March 1921, AGN/DT, Caja 274, Exp. 3.

[3] Barry Carr, *El movimiento obrero y la política en México, 1910–1920* (Mexico City: Ediciones Era, 1991), p. 19; Meyer et al., *The Course*, p. 451.

[4] Alan Knight, *The Mexican Revolution*, Volume 1: *Porfirians, Liberals and Peasants* (Lincoln: University of Nebraska Press, 1990), pp. 406–408.

Radicals – anarchists and anarcho-syndicalists in particular – landed in Tampico from Mexico City and European capitals. The oil industry too went into explosive growth, creating vast employment opportunities but exposing greater numbers of men to the harsh social and environmental realities of oil extraction in the tropical forest. The oil workers' response to the social, political, and environmental context they faced was unapologetic defiance. Between 1915 and until 1921, the Mexican oil workers became infamous for their confrontational culture and union life. They pushed the limits of official revolutionary discourse and practice and showed nothing but contempt for their bosses and the ecology that oil created. For eight years, the oil workers made Tampico and the Huasteca the site of one of the fiercest contests between international capital and Mexican labor, as class struggle replaced civil war. The results were mixed, with more losses than victories for the workers until the oil barons destroyed the movement in 1921. The oil workers were decimated; yet their legacy would prove positive not only for them but also for the nation as a whole.

A Class Born into Revolution, 1905–1914

Politics came with the territory for the first generation of Mexican oil workers. The artisans recruited from independent workshops and other industrial sectors like the railroads, as well as the hundreds of *enganchados* from the Mexican countryside, joined the oil companies, it turned out, just as the sun was beginning to set on the Díaz regime. In Tampico the new arrivals found men working for mostly foreign-owned businesses, with some organizational experience and plenty of energy to politicize and unionize fellow workers.[5] The first oil workers were quick to follow their lead. It did not take Mexican oil workers long to realize that as the Porfiriato, Mexico's modernizing regime, crumbled and the country descended into revolutionary chaos, their employers ascended in wealth and status, commanding attention not only locally but also internationally. Mexican oil workers ended up in the thick of the political battle, caught in the dangerous mix of oil and war. Yet by December 1914, the revolutionary crisis in the Huasteca had been all but resolved. Even

---

[5] The first Tampico labor groups formed in the late 1880s. They were artisans in foreign-owned businesses like the railroads, the power company, and the trolley system. Carlos González Salas, *Acercamiento a la historia del movimiento obrero en Tampico (1887–1983)* (Ciudad Victoria: Universidad Autónoma de Tamaulipas, 1987), pp. 11–13; Robles Saldaña, PHO/4/39; Román Cota, PHO/4/47.

though the oil workers were not part of the solution, they had been deeply marked by their experience.

Tampico workers in general and artisans in particular were well informed about the trouble brewing for President Díaz at the beginning of the century. They were avid readers of the clandestine opposition newspaper *Regeneración*. In its pages, workers found out about the great strikes in the mines of Cananea and the textile mills of Río Blanco in 1906. By 1907, the men were learning about anarchism as well. Increasingly radical in its attacks against Díaz, *Regeneración* introduced its readers to a new vocabulary and set of ideas. Workers started discussing notions like worker ownership of production, the dismantling of the state, the end of capitalism, and how to make it all possible through direct action tactics.[6]

Some men, in fact, were inspired to action by their reading and became involved in politics. In 1910, a group of longshoremen, railroad workers, and oil workers from the Waters Pierce refinery formed a political club in Doña Cecilia to support the candidacy of Francisco Madero against President Díaz.[7] When Madero was arrested in the summer and subsequently called for the Revolution to start on November 20, his working-class supporters in Tampico responded with a rally four days ahead of the appointed date. Local authorities reacted as well, arresting a number of participants and dampening further political agitation.[8]

Yet a series of unexpected events threw Tampico into upheaval. First, Díaz resigned and left for Paris in May 1911.[9] Second, a longshoremen-led, two-thousand-worker rally in celebration turned sour. As a breakaway group stormed the jail to liberate the Maderistas still imprisoned, the jailers opened fire on the crowd, killing six men and wounding several more. A melee ensued, with workers and soldiers fighting into the night. Merchants rushed to board up their shops, fearful that the "labouring men from Doña Cecilia, which has been the hotbed of the Maderistas,

---

[6] Interview with Mr. Andrés Araujo, conducted by Lief Adleson and María Isabel Souza on May 8, 1975 in Tampico, Tamaulipas, PHO/1/163; Bada Ramírez, PHO/4/91; James D. Cockcroft, *Intellectual Precursors of the Mexican Revolution, 1900–1913* (Austin: University of Texas Press, 1976), pp. 86, 160.

[7] Adleson, "Historia social," p. 180.

[8] Marcial Ocasio Meléndez, "Mexican Urban History: The Case of Tampico, Tamaulipas," Ph.D. Dissertation, Michigan State University, 1988, p. 199.

[9] Díaz embarked for Paris escorted by one of Pearson's executives. Pearson offered his place at Paddockhurst, England to the Díaz family in exile, but they politely declined. Mrs. Díaz preferred Paris. John B. Body to Lord Cowdray, Mexico City, June 3, 1911, P&S/HR, Box A: Mexican Political, 1911–1927.

would return at 10 a.m. to avenge the death of their comrades." Third, Tampico became an occupied city. Although merchant fears came to naught, city officials called on 150 federal troops to arrest more workers and patrol the streets to restore the peace.[10]

If the political front calmed down with the arrival of federal troops, the labor front did not. In 1911, the first oil workers' protests on record took place. The first involved a strike by the five hundred men from the Waters Pierce refinery. Although their demands are lost to history, the record shows they were attempting to follow in the footsteps of the fifteen hundred longshoremen who had successfully struck against their American employer for a wage increase, the eight-hour day, overtime pay, and union recognition.[11] The refinery men, however, were not so lucky. The provisional president, Madero, dispatched more federal troops to break the strike. The awakening was rude. By year's end, the Pierce workers found out why their erstwhile hero had betrayed them: rumors flew to the effect that the Madero clan "was buying oil lands in order to organize a new exploration and exploitation company, and any oil found would be refined at Waters Pierce."[12] Madero's loyalties, the men had discovered, were not with the workers who had supported him – a lesson they would encounter again soon. For now, that knowledge did not deter another group of oil workers from protesting. In November, several hundred workers building the Huasteca Petroleum refinery in Mata Redonda threatened to "revolt" because the foreign paymaster failed to arrive on time at the end of the long week. Although the sources do not say how that conflict was resolved, they make clear that Madero, in spite of himself, opened the door for "indocility" among the "lower classes," whose "disobedience to the mandates of authority" was "alarming" and "truly intolerable," as the Porfirian elite pointed out.[13]

Indeed, the year 1912 saw an increase in working-class organization in Tampico. The carpenters, many working for the oil companies then, formed a craft union, following the lead of the mechanics and the longshoremen. At the same time, the same labor groups opened schools for workers and their children. Boys and girls attended during the day, and illiterate adults, despite twelve-hour workdays, learned to read and write

[10] Quoted in Knight, *The Mexican Revolution*, Vol. 1, p. 217.
[11] Adleson, "Historia social," pp. 192–193.
[12] Ocasio Meléndez, *Capitalism*, p. 135. John Hart documents Madero's connections to the oilmen further in *Revolutionary Mexico: The Coming and Process of the Mexican Revolution* (Berkeley: University of California Press, 1989), pp. 245–246, 288.
[13] Quoted in Adleson, "Historia social," pp. 49–50.

at night. Their literacy kit included the political literature in circulation, particularly anarchist and socialist propaganda.[14] As workers etched their first letters, they formally came into contact with strains of critical social thought that helped them interpret their reality in the new world of industrial labor and told them there were alternatives to their current social, political, and environmental arrangements.

Outside the classroom, Tampico workers were learning lessons about international politics and the power of the foreign oil companies as well. When Madero announced the first tax on petroleum production in 1912, for example, the companies branded him as "anti-American."[15] Discontent with Madero's rule prompted the U.S. government to amass troops along the Río Grande in February. Yet when the longshoremen announced a mass rally against the United States for March 16, Madero obliged the request of the U.S. Consul for federal troops to forestall the protest. On the night of March 15, "the Mexican gunboat *Bravo*, stationed in the Pánuco, kept its search lights constantly over the town while the streets were combed by armed patrols of federal soldiers."[16]

The lessons went further. Although Madero had bowed to American pressure in the matter of taxes and protests, the oil barons were not satisfied. They demanded direct protection by the U.S. military, at the same time that they failed to protect their own workers. In 1912, a tank fire in the Pierce refinery destroyed workers' houses in Arbol Grande. Whereas no one came to the rescue of Pierce families, on November 3, American warships appeared off the Tampico coast. They were soon followed by the navies of Great Britain, Spain, France, Germany, and the Netherlands concerned about their citizens and their property.[17] In January 1913, moreover, U.S. gunboats crossed the sand bar and began cruising up and down the Pánuco "among the oil barges, tank steamers, and [Mexican] federal gunboats" as if they were in American territory.[18] Over the next nine years, "very fierce looking" American destroyers would become fixtures in the Gulf of Mexico in defense of foreign lives and property (see Table 5.1).[19] So it was that oil industry workers realized what capitalism and imperialism meant in practice. As they became acquainted with their assigned place in the social and environmental relations the oil companies

[14] Ibid., pp. 169, 172 (footnote 59), p. 216.
[15] Meyer, *México y los Estados Unidos*, p. 73.
[16] Ocasio Meléndez, *Capitalism*, p. 146.
[17] Ibid., p. 147.
[18] Brown, *Oil and Revolution*, p. 190.
[19] Diary of Tampico Crisis, October 23, 1914, SMU/ED, Box 207, Folder 6.

Table 5.1. *United States Warships in the Gulf of Mexico, 1912–1921*

Date	Triggering Event
Nov. 1912–April 1914, Tampico*	Labor and revolutionary unrest
April–Nov. 1914, Veracruz occupied	Revolutionary clashes in Tampico
March 1916–July 1917, Tampico**	Villa's attack on New Mexico
April 1920	Obregón's revolt against Carranza
July 1920	Tampico strikes
July 1921	Oil industry layoffs

* Before the U.S. occupation, there were navies from European countries as well.
** U.S. gunboats cruised the Pánuco River for the duration of the "punitive expedition" against Villa.
Sources: The New York Times, June 6, 1916 and July 11, 1917; Testimony of William F. Buckely, U.S. Senate Committee on Foreign Relations, *Investigation of Mexican Affairs,* vol. 2 (1920); The Secretary of the Navy to the Secretary of State, July 2, 1921, *Papers Relating to the Foreign Relations of the United States,* 1921, vol. 2 (1936); Paco Ignacio Taibo II and Rogelio Vizcaíno, *Memoria Roja: Luchas sindicales de los años 20* (Mexico City: Leega-Jucar, 1984); Macial E. Ocasio Meléndez, *Capitalism and Development: Tampico, Mexico 1876–1924* (New York: Peter Lang, 1999).

designed, Mexican workers also understood how international capital could affect revolutionary leaders and the life of the country at large.

The next two years proved key in that respect. The political reality of the nation became more complex with the overthrow of Madero in February 1913 and the subsequent emergence of different revolutionary factions. The civil war, in turn, turned Tampico and the Huasteca into a strategic region all parties sought to control. The increased importance of the riches of oil, moreover, meant that foreign intervention also escalated; yet all factors combined to stabilize local politics very fast and carve a definitive space on the left for Tampico's working class.

The collapse of Madero's government and his assassination in 1913 had direct repercussions on the lives of Mexican oil workers. Despite the turmoil, until then Mexican workers had been transforming the landscape without major interruptions, except for those the rains imposed. In May 1913, however, the camps and the Tuxpan terminals were raided for the first time by a revolutionary group allied with the northern hacendado, Venustiano Carranza. The loss of foodstuffs, money, and horses led

Doheny to create a private armed force.[20] Thinking that "the population of Mexico is largely composed of ignorant classes whose lack of civilized methods of warfare has been clearly demonstrated during the last several years," El Aguila and other companies did the same.[21] The white guards thenceforth became the enforcers of labor discipline, the muscle behind the ecology of oil in the Huasteca. They would be so much more zealous in doing the companies' dirty work than in pursuing revolutionaries that they would become despised figures in local history.

The fall of 1913 brought more surprises. After the summer floods receded, Carranza's *Constitucionalistas* advanced on Tampico forcefully. As they came near in October, President Woodrow Wilson ordered the evacuation of U.S. citizens from Mexico, including oil company employees. Suddenly, Mexican "assistants" found themselves in charge of the industry. They ran it through the worst of the fighting in the port, as Carrancista rebels, advancing from the south after taking Tuxpan, took the neighborhoods east of Tampico on December 10 and began attacking federal positions. The Mexican workers rose to the occasion as the *Federales*, returning fire from the river, accidentally shelled three barges, a wharf, one tank, and a warehouse. The workers contained the barge fires until they burned out, preventing a disaster of major proportions.[22] After three days of intense shelling, the Constitucionalistas retreated to Arbol Grande and Doña Cecilia, promising to burn down the Waters Pierce refinery – the only one fully operational then – upon their return.[23] By year's end, Americans were back in charge, Mexicans relegated to their "proper" place, and Tampico returned to normalcy.

Yet, what did normalcy mask in December 1913? The historical record is reticent in this regard, but new developments were clearly afoot. Mexican oil workers had tasted responsibility and independence on the job under extremely trying circumstances and had performed more than adequately. Surely that experience, although brief, must have been formative. At the same time, the presence of the revolutionary army in working-class neighborhoods must have had a political impact on both. What the record does show is that natural disaster brought workers and soldiers together: in January 1914, smallpox broke out among them. According

[20] Ocasio Meléndez, *Capitalism*, pp. 149–150.
[21] Memorandum for Captain Arthur Murray relative to conditions in Mexico, July 30, 1913, P&S/HR, Box A3.
[22] London, "Our Adventurers," p. 5.
[23] Ocasio Meléndez, *Capitalism*, p. 151.

to one account, 338 persons died between January 1 and March 11.[24] In all likelihood, the disease accounted for the peace in Tampico in the first trimester of 1914. Undoubtedly, the epidemic affected the level and quality of interaction among working-class and rebel leaders and civilian and military medical workers, if anything to coordinate the quarantine of the sick and contain the illness. For better or worse, Constitucionalistas and workers intermingled and came to know each other then. Even though it is impossible to reconstruct the course and effect of those relations, they surely affected the workers' political thinking.

The second rebel attempt to take Tampico had a direct impact on Mexican oil workers again. When the Constitucionalistas announced they were ready to lay siege to Tampico on March 28, the oil companies proceeded to shut down their operations for the second time. By April 2, the camps of the Huasteca were emptied out. Skeleton crews of Mexicans were left behind, however, giving them sole responsibility for keeping the oil flowing for the duration. Tampico, meanwhile, overflowed with jittery foreigners and evacuated Mexican oil workers none too happy to be unemployed and homeless on the eve of the rebel offensive. To add insult to injury, before the siege commenced on the morning of April 7, the multinational naval force stationed at Tampico since 1912 negotiated an exit for hundreds of foreigners aboard gunboats, oil tankers, and cargo ships, abandoning Mexican workers to their fate.[25] If Mexicans in the camps were gaining a sense of their own potential as leaders in the industry, those stranded in the streets of Tampico were seething. The slightest spark could blow their very short fuse.

Ironically enough, it was U.S. President Woodrow Wilson who opened the door for the full expression of Mexican worker sentiment in the port. After an aborted attempt to take Tampico, Wilson invaded Veracruz, ostensibly to bring long-term stability to Mexico but also to provide immediate protection for the oil companies.[26] Within hours of the bombing of Veracruz and the landing of the Marines on April 21, the streets of Tampico swarmed with outraged Mexicans. Despite the continuing Constitutionalist offensive on the port, thousands poured out in repudiation of the invasion. As an American witness recalled, "brown howling mobs,

---

[24] Gual, PHO/4/93.

[25] Carlos Gónzalez Salas, *Tampico, mi ciudad* (Mexico City: Grupo Unido de Alijadores de Tampico and Ediciones Contraste, 1981), pp. 128–129; E. DeGolyer, "The Petroleum Industry," SMU/ED, Box 107, Folder 5220; Ocasio Meléndez, *Capitalism*, pp. 152–154.

[26] Meyer, *México y los Estados Unidos*, pp. 66–71.

armed with clubs, stones and pistols" converged in the downtown, banging drums and tin pans and yelling "Death to the *gringos!*" while they "tore down and spat upon American flags." When the crowd marched past the Southern Hotel – where the Americans had "hoisted an old confederate flag of the [U.S.] Civil War" and huddled "like the Alamo" – moreover, the protesters "roared in the street and repeatedly attacked the doors with battering rams." The demonstrators also threw rocks at the hotel windows and dumped luggage on the sidewalk. The protesters were working class, and as the novelist Jack London pointed out, many "were the very employees of the gringos they wanted to kill."[27] The fury was unmistakable, but something more profound was in evidence on that day.

The march showed how the workers of Tampico in general and the oil workers in particular had integrated into a coherent ideology their schoolhouse and street lessons and their personal work experiences. Protesting was not new to port workers, and the fact that they did so in the middle of the Constitucionalistas' siege of Tampico demonstrated they were not intimidated by the revolutionaries.[28] On the contrary, workers were emboldened by the march of the Revolution itself. Its rhetoric of antidespotism and majority rule resonated with readers familiar with *Regeneración* and other writings. But, undoubtedly, the protest also displayed a significant dose of indignation born from the experience of personal humiliation at the hands of foreign bosses. That was certainly the reality for oil workers subject to systematic racism and discrimination on the job, but it was also an experience the rest of the workers shared. According to foreign observers, 90% of the city's 25,000-strong labor force worked for foreign employers; 70% for Americans alone – longshoremen, railroads, and oil.[29]

If individual humiliation at work was bearable because the men's needs were greater than their pride, national humiliation instigated by the same employers was simply intolerable. If pride of country and love of nation had not been foremost in the minds of Tampico workers before,

[27] London, "Our Adventurers," p. 7; Brown, *Oil and Revolution*, p. 194; Interview with Sam J. Hodgson, *Oklahoman*, March 13, 1914, SMU, Box 139, Folder 5823; Diary, IEAG/DW, Box 9; Testimony of Michael A. Spellacy, *Investigation*, vol. 2, pp. 946–947; PTO, Tape 103, pp. 17–18.
[28] The demonstrations against the U.S. invasion were not limited to Tampico, of course. In Mexico City, for instance, "there is unbound popular enthusiasm in favour of the defense of the country's rights," wrote El Aguila's R. D. Hutchinson to J. B. Body, Mexico City, April 23, 1914, SML/HR, Box 3A. No other city was under siege at the time, however.
[29] Cited in Brown, *Oil and Revolution*, 307.

as suggested by the fact that there is no record of protests against the presence of gunboats in the Pánuco since 1912, they certainly were the sentiments "inflamed" by the invasion, as London remarked. Perhaps the echoes of the U.S. invasion in the 1846–1848 war played loudly for Mexican workers too, and not just the Americans remembering El Alamo at the Southern Hotel. Even on the day after the protest, Mexican workers "spat upon and reviled" an oil company superintendent and his Texan aide when they "braved the streets" outside the hotel.[30] For weeks, as geologist DeGoyler recorded in his dairy, "friendliness [sic] towards Americans was very conspicuous by its marked absence."[31] Maybe the Americans were not going to lop off Mexican territory in 1914 as they had done in 1848, but they were taking Mexico's wealth just the same. No one knew that better than the oil workers. Class consciousness for them came wrapped up in a nationalism that was heavily laced with anti–Yankee imperialism as well. That was the sum total of a decade of experience working in the oil industry, revealed in the "rioting" of April 21.[32] As the political scene changed in Tampico and the Huasteca, the workers would find plenty of opportunity to nurture and cultivate their ideologies even more.

The worker protest of 1914 was the last one carried out under political uncertainty. Tampico fell to the Constitucionalistas on May 13 and remained under their control until the war ended in 1920, despite the revolutionary split into three factions – *Carrancistas* led by Venustiano Carranza, *Villistas* with Pancho Villa, and *Zapatistas* with Emiliano Zapata. Carranza controlled the port and filled his war chest with oil receipts from the Customs House, even though his relationship with the oil companies was strained (Chapter 6). A relative calm descended on the Huasteca camps as well. Even if anti-American sentiment remained "so strong" that when the foreign workers returned to the Golden Lane, they were not well received, Tuxpan was quiet under Carranza's son-in-law and provisional governor of Veracruz, General Cándido Aguilar.[33] The only snag in the end of hostilities in the Huasteca was the hacendado uprising started by Manuel Peláez in December 1914, discussed in Chapter 2.

---

[30] London, "Our Adventurers," p. 7.
[31] Diary of Tampico Crisis, April 20, 1914, SMU/ED, Box 207/Folder 6.
[32] Ibid.
[33] J. Body to Cowdray, Veracruz, June 8, 1914, P&S/HR, Box A3; Brown, *Oil and Revolution*, p. 198; Vidal Covián Martínez, *Cronología histórica de Tampico, Ciudad Madero y Altamira, Tamaulipas y de la expropiación petrolera* (Ciudad Victoria, Tamaulipas: Ediciones Siglo XX, 1969), p. 59.

Nevertheless, by keeping the factions from the camps and his royalties until 1920, Peláez brought peace to the region too.[34]

With the Carrancistas in Tampico and Peláez in the Huasteca, the oil industry thrived. More camps arose out of the rainforest in 1914 than any other year (Appendix II). Oil flowed freely across the landscape. Demand for fuel from the war machines of World War I would skyrocket as well and propel Mexican production to unprecedented heights, linking the region to an international economic network in one of the first truly global capitalist enterprises in history. By 1921 Mexico would reach its peak as the world's third-largest producer (Appendix V). To reach that level, the companies increased their refining capacity 400%. Before 1915 ended, Tampico had three new refineries (for a total of four), running twenty-four hours a day, seven days a week. Five years later, the total would be six (see Table 3.1).[35] Tampico and the Huasteca became an oil worker beehive.

A Politicized Culture

If until 1914 the oil workers were one group among several, thereafter they became a major presence in Tampico and the Huasteca. Their numbers alone made them important. Although there are no reliable employment figures for the Huasteca labor force during the early twentieth century, the estimates for some companies are illustrative of the type of growth involved. In 1915 the oldest refinery, Waters-Pierce, had between five hundred and seven hundred workers; the largest, El Aguila, counted up to eighteen hundred; the second largest, Huasteca Petroleum, had fifteen hundred men; and Transcontinental had another eight hundred to one thousand. Mexican Gulf and Texas Co. had seven hundred and five hundred workers, respectively, for some sixty-two hundred workers in six companies in Tampico.[36] Three years later, in 1918, Huasteca Petroleum and Standard Oil of New Jersey employed more workers than El Aguila: 3,000; 2,931; and 2,000, respectively. Mexican Gulf had grown to 1,858, while Texas Co. counted 1,331 workers.[37] That was a total of 9,262 oil workers in only five companies (there are no figures for Pierce in 1918).

34 Brown, *Oil and Revolution*, pp. 197–212.

35 PEMEX, *El petróleo*, p. 30; Meyer, *México y los Estados Unidos*, p. 21.

36 The number of workers are extremely rough approximations based on the incomplete Relación de personal, July 1-December 1917, AGN/DT, Caja 134, Exp. 20 and the Labor Inspector Report from Cayetano Pérez Ruíz, September 20, 1920, AGN/DT, Caja 220, Exp. 6.

37 Adleson, "Historia social," footnote 1, p. 470.

But there were hundreds of smaller oil companies in town, plus thousands of men working in camps throughout the Huasteca. Assuming Pierce still had seven hundred men in 1918, that meant that there were about ninety-nine hundred oil workers in six companies. Out of approximately eighty-six thousand Tampico inhabitants in 1918, the oil workers represented almost 11.5% of the city's population. Assuming, moreover, that about half the population of the port was made up of children, as was the case for the country in general, it is possible that the oil work force made up around 25% of Tampico's population, a significant proportion by any measurement. Whatever affected the oil workers, affected the city in general. Whatever the oil workers did affected the region as a whole. Given the level of political awareness and ideological formation the oil workers displayed by 1914, it is perhaps not surprising that the culture and politics they created were complementary and militantly leftist.

The sources of workers and the context they encountered in the Huasteca were important for their cultural and political development after 1914, nonetheless. Most new workers were *enganchados*, but not all. Other men who found work in the oil companies were Mexican refugees escaping the bloody fighting in the northern states and a steady stream of anarchist Russians, Spaniards, and other Europeans fleeing war and political persecution in their homelands.[38] Those workers met another tiny group of men who immigrated to the port in 1915 for political reasons, but not because they needed asylum. Rather, they were anarcho-syndicalists from the *Casa del Obrero Mundial* (COM) in Mexico City. As they described it, their mission was "the organization of workers into trade unions" and "direct action of worker against capitalists."[39] Like other anarcho-syndicalists, or revolutionary syndicalists, the COM activists believed that the state and capital and the workers were in "perpetual

---

[38] European radicals also migrated to the United States, Argentina, Brazil, and Chile in this period. They became the backbone of anarchist and anarcho-syndicalist organizations in those countries as well. See Hobart A. Spalding, Jr., *Organized Labor in Latin America: Historical Case Studies of Urban Workers in Dependent Societies* (New York: Harper Torchbooks, 1977), p. 8.

[39] Quoted in Cockcroft, *Intellectual Precursors*, pp. 223–224, 228–229. The COM also went to Tampico seeking volunteers to fight against Villa and Zapata, based on a pact the organization signed with Carranza's lieutenant, Alvaro Obregón, in February 1915. In exchange for printing presses and the freedom to proselytize among urban workers, the COM would raise "red battalions" against "conservative" rural folk like Villistas and Zapatistas. Since the oil companies offered jobs aplenty, better pay, and less dangerous work, few men chose to become Carrancistas, however. Jorge Fernández, Jorge Jaber, and Jorge A. Robles, "Alrededor de Febrero de 1915: La COM, los batallones rojos, Átl y las huelgas," in *Memoria del Segundo Coloquio*, pp. 440–442.

antagonism." Their goal was to destroy capital and the state through the organization of labor into unions and federations. The means to defeat class enemies was "direct action," that is, the strike. Their most powerful weapon was the general strike, which aimed at paralyzing the economy to bankrupt the capitalists and precipitate the collapse of the state.[40] As one scholar noted, "in reality, however, most syndicalists eventually came to recognize the state's immediate power. As a result, they sometimes called short-term strikes for local or limited demands that they believed would build the movement for the future."[41] Although COM migrants did not necessarily find jobs in the oil industry, they did organize trade unions that included oil workers. By November 1915, the Tampico COM had formed a federation with fourteen craft unions.[42]

The rapid and massive inflow of workers into Tampico and the Huasteca, fueled by the rising European demand for oil and political turbulence at home and abroad, meant that the region entered a period of economic expansion without historical precedent. *El auge* ("the boom") that the Mexican elite and the local hacendados had been hoping for since the nineteenth century was in full swing by 1915. As the oil companies grew immensely rich and the "juices of the earth" fed armies in nations thousands of miles away, Tampico and the Golden Lane became world famous. The region grew like never before. Its countless bars were open twenty-four hours a day. Its cabarets and theaters attracted performers from all over the world. Imported whiskey and silver and gold coin flowed almost as abundantly as oil, while brothels sprung by the hundreds like mushrooms after the rain. The Huasteca was also at the national forefront in hosting the latest technological wonders: airplanes, Ford model T's, and silent films.[43]

But rapid progress and international capitalist development also brought strains: a severe housing crisis, dangerous food shortages, and soaring inflation.[44] Working-class families felt the stresses most and more acutely than the benefits. As a native son of Tampico observed, "those who benefited were but a handful, while the people saw the ships go by

---

[40] Sabotage was also in the anarchist arsenal in theory, but the archives consulted never showed that Mexican anarcho-syndicalists in the oil industry advocated it or ever used it.
[41] Spalding, *Organized Labor*, p. 7.
[42] *Tribuna Roja*, November 27, 1915. They were masons, mechanics, electricians, day laborers, boilermakers, blacksmiths, painters, carpenters, river boatmen, restaurant workers, graphic artists, tailors, barbers, and drivers. The first nine had members in the oil industry.
[43] Torrea y Fuentes, *Tampico*, pp. 322, 326.
[44] Adleson, "Historia social," pp. 179, 252–254.

Figure 5.1. Mexican worker next to potential oil drilling site, 1910s. Negative #30874, courtesy Charles Laurence Baker Collection, American Heritage Center, University of Wyoming.

bursting with crude and the crumbs they received – even if they were paid in gold – ended up in the hands of opportunists and foreigners."[45] The response of oil workers to such conditions after 1914 was cultural and political, individual and collective, and always radical (see Figure 5.1).

Radical men, in fact, facilitated the flourishing of a vibrant and politicized Tampico working-class culture. The foreigners, whose nationalities, color, and skill entitled them to high wages and privileges in the oil industry, but whose notions of brotherhood and equality clashed with the superiority the oil companies granted them, reinforced radical notions that circulated in the port since the early 1900s. They called every workmate *compañero* and, after the Russian Revolution in 1917, they introduced "the very, very, very exotic word *comrade*."[46] Imbibing large quantities of cheap *caña* (cane alcohol) in the booming red light district, foreign radicals spent nights and early mornings excoriating capitalism, exalting the qualities of socialism, and speaking passionately about "equality among all the

[45] Gónzalez Salas, *Tampico es lo azul*, p. 260.
[46] Robles Saldaña, PHO/4/39.

classes" and "the equitable distribution of goods" to anyone who would listen.[47] In contrast to American oil workers, moreover, the radical foreigners learned Spanish and settled in working-class neighborhoods where they joined their Mexican counterparts in forming cultural-educational anarchist groups such as the *Hermanos Rojos* and *Grupo Germinal.* Together they set up schools, operated print shops, and produced propaganda in reams.[48]

One activity key for the politicization of workers was the Sunday "propaganda meeting," as oil worker Bada Ramírez described it. The event was outdoors and free of charge, a classic exercise in participatory political education that reinforced class consciousness and pride as well as nationalism, anti-imperialism, and anticapitalism. All family members participated: children declaimed poetry while wives, daughters, and sisters acted in political plays. Some of the titles staged in Tampico were *El Pan del Pobre, drama socialista en cuatro actos* ("The Bread of the Poor, a Socialist Drama in Four Acts"), "The Rich and the Poor," "Land and Liberty," and skits by "Emilio Zolá, Pedro Gorki, and Ricardo Flores Magón," one of the founders of *Regeneración.*[49] Working-class musicians also did their part, drawing from Mexican popular traditions like *corridos,* but with a twist. The song *Los IWW,* for example, was played to the music of the very popular revolutionary song, *La Adelita,* and went like this:

Here are the industrial [workers]	Join the union!
making war on Capital,	It is our freedom!
they are the Industrial Union	It is our mission to demolish
...From one continent to the next	The current political system
the exploited they will unite	And in its place put
and once triumphant, the world they will	The precious fruit of our ideal.
turn into a fountain of happiness	Follow the union, [follow] freedom...[50]

[47] *Excélsior,* January 18, 1919.
[48] Vega Soria, PHO/4/49; Robles Saldaña, PHO/4/39; Zogbaum, *B. Traven,* pp. 3–4; Paco Igancio Taibo II and Rogelio Vizcaíno, *Memoria roja: Luchas sindicales de los años 20* (Mexico City: Ediciones Leega/Jucar, 1984), pp. 33–34; Adleson, "Historia social," p. 352. Immigrants from Spain played a role in other sectors of the labor movement in Mexico, according to Barry Carr, "Marxism and Anarchism in the Formation of the Mexican Communist Party, 1910–1919," *Hispanic American Historical Review,* vol. 63, no. 2 (May 1983), pp. 277–305.
[49] *Tribuna Roja,* November 27, 1915; Miguel A. Velasco, *Del magonismo a la fundación de la CTM* (Mexico City: Ediciones de Cultura Popular, 1990), p. 17; Adleson, "Historia social," p. 355; Sierra Aguilar, PHO/4/94; Bada Ramírez, PHO/4/91.
[50] Paco Ignacio Taibo II, "Antología: la canción obrera mexicana de 1915 a 1937," *Historia Obrera,* Segunda época, vol. 5, no. 18 (January 1980), p. 12.

In addition to entertainment, the Sunday program had other features. One was the guest lecturer. Usually male, the speaker addressed current events, such as shortages or the cost of living, or gave theoretical-rhetorical speeches on "Marx . . . or imperialism," militarism and world peace, and other revolutionary themes. Those whose oratorical skills made the audience rise to its feet were the crowds' favorites.[51] The program also updated workers about strikes or marches and made appeals for donations in solidarity with fellow workers. In addition, the day included time for audience discussion and debate.[52] Thus, the whole community participated, exchanging ideas and information, and debating issues relevant to working-class families.

The Sunday program was a success. Gonzalo Bada Ramírez remembered with nostalgia that his gang of youthful refinery friends attended every Sunday religiously.[53] Indeed, in a city where the church crumbled in 1917 and was not rebuilt until 1931, political meetings replaced Sunday mass. Instead of priests and homilies, families heard neighbors and friends engage in "a little bit" of agitation. "In those days," explained the refugee from Dos Bocas, "that sort of thing went over well; it was not demagoguery, it was Truth."[54] Bold language and defiant expressions became acceptable public speech, and although certainly not everyone paid attention or adopted the worldview presented on stage, all workers became familiar and comfortable with a radical critical discourse. By 1916, it was mass currency. Ricardo Treviño, a carpenter at El Aguila and anarcho-syndicalist agitator, for instance, could argue by then that poverty was not a failure of individual effort or a mandate from heaven. Rather, it was a creation of "the bourgeoisie, the parasites, those that produce nothing useful for humanity, those who fill their treasure chests by the sweat of the brow of the poor, the capitalists, and in one word, that dark trinity: Capital, Clergy, and State."[55]

[51] Bada Ramírez, PHO/4/9.

[52] Velasco, *Del magonismo*, p. 17; Ruiz Carrillo, PHO/4/38; Adleson, "Historia social," p. 355; Volantes, April 1920, AHAT, Exp. n/n; Gual, PHO/4/93; Informe de la sección local de la Casa del Obrero Mundial de Tampico sobre la huelga general del 3 de abril de 1916," *Historia Obrera* 19, Segunda época, vol. 5 (May 1980), p. 3; Vega Soria, PHO/4/49.

[53] Bada Ramírez, PHO/4/9. "Religiously" comes from the language *Tribuna Roja* used to invite workers to the events, November 17, 1915.

[54] Bada Ramírez, PHO/4/93; Interview with Mr. Filogonio Olguín Rojo, conducted by María Isabel Souza and Lief Adleson, on May 9, 1975, in Tampico, PHO/4/46.

[55] *Tribuna Roja*, September 1, 1916.

At the same time, the workers also entertained alternatives to the status quo. Utopias were possible and, indeed, necessary and desirable. They softened the language, offered hope, and encouraged listeners and readers to imagine a country and a world without war and a workplace free of danger and denigration. Ramón Delgado, on "a propaganda tour through the oil camps" in 1916, for example, told the oil workers that he dreamed of a place

> where there are no slaves, nor enslavers, where the laborer works out of his own volition, where there is no misery, everyone is free and equal, all love each other as brothers. Science is for everyone, likewise with all types of food, clothing, just like air and sunshine, everything belongs to everybody and everyone works; there is no boss and all is peace. Illnesses are unknown save for those caused by old age; there are no jails, no barracks, and no churches, and yes [to] schools with playgrounds and workshops; parasites are unknown, so are vices. One generation follows the next, robust, happy, love without hate. This is the great human hive, this is Anarchist Society.[56]

According to Delgado, the workers responded to that vision with widespread enthusiasm and more than a little bit of sentimentality.[57]

Anarcho-syndicalists were successful in attracting oil workers not solely because they sponsored cultural activities or projected utopias, but also because they spoke to workers in a language they understood perfectly: gendered melodrama. To explain what worker ownership of the means of production meant, for instance, a contributor to the COM's official paper, *Tribuna Roja*, wrote a dialogue between a machine rendered as female and a worker assumed male. The piece was entitled *Lo que dicen las máquinas* ("What the Machines Say"). The *provocateur* machine told

---

[56] Ibid., May 3, 1916.

[57] Barry Carr argues, in fact, that Mexican anarcho-syndicalists interpreted European thought "superficially and vacuously" in *El movimiento*, pp. 54–55, 66–72. See also John M. Hart, *Anarchism and the Mexican Working Class, 1860–1931* (Austin: University of Texas Press, 1978), especially Chapter 1. But there is no question that the movement had momentum in Tampico. The sheer number of tabloids point to the interest aroused. Between 1915 and 1930, the following revolutionary syndicalist or anarchist titles were produced in Tampico and Doña Celicia: *Tribuna Roja* (1915–1916), ¡*Luz!* (1917–1919), *Germinal* (1917–1918), *Vida Libre* (1918–1919), *Fuerza y Cerebro* (1918–?) *El pequeño grande* (1919–1921), *Luz y Vida* (1921–1924), *Sagitario* (1923–1927), and *Avante* (1928–1930). Supported by reader donations, it is not surprising that publications folded because the editors ran out of money. However, some stopped printing because they were so effective that the Mexican government shut them down. That was the fate of *Tribuna Roja* in 1916, *Luz y Vida* in 1921, and *Sagitario* in 1927. See *Luz y Vida*, May 12, 1923; Librado Rivera, ¡*Viva Tierra y Libertad!* (Mexico City: Ediciones Antorcha, 1980), p. 25.

the worker that he was no different from "her" because the two worked for someone else. Thus from the onset the feminine voice suggested that the worker was emasculated by his employer, feminized and used like "her." Indeed, the machine proceeded to point out that "both were instruments," suggesting they were equal in their powerlessness, their femininity, and inhumanity. Then the machine said in a more defiant tone, "we produce fortunes that belong to you, but you never enjoy." Having provoked indignation, the machine revealed next that there was a simple way out of a situation constructed as uncomfortable and, indeed, unnatural: reclaiming manhood.

The machine became the classic damsel in distress, the female who promised endless pleasure if the worker acted like a man. "She" said,

> Worker: take power over me; pull me away from the arms of old man capital, your union to me is your only salvation. Stop being an instrument yourself so that the instrument may become yours. I want you as a master, not as an equal. Capital exploits me, only you make me fruitful. I want to be yours and yours alone.[58]

Thus, if the worker asserted his masculinity, he and the machine could take their proper places: as (male) master and (female) subordinate. They could overthrow the old oppressive order together and replace it with a bountiful "Anarchist Society," albeit without disturbing "natural" gender hierarchies. Despite the fact that the syndicalists did advocate gender equality actively and organized among women, in addressing industrial workers, they relied on understood meanings and cultural practices that resonated with a male audience.[59]

Radicals also used familiar gendered language for new purposes in relation to nationalist feeling. Although in theory anarcho-syndicalists

---

[58] The original reads: "Obrero, apodérate de mi; arráncame de los brazos del viejo capital, tu desposorio conmigo es tu única salvación. Deja de ser instrumento para que el instrumento te pertenezca. Te quiero amo, no compañero. El capital me explota, solo tú me fecundas. Solo a ti quiero pertenecer." *Tribuna Roja*, August 16, 1916, no. 25. Another example was more explicit: when the cathedral collapsed in 1917, *Germinal* described the structure as "the temple of human castration," a statement that workers agreed with, judging by the absence of men from church and the proliferation of bars and brothels. *Germinal*, October 4, 1917.

[59] *Tribuna Roja*, May 3, 1916. Delgado reported, for instance, that the day after he spoke to the oil workers in San Gerónimo a woman came up to him and told him that she "really liked" what he had said about women's rights. The COM, like anarcho-syndicalists elsewhere in the world, tried to organize the "unorganizable," which included women. In Tampico, the COM spent a good amount of time unionizing sectors dominated by female labor, like the *molineras* (corn millers).

rejected the nation-state in favor of class struggle across national boundaries, Mexican revolutionary syndicalists quickly recognized that nationalism was real among oil workers and tapped into it to reaffirm class consciousness and oppose capitalism. A 1916 article by Treviño illustrates the point. The carpenter began by defining the "motherland" (*la patria*) as the "piece of land where one was born," a sentimental popular phrase that evoked longing for a rural (and romanticized) past, in clear reference to the background of the intended audience. However, the writer then asked, what did Mexicans see when they looked at their land in 1916? "Hungry people" and workers producing wealth for others was the answer. He challenged his readers in an impassioned outburst, "if it is us, the proletarian, the disinherited, the poor, the workers, who enrich with our labor the motherland and it is us who have been and will always be the ones who have defended her and who will defend her, we have a right to own her!"[60] Treviño thus unabashedly confirmed the construction of the worker and the patriotic Mexican as male and nothing but male: the male protector, the male defender of the honor and integrity of the female motherland yesterday, today, and forever. The conclusion Treviño promoted therefore was that if the workers were real men, their collective task was to claim the motherland from capitalists and foreigners. She belonged to Mexican workers as part of the rightful order of majority rule over the minority and the "natural" order of masculine ownership of the feminine.[61] Class politics were male politics; male politics were nationalist politics; class and nationality thus merged through gender in anarcho-syndicalist language and ideology in the Huasteca. In the practice of Mexican oil workers, the convergence of class, nationality, and gender meant a workplace where a politics of masculinity prevailed and an ethos of defiance was the daily bread.

[60] Ibid., September 1, 1916.
[61] The propaganda was effective, in part, because it mirrored workers' lived experience, as the following shows. In 1922, oil worker Juan Torres Hernández wrote a letter to local authorities denouncing the superintendent at Tecomate, one "Mr. Mondi." The American nearly incited a riot when he shut down the celebration of Mexican Independence Day on September 16. The "lonches" and the ice cream were in the icebox and the band "was playing its fourth song" when the superintendent arrived and ordered everyone to go home. When the workers protested, the boss "began to remove the light bulbs, leaving the dance hall in the dark," something he felt entitled to do because the company owned the building. The workers were "indignant." As Torres Hernández put it, the men wanted "to lynch" the "foreigner who behaved like that" in a country that had been "welcoming" to him. Juan Torres Hernández to Junta Central de Conciliación y Arbitraje, September 19, 1922, AGEV/JCCA, Exp. 78.

Culture of Defiance

Beyond the fact that they came from the countryside, the record says little about Mexican workers before company recruiters packed them into boxcars and unloaded them in Tampico.[62] It is easier to find out what they became: men of "strong complexion; faces darkened by the heat of the tropics, and coarse in manner."[63] Their rudeness was of a particular kind, linked to their social, economic, environmental, and working conditions and the presence of radical organizers in their midst. In contrast to older segments of the Mexican working class, oil workers were not "orderly," "deferent," or "respectable."[64] On the contrary, they were defiant of authority and aggressive in defense of their manhood. In other words, Mexican oil workers forged their own fraternity, a brotherhood not so different from the roughnecks of Texas and Oklahoma or, for that matter, migrant oil workers anywhere.[65]

After 1914, Mexican workers challenged company men at every turn. Their individual actions ranged from general disrespect of authority and everyday acts of defiance to dangerous acts of transgression that undermined industrial discipline and put lives at risk. At its most inoffensive, for instance, workers' defiance amounted to no more than giving mocking nicknames to foreign bosses and Mexicans who did their dirty work, such as the English overseer who was atypically "enthusiastic about learning Spanish" and walked around with a dictionary. Because he failed to grasp the subtleties of the language, the workers renamed him. "Instead of saying 'I saw this, I saw that,'" recalled Cecil Knight Montiel, "he said, 'I discovered this, I discovered that.'" Mexican workers called him *Cristóbal Colón* (Christopher Columbus).[66] More biting was the name of the company agent who wrestled Cerro Azul from Eufrosina Flores, the Mexican Jacobo Valdéz. He was "the rat" for obvious reasons. Likewise, workers enduring the discipline the guard Juan de Dios (Juan of God) meted out renamed him Juan *el Diablo* (Juan the Devil).[67] Drawing lines between "us" and "them" through renaming was a satisfying and risk-free component

[62] Adleson, "The Cultural Roots," p. 41.

[63] *Excélsior,* January 17, 1919.

[64] Those were some of the adjectives the workers at the Cuahtémoc Brewery in Monterrey used to describe themselves since the late nineteenth century, for example, as Michael Snodgrass documents in *Deference and Defiance in Monterrey: Workers, Paternalism and Revolution in Mexico, 1890–1950* (Cambridge: Cambridge University Press, 2003).

[65] Boatright, *Folklore,* Chapters 10–11.

[66] Knight Montiel, PHO/4/35.

[67] Santos Llorente, *Episodios,* p. 41; Brown, *Oil and Revolution,* p. 331.

of oil worker culture that had been part of Mexican popular culture in general throughout the nineteenth century.[68] Thus, the oil workers were not inventing something new, only using a readily available cultural practice to defy the villains in a new context.

Less innocuous were the multiple ways in which individual Mexicans subverted industry discipline. The transgressions risked the men's jobs and often resulted in firings. The simpler cases involved relatively harmless acts of disobedience: "lacking respect... towards superiors," tardiness, "insubordination," talking too much, "disobeying," being "lazy, playful, and disrespectful," and generally "loafing around" – an (in)activity that was common enough for workers to have a special term for it, *hacer perra*.[69] Such behavior not only clashed with industry expectations, but also demonstrated the difficulty of shaping the first generation of workers according to a rigid pattern of social distinctions and labor hierarchies. It also showed that a deeper mechanism was at work, that is, Mexican oil workers were riding the tide of history and changing cultural norms. In the context of revolution and radical politics, submissiveness before social superiors was no longer acceptable. In the face of haughty foreigners, furthermore, deference was wholly unacceptable. As an El Aguila employee commented à propos of firing four Mexicans, "it is well known the arrogance with which the working classes proceed these days."[70] Class defiance was in; but that was not the half of it.

There were individual expressions of insubordination that were much more dangerous. It was not rare for Mexican workers to arrive to work inebriated and fall asleep on the job, or worse, take firearms and discharge them in "celebration."[71] In an industry flammable by nature, such

---

[68] On the use of humor as criticism in nineteenth-century Mexico, see William Beezley, *Judas at the Jockey Club and Other Episodes of Porfirian Mexico* (Lincoln: University of Nebraska Press, 1987). On the specific use of satire intended for working-class Mexicans, see María Elena Díaz, "The Satiric Penny Press for Workers in Mexico, 1900–1910: A Case Study in the Politicisation of Popular Culture," *Journal of Latin American Studies*, vol. 22, part 3 (October 1990), pp. 497–525.

[69] Rodolfo Usigli vs. Huasteca Petroleum, AGN/JFCA, 1928, Caja 22, Exp. 14/928/148; Félix Corona vs. Cortés Oil, AGN/JFCA, 1928, Caja 48, Exp. 15/928/749; Alberto Fernández vs. PennMex, AGEV/JCCA, 1922, Caja 30, Exp. 53; Juan Alcántara vs. El Aguila, AGEV/JCCA, 1928, Caja 72, Exp. 43; Guadalupe Morales vs. Huasteca Petroleum, AGEV/JCCA 1922, Caja 30, Exp. 52; Higinio Zúñiga vs. La Internacional, AGEV/JCCA, 1922, Caja 30, Exp. 47.

[70] Four (unnamed men) vs. El Aguila, AGEV/JCCA, 1921, Caja 17, Exp. 17.

[71] Martínez, Martínez, and Terán vs. Itamex Oil Co., AGEV/JCCA, 1927, Caja 59, Exp. 27. See also: Antonio Villareal vs. Transcontinental, AGN/JFCA, 1928, Caja 68, Exp. 15/928/1284; Francisco Medina vs. Mexican Sinclair, AGEV/JCCA, 1927, C. 62,

breaches of discipline risked not only the lives of the workers themselves, but also the fates of entire communities. As PennMex explained in a 1922 case involving the firing of a worker who slept instead of measuring the amount of oil entering a tank every half-hour, "there was a danger of the tank blowing up or breaking apart, and the oil spilling and, more than anything, the danger that the gas and the oil spread on the ground and put in danger the lives of the workers."[72] That was the case of Zeferino Gutiérrez, whom the Texas Company held responsible for the fire that burned down a pumping station in Quebrache, near Pánuco in the 1920s. Gutiérrez showed up to work drunk and fell asleep during his shift. While he slumbered, the fire started. Although he saved his life somehow, Gutiérrez lost his job.[73]

The workers' attitudes in cases where defiance led to accidents were ambiguous. They offered no excuses in their defense, but they showed no remorse either. Maybe the men reasoned that if the oil companies did not demonstrate concern for the safety and health of their workers or the communities where they were located, they were under no obligation to exert any more effort themselves. Harsh conditions and high labor demand worked to the workers' relative advantage. Workers fired for negligence or worse found employment in other camps or other companies. If the oilmen were not complicit in worker indiscipline, their labor needs and production practices went a long ways to facilitate it.

The same applies to another cultural development that took place among Mexican oil workers as part of, but different from, the subversion of discipline: the aggressive defense of manhood in response to racist foreigners. Because racism on the scale and mode the companies practiced was not part of their lived experience, Mexican workers did not identify it and name it as such.[74] Instead, Mexican men saw their experience through a gendered lens, interpreting the place the foreigners assigned to them and their daily hostility not as an expression of racism, but rather as a denial of the respect foreign males owed to them as men. That is, Mexican workers focused on the social divisions that were more familiar to them: nationality and class. And though the revolution opened up

Exp. 81; and Amparo de la Transcontinental re: Severo Ordoñez, Vicente Liquidano, y Luis Leyva, AGEV/JCCA, 1924, Caja 39, Exp. 4.

[72] Alberto Fernández vs. PennMex, AGEV/JCCA, 1922, Caja 30, Exp. 52.

[73] Zeferino González vs. Texas Co., 1928, AGN/JFCA, Caja 21, Exp. 15/928/94.

[74] In the oral histories and the official documents alike, the workers only referred to the overt manifestations of racism, that is, segregation and discrimination, but not to the racial ideology behind them.

possibilities to question the latter, as discussed below, the workers took it upon themselves to challenge individually what they presumed was the assumption that because they were Mexican nationals (rather than a "race"), foreign company men refused to recognize the fact they shared a common gender that merited respect. The oil industry therefore became the site of a serious contest over masculinity inextricably braided into the nationalist feeling expressed already in the 1914 U.S. invasion. Defense of manhood was defense of nation as well, the double helix of Mexican oil worker culture that the radicals noticed quickly but foreigners failed to recognize or simply ignored.

As the 1914 march had shown, Mexican workers could be vehement and passionate in a large group if provoked. They responded similarly to individual assaults. The oilmen might not have been an occupying force, but the industry was a violent environment. Industrial discipline more often than not came at the end of a fist. The Mexican oil workers responded in kind. The ways in which Mexican oil workers defined masculinity were specific, however. There were rules governing the territory. Violence was never the first line of action for a *macho* oil worker. Instead, it was a defensive reaction after stages of escalation on the offending man's part. The first unwritten rule in the oil workers' construction of masculinity was that a man had to exercise self-disciple in the face of adversity. This kind of control had nothing to do with the obedience the oil companies expected from the work force. On the contrary, self-control was a quality the men valued as a response to the daily indignities involved in capital-labor relations in the oil industry. *Aguantar* – "to put up with" – offensive treatment from foreigners without appearing submissive was the proper male behavior and always the first line of defense. Only when the other party crossed an invisible boundary was the Mexican worker to respond violently. Typically the line was drawn at physical contact, that is, striking of some sort. Thereafter the Mexican worker responded as he best saw fit to defend himself as a man.

Regino Torres' altercation with his American superior was a textbook case. Torres worked in Cerro Azul since "the beginning," probably 1913. By the late 1910s, he was an assistant to the tractor driver. As such, Torres "knew how to drive the tractor and could even repair it because I had examined the entire engine" out of sheer curiosity. Furthermore, "as a Mexican worker" proud of his work, he "kept the tractor shiny, as if it were mine," he noted. The American driver, however, ignored Torres' dedication and "always" "demeaned" him. "He humiliated me so much," Torres remembered, "that one day, feeling so offended in my own country by a foreigner, I cried and cursed my luck." Despite the double humiliation he was subjected to as a worker and a Mexican man, Torres put up with it (*aguantó*) not only because he needed the job, but also because he did not want his Mexican coworkers to call him *rajón* (a coward).[75] Manhood demanded enduring a certain amount of non-physical abuse. Torres obliged even after his supervisor almost ran him over, but "instead of being sorry," Torres noted, the American "got off the tractor in a fury...and insulted me." Torres "could not stand it anymore." Thus, he took a firearm to work, but did nothing. In the Mexican oil workers' emergent masculinity code, real men did not strike first.

One day, as Torres expected, his boss breached the physical contact boundary. "We were both in the tractor and he told me an obscenity," Torres recalled. "I, seething as I was, responded in the same language and maybe even worse. Since he hated me, he slapped me in the face." The anticipated breaking point had finally arrived. "*Ahora es cuando*" (now's the time), Torres told himself. He pushed the American off the tractor, jumped on top of him, and put the gun to his head. Torres, however, did not pull the trigger. He held back because the last unwritten rule of engagement was not fulfilled: the opponent was not worthy. The tractor driver, as Torres explained, proved to be "a coward." Instead of fighting back, he "opened his eyes this wide" and started "crying like a woman," begging for his life. Having so clearly emasculated his opponent, Torres "felt sorry" for the American and let him go.[76]

Torres' violent response to attack did not become lethal. In the contest over manhood, demonstrating a will to fight was more important than eliminating the opponent. Torres was satisfied that he had proven that he was the real *macho* between the two. He had exercised self-restraint in the face of denigration numerous times until the contender had crossed the line and struck first. Then, and only then, did Torres respond violently. Yet he controlled himself once more, refraining from meting out his private justice when he saw the American feminized through tears and begging. Thus, violent conflict between Mexican workers and foreigners were ritualized and gendered contests over "true" manhood, whereby Mexicans exposed the false assumptions of national/racial superiority foreigners enshrined in the labor hierarchy. If the point was lost in translation, Bulmaro Hernández made it explicit in another case. Upon his return from lunch with liquor on his breath one day, supervisor Johnstone [sic] ordered two guards to frisk him for weapons. Hernández became

---

[75] Quoted in Rodríguez, *El rescate*, p. 50.
[76] Ibid., p. 51.

furious, dropping his pants "to show all the sons of bitches the weapon he possessed."[77]

Foreign supervisors were not the only ones on the receiving end of Mexican oil workers' defensive violence, however. The Mexican company guards experienced more than their share. The archives are bloated with cases of guards ambushed, wounded, or killed in suspicious circumstances. The degree of hostility cannot be dismissed solely as instances of drunken brawls (although those were numerous as well), as the files often say. The enforcer role the guards played and the abuses they committed in their manifest loyalty to the companies must have been truer reasons for the "anonymous" attacks they suffered. They must have appeared as traitors in the patriotic eyes of Mexican oil workers, but there is no direct evidence to test that hypothesis. No one took responsibility for the misfortunes that befell the guards.[78]

The culture of defiance the oil workers nurtured on the job and the politicization of working-class culture that political radicals promoted since 1915 created not only a tense and vibrant atmosphere in oil country, but also facilitated the emergence of militant class struggle in the oil industry. A hypermasculine culture bridged individual work experience and collective class consciousness and action. The radical cultural life broke with Porfirian authoritarianism and encouraged workers to interpret their personal experience in social and political terms rather than as sheer individual luck. Without abandoning support for direct confrontation between workers and employers in the workplace, radical labor activists agitated for a political culture that sought collective solutions for the problems workers faced on the job and as a class generally. The oil workers as a group were receptive to the message. They brought the culture of defiance and defense of masculinity straight into the arena of collective political action, spawning an aggressive labor movement that replaced armed revolutionary combat with class war.

---

[77] Bulmario Hernández vs. El Aguila, AGEV/JCCA 1927, Caja 57, Exp. 15. It could be argued that there was also a subtext of homophobia in both of the cases described and many other confrontations recorded in the archives, as the men reacted to the (unsolicited) touching of their bodies by other males. An overwhelmingly male shop floor like that of the oil industry was ripe for homophobia and other behaviors, a topic waiting to be investigated.

[78] See, for example, the Letter to the Junta on the death of Herminio Jara, June 14, 1927, AGEV/JCCA, Caja 65, Exp. varios; Clippings from *El Pánuco. El Semanario de la Región Petrolera*, February 1927, AGEV/JCCA, Caja 64, Exp. 112; *LGO*, vol. 13, no. 86 (October 18, 1924); Otilia viuda de Villareal vs. Huasteca Petroleum, AGN/JFCA, 1929, Caja 78, Exp. 15/929/33.

Class War in Oil Country, 1915–1921

The politicization of defiant oil workers resulted in over two dozen walk-outs between 1915 and early 1921 (see Table 5.2).[79] Although their demands were typical of labor demands in the industrialized world at the time and reflected a rejection of the inequalities they faced in the oil industry, the results of their protests were mixed at best. After six years of intense struggle, the oil workers had less tangible gains than losses in terms of personnel incarcerated and organizations destroyed. The special location the oil workers occupied accounted for their defeats and, in addition to their militancy, for their resiliency, too. They were in the unusual position of working for an advanced capitalist industry with international economic ties in an overwhelmingly rural country largely disconnected from the oil companies themselves. The oil workers therefore were subject to developments that affected the oil industry internationally. By the same token, their actions could also have international repercussions, giving them political leverage most Mexican workers did not enjoy. The discourse the oil workers' movement adapted from anarcho-syndicalism (anticapitalist, antigovernment, and anti-imperialist), moreover, pitted them not only against a very powerful enemy, the foreign oil companies, but also against a weak but armed enemy, the Mexican revolutionary faction in control locally and eventually nationally, the Carrancistas. Mexican oil workers thus also felt the shifts in the military and political course of the revolution; but their actions too had the potential to make an impact

---

[79] In addition to the strike among workers fighting the fire at Potrero del Llano in the fall of 1914, there might have been a strike in 1914, in the Huasteca Petroleum camp at San Jerónimo. The only source that mentions it is Gonzalo Bada Ramírez, who participated in it, but his dates were confused. He remembered that it took place in late 1914, lasted eight days, and was organized with COM's assistance. COM, however, did not arrive in the area until 1915, which suggests the strike took place then. According to Bada Ramírez, their main demand was the eight-hour day. The strike was an environmental disaster, the worker acknowledged, because once the pumping station closed, the oil flowing north from the Juan Casiano wells had nowhere to go but into the Tamiahua Lagoon. Nonetheless, the men won the strike and the eight-hour day. The leadership of the strike, however, was fired, including Bada Ramírez and his brother. Thrown out of the camp, both men headed north to Mata Redonda, where the Huasteca Petroleum refinery was under construction. Before asking for a job, the men found out that the company had blacklisted the men who participated in the San Jerónimo strike. The same person who gave them that information advised they change their names if they wanted to work, which they did. They worked construction for a while, but then decided to return home. When they arrived, they realized the camp had new bosses who would not recognize them. They asked for jobs and were hired again, although he did not say if the workday was eight hours. Bada Ramírez, PHO/4/93.

Table 5.2. *Oil Workers' Strikes in Tampico and Northern Veracruz, 1911–1921*

Date	Company	Location
July 1911	Pierce	Arbol Grande, Tampico
Fall 1914	Huasteca Petroleum	Potrero del Llano, Veracruz
February 1915	Pierce	Arbol Grande, Tampico
April 1915	General strike	Tampico/Veracruz
May 1915	Transcontinental	Las Matillas, Veracruz
July 1915	Huasteca Petroleum	Mata Redonda, Veracruz
July 1915	El Aguila	Doña Cecilia, Tampico
April 1916	General strike	Tampico/Veracruz
April 1916	Huasteca Petroleum	Mata Redonda, Veracruz
June 1916	General strike	Tampico/Veracruz
December 1916	El Aguila	Doña Cecilia, Tampico
April 1917	El Aguila	Doña Cecilia, Tampico
May 1917	Pierce	Arbol Grande, Tampico
May 1917	Transcontinental	Las Matillas, Veracruz
May 1917	Texas Co.	Las Matillas, Veracruz
May 1917	Huasteca Petroleum	Mata Redonda, Veracruz
May 1917	La Corona	Las Matillas, Veracruz
July 1917	General strike	Tampico/Veracruz
October 1917	El Aguila	Doña Cecilia, Tampico
February 1918	El Aguila	Doña Cecilia, Tampico
March 1918	El Aguila	Doña Cecilia, Tampico
December 1918	General strike	Tampico/Veracruz
April 1919	Transcontinental	Las Matillas, Veracruz
May–June 1919	Pierce	Arbol Grande, Tampico
January–February 1920	Mechanics	Tampico/Veracruz
July 1920	All refineries	Tampico/Veracruz
August 1920	Camps (3 hours)	Pánuco, Veracruz
August 1920	La Corona	Pueblo Viejo, Veracruz
June 1921	General strike	Tampico

Sources: Informe de huelgas, 1918, Departamento del Trabajo, AGN, C. 118, Exp. 7; Informe de huelgas, 1919, AGN/DT, C. 169, Exp. 39; Unión de Mécanicos, AGN/DT, C. 213, Exp. 29; *The New York Times,* July 25–28, Oct. 8, 1917; *Excélsior,* June 8, 1921; Lief Adleson, "Historia social de los obreros industriales de Tampico, 1907–1919," Ph.D. Dissertation, El Colegio de México, 1982; Norman Caufield, "The Industrial Workers of the World and Mexican Labor, 1905–1925," M.A. Thesis, University of Houston, 1987.

on those same events. In the second half of the 1910s, then, the Mexican oil workers found themselves quite unwittingly in a singular position: in the forefront of capitalist industrial relations in a rural country undergoing a social revolution. That context made all the difference in what the oil workers tried to accomplish, lost, and managed to achieve.

The 1915–1921 period, as it turned out, was extremely fluid, unstable, and unpredictable at home and abroad, and so was the fate of the oil workers. Those years encompassed World War I, with its high demand for oil and, consequently, labor stability in production until its end in October 1918. Those needs would make the oil companies formidable adversaries, yet also willing to bend to workers' demands just enough to keep the oil flowing. Once the war was over, however, the companies ceased to be vulnerable to oil worker action and they became totally intransigent. The national political panorama was similarly in flux in the beginning of the period. The civil war and the "anarchy" of revolution opened up spaces for labor militancy that the oil workers exploited as best they could to improve their working conditions and strengthen their class in general. As Carranza gained the upper hand over his enemies, however, he turned the heat on radical workers, too. From 1918 on, the oil companies and revolutionary authorities coincided on the goal of eliminating revolutionary syndicalism from the ranks of the working class. Anarcho-syndicalism as a movement thus ceased to exist in 1921.

Pioneers of the Working Class: 1915–1916

Although little information on the 1915–1916 protests survives, the record reflects just how accelerated capitalist relations were in Tampico and the Huasteca already and how rapidly the oil workers claimed leadership among labor groups and beyond. The reaction of the oil companies and Mexican authorities, moreover, confirmed two items for the workers that pushed that atypical development further: the righteousness of their cause and the lack of true revolutionary commitment among Carrancistas.

The rash of strikes in the first half of 1915 started at Pierce, the oldest of the refineries with the most experienced workers. The demands on record are few: the eight-hour day, wages in U.S. currency, equal pay for equal work, and the hiring of Mexicans for supervisory positions in the oil industry.[80] In addition, the families from Arbol Grande protested Pierce's

[80] Adleson, "Historia social," pp. 445–446.

plans to add more oil tanks to the refinery despite the 1912 fire that
destroyed part of their neighborhood (see Chapter 4). The eight-hour
day was a staple demand among anarcho-syndicalists in industrialized
countries in that period, perfectly appropriate for an advanced capitalist
enterprise like the oil industry, but rather exotic in a rural nation like
Mexico. Payment in dollars likewise was a logical demand given the inte-
gration of Tampico and the Huasteca into global economic networks the
rest of the country did not necessarily experience. Since local merchants
preferred foreign currency to devalued national paper money, the workers' demand was a response to the economic pressures the oil industry
and the revolutionary war had created. It was also a patent rejection of
discriminatory policies in the industry, where foreigners were paid in U.S.
currency and nationals in pesos. The demands for equal pay for equal
work and Mexican supervisors was also an indictment of discrimination.
Their protest against the addition of oil tanks in their neighborhood
complemented the picture: in a vanguard industry like oil, Mexican oil
workers were positioning themselves as pioneers for working-class rights,
far ahead of their compatriots.

The response of the oil companies and Carranza to the 1915 strikes
confirmed the theses of revolutionary syndicalism regarding the eternal
enmity between workers and capital and the state. The capitalists did not
budge on the demands. Pierce, moreover, "mocked" municipal authorities, which included an El Aguila carpenter, Andrés Araujo, as city councilman, when they threatened to issue fines if the company built more
tanks in Arbol Grande. Carranza was even more inflexible. He used his
troops to put an end to the strikes and sent the men back to work.[81]

The results of the 1916 protests were more mixed because the circumstances grew tense. Early in the year, Tampico braced for U.S. intervention
again. In retaliation for President Wilson's support of Carranza, Pancho
Villa attacked a New Mexican town in March. Wilson then dispatched gunboats to Tampico and sent ten thousand soldiers into Mexican territory in
a "punitive expedition" against Villa.[82] The hunt would last for more than
a year and fail to capture him, but the immediate result, ironically enough,
was another exodus of foreigners from the oil camps. Fearful of a replay

[81] Ocasio Meléndez, *Capitalism*, p. 142; González Salas, *Acercamiento*, pp. 145–146.
[82] On Villa's raid of Columbus and Carranza's response, see James A. Sandos, *Rebellion in the Borderlands: Anarchism and the Plan of San Diego, 1904–1923* (Norman: University of Oklahoma Press, 1992), pp. 141–153.

of the 1914 wave of anti-Americanism, the oil companies evacuated their men. Mexican workers were left to carry on in their absence for the third time, an occurrence that no doubt boosted Mexicans' confidence in their leadership abilities and confirmed the correctness of their demand for increased responsibility within the industry.[83] At the same time, demand for fuel abroad was rising rapidly; consequently, the companies could not afford disruptions in production for any reason. The workers, therefore, really struck a sore spot when they followed the exodus of foreigners in March with a general strike in April. They had only one demand: payment in gold coin instead of worthless bills. The strike was a success: workers from all sectors participated, shutting down Tampico for the first time in its history.[84]

Carranza reacted first. The oil industry accounted for much of the revenue he was using to fight Villa himself, which meant the strike hurt his war effort, too.[85] Again, Carranza unleashed troops on the strike. This time the soldiers killed two or three men, wounded more, and arrested four anarcho-syndicalists, including El Aguila carpenter Ricardo Treviño.[86] To prevent "rioting and looting," moreover, Carranza "banned further gatherings, closed the town's saloons, summoned reinforcements and put patrols out on the streets." In response, the men marched in protest in June. The military broke up that march violently as well, warning that "troublemakers" would be shot.[87] Several foreigners were arrested and "exiled," a move the anarchist press lamented as the loss of "virile comrades."[88]

The oil companies by contrast were more conciliatory. Admitting in private that "the wages being paid were too low" given the cost of living in the region, Pierce and El Aguila promised to pay Mexican workers in silver and gold coin, while others raised the daily minimum wage to the equivalent of one peso gold (approximately 60¢). In addition, the companies agreed to open company stores to abate inflation (theoretically)

---

[83] E. DeGolyer, "The Petroleum Industry of Mexico," p. 30, SMU/ED, Box 107, Folder 5220; Precis of confidential memoranda by Mr. Brody to the Chief, re: American-Mexican crisis, P&S/HR, Box A3.

[84] González Salas, *Acercamiento*, p. 139.

[85] Meyer, *México y los Estados Unidos*, p. 94, footnote 35.

[86] Informe de la sección local de la Casa del Obrero Mundial de Tampico sobre la huelga general del 3 de abril de 1916, *Historia Obrera*, 19, Segunda época, vol. 5 (May 1980), pp. 3–5.

[87] Knight, *The Mexican Revolution*, vol. 2, p. 431.

[88] *Luz*, July 28, 1917.

and built cafeterias for Mexicans if they had not done so already.[89] The victory despite the repression was significant not only economically but also politically. The workers concluded that there were more continu- ities than ruptures between the Porfiriato and Carranza as far as labor was concerned. Therefore, they had to exercise "caution with those who call[ed] themselves revolutionaries" but acted otherwise.[90] At the same time, the men realized that direct action worked against foreign oil com- panies whose ties to the global economy made them more vulnerable to aggressive tactics than Mexican employers.[91] Those lessons led the oil workers to become more active the following year.

Militancy Ascendant: 1917

Building on their partial success, the oil workers accelerated the pace of the movement in 1917. The year would be the peak of anarcho-syndicalist

[89] Memorandum of Interview in Mr. Body's Office with Mr. Sidwell regarding his proposal to increase wages in the oil fields and at Tuxpam Bar, Tampico, February 10, 1916, P&S/HR, Box C45, File C45/5. Even the families of the most highly paid workers, the craftsmen, were going hungry. Their 4 pesos per day did not stretch far enough to pay 1.90 per kilogram of rice; 12 for a kilo of sugar, coffee, or beef; 3 per liter of beans, 3 per liter of corn, or 20 pesos per kilo of lard. To stave off famine and strikes, in fact, Doheny imported "beans by the carload" and distributed them to his Mexican workers. *El Luchador,* June 19, 1915; Primer Secretario de la Gran Logia de Tamaulipas, E. Tejeda al Jefe del Dpartamento del Trabajo, José I. Lugo, Tampico, July 1916, *Boletín* of the Archivo General de la Nación, Tercera Serie, vol. 5, no. 1 (15), (January–March 1981), p. 44. J.B. Body to Cowdray, New York, November 18, 1916, P&S/HR, Box A3; Editorial, BP, vol. 1, no. 6 (June 1916), p. 502; Jefe del Departamento del Trabajo, José I. Lugo to First Secretary of the Masonic Lodge of Tampico, August 11, 1916, *Boletín* of the Archivo General de la Nación, vol. 5, no. 1(15) (January–March 1981), p. 45; Anexo No. 1, AGN/DT, Caja 169, Exp. 40. The exchange rate is from 1918, as spelled out in the Descriptive statements of bandit outrages and holdups throughout the Tampico oil fields, chronologically arranged, Mexican Gulf Oil Co., May 17, 1918, in *Papers,* 1918, p. 677.

[90] *Germinal,* September 6, 1917. The Tampico mayor, the carpenter Tomás Morales, nev- ertheless released all the prisoners the troops had taken. He also set up an arbitration boards to consider individual worker grievances, but the oil companies voided it by refus- ing to recognize its jurisdiction. See S. Lief Adleson, "La adolescencia del poder: la lucha de los obreros de Tampico para definir los derechos del trabajo, 1910–1920," *Historias,* no. 2 (October–December, 1982), pp. 90–97.

[91] The simultaneous general strike in Mexico City, for example, not only made no gains for the workers, but also met a worse fate. Carranza called the leaders "traitors," had twelve of them arrested (including two women), and asked for their execution. In addition, federal troops occupied COM headquarters and destroyed its archives. Ricardo Treviño, *El movimiento obrero en México. Su evolución ideológica* (Mexico City: n/p, 1948), pp. 54– 62; Luis Aráiza, *Historia del movimiento obrero mexicano,* vol. 3 (Mexico City: n/p, 1964), pp. 144, 159; Knight, *The Mexican Revolution,* vol. 2, p. 433; *Luz,* July 7, 1917.

activity in Tampico before the collapse of 1921. Massive and violent worker confrontations against the companies and official revolutionaries alike took place, with mixed results once more. Differences between the British and American companies led to concessions for El Aguila workers, but not the rest. The response of revolutionary officials, however, did not vary much despite the advances in labor rights proclaimed in the new Constitution. Antagonism was becoming the rule.

The strike season began spontaneously, as was wont to happen with men who were not keen on industrial discipline and were just learning it in political life. On April 23, a small river-boatmen's local at El Aguila, affiliated with the International Workers of the World (the "Wobblies"), the COM's sister organization in the United States, went on strike. Within hours, the strike spread to the refinery. On April 25, the Pierce workers walked out in solidarity. To prevent "scabbing" at El Aguila, the men used direct action, assaulting the manager and a department chief who tried to keep the refinery open. At Pierce, too, some fifty strikers armed with clubs "compelled" the Americans to leave the premises.[92]

The demands of El Aguila and Pierce workers reiterated those from the previous June. The boatmen demanded a 50% wage increase; the eight-hour day; and payment in Mexican gold or U.S. dollars, as apparently the company had not fulfilled its commitment to do so.[93] The refinery workers added two familiar demands: the end to "despotic" treatment from supervisors and the replacement of foreign supervisors with Mexicans. They also included new ones: the dismissal of particular white guards; the end of arbitrary work assignments; and a stop to layoffs. Discrimination and mistreatment were obviously as important as wages to the workers, but to the companies other considerations were more important.[94]

The international importance of El Aguila during wartime worked to the workers' benefit. Worried about fuel for the Royal Navy, the British government prevailed on Pearson, by then a member of the House of Lords, to negotiate. At the end of April, El Aguila agreed to the eight-hour day (with half-day on Saturday), a salary increase, and a joint worker-company committee to "deal with labour questions."[95] Although El Aguila did not recognize the union, the joint committee acknowledged

[92] Consul Dawson to the Secretary of State, May 2, 1917; Consul Dawson to the Secretary of State, July 16, 1917 in *Papers*, 1917, pp. 1021–1023, 1028.
[93] Ibid., p. 1021.
[94] Adleson, "Historia social," p. 452.
[95] A. E. Chambers to Body, Tampico, June 3, 1917, P&S/HR, Box A4; Cuestionario sobre conflictos por cuestión de salarios, 1918, AGN/DT, Caja 118, Exp. 7.

de facto that the workers had the power to disrupt a strategic industry at a critical time. The committee was also a partial affirmation of anarcho-syndicalist tactics, though contradicted by the fact that it would have a mediator appointed by the governor. Still, El Aguila extracted revenge by firing two Wobblies.[96]

The success at El Aguila encouraged the rest of the oil workers to walk off the job and join the Pierce men still on strike. In May, workers at Transcontinental, Texas Co., Huasteca, and La Corona walked out in the first mass oil workers' strike. In July, moreover, the COM led a general strike across Tampico. The river boatmen at El Aguila, led by Spanish and Portuguese sailors, went out in solidarity. Thousands of defiant workers waving anarcho-syndicalist red-and-black flags marched downtown, fists raised, yelling slogans and wrapping up the rally with rebel-rousing speeches.[97] As usual, Americans were subject to vituperation: "ugly remarks could be heard about the family tree of all 'gringos,'" reported an employee.[98]

Despite the show of force, the workers were routed. The Americans were unwilling to bend. Standard Oil of New Jersey had purchased Transcontinental and Pierce, while the United States had entered the war. Stability in the Mexican oil industry now became a matter of U.S. national security – something the companies tried to leverage by mobilizing their friends in the State Department and the Congress to pressure Wilson to overthrow Carranza.[99] The State Department became actively involved in opposition to the walkouts, as the Ambassador in Mexico City charged that German spies were behind the strikes, a tactic the U.S. government was using quite effectively against the IWW at home at the time.[100] The U.S. Consul in Tampico went as far as to demand that the "ignorant" and "semi-savage" military commander protect foreign employees trying

---

[96] At the same time El Aguila assured deliveries for the English Navy by bringing on line its Tuxpan plant at the end of May. Weekly News Summary from Body to C. Reed, New York, June 11, 1917, P&S/HR, Box A4.

[97] Consul Dawson to the Secretary of State, July 16, 1917; Consul Dawson to the Secretary of State, July 22, 1917, in *Papers*, 1917, pp. 1028–1029; Norman E. Caufield, "The Industrial Workers of the World and Mexican Labor, 1905–1925," M.A. Thesis, University of Houston, 1987, pp. 80–85.

[98] Robert Nock to DeGolyer, Tampico, August 12, 1917, SMU/ED, Box 117, Folder 5388.

[99] Jonathan C. Brown, "Why Foreign Oil Companies Shifted their Production from Mexico to Venezuela during the 1920s," *The American Historical Review*, vol. 90, no. 2 (April 1985), p. 370; Brown, *Oil and Revolution*, p. 281.

[100] Hamilton, *Early Day*, p. 177; Melvyn Dubofsky, *We Shall Be All: A History of the IWW, The Industrial Workers of the World* (New York: Quadrangle/The New York Times Book Co., 1969), pp. 376–378.

to keep the refineries open, lest he call on the warships patrolling the Gulf coast for help.[101] Doing their own part, the companies began making "blacklists" of anarcho-syndicalist workers. The first to go were the carpenters affiliated to the COM.[102]

Soon enough, Mexican authorities bent to U.S. pressure. The governor personally led 500 soldiers into Tampico on July 15, ordered the strikers back to work at gunpoint, and arrested seventeen organizers, including Treviño, Araujo, and longtime activist Alejandro Berman.[103] Scouring for German agents and other "pernicious foreigners," the authorities also detained three Catalans and two Cubans and deported them.[104] In response, a satirical syndicalist press lauded "Rockefeller, that laborious Mexican (who was never in Mexico) who through his work and efforts transformed vast arid terrains into wells of the richest production, under whose shade millions of ungrateful workers live lazily without knowing how to say thank you."[105]

Unable to gain concessions from the Americans, workers turned to national issues in the fall. In October Tampico hosted the Second Labor Congress. The first had taken place in 1916, leaving the participants split between those who favored direct action, like the Tampico delegation, and those who preferred a "multiple action" approach that embraced electoral politics and alliances with revolutionary officials.[106] The 1917 hosts included luminaries of Tampico anarcho-syndicalism. They promised a spirited debate.[107]

Tempers flared from the start of the session, indeed. One of the Mexico City delegates, the typesetter José Barragán Hernández, was shot by a soldier as he left for Tampico. In addition, the local press attacked the hosts, accusing them of being German agents, or worse, Villistas. Meanwhile, the "entire military apparatus" poured onto the streets for "crowd control." On the third day of meetings, moreover, an explosion and fire rocked the Pierce refinery, underscoring the tinderbox quality of the

---

[101] Consul Dawson to the Secretary of State, Tampico, April 28, 1917, in *Papers,* 1917, pp. 1021–1023.

[102] Adleson, "Historia social," pp. 434, 465.

[103] Treviño, *El movimiento,* p. 67.

[104] *The New York Times,* July 25, 28, 31, 1917; *El Universal,* August 12, December 20, 1917; Chargé Summerlin to the Secretary of State, July 15, 1917, in *Papers,* 1917, p. 1029; Ricardo Treviño, *El espionaje comunista y la evolución doctrinaria del movimiento obrero en México* (Mexico City: n/p, 1952), p. 96.

[105] *Germinal,* August 9, 1917.

[106] González Salas, *Acercamiento,* pp. 48–51.

[107] *Luz,* September 5, 1917.

entire event.[108] Inside COM headquarters, the discussions became heated over labor's response to the Constitution proclaimed in February. The "pragmatists," led by an electrician named Luis Morones, saw the Constitution – and especially Article 123 pertaining to the rights of labor – as evidence that the revolutionary leadership was *obrerista* (pro-labor) and should be supported by the workers. The Tampico delegates, the "utopians," did not trust the framework official revolutionaries proposed and argued for total labor independence instead.[109]

The Constitution was a contradictory document, the creation of men experienced in leftist politics as well as many political conservatives.[110] Article 123 was no exception. It granted labor wide-ranging rights, including the eight-hour day, a minimum wage, the right to unionize and to receive "the same compensation ... for the same work, without regard to sex or nationality," compensation for "labor accidents and occupational

---

[108] "Prometeo," 1918; Aráiza, *Historia*, vol. 3, p. 178; *Luz*, November 7, 1917; González Salas, *Acercamiento*, p. 100; Superintendent General of Pierce Oil to the Municipal President, October 16, 1917, AHAT, Exp. 140–1917.

[109] *Germinal*, August 9, 1917; *Luz*, November 18, 1917.

[110] The conservatives were the minority faithful to Carranza, dubbed as *las derechas* (the right). The majority were the "socialists" or "Jacobins." These included a nucleus experienced with anarcho-syndicalism and oil. They included Veracruz governors Cándido Aguilar and Heriberto Jara; Carlos L. Gracidas from the COM; and a former writer for *Regeneración* and ex-Tampico Customs Officer, Francisco Múgica. Múgica was the president of the Constitutional Convention. His experience at Customs in 1914–1915 included confronting the oil companies on issues ranging from tax evasion to their legal status as corporate entities. In 1915, when Carranza appointed him provisional governor of Tabasco, Múgica discovered that El Aguila already controlled approximately 150,342 hectares (375,855 acres) of state rainforest. Heriberto Jara also had been an active participant in the strikes that rocked the Río Blanco textile factories in 1908. Also present as representative from Tamaulipas was the military commander, Emiliano Nafarrete, a member of the conservative faction who had many run-ins with the companies nonetheless. See José Napoleón Guzmán A., *Francisco J. Múgica: Semblanza de un revolucionario michoacano*, Series Personajes Michoacanos Ilustres (Morelia: Gobierno del Estado de Michoacán, 1985), pp. 2, 5; Magdalena Mondragón, *Cuando la revolución se cortó las alas (Intento de una biografía del General Francisco J. Múgica)* (Mexico City: B. Costa-Amic, 1966), pp. 74–75; Heather Fowler Salamini, "Revolutionary caudillos in the 1920s: Francisco Múgica and Adalberto Tejeda," in *Caudillo and Peasant in the Mexican Revolution*, edited by D. A. Brading (Cambridge: Cambridge University Press, 1980), pp. 172–174; *Excélsior*, May 16, 1921; Randolf Melgarejo and J. Fernández Rojas, *El Congreso Constituyente de 1916 y 1917* (Mexico City: Talleres Gráficos de la Secretaría de Fomento, Colonización e Industria, 1917), pp. 144–145; Djed Bórquez, *Crónica del Constituyente* (Mexico City: Comisión Nacional Editorial del Comité Ejecutivo Nacional del PRI, 1985), pp. vi-viii, 161; Corián Martínez, *Cronología*, p. 59; González Salas, *Acercamiento*, pp. 48–49; Spender, *Weetman*, pp. 151–152; Silvia González Marín, *Heriberto Jara, luchador obrero en la Revolución mexicana, 1879–1917* (Mexico City: El Día, 1984), pp. 36–37, 50–51, 166–167, 179–203.

diseases," three-months severance pay, profit-sharing, and more. But the article also clashed with revolutionary syndicalism in fundamental ways. The Constitution did not intend to overthrow capitalism at all. Rather, Article 123 sought to "achieve equilibrium between the various factors of production, harmonizing the rights of capital and labor."[111] The rights enshrined in the article provided a legal framework for class struggle, instead of pursuing the abolition of classes. The Constitution envisioned the institutionalization and management of class struggle, making the state the mediator and arbiter that would guarantee "equilibrium" between the classes. Article 123, in fact, provided a mechanism to do just that: the conciliation and arbitration board (*junta de conciliación y arbitraje*), whose jurisdiction included individual and collective claims, as well as the authority to declare strikes legal or illegal. Those provisions granted more power to the state than to labor and, as one contemporary observer pointed out, "implied grave threats to the rights of the workers and opened the door to government domination of the labor movement."[112] The Tampico delegates recognized those dangers and emphasized them; the "realists" minimized them and focused on the rights guaranteed instead. The labor congress closed with a defeat for the utopians. The majority of the delegates approved the rapprochement with Carranza that Morones favored.[113]

Outside the Congress, the Tampico radicals suffered more setbacks. A demonstration to protest the murder of Barragán Hernández almost ended in a bloodbath when the military commander ordered his troops to open fire on the crowd, an order the troops refused for reasons unknown.

---

[111] Article 123 in *The Mexican Constitution*, translated by H. N. Branch, and reproduced in Ackerman, *Mexico's Dilemma*, Appendix B.

[112] Robert p. Millon, *Zapata: The Ideology of a Peasant Revolutionary* (New York: International Publishers, 1995), p. 129. Millon attributes the analysis to Zapata.

[113] Morones proposed the labor movement forge another alliance with revolutionary officials to fulfill the promises of Article 123. The radicals rejected that idea as tried and untrue. They argued that Constitutions were by definition conservative documents that stifled new ideas and aspirations. Instead, the radicals listed their alternatives: revolutionary syndicalism as the means of struggle, and the communalization of the means of production and consumption as the final objective; abolishing rules, regulations, and quotas for union membership; abolishing leaders; opening schools and libraries; focusing more on the final objectives than on immediate economic gains; never going on strike to obtain something that contradicted the interests of the entire working class, placing those interests above all others; preparing workers for the conquest of property and its transformation into common property through education; and ending the practice of having paid union leaderships. *Germinal*, August 9, 1917; *Luz*, November 18, 1917.

A follow-up general strike was also undone by authorities. So was a political strike called for November 16 to demand the release of incarcerated labor leaders.[114]

Why the reversals after such promise at the beginning of 1917? The fact was that the context for the oil workers' movement was changing very fast. And although some factors favored the workers, like England's need for labor peace at any cost, more were against them. The United States had become more deeply involved in Mexican affairs on account of the war; and unlike Britain, it had the military might and, by an accident of geography, the location to deliver on its threats. American oil companies therefore felt less vulnerable to worker unrest and more willing to resort to repression at the first signs of discontent. At the same time, Carranza had defeated his rivals politically with the proclamation of the Constitution, becoming provisional president with the support of labor through Morones. Full stability could be achieved only if everyone submitted to the legal framework the Constitution provided. That included the oil workers.

Revolutionary Syndicalism on the Defensive: 1918–1920

The siege on the oil workers started in earnest in 1918, as the revolutionary government presided by Venustiano Carranza declared open season on anarcho-syndicalism in general. A combination of local, national, and international factors combined to put radical workers on the defensive. Despite intermittent attempts to reverse the trend, the workers found they could not overcome the companies or revolutionary officials. Their successes paled in comparison to the defeats.

At the local level, the space the radicals had enjoyed to politicize and organize in 1915 formally ended. In January 1918, the mayor of Tampico, a Carrancista, banned meetings and speeches with "political themes," placed the downtown off-limits for marches, and sponsored cultural activities to compete with the radical Sunday program.[115] At the national level, Carranza's lieutenant, General Alvaro Obregón, made great progress integrating labor into the official revolutionary fold. In May, the Third Labor Congress met and formed the *Confederación Regional Obrera Mexicana* (CROM), with Luis Morones as secretary

---

[114] The Acting Secretary of State to Ambassador Fletcher, November 16, 1917, Department of State, *Papers*, 1917, p. 1030.

[115] *Excélsior*, April 15, June 7, 11, 1919; *Fuerza y Cerebro*, June 15, 1918; Sociedad Cultural Amado Nervo to Municipal President, March 20, 1920, AHAT, Exp. 90–1920; González Salas, *Acercamiento*, pp. 149–155; Adleson, "Historia social," pp. 295–296, 320.

general and defector oil worker Ricardo Treviño in the executive committee. Morones, the most powerful labor leader for the next two decades, immediately swore loyalty to the revolutionary government, isolating the Tampico radicals altogether. The only traces of the CROM's revolutionary syndicalist roots were the red-and-black flag and the motto, "health and social revolution."[116]

Internationally, the moment was no better. Attacks on revolutionay syndicalists in the United States escalated with the first "red scare" of 1918, as the German-baiting of syndicalists shifted to red-baiting upon the triumph of the communists in Russia in late 1917.[117] The mood of intolerance against dissent spread to Mexico explicitly in November 1918, when the CROM and the American Federation of Labor met in Texas and formally denounced the IWW, anarchism, socialism, and communism.[118] To make matters worse, Tampico and Huasteca workers felt the brunt of nature that fall as well. The floods submerged everything, and the influenza pandemic reached the port. Gonzalo Bada Ramírez, who caught the flu himself but survived, remembered that at the Huasteca refinery in Mata Redonda where his family lived, many workers' houses were left "locked up" or with doors "wide open" as entire families died of the flu. The scene was "disconsolate," wrote Andrés Araujo, as victims were loaded onto vegetable carts, taken to the cemetery, doused with "petroleum or gasoline," and cremated to stem the contagion.[119]

Worker militancy plummeted. Only one strike was reported for all of 1918, at El Aguila.[120] The two working-class protests on record, moreover,

[116] *Lucha Social*, April 11, 1918, May 5, 1918; *Luz*, January 15, 1919; Taibo II and Vizcaíno, *Memoria*, pp. 39–44; Treviño, *El movimiento*, pp. 78, 81.

[117] Dubosfky, *We Shall Be All*, p. 424.

[118] Taibo II and Vizcaíno, *Memoria*, p. 45. *The New York Times* reported that "anti-American sentiment" in Tampico was attributed to the Germans, for instance, on February 25, 1918.

[119] Bada Ramírez, PHO/ 4/91; Sierra Aguilar, PHO/4/94; *Luz*, October 23, 1918. See also, Interview with Mr. León Vargas Domínguez, conducted by Lief Adleson on February 7, 9, and 11, 1974 in Ciudad Madero, Tamaulipas, PHO/4/27.

[120] Taibo mentions a second strike at El Aguila at mid-year, either June or July, citing the newspaper *El Pueblo*, but I found no such strike in the archives. Taibo II and Vizcaíno, *Memoria*, p. 44; Avisos e informes sobre huelgas, paros y accidentes en el trabajo, 1918, AGEV/JCCA, Caja 6, Exp. n/n/2. The strike documented involved the mechanics and the day laborers at El Aguila. Two thousand men were picketing on the first day, March 20, but all were back within two weeks because the company refused to negotiate. Details of the defeat are in *Fuerza y Cerebro*, March 30, 1918 and Informe sobre la huelga de El Aguila, 1918, AGN/DT, Caja 118, Exp. 7. The defeats were reflected in the decline of the syndicalist press as well. Two papers had shut down by mid-year, and others pooled resources for an aptly named new single sheet, *El Pequeño Grande* (The Little Big One). *Luz*, January 31, 1919; *Fuerza y Cerebro*, June 15, 1918.

reflected the prostration of revolutionary syndicalism in general. The first was a political protest in February to denounce the persecution of the IWW in the United States. As they marched past the American consulate, the men accused Wilson and Carranza of forging "a co-alliance to persecute revolutionary syndicalists, socialists and anarchists in both countries."[121] That both were of one mind on that issue became clear in the meeting between the CROM and the AFL in November; in February, the demonstration ended with the arrest of the organizers and a decree banning IWW outdoor gatherings.[122] The second protest took place in December, for similar reasons. The longshoremen led a twenty-four-hour general strike as part of a worldwide repudiation of the trials of Wobblies throughout the United States.[123]

By 1919, workers were totally on the defensive. The red-baiting that started in the United States the year before crossed the southern border in January. An alarmed "special correspondent" from Mexico City "warned" readers that Tampico was "the cradle of bolshevism" in the country. He wrote that red posters announcing the forthcoming newspaper *El Bolsheviki* were plastered across Tampico walls, while workers awaited the first edition "eagerly."[124] But as the anarchist José Angel Hernández reported a few days later, the new paper never saw the light of day. The military confiscated the first issue. They also stormed a small shop that had just begun to publish *El Pequeño Grande*, removed the printing press, and deported a Russian "agitator."[125]

Other changes affected the oil workers directly. Pearson sold a large chunk of El Aguila to Royal Dutch Shell and transferred all management responsibilities to the new company.[126] From then on El Aguila workers, like those at Pierce and Transcontinental, would have to confront a truly multinational oil giant. At the same time, Mexico's profile in the world petroleum market rose owing to the suspension of oil work in the Caspian Sea because of the Russian Revolution and the shifts in markets and products that took place in the aftermath of World War I. As the European war machine stopped in October 1918, the largest consumers

---

[121] *Luz*, September 11, 1918.
[122] Adleson, "Historia social," pp. 299–300, 320.
[123] *Luz*, December 18, 1918; see also Dubofsky, *We Shall Be All*, Chapter 17.
[124] *Excélsior*, January 17, 1919.
[125] Adleson, "Historia social," p. 503. The governor of Tamaulipas, Andrés Osuna, also confiscated the printing press of an anarchist group in the capital, Ciudad Victoria, to end the publication of *Alba Roja*, according to *Excélsior*, June 28, 1919.
[126] Yergin, *The Prize*, p. 232.

of petroleum products became the civilian American automobile industry.[127] That meant that the recession that followed World War I and lasted until 1920 did not affect the Mexican oil industry and that American oil companies and interests rose further in importance compared to that of the Europeans.

With the odds against them and after a year of inactivity, the oil workers tried to recover terrain in 1919 to avoid the role of "eunuchs" the syndicalists accused Morones of accepting.[128] They did so by making organizational leaps. The workers formed the first refinery-wide unions to replace trade unions. The change was important ideologically and pragmatically. A single union in a refinery advanced the revolutionary syndicalist idea of "One Big Union" as the ideal unit of social organization. Uniting refinery workers scattered across craft unions and incorporating unorganized workers into a single organization also made communication and coordination faster, increasing the potential for success. In other words, a single refinery-wide union had more power than discrete groups within an installation.

Pierce and Transcontinental workers were the first to form refinery-wide unions. To consolidate the organizations, they drafted a collective contract to present to the companies in April. The demands from the Transcontinental men are not on record, but those the Pierce workers drew up survived. The men wanted union recognition, a 25% wage increase to cope with continuing inflation, the "abolition" of the company store that ate up their wages, protection against reprisals for striking, and compliance with Article 123. If the contract were signed, Pierce oil workers would be the first men in Mexico to enjoy such benefits. If the company did not negotiate, the men would walk out a month later, on May 24.[129]

The showdown between the union and the company started at Transcontinental, however. Standard Oil gave notice to two leaders upon hearing they had formed a refinery-wide union. Although the men had chosen May Day as the start of their strike if contract negotiations failed, they walked out immediately in support of their union leaders, on April 16. They demanded that the company employ union members first

---

[127] Ibid., pp. 183, 194–195, 238.
[128] *Luz*, January 19, 1919.
[129] Informe de huelgas, 1919, AGN/DT, Caja 169, Exp. 40. The dates for the Pierce strike are confused in several of the sources, including some primary ones. The recounting that follows here is based on the dates that appeared in the newspapers and the report from the Department of Labor.

and that instead of giving eight-days notice they pay eight-days salary to fired workers.[130] The strike lasted one week, but the military protected foreign employees who maintained operations, while a municipal conciliation and arbitration board studied the demands. On April 23 the board ruled that Transcontinental need not give preference to union members in hiring, but it could not dismiss workers for being union leaders. Pleased with that "balanced" ruling, the company sent the men back to work. The collective contract never came up.[131]

But Transcontinental was only the first round in the workers' efforts to regain the offensive. Another conflict broke out among railroad workers, who called for a general strike for May 7. The oil workers pledged their support, threatening to shut down the port like they had done in 1916. The companies cried foul and asked for government protection. The port awakened "militarized" the Wednesday of the general strike. Troops occupied the streets, blocking what the mainstream press misnamed a "Bolshevik demonstration."[132] On May 24 the Pierce union walked out as planned. The men were better prepared this time. Pierce men secured not only solidarity pledges from workers at El Aguila, Huasteca, Mexican Gulf, and Texas Co. in the event of a general strike, but also a promise of financial support from the most powerful union in Tampico, the longshoremen.[133] The workers had laid out the groundwork for a successful action as best they could, showing they had indeed made qualitative advances in their organizational strategy.

The strike went on as planned for ten days, without reported incidents. Then on June 3 the strikers organized a protest march to highlight their continuing struggle against international capital, in defiance of the mayor's ban on demonstrations. Somewhere along the route, the union men ran into strike-breakers. A violent clash ensued, but apparently the authorities did not intervene.[134] Tensions escalated, as the Pierce men took the next step: a general strike for June 15 and a mass demonstration on June 16. The general strike was a success. Nothing moved on June 15. That night, however, an oil worker confronted a soldier guarding one of the wharves and was shot dead. The next day's march was ripe for further violence. As ten thousand angry workers marched from Llanos del Golfo to downtown Tampico, a major tried to use a trolley car to block

[130] Informe de huelgas, 1919, AGN/DT, Caja 169, Exp. 39; *Excélsior*, April 8, 23, 1919.
[131] Informe de huelgas, 1919, AGN/DT, Caja 169, Exp. 39.
[132] *Excélsior*, April 29, May 7–8, 1919; Taibo II and Vizcaíno, *Memoria*, p. 31.
[133] González Salas, *Acercamiento*, pp. 174–175.
[134] *Excélsior*, June 4, 9, 1919.

the march. A group of workers lunged at him and wrestled him for his 45-caliber pistol. In the scuffle, the weapon fired, killing the major and injuring a captain. Soldiers then opened fire on the crowd, killing four and wounding others. By the end of the day, the military occupied the unions' headquarters, the COM hall.[135]

But working-class defiance did not end there. The following day, June 17, Tampico remained closed. No one returned to work. Soldiers closed the Customs House and patrolled the streets as if in a state of siege. At mid-morning a crowd began to gather: men, women, and children. Numbered at around five thousand, they trailed the coffins of the dead workers on their way to the cemetery. As they filed past the police station, they stopped. Anarcho-syndicalist union leaders Andrés Araujo, Alejandro Berman, and José Angel Hernández addressed the crowd, "violently" attacking "revolutionary" authorities. A few hours later, a full-fledged political funeral took place. As widows, children, and comrades lowered bodies to the ground, workers stepped forward to "pronounce furious oratory pieces."[136]

Neither the Pierce strike nor the general strike had been resolved, however. Pierce had been on strike for twenty-six days. The rest of the companies had been out for four days. Under pressure from the companies, the governor sent additional troops to escort foreign employees and Mexican strike-breakers into the refineries. On June 19, moreover, officers arrested fifteen men and put them on a westbound train, including the secretary general of the Transcontinental union, Andrés Araujo; the secretary general of the Pierce union, Fernando Bolaños; two members of Pierce's executive committee, Antonio Sánchez and Francisco González; and the union lawyer, Emilio Portes Gil. The general strike collapsed the next day.[137]

Pierce workers held out three more days, but finally folded. With their leadership exiled, the union met on a rainy Sunday, June 22, at 10 a.m. to discuss options. As the union's letter to the company said, "after much debate" the men decided to end the strike, but they "reserved the right" to call for another action when "a better opportunity" presented itself.[138]

---

[135] The military also confiscated their files and never returned them – a true loss for historians. Report on the Events of June 16, 1919, AGN/DT, Caja 169, Exp. 40; *Excélsior*, June 17, 23, 1919.

[136] González Salas, *Acercamiento*, p. 176.

[137] Ibid.; *Excélsior*, April 16, 1919.

[138] Trabajadores Unidos de la Pierce Oil Corporation to the Company, Tampico, June 22, 1919, AGN/DT, Caja 169, Exp. 40.

By the end of the day, the rain had become torrential and the Pánuco had overwhelmed its banks. Refineries and working-class neighborhoods were underwater again. The installations thus remained closed for days, in a "natural" prolongation of the strike no one had planned.[139]

In the meantime, a group of anarchist women from Doña Cecilia picked up where the men had left off. On June 24, they organized a march to the local garrison to demand the military return the COM hall. When the officer denied the request, the women asked for the red-and-black flag. Upon their return to the neighborhood, the radical women used the banner to wrap the body of another dead worker. According to a reporter, "numerous" workers and their families then gathered for the second political funeral in seven days. This one resembled "a parade of red-and-black flags."[140]

There were no more oil worker actions for 1919. As the general manager of Pierce, William Mealy, wrote to President Carranza on July 22, "the behavior" of local officials "cannot be praised enough. Their actions have created a situation that I believe will avoid difficulties in the future and will bring a lasting peace to the Tampico region."[141] The repression from revolutionary authorities succeeded in halting the movement. The collective contracts were not discussed, the workers lost the strikes, and the Pierce and Transcontinental unions lost their leadership. Moreover, at least six workers were murdered by soldiers as police occupied the union hall. The defeats of 1919 were undeniable.

Yet not all was lost. The organizational advances were real. Transcontinental and Pierce workers still had refinery unions. The workers recovered the COM hall before the year ended, allowing them to pursue their cultural, educational, and political activities. Compared to anarcho-syndicalists elsewhere, the Tampico workers had not fared as badly. The Mexico City COM, for instance, never reopened its hall, and revolutionary syndicalists in Latin American cities were deported or isolated to the point of irrelevance.[142] In the United States, likewise, hundreds of IWW members languished in prison. Those still free were hunted in police raids or worse: in 1919, a "patriotic" mob attacked an IWW hall and lynched its leader after castrating him.[143] By year's end anarcho-syndicalism was

[139] *Excélsior*, June 23, 1919.
[140] Ibid., June 25, 1925.
[141] William Mealy to León Salinas, Subsecretario Encargado del Despacho de la Secretaría de Industria, Comercio, y Trabajo, July 22, 1919, AGN/DT, Caja 169, Exp. 40.
[142] Spaulding, *Organized Labor*, pp. 31, 33, 55.
[143] Dubofsky, *We Shall Be All*, p. 455.

history in the United States and Latin America. Not so in Tampico, where the movement enjoyed a brief moment in the sun in 1920 before the shock of mid-1921.

The year 1920 turned out to be as unpredictable as any since the Mexican Revolution started. The twists and turns in the lives of the nation and the oil workers intertwined once more, as the workers took advantage of the political opportunities revolutionary leaders offered, unwittingly or not, to press their agenda on the oil companies. The results of the new skirmishes in the class war that rocked Tampico and the Huasteca since 1915 were, yet again, mixed.

The Mechanics' Union started the 1920 mobilizations. As one of the oldest organizations with over two decades of existence, the mechanics had taken up the banner for recognition that the Pierce and Transcontinental unions had raised to no avail in mid-1919. They began circulating a petition for union recognition among the companies in October 1919, but received no response. Disgusted, the mechanics went out on strike on January 21, adding a wage increase to their demands.[144] The companies reacted by moving mechanics from the camps to Tampico as strike-breakers during the first week of February. When the mechanics arrived, however, the strikers intercepted them and "convinced" them not to work.[145] Undoubtedly intimidation was the better part of the convincing, but the strikers may also have pointed out that if they won, the victory would apply to every mechanic because all the companies were involved. The strikers, moreover, offered the camp mechanics room and board in a hotel until the strike was resolved, a true sign of the strength of the union irrespective of their persuasive abilities. The would-be scabs accepted the "vacation" and refused to work.[146] That meant, in effect, that the walkout extended to the camps as well, affecting production from Tampico to Tuxpan. This time, the companies agreed to negotiate. Although the record does not explain why, the limited quality of the strike and its territorial expanse made repression unworkable in this case. Negotiation was easier. The strike thus ended a month after it started, on February 21. The companies did not recognize the union, but did agree to increase wages.[147]

The success of the mechanics might have reverberated among other oil workers sooner had national events not overtaken them. Just two months

[144] Unión de Mecánicos to all companies, January 20, 1920, AGN/DT, Caja 213, Exp. 29.
[145] *El Universal*, February 6, 1920.
[146] Ibid., February 9, 1920.
[147] Ibid., February 23, 1920.

after the strike, in April, Tampico was under high alert, with U.S. gunboats patrolling the waters off shore. The reason was Obregón's revolt against Carranza when the latter refused to select the former as presidential candidate for the upcoming elections. Fearing that Tampico workers would support the revolt, policemen loyal to Carranza stormed the COM hall a second time. When workers inside resisted, the police opened fire. Two men were killed and two wounded. As another wave of political funerals filled Tampico streets, rumors circulated that Carranza was on the run, heading for Veracruz and possible exile. He never arrived. The president was assassinated en route on May 21, 1920.[148]

Taking advantage of the political turmoil that followed the death of the president, the oil workers went out on a massive strike. The tank builders and smiths started the mobilization in July. Only one demand survives in the record: equal pay for equal work. The difference was glaring in that category: six to eight pesos for nationals, sixteen dollars for foreigners.[149] Given the continuing inflationary pressures on the peso and the fluctuation in the exchange rates, the gap was enormous. But that was not the only significance of the demand. The two unions were also making political and ideological claims that reaffirmed their politicized culture and radical discourse at a time of national political uncertainty. To begin with, by proclaiming their equality with foreigners, the men rejected the discrimination and racism the oil companies built into the labor hierarchy. In addition, in the context of the 1917 Constitution, the demand for equal pay for equal work meant the men were also demanding that the oil companies respect the law of the land. Thus, the workers reaffirmed both nationalism and anarcho-syndicalist egalitarian ideals before foreign capital and nationals of dubious revolutionary credentials. The message could not have been lost on Obregón and Morones, especially when a general oil worker strike took place a few days later: between ten thousand and twenty thousand oil workers participated, closing down all the refineries in the port again.[150]

Unfortunately, the historical record is silent on the results of the strikes. Given that revolutionary officials were preoccupied with the political crisis stemming from Carranza's death, repression was unlikely this time around. For the same reason, the possibility that the companies made some concession cannot be discounted. Although Mexican smiths and

---

[148] González Salas, *Acercamiento*, p. 164.
[149] A. Lartigue to Municipal President, July 5, 1920, AHAT, Exp. 78–1920.
[150] *The New York Times*, July 15, 1920; González Salas, *Del reloj*, pp. 206–208.

tank builders never made the same wages as their foreign counterparts before nationalization, they might have received a wage increase like the mechanics. If so, that would have been the last partial victory the oil workers enjoyed under the banner of anarcho-syndicalism.

The "Bust" of 1921

In 1920 and 1921 the oil workers faced an uncoordinated but joint frontal attack from their eternal class enemies: the state and capital. The workers lost. The Mexican state-in-gestation attacked first. Obregón became president in 1920, ending the civil war. He settled with the Zapatistas, persuaded Villa to retire, and convinced Peláez to abandon arms in the Huasteca and return to his oil deals. Peace descended over Mexico at last after ten years. But the task of reconstruction was not easy. One problem had emerged as intractable already: ownership rights over Mexico's subsoil in the aftermath of the 1917 Constitution. As the next chapter will discuss, Article 27 made changes to Porfirian legislation that displeased the oil companies. Obregón correctly feared that continued oil worker activism would compound the problem and affect U.S. recognition for his government. One of the top items in his agenda upon becoming president, therefore, was to make the CROM the sole labor representative in the country. Those who refused to join would be destroyed.[151] Men mixed up with anarcho-syndicalists, like the oil workers, were the first targets of the new policy. Thus, the COM hall that the police occupied in May 1920 in Tampico was closed permanently. Foreign anarchists were deported, and union leaders who did not submit to Morones were marginalized.[152]

Perhaps the oil workers could have weathered the persecution of their leadership and the deportation of foreign radicals. They had enough accumulated political experience to replace both. They were not prepared, however, to avert the blow capital delivered. In response to Obregón's attempts at regulation (see Chapter 6), the companies locked out the industry between June and July, suspending all production and shipping, closing down Puerto Lobos, and dismissing about 50% of the Mexican labor force. Almost overnight, the companies fired anywhere from ten thousand to twenty-five thousand men.[153] The oil workers were

---

[151] Carr, *El movimiento*, pp. 132–135.
[152] Ibid., pp. 136, 138–140.
[153] *The New York Times*, July 4, 6, 1921; *Excélsior*, July 2–6, 1921; Meyer, *México y los Estados Unidos*, p. 176.

blindsided. The suddenness of the crisis left them without means to react effectively, not even violently. The Mexican press reported only one case of a melee between Mexican and American workers in Zacamixtle, as thousands of men, women, and children evicted from company housing began walking toward Tampico from the Huasteca. In the port countless families camped out in parks and plazas – causing an outbreak of bubonic plague in the process. Men by the hundreds vied for day labor at the refineries' gates.[154] Hundreds more walked upstream, hoping to work in Cacalilao, Buena Vista, Chapacao, and newer camps. The companies did not miss a beat: they reduced wages up to 20% for all Mexican nationals.[155]

The avenues open to the workers under the magnitude of the crisis were few. The entire region was militarized quickly as Obregón, caught by surprise as well, dispatched fifteen hundred to two thousand soldiers to protect company property and prevent "disturbances." A general strike in Tampico to protest the firings came to an abrupt halt when two U.S. Navy cruisers appeared at the sand bar.[156] In Mata Redonda, 146 men fired from Puerto Lobos sites organized a "moderate manifestation of protest" on August 18, then dispersed to return the same night and crowd around tank no. 19. Fearing the first act of worker sabotage ever was about to take place, soldiers ordered the workers to disperse. The men responded with gunfire, escaping without further incident.[157] "Not listening to supplications nor promises of aid," wrote a Mexican official, workers came up with a solution: free train tickets to leave oil country.[158] They became vociferous when a hurricane struck in September and the companies dismissed several thousand more men from flooded upstream camps. Families poured back into Tampico, itself reeling from the storm's destruction. Checkmated by the companies and nature, Obregón gave in to workers' demands. He ordered free passage for all the workers the railroad could carry. Thousands upon thousands of men, women, and children departed in September, October, and November.[159]

[154] *Excélsior*, July 8–9, 1921.
[155] Informe sobre emigración obrera, July 23, 1921, AGN/DT, Caja 329, Exp. 30; Mr. Frederic N. Watriss to the Under-Secretary of State, July 7, 1921, in *Papers*, 1921, vol. 2, p. 449; Ocasio-Meléndez, "Mexican Urban History," p. 269.
[156] *The New York Times*, July 6, 11, 1921; Meyer, *México y los Estados Unidos*, pp. 176, 201.
[157] Amplía informe acerca de motín en Mata Redonda, Tampico, August 21, 1921, AGN/DT, Caja 329, Exp. 30.
[158] Movimiento de personal en las compañías petroleras, November 10, 1921, AGN/DT, Caja 326, Exp. 5.
[159] *The New York Times*, October 9, 1921; Telegram from the Municipal President to the State Governor, October 17, 1921, AHAT, Exp. 83–1921; Inspector Eliseo Garza to the Chief,

Those who held on to their jobs tried to respond by advancing their organization further. They discussed the formation of a single industry-wide union, the *Gran Unión de Trabajadores Petroleros*.[160] September 1921, however, was not the historical moment for such a leap. The workers were under siege like never before. In addition to firings and wage cuts across the board, the companies changed hiring policies. Labor-intensive tasks, drilling, and construction were spun off to contractors who, in turn, subcontracted men as temporary workers one project at a time. Subcontracted men lost the concessions the unions had squeezed from the companies. Blacklisted "troublemakers," often men with years of work and political experience, lost all possibility of employment. Faced with overwhelming oilmen power, the idea of an industrial union did not get off the ground. The most the unions could do was to demand that dismissed workers receive the severance pay they were entitled to according to law.[161] After a decade of class conflict, the oil workers were finally unequivocally crushed.

Nevertheless, the workers scored a victory. As the following chapter will show, one of the results of the dismissal of half the work force was a change in the terms of the debate. Taking advantage of the fact that the whole nation was focused on their plight, the workers delivered a black eye to the companies. They helped bring to light the worst environmental and social practices of the oil companies and thus played a key role in discrediting the notion that the oil industry was synonymous with progress.

Most scholars regard the decade from 1910 to 1920 as a period of failure for Mexican labor in general. The reasons they give include the destruction of the COM, the loss of most strikes, the lack of union recognition across the country, and the lack of effectiveness of Article 123.[162] The demise of the oil workers in 1921 certainly fits the pattern, but the legacy of anarcho-syndicalism was significant. The distrust of authority, political parties, and politicians inscribed in revolutionary syndicalism advanced the cause of Mexican workers at large, as no revolutionary official could dismiss them as a sector – a fact that remains true to this day. Likewise,

Department of Labor, November 10, 1921, AGN/DT, Caja 326, Exp 5. Thousands of passes granted to oil workers and their families can be found in AGN/DT Cajas 313–316.

[160] Taibo II and Vizcaíno, *Memoria*, p. 134.

[161] de Gortari, "Petróleo y clase obrera," pp. 148–150.

[162] See, for example, Mirna A. Benítez and Leopoldo Alafita Méndez, "La industria petrolera como frontera interna en el estado de Veracruz: 1900–1930," in *Veracruz, un tiempo,* pp. 9–20; Jonathan Brown, "Foreign Oil Companies, Oil Workers, and the Mexican Revolutionary State in the 1920s," in *Multinational Enterprise in Historical Perspective,* edited by Alice Teichova, Maurice Lery-Leboyer, and Helga Nussbaum (Cambridge: Cambridge University Press, 1986), p. 264; Celis Salgado, *La industria,* pp. 192–193.

anarcho-syndicalist discourse and practical demands played an important role in gaining rights for labor through their influence on the men who drafted Article 123. The article became an important rallying point and political tool for workers, an opportunity for advancing the organization and politicization of Mexican workers. Syndicalism also accounted for the powerful streak of independent unionism not only among oil workers, but also in railroad workers and longshoremen. Their critical thought and radical critique would continue to test official revolutionary leadership in the postrevolutionary period. In addition, the radicals helped the oil workers in particular to develop a culture of defiance that challenged foreigners' prejudiced view of Mexicans and encouraged anti-interventionist sentiment. In so doing, this curious bunch of internationalists nurtured a profound feeling of nationalism among Mexican oil workers and others.

The red-and-black roots of the oil workers, in fact, would show vividly in the final years of the foreign oil industry, years after anarcho-syndicalism was dead and buried. As official revolutionary leaders made the transition from war to reconstruction, the oil workers continued to make use of radical ideas and direct-action tactics to advance their interests as well as to contest the meaning of the Mexican Revolution. Thus, trace elements of revolutionary syndicalism informed all oil union struggles of the prenationalization period and hence one of the most important hallmarks in the history of modern Mexico: the 1938 nationalization. Even in defeat, therefore, anarcho-syndicalists exerted an influence far exceeding their numbers.

If the set of changes that comprised the ecology of oil remained on course into 1921, it was not because the oil workers had not done their utmost to derail them. Mexican oil workers were not thinking about ecology or the environment per se. To the degree that they drank deep from the well of early twentieth-century revolutionary syndicalism, they accepted visions of progress that proclaimed nature as an entity that had evolved for the service of man. They shared that view with the Porfirians and the revolutionaries. However, because the workers literally created the wealth men extracted from nature but did not receive any of the riches, they wanted redistribution to obtain their fair share of the wealth, just as the foreigners did, at least. To achieve those goals, they fashioned a culture of defiance and a practice of militant unionism that confronted the companies in every way. They resisted industry discipline, defied labor hierarchies and discriminatory practices, and agitated tirelessly against a capitalist development model. Taking advantage of the chaos of revolution, the oil workers tried hard to turn vague dreams into tangible realities, challenging official revolutionaries just as much as they defied their foreign employers in discourse and in action. But simultaneously taking on powerful international capital and even a weak state was more than the oil workers could handle. The companies and the revolutionary leadership coincided in assaulting precociously politicized men with utopia in the brain and direct-action tactics at hand. The defeat was perhaps inevitable, but not readily predictable. Even if they shared their distaste for radical syndicalist workers, the companies and the revolutionary leadership did not agree on much else. That conflict also revolved around the changes the companies introduced to the region: it represented the official revolutionary challenge to the ecology of oil.

6

REVOLUTIONARIES, CONSERVATION, AND WASTELAND

¿Qué acontecerá, digo yo, con esos campos en que las emul-
siones de chapopote y agua han dejado inútiles millares de
hectáreas? Acaso es el propietario el que única y exclusiva-
mente resiente los perjuicios? No, es el Estado también pues
aún suponiendo que esos charcos fuesen quemados, las tierras
habrán perdido por dicha causa el resultado de su beneficio
agrícola, único índice de riqueza estable en el país.

M. Méndez, February 1, 1937

Oil exploitation is not always a benefit, for it has imperiled the
progress of some Mexican regions, among them Las Huastecas,...says Ing. José D. Baez, chief of the petroleum department. He sees "desolation, ruin and degeneration" among the
inhabitants of this region as a result of petroleum exploitation... "Fantastic wealth extracted from the subsoil not only
evaporates without hardly a trace, but is destructive, for it has
ruined numerous communities of people who loved work and
the land."

Enclosure to dispatch number 3862 of August 24, 1936,
from the American Embassy, Mexico City

If the rude men directly affected by the changes and processes of the
ecology of oil responded by fashioning and nurturing a confrontational
culture and politics, they were not alone. The national revolutionary leadership also expressed its discontent with the oil apparatus the moment the
bullets started flying across the Huasteca. As soon as they could, the revolutionaries began building institutions and emitting decrees aimed at regulating the industry. An explicit ethic of conservation drove their efforts,
but the weakness of the revolutionary state-in-formation and the strength
of the oil companies thwarted them. Patently defeated by the mid-
1920s, the revolutionaries nonetheless changed the terms of the debate.
After 1921, foreign oil ceased to be associated with progress. A narrative

of wasteland emerged in Mexican national discourse instead. It would remain dominant through the 1938 nationalization and into the present. Likewise, new agrarian policies born out of Article 27 of the 1917 Constitution allowed the indigenes of the Huasteca to reemerge as actors to claim ownership of a radically changed landscape. The results of their efforts were more mixed, as the impetus for land reform ebbed and flowed with successive administrations. The Mexican government nevertheless continued trying to erode the power of the oil companies and reconfigure their practices into the late 1930s. Again, the efforts failed. The emergent revolutionary state simply was not strong enough to impose its priorities on multinational oil.

The Regulatory Impulse

The first step the revolutionary leadership took to address what it saw as excessive oil industry power was to exert state authority over production through taxation and regulation. President Francisco Madero inaugurated the trend in 1912 with a modest 20 Mexican cents on production per barrel, but failed. General Cándido Aguilar made similar efforts at the local level. In 1913 Aguilar decreed his own tax on oil production. He was as unsuccessful in collecting as Madero, however. Upon gaining control of Tampico in 1914 and becoming provisional governor of Veracruz, Aguilar tried again, shifting focus to the issue of land leases and sales. Accusing the companies of

> all kinds of abuses and crimes, including the falsification of land titles, marriage certificates, birth certificates, and all sorts of documents, falsification of signatures of those who could not write, supplying sons and heirs that did not exist or suppressing those who did, burning down houses and *potreros*, and homicides,

he decreed in August that parties to leases and sales had to apply for state permits before concluding new deals.[1] The penalty for circumventing the permits was unequivocal: the lots in question would be confiscated.[2]

---

[1] Cándido Aguilar, *El génesis del conflicto petrolero en nuestro país* (Mexico City: Editorial de Izquierda de la Cámara de Diputados, 1949), p. 8.

[2] Decreto No. 3, LGO, tomo I, no. 2 (September 10, 1914). As Meyer documents, the decree also declared null and void all contracts made while Huerta was in power. Although the companies were outraged at that and enlisted Washington's support in its opposition, the fact of the matter was that most contracts in the Huasteca had been signed by 1906 rather than between 1913–1914. Meyer, *México y los Estados Unidos,* pp. 94–95.

Thus Aguilar attempted to slow down the wholesale alienation of rainforest from native owners to the oil companies. As was becoming customary, however, the Americans complained to Washington and refused to comply with the decree. Needless to say, Aguilar was unable to enforce his own laws once again. Undeterred, in 1915 the governor imposed a two-cent tax (Mexican) on each barrel of crude. This time he met with more success, as he threatened to shut down the pipeline of noncompliers just as the demand for petroleum in Europe was in apogee.[3]

Aguilar's actions at the state level were not isolated. On the contrary, they merely anticipated the vision and work the leader of the revolutionary faction in control of Tampico, Venustiano Carranza, had for the future of the industry at the national level. Between 1915 and 1916 Carranza began laying the groundwork to regulate many aspects of the oil industry. In January 1915, as "First Chief of the Constitutionalist Army, Acting as the Executive of the United States of Mexico, and Chief of the Revolution," Carranza decreed that oil exploration and exploitation was suspended until the revolutionary government had the opportunity to establish regulatory laws. The goal was deceptively simple: conservation.

Conservation

The first chief justified the suspension of oil production on environmental grounds. The 1915 decree argued that the companies' practices caused "great damage to agriculture and to the waterway communications of the country." The new law also declared that the industry left benefits neither "to the nation [n]or the government."[4] In practice the decree did not stop production. Carranza lacked the power to enforce the decree, but it demonstrated that the revolutionary leadership was not ignorant of the environmental impact of oil development. Exactly what it intended to do about it became clear soon.

Despite the fact that Carranza was not assured of victory over rival revolutionary factions, he initiated the reconstruction of the state apparatus early in 1915. He knew that he could not advance the regulatory impulse solely by decree. Institutions were necessary. To address oil matters specifically, Carranza organized the *Comisión Técnica del Petróleo* two months

3 Ricardo Corzo Ramírez, José G. González Sierra, David A. Skerritt,... *nunca un desleal: Cándido Aguilar, 1889–1960* (Mexico City: El Colegio de México and El Gobierno del Estado De Veracruz, 1986), pp. 100–101.
4 Decree of January 7, 1915, in *Papers*, 1915, pp. 872–873.

after the January decree. He placed his son-in-law Cándido Aguilar at the political helm. The staff was composed of young engineers, middle class professionals with revolutionary leanings and strong nationalist feelings. Their assigned task was to "study the industry and propose laws for its regulation." One of the *técnicos*, engineer Pastor Rouaix, became Carranza's secretary of industry later in the year. In that position, he quickly set up the Department of Petroleum and began publishing the *Boletín del Petróleo*. The first issue spelled out the view of the nascent revolutionary government unambiguously. The editorial declared that "Mexican petroleum ought to be considered like a great, but exhaustible, national wealth and for that reason the State ought to care for its conservation and best utilization."[5] Conservation thus was the official policy of the revolutionary leadership as early as 1916. The notion became a mantra in the *Boletín*. By the fall of 1916, open criticism of the way the companies conducted business was commonplace. The flares burning off natural gas in the Juan Casiano wells, for example, were labeled "*un despilfarro*" (a prodigal wastefulness) or worse, a "crime."[6]

To further the goal of state formation and tighten control over key economic sectors, Carranza emitted another decree in August. This one annulled all state laws under the purview of the secretary of industry – oil, mining, banking, forestry, and waterways under federal jurisdiction – and shifted that authority to the federal government. Thereafter state governors, like Aguilar, no longer had the formal authority to issue regulatory decrees of any kind. Decrees already issued, moreover, were null and void. Although it may appear that Aguilar and Carranza were working at cross-purposes, they were not. The justification for the centralization of power spelled out in the law shows they shared the same goals. The revolutionary leadership identified closely the future of the nation with state control over nature. Reflecting on petroleum specifically, the decree argued that hydrocarbons constituted a "source of wealth" that was "immense in quantity and incalculable in value." That potential wealth compelled the "General Government" to "guard jealously" the "conservation of national riches, avoiding as much as possible their deterioration or diminution." Conservation of such "riches," argued Carranza, increased the chances of peace and stability in the country.[7] A *Boletín*

---

[5] Quoted in Brown, *Oil and Revolution*, p. 220.
[6] BP, vol. 2, no. 3 (September 1916), p. 206 and no. 5 (November 1916), p. 419.
[7] Documento 5, "La Legislación petrolera en México, 1887–1927," *Boletín* of the Archivo General de la Nación, Tercera Serie, Tomo VII, Vol. 3–4 (July–December 1983), p. 23.

article several months later explained the idea further. The oil pools, noted the writer, were exhaustible, given that their life "geologically speaking" was truly "ephemeral." For that reason, it behooved the government to protect the country's underground oil rivers; therein lay the future economic independence of Mexico.[8] In other words, state control of nature and the conservation thereof were ultimately issues of national sovereignty.

Article 27

Yet through 1916, the revolutionaries were still operating under Porfirian laws that had granted landowners property rights over the subsoil. Until those were overturned, the companies had the law on their side as they transformed the social fabric and the environment of the Huasteca. That legality came into question with the proclamation of the 1917 Constitution. On the question of petroleum, Article 27 was key. The article reversed Porfirian legislation and returned to the Spanish colonial legal tradition that established the nation as the depository of ownership over the country's territory, surface and subsurface alike. Specifying that rivers, mountains, lakes, "beds of precious stones, rock salt, and salt lakes," as well as "solid mineral fuels; petroleum and all hydrocarbons – solid or gaseous" belonged to the nation, Article 27 reclaimed the ownership of nature for the nation as a matter of principle.[9]

Article 27, however, did not eliminate private property. On the contrary, the article stipulated that the nation had "the right to transmit title thereof to private persons." Private ownership of nature, therefore, was recognized and secured, but only as an artifice that emanated through a concession from the nation. As such, private property could be subjected to the state's regulatory powers. The first regulation was included in the article itself: only Mexican enterprises, nationals, or naturalized citizens could become property owners.[10] Foreigners and foreign companies could enjoy limited concessionary rights only. Under no circumstances, moreover, could foreigners "acquire direct dominion" over lands

[8] BP, vol. 3, no. 1 (January 1917), p. 23.
[9] Article 27, reproduced in L. J. de Bekker, *The Plot Against Mexico* (New York: Alfred A. Knopf, 1919), p. 203.
[10] In December 1916 Carranza had decreed that all foreigners had to become naturalized Mexican citizens to acquire property, so Article 27 only reaffirmed the principle. For the oilmen, the decree and the article meant they had to incorporate their companies in Mexico instead of the United States or Europe. BP, vol. 3, no. 2 (February 1917), p. 135.

or waters within fifty kilometers from the coasts of the country. Furthermore, Article 27 stated that

> the nation shall have at all times the right to impose on private property such limitations as the public interest may demand as well as the right to regulate the development of natural resources, which are susceptible of appropriation, in order to conserve them and equitably to distribute the public wealth.[11]

The implications for the oil industry were enormous. By reinserting the nation into the property equation, the revolutionary leadership undid the absoluteness of private ownership of nature. It voided the notion that nature was but a commodity that could be negotiated as a simple matter of contracts between individual private parties. The state not only decided who could own property, but also reserved the right to regulate all contractual negotiations involving the transfer of property and to reverse them altogether under specific circumstances. That meant that the changes in land tenure patterns central to the ecology of oil that had been taking place in the Huasteca since 1900 were neither final nor secure once the Constitution became effective on May 1, 1917. On the contrary, they were "susceptible" to state intervention and even to "expropriation for reasons of public utility." If the state found that the oil companies did not fulfill the definition or requirements of public utility (a concept left undefined in Article 27), it could retrieve nature from those who held title to it. The future of almost six million acres of company controlled land throughout Mexico thus hung in the balance.

But that was not all. Article 27 also brought land use into question explicitly. It declared that the state could regulate the exploitation of "natural resources" specifically to "conserve them." Overseeing the uses of nature and ensuring their conservation were now the direct responsibility of the state. There is no doubt that the oil industry had been a source of inspiration for the decree. The lead author of Article 27 was Pastor Rouaix, the founder of the Department of Petroleum and secretary of industry. His two-year experience as an industry observer had convinced him that the companies, concerned primarily with profits, could not be trusted to protect the country's fossil fuels. That responsibility had to rest with an entity motivated by goals and a vision broader than quarterly returns on investment – that is, the nation. But since the revolutionary leadership had decided not to eliminate private property, the best means

---

[11] Article 27, in de Bekker, *The Plot*, p. 203.

to prevent the exhaustion of the oil mantles was not only to nationalize the subsoil once more, but also to scrutinize the uses of private land and regulate them as necessary.[12]

Neither the revolutionary leadership in general nor Article 27 in particular was concerned with ecology per se. Neither was environmentalist in outlook or principles; that is, neither the professionals at the Petroleum Department nor the Carrancista leadership was preoccupied with protection of nature itself or for itself. They did not oppose changes in the landscape, changes in land use, or even habitat destruction and the accompanying transformations of the ecology of oil specifically. Even Miguel Angel de Quevedo, one of Mexico's first and most committed conservationists and the man directly responsible for a "conservation plank" in the Constitution according to one historian, advocated for the preservation of nature – that is, nonhuman use of the environment, the more common alternative to conservation at the time. As one historian argues, Quevedo did not "espouse the view that nature had an intrinsic right to exist irrespective of whether that existence served people."[13] No one in the revolutionary leadership, moreover, ever considered indigenous ecological knowledge and land use practices as an alternative land-based ethic or approach to development.[14] That generation of revolutionaries was utilitarian instead: what they objected to was the "Waste of Natural Resources," as the title of a *Boletín* article explained.[15]

In other words, the middle-class professionals and revolutionary leadership, like their nineteenth-century predecessors, believed in progress, development, modernization, and the exploitation of nature. They, like the Científicos and the oil barons, saw nature as a resource. They recognized that wealth resided in exploitation and for that very reason, objected to "wasteful" practices. Their nationalism and familiarity with radical ideologies like socialism and anarchism, however, distinguished them from the Porfirians and the oil magnates. The revolutionaries envisioned nature as a collective good whose exploitation required conscientious management. The managers of nature would be men like

---

[12] Editorial, "La nacionalización del petróleo," BP, vol. 3, no. 5 (May 1917), pp. 401–403.

[13] Lane Simonian, *Defending the Land of the Jaguar: A History of Conservation in Mexico* (Austin: University of Texas Press, 1995), pp. 77–79.

[14] Even Zapata, the revolutionary leader most closely associated with concern for the land and peasant practices, seems to have been partial to agroindustrial tendencies nowadays criticized by environmentalists as ecologically destructive. Millon, *Zapata*, pp. 51–57. However, no one has yet researched Zapata's environmental views or the ecological implications of his demands and programs.

[15] BP, vol. 2, no. 5 (November 1916), p. 415.

themselves: middle class and national in vision, capable of articulating what was best for the country as a whole. Within that framework, the professionals who drafted Article 27 believed that conservation was the best means to prolong the exploitation of exhaustible resources. Thus, they could guarantee that nature would yield riches for the long-term benefit of the nation in its entirety, rather than for the short-term return on private investment. As engineer Santiago González Cordero wrote, conservation did not mean "keeping this [oil] resource underground for an indefinite time, rather, [it meant] not wasting it, not failing to take advantage of it selling it at a minimum price; rather [it meant] getting the most from it" for all of Mexico.[16]

Nevertheless, conservation could have environmental benefits. Although it would not eliminate habitat loss nor reverse the ecological damage that wells like Dos Bocas, Potrero del Llano No. 4, or Juan Casiano Nos. 6 and 7 had caused by 1917, the conservationist ethic of Article 27 promised to avert further devastation on the same scale if the elimination of "waste" alone were successful. Prevention of spills and fires; development of uses and markets for natural gas; prevention of evaporation; regular and systematic maintenance of pipeline and facilities; proper tubing, cementing, and closing of wells; and similar conservationist measures could certainly slow down the rate of environmental destruction in the Huasteca.[17] Likewise, conservationist measures would not eliminate malaria, tuberculosis, and hydrocarbon poisonings among oil workers, but they could decrease the number of accidents that plagued the industry and destroyed men's health and bodies. Conservation would not reverse the alienation of the rainforest from its Teenek owners, nor would it prevent their marginalization and the disappearance of their ecological knowledge; but it did promise containment of the physical devastation that might give indigenous owners an opportunity to restore their ecology under more propitious political circumstances.

Article 27, however, did threaten to destabilize the ecology of oil. Both articles opened up a new battlefront for the oil barons. As the companies correctly argued, Article 27 represented an assault on their extractive practices, core beliefs, and conception of nature. By eliminating the absolute right to private property and instituting state tutelage over land use,

<hr />

[16] Santiago González Cordero, "El Derecho de los Trajadores Petroleros Huelguistas y el Derecho de la Nación," October 1937, AGN(AHH, Legajo 1857–117, Legajo #2.
[17] See, for example, Max. W. Ball, "La conservación del petróleo," translated and reviewed by engineer José Vázquez Schiaffino, BP, vol. 3, no. 3 (March 1917), pp. 232–236, 256–262.

Article 27 brought into question not only the practices of the industry, but also the existence of the companies themselves. Their distrust was confirmed by the decrees the provisional government began emitting as soon as the Constitution became effective. In April 1917 Carranza imposed a tax on petroleum wastes (*desperdicios*) that included spills. Shortly thereafter, a "fire prevention" decree delineated the distances that government experts believed should be maintained between tanks and other structures. In August the Department of Petroleum sent out *Circular* #1 advising the companies that "as a conservation measure" drilling could take place only in lots measuring a minimum of four hectares. Weeks later, another circular stipulated that all storage tanks were to be painted pearl gray or white to minimize evaporation.[18] By November, the companies found even less comfort in the fact that Cándido Aguilar and Pastor Rouiax were drafting the statutory law (*ley orgánica*) that would implement Article 27 specifically.[19]

"The Squeeze by Decrees"

The revolutionaries turned up the legislative heat against the companies in 1918 and 1919. The most surprising decree came out of the Veracruz legislature, despite the fact that their authority in oil matters had been removed in 1916. Impatient with the pace of oil legislation at the national level given the social and environmental costs of oil production in their midst, the state Congress passed a law "recovering all the rights to the subsoil of all the lots that through any title are held by or might be held by, and all other rights of any type whatsoever . . . , misters Pearson and Son Limited." That was not all. The state legislators also included punitive measures, demanding that

> misters Pearson and Son Limited and the company or companies they
> might have organized, or [might] organize and their associates will
> return to the state executive, in cash, the entire value of all petroleum
> and carbons or hydrogen hydrocarbons and their derivatives that they
> might have extracted since 1906.[20]

---

[18] BP, vol. 3, no. 6 (June 1917), p. 517; *The Mexican Review*, vol. 1, no. 8 (May 1917); Circular #1, BP, vol. 4, no. 2 (August 1917) p. 182; *El Pueblo*, July 24, 1917, SMU/ED, Box 102; File Folder 5138; Circular #3, BP, vol. 4, no. 3 (September 1917), p. 245.

[19] "Iniciativa de ley órganica del Artículo 27 Constitucional presentada por el C. Gobernador del Estado de Veracruz," November 19, 1917, in *Legislación petrolera mexicana: Documentos*, Tomo 1 (Mexico City: Secretaría de Industria, Comercio y Trabajo, 1919), pp. 281–330. For a copy of the proposed law, see Argument of General Cándido Aguilar in support of the petroleum bill, in *Papers*, 1918, pp. 689–708.

[20] Quoted in Corzo Ramírez et al., . . . *nunca*, p. 210.

In one fell swoop the state of Veracruz effectively sought to expropriate El Aguila without using the term. As one scholar noted, Pearson and Son "did not take it lying down" and set their lawyers on the case. The "squeeze by decrees," as Standard Oil dubbed the process, continued into 1918. In February Carranza emitted a decree requiring all title holders and aspirants to oil rights to register or apply for their rights, a procedure called *denuncio*, before any drilling could commence or continue. Thus, the government hoped to figure out who was drilling where and to gain some control over the process. In addition, the decree demanded the companies pay rent and royalties owed.[21]

Nevertheless, the oilmen and the revolutionary leaders both knew full well that no such monster as a revolutionary state existed. Not only did the Veracruz Congress pass oil laws despite Carranza's explicit prohibition, but also Carranza himself emitted more decrees extending the deadlines for the companies to comply with previous decrees than actual new ones. When the industry protested the February 19 law, for example, Carranza decreed an extension in May and another one in July. The only other new law proposed in 1918 was the regulatory decree Aguilar and Rouaix had been drafting since late 1917. It reached the Congress in August, but apparently died there.[22] Similarly, the Department of Petroleum complained time and again that the companies dismissed their regulations and blatantly ignored their earnest antiwaste campaigns.[23] Not even threats of outright "confiscation" of wells and destruction of work if the companies did not file drilling permits brought compliance. Neither did the actual sending of troops to stop oil drilling in 1919, surely an act born of utter frustration on Carranza's part.[24]

Indeed, the revolutionaries did not have military control over the Huasteca. Manuel Peláez did. The hacendado, predictably, rejected Article 27.[25] The article put at risk hacendados' royalties. Since they no longer

[21] Standard Oil Company (N.J.), *Confiscation or Expropriation? Mexico's Seizure of the Foreign-Owned Oil Industry* (New York: Standard Oil Company, N.J., 1940), p. 14.

[22] *The Mexican Oil Controversy as told in Diplomatic Correspondence Between the United States and Mexico* (n/p, October 1920), p. 30.

[23] BP, vol. 4, no. 3 (September 1917), p. 245; Editorial, BP, vol. 5, no. 1 (January 1918), pp. 1–3; BP, vol. 5, no. 6 (June 1918), p. 568; BP, vol. 6, no. 2 (August 1918), p. 150; José Vázquez Schiaffino, Joaquín Santaella, and Aquiles Elorduy, *Informes sobre la cuestión petrolera* (Mexico City: Imprenta de la Cámara de Diputados, 1919), pp. 7, 10.

[24] *The Mexican Oil Controversy*, p. 31.

[25] Article 27 had the "agrarian question" in mind beyond the oil industry. As such, it would become the basis for all land reform efforts during subsequent revolutionary governments, something that would affect the hacendados directly. Jorge Sayeg Helu, *Pastor Rouaix*. Series: El pensamiento de la Revolución (Mexico City: Secretaría de Educación, 1968), p. 53; Brown, *Oil and Revolution*, p. 255.

owned the subsoil, they could not assume that the embryonic revolutionary state Carranza represented would sanction the contracts they had
made with the companies. On the contrary, opposition was the best option
to secure their own interests, too.

La Reacción – Backlash

Working in tandem, if not actually in coordination, Peláez and the companies led the opposition to Article 27 in the Huasteca. Peláez pronounced
his opposition to the *Magna Carta* and the first chief in May and again in
December 1917. All the while he praised the oil companies financing him
"because it is our duty as Mexicans to grant protection and give hospital-
ity to all foreigners who, attracted by our institutions and the richness of
our land, have come with their wealth, labor, capital and civilization to
take part in our life."[26] Such Porfirian worldview appealed to the deposed
dictator's nephew, Félix Díaz, who became an ally in early 1918. Peláez's
brimming war chest – which bought him two thousand "perfectly armed"
men, although he claimed to have 30,450 troops commanded by thirty-
nine generals – combined with Díaz's flagging efforts nonetheless meant
the alliance did not survive the year. By September, Peláez had abandoned
Díaz and was seeking command of the avowed anti-Carrancistas, the Zapatistas. By mid-1919, moreover, the hacendado was secure enough in his
own position in the Huasteca to compete for the leadership of the movement against Carranza at the national level. True to hacendado interests,
if not to his rebel allies, Peláez sought out anti-Carrancistas until the end.
In 1920 he selected Obregón over Carranza and ended on the winning
side when the first chief was assassinated and his former subordinate
became president. At last aligned with a clear winner, Peláez abandoned
the armed struggle and after a number of diplomatic posts abroad, settled
into the oil business until his retirement.[27]

Still, for as long as it lasted, the hacendado "oil-rich rebellion" was
wholly dependent on the companies' largesse. They were the truly powerful party in the dispute and the ones called on to do the heavy lifting
in the confrontation with Carranza. As such, they spared no expense in

[26] Quoted in Brown, *Oil and Revolution*, p. 274. Such adherence to the past may also have
alienated indigenous landowners hurt by the legislation that Article 27 overturned and
might have convinced them to stay away from his movement – not that Peláez needed
them anymore by 1917.
[27] Womack, Jr., *Zapata*, pp. 301, 310, 313, 319, 340–342, 360. The figures on the number
of troops are from Brown, *Oil and Revolution*, pp. 265, 277.

Mexican and American law firms to overturn Article 27 or, short of that, to make sure it did not apply to them. As historian Lorenzo Meyer has documented, the companies fought tooth and nail against Article 27 from the moment it came under discussion during the Constitutional Convention in late 1916 and pursued the same course with every regulatory decree thereafter. Each move Carranza made the companies countered with a barrage of lawsuits, diplomatic pressure from U.S. officials, and propaganda campaigns, until the first chief was shot dead.[28] Thus, the first revolutionary president had confronted the companies and lost at every turn.

Ironically, by the time of Carranza's murder, Pearson himself favored regulation – at least in his native country. On November 6, 1918, Pearson (Lord Cowdray) addressed the British House of Lords on the topic of drilling for oil in England. After posing the question in a decidedly unflattering manner, "what happens from promiscuous, uncontrolled drilling?" he recited a litany of dangers and losses of oil, which he argued he had "seen in the United States." He had seen them also in Mexico since his well at Dos Bocas had blown up in 1908 and Potrero del Llano in 1914, but Pearson chose not to acknowledge them. The destruction, the oil Lord concluded, led him to refuse drilling in England unless the state regulated the industry. He explained, "I mean controlled it – regulate the number of wells that should be put down and the method in which they should be put down."[29] If Pearson's change of heart protected his native England, it came too late for Mexico. Only a couple of weeks earlier he had transferred management of El Aguila to Royal Dutch Shell, and so his clamor for regulation at home did not extend past the eastern shores of the Atlantic.

The Americans, by contrast, were more consistent. They were opposed to regulation wherever they operated, beginning with the United States. Since the nineteenth century and until the Great Depression, the "rule of capture" remained the law of the land north of the border. Whoever "captured" the oil first, even if the action depleted an adjacent field, was the rightful owner. Conservation and government regulation was anathema to these masters of nature, and the oil companies fought them accordingly and successfully in the United States throughout the 1920s.[30]

---

[28] Meyer, *México y los Estados Unidos*, pp. 107–149.
[29] Spender, *Weetman*, p. 213.
[30] Yergin, *The Prize*, pp. 212, 220–222, 228, 256. Yergin adds that the rule of capture was not overturned by U.S. courts until 1933. The battle over conservation and environmental

The double standard of laissez-faire ideology predominated among oil moguls, who rejected regulation of their activities but demanded state intervention on their behalf at home and abroad. Few were the state or federal officials in the United States who dared to speak of restrictions on capital, even timid ones like ending wasteful practices, throughout the "roaring 1920s." The oilmen enjoyed the full support of powerful figures like the mining mogul and intimate friend of Edward L. Doheny, Senator Albert B. Fall, and the Republican elected president in 1920, Warren G. Harding.

Regulation Postponed

Yet in revolutionary Mexico, the leadership of the state-in-formation proved to be as stubborn as the companies, if not as powerful. Despite the bitter and murderous disagreements among them, they did agree on Article 27 and the need for conservation. Alvaro Obregón was no exception. One of Obregón's first acts upon becoming president after the assassination of Carranza in 1920 was to reassert the legitimacy and validity of his predecessor's decrees. In January 1921 he announced that "drilling permits could be granted only to those individuals and companies who had complied with Carranza's earlier decree to apply for concessions." His first and second decrees, issued on May 24 and June 7, imposed taxes on petroleum production; he thus aimed at conservation, like Carranza before him, and justified these aims on environmental grounds more forcefully than ever.[31]

The results of hyperexploitation were undeniable by 1921. The companies had alerted Carranza to the presence of saltwater intrusion and other signs of exhaustion in Tepetate already in January 1920.[32] On March 11, 1921, furthermore, Pearson had admitted to the Mexican press that the Huasteca wells were at risk because of the "manner in which they have been exploited."[33] The worst fears of the professionals at the Department of Petroleum were coming true. They could find little comfort in the fact

protection, of course, still rages. See Martin V. Melosi, "Energy and Environment in the United States: The Era of Fossil Fuels," *Environmental Review*, vol. 11, no. 3 (Fall 1987), pp. 167–188.

[31] Hall, *Oil, Banks, and Politics*, pp. 26–27, 109.

[32] Mr. T. J. Ryder to Señor Rodolfo Montes, New York, January 14, 1920, in *Papers*, 1920, vol. 3, pp. 204–205.

[33] *Excélsior*, March 11, 1921.

that they had sounded the alarm since 1919, when they had editorialized that

> most of the companies try to drill guided only by an unbridled greed, by an intense rivalry and commercial competition, by a struggle in which they try to steal from each other that which they consider their own, without worrying in the least about exploiting such wealth rationally and carefully, without caring nor taking into account the future of the Mexican nation, and without regard for those who inhabit the land where they extract their riches.[34]

The actions of President Obregón, although justified by the scientific evidence, had devastating political results nevertheless. As the previous chapter noted, the companies responded to the 1921 regulations and taxes by stopping production, firing half the Mexican work force, and precipitating a social crisis in the Huasteca. Obregón was forced to retreat. He reduced the June tax by 50–60%. He also wrote two letters to President Harding, the friend of the oilmen who had yet to grant diplomatic recognition to Obregón as the legitimate ruler of Mexico. Dated July 21 and August 18, the letters assured Harding that Article 27 was not retroactive. That is, the rainforests and subsoil rights the companies had acquired before May 1, 1917 were exempted from the renationalization of nature the Constitution postulated.[35]

Obregón's private rapprochement with the United States soon became open and public capitulation to the oil companies' position. On August 30, 1921 the Mexican Supreme Court ruled on the Carranza decrees the companies had challenged. They were all overturned. Echoing Obregón's reassurances to Harding, the Court declared that Article 27 was not absolute in its application. It did not apply in cases where the interested parties could show a "positive act" undertaken to stake their claims. Since by 1921 the oil companies had opened up camps throughout the Huasteca, the 5,892,665 acres of rainforest they controlled became exempt from the law of the land.[36]

Under severe pressure from the companies, Obregón had decided to gamble. Maybe rescinding the nation's claim of absolute ownership over nature as the companies wanted would win American recognition for his government. If that were the case, Obregón would have a better chance

[34] BP, vol. 3, no. 1 (July 1919), p. 4.
[35] Hall, *Oil, Banks, and Politics*, p. 28; Meyer, *México y los Estados Unidos*, pp. 173, 177.
[36] Clagget and Valderrama, *A Revised Guide*, p. 287.

to protect the integrity of the postrevolutionary state-in-formation, as his rule would be legitimized internationally. Although compromising or abdicating on the application of Article 27 was in itself a blow to the revolutionary state, revealing its weakness vis-à-vis foreign capital, Obregón clearly felt that the continuous confrontation with the companies and the United States threatened to stunt the development of the new state in ways that may be more detrimental to Mexico in the long run. The immediate reward for the capitulation might have confirmed that analysis. Settling the crisis over Article 27 in the companies' favor meant that production began in earnest again. Despite the impending exhaustion of the Golden Lane, the companies reached their peak of extraction in Mexico in 1921 at close to two hundred million barrels. Moreover, with only half the work force, the companies continued to produce over one hundred million barrels annually through 1925 (Appendix V). Diplomatic recognition for Obregón's government, however, took time to achieve. Two more years of substantial private negotiations with U.S. officials, oilmen, and bankers passed before it finally arrived in September 1923. The concessions Obregón agreed to in the process included further guarantees to the oil companies over their land holdings; the creation of mixed, state-oil, commissions for the resolution of disputes and claims; and the establishment of the principle of compensation in case of expropriation, a package known as the Bucareli agreements.[37]

The price of stability must have been deeply disappointing for the young professionals at the Department of Petroleum. In their 1919 reports to the Mexican Congress they had argued forcefully against the retroactivity issue, that is, against the notion that Article 27 did not apply to legislation in place before 1917. The position of the nationalists who aspired to become the managers of nature was that a Constitution by definition replaced all previous laws in the name of the nation as a whole and to benefit the nation itself. The private sector could not pick and choose which articles of the Constitution applied to them and which did not. That defeated the very purpose of a Constitution in the first place.[38] Nonetheless, they kept their disappointment off the pages of the *Boletín* and opted for another course. They joined the bandwagon to overturn the narrative of progress.

---

[37] Meyer, *México y los Estados Unidos*, pp. 203–214.
[38] Documento 1, Retroactividad de la Constitución de 1917 de la Legislación del Petróleo, "La legislación," *Boletín* of the Archivo General de la Nación, pp. 45–49.

The Narrative of Wasteland

Despite the political defeat the companies inflicted on the Mexican government in 1921, the industry did not emerge unscathed from the fray. On the contrary, their 1921 offensive shattered once and for all the notion of civilization and progress the companies had cultivated since the Porfiriato. At the moment of their greatest triumph against the emergent revolutionary state and the oil workers, the companies lost the ideological struggle. Suddenly, a new oil narrative was born: a narrative of wasteland. Although the Teenek, the Mexican oil workers, the revolutionary leadership, and the middle-class professionals at the Department of Petroleum shared a discontent with the practices of the oil companies, until 1921 they had never been in the same place at the same time to express it. The opportunity finally came in mid-1921, upon the firing of half the Mexican work force from the northern Veracruz oil fields. In June and July the aggrieved parties met for the first time and changed the public perception of the foreign oil industry from harbingers of progress to perpetrators of destruction. The idea of wasteland was so powerful that it remained the dominant narrative of foreign oil in Mexico until the end of the twentieth century.[39]

When the companies shut down production and dismissed the Mexican work force in June and July 1921, Obregón sent his secretary of *Gobernación*, Plutarco Elías Calles, to the Huasteca to investigate. Calles had an important tour guide: Joaquín Santaella, one of the engineers from the Department of Petroleum responsible for the 1919 reports to Congress alerting the members to the wasteful and reckless practices of the industry. With the press in tow, Santaella showed Calles through Zacamixtle, Amatlán, Chinampa, Toteco, and other areas that at first sight "gave the impression of prosperity and abundance," but upon closer inspection revealed a darker reality. The flares of burning natural gas that illuminated the tropical night skies were a "waste." "Immorality," "scandals," and "grave crimes of blood" permeated the Huasteca. Local authorities were powerless. With the disappearance of Peláez, real power had passed not to state or municipal authorities but rather to the companies' white guards.[40]

[39] This interpretation of the foreign oil industry permeated not only the writings of the participants and many observers, but also works of fiction written up to 1986. See, for example, Icaza, *Panchito Chapopote*; Beals, *Black River*; López y Fuentes, *Huasteca*; Nájera, *Poza negra*; Moreno, *México negro*; Paco Ignacio Taibo, *De Paso* (Mexico City: Leega Literaria, 1986).

[40] *Excélsior*, May 21, 1921.

As Calles met with the diverse Huasteca groups, the criticisms and grievances different social segments had accumulated over two decades became front-page news. The oil workers showed the secretary that the oil companies had imported segregationist and discriminatory policies to Mexico. They showed Calles that their quarters were overcrowded and in "poor hygiene," prompting the secretary to declare that the health conditions the workers endured were "truly atrocious." The oil companies, Calles claimed, mistreated Mexican workers so badly that they had sent back to the countryside over thirty thousand "disabled" men in only six months. Similarly, indigenous landowners took advantage of the opportunity to denounce company land agents and lawyers, accusing them of dispossession and fraud. The Department of Petroleum inspectors stationed in Tampico chimed in, charging that the companies failed to pay any taxes on the oil they exported through the underwater pipelines at Puerto Lobos.[41]

In the first week of July, Calles made his final declarations to the press. Mincing no words, the secretary decried industry abuse of workers and indigenous people alike. He argued that the oil industry hurt small businesses, which could neither compete with the monopolies nor use their road system for transport. Furthermore, he accused the companies of "wasting" oil, "throwing away" natural gas, and "ruining the land." In two short decades, he emphasized, the companies had extracted the oil and abandoned the land, leaving the terrain "useless for agriculture." The communities emptied out, said Calles, leaving "nary a weed nor a living being."[42] Oil, in sum, had turned the Huasteca into a wasteland.

For the first time, disparate Mexican social segments touched by the industry had united in denouncing the changes and processes encapsulated in the ecology of oil. Together, the multiethnic and multiclass chorus of revolutionary leaders, indigenes, workers, and professionals created a new interpretation of the historical meaning of the industry. The new narrative was an open rejection of Díaz's nineteenth-century love affair with foreign investors. It also represented a reassertion of discursive nationalism in the face of political weakness. If Mexicans could not impose their priorities on the industry, they could at least deflate the claims to progress the oilmen and the nineteenth-century Mexican elite had shared and expounded. As a group, multiple voices in a revolutionary

[41] Ibid., June 12, July 5, 1921.
[42] Ibid., July 6, 7, 1921.

Mexico argued instead that the foreign oil industry meant exploitation at multiple levels: labor, nature, aborigines, and the nation as a whole.

A critique of the industry, however, did not mean a wholesale rejection of old-fashioned notions and practices. Revolutionary leaders and the professionals at the Department of Petroleum did not reject the progress and modernization propounded since the Liberals gained power in the mid-nineteenth century. On the contrary, they considered themselves the true heirs of that Liberal legacy, which in their interpretation Díaz had betrayed with his dictatorial powers and infatuation with European and American investors.[43] Where the revolutionary leadership differed from the companies was in espousing a nationalist version of progress narrowly defined. That is, they wanted to continue creating wealth from the exploitation of nature and modernizing the country further along a capitalist model, but they wanted to be more conservative in their environmental practices and distribute the benefits of those riches in a more equitable manner. Insofar as oil was concerned, they wanted to extract it conservatively and keep the wealth it generated within the country for reinvestment and national capitalist development. A 1927 poem entitled "Song of Tampico," reproduced in the daily *El Mundo*, captured the sentiment thus:

> I dream that tomorrow
> your soul, more than ever will be Mexican!
> that your geysers
> of liquid black gold, will not bring you
> streaks of tragedy, nor winds of death,
> nor accursed wars, nor historic ills,
> and before losing you they shall know how to protect you
> because they are the blood of your strong motherland
> that open up, smiling, immortal veins![44]

The goals of the revolutionary leadership to "protect" nature and make it "Mexican" were spelled out in the Constitution already, and the new narrative contradicted none of them. Therefore, despite the changes in the narrative, the solution Calles proposed to the crisis of 1921 was simply to pass legislation enabling Article 27.[45]

---

[43] Charles A. Hale, "The Political Myths of the Mexican Nation: Liberalism and the Revolution," Unpublished Paper, n/d.

[44] Enrique Pérez Arce, "Canto a Tampico," *El Mundo*, April 10, 1927.

[45] *Excélsior*, July 7, 1921.

Yet, even that mild suggestion was more than the newborn state could handle. Having yielded on the application of Article 27, the president did not back the statements of his secretary, nor did he support Santaella when he justified to the press the tax that precipitated the crisis. Instead, Obregón rebuffed both. Before the Mexico City press he argued that the numbers of fired Mexicans were "exaggerated." At the same time, he ordered federal troops to the region to contain the oil workers, despite the fact that Calles had told the men that the army "was not necessary."[46]

In private, moreover, Obregón reassured Washington as much as he could. He showed frank enthusiasm about a proposal for a joint oil venture with the Mexican government to undertake new exploratory work given the apparent exhaustion of the Golden Lane. The presence of the Mexican government in a joint development company could satisfy both parties. It would turn moot the question of subsoil rights without violating nationalist principles beyond the acceptable in a revolutionary state. The negotiations fell apart, however, because the oil companies ultimately refused to give up their claims to subsoil rights as a matter of principle.[47] It would be another decade before the Mexican government would try a similar experiment again. Nevertheless, even if the narrative of wasteland inaugurated in 1921 did not change the balance of power between the oil companies and the revolutionary leadership and did not reject progress and modernization at the expense of nature, it did open the doors to competing claims on the land and its uses. The first to take advantage of the opportunity were the Teenek.

Restoring the Indigenous Ecology?

Upon the workers vacating of the camps, the native population of the Huasteca regrouped to reclaim the lands they had alienated to the oil companies. Although the narrative of wasteland provided them with the language to make their demands, it was Article 27 that made the process possible. One of the promises of the article was land reform. Carranza had begun to address the issue in tandem with oil industry regulation, decreeing an Agrarian Reform Law in 1915 that promised the "restitution of lost lands," later absorbed into Article 27. In 1920 the governor of Veracruz, Adalberto Tejeda, followed up with legislation of his own, enacting the Law of Idle Lands. The purpose of the law, as its name suggests, was to pressure landowners into putting uncultivated areas into circulation

[46] Ibid., and July 9, 13, 1921.
[47] Hall, *Oil, Banks, and Politics*, pp. 32–34.

among those who lacked access to land. As such, the law was a perfect fit for the Huasteca, where hacendados held land as speculative capital in case oil were discovered.[48] As part of the effort to build institutions for the revolutionary state, the federal government had also organized a National Agrarian Commission to survey the countryside, report on land availability, and rule on petitions.[49]

In Veracruz, the new laws propitiated renewed armed revolt in the countryside. Peasants in central and southern Veracruz were the first to rebel. In the Huasteca only one incident of armed takeover of land was reported. It took place in Amatlán, where according to a newspaper account twenty armed *"bolcheviques"* occupied an hacienda in May 1922.[50] Most Teenek followed a different path: they sued the companies individually to recover their property or formed organizations that petitioned the Agrarian Commission for *ejidos*, communal lands that followed traditional indigenous land tenure systems.[51]

The environmental degradation of the Huasteca, however, affected the claims. In El Alamo, Zacamixtle, El Humo, and Potrero del Llano, for example, petitioners found that the forest they once owned "was sterile because they [the companies] converted it into a savannah."[52] Hacendados, moreover, defended themselves against claims by using the narrative of wasteland in their favor. In 1923, for example, Josefa Nuñez de Llorente refuted claims to her hacienda in El Alamo by arguing that PennMex had not only failed to pay royalties, but also ruined the forest. In a letter to the Agrarian Commission, she wrote:

> All the people who established themselves in the oil camps used and abused the natural products they could get their hands on, carrying out immoderate deforestation of precious woods such as zapote, cedar, and other hardwoods for such trivial uses such as the construction of housing and the feeding of fires... [They] used the most primitive and cruel methods of fishing in the rivers, streams, and lagoons, destroy[ing], due to their lack of moderation, the species they hunted.

[48] LGO, vol. 10, no. 775 (July 22, 1922); Corzo Ramírez et al.,... *nunca*, p. 85.
[49] Like the Department of Petroleum, the Agrarian Commission attracted young professionals committed to the revolution, but in this case the participants were agronomists and anthropologists. Hart, *Revolutionary Mexico*, p. 341.
[50] *El Dictamen*, May 17, 1922.
[51] Some of the organizations included the Sociedad Cooperativa de Campesinos de Galera, Tantoyuca, the Unión de Campesinos Agricultores de San Antonio Chinampa, and the Agrupación Agraria del Municipio de Amatlán. See AGEV/JCCA, Caja 48, n/n, 1925; Caja 67, Exp. 8, Amatlán, 1928; Caja 84, n/n, 1929.
[52] Letter to Agrarian Commissioner, El Humo, September 15, 1928, AGEV/CAM, Exp. 828, El Humo, Tepezintla.

The Agrarian Commission investigators confirmed the description, noting that out of 1,687 inhabitants, only 12 still cultivated corn "for personal consumption." El Alamo had disappeared as a tropical forest altogether. Based on those findings, the Commission ruled against the petitioners in September 1923.[53]

Other cases confirm the pattern. Thirty-five heads of household of "the indigenous race," for example, petitioned in 1929 for the unpolluted parts of the Tierra Amarilla and Palma Real haciendas belonging to Ana Gorrochotegui of the Peláez clan. According to the Agrarian Commission topographer, the land was deforested and the soil was "not very good." In order for those families to make a living by farming, they would require not the typical five hectares per household of yesteryear, but ten instead. Whether they actually received an ejido even in degraded land, however, was not clear from the record.[54] Likewise, in 1921 "a large number of indigenes" from Zacamixtle organized to petition for Lot No. 19, the only one not severely polluted because the oil company that owned never exploited it. The case was not resolved until 1963, when the descendants of the original petitioners finally received their ejido. In this case, nonetheless, the record makes no mention of what the Zacamixtle landscape looked like by the 1960s.[55]

Inhabitants of Juan Felipe who had lost their land to the Huasteca in 1902 similarly organized to reclaim the land in 1930. Because the company still had several wells in the area protected by the positive-act test of 1921, the Agrarian Commission granted 672 hectares in adjoining lands in 1932. The ruling reminded the eighty-four *ejidatarios* that they were "obligated to conserve, restore, and propagate forests and trees that might be contained in the property" still, something the restored owners explicitly said they intended to do.[56] That success inspired another thirty-four heads of household to request the neighboring Moyutla hacienda, which belonged to El Aguila since 1913 but apparently never went into production. El Aguila had sold a twenty-two-meter strip through the lot to Huasteca Petroleum for a pipeline instead. By the time the thirty-four inhabitants made their claim in 1932, however, Moyutla was no longer a

[53] Letter from Josefa Nuñez de Llorente to the Agrarian Comission, August 4, 1923, and Informe de la Comisión, AGEV(CAM, Exp 244, Alamo, Temapache.

[54] Topographer's Report, 1919, AGEV(CLA, Exp. 887, Ranchería Tierra Amarilla, Municipio Temapache; LGO, vol. 21, no. 47 (April 18, 1929).

[55] *Excélsior*, March 3, 1921; LGO, vol. 27, no. 47 (April 19, 1932).

[56] Petition, January 30, 1930, AGEV/CAM, Exp. 1120, Municipio Tepetzintla, La Loma.

Table 6.1. *Huastec Speakers in Northern Veracruz, 1921–1950*

Language	1921	1930	1940	1950
Huastec	18,843	22,437	29,826	36,756

Sources: Instituto Nacional Indigenista, *Memorias. Densidad de la Población Indígena en la República Mexicana* (Mexico City: Instituto Nacional Indigenista, 1950) and *Memorias. Realidad y Projectos. 16 años de trabajo*, vol. 10 (Mexico City: Instituto Nacional Indigenista, 1964); Secretaría de Economía de la Dirección General de Estadística, *Séptimo Censo General de Población, Estado de Veracruz* (June 6, 1950).

forest: it was a *potrero*, grassland dotted with palm trees and remnants of tall trees. Despite their best intentions, the petitioners had little chance of recreating the indigenous ecology in any case. Their petition remained unresolved through 1951.[57]

Thus, the changes in discourse and land reform policies allowed a few Teenek families to reclaim their traditional lands after 1921. As Table 6.1 shows, the numbers of Teenek speakers in the Huasteca remained stable through 1950, suggesting the community either did not emigrate or some who had done so returned. However, the landscape they occupied was altered beyond recognition. Only "tiny little forests" remained in the Huasteca by then, too miniscule to restore the ecology of 1900.[58] Even the indigenous farmers who recovered land were unable to produce as much as they needed. Without the rainforest to capture and cycle nutrients, the ejidos were too small and degraded to support agriculture. Additional land was necessary even for a few seasons of corn, but it would not be forthcoming. By 1929 it was clear that the hacendados disengaging from oil production were moving in a different direction altogether: they were returning to the nineteenth-century plan for cattle ranching. Indigenous farmers with claims before the Agrarian Commission would spend decades trying to acquire as much land as they needed in a degraded environment. Meanwhile, the hacendados shifted gears, turning denuded forests and less-polluted lands into grasslands,

[57] Petition for ejido, June 10, 1932, AGEV/CAM, Exp. 1912, Moyutla, Tepetzintla.
[58] Williams, *Introducción*, p. 37.

just as they had begun to do one hundred years prior.[59] Ironically, the oil industry ended up facilitating the success of a plan for ecological trans- formation that Teenek farmers had defeated generations earlier. In the aftermath of oil, even the best efforts of the nascent revolutionary regime could not restore the landscape or the people.

Calles: The Failed Regulator

Focused on conservation of natural resources rather than on ecological change, the revolutionary state continued searching for ways to rein in the oil companies. Despite Obregón's retreat on Article 27, the nation's grow- ing middle class was becoming more and more concerned about conser- vation. Miguel Angel de Quevedo, for example, founded the *Sociedad Fore- stal Mexicana* in 1922 to lobby against deforestation and in favor of forest conservation in general. It enjoyed official approval: President Obregón and Pastor Rouaix were honorary members.[60] Also, the Department of Petroleum followed Calles' admonition to prepare the statutory law to implement Article 27. A first bill was ready by July 6, 1922. Its tone was firm but subdued: the problem was the "competition among the compa- nies that led to the unbridled exploitation and the premature exhaustion" of the wells. The goal was "a more rational exploitation" of the oil fields. The recommendations focused on two points: spacing between wells (200 meters/656 feet) and around wells (four hectares/ten acres per well); and restriction of production, particularly for gushers.[61] Conservation was the assumption throughout.

The bill made slow progress toward Congress for two reasons. First, the professionals were busy inspecting abandoned wells and drafting reg- ulations for their proper closure. As Chapter 3 noted, improperly closed wells sometimes leaked gas and caused explosions.[62] Second, the U.S. State Department and the companies obtained copies of the bill and made their objections known to Obregón. Neither was prepared to let

---

[59] Alberto J. Olvera R., "La estructura económica y social de Veracruz hacia 1930. Un análisis inicial," *Anuario* III, p. 17.

[60] *México Forestal*, vol. 1, no. 1 (January 1, 1923), p. 8 and no. 11–12 (November–December 1923), p. 9. According to a Forestry Society survey, in 1910 Mexico had twenty million hectares of forests (forty-eight million acres). A "good part" of that acreage was in the tropical rainforests of the southeast. Ibid., vol. 8, no. 3 (March 1930), p. 36.

[61] Proyecto de reglamentación tendiente a obtener una más racional explotación de nuestos campos petrolíferos, AGN/DP, Caja 41, Exp. 11, 316(02)/9, 1922.

[62] Proyecto de instrucciones relativas al taponamiento de pozos, AGN/DP, Caja 40, Exp. 9, 310/11, 1923; BP, vol. 15, no. 4 (April 1923), p. 307.

the revolutionary government pass legislation that restrained the companies in any way.[63] Thus, Obregón finished his term without a petroleum
law. The responsibility for implementing Article 27 passed to President
Calles.

Calles gave immediate priority to the regulation of the industry. Upon
his inauguration, a Congressional subcommittee began meeting to chisel
out the elusive Petroleum Law. The president's man in the subcommittee
was his tour guide in the Huasteca, Joaquín Santaella. The meetings took
place between February and March 1925 and reaffirmed the commitment
of the revolutionary state-in-formation to the principle of national ownership of the subsoil and conservation in the oil industry. But the law also
made clear its intention to encourage the continued development of the
industry, albeit along rules grounded in "technology and science" rather
than "monopoly" capitalism intent on "enormous profits."[64] In practical terms, the subcommittee members referred to questions of spacing
between wells, the amount of oil that could be extracted from each well,
the prevention of gushers, the proper capping of exhausted wells, the utilization of natural gas, the exploration of fields already under production,
and other technical matters.[65]

The discussions also confirmed that despite its confrontations with
the industry, the Mexican revolutionary leadership was committed to
oil extraction at the expense of the environment. The conservation of
resources did not mean legal environmental protection or opposition to
ecological transformations in the practice. On the contrary, the subcommittee proposed including an article in the law declaring that the state
would prioritize oil as an economic activity in any area where it might be
found. Insofar as "the surface of the terrain" was concerned, the members wrote, the petroleum industry "will enjoy preference over all other
uses." Knowing that such a decision would mean that "those lands will
not be able to be used for cattle ranching or agriculture," the committee
members discussed the options for landowners. Anticipating resistance
from indigenous farmers, hacendados, and the companies alike, the
final bill incorporated two solutions: expropriation and compensation.

---

[63] Meyer, *México y los Estados Unidos*, pp. 194–197.

[64] José Colomo, "The Mexican Petroleum Laws: Its Basis and Its Aims," (Mexico City: Secretaría de Industria, Comercio y Trabajo, 1927), p. 5; Vázquez Schiaffino, Santaella, and
Elorduy, *Informes*, p. 52.

[65] Acta de la Cuarta Sesión de la Junta Consultiva para la formación de la Ley Orgánica
del Artículo 27, March 10, 1925, "La legislación," *Boletín* of the Archivo General de la
Nación, p. 60.

Theoretically, compensation would cover not only the loss of land, but also the "damages and injuries" the members recognized as inherent in the ecology of oil.[66] Revolutionary nationalism and Article 27 only went so far.

At Calles' insistence, the Congress approved the Petroleum Law in November 1925. It went into effect on December 26. The response from the companies was fast and forceful. They disapproved of six specific points the law made that abolished the idea of absolute private ownership: that landholders must confirm their rights by registering their concessions with the state; that concessions were not in perpetuity but rather only for fifty years; the narrow definition of what a positive act entailed; the stipulation that no foreigner could appeal to his home government in case of conflicts with Mexican officials; the reaffirmation of the Constitutional principle that no foreigner could own land along the coastline and the international borders; and proof of having complied with Carranza's decrees for the confirmation of concessions. To derail the legislation, the companies immediately filed sixty injunctions (*amparos*) before the Mexican courts, as they retaliated with a production boycott. By 1927 production had plummeted to sixty-four million barrels, a downward trend that continued until nationalization (Appendix V).[67]

The State Department also reacted to the Petroleum Law. Washington protested the abrogation of the Bucareli agreements the law supposedly represented because it applied Article 27 "retroactively" and "confiscated" oil company landholdings with its restrictions. Mexico and the United States exchanged over 250 pages of correspondence over the disputed sections of the law, to the point where the Americans threatened to withdraw recognition for Calles altogether if he did not change them.[68]

Calles resisted stubbornly. His men in the *Boletín* actively promoted the narrative of wasteland. They wrote historical articles reconstructing the recent past as unequivocally destructive. Dos Bocas, for instance, was referred to as "a forest of the dead" and "gushers" as "true cataclysms." The "inheritance" the industry left to Mexico, the professionals wrote, was "salt fields, ruined camps, and devastated regions." The editorials in the *Boletín* defended the Petroleum Law vigorously, citing the conservation

[66] Acta de la Quinta Sesión de la Junta Consultiva para la formación de la Ley Orgánica del Artículo 27, March 14, 1925, and Proyecto de ley reglamentaria del Artículo 27 Constitucional en el Ramo del Petróleo, Ibid., pp. 61, 75–76.

[67] Meyer, *México y los Estados Unidos*, pp. 229, 235, 237.

[68] Ibid., p. 236.

debates taking place in the United States at that very moment to support Mexico's "more advanced" legislation.[69]

At the same time, the Department of Petroleum continued developing the petroleum legislation. Once Congress adopted the Petroleum Law, the legislators submitted it to the Department to establish the code that would implement its stipulations. That document was called the "Regulations for Petroleum Works," and it was approved in April 1926. The Regulations were the revolutionary government's most comprehensive attempt to change the way the companies did business. In addition to conservation, it addressed environmental and labor issues directly for the first time. The code held the companies responsible for pollution on land, rivers, and oceans and for damages to fishing and agriculture under penalty of fines. That responsibility, moreover, did not end with the exhaustion of any given field. The works the companies had to undertake included everything necessary to leave the terrain "in good sanitary conditions."[70]

As the document read, moreover, one of its goals was to gain "respect for all the rights to life and to health for those who work in the industry or come into contact with it." Hence, the Regulations included far ranging protections for labor that exceeded Article 123. The code, for instance, held the companies directly responsible for the health and safety of workers, including those subcontracted, and listed article after article designed to prevent fires, poisonings, accidents, gas leaks, spills, and toxic air emissions harmful to workers and their families. It went so far as to prescribe the wholesale redesign of refineries and workshops and the location of working-class housing to make them safer and healthier, as well as the upgrading of existing equipment and the incorporation of the latest technologies in firefighting and pollution control.[71] Although neither the Regulations nor the *Boletín* explained the reasons for incorporating labor rights into the code, it was clear that the oil workers' successful unionization drives of 1924–1926, discussed in the following chapter, had made an impact at the national level.

With the Regulations in hand, moreover, the Department went on to draft more restrictions for Calles to sign. On July 21, 1926, for instance, Calles circulated a directive banning simultaneous drilling of wells within

---

[69] BP, vol. 19, no. 1 (January 1925), p. 29.
[70] Secretaría de Industria, Comercio y Trabajo, *Reglamento de Trabajos Petroleros* (Mexico City: Talleres Gráficos de la Nación, 1927), *passim*.
[71] Ibid.

sixty meters of each other as a fire prevention measure. In 1927 the Department followed up with recommendations for the regulation of storage tanks and the elimination of the remaining earthen dams.[72]

When President Calles moved aggressively to enforce the Petroleum Law and its code for petroleum works, however, a new oil crisis arose. Effective law enforcement had not been a hallmark of the revolutionary state-in-formation. Attempts had been null, weak, or generally futile inso-far as the oil industry was concerned, but Calles was determined to make changes. The consolidation of the postrevolutionary state demanded as much. Thus, Calles put muscle into the Petroleum Law by authorizing the Department of Petroleum to suspend drilling permits, impose fines for violations of the law, and, in some cases, actually to shut down wells drilled without permission. The companies became predictably incensed, yet Calles did not budge. On the contrary, in June 1927 Mexican Gulf and Standard Oil's Transcontinental received notification that they had lost all their concessionary rights on account of their violation of the law. The reaction from the industry as a whole was unequivocal: with the agreement of the U.S. ambassador in Mexico City, they requested direct military intervention to resolve the oil question once and for all. Calles prepared for the worst: he ordered the military commander of the Huasteca, Lázaro Cárdenas, to prepare for the invasion. Upon the landing of the Marines, Cárdenas would respond by setting the oil fields ablaze.[73]

Although Calles was willing to engage the companies and the United States in the ultimate confrontation, or perhaps because of that resolve, the crisis of 1927 found resolution through negotiation. The United States sent a new ambassador to Mexico, Dwight Morrow, with explicit instructions to move the two countries away from war. On November 17, 1927, only weeks after the first meeting between Calles and Morrow, the Mexican Supreme Court overturned the six points the companies had found most objectionable in the Petroleum Law. The modifications required, moreover, were not penned by the professionals at the Department of Petroleum. Instead, they were negotiated directly between the companies and the former CROM leader, Luis Morones, the new secretary of industry. Thus, the company-revised law went into effect in 1928.

---

[72] BP, vol. 22, no. 3 (September 1926), p. 195 and no. 6 (December 1926), pp. 393, 400, 428–458; BP, vol. 23, no. 2 (February 1927), pp. 73, 76–79 and no. 3 (March 1927), p. 188.

[73] Meyer, *México y los Estados Unidos*, pp. 252–255, 261–262.

A period of "peaceful coexistence" between the government and the companies ensued.[74] Despite Calles' bravado, the companies had not only jettisoned all regulatory efforts, but also, writing their own legislation in Mexico, had finally exempted themselves from Article 27. The modified law restored the principle of absolute private property to the companies, granting them total ownership and mastery over nature once more.

The Great Depression and Conservation

The revolutionary government's total capitulation to the oil companies had mixed results. The companies did not increase production in part because new discoveries in the late 1920s glutted the market, but also because the Great Depression hurt global demand. At the same time, the market for Mexican oil shifted from abroad to internal consumption. As the revolutionary state promoted national development, Mexico's own fuel needs grew and offset some of the negative effects the Depression had on both the industry and the country. Simultaneously, El Aguila made a major discovery immediately south of the Huasteca near the properties that once belonged to Percy Norman Furber. To reflect its wealth, the field became known as Poza Rica (rich well). By 1936 that combination of factors allowed the Mexican government to make one last effort to regulate oil production and put conservation back on the agenda.

The Great Depression had an important impact on the oil industry in Mexico. The prices for crude had been dropping fast since 1926 with discoveries in Oklahoma, Texas, New Mexico, and Venezuela.[75] As demand dropped world wide, moreover, the companies curtailed production. The Mexican professionals at the Department of Petroleum decried that decision on new grounds. Their conservationist critique broadened to include concerns for the fate of Mexico's temperate forests, which had made more headway on the national agenda than their tropical counterparts. In 1926 Calles had passed a forestry law aimed at slowing down the rate of deforestation in the temperate forests occurring partly because of the extensive use of charcoal as fuel.[76] On the eve of the Great Depression, the Department of Petroleum had arrived at the conclusion that the oil industry could reduce waste and save the nation's temperate forests at the same time: instead of burning off the natural gas the wells released,

[74] Ibid., pp. 270–275.
[75] Yergin, *The Prize*, pp. 223, 233–237.
[76] Simonian, *Defending*, pp. 82–83.

the companies could sell it for household use. Then, instead of using charcoal or wood for cooking, Mexican families could switch to gas or, at least, kerosene stoves. The change would protect trees, make full use of the products of the oil fields, and expand the national market for the oil industry as a whole.[77] However, despite the exhortations in the *Boletín* that began in 1928, there is no evidence that the companies made efforts to tap into the household fuel consumption market. Estimating that the companies had burned one billion cubic feet of natural gas between 1911 and 1927, the highest ranking Mexican in the oil industry, the engineer Ezequiel Ordoñez, ventured as an explanation for such inaction that "no one wanted to be adventurous and spend on [gas] pipeline and guarantee its consumption."[78]

Nevertheless, El Aguila's parent company, Royal Dutch Shell, did change production practices in the oil field they opened in 1932: Poza Rica. Touted as richer than the Golden Lane, the field in the Totonaca-pan of old came into production while the world price of crude was still dropping. Without an economic incentive to produce at high speed or in great volume, El Aguila decided to give a chance to the most mini-mum of conservation measures: the company designed a "spacing pro-gram" for Poza Rica. It meant leaving 750 meters (2,460 feet) between wells. To protect itself, moreover, the Royal Dutch Shell subsidiary con-vinced its tiny local rivals to agree to keep the same distances. The spac-ing program thus guaranteed El Aguila monopolistic control over the wells of Poza Rica, but it also started local operators on the road to conservation.[79]

The opening of such a rich new field during a time of world economic crisis coincided with another change: the expansion of Mexico's own oil consumption. The growth of railways and roads as a result of state invest-ment and the promotion of small industry increased internal demand for petroleum products. So did the country's growing fleet of buses, taxis, and individual automobiles. The happy coincidence led El Aguila to turn its back on the global market and sell Poza Rica's production nationally. Huasteca Petroleum and others followed suit, and – amidst the Great Depression – Mexico's consumption of oil rose to the all-time high of

[77] BP, vol. 21, no. 2 (August 1928), p. 456; BP, vol. 27, no. 1 (January 1929), pp. 24, 36; BP, vol. 29, no. 6 (June 1930), pp. 681–682.

[78] Ordoñez, *El petróleo*, p. 71

[79] Guillermo Salas, "Geology and Development of Poza Rica Oil Field, Veracruz, Mexico," *Bulletin* of the American Association of Petroleum Geologists, vol. 33, no. 8 (August 1949), p. 1390.

40% of production.[80] The concomitant environmental transformations inherent in oil extraction thus moved beyond the Huasteca. El Aguila built a refinery in Poza Rica and embarked on a pipeline project that stretched several hundred kilometers west to Mexico City. At the gates of the metropolis, in Atzcapotzalco, a second, massive refinery underwent construction as well. There the crude from the Totonac tropical rainforest would be converted into gasoline, diesel, kerosene, motor oil, and all the other riches of the hydrocarbon age that eventually contributed its share to making Mexico City one of the most polluted cities in the world.[81]

Despite the Depression, the oil companies remained politically and economically strong in Mexico. As they gained a new market in the national Mexican economy, they also became an essential source of revenue for the Mexican treasury. Between 1931 and 1932 alone, for example, the government borrowed ten million dollars in tax advances from the companies to meet basic expenses. That loan indebted the state to the foreign oil companies and created a vested interest in making sure the companies maintained and, if possible, increased production. The Mexican revolutionary government, therefore, not only guaranteed the companies a profit through increased national consumption, but also depended on those profits for revenues. Under those circumstances, regulation took a decided back seat in the revolutionary agenda, even as conservation became less taboo in oil circles.[82]

Nonetheless, the Mexican government continued trying to gain advantages from the accommodation with the companies after the modifications to the Petroleum Law in 1928. Calles brought political continuity to the Mexican revolutionary government as he prolonged his rule. In a manner similar to Porfirio Díaz, Calles extended his official rule past 1928 via a series of presidents he personally selected through 1934. That habit won Calles the nickname of *jefe máximo* (supreme chief) and gave the name of *maximato* to his decade of rule, 1924–1934. Even if such continuity did not translate into political stability or peace for the country – not to mention democracy – it did allow the government to gnaw at the edges of the oil behemoth. In late 1933 and early 1934, for example, President Abelardo L. Rodríguez surveyed the industry to see if he could

[80] Lorenzo Meyer, *El conflicto social y los gobiernos del maximato,* Serie Historia de la Revolución Mexicana, 1928–1934, vol. 13 (Mexico City: El Colegio de México, 1980), pp. 20–21, 51.
[81] Bases sobre las cuales se regirán los trabajos de la refinería de Atzcapotzalco, D.F, 1930, AGN/JFCA, Caja 233, Exp. 15/931/702; *El Dictamen,* June 15, 1932.
[82] Meyer, *México y los Estados Unidos,* p. 296.

resuscitate Obregón's idea of a joint company between the state and the oil companies. The multinationals declined. Rodríguez then approved the creation of a state petroleum company, Petromex. The lack of capital crippled Petromex from the beginning, but nevertheless it gave the professionals at the Department of Petroleum a place to acquire a smidgeon of badly needed field experience. Harmonious relations with the companies allowed the government to place a small number of newly minted Mexican engineers in their exploration departments for practical training, extending to Mexican nationals the privilege the companies had granted to U.S. graduates since the early 1910s. Despite the limited number of men who benefited from these efforts, Rodríguez was on the right track: that handful would become very important in the aftermath of the nationalization decree.[83]

The Final Effort at Conservation and Regulation

In 1934 Mexicans elected a new president, Lázaro Cárdenas. Intimately acquainted with the ecology of oil from his experience as military commander in the Huasteca during the mid-1920s, the general was deeply concerned about the use and conservation of natural resources. Like his predecessors, Cárdenas was committed to progress and development, but he believed that "conservation and development were complementary goals."[84] His journal entries testify to the importance he gave to national control over nature. In March 1938, for example, he wrote that "unity among Latin American countries for the defense and the development of their natural resources would be the solution to many of our problems; but," he recognized immediately, "it is a long way to achieve it."[85] Nevertheless, as soon as he came to power Cárdenas began to advance Mexico's control over its natural environment and the consolidation of the revolutionary state simultaneously.

One of Cárdenas' first acts as president was to create an institution charged with the explicit task of conservation. In 1935 the Department of Forestry, Fish, and Game opened its offices. At the helm was Mexico's main spokesman for forest conservation, the founder of the Forestry Society, Miguel Angel de Quevedo. At the ceremony inaugurating the

---

[83] Ibid., pp. 298–299.
[84] Simonian, *Defending*, p. 86.
[85] Quoted in Adolfo Gilly, *El cardenismo, una utopía mexicana* (Mexico City: Cal y Arena, 1994), p. 41.

Department, Cárdenas pronounced the most environmentally conscious words a Mexican president had ever emitted. He declared that he knew "the Mexican people, conscious of the great benefits provided by forests and fauna, will cooperate enthusiastically and faithfully with the work of salvation and protection of nature, the true work of national conservation."[86] As the Department began to interact with fishing communities along the Gulf coast, the deleterious effects of oil pollution on the fishermen of Tampico and the Huasteca found their way into the historical record (see Chapter 3) and contributed to the narrative of wasteland. Saving and protecting nature in practice, however, proved to be extremely difficult work.

The oil industry was the perfect example. In this case, Cárdenas intended to take the initiative from the beginning. The six-year plan he made public on the campaign trail called for the "effective nationalization of the subsoil" and "true regulation" in the oil industry. That included preventing the "hoarding of petroleum deposits" and increasing known reserves. The plan also emphasized the desirability of more active governmental participation in the industry and the need to "maintain a rhythm of production in accordance with the volume of reserves." In addition, the plan included another component: the banning of the export of crude oil altogether. Only refined products would be allowed to leave the country.[87] The idea was not new, only revised. The professionals at the Department of Petroleum had argued since 1917 that exporting oil was wasteful in and of itself because it robbed Mexico of the benefits of its own natural resources.[88] Cárdenas echoed that concern and translated it into a concrete proposal that advanced the cause of Mexican industrialization and added value to its export products. In other words, candidate Cárdenas envisioned the creation of a national petrochemical industry. As president, however, he had little opportunity to put the plan into effect as programmed. As the next chapter will show, by the time Cárdenas was inaugurated in January 1935, the oil workers were already on the offensive, making far–more-radical demands.

As political and labor turmoil mounted during his administration, Cárdenas used the occasion to try to extract concessions from the oil companies. In late 1937 he came very close to succeeding where other revolutionary presidents before him failed, but in the face of company

---

[86] Quoted in Simonian, *Defending*, pp. 86–87.
[87] Quoted in Meyer, *México y los Estados Unidos*, p. 307, footnote 18.
[88] Julio Baz, opinion piece, BP, vol. 3, no. 5 (May 1917), p. 518.

intransigence his efforts too were ultimately fruitless. What Cárdenas managed to pull off momentarily was a historic agreement between El Aguila and the government to exploit the Papantla fields jointly (Poza Rica, the largest, plus Poza de Cuero, Troncones y Potrerillo, and Coazintla). The agreement was signed on November 11, 1937 and even though it failed, it was important for two reasons. It not only created a rift between the American and British companies at a time of intense labor strife, as the historiography points out, but the agreement also took the principles and the letter of Article 27 the furthest in the most productive oil field in the country. At the time of the agreement, domestic consumption of oil had risen to 70% of total production, with Poza Rica alone accounting for 45% of all Mexican production. The district in fact was "the second most important field in production in the world, after Richfield in Texas."[89] Given that the companies controlled some twenty-four million acres (ten million hectares) across the country, the repercussions of a joint state-El Aguila venture would have been felt throughout the industry and the nation.

The terms were unprecedented. In exchange for thirteen thousand acres (5,263 hectares) with an estimated five hundred million barrels of crude, Royal Dutch Shell committed itself to major concessions on principle and in practice. First of all, the company finally accepted Article 27. The company gave up the idea of absolute private ownership and recognized the Mexican nation as the owner of the subsoil with the right to regulate private property and concessions. Second, Royal Dutch Shell also recognized the Petroleum Law and its Regulations. Third, the company agreed to give the state control over 15 to 35% of production, pegged at a minimum of 12,580 barrels per day. Last but not least, the company agreed to adhere to the strictest conservationist practices then in use to protect the life of the wells. Among these were the minimum of 750 meters (2,460 feet) between wells, and acceptable levels of gas-oil ratios and percentages of water intrusion.[90]

Moreover, the president's efforts to reconfigure the relationship with the oil companies in the state's favor did not stop with Royal Dutch Shell. Cárdenas had two other schemes underway. The first was a second joint

[89] Olvera, "The Rise," p. 64; Mario A. Román del Valle and Rosario Segura Portilla, "La huelga de 57 días en Poza Rica," *Anuario* V, p. 65; Brown, "The Structure of the Foreign-Owned Petroleum Industry," p. 23.

[90] Brief Abstract of Contract Between the Mexican Government and the Aguila Covering Development of Lands in the Poza Rica District, enclosure to T. R. Armstrong to Sumner Welles, New York, December 28, 1937, RG 59, Roll 131, File 812.6363/3056.

venture with a consortium of small English firms. Under negotiation was a plan more favorable to the state than to El Aguila. The oilmen would build three new refineries, purchase ten tankers, drill thirty to forty wells, and turn over 50% of production to the government, on top of a five-million-dollar loan in exchange for acreage and legal guarantees on the concession. The second project was in its preliminary stages: Cárdenas extended a formal invitation to "accept the Mexican government as an associate" to the American companies.[91]

Cárdenas' maneuvers were not only economically sound but also eminently political: the companies and the oil workers had been locked in fierce combat over collective bargaining since 1935. The government was acting as mediator (Chapter 7). Cárdenas' proposals therefore offered the companies a resolution to their irresolute labor problems. If the Americans accepted similar terms to the Europeans, the government would guarantee the companies' rights to private ownership and might bring the two-year labor conflict to a conclusion, achieving a lasting labor peace and establishing "equilibrium" in labor-capital relations in the oil industry at last. At the same time, Cárdenas would achieve two more goals: instituting up-to-date conservation practices in the most productive oil field and, most importantly, a political victory that would go a long ways toward the consolidation of the revolutionary state.[92]

Given the continuing global economic crisis, the offer was attractive enough for the Europeans. But not so for the Americans. The Americans never even bothered to respond to Cárdenas' invitation. Then, in December 1937, in retaliation for a court decision in favor of the workers in the dispute over contract negotiations, Royal Dutch Shell pulled out of the Poza Rica deal.[93] Accustomed to a weak Mexican state, the multinationals closed ranks and decided to use their power to defy Mexican institutions and bend the revolutionary state to their will yet again. They were confident they would prevail. They had lost the ideological battle since 1921 and no one besides them believed that they were the paragons of progress and civilization. The narrative of wasteland and the global economic depression had them on the defensive in general, but the companies were betting that the revolutionary state was not strong enough to command their submission to Mexican law. Until the end of

---

[91] Meyer, *México y los Estados Unidos*, p. 326.
[92] Nora Hamilton, *The Limits of State Autonomy: Post-Revolutionary Mexico* (Princeton: Princeton University Press, 1982), p. 119.
[93] *Mexican Labor News*, December 19, 1937.

1937, that logic was sound. History was certainly on the side of the companies. But then again, radical Mexican oil workers were convinced that History was on their side. Acting on that belief, the oil workers produced from below what the state alone could not do from above: a revolution, that is, the nationalization of the oil industry.

For two decades, from 1912 through 1937, the Mexican revolutionary leadership tried time and time again to regulate the foreign oil industry to protect the nation's natural resources. The revolutionaries recognized nature as the fountain of wealth for humanity, and for that same reason believed that its usage must not be left up to individual private parties whose economic motives trumped all others. As nationalists, revolutionary leaders of the period sought to impose a conservative approach to oil production, one that placed the long-term interests of the nation as a whole at the top of the agenda. Thus, successive administrations passed laws and handed down decrees that limited the untrammeled capitalist ways of the foreign oil companies, but to no effect. The companies were simply stronger than the revolutionary state and remained so in spite of the Great Depression of the 1930s. The most the revolutionary leadership managed to achieve through 1937 was to change the terms of the debate, stripping the companies of their civilizing image and revealing them as exploiters of men, nature, and nation. It was a price the companies were willing to pay. Yet there was reason for hope among the Mexican leadership: the Great Depression did affect company practices. Royal Dutch Shell became convinced that conservation was not intrinsically incompatible with profit making and shifted gears in that direction. Under Cárdenas the company seemed willing to go further and cement its position in Mexico by submitting to the provisions of the Mexican Constitution at last. In rejecting that option a short month after entertaining it, however, the Europeans as well as the Americans unknowingly jettisoned the last possible solution favorable to their interests. For if in the decades of conflict with the revolutionary leadership and the oil workers alike the former had been willing or forced to compromise, the latter had not. Despite the failures of the 1910s and the devastating blow of 1921, the oil workers rose from the mat for more rounds until they finally won.

7

REVOLUTION FROM BELOW

THE OIL UNIONS, 1924–1938

Property owned by foreigners, enterprises conducted by foreigners, will never be safe in Mexico so long as their existence
and the method of their use and conduct excite the suspicion
and, upon occasion, the hatred of the people of the country
itself.

President Woodrow Wilson, October 1916

You understand that what we are interested in is extracting
Mexico's oil; we are here exclusively for that. That is why I,
and the other managers, have suffered through these climates
for years. The companies . . . are not charity organizations.

El Aguila Personnel Manager, Hume, 1937

If the challenges to the ecology of oil posed by the revolutionary state
did not yield fruit, it would seem that a labor force devastated since 1921
could hardly do better. That impression, however, is mistaken. Ten years
of intensive political education had left a deep imprint in the workers
and their work culture. At the same time, the weakness of the revolutionary state meant that even if Mexico City had lost patience with radicals,
local authorities could be flexible. Thus, workers who survived the 1921
debacle returned to the offensive in the mid-1920s. They made organizational advances and unionized the labor force at last. The emergence of
political differences among the unions, however, meant that a significant
minority failed to negotiate contracts and experienced the dissolution of
their unions in the late 1920s. Key to the victories and the defeats were several local officials: the lawyer Emilio Portes Gil, the governor of Veracruz,
Adalberto Tejeda, and the general Lázaro Cárdenas. Their intervention
would have long-lasting consequences in the life of the unions.

The economic depression that engulfed the Mexican oil industry in
the second half of the 1920s and merged into the Great Depression of the

1930s affected union activity as well. The unions split internally between those who wanted stability and a fringe that agitated for militancy. The Depression became a period of intense intraunion struggle in Tampico and the Huasteca, while a militant second generation of oil workers took over union leadership in new production sites in the Isthmus of Tehuantepec, Poza Rica, and Atzcapotzalco. In northern Veracruz the radicals' rise to leadership coincided with the ascent of Lázaro Cárdenas to the presidency in 1935. That convergence made possible the organization of the industry-wide union, the *Sindicato de Trabajadores Petroleros de la República Mexicana* (STPRM).

The battle over the collective contract that followed the formation of the STPRM became the worker offensive that led Cárdenas to nationalize the industry in 1938. The demands the companies refused to accept show the oil workers drawing from their radical origins, adhering stubbornly to notions of workers' control over production that clashed with early twentieth-century capitalist practice. At the same time, the workers demonstrated political pragmatism vis-à-vis the state. They were quick to propose expropriation as the solution to labor conflicts in the oil industry, making explicit their belief that class interests were national interests and that there was no contradiction between the two. The nationalism and class consciousness the Mexican oil workers had displayed since 1914 was as alive as ever in their battle against the oil companies in the 1930s. The element that was new in their ideological arsenal was environmental. By the mid-1930s, the oil workers embraced conservation as a working-class value befitting nationalist economic planning. Relentless in their pressure against the companies and the government from 1936 to 1938, the oil workers were directly responsible for the culminating act of the Mexican Revolution: Lázaro Cárdenas' nationalization of the foreign oil companies on March 18, 1938. After three decades of intense struggle against capital and the state, the oil workers achieved one of their goals: landing a fatal blow to one of the most powerful multinational conglomerates in the world. They also delivered, ironically enough, a tremendous victory to the Mexican state, one that would allow it to become one of the strongest in Latin America in the twentieth century. In either case, the oil workers changed the course of Mexican history.

The Revival of the Unions, 1924–1925

After the oil companies cut the Mexican work force in half in 1921, the still-employed oil workers had little choice but to retrench. Their unions were in tatters, their salaries slashed, and their gains null. But their combative spirit survived and revived in the mid-1920s. A tidal wave of strikes in 1924 and 1925 resulted in significant organizational advances, new ideological developments, and the first collective contracts in the history of the industry. In two years, the oil workers had formed nearly thirty unions organized by company and location, rather than trades. One group of unions, moreover, had formed the first oil union federation on record.

Yet the gains were uneven. All but two companies signed contracts. The reasons for the success of the majority and the failure of the minority were complex, but they point to changes in the historical moment that some oil workers were able to exploit better than others. Although all the workers used aggressive direct action tactics, El Aguila's union – the first to win a contract – adjusted its ideological stance toward capital and the state enough to broker a deal and consolidate its organization independently of the national confederation, the CROM. The unions at Huasteca Petroleum and Mexican Gulf, in contrast, held on to anarcho-syndicalist discourse and paid the price. Nevertheless, the mid-1920s were an important period for the oil workers, a time of gains as well as false starts and loss of opportunities that would bear fruit a decade later, as the workers stayed to the left of the emergent revolutionary state, firmly planted in the miniscule ranks of independent Mexican unionism.

Success at El Aguila

The 1924 strike by the *Sindicato de Obreros de la Compañía Mexicana de Petróleo El Aguila* was long and hard fought. The men were out for four months, from March 23 to July 28, until Royal Dutch Shell signed the first collective contract in the industry. Multiple factors contributed to the victory, but all of them centered on the new language the union used to justify the strike and convince the community at large of the righteousness of their cause. Without abandoning a revolutionary vision that challenged laissez-faire capitalism, El Aguila workers embraced the Mexican Revolution and its nationalism with a passion that co-opted both for labor. That approach helped them build an impressive solidarity apparatus, which, in turn, was critical in blocking a hostile takeover by the CROM and achieving a precedent-setting victory that all oil unions would follow.

The 1924 El Aguila strike was precipitated by a walkout at the Tampico power company in November 1923.[1] No electricity meant the refineries

---

[1] The strike is discussed in detail in Adleson, "Coyuntura," pp. 641–649.

Figure 7.1. Mexican workers at El Aguila's refinery in Doña Cecilia, 1920. From the Pearson & Son Photographic Archives at the Science and Society Picture Library in the Science Museum in London.

could not function, so El Aguila sent its two-thousand-plus Mexican workers on "vacation." Worried about layoffs, the craft unions met clandestinely and formed a refinery-wide union, as Pierce and Transcontinental had done in 1918. A spy in their midst informed the company, however, and the morning after the meeting El Aguila dismissed the 160 men involved. The new union demanded the rehiring of the men and recognition, but the general manager, Alfred Jacobsen, allegedly replied that if they walked out, "they'd be eating the soles of their shoes in a week."[2] When the lights came back on in February, the company refused to pay salaries for the four months of the blackout. Outraged, El Aguila men walked out (see Figure 7.1).

Although the strike arose from very specific grievances, its trajectory shows that the workers had shed the anarcho-syndicalist discourse of the late 1910s in favor of more conciliatory ideas. A full-page advertisement the union placed in *El Mundo* described the change as a desire to "move from being an anonymous mass without rights to being a respectable

[2] Quoted in Rodríguez, *El rescate*, p. 57.

corporation."[3] The search for respectability meant taking the words of the Mexican Revolution at face value and using them as weapons. The workers demanded full compliance with the letter of Article 123 of the 1917 Constitution. In addition, the workers raised old issues, such as the end of discrimination and the replacement of foreigners with qualified Mexicans, and made new demands: specific health and safety measures to protect them from the dangers of oil work in the tropical rainforest. The company deemed all the demands "most unreasonable."[4]

Although the proposed contract exceeded Article 123, the men did not consider the list unreasonable. On the contrary, by 1924 the first generation of oil workers had broadened their analysis of their relationship to capital. The narrative of wasteland they had helped bring about in 1921 had led the men to connect labor and nature in a chain of exploitation perpetrated by the companies, which "are not only happy with wringing the entrails of the earth, they also suck the blood and energies of the worker."[5] Just as the companies destroyed the landscape, they stole "the most sacred [years] of youth," leaving sick and battered bodies behind.[6] The high rates of disease, accident, and death in the industry meant that Mexican oil workers did not simply sell their labor power, they also placed their lives in the hands of the oil companies: oil work, argued a worker, was equal to "the material annihilation of the worker."[7] Therefore, using

---

[3] *El Mundo*, March 25, 1924.

[4] Pliego petitorio, January 1925, Sindicato de Obreros de la Huasteca, Cerro Azul, AGEV/JCCA 1925, Caja 48, Exp. n/n; Pliego petitorio, Sindicato de Obreros Unidos de The Texas Co., Terminal de Matillas, AGEV/JCCA 1924, Caja 40, n/n(134); Pliego petitorio, Sindicato de Obreros de la Trancontinental, reprinted in *Excélsior*, October 3, 1924; *The New York Times*, February 21, 1924. Some occupational health demands were extremely detailed. The Texas Company refinery workers cited above, for example, listed as demand #13 that "no order will be given to the boilermakers, pipe-layers, masons, or cleaners to enter the boilers or stills when the temperature reaches 60oC; and when it is absolutely necessary to undertake tasks in temperatures between 500 and 600C, double time will be paid; similarly, double time will be paid to those who clean the interior of tanks, places where there are gases, and those who work submerged in water . . . , including payment for the small rest periods the workers might need on account of the special nature of their work." The response to the petitions is in W. E. McMahon, *Mexico's Expropriation of American Oil Properties* (Dallas: Institute of Public Affairs, Southern Methodist University, 1938).

[5] *Sagitario*, October 25, 1924.

[6] Esteban Sánchez to the Junta Central, July 1928, AGEV/JCCA 1928, Caja 72, Exp. 47.

[7] The idea of "annihilation" appears regularly. See Frank Kemper vs. El Aguila, AGEV(JCCA 1928, Caja 68, Exp. 13; Gonzalo Arvizo to the Junta Federal, November 19, 1927, AGN/JFCA 1927, Caja 13, Exp. 15/927/318; and Tomás Green to the Junta Central, December 18, 1918, AGEV/JCCA 1918, Caja 1, Exp. 5.

capitalist logic, the men argued, the oil companies should have to pay for what they consumed, that is, the workers' entire lives. As worker José Ramírez reasoned, "Well, doesn't the businessman or owner pay from his own pocket the repairs that have to be done to the machines when these wear out in the production process?"[8] The same ought to be true for the workers.

Nevertheless, the shift away from absolute opposition to capital did not mean that El Aguila workers accepted the idea of harmony between labor and capital proposed in Article 123, nor the welfare capitalism the companies were experimenting with in the United States at the time.[9] Instead, the union concluded that with the revolutionaries in power and a narrative of wasteland surrounding the oil industry, labor might be able to accelerate the pace of change in their favor if they did not alienate the revolutionary leadership. Thus, the union adopted nationalism as official discourse. El Aguila strikers justified their militancy on "the postulates and principles of the revolution," brought about by a labor movement "whose achievements have drenched in blood the national territory."[10]

Despite demanding unprecedented concessions, El Aguila workers not once mentioned class struggle; rather, they argued they were defending the Revolution, the Constitution, and the nation itself. The union made the connections in an ad: company managers "mistreat" and "humiliate" Mexicans, "olympically laughing at our misery from their offices" and using "disparaging and injurious words towards our laws." Winning the strike against "ORGANIZED CAPITAL," therefore, meant "the laws of our country" would be "victorious." Defending their rights as workers was the same as "defending the interests of the Motherland."[11] Thus, El Aguila workers repositioned themselves as the revolutionary mainstream without subsuming class under nation. They turned nationalism into a synonym of class struggle, reaffirming the class nature of the Revolution itself and the role of labor in forging it at a time when Obregón was rebuilding the Mexican state at very high costs for the revolutionary ideal – costs

---

[8] José G. Ramírez vs. East Coast Oil Company, AGN/JFCA 1928, Caja 22, Exp. 15/928/130.

[9] In the 1920s Standard Oil was among the first companies to introduce an "Industrial Relations Plan" that accepted just enough worker demands and benefits to neutralize unionization. Paul H. Giddens, *Standard Oil Company (Indiana) Oil Pioneer of the Middle West* (New York: Appleton-Century-Crofts, Inc., 1955), pp. 348–358; "In the Domain of Standard Oil," *The Industrial Pioneer*, vol. 1, no. 6 (October 1923), pp. 17–19.

[10] Sindicato de Obreros y Empleados Unidos de la Cía. Transcontinental to Federal Inspector, July 26, 1927, AGN/JFCA, Caja 14, Exp. 15/927/330.

[11] The capitals are in the original, *El Mundo*, March 24, 1924; Robles Saldaña, Fourth Interview, March 20, 1975, PHO/4/39.

incurred, in no small part, by the oil industry's refusal to submit to the Constitution. According to the strikers, nationalism and revolution meant working-class victories.

The new language El Aguila unionists used struck a chord in an overwhelmingly working-class city like Tampico. The union mustered unprecedented solidarity across the port, making its direct action tactics remarkably effective. The strike did not start with a majority. When the strike vote was held, only five hundred men authorized it, less than a third of the twelve hundred who had signed on to a contract proposal. To prevent strike-breaking, the committed took the refinery by storm at 11 p.m. on March 23, the night before the official strike date, holding Superintendent Roberts at gunpoint and expelling all foreigners on duty. The next morning, with the red-and-black flag draped over the refinery gates, many more men joined the takeover.[12] When General Manager Jacobsen announced he had asked Obregón to send troops a week later, however, the strikers decided not to alienate the president and gave up the plant.[13]

Although the union showed political prudence, it did not renounce its confrontational culture and tactics. On the contrary, the union escalated direct-action tactics further than ever, gaining favorable national attention in the process. The strikers not only ambushed, beat, and "bathed" strike-breakers in oil waste canals, but also used the boycott for the first time. The response was overwhelming. No one in Tampico bought El Aguila products. The truck drivers' union refused to haul company goods out of town. The CROM got into the act also, taking the boycott across the country and floating the idea of spreading it north of the border through the American Federation of Labor.[14] Presidential candidate Calles jumped on the bandwagon as well. Campaigning in Tampico in April, he declared that

> I have always been, and always will be on the side of the worker, not to destroy capital...but to effect the betterment of the worker – the producer; to put into effect the victories of the Revolution; in one word, that workers be treated in the manner that they justly merit, and not like animals.[15]

[12] Adleson, "Coyuntura y conciencia," p. 654; *The New York Times*, March 26, 1924.

[13] *The New York Times*, April 28, 1924; José Esteves Torres, "Las principales huelgas de los trabajadores petroleros en México en el año de 1924," B.A. Thesis, Universidad Nacional Autónoma de México, 1983, p. 37.

[14] *The New York Times*, March 27, April 6, 1924; Esteves Torres, "Las principales huelgas," pp. 44–45, 72.

[15] Quoted in Consul Stewart to Secretary of State, April 22, 1924, RG 59, File 800.

With such widespread support and Calles echoing the union's language, the workers had the moral high ground. Yet, in the face of a company that refused to negotiate, what the men needed was material support.

The port's population rallied around the workers. Men unrelated to the strike volunteered on the picket lines. The unions – oil workers, long-shoremen, railroad workers, electric company workers, masons, shoe-shiners, street sweepers, barbers – raised funds for the strike. So did sectors dependent on workers for their livelihood: storekeepers, mom-and-pop shops, and farmers.[16] Surviving anarchist cultural groups did the same with dramatic plays. Even a group of "Catholic Ladies" raised money for the strike.[17] The most revealing fund-raising episode involved an hacendado named Bartolo Rodríguez, "Bartolo the Bourgeois." The union approached Rodríguez for support with an appeal to masculinity that emphasized national identity and nationalist sentiment. According to a worker, they told the hacendado:

> You must understand us. We are Mexican men defending the bread of our children and our rights. If people like you who can help us do not, we will starve because we prefer to do that than to sacrifice our dignity as men and as Mexicans.[18]

Although Rodríguez donated sixteen cows, no one could support two thousand idle workers indefinitely. Donations faltered in late spring, opening the door for the CROM to hijack the process and try to take over the union. Luis Morones and Ricardo Treviño chiseled out a contract with the company and presented it to the workers on June 10, after two-and-a-half months without a paycheck. In a raucous meeting, however, Serapio Vanegas, the union's secretary general, denounced the contract as a "sweetheart deal" and swore "he would shoot himself in the head" rather than accept it.[19] Pandemonium ensued and deadly weapons surfaced all

---

[16] Adleson, "Coyuntura," p. 655; *The New York Times*, April 17, 1924.

[17] Esteves Torres, "Las principales huelgas," p. 47.

[18] In exchange for his gift, Rodríguez hoped the men would quit calling him *el burgués Bartolo*, but asked only for a letter of recognition signed by the entire Executive Committee of the union. Upon receiving it, he allegedly remarked that "this is worth more than 16 cows!" and proceeded to frame it and display it "prominently" in his office. Quoted in Rodríguez, *El rescate*, p. 58.

[19] The proposed contract included neither payment for the months spent on strike nor severance pay in case of layoffs, and it let the company decide who could return to work as a full-time worker and who could be sloughed off as "temporary" or subcontracted. Esteves Torres, "Las principales huelgas," p. 58; María Luisa Serna, "Cronología: las luchas obreras en 1924," *Historia Obrera* 21, Segunda época, vol. 6 (January 1981), p. 16; Adleson, "Coyuntura y conciencia," p. 657.

around. The strikers accused the CROM of betrayal; the CROM shouted back, calling the workers anti-Obregón "reds."[20] When the votes were counted, nevertheless, the contract was dead. According to the Xalapa daily, *El Dictamen*, the workers had rejected a "model" contract, one patterned on the welfare capitalism of the "English or Americans." The men's error, the editorial noted, was due to the fact that "the proletariat is poorly instructed and believes it ought to win its demands."[21]

Poorly instructed or not, the decision to reject the contract carried risks. Morones acted with Obregón's blessing. Defying Morones, therefore, meant challenging the president as well. For that reason, the union pronounced its support for Obregón publicly on July 1, but they were too late. The next day the army occupied the refinery. With the strike on the verge of collapse, all parties tried to gain the upper hand. Thirty-six organizations protested Obregón's actions. Royal Dutch Shell removed El Aguila's general manager. The CROM cancelled food donations and aid for the families and held another session with the union to convince the men to sign their contract. The night ended, however, with Morones, Treviño, and other *cromistas* chased out of town.[22] The solution had to come from somewhere else before Obregón resorted to repression.

The strike ended on July 28. The man who resolved the conflict was Emilio Portes Gil, the lawyer exiled in the 1919 Pierce strike. Portes Gil was running for governor of Tamaulipas and needed votes. He was also a personal enemy of Morones. Therefore, when the union asked him to mediate, he did not hesitate. The first collective contract between a Mexican union and a foreign oil company was signed.[23] When Portes Gil became governor later in 1924, he kept the CROM at bay. Pierce and El Aguila unions thus remained independent from the CROM (if not from Portes Gil as discussed below) through the 1938 nationalization.[24]

---

[20] Calvillo Uvalle, Second Interview, PHO/4/90; *El Dictamen*, June 21, 1924.

[21] *El Dictamen*, June 21, 1924.

[22] Calvillo Uvalle, Second Interview, PHO/4/90; Serna, "Cronología," pp. 17–18; Paco Igancio Taibo II, *Bolshevikis: Historia narrativa de los orígenes del comunismo en México (1919–1925)* (Mexico City: Editorial Joaquín Mortiz, S.A., 1986), p. 250.

[23] Report from the Junta Central de Conciliación y Arbitraje, December 1924–June 1925, AGEV/JCCA 1926, Caja 50, Exp 3; Report from the JCCA, April 1925, AGEV/JCCA 1925, Caja 40, Exp. 3.

[24] Emilio Portes Gil, *Quince años de política mexicana* (Mexico City: Ediciones Botas, 1941), pp. 105–106, 446–447. It was not until 1949 that the national oil workers union was finally subjugated by federal authorities. See Angélica Cuello Vásquez, "El movimiento del sindicato de trabajadores petroleros de la República Mexicana en 1949," *Memorias del encuentro sobre historia del movimiento obrero*, vol. 2 (Mexico City: Editorial de la Universidad Autónoma de Puebla, 1980), pp. 389–400.

The company did not accept every demand. However, as Royal Dutch Shell admitted, times had changed and certain demands were becoming standard practice in the industrialized world: the eight-hour day; minimum wage (4 pesos per day); a day of rest per week; paid holidays; severance pay; no reprisals against union members or strikers.[25] There were other gains El Aguila workers celebrated: ground-breaking health and safety provisions such as company-issued safety equipment; the end of mandatory work inside confined spaces with temperatures over 55°C (131°F); double pay for jobs inside oil tanks; full salary for men injured on the job; death benefits for families of men killed on the job; access to prosthetics for accidents on the job; and disability payments in case of injury or loss of limbs, a category that listed thirty-five common injuries.[26] If the contract did not pay for the full cost of labor, it promised more protection against bodily harm than ever before, in addition to paying for the multiple ways in which men's bodies took a beating extracting oil.

Although discrimination and segregation remained, the victory was unquestionable and collective. As the union acknowledged, the contract was made possible by the "moral and pecuniary" support of "sister organizations." That solidarity, the union wrote, "will not be erased from the minds of each and every one of our members." Thus, they pledged to "be now and forever be" equally supportive "in everything and for everything" of those who stood by them throughout the strike.[27] The promise was not idle: a tsunami of strikes followed (Table 7.1). Each refinery and every camp across northern Veracruz organized its own union and demanded a contract. Faced with a new reality, the Association of Petroleum Producers resigned itself to collective bargaining. By early 1925, most unions had contracts promising some of the best working conditions in the country.[28] In addition, the socialist governor of Veracruz, Adalberto Tejeda,

[25] de Gortari, "Petróleo y clase obrera," p. 217.
[26] This information comes from the contracts El Aguila signed with its seven unions in southern Veracruz. I could not locate a copy of the contract with the northern refinery. However, most of the contracts were nearly identical. Convenio colectivo entre El Aguila y agrupaciones de Minatitlán y Puerto México, June 3, 1926, AGEV/JCCA 1925, Caja 48, Exp. n/n; Convenio colectivo entre El Aguila y agrupaciones de Minatitlán y Puerto México, July 16, 1926, AGEV/JCCA 1927, Caja 58, Exp. 21; Reglamento Interior del Trabajo entre los Obreros y Empleados de la Compañía de Petróleo Mexican Sincalir Petroleum Corporation y la misma, April 20, 1925, AGN/JFCA, Caja 66, Exp. 15/928/1221.
[27] Quoted in Adleson, "Coyuntura," p. 660.
[28] That included Pierce, Transcontinental, La Corona, Sinclair, and nearly thirty smaller unions. Sindicato de Obreros Unidos de The Texas Co., AGEV/JCCA 1924, Caja 40,

Table 7.1. *Selected Oil Workers' Strikes in Tampico and Northern Veracruz, 1924–1926*

Date	Company	Location
March–July 1924	El Aguila, refinery	Villa Cecilia, Tamaulipas
May 1924	El Aguila, camp	Toteco, Veracruz
August–September 1924	Huasteca, refinery	Mata Redonda, Veracruz
August 1924	Pierce, refinery	Villa Cecilia, Tamaulipas
September–February 1924–25	Mexican Gulf, terminal	Las Matillas, Veracruz
September 1924	Tanscontinental, refinery	Las Matillas, Veracruz
October–December 1924	La Corona, refinery	Pueblo Viejo, Veracruz
October 1924	General strike	Tampico/Villa Cecilia
February 1925	Huasteca, camps	Chapopote Nuñez, La Laja Juan Casiano, Tancoche, Cerro Azul, San Jerónimo, Horconcitos, Garrapatas, Tres Hermanos, Veracruz
May–June 1925	Huasteca, refinery	Mata Redonda, Veracruz
May–June 1925	Huasteca, camps	Huasteca, Veracruz
August 1926	El Aguila, camp	Potrero del Llano, Veracruz

Sources: Junta Central de Conciliación y Arbitraje, "Dificultades: Mexican Gulf," C. 40, Exp. n/n, 1924, "Huelga de la HPC en Cerro Azul," 1925, C. 48, Exp. n/n; Mirna Alicia Benítez Juárez, "Organización y lucha sindical de los petroleros en Veracruz: 1918–1928," B.A. Thesis, Universidad Veracruzana, 1983; José Esteves Torres, "Las principales huelgas de los trabajadores petroleros en México en el año de 1924," B.A. Thesis, Universidad Nacional Autónoma de México, 1983; María Luisa Serna, "Cronología: las luchas obreras en 1924," *Historia Obrera* 21, Segunda época, vol. 6 (January 1981); *Sagitario*, September 11, 1926.

legitimized workers' health and safety demands by approving the *Ley sobre riesgos profesionales* (Law on Occupational Risks) in August 1924. The law classified asphyxia, anemia, chronic respiratory illness, conjunctivitis, skin rashes, ulcers, and "benzinitis" as occupational diseases among oil workers. In Veracruz, the companies were thenceforth responsible for "paying for doctors, medicines, and compensation" in all those cases.[29] Changing discourse but not tactics, El Aguila's union had not only won a contract

Exp. n/n (134); Informe de la JCCA, December 1924–June 1915, AGEV/JCCA 1926, Caja 50, Exp. 3; Informes, AGEV/JCCA, 1925, Caja 48, Exp. n/n.
[29] *LGO*, Tomo XIII, No. 58 (August 14, 1924).

and inspired the formation of nearly thirty oil unions but also made legal gains for oil workers beyond the Tamaulipas' state border.

Failure at Huasteca Petroleum and Mexican Gulf

If the oil companies recognized that organized labor was a fact of life, why did Mexican Gulf and Huasteca Petroleum fail to negotiate contracts? The answer is simple: their unions remained adhered to anarcho-syndicalist discourse. Neither the companies nor the state resigned themselves to that much independence. Huasteca Petroleum created a competing company union, while the Mexican revolutionary government continued to repress the left-wing competition revolutionary syndicalist remnants represented. When Mexican Gulf and Huasteca unions joined the *Confederación General de Trabajadores* (CGT), the anarcho-syndicalist confederation that formed in 1921 with pieces from the shattered COM, their fate was sealed.[30]

Although the Huasteca Petroleum union would end up eviscerated in 1925, the men made organizational strides and demands that, ironically enough, advanced the cause of labor further than El Aguila's union, if only in the long term. The *Sindicato de Obreros del Petróleo de la H.P.C.* (Oil Workers' Union at HPC) at the Mata Redonda refinery went out on strike in August 1924, after the settlement at El Aguila. By September they had a contract virtually identical to El Aguila's. The demands rejected were also similar, with an important exception. The Huasteca union had demanded "workmen's councils" to manage the plants jointly with the company. The notion of worker comanagement was a testament to the resiliency of the anarcho-syndicalist idea of worker management among union leaders, modified to fit the reality that capitalism in Mexico was not going away despite the revolution. Even though the company dismissed the concept altogether in 1924, it would stay with the union and resurface a decade later. Victorious for the first time in a decade or organizing, moreover, the Huasteca Petroleum men rushed to extend their benefits to all company installations in northern Veracruz. By early 1925, they had formed eleven Huasteca Petroleum unions in the camps and gathered them in the first oil union federation, the *Federación de Sindicatos del Petróleo* (Oil Unions' Federation). The twelve unions had 2,825 members.[31]

[30] Taibo II and Vizcaíno, *Memoria*, p. 115.
[31] The camps organized were Garrapatas, Horconcitos, La Laja, San Jerónimo, Juan Casiano, Tres Hermanos, La Dicha, Esperanza, Cerro Azul, Chapopote Nuñez, and

The potential power of the Federation was not lost on the company's general manager, William Green. The ex-Marine decided to get rid of the "red" union by forming a "white" company union. He assigned the task to the head of the white guards, Ventura Calderón, who formed the *Sindicato Único de Obreros y Empleados de la H.P.C.* (The Only Union of Workers and Employers at HPC).[32] Before the inevitable confrontation between the two unions took place, however, Mexican Gulf workers snatched the headlines with their own strike.

The strike at Mexican Gulf began like all others, but ended in repression. The walkout quickly degenerated into violence because Obregón was disinclined to leniency toward CGT unions after the defeat of the CROM in Tamaulipas. But Veracruz, the location of Mexican Gulf, had labor laws not existent in Tamaulipas that permitted state officials to intervene in union conflicts. In this case Governor Tejeda used that authority to block the CROM and act as a buffer between the union and the presidency – to no avail. Although his efforts promised broad solutions, the companies balked and Obregón imposed his will through force.

On September 9, 1924, Mexican Gulf workers walked off their jobs to win a contract. The company had a pumping station and terminal in Las Matillas, eight kilometers upstream from Tampico in Veracruz. Its 250 workers lived in the port and traveled to the terminal daily. The strike, however, involved only 122 men, four short of the majority, which under Veracruz law made it illegal. The men, however, flaunted the law. Faithful to anarcho-syndicalist discourse, they argued that the law "[was] as unjust as the regime on which it [was] based."[33]

The union's position opened the door for repression. Obregón dispatched troops to the terminal immediately to escort nonunion workers and foreigners across the picket lines. In response, the Tampico CGT organized a protest. About five hundred men navigated to Las Matillas on October 2, armed with "rocks, sticks, and iron bars." The troops opened fire, killing the union secretary general, Anastasio Carrillo, and wounding eleven. The confrontation escalated within seventy-two hours, as thousands marched in Carrillo's funeral procession and the CGT organized a general strike. Tampico shut down: twenty-five thousand workers took

Cacalilao. *Sagitario*, November 8, 1924; Mirna Benítez Juárez, "Organización y lucha sindical de los petroleros en Veracruz: 1918–1928." B.A. Thesis, Universidad Veracruzana, 1983, pp. 134–145.

[32] Bada Ramírez, Continuation of the Second Interview, PHO/4/91.

[33] Quoted in Esteves Torres, "Las principales huelgas," pp. 128–157.

the streets. Among them were Huasteca men carrying a sign that read "Government, Capital and Clergy: Herein are your Victims!" The Mexican Gulf union banner called for "Death to those whose despotism cause ill to the collectivities."[34] Obregón sent more troops. They killed two more men and detained five "Bolsheviks."[35]

After three dead, eleven wounded, and five arrests in three days, Veracruz governor Adalberto Tejeda stepped in. Around October 10, he called the unions and the companies to a joint meeting to find a common solution. It was an unprecedented move, an attempt to reach industry-wide solutions to all the conflicts. Given that the Huasteca Petroleum Federation pointed in a similar direction, the unions recognized the potential immediately. As soon as the twenty companies that responded sat across the table, the unions presented their solution: an industry-wide contract, with Tejeda as the mediator. The companies demurred, saying they lacked the authority to discuss such a proposal before consulting with their superiors abroad. They were willing, nonetheless, to consider standard minimum wages. The unions replied they would wait for an answer to their idea and continue with individual strikes in the meantime. Although the workers were ready to negotiate on a much larger scale, the companies were not willing to face a unified labor force. The unions had to wait literally a decade for their plan to reach fruition.[36]

In December the picket lines at Mexican Gulf were still in place and the revolutionary leadership was losing patience. President-elect Calles asked the new governor, Heriberto Jara, to put an end to the strike. Tejeda realized that the workers were in a losing battle and gave Mexican Gulf workers one last piece of advice: break with the CGT and accept Jara, one of the architects of Article 123, as mediator. Three months into the strike, the workers disaffiliated from the CGT. But Mexican Gulf refused to negotiate. Backed by troops, the company now locked out the union

[34] *Sagitario*, October 11, 1924.

[35] Bada Ramírez, Continuation of the Second Interview, PHO/4/91; Robles Saldaña, Fourth Interview, March 20, 1975, PHO/4/39; Report from the Municipal Secretary on difficulties at Mexican Gulf, October 1924, AGEV/JCCA, Caja 40, Exp. n/n; *Excélsior*, October 2–4 and November 8, 1924; *The New York Times*, October 3, 1924.

[36] Junta general convocada por el Gobernador del Estado para solucionar dificultades existentes en la región petrolera, October 21, 1924, AGEV/JCCA, Caja 40, Exp. n/n. In late October the outgoing secretary of Industry, Commerce, and Labor echoed its support for the unions' proposal, but the new secretary, Luis Morones, did not pursue it, according to *Excélsior*, October 10 and 18, 1924.

for two months, then fired the unionists in February 1925.[37] The strike was a total loss.

The early intervention of the federal government and the late flexibility of the union combined to defeat the workers. Miniscule in comparison to El Aguila, the Mexican Gulf union was on the defensive as soon as the strike started, given that the military facilitated the entrance of strike-breakers. At the same time, the leaders committed a strategic error in not convincing four more men to their side to have an official majority. Had they done so, the Veracruz arbitration board would have declared the strike legal. That judgment, in turn, would have permitted Tejeda to pressure the company into negotiations and made it difficult for Obregón to use repression. By the time the union accepted mediation, they were already too weak. Thus, Obregón and Calles colluded with the company and destroyed the union.

Gulf workers paid dearly for their errors. The strike-breakers not only ended up doing the work of twice as many men, but also became Gulf captives. General Manager H. K. V. Tompkin, convinced that the Mexican workers were "an ignorant class who afford[ed] fertile field for agitators," designed a plan to keep organizers from "contaminating" his men again. The design called for "a certain amount of geographical isolation." Thus, he assigned "detectives" to convince workers to leave "their fever-ridden slums" in Tampico and move to Las Matillas. By 1926 Gulf's workers enjoyed U.S.-style segregation inside the terminal, with forty houses, "sufficient" outhouses, a grocery store, a school, and a hospital – surrounded by a high cyclone fence and patrolled by armed guards.[38] Mexican Gulf never formed a union again before 1938.

In late 1924, however, the Gulf strike did not necessarily look like a disaster for the reds. They had lost strikes before. What seemed more important was the extraction of a contract from Huasteca Petroleum's

[37] *Sagitario* reported that the negotiations with "municipal authorities from Pueblo Viejo" began since October, in the October 25, 1924 issue. Report on Gulf strike, August 1924, AGN/DT, Caja 724, Exp. 6; Telegram from President- Elect Calles to the Governor of Veracruz, December 22, 1924 and Telegram from Luis Morones to General Jara, December 26, 1924, AGN/JCCA, Caja 40, Exp. n/n; *Excélsior*, October 14 and 17, 1924. Through May 1925, a number of strikers were still fighting to win their jobs back, using all state channels at their disposal, including the CROM. Morones, however, did not respond to their letters. Benítez Juárez, "Organización," pp. 115–116.

[38] H.K.V. Tompkins to Underwood Nazro, February 13, 1924, RG 59, File 850.5; Hamilton, *Early Day*, pp. 235–239; Report on the Inspection of Mexican Gulf, May 19, 1926, AGN/DT, Caja 990, Exp. 5.

manager, the "abominable Green."[39] Yet the union paused to analyze the Gulf defeat and became more flexible in its stance toward Veracruz authorities, including the new military commander Lázaro Cárdenas. Thus, the 1925 Huasteca strikes were more conciliatory, but President Calles took no note of that.

The main objective of the Huasteca Federation leadership in early 1925 was to extend the 1924 refinery contract to the camps. To guarantee majority support for the strike that would win the contract, the Mata Redonda union prepared the groundwork carefully. The leaders convened all Huasteca workers to discuss the problems that confronted the union, "which we love like a great and beautiful thing, like a son loves his parents." They explained to the men that theirs was more than "a struggle between two classes"; it was a struggle between two principles: "authority and freedom." The appeals paid off. In February the Federation walked out with majority support.[40] The legality of the strike was guaranteed.

Complications arose immediately, however. The company reacted through Calderón, who claimed his white union was the majority and requested the CROM remove the agitators. Governor Jara stepped in first, however, and blocked Morones by proposing a census to determine which union represented the majority. More flexible than usual, the reds accepted the plan. The strike ended around March 8, while the census was prepared.[41] Irritated by Jara's maneuvers, President Calles initiated his own preparations to deal with Huasteca workers. On March 1, he appointed Cárdenas as his own man in the Huasteca.[42]

---

[39] Sindicato de Obreros Panaderos de Tampico y Villa Cecilia to the President of the Republic, June 24, 1925, AGN/DT, Caja 725, Exp. 2.

[40] *Sagitario*, November 8, 1924.

[41] Sindicato Único de Obreros y Empleados de la Huasteca, Sucursal Juan Casiano to President Calles, February 23, 1925, AGN/DT, Caja 725, Exp. 2; Sindicato Único de la Huasteca, Sucursal Tierra Blanca to President Calles, February 23, 1925, AGN/DT, Caja 725, Exp. 2; Sindicato Único to Morones, March 12, 1925, AGN/DT, Caja 725, Exp. 2; *El Dictámen*, February 24, 27, March 8, 1925; Mirna Benítez Juárez, "La lucha de los petroleros de la Huasteca Petroleum Company en el norte de Veracruz: 1926–1931." M.A. Thesis, Universidad Autónoma Metropolitana, Iztapalapa, 1987, pp. 45–46; Benítez Juárez, "Organización," pp. 139–148.

[42] Enrique Krauze, *Lázaro Cárdenas: General misionero* (Mexico City: Fondo de Cultura Económica, 1987), p. 25. In 1970 Cárdenas wrote that he had been in the Huasteca during 1918–1920, but he did not describe the nature of his activities beyond saying they were "military." That suggests he was part of the Constitutionalist forces that failed to wrestle the area from Peláez, undoubtedly a first lesson on the politics of oil and revolution. Lázaro Cárdenas, *Apuntes* (Mexico City: Universidad Nacional Autónoma de México, 1972), vol. IV, p. 182.

Cárdenas would spend three years learning about foreign capital and class struggle as an observer and a participant. General Manager Green welcomed him with $50,000 and a "beautiful Packard sedan," which Cárdenas politely declined.[43] In his "dilapidated" Hudson shortly thereafter, Cárdenas experienced a less welcoming side of Huasteca Petroleum. Taking his good friend Francisco Múgica for a ride, he ran into a locked gate between Cerro Azul and Potrero del Llano. The two generals had to wait one hour before company guards let them through. Incredulous, Cárdenas commented, "that is what happened to the commander of the Military Zone himself."[44] But Green was not called a master of men in vain. He sent a group of workers with a bathtub. According to one of them, the general was out, but his wife accepted the relief from the heat and the humidity the tub promised. By the time Cárdenas returned, the men were busy with the installation. For the next two weeks, the general watched the men work, asking them about the oil industry. One of the workers who answered his questions was Gonzalo Bada Ramírez, the same child who had escaped from Dos Bocas on horseback and became a lunch boy at age eight. He was now an anarcho-syndicalist union leader. Following a more relaxed attitude toward revolutionary officials, the workers invited Cárdenas to union meetings. This general accepted the invitation.[45]

At the same time, Huasteca Petroleum changed owners. On April 1, Doheny sold out to Standard Oil of Indiana.[46] Deeply embroiled in the Teapot Dome bribery scandal over oil concessions at home, Doheny had no desire to fight on two fronts at once. Thus, Rockefeller, the "greatest North American shark," inherited the misnamed Mexican *bolshevikis.*[47] Green remained at the helm, however, so business continued as usual. On the morning of May 11, armed whites drove a company truck to where the red Miguel Padrón and his crew were repairing a pipeline. The whites taunted the reds until tempers flared, and the *blanco* Aurelio Villacaña shot and killed Padrón. By noon, 1,315 refinery workers had walked out in protest, while several "committees" of three or four men hunted Villacaña with the intention "not to bring him back alive." Bada Ramírez and two others searched every departing railroad car for three

[43] William Cameron Townsend, *Lázaro Cárdenas: Mexican Democrat* (Ann Arbor, Michigan: George Wahr Publishing Co., 1952), p. 43.
[44] Quoted in Krauze, *Lázaro*, p. 30.
[45] Bada Ramírez, Continuation of the Second Interview, PHO/4/91.
[46] Davis, *Dark Side*, pp. 186–187.
[47] *Sagitario*, August 16, 1925.

days. Failing in their "delicate mission," the men organized wildcat strikes across all Huasteca installations as the CGT called for a general strike.[48]

President Calles was furious. He "appointed himself mediator," declared the strike illegal, and gave the workers fifteen days to return to work. Those who remained on the picket line at the end of May would be fired at Green's discretion and their severance pay denied.[49] In addition, Calles ordered Cárdenas to prevent the general strike.[50] Cárdenas went to Mata Redonda and personally directed the troops. He also spoke to Green about his own safety. Green had received enough death threats from the union to prompt him to "take precautions." Cárdenas insisted on providing the general manager with his own security detail, a gesture the U.S. consul and Green interpreted as a demonstration of Calles' support.[51] Calles, indeed, ordered Cárdenas to "give all types of protection and guarantees" to the company and to "take all measures you might consider appropriate to guarantee that order not be altered."[52]

The confrontation escalated on all sides. The Federation repudiated Calles with "*bravura*" (bravery), a string of unprintable epithets, and continued the strike past the ultimatum. Green fired the men, who numbered slightly more than two thousand, while Cárdenas protected strikebreaking whites. Taking his cue from Gulf, moreover, Green erected a fence two meters high around the refinery.[53] Open warfare between *rojos* and *blancos* followed. For three months, the reds ambushed whites, tarred and feathered them, and "bathed" them in oil-waste canals, as shoot-outs sent women and children scrambling for cover in the streets. In August, the strike finally collapsed: the unions had run out of funds. With so many men out of work for four months after so many strikes in succession, no

[48] Bada Ramírez, Continuation of the Second Interview, PHO/4/91; Telegram to Chief of Department of Labor, May 14, 1925, AGN/DT, Caja 725, Exp. 2. Villacaña was promoted within days, according to *Sagitario*, May 16, 1925.
[49] Bada Ramírez, Continuation of the Second Interview, PHO/4/9; Report from Inspector Andrés Araujo to Chief of Department of Labor, July 22, 1915, AGN/DT, Caja 725, Exp. 2. A more conciliatory view of Calles' intervention in the 1925 strike is in Gilly, *El cardenismo*, pp. 236–237.
[50] *The New York Times*, May 16 and 19, 1925.
[51] Consul Charles A. Bay to the Secretary of State, June 29, 1925, RG 59, File 800B; *The New York Times*, July 2, 1925.
[52] Quoted in Benítez Juárez, "Organización," p. 151.
[53] Bada Ramírez, Continuation of the Second Interview, PHO/4/91; Vega Soria, PHO/4/49. In some camps, perhaps hearing the news about Mata Redonda, the opposite took place: the reds moved quickly to occupy all the homes in the Mexican quarter, sending the whites and their families scampering out to company tents elsewhere. Telegram from J. J. Peña to H. N. Branch, Tampico, August 11, 1925, AGN/DT, Caja 725, Exp. 2.

amount of melodramas could raise the funds needed to keep the families afloat.[54]

Years later, oil workers Gonzalo Bada Ramírez and Gonzalo Ruiz Carrillo recalled that the unions had confronted Cárdenas about his role in the strike. The men marched to the general's headquarters with banners reading, "If justice is denied, and our patience runs out, what shall we do?" But the army blocked the demonstrators, allowing only a select few to enter the base.[55] Bada Ramírez and Ruiz Carrillo were among them. According to them, Cárdenas' reply was that he was under orders "directly from the presidency" to protect the company. "But that doesn't mean that I have stopped being a friend of yours," he allegedly added.[56]

Throughout the strike, Cárdenas played a critical buffer role like Tejeda and Jara. First, he held back the troops, limiting their response to breaking up fights near the refinery. Second, he attended daily union meetings "*a lo macho*," recalled Alejo Calvillo Uvalle, but did not intervene.[57] Third, when Cárdenas executed orders to evict fired workers and their families from company housing, he did so without further violence. Lastly, the general used his military budget as a de facto strike fund, distributing money among the evicted to help the families in the short term. In the medium term, he convinced Green to give away train tickets for those wishing to emigrate. Over eight hundred men and their families left, as Green announced that he would rehire only 627 workers, preferably younger. Another six hundred became part of the longest oil industry blacklist in history. In the longer term, Cárdenas' gestures toward the vanquished reds did not erase the memory of his role in the strikes, but it did win him genuine gratitude and a degree of moral authority among workers used to harsher treatment from military officers. That complicated

---

54 Even the large unions supporting the strikers – the longshoremen, Pierce, El Aguila, electric company workers, railroad workers, and tramway operators – had depleted their coffers. Atilano Chávez Hernández to President Calles, February 25, 1925, AGN/DT, Caja 725, Exp 2; Sindicato Único de los Trabajadores de la Huasteca Petroleum Company to Governor Jara, June 27, 1925, AGN/DT, Caja 725, Exp. 2; Bada Ramírez, Continuation of the Second Interview, PHO/4/9; Vega Soria, PHO/4/49; Ortega Infante, Second Interview, February 19, 1974, PHO/4/28; Esteves Torres, "Las principales huelgas," p. 72.

55 Gilly, *El cardenismo*, p. 237.

56 Bada Ramírez, Continuation of Second Interview, PHO/4/91; Ruíz Carrillo, PHO/4/38.

57 Calvillo Uvalle, Continuation of the Fourth Interview, November 25, 1978, PHO/4/90. According to Bada Ramírez, Cárdenas listened attentively and participated only to ask the "*muchachos*" (young men) to stop tossing "whites" into the Pánuco River. His request went unheeded, however, and the practice spread like wildfire among unionists of all companies and lasted into 1938. See, for example, Andrés Guniseh vs. Huasteca, AGN/JFCA, Caja 136, Exp. 15/929/1573.

relationship would resurface nine years later, when Cárdenas became president.[58]

In August 1925, the *rojos* put on one final performance before scattering to the winds. They gathered in a "giant" assembly and held their last "prolonged and violent discussions," reported a journalist.[59] Afterwards they marched to CGT headquarters and deposited their red-and-black flags in public acknowledgment of defeat. Then the closing act took place. The ex-unionists unfurled a "very large" Mexican flag and gathered around it. One by one, hundreds of reds pricked their fingers with a pin and let their blood drip onto the white middle stripe of the flag around the eagle and the serpent. Bada Ramírez, retelling the story as an octogenarian, asked dramatically: "How many hundreds signed it? How many thousands? I couldn't tell you, but [the white] was covered . . . with our blood."[60] Thus the men officially dissolved the last anarcho-syndicalist oil union and the first oil union federation. If the switching of flags marked the death of anarcho-syndicalism in favor of nationalism, it was obvious that these men felt that revolutionary Mexico still owed a great debt to its workers. Article 123 notwithstanding, the prospects that it would be paid appeared mixed at best.

The Long Depression, 1927–1934

The flush of victory was fleeting for the unions. Labor conditions changed in the post 1925 period, but they were not for the better. Just as the multinationals worked out an arrangement with Calles reminiscent of the Porfiriato, they gained the upper hand over the unions. In 1927 the companies began consolidating their Mexican operations and slashing the labor force again. Tampico and the Huasteca faced a prolonged economic depression. Confronted with the erosion of their gains, the oil workers diverged in their response. By the early 1930s, El Aguila's union had become paragon of accommodation and patron-client politics. The second generation of oil workers, however, took a different road. They threw their lot with the dissenting fringe leftover from the mid-1920s and unleashed a critical battle for union control. Violence was the order of the

[58] Among those departing was a Nicaraguan gasoline dispatcher from the Cerro Azul camp, Augusto César Sandino, who went home to start a revolution of his own. Bada Ramírez, Continuation of the Second Interview, PHO/4/91; *El Mundo*, July 15, August 21, 22, 26, 1925; *Sagitario*, August 22, 1925; *El Mundo*, January 15, 1928.
[59] *El Mundo*, August 16, 1925.
[60] Bada Ramírez, Continuation of the Second Interview, PHO/4/91-INAH.

day in the Huasteca once again as Cárdenas emerged as the presidential candidate in 1934.

In the late 1920s the multinational oil conglomerates began streamlining their Mexican operations. With a global vision, friendlier production sites than Mexico, and a glutted petroleum market, the oil empires had no need for multiple installations in Mexico. Thus, Rockefeller cut 50% of its personnel at Huasteca Petroleum in 1927 and eliminated the Transcontinental refinery in 1928. The next year the companies dismantled Puerto Lobos altogether. In October, the stock market crashed in New York and the depression the oil workers were experiencing merged into the Great Depression. In 1931 Royal Dutch Shell closed down La Corona. In 1932 it dismantled the gas plant at Los Naranjos, dismissed 40% of El Aguila's work force, and reduced wages. Only three refineries remained open in 1932: Huasteca, El Aguila, and Pierce. Together these employed 2,745 workers: 581 at Huasteca; 1,916 at El Aguila; and 248 at Pierce, many of the workers being young men considered disciplined and free of "vices."[61] Including the men at Mexican Gulf, smaller companies, and the camps, the Huasteca and Tampico had no more than four thousand oil workers, less than a third of the estimated 13,200 employed in the industry throughout the country in 1931.[62]

The unions were hollow. The companies turned them into contractors, effectively nullifying collective contracts.[63] Calles corralled them as well. He removed labor conflicts in key sectors – mining, railroad, electricity, textiles, and oil – from state jurisdiction and moved them to the federal arbitration board in 1927. The president then placed the Junta Federal under his minister of industry, the foe of the oil workers, Luis Morones. In 1931 the new Federal Labor Law voided state laws giving labor autonomy, tightening control over oil workers, too.[64]

---

[61] Celis Salgado, *La industria*, p. 235; Knight Montiel, PHO/4/35; Rocha Juárez, PHO/4/92; Ortega Infante, Continuation of the First Interview, PHO/4/28; Vargas Domínguez, PHO/4/27; *Revista Huasteca*, no. 11 (July 1926).

[62] Meyer, *El conflicto social*, pp. 51–52; Celis Salgado, *La industria*, pp. 189, 235.

[63] Calvillo Uvalle, Continuation of the Fourth Interview, PHO/4/90. Working for union contractors was a better proposition for workers than working for independent contractors, some of whom never paid their workers, according to *El Mundo*, January 24, May 20, June 6, August 14, 1927, March 9, 19, 1928.

[64] Decreto del ciudadano Presidente Constitucional de los Estados Unidos Mexicanos, expidiendo el Reglamento de las Juntas Federales de Conciliación y Arbitraje, BP, vol. 24, no. 4 (October 1927), pp. 419–421. The only oil strike of the Great Depression, at La Imperial in 1932, was declared "illegal" by the Junta Federal under the new law, for example. *El Machete Ilegal*, no. 231 (July 10, 1932) and no. 232 (July 20, 1932).

The crisis was severe. Because "practically every commercial establishment here, from the large concern which sells heavy machinery and supplies for use in the oil fields and the refineries, to the small Chinese
grocery store which sells foodstuffs to the workers, derives its income
either directly or indirectly from the oil companies," Tampico was a
"graveyard."[65] By 1930, the population had dropped to 70,303 from its
1920 peak of 120,000.[66] Huasteca Petroleum admitted that working-class
neighborhoods were a spectacle of

> miserable hovels made out of rotten wood, semi-nude children
> with starved bodies, meat stores with a couple of slabs covered by
> flies... immobile men seating by the side of the road; misery, filth, indo-
> lence. On the other side of the river, houses that used to be two or three
> stories high, abandoned and crumbling, boilers turned upside down,
> walls falling part, broken storage tanks.[67]

The port was disintegrating. Terrific 1927 floods eroded the jetties,
clogged the Chijol Canal, and deposited tons of silt at the bottom of
the Pánuco. By 1930, the sandbar at the mouth of the river had risen to
levels not seen since the 1910s, but no one had plans to dredge it.[68]

To make matters worse, in 1933 twin hurricanes struck northern
Veracruz on September 15 and 24, causing the worst floods of the century.
The Pánuco River rose so high it joined the Chairel and the Pueblo Viejo
Lagoons from north to south. Refineries and neighborhoods were sub-
merged below.[69] A *corrido* writer described the "*Catástrofe ciclónica*" thus:

> From Altamira, Arbol Grande and Miramar Llanos del Golfo to El Aguila
> and Cecilia, all the landfill of Cascajal and even Espartal, all that zone
> by water was invaded...
>   When the fury of the hurricane was ending, in the afternoon, on
> the 15th at dusk, rubbish and many cadavers floated over the waters
> everywhere.
>   A sinister spectacle was obvious, everything was mourning, ruin, and
> desolation because so many dead and injured were found among the
> destruction caused by the cyclone.
>   Nine days later it returned, madder than ever, the deluge, causing
> Tampico a great national mourning.[70]

[65] Consul C. E. Macy to Secretary of State, Tampico, September 2, 1931, RG 59, Roll 20, File
    LC 812.00 Tamaulipas/40; Consul L.S. Armstrong, March 4, 1938 to James B. Stewart,
    American Consul General, Tampico, RG 59, Roll 66, File 812.5054/703.
[66] *El Mundo*, May 18, 24, 1930.
[67] *Fanal* (March–April 1937), p. 8.
[68] *El Mundo*, January 13, 1928, June 2, 1930.
[69] Torrea and Fuentes, *Tampico*, pp. 419–420; Robles Saldaña, PHO/4/39-INAH.
[70] "Catástrofe ciclónica," in *Corridos Tamaulipecos*, collected by Francisco Ramos Aguirre,
    n/p, n/d, pp. 68–69.

The landfill foundation of working-class neighborhoods dissolved like sugar under the rushing water. Houses washed out into the Gulf. So did wildlife, cattle, domestic animals, pipelines, trees, and people. Oil ships were "either sunk or stranded."[71] Over fifteen thousand people were left homeless. In total, the American vice-consul estimated that the hurricanes caused ten million dollars in damage to Tampico alone, but the destruction extended to Tuxpan.[72]

The decay was reflected in working-class bodies. In 1927 vapors leaking from Pierce's crumbling towers killed two people.[73] At El Aguila, a corroded boiler exploded, killing the Russian supervisor and an Estonian worker, and burning a dozen Mexicans, including the supervisor's son, Pedro Rabishkin Masloff.[74] In 1928 the daily *El Mundo* shocked the port with reports that deaths from tuberculosis had surpassed malaria in the past year by a significant number: 368 to 287. Dr. Alfredo Gochicoa estimated that twenty-five hundred persons had active tuberculosis, while Dr. Juan Vela argued that probably 10% of the working-class population required "isolation" to avoid spreading the bacillus. By 1930, *El Mundo* figured that the number of fully symptomatic men, women, and children had risen to four thousand.[75] In 1931 medical experts feared that Tampico had become "the TB capital of the country." Refinery workers in enclosed spaces reported bloody coughs.[76] One doctor who examined Camilo Román Cota's crew at a windowless Huasteca shop, for instance, found sixty-seven men with advanced tuberculosis.[77] The "consumption" of workers' bodies that the men had demanded payment for in 1924 was truer than ever. Structures and people were disintegrating all around, confirming further the idea that the oil industry left a wasteland in its

[71] Report to the Directors and Accounts, to 31st December 1933, P&S/HR, Box C44, File C44/1.

[72] *El Machete Ilegal*, September 30, October 10, 1933; Chávez Padrón, *Testimonio*, pp. 82–84; Reginald S. Carey, ViceConsul to Secretary of State, Tampico, September 30, 1933, RG 59, Roll 20, File 812.00-Tamaulipas/122; Consul C. E. Macy to Secretary of State, Tampico, December 1, 1933, RG 59, Roll 20, File 812.00-Tamaulipas/131; Consul C. E. Macy to Secretary of State, Tampico, September 3, 1933, RG 59, Roll 20, File LC 812.00 Tamaulipas/40.

[73] *El Mundo*, March 4, 1927.

[74] Rabishkin Massloff, PHO/4/87; Calvillo Uvalle, Third Interview, PHO/4/90.

[75] Only infant diarrhea accounted for more dead, at 1,017 children in 1927 alone. *El Mundo*, June 7, 1928, December 1, 1930.

[76] Dr. Donato G. Alarcón, "La TB en la República Mexicana," 1931, AGN/DGG, Caja 71, Exp. 24, 2.017(24)10, n/p.

[77] Román Cota, PHO/4/47. See also complaints from Herculano Rivera vs. Mexican Sinclair, AGEV/JCCA 1927, Caja 62, Exp. 67; Alejo Salazar to the Junta Federal, December 10, 1927, AGN/JFCA, Caja 10, Exp. 15/927/237.

wake. Given the history of the oil workers, it was not typical of them to watch impassively. But with so few in number, what actions could they take? The answer depended on whether the men worked for El Aguila or not.

The Model Union vs. the Dissenting Fringe

Two responses to the crisis of the late 1920s and early 1930s emerged among oil workers. El Aguila's *Sindicato de Obreros* became the "model" union. It scuttled confrontation in favor of social and civic activity closely allied to Emilio Portes Gil as governor (1924–1928) and as provisional president (1928–1930) in a classic patron-client relationship typical of the CROM and other Latin American countries in the 1930s and beyond.[78] The other response was to agitate on the margins, often unemployed and persecuted, but always ready to battle another day.

To weather the long depression, El Aguila's union became an ally of the mediator in the 1924 contract negotiations, Emilio Portes Gil. With financial support from Portes Gil, the union turned its back on class struggle, undertaking a myriad of social works and activities instead. Between 1927 and 1931, the union built a library and a school, paved a street, installed the city's first potable water and sewage systems, sponsored an evening adult literacy program, organized a musical band and a baseball team, managed a consumer cooperative and a farm for its members, and became one of the sponsors of the Lenten carnival.[79] In return for Portes Gil's largesse throughout, the union shunned "politics," that is, it supported Portes Gil's candidates for municipal and state offices.[80] The

---

[78] Hugo Pedro González, *Portesgilismo y Alemanismo en Tamaulipas* (Ciudad Victoria: Universidad Autónoma de Tamaulipas, 1984), pp. 19–53; Ezequiel Padilla, *Los nuevos ideales en Tamaulipas* (Mexico City: Talleres Gráficos de la Nación, 1929), pp. 22, 56, 59–60, 62, 82–83.

[79] Adolfo Roldán, Personal Secretary to Portes Gil to Eustacio Valencia, Coop. Director, November 6, 1929, AGN/PEPG, Exp. 6/603, Registro 144421, Año 1929; El Aguila's Union to Portes Gil, March 19, 1929, El Aguila's Union to Portes Gil, June 4, 1929, and El Aguila's Union to Portes Gil, August 16, 1929, AGN/PEPG, Exp. 3/234, Registro 5225, Año 1929; *El Mundo*, February 23 and March 2, 1927, March 7, 1928, January 1, 20, March 12, May 4–5, June 28, August 4, 13, 26, 1930, January 1, February 16, 1931.

[80] A critique of the alliance between Portes Gil and the state's labor organizations can be found in Juan Guerrero Villareal, *La historia como fue. Comentarios políticos* (Mexico City: Universidad de Tamaulipas and Miguel Ángel Porrúa, 1979). For a more laudatory view, see Francisco Cervantes López, *La organización obrera y el presidente provisional: la organización obrera y campesina en Tamaulipas* (Mexico City: n/p, 1929); and Portes Gil, *Quince años*.

men lost their voice: the 1931 May Day march the union led was silent. The "mute" workers, *El Mundo* wrote, were "orderly and brilliant."[81] In the eyes of other Mexicans, the oil workers had become "Americanized," partial to "the ideology of efficiency, discipline, order, responsibility, and honesty."[82] But appearances were deceiving.

Although the majority of oil workers followed the example El Aguila's union set, a tiny but loud group of nonconformists continued foment-ing disenchantment with company practices and questioning union inac-tion.[83] Although they lacked union jobs, individual syndicalists remained linked to the local scene by family ties – not the least of whom were younger siblings in the oil industry.[84] Some worked in the state bureau-cracy. The carpenter Andrés Araujo, for example, became a labor inspec-tor.[85] The Huasteca syndicalist Gonzalo Bada Ramírez was elected city councilman.[86] Others attempted to reverse the "proletarianization" pro-cess and tried agriculture for the first time, while some relied on the sympathy of the railroad union and the longshoremen for day labor.

[81] *El Mundo*, April 30 and May 3, 1931.
[82] Leopoldo Alafita Méndez, "La administración privada de las empresas petroleras: 1880–1937," *Anuario* V (July 1988), p. 44.
[83] At the same time, the CGT showed "signs of discouragement and wear and tear in its revolutionary zeal" in 1928 and "seemed to lose its sense of direction" altogether in 1929, according to Hart, *Anarchism*, pp. 173–175. See also Carr, *El movimiento obrero*, pp. 194–212.
[84] Bada Ramírez's younger brother, for example, was offered a job at Huasteca after two older siblings were expelled from the refinery for organizing the 1924–1925 strikes. The family decided the young man should take the job so their mother could continue living in company housing, even though the two eldest were banned from the premises. Bada Ramírez, Continuation of the Second Interview, PHO/4/91.
[85] The incorporation of oil workers into local political offices was much more pronounced in Minatitlán, in southern Veracruz, where El Aguila workers began running for and winning municipal posts since 1924. See *El Dictamen*, June 10, 1929 and Julio Valdivieso Castillo, *Historia del movimiento sindical petrolero en Minatitlán, Veracruz* (Mexico City: 1963). Another example is Tuxpan, where an oil worker became the labor inspector in 1926; see Xavier Icaza Jr. to the Junta Central, March 22, 1926, AGEV/JCCA, Caja 38, Exp n/n, "Asuntos varios." In Tampico the oil workers lagged behind in municipal or even state jobs for several reasons. First, the radicals refused to participate in electoral politics, which they considered corrupt. Second, other unions, particularly the longshoremen, were stronger and had more possibilities in that arena. See "Editorial de libertad," March 7, 1925 and "Manifiesto de la Federación Local de Tampico," reprinted in González Salas, *Acercamiento*, pp. 189–194 and *El Mundo*, March 7, 1930. Araujo himself was such a strong labor advocate that he appeared in the Tampico Consul's list of troublemakers into 1935. See Araujo, PHO/4/163; Consul C. E. Macy to the Secretary of State, Tampico, April 29, 1935, RG 59, Roll 59, File 812.5045/214.
[86] He resigned, however, because the city could not meet its payroll for months at a time. Bada Ramírez, Continuation of the First Interview, PHO/4/90; *El Mundo*, May 7, 1931.

Among the latter, some thirty to fifty men, like Mario Ortega Infante, Francisco Vega Soria, and Gonzalo Ruiz Carrillo, volunteered their time in clandestine printing presses. From their hideouts in Villa Cecilia, they cranked out anticompany flyers and a "little workers' newspaper," which they "sneaked into" the refineries whenever they could.[87]

In addition to their papers, the radicals kept sponsoring cultural activities, albeit on a much smaller scale. They staged dramas and organized fund-raising dances for destitute families and comrades, including one in 1928 in Cerro Azul for former gasoline dispatcher Augusto César Sandino, who was leading the resistance against the U.S. occupation of Nicaragua.[88] Such activities met with disapproval of Portes Gil, who sent the police after troublemakers in his jurisdiction. Veracruz governors, by contrast, were more sympathetic.[89]

As the depression took hold, second-generation oil workers began to agree with the radicals that the unions were part of the problem. The contempt the rank-and-file felt toward the union leadership showed in a 1929 handwritten letter to Calles. The letter referred to Huasteca Petroleum's white union, and its authors were from the camps instead of the refinery. Their language echoed the universe of syndicalist ideology even though the spelling and grammatical errors pointed to a barely literate pen. The letter accused the whites of

> triplicating the Foreign Companies' treasures, through treasons they perpetrate on their class, Race, and socialist brothers, without adopting their role as Mexican[s], and without taking into consideration that that money that that worker lacking in consciousness helps the Foreigner hoard is none other than the Richest National treasure; and those individuals without consciousness and without a drop of Mexican blood, because they praise the fact that the most fabulous profits or capital stolen from us go Abroad and do not benefit our Motherland; and without thinking about how the Foreigner is the most powerful enemy of our Motherland, as in U.S. Americans who have always dreamed and dream still that this dear Mexico be under their feet, Governing us the ambitious *yanqui* that [is] nothing less than an octopus because they only want to suck our arteries to leave us rickety and in misery, trampl[ing] the law underfoot.[90]

[87] Vega Soria, PHO/4/49; Ortega Infante, PHO/4/28; Ruiz Carrillo, Second Interview, PHO/4/38; *El Mundo*, August 18, 1929.

[88] Ruiz Carrillo, Second Interview, PHO/4/38; Román Cota, PHO/4/47; *El Mundo*, January 15, March 22, 1928, July 7, 1929.

[89] Calvillo Uvalle, Continuation of the Fourth Interview, PHO/4/90.

[90] Sindicato de Obreros Congregación 1° de Mayo to President Calles, June 29, 1929. The Spanish original reads as follows: El Único "le cuidan y le triplean los tesoros a las Empresas Extranjeras por medio de las traisiones que les juegan a sus hermanos de Raza de

As decay gripped the industry, the union leadership appeared increasingly stale to younger men who had grown up in the hypermasculine, nationalist culture of oil work in the middle of a revolution. A restless second generation of workers thus joined a handful of old radicals to take over the unions once more.

Rojos vs. Blancos: 1931–1933

While the companies enjoyed harmony with the state, old radicals and young oil workers joined forces to spur the resurgence of revolutionary unionism in Tampico and the Huasteca. The revolt began in 1931, at El Aguila, where Serapio Vanegas was in his seventh year as secretary general. At a meeting in June, the membership voted to expel Vanegas from the union for failing to stop the hemorrhage of workers at the refinery. Even the conservative *El Mundo* acknowledged that the dissatisfaction with Vanegas was overwhelming, but the union leader blamed the vote on "communist agitators." The union split into two factions: the majority red, and Vanegas' minority loyalists, white. The acrimony that followed cost Vanegas his life. He was murdered by unidentified assailants on May 1, 1932.[91] The demise of the secretary general unleashed a minor war, as the younger generation tested their manhood trying to wrestle union control from their elders through street violence. Through 1933, ambushes of vehicles, shoot-outs in trolley cars, and fistfights sent families fleeing for cover in Ciudad Madero, the city that now comprised the working-class neighborhoods east of Tampico.[92] According to *El Mundo*, however, it was clear by March that the reds were the overwhelming majority at El Aguila's refinery, twelve hundred to six hundred. Even if the minority

clase y de socialismo sin ponerse a la altura de su deber como Mexicano, ni considerar que aquel dinero que ese obrero inconsciente le ayuda a acaparar al Extrangero es nadamenos que el Riquísimo tesoro Nacional; y estos indibidos sin consiensia y que sin gota de sangre Mexicana porque elogian el que las utilidades o capitales mas fabulosos y urtados a nosotros mismos sean para el Extrangero y no para el beneficio de nuestra Patria; y sin ponerse a considerar que el Extrangero es el aserrimo enemigo de nuestra Patria como es E.U. Americanos que estos siempre an soñado y sueñan que este México querido esté vajo sus plantas Gobernandonos el ambisioso yanqui que nadamenos que un pulpo porque tan solo quieren chuparnos nuestras arterias para quedar raquíticos y en la miseria, pisotean la ley."

[91] *El Machete Ilegal*, no. 203 (July 10, 1931) and no. 226 (May 20, 1932); Vice Consul Walter P. McConaughy to Secretary of State, Tampico, June 10, 1932, RG 59, Roll 20, File 821.00 Tamaulipas/70; Maureen Grace Wilson, "Mexico's Oil Workers: Incorporation and Insurgency," Ph.D. Dissertation, University of Toronto, 1986, pp. 160–161.

[92] *El Mundo*, March 5, 28, 1933, September 26, 1931, and April 1, 15, 1933.

refused to relinquish leadership to a new generation, the fact was that the union did not belong to them anymore.[93]

Elsewhere in the industry, the process was similar but not as violent, as increased national demand for oil products spurred the growth of new fields and installations. At Huasteca Petroleum, the white union split after a troop hired to renovate the crumbling Mata Redonda refinery in 1931 became members and demanded new elections. PennMex workers in El Alamo fared better: militant workers won elections in 1931 unopposed.[94] In mid-1933, the thirteen hundred workers at the new Poza Rica sites unionized and affiliated to the El Aguila refinery's red union as a sub-local with encouragement from radicals such as Esteban Méndez, who had migrated from the port and proselytized tirelessly.[95] In late 1933, as well, the men hired to rebuild the Huasteca Petroleum's camp the twin hurricanes razed in Cerro Azul deposed the company union, influenced by Bada Ramírez and others who had found work there.[96] In Tehuantepec Isthmus in southern Veracruz, where Royal Dutch Shell opened a half-dozen camps in 1932, the process repeated itself. Old syndicalists like Raymundo Piñones Méndez moved in and dispensed propaganda in reams. In addition, the south attracted communists eager to establish a presence among oil workers. By 1933, more than four thousand men in the southern fields and the refinery at Minatitlán were organized.[97] Lastly, the 380 workers at El Aguila's refinery in Atzcapotzalco outside Mexico City also unionized in the same year, as did the

---

[93] *El Mundo*, March 22–23, 1933; Jonathan C. Brown, "Labor and the State in the Mexican Oil Expropriation," Paper No. 90-10 of the Series: Texas Papers on Mexico, Institute of Latin American Studies, University of Texas at Austin, pp. 12–14.

[94] Consul C. E. Macy to Secretary of State, Tampico, March 5, 1935, RG 59, Roll 23, File 812.001-Cárdenas, Lázaro/40; *El Mundo*, October 13, 16, December 16, 1931; Unión de Obreros y Empleados de la PennMex Fuel Company to Junta Regional Permanente no. 4, September 20, 1931, AGN/JFCA, Caja 277, Exp. 15/931/2306.

[95] Social and environmental conditions in Poza Rica were a carbon copy of Huasteca in the 1910s: segregation and squalor for Mexican workers and their families, luxury and amenities for a handful of foreign employees. The "Ethiopian colony," as the English dubbed Mexican quarters, was "a blackened stain; lots of miserable and crowded hovels surrounded by swampy canals carrying sewage from the aristocratic 'american colony' [sic]" on the hill, wrote Vargas, *Lo que ví*, p. 23. On unionization, see Olvera, "The Rise" pp. 64–65; Ella Fanny Quintal, "La Sección 30 del STPRM (Poza Rica)," in *Los sindicatos nacionales en el México contemporáneo: Petroleros*, vol. 1, edited by Javier Aguilar (Mexico City: GV Editores, 1986), pp. 291–300; González Salas, *Acercamiento*, p. 118.

[96] Bada Ramírez, Continuation of the Second Interview, PHO/4/91.

[97] Palma Alor, *Las Choapas*, p. 31–32, 81, 115; Valentín Campa, *Mi testimonio: Memorias de un comunista mexicano* (Mexico City: Ediciones de Cultura Popular, 1985), p. 143; Velasco, *Del magonismo*, p. 30.

230 workers at Huasteca Petroleum in the refinery at Ebano, in San Luis Potosí.[98]

The Recovery, 1934–1936

By 1934 the Mexican oil industry had changed. Mexico was a minor piece in a global chess game controlled by multinationals. And although no single company depended on Mexico for its profits, the repercussions of political developments in Mexico could have global implications. Mexico's own energy consumption had increased, making the economy much more sensitive to fluctuations in production and hence to disruptive union activities. New production and refining sites expanded the labor force beyond the confines of Tampico and the Huasteca. Federal labor law likewise sidelined Tamaulipas and Veracruz in oil matters, as the president became the principal arbiter in industry conflicts. As a result, the industry became even more of a national concern, apt to grab headlines as each new vicissitude provoked presidential reaction. With the entire labor force unionized, what the oil workers did or failed to do now affected the entire country. That became obvious from mid-1934 through mid-1936, as workers put the companies back on the defensive and the federal government reversed its position on militant unionism. The state-labor-oil company equation began to change, with increasingly serious political consequences for all parties, including the newly elected President Cárdenas and the revolutionary state in general.

Oil workers' challenge to Depression-era conditions and the apparatus of the ecology of oil in general did not begin in the Huasteca. It started in the Royal Dutch Shell fields of southern Veracruz (see Table 7.2). The five separate unions formed in 1933 joined into a federation, the second in the history of the industry, the *Federación de Sindicatos de Trabajadores del Petróleo y sus Derivados* (Federation of Oil and Oil Products Workers' Unions). The Federation included the "socialization" of the industry under workers' management as an objective, a concept with decades of history in the northern fields and refineries.[99] The Federation

---

[98] The exact date for the unionization of the Atzcapotzalco workers is not recorded in the Libro de Registros de Sindicatos, but given that their first strike was in mid-1934, it is likely that it took place shortly before that. El Ebano formed its union in 1933. The Registro is reprinted in Celis Salgado, *La industria*, p. 249.

[99] The Federation included Nanchital, Las Choapas, Agua Dulce, Francita, and the Minatitlán refinery, which was divided into two warring factions. Report on the Inspection in Francita, July 30, 1928, DT, Caja 1411, Exp. 12-13; Rodolfo Zavala Montejo, "Relaciones sociales y problemas regionales en una zona petrolera (El caso de Las Choapas, Ver., 1930–1940)," B.A. Thesis, Universidad Veracruzana, 1987, pp. 67, 86, 89.

Table 7.2. *Selected Oil Workers' Strikes, 1934–1937*

Date	Company	Location
May–June 1934	El Aguila	Minatitlán (Isthmus)
		Agua Dulce (Isthmus)
		Puerto México (Isthmus)
		Nanchital (Isthmus)
		Las Choapas (Isthmus)
		Francita (Isthmus)
June 4–9, 1934	El Aguila	Atzcapotzalco (Mexico City)
October 1934	Huasteca	Mata Redonda
January 1935	El Aguila	Atzcapotzalco (Mexico City)
January 9–25, 1935	Huasteca	Mexico City (Sales office)
January 1935	Huasteca	El Ebano (San Luis Potosí)
January 1935	El Aguila	Agua Dulce (Isthmus)
Jan. 12–26, 1935	Huasteca	Huasteca camps
Jan. 23–May 31, 1935	Huasteca	Mata Redonda
March 1935	El Aguila	Agua Dulce (Isthmus)
April 1935	El Aguila	Ciudad Madero
April 1935	Pierce	Arbol Grande
June 1935	Huasteca	El Ebano (San Luis Potosí)
Jan.–July 1936	Huasteca	El Ebano (San Luis Potosí)
April 1936	Huasteca	Cerro Azul
July 1936	Pierce 24-hrs	Arbol Grande
July 1936	El Aguila 24-hrs	Ciudad Madero
July 1936	Huasteca 24-hrs	Mata Redonda
Oct.–Nov. 1936	Pierce	Arbol Grande
October 1936	El Aguila	Ciudad Madero
January 1937	El Aguila 24-hrs	Ciudad Madero
May 13–June 2, 1937	16 companies	National Oil Strike
July–September 1937	El Aguila	Poza Rica
October 1937	El Aguila 24-hrs	Poza Rica
December 1937	various 24-hrs	Veracruz

Sources: El Machete Ilegal, July 10 and 20, 1932; El Aguila and other strike movements in Mexico, June 11, 1934, RG 59, Roll 58, 812.5054/168; *El Mundo,* January 6, 10, 27–28, 1935; C. E. Macy to Secretary of State, April 30, 1935, RG 59, Roll 20, 812.00-Tamaulipas/187; Telegram, June 26, 1936, Dirección General de Gobierno, Caja 36-A, Exp. 27, 2.331.8(20); C. E. Macy to Secretary of State, October 31, 1936, RG 59, Roll 20, 812.00-Tamaulipas/283; *Mexican Labor News,* June–September 1937; Josephus Daniels to Secretary of State, March 4, 1938, RG 59, Roll 57, 812.504/1717.

tested its muscle by demanding a collective contract to replace individual ones. El Aguila, however, refused to renegotiate before the contracts expired, threatening to close down its Isthmus fields instead. Given the closings in northern Veracruz and Tampico, the threat was not idle, but the Federation was not cowered. If the company left, the Federation proposed, President Abelardo L. Rodríguez should turn the fields into workers' cooperatives, socializing them. Defiant, the Federation went on strike on May 10, 1934.[100] The red El Aguila unions at the refineries in Ciudad Madero and Atcapotzalco immediately announced solidarity strikes for June 6. If carried out, the strikes would paralyze most of the industry.

The president intervened. Eschewing repression in favor of institutional solutions that would advance the consolidation of the revolutionary state, Rodríguez averted the solidarity strikes with promises of a prompt, legal solution. On June 9, he delivered. Following the Federal Labor Law of 1931 to the letter, Rodríguez ruled favorably to labor on most demands, including the most controversial: the closed shop.[101] That decision, as the U.S. consul wrote, "amount[ed] to this: the company [could not] hire, discharge, transfer or promote employees without the approval of the union. In cases of definite vacancies and jobs newly created, the company [was] obligated to fill the same with the members of the union."[102] Moreover, none but the highest administrators and professionals were to be exempt from union membership. The implications of that decision, of course, were lost neither on the unions nor the company: the ruling reduced managerial privilege. Adding to the tensions, on June 14 *El Mundo* reported rumors that presidential candidate Cárdenas, on the campaign trail with his old acquaintances at the Huasteca union, had promised to make the closed shop the rule throughout the country should he be elected. Two weeks later, Cárdenas confirmed the rumors publicly.[103]

[100] Zavala Montejo, "Relaciones," pp. 78–79.

[101] *Excélsior*, May 10–16, 1934; *El Dictamen*, May 28–31, June 5, 1934; *El Machete Ilegal*, no. 291 (May 10, 1034), no. 292 (May 30, 1934); Abelardo L. Rodríguez, *Laudo Arbitral en la Huelga del Istmo contra la Cía. Mexicana de Petróleo El Aguila, S.A.* (Mexico City: Royal Dutch Shell, 1934); on El Aguila and other strike movements in Mexico during May, see John S. Littell, American Vice consul, Mexico City, June 11, 1934, RG 59, File 812.5054/168

[102] Consul C. E. Macy to Secretary of State, Tampico, March 5, 1935, RG 59, Roll 23, File 812.001-Cárdenas, Lázaro/40.

[103] *El Mundo*, June 14, 1934; Joe Ashby, *Organized Labor and the Mexican Revolution under Lázaro Cárdenas* (Chapel Hill: University of North Carolina Press, 1967), p. 20.

As could be expected, Rodríguez's ruling turned up the temperature on the oil conflict. Royal Dutch Shell refused to comply with the ruling, sloughing off workers instead. Federation locals responded with wildcat strikes into 1935. In the north, workers did the same. Mata Redonda and El Ebano walked off the job in October, demanding Standard Oil incorporate the closed shop into existing contracts. Both were successful. In Ciudad Madero, El Aguila men decided to strike for a new contract altogether. At Atzcapotzalco, the union walked off the job in January 1935 for its first contract. Within days, Mata Redonda had joined them in solidarity.[104] Thus, when Cárdenas became president in January 1935, three oil unions were on strike.

The oil workers' renewed militancy had unexpected political consequences. Their activism contributed in no small measure to the rift between Calles and Cárdenas. Since 1928, Calles had selected the presidential candidates and exercised power behind the scenes. Cárdenas, whom Calles had appointed as military commander in the Huasteca in 1925, was no exception. When Cárdenas emerged as his own man in early 1935, therefore, Calles lashed out. He challenged the president in public, again placing in jeopardy the stability of the country at large. The oil workers helped precipitate the crisis unwittingly. When Cárdenas moved into the presidential palace in January 1935, five oil union strikes were in progress (Table 7.2). Not surprisingly, one of Cárdenas' first acts in office was to attend to them. The president chose a symbolic place for his first visit: Huasteca Petroleum at Mata Redonda, the union he had helped destroy in 1925. Between February 27 and March 4, Cárdenas met several times with both the reds and the remnants of Ventura Calderón's white union. There is no record of the topics discussed, but Cárdenas did not call publicly for an end to the strike.[105] The companies concluded that meant that

[104] *El Machete Ilegal*, no. 253 (June 30, 1934), no. 298 (July 30, 1934); *Excélsior*, October 13, 1934; *El Mundo*, February 3, 5, May 4, 1935; Celis Salgado, *La industria*, pp. 255–257; Valdivieso Castillo, *Historia*, p. 68. On October 10, 1934 Rodríguez ruled on the application of the *laudo* to Huasteca Petroleum, conceding the closed shop to the union. Consul C. E. Macy to Secretary of State, Tampico, March 5, 1935, RG 59, Roll 23, File 812.001-Cárdenas, Lázaro/40. The strike at El Ebano was declared illegal by the junta federal, however, because the company agreed to comply with the ruling. *El Mundo*, January 27, 1935.
[105] *El Mundo*, February 27–28, March 1–4, 1935.

"government officials from the president down want to give in to the workmen."[106]

The companies accurately sensed that changes were afoot. State-labor relations were not as antagonistic as before, and that spelled trouble for the oil industry. Testing their hypothesis, Standard Oil let the rumor spread before Cárdenas left town that it might close the refinery altogether. Cárdenas ignored the challenge, but the union did not. Upon the president's departure on March 6, the Huasteca union responded to the rumors. If the company left, the refinery should become a "cooperative society."[107] In a "strictly confidential" memorandum to the State Department dated April 11, the consul sounded the alarm: the "real object" of the strike was the "monopolistic control" of the industry by the unions.[108] Although there is no evidence to support such a broad claim, the thawing of state-labor relations signaled by Rodríguez's late 1934 ruling had increased discussions about worker control and ownership in northern and southern Veracruz. Testing their own independence, the unions at Atzcapotzalco, Pierce, and Ciudad Madero staged solidarity strikes in April – despite telegrams from Cárdenas urging them to desist.[109] By May, five months into the Mata Redonda strike, Huasteca Petroleum pleaded with Cárdenas to intervene as he had done in 1925. Selectively using the language of Mexican law, the company wrote that

> this company is disposed to cooperate with the Government in the best manner possible to the end of affording the laborers all the advantages granted them by presidential decisions... In a few words, Mr. President, this Company desires to be permitted to work in peace in strict accordance with the presidential orders (*laudos*); to be freed from the action of the leaders, which is unceasing and insatiable;... to be protected against the persistent hostility of the syndicates, which appear to have forgotten that complete harmony should reign between the factors of production for the latter to exist and prosper.[110]

[106] Visit of President Cárdenas to Tampico and its Effects on Local Strike Situation, Enclosure #1, C. E. Macy to Secretary of State, Tampico, March 5, 1935, RG 59, Roll 23, File 812.001-Cárdenas, Lázaro/40; Consul C. E. Macy to Secretary of State, November 27, 1936, RG 59, Roll 59, File 812.5045/346LH.

[107] *El Mundo*, March 4, 6, 1935.

[108] Consul C. E. Macy to Secretary of State, Tampico, April 11, 1935, RG 59, Roll 59, File 812.5045/204.

[109] *El Dictamen*, April 26–27, 1935; Consul C. E. Macy to the Secretary of State, Tampico, April 30, 1935, RG 59, Roll 20, File 812.00-Tamaulipas/187 LG.

[110] Huasteca Petroleum Company, Translation of Memorandum for the President of the Republic, General Lázaro Cárdenas, enclosure to letter from Charge d'Affaires

Yet the terms of "harmony" were shifting. On May 30, the strike finally ended, but not because the workers had been defeated. Rather, the Federal Arbitration Board awarded "practically all the [union] demands."[111]

Calles was as alarmed as the companies with the reversal in labor policy. In June Calles chastised Cárdenas, publicly questioning the wisdom of allowing strikes all over the country. He saved his bitterest comments, in fact, for the Huasteca union. Echoing the company's telegram, Calles declared that "in Mata Redonda...no sooner had President Cárdenas come into office when new and insatiable appetites laughed at [the 1934] award and started another strike."[112] Labor activism, Calles feared correctly, threatened the "peaceful coexistence" with the oil companies he had attained in 1927. He coincided with the industry's appraisal regarding "the extreme radical direction of the Mexican Government's labor policy" and decried "agitators" who were "risking the economic life of the country."[113] Having ordered Cárdenas to crush the Huasteca union specifically in 1925, Calles took their resurgence as a personal affront. "I know the history of all these organizations since they were created," Calles told the press, "I know their leaders, both old and new," and they were not merely "ingrates" but "traitors."[114]

The revolutionary state had reached a turning point. Like Carranza in 1916, Calles in 1935 saw class and national interests as contradictory. He believed in harmony between labor and capital so long as that meant subordinating the majority (labor) to the minority (capital). He interpreted class struggle as sectional and antinational, hence treasonous. Like others in the revolutionary generation, Calles subscribed to a capitalist development project for Mexico as spelled out in the 1917 Constitution, with class conflict minimized through state management. He was unable to conceive of an alternative interpretation of the Constitution, much less the notion that workers represented the national interest. That was the crux of the stabilization of the revolutionary Mexican state in the 1930s: whose interests should prevail in a nationalist, revolutionary society?

R. Henry Norweb to Secretary of State, Mexico City, May 14, 1935, RG 59, Roll 59, File 812.5045/221 LH.

[111] Huasteca Petroleum Company, *Mexico: Labor Controversy: 1936–1938. Memoranda on the Controversy Arising Out of Mexico's Impositions on Foreign Oil Companies in Mexico Leading up to the Expropriation Decree of March 18, 1938*, n/p, n/d, pp. 20–21.

[112] *El Mundo*, June 12, 1935.

[113] Quoted in Huasteca Petroleum, *Mexico: Labor Controversy*, p. 20.

[114] Quoted in Ashby, *Organized Labor*, p. 26.

Cárdenas had some ideas. In some ways, they did not differ fundamentally from Calles'. Cárdenas did not envision the destruction of capitalism, only the end of what he called the "colonial economy." In 1934 he had declared that

> the formation of our own economy will liberate us from *that kind* of capitalism that does not even care to reinvest its profits in Mexico, that becomes a danger to our nationality in times of misfortune, and that leaves behind nothing but infertile lands, impoverished subsoils, starvation wages, and uneasiness that forebodes public intranquility [emphasis mine].[115]

Where Calles had used the state to control the labor side of the labor-capital divide to pave the way for capitalist development, Cárdenas intended to strengthen the state to redirect capital toward a different kind of capitalism.[116] Thus, in response to Calles, Cárdenas argued that

> the labor problems that have occurred ... are the consequence of the [re]adjustment of the interests of both factors of production; [but], if they cause malaise and even momentarily harm the national economy, resolved in a reasonable manner and within a spirit of equity and social justice, they will contribute in time to make the economic situation more solid, as their correct solution consequently brings betterment to the workers if obtained in relation to the economic possibilities of the capitalist sector.[117]

Both Calles and Cárdenas believed in the principle of equilibrium of production set in the Constitution. Their methods to achieve that balance, however, differed substantially. Whereas Calles compromised with capital and squeezed labor, Cárdenas believed equilibrium could only be reached by guaranteeing workers' rights.[118] Without a level of "equity and social justice," the stability development required would be elusive, as the Porfiriato itself had ultimately shown. In a variant of the reinterpretation of capitalism the oil workers had made during the mid-1920s, Cárdenas envisioned what could be called a socially responsible capitalism. Insofar as he spelled out his "Mexican utopia," as the historian Adolfo Gilly has

---

[115] Lázaro Cárdenas, *Mensajes, discursos, declaraciones, entrevistas y otros documentos: 1928–1940* (Mexico City: Siglo XXI Editores, 1978), pp. 132–133.

[116] Hamilton, *The Limits*, pp. 121–123.

[117] Quoted in Luis González, *Los días del presidente Cárdenas, 1934–1940*, Serie Historia de la Revolución Mexicana, vol. 15 (Mexico City: El Colegio de Mexico, 1981), p. 41.

[118] Mexican Correspondent Report, February 1936, International Labor Organization Historical Archives (ILO), Box: Mexique 334, C 41/1935–1937, Bundle C 41/1936, File C 3303/10.

called it, Cárdenas suggested certain changes: investing profits in Mexico, rewarding labor proportionally to business profitability, conserving and protecting natural resources, and using science and technology for the good of the majority.[119] That kind of capitalism was unrecognizable to many, including Calles and the oil companies. It was not clear, moreover, that the oil workers envisioned the same future either.

Revolution from Below, 1936–1938

At the end of 1936 the oil workers presented their proposal to the companies for an industry-wide collective contract. The demands were not modest: with Cárdenas espousing economic nationalism and opening the door to national mobilizations of labor and peasantry, the workers acted from a position of strength. They aimed for a measure of workers' control the companies would not accept. When the workers refused to relent, however, the revolutionary state intervened as mediator. The workers thus precipitated an impossible three-way tug-of-war with the companies and the state. They proposed expropriation again as a solution, but it was by no means a foregone conclusion.[120] On the contrary, the March 1938 decree was a measure of last recourse for Cárdenas, the last option left after all others had failed and the alternatives seemed worse. Under rapidly changing circumstances, the oil workers did what they had done well historically: take the initiative, go on the offensive, take advantage of the political moment, and push the revolution from below. In 1938 their perseverance and stubbornness finally paid off: the nation became the unequivocal owner of its natural oil bounty at last.

Unification Amidst "Disequilibrium"

Despite what Calles and the oil companies said, the oil workers familiar with Cárdenas did not see him as red. When he proposed the unification of the forty-odd oil unions into an industry-wide organization, therefore, the men rejected his entreaties.[121] The first effort to unify the oil workers in May 1935 at the behest of the Labor Department

[119] Gilly, *El cardenismo*, pp. 41, 96. See also Simonian, *Defending*, pp. 85–110.
[120] See Alan Knight, "The Politics of the Expropriation," in *The Mexican Petroleum Industry*, pp. 90–128, and Gilly, *El cardenismo*, pp. 17–20.
[121] Cárdenas made a plea for unification in Minatitlán when he toured the town as presidential candidate. The southern Veracruz refinery was divided along ideological lines in a manner very similar to Huasteca's union. Valdivieso Castillo, *Historia*, p. 62.

thus failed. Although the southern federation attended, the northern unions (El Aguila, Huasteca, and Pierce) boycotted the meeting, arguing the organizers "were not workers." After months of acrimony, the northerners led a second "great convention" of oil workers and formed the *Sindicato de Trabajadores Petroleros de la República Mexicana* (STPRM) in December 1935, totally independent of the state.[122] Nevertheless, the locals remained weary of the federal government and deeply suspicious of each other. Whereas the American consul in Tampico interpreted such misgivings as the result of the "selfishness of paid radical leaders who [saw] at the worst outright loss of their present jobs and at best diminution of their power and influence," the men as a group had historical reasons to harbor distrust.[123] Three decades of experience with revolutionary authorities, including Cárdenas, made the Tampico and northern Veracruz locals reluctant to surrender their right to autonomous action. The ease with which unions like El Aguila had made the transition from "red" to "model" in the late 1920s also made unionists distrustful of each other and unwilling to tie their destiny to a larger collective of dubious staying power. The strong tradition of autonomy among the northern unions and their history of militancy likewise made the yielding of power to brand-new and politically untested unions a preposterous proposition. By the same token, the fervor of the newly converted that was prevalent among the southern unions made them suspicious of the established northern organizations. The Isthmus Federation, in fact, refused to join the STPRM until August 1936. Deeming each other not radical enough, no union local was willing to hand over control to a "*líder máximo*" in Mexico City union headquarters.[124]

The nominal unification of the oil unions in the STPRM, therefore, did not produce equilibrium in labor-capital or labor-state relations. On the contrary, in January 1936, the Huasteca Petroleum workers at El Ebano walked out without consulting the national union, the first of many wildcat strikes (see Table 7.2). Thus, the workers demonstrated their unwillingness to submit to a national union and their predisposition to

---

[122] *El Mundo*, May 20, December 23, 28, 1935; Celis Salgado, *La industria*, pp. 266–279, 290–300.

[123] Political Report for the Month of September, Consul C. E. Macy to the Secretary of State, Tampico, September 30, 1935, RG 50 Roll 20, File 812.00-Tamaulipas/224.

[124] Robles Saldaña, Eighth Interview, PHO/4/39; Celis Salgado, *La industria*, pp. 300–304; Zavala Montejo, "Relaciones," pp. 90–93. Oil worker García Herrera argued that the workers feared the national union would be a "failure," although he did not explain exactly what that meant. García Herrera, *Memorias*, p. 33.

challenge Cárdenas. El Ebano workers argued that the company exploited both the country and the workers and "neither the salary paid to
its personnel nor the taxes paid to the country" would "ever be enough" to
compensate for what they extracted.[125] Echoing the anarcho-syndicalist
analysis of 1924 that exposed the joint exploitation of labor and nature,
the workers reiterated that capital could never reach a state of "equilibrium" with workers or the nation. The costs of extraction were so high
that the companies could never possibly pay their full price. Likewise, the
workers revealed they made a connection between job security and the
protection of natural resources the president himself might have over-
looked. As Bada Ramírez explained, the union wanted permanent positions for maintenance work, including specialized crews whose sole task
would be to maintain productive wells and prevent premature exhaustion. The union demanded those positions not because the labor leaders had a "mania" for creating new jobs, as the U.S. consul argued, but
because a conservationist approach to production meant long-term job
protection.[126] Although the workers were not explicit conservationists
like the professionals in the Department of Petroleum or Cárdenas, their
manifest concern for instituting maintenance as an integral part of production suggests the incorporation of conservation into working-class values. That is, the oil workers approached conservation more from a practical than a theoretical perspective: they tied their needs for job security
to the long-term protection of the resource they extracted. Their starting point for wanting conservation was different from the professionals
and the president, but the endpoint was the same: careful management
of nature for the benefit of the majority, workers and nation. Questions
regarding management, however, would become one of the breaking
points in the collective contract talks with the companies over the next two
years.

The political moment in late 1935 and half of 1936 paralleled the
"disequilibirum" workers saw in the relations between the companies and
labor, nature, and nation, as they witnessed Calles and Cárdenas confront
each other over the course of the Mexican Revolution. Calles conspired to
depose Cárdenas and sought to control the center of national industry,
Nuevo León, by running his son for governor. In response, Cárdenas

[125] José Rivera Castro, "El conflicto obrero-patronal en la Huasteca Petroleum Company
en 1936," *Anuario* V (July 1988), pp. 49–53.
[126] Consul C. E. Macy to Secretary of State, Tampico, October 5, 1935, RG 59, Roll 59, File
812.5045/244 LH; Bada Ramírez, Continuation of the Second Interview, PHO/4/91.

annulled the Nuevo León elections, prompting the deeply conservative *regiomontano* elite to organize a lockout. On February 6, 1936, the
Monterrey industrialists shut down their city to condemn "communism
and Russian influence" in Mexico. Cárdenas counterattacked. He went
to Monterrey and, after restating his commitment to the "attainment
of social equilibrium on the basis of just relations between capital and
labor," he gave his famous "fourteen points" address.[127] In it, Cárdenas
spelled out the alternative to negotiating with organized workers: "the
entrepreneurs who feel tired by the social struggle may turn over their
industries to the workers or the Government. This would be patriotic;
not so the lockout."[128] If socially responsible capitalism was exhausting
for the private sector, state and worker ownership had become not only
official options but also patriotic ones.

If the oil workers thought Cárdenas had adopted their positions, they
were mistaken. Leaving Monterrey to stew, the president traveled to El
Ebano, Tampico, and Ciudad Madero to meet with the unions again.
Cárdenas reiterated that his government sought "equilibrium" between
capital and labor. He told the workers that "in order for that equilibrium to be stable," however, its base had to be not the subordination of
labor to capital, but rather "social justice." In their specific case, Cárdenas
"assure[d]" the men that he knew the companies had the means to meet
their demands and "therefore, they cannot be considered disproportion-
ate."[129] Without retreating from his support for worker management as
an alternative to class struggle, Cárdenas was nevertheless trying to stake
a middle ground between the men and the companies, advising both
that despite their historical ties, Cárdenas was not Calles, and the 1930s
were not the 1920s. In a revolutionary Mexico, organized labor was to be
a permanent force. Capitalism would not be overthrown, but capitalists
needed to learn to compromise with labor.

In order to make capitalism responsive, however, Cárdenas needed to
confront Calles' challenge once and for all. Throwing his full support
behind a new national labor confederation formed in February, the *Confederación de Trabajadores Mexicanos* (CTM), and lifting all restrictions on
the Communist Party to organize and participate in civic and political life,
Cárdenas took a big risk. He exiled Calles and Morones to Los Angeles,

[127] Mexican Correspondent Report, February 1936, ILO, Box 334, C 41/1935–1937, Bundle C 41/1936, File C 3303/10.
[128] Lázaro Cárdenas, *Ideario político* (Mexico City: Ediciones Era, 1991), pp. 24–25, 189–191.
[129] Mexican Correspondent Report, February 1936, ILO, Box 334, C 41/1935–1937, Bundle C 41/1936, File C 3303/10.

California in April 1936. "Millions" cheered the demise of the *jefe máximo* and his faithful Morones.[130] Calles' warning upon his arrival in the United States that a "communistic group in Mexico has the support of the government" and that it intends "to provoke the immediate socialization of all the sources of production, to then implant a communistic dictatorship," failed to arouse the majority of Mexicans.[131] Cárdenas thus gained legitimacy among ordinary Mexicans and the political support he needed to promote reform. And although the state did take over the oil industry two years later, the process disproves Calles' theory of a plot, communist or otherwise. Cárdenas did not share the eagerness oil workers had to socialize their work centers.[132] On the contrary, he did everything possible to avoid drastic action. Yet despite the fact that Cárdenas placed the responsibility for nationalization squarely on the shoulders of the companies, it was the oil workers who ultimately led him to expropriation.

Negotiation and Insurrection

The last two years of foreign oil in Mexico were a fierce battle of wills among the companies, the workers, and the president, an oil workers' insurrection in the context of negotiations over the first industry-wide collective contract. The political maneuvering was unpredictable and fast, more like a full-contact sport than a methodical and calculating game of chess. All three contestants were skillful, savvy, and determined or even ruthless, but in the end someone had to lose. For the first time in over a decade, it was not the oil workers whose backs landed on the mat.

The contest began in November 1936, when the STPRM announced a nationwide strike for a single industry-wide collective contract, a 160-page document with twenty-four chapters and 250 clauses. As an initial show of force and unity, the STPRM carried out a twenty-four-hour walkout on November 25. On the 26th, Cárdenas advised the STPRM that a nationwide strike was "totally inconvenient," for it jeopardized his first major attempt at land redistribution then underway in La Laguna, in northern Mexico. Despite opposition from southern locals, the STPRM

---

[130] Mexican Correspondent Report, February 1936, ILO, Box 334, C 41/1935–1937, Bundle C 41/1936, File C 3303/10; Alex M. Saragoza, *The Monterrey Elite and the Mexican State, 1880–1940* (Austin: University of Texas Press, 1988), pp. 170–181.
[131] Quoted in Huasteca Petroleum, *Mexico: Labor Controversy*, p. 22.
[132] Ambassador Josephus Daniels to the Secretary of State, Mexico City, March 4, 1938, RG 59, Roll 57, File 812.504/1717.

conceded and postponed the strike for 120 days for negotiations.[133] As the oil workers' history showed, however, compromise was not one of their strengths. Their demands, as observers noted, went "beyond the customary."[134] In addition to improvements in wages, hours, and living conditions, the workers wanted guarantees in matters of health and safety and input into "basic principles of administration." Nevertheless, the first set of demands, 70% of the clauses, was resolved before negotiations broke down in May 1937. Demands for health, safety, and workers' control were beyond compromise.[135]

Collectively, the disputed clauses demanded the companies pay for the bodily damage that the ecology of oil did to workers while denying them exclusive control over those same bodies. In other words, the union demanded unprecedented decision-making power over hiring, firing, and disciplining workers and defining work categories and assignments. Clauses 26 and 27, for instance, changed the definition of permanent work (*trabajos de planta*) and temporary work (*obra determinada*). The companies defined maintenance, dismantling, repairs, road construction, exploration, and even drilling as temporary work, hence subcontracted. The union, by contrast, wanted to classify all but new construction as permanent work, to be performed by union men, thus gaining effective control over the work force.[136] Nowhere was that intention clearer than in the clauses that shrunk the number of foreign and nonunion employees. Clause No. 3 was the crucial one. It set at 114 the total number of employees "exempt from union domination," down markedly from the 1,100 such positions in existence at the time of negotiations.[137] That

---

[133] Valdivieso Castillo, *Historia*, p. 84; Confederación de Trabajadores Mexicanos, *CTM: 1936–1941* (Mexico City: CTM, n/d), pp. 349, 532; Samuel León and Ignacio Marván, *En el cardenismo*, Serie la clase obrera en la historia de México (Mexico City: Siglo XXI Editores, 1985), p. 234; García Herrera, *Memorias*, p. 35.

[134] Mexican Correspondent Report, November 1936, ILO, Box 334, C 41/1935–1937, Bundle C 41/1936, File C 3303/19.

[135] Memorandum Concerning Provisions of Proposed Standard Contract (Contrato-Tipo) in the Mexican Oil Industry, Enclosure No. 1 attached to Consul C. E. Macy to the Secretary of State, Tampico, November 27, 1936, RG 59, Roll 59, File 812.5045/346LH. The disputed clauses are included in Mexican Correspondent Report, May 1937, ILO, Box 334, C 41/1935–1937, Bundle C 41/1937, File C 3303/24.

[136] Government of Mexico, *Mexico's Oil*, p. 749; Compañía de Petróleo El Aguila, S.A., *The Mexican Oil Strike of 1937 (May 28–June 9)*, n/p, n/d, p. 26.

[137] The proposed distribution of nonunion employees was as follows: thirty-five for El Aguila, eleven for Huasteca, ten for La Imperial, four for Pierce, and less for the smaller companies. Mexican Correspondent Report, November 1936, ILO, Box 334, C 41/1935–1937, Bundle C 41/1936, File C 3303/19.

demand meant that key men, including drillers, accountants, and "important executives such as assistant general manager, assistant general sales manager, assistant manager of production," and all but the chief geologist, would be card-carrying union members, subject to union rules, discipline, and protection in cases of conflict with the companies.[138]

If the demands meshed with Cárdenas' ideas of equilibrium between labor and capital, they certainly did not fit contemporary notions of capitalist management. Sharing power with workers, that is, altering established social hierarchies, was nothing short of "communism" for the companies. As Huasteca Petroleum argued, the subtext to the conflict was "a revolutionary social theory that the workmen are somehow entitled to control the business in which they work and that the employer is in the nature of a usurper depriving the workmen of their natural rights."[139] Indeed, the companies were correct in arguing that Article 123 did not support such a radical interpretation. The Constitution granted substantial rights to workers, but it did not entertain worker management. Cárdenas' openness to labor organization in fact presented risks to the role revolutionaries had envisioned for the state: managing the class struggle. Although, as Cárdenas knew, the Mexican working class as a whole was too small and weak to pose a threat to capitalists, the segment the oil workers represented was different. They were taking advantage of the moment to push the revolutionary agenda as far left as possible. The companies, however, missed the point. They erroneously believed that Cárdenas and the workers were interchangeable and refused to compromise further.[140] Thus, the 120-day cooling off period expired without a contract.

The unified oil workers went on the offensive. On May 28, 1937, the eighteen thousand *petroleros* staged the first industry-wide strike in history. For thirteen days, red-and-black flags covered the gates of the 178 oil company installations that dotted Mexico from El Ebano and Tampico to the Isthmus of Tehuantepec and Atzcapotzalco. The scent of victory,

---

[138] Roscoe B. Gaither, *Expropriation in Mexico: The Facts and the Law* (New York: William Morrow and Company, 1950), p. 10.

[139] Huasteca Petroleum, *Mexico: Labor Controversy*, p. 13.

[140] Certainly in retrospect the companies argued that the oil workers and the president had been working in tandem to "squeeze" the companies progressively until the industry had "no alternative but to cease operations." The strikes were the "excuse" the president needed to expropriate. Standard Oil, *Confiscation or Expropriation?*, pp. 20–21. See also Gilly, *El cardenismo*, p. 249.

moreover, inspired the rank and file to spread the insurrection: they sent out a call for a national general strike in solidarity.[141] Cárdenas reacted immediately, advising the STPRM and the CTM against the general strike. Arguing that state channels were the best means for workers to achieve their goals – and cement the revolutionary state in the process – Cárdenas proposed a way to break the stalemate. The 30% of the contract in dispute could be submitted to arbitration as a *conflicto económico,* a new legal tool created in 1934 to resolve labor-capital conflicts.

The *conflicto económico* was a risky alternative to direct action. It entailed the appointment of a special panel to determine whether the defendant, that is, the oil companies, had sufficient economic resources to meet the plaintiff's demands. It was up to the panel as well to make recommendations for a settlement to the Federal Arbitration Board for a final ruling.[142] The whole process, therefore, depended on the decisions of government officials, the managers of class struggle in revolutionary Mexico. Although the STPRM leadership deferred to Cárdenas for a second time, it did so reluctantly. As one delegate pointed out to the president, his local "would kill him" when he announced the decision to them. From the twenty-five locals that made up the STPRM, only eighteen accepted the moratorium on strikes for the duration of the *conflicto económico.*[143] The insurrection underway could not be stopped: between November 1936 and the ruling of October 1937, the companies tallied ninety-one wildcat strikes.[144] At the same time, the men refused to obey supervisors, reported in sick, slowed down production, and attempted strikes that the government diffused.[145]

One local in particular emerged as combative and ready to push the nationalization alternative. Poza Rica Local 30 went on strike in July 1937 to protest the fact that El Aguila had abrogated the existing contract in the light of the one under negotiation. In August a worker committee intercepted Cárdenas in Yucatán with a petition: to expropriate Poza Rica and sell the field to the union as "a cooperative." They pledged to pay

---

[141] CTM, *CTM,* p. 396; Editorial, *Futuro,* July (1987).

[142] Government of Mexico, *Mexico's Oil,* pp. 517–519.

[143] García Herrera, *Memorias,* p. 55.

[144] Telegram from Ambassador Josephus Daniels to the Secretary of State, Mexico City, October 20, 1937, RG 59, Roll 63, File 812.5045/576 LH.

[145] Lázaro Cárdenas, "Mensaje que dirigió al sindicato de trabajadores petroleros de la República Mexicana," (Mexico City: Talleres Gráficos de la Nación, 1937), p. 2; Gilly, *El cardenismo,* pp. 245–246.

the twenty-five million pesos the company estimated as its worth within twelve months, promising to protect the "source of natural riches" the field represented. But Cárdenas was reluctant to go that far. According to committee member Eduardo Pérez Castañeda, the president declined the petition, but called the idea "interesting."[146] The Poza Rica men showed once more that the oil workers linked the interests of labor to the protection of natural resources and that worker control meant reorienting production to meet the nation's long-term interests, reaffirming the notion that worker management, worker ownership, and working-class interests coincided with national interests.

The pressure on Cárdenas increased. On September 6, the Mexican Chambers of Commerce sent him a telegram announcing they would lay off forty thousand workers if the Poza Rica strike continued.[147] The businessmen's ultimatum reflected how much the Mexican economy depended on petroleum by 1937. Mexico consumed 16.86% of the heavy oil, 43.50% of the refined products, and a whopping 99.9% of the light crude produced in the country.[148] Poza Rica in fact supplied all of Mexico City's gasoline. As supplies dwindled and gas lines stretched for blocks, the capital's businessmen awakened the nation to another reality: the oil workers held the country's economy in their hands. That unprecedented power shift refocused the oil conflict: it put the workers at odds with Cárdenas.

Cárdenas chastised the oil workers publicly. In a press conference, he pointed out that "the lack of cohesion" in the STPRM and the "partial" attitudes of some locals made it seem as though the workers "conspired" with "capitalist interests." Furthermore, Cárdenas questioned the men's patriotism, reminding them that "they are not living within a conservative state" and should "collaborate with the government." Failure to do so

---

[146] Del Valle and Segura Portilla, "La huelga de 57 días," pp. 77–83. The president refused a similar request for nationalization from the Mexican Light and Power Company workers in 1936, according to Ambassador Josephus Daniels to Secretary of State, Mexico City, March 4, 1938, RG 59, Roll 57, File 812.504/1717. The idea did not go away, however, and in December 1936 a number of Poza Rica workers proposed that the drilling equipment belonging to foreign contractors be "expropriated" as "national patrimony." See *La Palabra*, December 20, 1936, in AGN/DGG, Caja 87, Exp. 43, File 2.017(26)15901.

[147] Charge d'Affaires, Pierre de L. Boal to the Secretary of State, Mexico City, August 3, 1937, RG 59, Roll 60, File 812.5045/488; Ambassador Josephus Daniels to the Secretary of State, Mexico City, September 8, 1937, RG 59, Roll 63, file 812.5045/548 LH; Hamilton, *The Limits*, pp. 223–224.

[148] Mexican Correspondent Report, August 1937, ILO, Box 334, C 41/1935–1937, Bundle C 41/1937, File C 3303/27.

was "suicidal."[149] As *El Mundo* reported, the speech fell like "a bomb" among the workers.[150] They felt the responsibility was the reverse: the state should collaborate with the union. Unrepentant, Local 30 returned the accusation, arguing it was Cárdenas who was playing into the hands of *la reacción.* They remained on strike. Two weeks later, Cárdenas promised that the Labor Department would review the Local's demands and the workers lifted the strike. After fifty-seven days, the president had given in first. Still, the men staged more wildcat strikes "to force the company to acquiesce" to their demands, as they said, but undoubtedly to keep the heat on Cárdenas as well.[151]

In the next three months, the conflict over the collective contract kept the three parties on the front pages of the national newspapers. After touring the Isthmus, Tampico, and northern Veracruz, the experts presented their report in September. Even though the STPRM filled seventy-two pages with objections, the workers were the undisputed winners on health and safety as well as in their bid for control over large segments of the labor force.[152] The report then passed to the Federal Arbitration Board for a final ruling. Convinced that the Board would only rubber stamp the conclusions, the companies rattled their sabers, canceling contracts, packing files, and laying off hundreds of temporary workers in the Huasteca and Tampico.[153]

In November, Cárdenas made a surprise move. He announced that Poza Rica would be a joint venture between the state and Royal Dutch Shell (see Chapter 6). The news "caused a distinctly unfavorable impression in labor circles," according to the labor press. The decision to reject expropriation and cooperatives in favor of collaboration with a multinational confirmed the workers' opinion that Cárdenas was playing the capitalist game.[154] The unions struck back. On December 10, the northern Veracruz and Tampico locals called for a twenty-four-hour "protest against the authorities" for letting three months elapse without a ruling on the experts' report. The strike was a local idea, unauthorized by the STPRM, and even though the workers vehemently

[149] Cárdenas, "Mensaje," p. 3.
[150] *El Mundo,* September 13, 1937.
[151] Olvera Rivera, "The Rise," p. 71; Román del Valle and Segura Portillo, "La huelga de 57 días," pp. 84–93.
[152] Most of the objections centered on the numbers of nonunion employees the panel of experts allowed. The union wanted less, of course. Mexican Correspondent Report, August 1937, ILO, Box 334, C 41/1935–1937, Bundle C 41/1937, File C 3303/27.
[153] *El Dictamen,* August 17, September 3, 1937.
[154] *Mexican Labor News,* November 18, 1937.

denied that Cárdenas was their target, the president knew otherwise. He warned the men that "the Executive would regard this act as one of open hostility against the Revolutionary Government" and held them responsible for the consequences.[155] No matter. The protest strike took place.

Royal Dutch Shell, for its part, wavered between the joint venture and the Americans who saw Cárdenas as a communist. The test of loyalties came on December 16: the Arbitration Board ruled that the recommendations of the panel of experts stood in their entirety. Closing ranks, Shell joined the other corporations in requesting an injunction from the Supreme Court to stop implementation of the Board's decision. Cárdenas' efforts to broker a separate peace with El Aguila had come to naught. The collective contract and the future of workers' control were in the hands of the Mexican Supreme Court. Given the Court's history, the companies had a chance. To raise the odds in their favor, the multinationals withdrew their deposits from Mexican banks, encouraging others to do the same. As intended, the ensuing run on the banks worsened an already critical economic situation.[156]

The workers confronted the challenge head on. On February 3, 1938, the STPRM sent out an "urgent" and "strictly confidential" memo to all locals instructing them to prepare to take over the industry if the companies left the country.[157] At the end of the month the union raised the issue publicly. Speaking at the first national congress of the CTM on February 21–25, 1938, its secretary general, Vicente Lombardo Toledano, told the crowd he felt "positively sure" that the Supreme Court would rule in favor of the STPRM. But "once the sentence is handed down," he asked, "what is going to happen?" The "unavoidable moment will arrive," Toledano predicted, "when the oil companies will have to be replaced" by the state and the workers. He asked, "are we willing to assume the technical, economic, legal, moral, and historical responsibility" that entailed? The response was, of course, a resounding "yes." It was confirmed a few days later at the national oil workers' congress.[158] Thinking that the companies would leave and the industry end up nationalized by default, the union did not

[155] Mexican Correspondent Report, December 1937, ILO, Box 334, C 41/1935–1937, Bundle C 41/1937, File C 3303/31.
[156] Mexican Correspondent Report, February 1938, ILO, Box 335 C 41/1938–1941, Bundle C 41/1938, File C 3303/33; *Mexican Labor News*, December 13, 1937.
[157] Quoted in Gilly, *El cardenismo*, pp. 26–27.
[158] Mexican Correspondent Report, February 1938, ILO, Box 335 C 41/1938–1941, Bundle C 41/1938, File C 3303/33.

demand expropriation outright, but the actions of the membership over the next two weeks led down that road.

The first two weeks of March were as agitated as any in the course of the Revolution. On the 1st the Court ruled against the companies. On the 4th and again on the 7th, the companies and Cárdenas met to discuss the ruling. The companies were willing to bend on health and safety, period. Their opposition to workers' control was total and final. Union locals, meanwhile, met to determine which workers would manage which departments.[159] On the 9th, Cárdenas had a long meeting with his old friend Francisco Múgica and asked him to prepare the nationalization decree in case the companies flaunted the ruling of the Supreme Court.[160] Five days later the companies obliged, announcing that they "were unable to meet the terms of the decision."[161] Before Cárdenas reacted, Mata Redonda had taken over the streets. Upon hearing the news, the men walked out of the Huasteca Petroleum refinery. By the 16th, the strike had spread to El Aguila and Pierce. Conscious of the effects of the strike on the economy, however, the men suspended only export-related work.[162] The companies sought another meeting with Cárdenas, but he declined. Through diplomatic channels, he recommended the companies return to the Arbitration Board.[163] The companies ignored the advice. The Board met instead with the STPRM, which requested the voidance of standing contracts. The Board did so on the 18th and the STPRM announced a strike for midnight. The CTM immediately called for a general strike and march on the 23rd to support "the oil workers and the Mexican people and government in their struggle against foreign imperialism."[164]

Cárdenas had reached the end of the line. The companies were defying the law as usual, but the strikes planned were a double-edged sword. Although they repudiated the companies, they also tested Cárdenas. The crisis was real. By 1938 the polarization that Calles precipitated and Cárdenas deepened with his fourteen points had reached alarming proportions. Mexico's homegrown fascist movement was clashing in the

---

[159] Gilly, *El cardenismo*, pp. 59, 62–64, 93; *El Dictamen*, March 7, 1938.
[160] Gilly argues that Cárdenas made up his mind to nationalize the industry on March 14. All he needed was the right moment. The oil workers certainly provided that. *El cardenismo*, pp. 16–17, 42.
[161] Mexican Correspondent Report, February 1938, ILO, Box 335 C 41/1938–1941, Bundle C 41/1938, File C 3303/33.
[162] *El Dictamen*, March 15, 17, 1938.
[163] Gilly, *El cardenismo*, p. 59.
[164] *Mexican Labor News*, March 17, 24, 1938; Government of Mexico, *Mexico's Oil*, pp. 697–872.

streets with organized labor, while rumors of armed right-wing rebellion flew. The economy reeled not only from the Great Depression but also from worker and peasant militancy and capitalist resistance. In fact, on the morning of March 18 Cárdenas told his Cabinet that the oil workers' strike in the Huasteca alone "was already causing very serious disruptions in the national economy" and threatened to paralyze the country.[165] If the strike expanded across the industry and the CTM carried out a general strike nationwide, the revolution being led from below by the oil workers might embolden *la reacción* into counterrevolutionary violence.[166] The options were narrow. Using military force against the oil workers was one alternative. Repression of oil strikes had a long history, as Cárdenas knew from personal experience. But given his commitment to social justice, that avenue was not only repugnant but also politically dangerous. The oil workers had the sympathy of the nation on their side, which meant that Cárdenas risked sacrificing his entire reform project if he turned his back on the workers now. Furthermore, he risked the legitimacy of the entire revolutionary apparatus he was trying to consolidate if he allowed the foreign oil companies to disregard Mexican law and institutions yet again. For the sake of the stability of the nation and the consolidation of the state after four decades of upheaval, Cárdenas chose the last option the oil workers' movement had left him and, indeed, proposed since 1934.

Nearly twenty thousand oil workers and their families were waiting for the clock to strike midnight to unfurl their red-and-black flags on March 18, 1938, when at 10 o'clock the radio interrupted its regular programming for an important message from President Cárdenas. Because the companies' refusal to abide by the ruling of the Supreme Court had as its "inevitable consequence the total suspension of activity in the oil industry," and because "in those conditions it is urgent that the public administration intervene with measures [that are] adequate to prevent... grave internal disturbances," Cárdenas read out slowly, the "machinery, installations, buildings, pipelines, refineries, storage tanks,

[165] Quoted in Gilly, *El cardenismo*, p. 70.
[166] Toledano had raised the issue at the CTM Congress in February, calling on the "million men and women" members to be prepared for a right-wing uprising led by Saturnino Cedillo, former Cabinet member and strongman from San Luis Potosí. Cedillo began making military preparations against Cárdenas in September 1937. A month and a half after the nationalization, on May 15, 1938, Cedillo revolted. His band put up resistance in San Luis Potosí, Puebla, Guanajuato, and Michoacán until Cedillo died in battle in early 1939. Meyer, *México y los Estados Unidos*, pp. 350–351.

means of communication, tankers, distribution stations, ships, and all other properties" of the foreign companies were thereby expropriated.[167] At midnight on March 19, 1938, the oil industry became Mexican.

The revolutionaries' idea of achieving equilibrium between labor and capital proved to be a chimera. The companies had risked it all and lost. The oil workers were "euphoric," "jumping" for joy in the Huasteca and Isthmus camps, Tampico, Ciudad Madero, and the metropolis. As soon as Cárdenas finished speaking, hundreds of men, women, and children began marching from their union halls toward their work sites. Yelling "¡*Viva Cárdenas!*" they rolled up the red-and-black banners and, upon reaching their installations, hoisted the Mexican flag instead.[168] In their eyes, that single act summarized and justified decades of bloody class struggle: their militancy had made the industry Mexican.[169]

The decree also demonstrated that the working class indeed represented the nation's interests. The starkest proof was in Las Matillas. Mexican Gulf workers had literally nothing to celebrate. The manager's 1924 sequestration plan had succeeded beyond his wildest expectations. Isolating the men behind "electrified" fences and armed guards who kept union organizers at bay, the company had fought off the STPRM successfully. The absence of the union meant that Gulf had not been a party in the contract negotiations, the Supreme Court ruling, or the strike threats that led to nationalization. Mexican Gulf therefore was not included in the decree.[170] But despite the exhilaration of the moment,

---

[167] Decreto de la Expropriación de la Industria Petrolera, Box 335, ILO, C 41/1938–1941, Bundle C 41/1938, File C 3303/34.

[168] Ortega Infante, Continuation of the First Interview, PHO/4/28; Vargas Domínguez, Third Interview, PHO/4/27.

[169] Over the course of the formation of the STPRM and the contract negotiations, the oil workers reaffirmed their radical tendencies time and again, voting for communist candidates for union leadership positions whenever possible. The oil workers, in coalition with the railroad workers, miners, electric company workers, tramway drivers, and teachers, voted for the Communist Party member, Miguel Velasco, in the CTM elections that pitted him against Fidel Velázquez in 1936. When unions that had been closely affiliated to Morones threatened to withdraw from the CTM if a communist was seated in the leadership, Velasco renounced his position in the interest of working-class harmony. A second vote ensued and Velázquez was elected instead, a decision more than one worker later regretted. Velázquez stayed in the leadership of the CTM for the next sixty-one years, until his death in July 1997. See Hamilton, *The Limits*, pp. 154–155.

[170] STPRM to Lázaro Cárdenas, June 29, 1937, November 16, 1937, February 1, 1938, AGN, Presidentes: Lázaro Cárdenas (P/LC), 432/401; STPRM to Chief of Departamento Autónomo del Trabajo, December 31, 1936, AGN/DGG, Caja 46-A, Exp 8. 2.331.8(26)17/90; Consejo Permanente de Agrupaciones Obreras de la Región to President Cárdenas, AGN/P/LC, Exp. 431/401.

the STPRM did not forget their Gulf brothers. In the weeks following the nationalization the union launched a boycott of Gulf products, pressuring the government to extend the decree to the company.[171] Their efforts were in vain, however, as Cárdenas adhered strictly to the legality of the case. Thus, the president himself confirmed that the victory over the oil companies rightly belonged to the Mexican oil workers. Although the nationalization might not have taken place without Cárdenas in the presidency, there can be no question that without the oil workers, the industry would have not become Mexican. It was the revolution from below that made all the difference.

Nevertheless, the decree left questions pending. The oil workers had not gained anything materially. They had no contract. They had no employer. Half of the anarcho-syndicalist dream had come true – the capitalist boss had been eliminated – but the future was uncertain. The workers had much to negotiate with the state, beginning with who owned the industry. Would the workers have their cooperatives? Would the state run the industry, with the oil workers as government employees? Or, would the state transfer the industry to the Mexican private sector? The battle over the ownership of nature, the uses of national territory, the exploitation of resources, and the conditions of labor was far from over – it was only in a state of suspended animation, left for tomorrow while the *mariachis* played into the tropical night.

The oil workers traveled far between the mid-1920s and 1938. After impressive displays of working-class power and solidarity, the men won their first collective contracts in 1924–1925. As the industry consolidated and the Great Depression took hold, however, hundreds lost their jobs and gains. Social and environmental conditions worsened, making the second generation of oil workers restless. Joining forces with anarcho-syndicalist relics holding fast on the margins of working-class culture, the adolescent boys who had matured in the industry began claiming leadership in Tampico and northern Veracruz in the early 1930s. When Lázaro Cárdenas became president in 1934 and opened the door to labor organizing nationally, the oil workers were already on the march. Labor mobilization, however, brought to the fore contradictions within official revolutionary circles and led to a rupture between Calles and Cárdenas in 1935. For the next three years, the state, capital, and labor wrestled

---

[171] STPRM to President Cárdenas, June 1938 and July 2, 1938, AGN/P/LC, Exp. 432/401. Mexican Gulf remained foreign until 1951, when it sold out to PEMEX. Hamilton, *Early Day*, p. 239.

for the heart and soul of the Mexican Revolution. Cárdenas sought to consolidate the Mexican state into an entity strong enough to refashion capitalism into a system responsive to peasants and workers. The oil companies resisted the attack on their privileges at every turn, while the oil workers staged an insurrection. As the companies' defiance of Mexican law exposed them to drastic measures if the government had the will, the oil workers challenged Cárdenas to take the dare. Threatening to use the most powerful weapon in the working-class arsenal – the general strike – the oil workers rallied the entire country to their side and against the oil companies. Before the men brought the country to a standstill and potential violence, however, the former commander of military operations in the Huasteca nationalized the industry and averted the crisis. Although many issues were unresolved still, the chapter of foreign oil in Mexican history had come to a close.

CONCLUSION

As headlines alert us to "the end of cheap oil" and scientists begin publishing books about running *Out of Gas*, it seems appropriate to ask, "What exactly did petroleum extraction entail?"[1] The case of northern Veracruz from 1900 to 1938 provides a template: oil produced its own ecology. That is, the oilmen, those who owned and conducted the industry, carried out major social and environmental changes in the sites where they operated, unwittingly or not. The transformations encompassed three broad areas: land tenure systems, land use, and the social composition in the territories under production.

The transformation of social groups and land tenure and usage included further changes, connected to the broader processes like aftershocks to an earthquake. The shifts in land tenure the oilmen wrought meant they accumulated land and concentrated it under their control, displacing the local owners, indigenous Huastecs and hacendados alike. The purpose of securing power over the land, in turn, was to change its uses. Local patterns of production, indigenous small-base subsistence farming, and hacendado cattle ranching gave way to oil extraction, transportation, and refining. Building the infrastructure for the petroleum industry, moreover, entailed extensive changes in the land, often radical enough to eradicate existing ecosystems altogether. In the Huasteca that meant degrading or destroying estuaries, marshes, mangrove forests, sand dunes, and the northernmost tropical rainforest in the Americas. Oil extraction and refining, as well, led to chronic pollution. The air, land, and water of the Huasteca became tainted with and by hydrocarbons and other toxic compounds, as spills and fires spread over the landscapes

---

[1] Tim Appenzeller, "The End of Cheap Oil," *National Geographic*, vol. 105, no. 6 (June 2004), pp. 80–109; David Goodstein, *Out of Gas: The End of the Age of Oil* (New York: W.W. Norton, 2004). See also Richard Heinberg, *The Party's Over: Oil, War and the Fate of Industrial Societies* (Gabriola Island, Canada: New Society Publishers, 2004).

of northern Veracruz, southern Tamaulipas, and the open waters of the northwest curve of the Gulf of Mexico. All living organisms in the area felt the effects deeply, as nothing had caused such dramatic environmental disruption since the arrival of the Spaniards in the fifteenth century.

Social changes were also part and parcel of oil production. The labor demands of mounting an enterprise of such scale required importing workers by the thousands. The rapid arrival of immigrants in high numbers resulted in the displacement and marginalization of the indigenous population, reducing their social and political weight and participation and, hence, their opportunity to reap rewards from the wealth oil created. New social groups, moreover, entailed new social relations. In the Mexican oil industry those relationships were determined by capitalism and racism. That is, the oilmen introduced rigid class divisions to the Huasteca, which were reinforced further by nationality or "race." The industrialists reserved the executive and managerial levels of the labor hierarchy for Europeans and Americans, entrusted supervisory and foremen positions to foreign "white" workers, and limited the roles of Mexicans to the lowest rungs of the hierarchy. Drilling work, the most important task in an era of low technology in general, was closed to Mexicans altogether.

Part and parcel of the changes in environment and social relations the oil companies generated in northern Veracruz were also differences in the human experience in and of nature. That is, in the ecology of oil nationality and class determined the relationship between humans and their surroundings. Those at the top of the social ladder lorded over nature in multiple ways. They caused environmental destruction not only to produce oil, but also for aesthetic and recreational reasons. The men at the bottom of the hierarchy, Mexicans, by contrast, carried out the physical work of changing and destroying nature and were the most exposed to its dangers. The risks Mexican men endured ranged from occupational hazards in an inherently flammable and poisonous industry, to high disease rates bred in a tropical climate, to chronic exposure to industry pollution in their neighborhoods.

The package of changes that was the ecology of oil was buttressed by a powerful set of ideas. The premises that served as its foundation were unquestioned: control of nature and control of men. Both were assumptions and practices deeply rooted in notions of progress, modernization, and capitalism shared by elites in Latin America, the United States, and Europe in general at the turn of the century. Such elites considered the creation of wealth as good and positive without much attention to the process or the consequences. The men who led the capitalist revolution were considered "pioneers," harbingers of civilization wherever they went. The justification for the profound changes such men produced were truisms: rainforests were "Edenic" but unproductive, indigenous peoples were backwards, and workers were lazy and ungrateful. The privileged few, therefore, were free to make decisions for the many and shape nature and men according to their vision.

There were inherent contradictions in the ecology of oil, however. The dynamics of the processes bred resistance: commanding capital was easier than controlling nature or men. The tropical environment hurt the oil industry: the weather eroded and destroyed infrastructure; microorganisms attacked the labor force; toxic compounds threatened lives; and gusher wells turned wealth and life into cinders. Men also rebelled. Indigenous peoples sought ways to resist the changes in the land the oilmen unleashed; hacendados found the means, including force of arms, to extract benefits from the companies. But it was the men at the bottom of the labor hierarchy, those most vulnerable to the forces of nature and the ideologies of oilmen, who posed the greatest challenge to whole enterprise.

The Mexican Revolution was critical for the development of the oil workers' struggle against the petroleum companies. The industry was founded under the Porfiriato, with its nineteenth-century Liberal assumptions, outlook, and laws. The Mexican oil workers were a product of the early twentieth century and its challenges to the thirty-year rule of Porfirio Díaz. A radicalism – watered down, mistranslated, or melodramatized, it does not matter – informed their formation. The Mexican Revolution thus highlighted the contradictions inherent in the ecology of oil as it unleashed unprecedented questioning of the status quo. Mexican oil workers took revolution seriously. They did not take up arms, but they accepted the mission of social transformation with the faith of the newly converted. Their culture, their rhetoric, and their vision became infused with notions lifted from European anarcho-syndicalist thought mixed with nationalism and the defense of masculinity. The result was a labor force defiant of authority, aggressive individually and collectively, and prone to organization to achieve its goals.

The chaos of a decade of war, furthermore, produced a situation without precedent in the Huasteca: strong workers and a weak state. That meant that the Mexican oil workers could, and did, shape the revolutionary agenda, as their resistance to exploitation included a healthy dose of opposition to governmental officialdom in keeping with anarcho-syndicalist discourse. The militancy of the oil workers, together with other radical segments of Mexico's small working class, influenced the drafting of the 1917 Constitution. Article 123 was the product of that movement, even if its blueprint for Mexican society was not radical in the long term. Thus, the peace achieved in 1920 found oil workers to the left of official revolutionaries, with a list of martyrs, plenty of enemies among the revolutionary leadership, and no material gains.

At the same time, revolutionary officials had their own troubles with the companies during the war decade of 1910–1920. The nationalism the leaders of the revolution shared and the resulting desire to regain control over the country's natural resources meant the companies eyed the revolution with suspicion from the start. Distrust turned into outright enmity in 1917, when Article 27 of the Constitution designated the state as the unequivocal steward of nature, assigning it the task of conservation and granting it the power to expropriate private owners and nationalize whatever resources were considered vital for the nation. Such provisions challenged the supremacy of the oilmen and the arrangements and assumptions of the ecology of oil, threatening the companies' control over land and their freedom to change it according to their needs. Governmental efforts to regulate the industry thus generated serious political conflicts between the companies and revolutionary authorities and affected Mexico–U.S. relations negatively. American administrations refused to recognize Mexican heads of state until the demands of the oil companies to suspend the application of Article 27 to their case were met. That did not happen until 1923.

The efforts to reconstruct the Mexican state in the 1920s ended up protecting the ecology of oil, even though a new narrative came into being. When the companies dismissed half the Mexican work force in 1921, high officials from Mexico City traveled to the Huasteca and met for the first time with workers and dispossessed indigenous families. As a result, the discourse about oil changed. The companies ceased to be the progressive force of the Porfiriato and became the epitome of exploitation: wasteland was what they left in their path. The new narrative of foreign oil befitted the Mexican revolution. It confirmed the revolutionaries' rejection of the Porfiriato with its perceived favoritism toward foreign capital at the expense of Mexicans and the nation. But the translation of the theory into alternative policies did not take place. On the contrary, the companies were stronger than the nascent revolutionary state. Thus, they exempted themselves from offensive legislation and drafted their own. In practice the relationship between the Mexican government and the oil companies in the 1920s was more reminiscent of the Porfiriato than exemplary of a revolutionary society.

By the same token, the agreement on a new narrative did not mean that sympathy was the dominant sentiment in worker-state relations in the 1920s. Insofar as national stability and peace between the companies and the revolutionary government entailed acquiescing to the former, labor militancy required containment. If the oil workers succeeded in unionizing and signing collective contracts, it was because they had built a strong base of local support that state governments could not ignore. Local political leaders thus supported the oil workers' unions in their efforts to change the unequal social relations inscribed in the ecology of oil, but they failed. They were either ahead of their time or swimming against the revolutionary tide represented by President Plutarco Elías Calles in Mexico City. Repression, another infamous Porfiriato practice, was the common response the federal government gave to oil worker militancy until the end of the *maximato* in the mid-1930s.

In 1938 the foreign oil industry ended. The nationalization decree Lázaro Cárdenas pronounced on March 18, however, was the product of contingency rather than the logical conclusion of the Mexican revolutionary process. A second generation of oil workers opened the decade in the tradition of their fathers: organizing and practicing radical union politics. The individuals had changed, but not the commitment to revolution. The oil workers, in fact, made their goals more concrete and explicit in the 1930s: they aimed for worker control over the industry, were positively disposed toward nationalization, and revealed an appreciation for conservation as the appropriate national policy on petroleum matters. The workers thus posed the most articulated challenge to the ecology of oil until then, proposing alternative ways of land ownership, land usage, and social relations. By contrast, the position of the oil companies varied little: they had accepted the inevitability of collective bargaining to negotiate labor conditions, but did not intend to give up management prerogatives to anyone. The two parties remained enemies, deadlocked in class struggle.

What changed in the 1930s was the position of the revolutionary state under formation. Upon becoming president in 1934, Cárdenas rekindled the fire of revolutionary change in Mexico. Shaking off the ghost of Porfirio Díaz inhabiting Calles and the body politic, Cárdenas tried to breathe life into the 1917 Constitution and the promises for majority rule it contained. The interests of the great Mexican majority moved to the foreground. The oil workers took advantage of the political opening to try to capture a piece of the oil industry, testing their ideas about worker control and nationalization on the president. Cárdenas, however, did not believe that capitalist enterprises needed to be replaced by state or workers' ownership. There was room for variety in his revolutionary universe: capitalists need not fear for their future if they were socially responsive to the needs of their workers and respectful of the laws of the land. The convergence of official revolutionary authority and oil workers was not strategic: it hinged on the behavior of the oil companies.

Knowing their historical adversaries well, the workers tested the companies, the muscle behind the laws of the land, and the president's commitment to the revolution. The battle over the industry-wide collective contract became emblematic of the entire struggle over the revolutionary project and the relationship among the state, labor, and capital. The oil workers persevered, not taking the revolutionary state at its word but stubbornly agitating from below, in essence pressuring Cárdenas to move to the left. In the end he did because the companies behaved normally, flaunting Mexican law, as the oil workers threatened to undermine Cárdenas' own project with their rebellious and independent stance. To bring back the nation from the brink of internal chaos, the president risked a negative international reaction and expropriated the foreign oil companies. In so doing, he unified the bulk of the nation behind him as no other Mexican leader in history. Mexicans embraced the expropriation as the triumph of the people and the Revolution, guaranteeing Cárdenas' place in the pantheon of heroes for generations and transforming the country's oil into their most precious national possession to date.

The fate of the ecology of oil was left in the hands of the oil workers and the revolutionary state. Although the men never intended to give the state a victory with their militancy, that is also part of what they accomplished in 1938. As the population rallied behind the president, the revolutionary state gained strength at the expense of the oil companies and the workers alike. Thanks to their own doing, the Mexican oil workers would have to negotiate the future of the industry from a position of relative weakness. They had changed Mexican history, as well as their own future, too.

EPILOGUE

> The Mexican cannot develop their own oil industry. They have neither the money, the constructive or mechanical ability, the inclination to follow sound technical advice nor the necessary practical sense.
>
> Geologist Charles Laurence Baker, 1926

> El presidente de la Confederación Patronal de la República Mexicana, Alberto Fernández Garza, se lanzó de lleno ayer, al sostener que se tiene que privatizar PEMEX... México, dijo, debe quitarse la "falsa máscara de la soberanía" o se quedará pobre.
>
> *La Jornada*, July 29, 1999

> ¿Por qué vamos a creerle a funcionarios del PEMEX privatizado, si toda la perforación de Campeche y Tabasco los extranjeros han desplazado a los mexicanos? ¿Qué las contrucciones y reparaciones se las dan a los extranjeros asiáticos, corriendo a los mexicanos con la complicidad de los líderes? ¿Qué la inmensa riqueza en gas de la Cuenca de Burgos se la dieron a españoles y norteamericanos, dejando a los petroleros de Reynosa las migajas?
>
> Pedro Aníbal Ramírez and Eduardo Carrillo R.,
August 12, 2004

As dawn approached on March 19, 1938, the future was a mystery. Cárdenas had analyzed the situation in Europe correctly, figuring that the rise of fascism and its drums of war would preclude foreign military intervention to rescue the oil companies. He was less forthcoming, however, on what he had in mind for the nationalized industry.[1] The workers, by contrast, took control of daily industry operations immediately and

---

[1] The companies believed they had sufficient political muscle to provoke an international crisis that would force Mexico to return the industry. The fragile state of peace in Europe,

assumed that workers' management would be the rule.[2] Given the history of relations between the oil workers and the Mexican revolutionary state, however, a long lasting agreement was highly unlikely. Thus, it was no surprise that the joy of March 19, 1938, was short-lived. The central issue of contention was the same that had deadlocked contract negotiations between the companies and the STPRM, namely, workers' control.

Friction between the workers and the government over industry control began within a month of expropriation. While they made every effort to keep the industry running despite a lack of spare parts and the companies' international boycott against the Mexican industry, workers protested the number and quality of officials appointed to management positions.[3] Tensions reached the breaking point in July when Cárdenas created the state oil monopoly, *Petróleos Mexicanos* (PEMEX).[4] Although the STPRM was included in the new administration, it played a minority role: three out of nine positions on the PEMEX board were theirs. Protests from locals like Poza Rica and the ex-El Aguila and Pierce refineries notwithstanding, the government eliminated workers from management promptly.[5] There were several reasons for the decision. The workers knew the daily functions of the industry. With ingenuity and experience, moreover, they could innovate parts and materials for the maintenance and repair work the industry badly needed.[6] But, by company design, they had little scientific knowledge. They also lacked management and planning experience. The workers recognized those realities and knew that the industry could not run without personnel trained in such matters. Their objections were to appointees who were not experts themselves.[7]

---

however, made such a scenario impossible, even if the British did break diplomatic relations with Mexico and the companies imposed a world-wide boycott of Mexican oil products that lasted several years. Meyer, *México y los Estados Unidos*, pp. 370–393; Gilly, *El cardenismo*, p. 43.

[2] Such was the case in the railroads, which had been nationalized in 1936 and run by the unions. González, *Los días*, pp. 167–171.

[3] Vargas, *Lo que vi*, pp. 52–53; Chávez Padrón, *Testimonio*, p. 107; Gallegos Martínez et al., *Testimonios*, pp. 37, 62, 64, 73. In addition, company employees emptied their technical files before leaving, assuming Mexicans would not be able to run the industry without maps, geological reports, and such. See Rodríguez, *El rescate*, pp. 115, 125–128.

[4] Pierre de L. Boal, Chargè d'Affairs ad interim,to the Secretary of State, Tampico, May 9, 1938, RG 59, Roll 137, File 812.6363/3936.

[5] Ruth Adler, "Worker Participation in the Administration of the Petroleum Industry, 1938–1940," in *The Mexican Petroleum Industry*, pp. 134, 137–139.

[6] Gallegos Martínez et al., *Testimonios*, pp. 37, 62, 64, 73.

[7] Petitions from Local #1 (El Aguila, Ciudad Madero) of the STPRM, June 1939, AGN/P/LC, Exp. 432/1088, 1939.

Cárdenas assigned the scientific and technical aspects of the industry to the Department of Petroleum and university graduates whose practical experience was indeed quite limited.[8] Even the CTM leader and loyal Cardenista, Vicente Lombardo Toledano, complained about the political nature of many appointments.[9] It quickly became clear that what drove the decisions was the fact that neither the professionals nor the state had "faith in the capacity of the union to administer the industry."[10]

Cárdenas and the professionals did not express the distrust they felt toward the workers explicitly. Instead, the president justified the removal of workers from management positions on nationalist grounds, as he asserted state control over nature and labor alike without distinction. The choice Cárdenas gave the workers was stark: patriotism or treason. The first meant yielding on worker control; the second meant insisting on it. In other words, Cárdenas argued that the workers represented their own narrow self-interest, not the interests of the nation. Only the state could do that as impartial owner and steward of nature. Therefore, only the state apparatus was qualified to run the nationalized industry. The corollary to that notion was that nationalization dissolved class struggle. Contradictions between labor and the state were not only counterproductive, but also antinational.

Riding the wave of nationalism the expropriation inspired across the country, the president put the workers on the defensive. In February 1940, Cárdenas called "erroneous" the union's opposition to the government's plan for reorganizing the industry, accusing them of "forgetting

[8] Meléndez de la Cruz, Juan. "Industria petrolera: El personal calificado ante la nacionalización," *Anuario* V [1988], pp. 230–235.

[9] Consul William P. Blocker to Secretary of State, Tampico, May 9, 1938, RG 59, Roll 137, File 812.6363/3871; Pierre de L. Boal, Chargè d'Affairs ad interim to the Secretary of State, Tampico, April 27, 1938, RG 59, Roll 136, File 812.6363.3773.

[10] Adler, "Worker Participation," p. 144. See also Gallegos et al., *Testimonios*, p. 63. Distrust of labor had been latent in the editorials of the *Boletín del Petróleo* since the 1910s. Ignoring or ignorant of oil worker militancy, a 1917 editorial, for example, called for a "change ... in the state of servitude of the Mexican [oil] worker, [by] awakening in him a desire for progress and an active and efficacious cooperation," BP, vol. 3, no. 2 (February 1917), pp. 105–108. In 1939, the attitude had not changed much. The general manager of PEMEX in Tampico, for example, wrote to the president on August 30, 1939, telling him in a tone of exasperation that it was "necessary to put an end [*poner un hasta aquí*] to the indiscipline" of workers' representatives in the administrative council. Vicente Cortés Herrera to Lázaro Cárdenas, AGN/P/LC, Exp. 432/1088. In his book on oil, Silva Herzog, one of the experts who decided in the workers' favor in 1937, was more explicit in naming "worker inability" as one of the industry's early problems, though the examples he cites refer to purchase agents, rather than production workers. Jesús Silva Herzog, *Petróleo Mexicano* (Mexico City: Fondo de Cultura Económica, 1941), p. 218.

the Nation" in their antagonism. What they ought to do, the president said, was "to place above all individual interest a high sense of responsibility and of collective solidarity, indispensable for Mexico's good name."[11] At the same time, the secretary of communications circulated a pamphlet calling the oil workers "bad revolutionaries," "bad Mexicans," and even "traitors to the homeland" for objecting to their minority position on the PEMEX board.[12] In July, relations reached a low point as the government filed its own *conflicto económico* suit against the STPRM to impose the restructuring plan on the union. The decision of the Junta Federal was never in question. When the ruling came down in November, PEMEX began dismissing workers, arguing that it faced unsustainable losses owing to a drop in production.[13]

The oil workers responded to the government onslaught in kind. "Hurt" in their "patriotic love" and not reconciled to the idea of losing control of the industry, the union placed the blame for the administrative chaos and high expenditures on PEMEX management.[14] In a letter to the labor board, the STPRM argued that "the real problem in the petroleum industry is the obvious incapacity of the administrators, the exorbitant salaries of functionaries, burdensome sales contracts, loss of markets, lack of attention to the domestic market, and ruinous purchase of materials."[15] Who else could be responsible, given that the workers did not run the industry?

Cárdenas, however, was reaching the end of his presidential term under severe pressure from national capital. The expropriation of the oil industry, the agrarian reform program, and other nationalizations convinced the Mexican private sector that the country was teetering on the edge of a socialist precipice. Following the steps of the oil companies, Mexican capitalists withdrew their bank deposits en masse, seriously destabilizing the Mexican economy.[16] Unable to exert the control over

[11] Lázaro Cárdenas, "A todos los trabajadores de la Secretaría de Comunicaciones y Obras Públicas" (Mexico City: Secretaría de Comunicaciones y Obras Públicas, 1940), pp. 5–6.
[12] Adler, "Worker Participation," p. 147.
[13] Ashby, *Organized Labor*, p. 262.
[14] Gallegos et al., *Testimonios*, pp. 62–63.
[15] *Mexican Labor News*, August 25, 1940.
[16] Alicia Hernández Chávez, *Historia de la Revolución Mexicana: Período 1934–1940. La mecánica cardenista*, vol. 16 (Mexico City: El Colegio de Mexico, 1979), pp. 190–193. Scholars have pointed out that after the nationalization, in fact, more than a few national groups "silently and covertly" wished to see Cárdenas fail. See Alan Knight, "The Politics of the Expropriation," in *The Mexican Petroleum Industry*, pp. 114–120. The classic study of the matter is Hamilton, *The Limits of State Autonomy*.

capital he hoped, the president appealed to Mexican workers instead. Upon the occasion of a banquet in his honor organized by the CTM on November 25, 1940, Cárdenas asked that labor choose "nationalism over class warfare," implying that the worker who did not focus on production was, in fact, a "traitor" to his class.[17] Although the CTM largely, if ruefully, followed Cárdenas, the oil workers held on to their independence through the end of the presidential term.

Not until a military occupation of the Atzcapotzalco refinery in 1946 – twenty-one years since the last and six years after Cárdenas left office – did the oil workers resign themselves to the notion that only the state represented national interests.[18] In the aftermath of repression, moreover, Cárdenas became a true oil worker hero. An outright amnesia regarding the conflicts between the workers and Cárdenas in 1939 and 1940 descended like a curtain over the minds of the oil workers. Instead, they remembered him, as David Robles Saldaña put it, as "*obrerista a su máximo*" (pro-labor to the hilt).[19] In retrospect, it seemed to the workers that Cárdenas, more than any other revolutionary leader, had made a tangible difference in their lives and the lives of thousands of Mexican working families.[20] To elderly oil workers interviewed in the 1970s, having lost control of the industry meant losing a battle after having won the war: thanks to their activism, the oil industry belonged to Mexico.

The ecology of oil changed little over time, however. Although the oil workers made enough gains in compensation, benefits, and health and safety to be regarded as the aristocracy of labor in Mexican popular

---

[17] Albert L. Michaels, "The Crisis of *Cardenismo*," *Journal of Latin American Studies*, vol. 2, no. 1 (May 1970), pp. 69–70.

[18] Cuello Vázquez, "El movimiento, pp. 389–401.

[19] Robles Saldaña, Ninth interview, PHO/4/39. None of the testimonies include commentary, description, or even mention of the conflicts with Cárdenas between 1939 and 1940. See, for example, García Herrera, *Memorias*, p. 102, and Barragán Camacho, *Memorias*, pp. 178–182. Scholars Olvera Rivera and Adleson, furthermore, note explicitly that the men they interviewed ignored or refused to consider criticisms of Cárdenas. See Alberto Olvera Rivera, "Los obreros y la nacionalización de la industria petrolera en México," *Historia y fuente oral*, no. 1 (1989), p. 146 and comments by Adleson in the interview with Felipe Neri Romero Osorio, PHO/4/86.

[20] Compare the oil workers' memories and experiences with those of other sectors, as analyzed in a series of works on cardenismo, including Adrian A. Bantjes, *As if Jesus Walked on Earth: Cardenismo, Sonora, and the Mexican Revolution* (Wilmington, Delaware: Scholarly Resources, 1998); Marjorie Becker, *Setting the Virgin on Fire: Lázaro Cárdenas, Michoacán Peasants, and the Redemption of the Mexican Revolution* (Berkeley: University of California Press, 1995); and Ben Fallaw, *Cárdenas Compromised: The Failure of Reform in Postrevolutionary Yucatán* (Durham, North Carolina: Duke University Press, 2001).

perception, scholars and the critical media dispute the idea, arguing that marked social hierarchies and their contingent experiences of nature persist under PEMEX management.[21] Similarly, as the 1925 Petroleum Law contemplated, oil extraction and processing had priority over all other land uses. Land ownership, therefore, has conformed to national oil development objectives, irrespective of the opinions of local populations. Continuity rather than rupture became the rule between PEMEX and the foreign oil companies as far as social relations and land tenure and uses.

In addition, although conservation was official state policy since PEMEX was formed, economic imperatives have taken priority in management. Until the discovery of the "extension" of the Golden Lane in the 1950s, conservation was only a goal. Since production resumed fully in the 1950s, the concept has meant minimizing waste, recovering the last drop of oil from wells past the runaway stage, spacing wells "according to a scientifically developed pattern," capturing as much natural gas as possible to avoid burning it into the atmosphere, and not dipping into Mexico's strategic reserves more than the state deems necessary at any given time.[22] PEMEX practice thus recalls the "wise-use" position first proposed in the late nineteenth century in the United States. Without questioning social and environmental necessity, costs, or trade-offs of oil extraction or processing, PEMEX echoes the argument that "sustained economic growth" is the nation's primary objective, achieved through "wise use" of natural resources that avoid "rampant squandering."[23] Like the wise-use proponents but in contrast to its origins in the Department of Petroleum, PEMEX has ignored the social and environmental consequences not only of oil extraction but also of petrochemical production, which began in the 1970s. Today, despite advanced legislation on environmental protection, wherever PEMEX goes, illness, pollution, deforestation, degradation of

---

[21] See, for example, Victoria Novelo, *La difícil democracia de los petroleros: Historia de un proyecto sindical* (Mexico City: CIESAS and Ediciones El Caballito, 1991) and Claudia Canales, "El caso de los trabajadores petroleros transitorios. Una aportación de la historia oral a la historia del movimiento obrero," in *Memorias del encuentro*; Rafael Loyola Díaz, "Los petroleros bajo la industria nacionalizada: 1938–1946," *Anuario* V [1988]; Augusto Palma Alor, "Testimonio: Los trabajadores eventuales y la expropiación petrolera," *Anuario* V [1988]; and Meléndez de la Cruz, "Industria petrolera," pp. 236–243.

[22] J. Richard Powell, *The Mexican Petroleum Industry, 1938–1950* (Berkeley: University of California Press, 1956), pp. 66–67; Javier Lozada, *Temple y destello* (Mexico City: PEMEX, 1988), pp. 115–117, 355; Antonio J. Bermúdez, *The Mexican National Petroleum Industry: A Case Study in Nationalization* (Stanford: Stanford University Press, 1963), pp. 53–56.

[23] Melosi, "Energy and Environment, p. 167.

land, elimination of ecosystems, destruction of wildlife, toxic neighbor-hoods, and acid rain follow.[24] The state's decision to make PEMEX the engine of national economic growth has meant that oil remains one of the most destructive forces unleashed on Mexico's environment.

The definition of what the national interest entails in relation to the oil industry has come back to the political front burner as well. In 1996 the Mexican government changed Article 27 to be able to reprivatize the oil industry piecemeal.[25] As a result, in 2005, the ExxonMobil logo appeared in petrochemical plants in Tuxpan, and the state continues seeking partners for joint ventures with PEMEX. Another chapter of for-eign oil is being written. Mexican oil workers have their work cut out for them: with the STPRM wholly discredited, without roots or national respect, the only virtue Mexicans recognize in the oil workers is their opposition to the privatization of the industry. The continuities between the twenty-first and the nineteenth centuries in Mexican history begin to emerge, persistent like the ecology of oil itself.

[24] On some of the environmental problems PEMEX has caused, see Armando Báez, *La calidad del aire*, Serie Medio Ambiente en Coatzacoalcos, vol. 2 (Mexico City: Centro de Ecodesarrollo, 1986); Lorenzo Bozada and Margarito Páez, *La fauna acuática del río Coatzacoalcos*, Serie Medio Ambiente en Coatzacoalcos, vol. 8 (Mexico City: Centro de Ecodesarrollo, 1987); Joel Simon, *Endangered Mexico: An Environment on the Edge* (San Francisco: Sierra Club Books, 1997), Chapter 6; "Cárdenas González: 'el derrame del Ixtoc es bueno para los peces'," *Proceso*, no. 145 (August 13, 1979), p. 10; "Pemex despoja, contamina y quiebra un modo de vida," *Proceso*, no. 140 (July 9, 1979), pp. 11–12; "Pemex rompe récord de muertos en 1998," *El Financiero*, December 29, 1998; Iván Restrepo, "La historia negra de las petroquímicas," *La Jornada*, November 13, 1995. One example will suffice: in 1996 Tabasco residents (including some from a neighborhood named "Lázaro Cárdenas") living adjacent to PEMEX drilling sites and petrochemical plants reported health effects ranging from skin rashes to high rates of leukemia among children. In testimony that could have been taken in the 1910s, a teacher declared that "everyday at 4:00 a.m., the oil wells – drilled just 50 meters from people's homes – released gas that had such a strong smell that the people woke up coughing and vomiting. In the wells where we get drinking water, there is a foam so thick on the surface that you have to remove it with your hand." Global Exchange, "Human Rights and Environment in Tabasco: Report from an International Delegation" (San Francisco, 1996), pp. 3, 6.

[25] Anthony DePalma, "Mexico Renews Its Intention to Sell Parts of Oil Monopoly," *The New York Times*, February 13, 1996.

APPENDICES

Appendix I. *Selected Land Transactions Between Hacendados and Oil Companies, 1881–1927**

Year	Owner	Hacienda	Hectares	Oil Company
...	Herrera/Llorente	Chila Cortaza	...	...
...	Basáñez/Hernández	Castillo de Teayo	10,653	...
...	Herrera/Llorente	San Nicolás	130	R. Thomas→Huasteca/El Aguila (1906)
...	Herrera	Tampaca	...	Espuela Oil
...	Herrera	Mecapala	693	R. Thomas → ...
...	Herrera/Ostos	La Laja	...	Huasteca Petroleum
...	Nuñez/Basáñez	San Isidro	...	PennMex
...	Sánchez	Tamatoco	...	El Aguila
...	Nuñez	Tierra Blanca	...	Huasteca Petroleum
...	German/Borbolla	Tlacolula	26,280	United Oil → El Aguila (1912)
1881	Herrera/Nuñez	Chapopote	3,420	G. Glidden→Huasteca/El Aguila (1906)
1881	Cárdenas/Pesqueira	Juan Felipe	19,000	Huasteca (1906); AGWI (1922)
1892	Sánchez	Tanhuijo	...	G. Glidden→El Aguila
1895	Cárdenas	Moralillo	...	G. Glidden → ...
...	Chao/Núñez	Agua Nacida	1,220+	PennMex
1899	Gorrochótegui/Basáñez	Cerro Viejo	7,000	London Trust→Huasteca, El Aguila, and Tuxpan (1906)
1900	Guzmán/Zúñiga/Ugarte	Buenavista	...	Mexican Gulf, PennMex, International Petrol, New England Fuel Oil, and Panuco Boston
1900	Meade	El Naranjo	4,000	Huasteca Petroleum
1900	Sáinz Trapaga	El Tulillo	113,200	Mexican Petroleum

(continued)

357

Appendix I *(continued)*

Year	Owner	Hacienda	Hectares	Oil Company
1900	Sáinz Trapaga/Meade	Chapacao	66,118h	Mexican Petroleum
1901	Cárdenas	Cerro Azul	5,000	Barber Asphalt→Huasteca
1906	Gorrochótegui/Peláez	Cuchilla del Pulque	672	El Aguila and Tuxpan Co.
1906	Ortíz	Tierra Nueva	. . .	El Aguila
1906	Gorrochótegui/Peláez	Buenavista	6,343	El Aguila
1906	Manuel Saldívar	La Pitahaya	2,000	Huasteca Petroleum
1907	Herrera	Peceros	5,260	. . .
1907	Rivera	La Calzada		El Aguila
1907	Sánchez	Tamemas		El Aguila
1908	Herrera	SanAntonioTamijui		El Aguila
1908	Herrera	Tumbadero		El Aguila
1908	Harper	Tuxpan		. . .
1909	Peláez/Peralta	Potrero del Llano	2,200	El Aguila
1909	Peláez	Llano Grande	2,352	El Aguila
1909	Gorrochótegui/Peláez	Cuchilla de Cal	. . .	El Aguila
1909	Peláez	Tierra Amarilla	1,920	El Aguila
1909	Nuñez/Llorente	El Alamo	225+	J.W. Leonard→PennMex
1910	Gómez	Alazán	2,470	El Aguila
1911	Francisco Cárdenas	Rancho Cárdenas	. . .	Huasteca Petroleum
1912	Nuñez	Palo Blanco	13,000	Huasteca/Aguila/PennMex
1912	Nuñez	Jardín	3,755	J.W. Leonard→PennMex
1912	Nuñez/Llorente	El Molino	1,300	J.W. Leonard→PennMex
1913	Herrera	Moyutla	223	El Aguila
1914	Sánchez	Potrero de la Isleta	14	G. Casabon→El Aguila (1917)
1917	Pérez	Tampuche	18	El Aguila
1920	Cárdenas	Tancoco	. . .	. . .
1927	Herrera	La Mesa		El Aguila

* Information missing in the records is marked by ellipses (. . .).

Sources: Ana María Graciela Gutiérrez Rivas, "La Familia Herrera, Miembro del Grupo de Poder del Norte de Veracruz, 1743–1890," M.A. Thesis, Centro de Investigaciones y Estudios Superiores en Antropología Social, 1998; Antonio Escobar Ohmstede, *Ciento cincuenta años de historia de la huasteca* (Veracruz: Instituto Veracruzano de Cultura, 1998); Robert G. Cleland, *The Mexican Yearbook 1920–1921* (Los Angeles: Times-Mirror Press, 1922); *Boletín del Petróleo*, 15:3 (March 1923), 25:3 (March 1928); PanAmerican Petroleum and Transport Company, *Mexican Petroleum* (New York, 1922); Jorge García Granados, *Los veneros del diablo* (Mexico City: Ediciones Liberación, 1941); Southern Methodist Univesity, The Papers of Everett Lee DeGolyer, Sr. Mss 60; S. Pearson & Son, Ltd., Historical Archives; Linda B. Hall, *Oil, Banks, and Politics: The United States and Postrevolutionary Mexico, 1917–1924* (Austin: University of Texas Press, 1995); Mexican Senate, *El Petróleo: La más grande riqueza nacional* (Mexico City: Mexican Senate, 1923).

Appendix II. *Oil Fields Opened for Exploitation in the Huasteca, 1901–1921*

Date of Construction	Field	Location
1901	La Dicha	Pánuco, Ozuluama
1903	Cerro de la Pez	Pánuco, Ozuluama
1906	Juan Casiano	Chinampa, Tuxpan
1907	San Diego de la Mar	Tantima, Ozuluama
1909	Potrero del Llano	Temapache, Tuxpan
1909	Chijol	Pánuco, Ozuluama
1909	Méndez	Pánuco, Ozuluama
1909	Tepetate	Tantima, Ozuluama
1910	Juan Felipe	Tepetzintla, Tuxpan
1910	Tanhuijo	Tamiahua, Tuxpan
1910	Tierra Amarilla	Temapache, Tuxpan
1910	Cerro Azul	Tepetzintla, Tuxpan
ca.1910	Soledad	Chinampa, Tuxpan
1910	Topila	Pánuco, Ozuluama
ca. 1911	San Pedro	Pánuco, Ozuluama
1911	Salinas	Pánuco, Ozuluama
1912	Alazán	Temapache, Tuxpan
1912	Chapopote	Temapache, Tuxpan
1913	San Sebastiaán	Tamiahua, Ozuluama
1913	San Marcos	Tamiahua, Ozuluama
1913	Los Naranjos	Amatlán, Tuxpan
1913	Alamo	Temapache, Tuxpan
1913	Llano Grande	Temapache, Tuxpan
1913	Tlacolula	Tlacolula, Tantoyuca
1914	Salvasuchi	San Isidro, Tuxpan
1914	Tierra Blanca	Temapache, Tuxpan
1914	San Antionio y Tamijui	Tamalín, Ozuluama
1914	Potrero del Zacate	Pánuco, Ozuluama
1914	Toteco	Temapache, Tuxpan
ca. 1914	Empalizada	Chinampa, Tuxpan
ca. 1914	Juárez	Tepetzintla, Tuxpan
ca. 1914	Tamatoca	Tepetzintla, Tuxpan
ca. 1914	Rancho Abajo	Tepetzintla, Tuxpan
ca. 1914	Caracol	Pánuco, Ozuluama
ca. 1914	Chila	Pánuco, Ozuluama
ca. 1914	El Gallo	Amatoco, Tuxpan
ca. 1914	Quebrache	Pánuco, Ozuluama
ca. 1914	Pithaya	Tepetzintla, Tuxpan
1917	Chiconcillo	Tantima, Ozuluama

(continued)

Appendix II *(continued)*

Date of Construction	Field	Location
1917	Chinampa del Sur	Chinampa, Tuxpan
1919	Zacamixtle	Tancoco, Tuxpan
1920	San Jerónimo	Tamalín, Ozuluama
1920	Cerro Viejo	Temapache, Tuxpan
1921	Cacalilao	Pánuco, Ozuluama
1921	Corcovado	Pánuco, Ozuluama
ca. 1921	El Barco	Pánuco, Ozuluama
ca. 1921	Paciencia y Aguacate	Pánuco, Ozuluama
ca. 1921	Reventadero	Pánuco, Ozuluama
ca. 1921	Tempoal	Pánuco, Ozuluama
ca. 1921	Chapopote Nuñez	Temapache, Tuxpan
ca. 1921	Tecomate	Pánuco, Ozuluama

Sources: Joaquín Meade, *La Huasteca Veracruzana,* vol. 1 (Mexico City: Editorial Citaltépetl, 1963); Government of Mexico, *Mexico's Oil. A Compilation of Official Documents in the Conflict of Economic Order in the Petroleum Industry, with an Introduction Summarizing Its Causes and Consequences* (Mexico City: 1940); Ezequiel Ordoñez, *El petróleo en México: Bosquejo histórico* (Mexico City: Empresa Editorial de Ingeniería y Arquitectura, 1932); *Boletín del Petróleo,* 7:6 (June 1919), 14:1 (January 1922), 10:3 (September 1920), 15:3 (March 1923).

Appendix III. *Selected Oil Industry Accidents in Tampico, 1912–1929*

Year	Accident	Company, Neighborhood
May 1912	Storage tank/homes on fire	Pierce, Arbol Grande
June 1912	Tank on fire	Pierce, Arbol Grande
August 1914	Tank #175 on fire	El Aguila, Doña Cecilia
August 1914	Tank on fire	Pierce, Arbol Grande
August 1916	Three tanks on fire	East Coast, Las Matillas
August 1916	Barge collision	Pánuco River
August 1916	Two barges on fire	Texas Co., Las Matillas
August 1916	Tank on fire	Texas Co., Las Matillas
1916	Tank #1009 on fire	Mexican Gulf, Las Matillas
1916	Three tanks on fire	Pierce, Arbol Grande
July 1917	Tank on fire	Mexican Gulf, Las Matillas
October 1917	Refinery fire	Pierce, Arbol Grande
November 1917	Main Depot fire	El Aguila, Doña Cecilia

Year	Accident	Company, Neighborhood
November 1917	Barge on fire	El Aguila, Doña Cecilia
1917	Tank on fire	Huasteca, Mata Redonda
March 1918	Tank on fire	Texas Co., Las Matillas
March 1918	Refinery fire	El Aguila, Doña Cecilia
1918	Tank #D on fire	Huasteca, Mata Redonda
1918	Tank #21 on fire	Huasteca, Mata Redonda
1918	Tank on fire	Pierce, Arbol Grande
1918	Launch burns and sinks	Sinclair, Tamesí River
May 1919	Refinery explosion and fire	Pierce, Arbol Grande
May 1919	Tank #106 on fire	MexFuel, Tampico
September 1919	Two barges on fire	Texas Co., Las Matillas
September 1919	Tank fire	Texas Co., Las Matillas
June 1920	Tank #106 on fire	El Aguila, Doña Cecilia
June 1920	Tank on fire	La Corona, Tampico
June 1920	Tank #1006 on fire	Mexican Gulf, Las Matillas
September 1920	Five tanks on fire	El Aguila, Doña Cecilia
November 1920	Three tanks on fire	El Aguila, Doña Cecilia
1920	Tank on fire	Pierce, Arbol Grande
January 1922	Refinery explosion and fire	Huasteca, Mata Redonda
January 1923	Barge on fire	El Aguila, Pánuco River
August 1923	Refinery explosion and fire	Pierce, Arbol Grande
January 1927	Tanker burns and sinks	El Aguila, Pánuco River
February 1927	Wharf spill	Pánuco River
March 1927	Tanker spill	Pánuco River
June 1927	Refinery fire	Huasteca, Mata Redonda
July 1927	Tank fire	Tampico
July 1927	Tanker spill	Pánuco River
July 1917	Wharf spill	Pánuco River
October 1927	Tanker sinks and spill	Pánuco River
October 1927	Barge fire	Pánuco River
1928	Refinery explosion and fire	El Aguila, Doña Cecilia
October 1929	Tanker crash and spill	El Aguila, Pánuco River

Sources: Archivo Histórico del Ayuntamiento de Tampico, Exp. 5, No. 5113, 1916, Exp. 140, 1917; Archivo General de la Nación, Junta Federal de Conciliación y Arbitraje, Caja 69, Exp. 928/1305, Sindicato de Obreros y Empleados de la Pierce to the JFCA, September 28, 1928; *Petroleum Review,* New Series, No. 35 (Sept 30, 1916), p. 742; *Boletín del Petróleo,* 5:5 (May 1918), 10:3 (Sept 1920), 9:5 (June 1920), 10:5 (Nov 1920), 24:5 (Nov 1927); *Excélsior,* May 1919; *El Mundo,* Jan 20, Feb 20, March 9, July 2, July 7, July 16, Oct 15, Oct 13, 1927; S. Pearson & Son Ltd., Photographic Records, P10/9–13, P1/91–97, P18, P/6/94–97; S. Pearson & Son Ltd., Historical Records, Box C48, File C 48/2, C 48/10; Southern Methodist University, The Papers of Everette Lee DeGolyer, Sr. Mss 60, Box 108, Folder 5246, Box 190, Folder 5273; International Archive of Economic Geology, W. L. Connelly Collection, Acct. 1722, Box 1, Diaries.

Appendix IV. *Selected "Gusher" Wells and Fires in the Huasteca, 1901–1927*

Date	Well, Type	Place
May 1901	La Dicha No. 4, spill	El Tulillo, Pánuco
April 1904	Cerro de la Pez No.1, spill	Chapacao, Pánuco
July–August 1908	Dos Bocas No. 3, fire	San Jerónimo,Tamalín
June 1910	Potrero del Llano No. 4, spill	Temapache
September 1910	Juan Casiano No. 6, spill	Chinampa
September 1910	Juan Casiano No. 7, spill	Chinampa
1912	La Corona No 5, spill/fire	Pánuco
August 1914	Potrero del Llano No. 4, fire	Temapache
August 1914	Tepetate No. 5, spill	Amatlán
October 1914	Los Naranjos No. 1, spill	Amatlán
February 1916	Cerro Azul No. 4, spill	Tancoco
May 1918	Juan Casiano No. 7, spill	Chinampa
May–July 1918	Pazzi No. 1, spill	Amatlán
May–August 19, 1919	Amatlán No. 2, spill	Amatlán
August 1919	Chinampa No. 1, spill	Amatlán
November 2, 1919	Los Naranjos No.10, spill	Amatlán
1920	Toteco No. 1, spill	Tancoco
October 1920	Transcontinental No. 4, spill	Chinampa
October 9, 1920	Los Naranjos No. 14, spill	Amatlán
October 23, 1920	Zacamixtle No. 1, spill	Zacamixtle
April 1921	Amatlán No. 4, spill	Amatlán
April 26, 1921	Amatlán No. 13, spill	Amatlán
July 1921	Díaz No. 5, fire	Amatlán
July 1921	Buckley No. 5, spill	Amatlán
July 1921	Eschuasier No. 3, spill	Amatlán
August 1921	Amatlán No. 29, fire	Amatlán
September 1921	Toteco No. 4, fire	Tancoco
October 1921	Cacalialo No. 1, spill	Pánuco
July 1922	Merriwether No. 3, fire	Amatlán
July 1922	Morrison No. 5, fire	Amatlán
April 1923	Freeport No. 2, spill	Pánuco
November 1923	Richmex No. 3, fire	Pánuco
1924	Quebrache No. 2, spill	Pánuco
September 1924	Cacalilao No. 99, spill	Pánuco
March 1925	Tierra Blanca No. 44, spill	Alamo
September 1926	Cacalilao No. 99, spill	Pánuco
December 1926	Cacalilao No. 6, fire	Pánuco
May 1927	La Dicha No. 152, fire	El Tulillo, Pánuco
May 1927	Midway No. 70, fire	Pánuco
October 1927	Tierra Blanca No. 98A, spill	Alamo

Sources: Archivo General de la Nación, Departamento del Petróleo, Caja 16, Exp. 10, 101(04)1920, Telegrama de la Agencia de Tuxpan; Caja 7, Exp. 10, 032(02)/3, Informe del Inspector en Tampico, 1918; AGN, Departamento del Trabajo, Caja 329, Exp. 30, Chief of Inspectors to Chief of Labor, August 21, 1921; *Boletín del Petróleo,* 5:5 (May 1918), 4:5 (Nov 1917); 7:5 (June 1919), 9:6 (June 1920), II:1 (March 1921), 12:5 (Nov. 1921), 13:2–3 (Aug–Sept 1921), 23:2 (Feb 1927); *Excélsior,* June 25, 1919; *El Mundo,* May 7–8, 1927, May 5, 1929; *The Petroleum Review,* 34: 718, new series (April 22, 1916), p. 341; Southern Methodist University, The Papers of Everette Lee DeGolyer, Sr. Mss 60, Box 101, Folder 5099, Box 103, Folder 5149, Box 108, Folder 5246.

Appendix V. *Mexican Oil Production, 1901–1937*

Year	Barrels
1901	10,345
1902	40,200
1903	75,375
1904	125,625
1905	251,250
1906	502,500
1907	1,005,000
1908	3,932,900
1909	2,713,500
1910	3,734,080
1911	12,552,798
1912	16,558,215
1913	25,692,291
1914	26,235,403
1915	32,910,508
1916	40,545,712
1917	55,292,770
1918	63,828,326
1919	87,072,954
1920	157,068,678
1921	193,397,587
1922	182,278,457
1923	149,584,856
1924	139,678,295
1925	115,514,700
1926	90,420,973
1927	64,121,142
1928	50,150,610
1929	44,687,887
1930	39,529,901
1931	33,038,853
1932	32,805,496
1933	34,000,830
1934	38,171,946
1935	40,240,563
1936	41,027,915
1937	46,906,605

Source: Lorenzo Meyer, *México y los Estados Unidos en el conflicto petrolero, 1917–1942* (Mexico City: El Colegio de México, 1981).

A NOTE ON THE SOURCES

The sources for this work were varied. Much of the material on the landscape and the environment came from travel journals, the writings of anthropologists and oilmen, and the reports of American geologists and Mexican engineers. The American Heritage Center at the University of Wyoming in Laramie has an excellent collection of the last two in the International Archive of Economic Geology. Equally important were the DeGolyer Archives at Southern Methodist University in Dallas, which include a great deal of information about the social life of the American colony in Tampico, which still needs to be investigated in depth. The Pearson & Son Archives in the Science Museum Library in London were indispensable for practically every aspect of this work, including vivid descriptions of gushers, fires, and spills. They contain material that will be useful for researchers looking at southern Veracruz and the Isthmus of Tehuantepec in the early twentieth century as well. The Bancroft Library at the University of California at Berkeley has a significant and extensive Mexican oil collection, including materials produced by the oil companies, the American press, and the official *Boletín del Petróleo* that documented much of the environmental destruction the oil industry caused.

Labor information came from several different collections. The most important sources were the two Departmentos del Trabajo and the local and federal Juntas de Conciliación y Arbitraje in the Archivo General de la Nación in Mexico City, as well as the Archivo General del Estado de Veracruz in Xalapa. They are bursting with complaints from Mexican workers, complaints that contain information not only about working conditions, but also about working-class thought. I also made extensive use of the oral histories of Mexican oil workers that Leif Adleson collected in the 1970s and deposited in the Instituto Nacional de Antropología e Historia in Mexico City and the American oil workers' oral histories at the University of Texas at Austin. The underutilized Archivo Histórico del Ayuntamiento de Tampico is rich in material for the history of

Tampico labor during the 1920s and beyond. Equally underexploited is the International Labor Organization Historical Archives in Geneva, which provided detailed information on the labor scene in Mexico during the 1930s. The collection of Mexican anarcho-syndicalist press is in microfiche at the International Instituut voor Sociale Geschiendenis in Amsterdam, with a small cache of newsprint carefully tended at the Centre International de Recherches Sur L'Anarchisme in Lausanne, Switzerland. All of these sources contain rich veins of Mexican social and political history that will prove fruitful for other labor historians.

Finding information on the indigenous communities of northern Veracruz was a more challenging task. The agrarian archives at the Archivo General del Estado de Veracruz were invaluable in this area. They complemented Mexican government census reports as well as the published work of anthropologists and historians, plus the memoirs of oilmen and geologists. Much work still needs to be done on this topic, not only to document fully the histories of indigenous people in the Huasteca but also to analyze the effects of oil production on the Totonacas of Poza Rica and the aboriginal communities of the Isthmus of Tehuantepec.

Other less traditional sources were very useful for this investigation. Period oil novels – many of them veiled memoirs – confirmed the historical sources and brought to life a lively humanity. Photography was an important source for the reconstruction of the landscape in this work as well. In this respect the Pearson Photographic Albums in London were irreplaceable and delightful. The photos of Everett Lee DeGolyer and his wife Nell in Dallas were also exciting and a nice complement to those routinely reproduced in the *Boletín del Petróleo*. These collections offer wonderful possibilities for the environmental history not only of Tampico and northern Veracruz, but also the Isthmus of Tehuantepec and other oil regions.

Record Group 59, the Records of the Department of State Relating to the Internal Affairs of Mexico at the National Archives in College Park, Maryland, will continue to surprise historians analyzing the 1930s in Mexico for a long time to come. Their volume, wealth of detail, and breadth of topics at least prove that American diplomats in Mexico earned their pay, observing every move the labor movement and the Mexican government made and filing numerous reports about them.

There is one archive I was told exists but was not able to locate and examine. That is the material the foreign oil companies left behind upon their abrupt departure in March 1938. Although the companies admitted they had taken their technical files before leaving to make sure the

Mexican government knew nothing about future exploration sites and potential oil reserves, they did not take their personnel files and whatever else they kept in 178 installations across Mexico. Rumors had it that PEMEX, who inherited that information, filled boxes with the files the companies left and put them in storage somewhere. If such an archive does exist, it is not open to the public, and that is a real pity.

I said it before, but it bears repeating that the archivists and librarians in each of the places I was lucky to work in were not only experts in their craft but also courteous and genuinely enthusiastic about sharing with me the treasures they guard so carefully. To them I am most grateful.

ARCHIVES CONSULTED

Archivo General de la Nación (AGN), Mexico City
DT   Departamento del Trabajo
DAT   Departamento Autónomo del Trabajo
DP   Departamento del Petróleo
DGG   Dirección General de Gobierno
AHH   Archivo Histórico de Hacienda
JFCA   Junta Federal de Conciliación y Arbitraje
P/LC   Presidentes: Lázaro Cárdenas

Archivo General del Estado de Veracruz (AGEV), Xalapa, Veracruz
JCCA   Junta Central de Conciliación y Arbitraje
CAM   Comisión Agraria Mixta
CAL   Comisión Agraria Local

RG 59   Record Group 59, General Records of the Department of
          State, Records of the Department of State Relating to Internal
          Affairs of Mexico, 1930–1939, National Archives, College
          Park, Maryland

Science Museum Library, London, England
P&S/HR   S. Pearson & Son, Ltd., Historical Records
P&S/PA   S. Pearson & Son, Ltd., Photographic Albums

Southern Methodist University (SMU), Dallas, Texas
ED   The Papers of Everett Lee DeGoyler
ND   Nell Goodrich DeGoyler Collection

International Archive of Economic Geology (IAEG), American Heritage
Center, University of Wyoming, Laramie
CB   Charles Laurence Baker Collection
EL   Edward D. Lynton Collection
CC   Chester Cassel Collection

KW   Kessack D. White Collection
WC   W.L. Connelly Collection

PHO   Proyecto de Historia Oral, Petroleros, Instituto Nacional de
          Antropología e Historia, Castillo de Chapultepec, Mexico City
ILO   International Labor Organization Historical Archives,
          Geneva, Switzerland
AHAT   Archivo Histórico del Ayuntamiento de Tampico, Tamaulipas
DMC   Doheny Mexican Collection, Occidental College, Los
          Angeles, California
DC   Doheny Collection, University of Southern California, Los
          Angeles, California
PTO   Pioneers in Texas Oil, Oral History of the Oil Industry,
          University of Texas, Austin

Newspapers

El Dictamen (Veracruz), 1922–1938, Biblioteca del Instituto de
  Antropología de la Universidad Veracruzana, Xalapa
Excélsior (Mexico City), 1919–1938, Hemeroteca Nacional, Mexico City
La Gaceta Oficial (LGO) (Veracruz), 1910–1924, AGEV
The Industrial Pioneer, 1923–1925, University of California, Berkeley
  (UCB)
El Machete, 1924–1928, UCB
El Machete Ilegal, 1929–1932, UCB
Mexican Labor News, 1937–1940, UCB
El Mundo (Tampico), 1924–1937, Hemeroteca
The New York Times, 1917–1925, UCB
La Opinión (Los Angeles), 1931–1933, UCB
El Universal (Mexico City), 1917–1920, Hemeroteca

Other Serials

Boletín del Petróleo (BP) (1916–1929), UCB
Boletín del Departamento Forestal de Caza y Pesca (1937–1938), UCB
Fanal (1937–1938), Huasteca Petroleum Company, Hemeroteca
Fuerza y Cerebro, 1918, Centre International de Recherches Sur
  L'Anarchisme (CIRSA), Lausanne, Switzerland
Germinal, 1916, International Instituut voor Sociale Geschiendenis
  (IISG), Amsterdam, Holland

Germinal, 1917–1918, CIRSA
Journal of Forestry, 1930–1935, UCB
Libertario, 1919, IISG
Lucha Social, 1917, IISG
Luz, 1917, CIRSA; 1917–1919, IISG
Luz y Vida, 1921, IISG
México Forestal (1930–1935), UCB
Protección a la naturaleza (1935–1938), UCB
Revista Huasteca (1925–1926), Hemeroteca
National Geographic (1910–1920), UCB
Sagitario, 1924–1927, IISG
El Sindicalista, 1913, IISG
Tribuna Roja, 1915–1916, IISG
Vida Libre, 1918, IISG

SELECTED BIBLIOGRAPHY

Primay Sources

Ackerman, Carl W. *Mexico's Dilemma.* New York: George H. Doran Company, 1918.
Aguilar, Cándido. *El génesis del conflicto petrolero en nuestro país.* Mexico City: Editorial de Izquierda de la Cámara de Diputados, 1949.
Alegatos. Mexico City: Imprenta Escalante, 1919.
Alejandre, Marcelo. *Cartilla huasteca.* Mexico City: Oficina Tipográfica de la Secretaría de Fomento, 1889.
Asunto Nuñez y Rocha vs Penn Mex Fuel Company. Mexico City: n/p, 1925.
Barragán Camacho, José. *Memorias de un petrolero.* Mexico City: n/p, 1983.
de Bekker, L. J. *The Plot Against Mexico.* New York: A. A. Knopf, 1919.
Bermúdez, Antonio J. *Doce años al servicio de la industria petrolera mexicana, 1947–1958.* Mexico City: Editorial Comaval, 1960.
Boatright, Mody C. *Folklore of the Oil Industry.* Dallas: Southern Methodist University Press, 1963.
Boatright, Mody C., and Owens, William A. *Tales from the Derrick Floor: A People's History of the Oil Industry.* Garden City, NY: Doubleday & Co., Inc., 1970.
Campa, Valentín. *Mi testimonio: Memorias de un comunista mexicano.* Mexico City: Ediciones de Cultura Popular, 1985.
Canby, Thomas Y. "After the Storm." *The National Geographic.* Vol. 180. No. 2 (August 1991).
Cárdenas, Lázaro. *Mensaje que dirigió al sindicato de trabajadores petroleros de la República mexicana, el ciudadano presidente, General Lázaro Cárdenas.* Mexico City: Talleres Gráficos de la Nación, 1937.
Cárdenas, Lázaro. *Discurso al Pueblo de Tampico, 10 de junio de 1938.* Mexico City: Talleres Gráficos de la Nación, 1938.
Cárdenas, Lázaro. *Discurso pronunciado por el Sr. Presidente de la República, con motivo del Aniversario de la Expropiación Petrolera.* Mexico City: Talleres Gráficos de la Nación, 1939.
Cárdenas, Lázaro. *A todos los trabajadores de la Secretaría de Comunicaciones y Obras Públicas.* February 28, 1940. Mexico City: Secretaría de Comunicaciones y Obras Públicas, 1940.
Cárdenas, Lázaro. *Mensajes, discursos, declaraciones, entrevistas y otros documentos: 1928–1940.* Mexico City: Siglo XXI Editores, 1978.
Cárdenas, Lázaro. *Ideario político.* Mexico City: Ediciones era, 1991.

Campbell, Reau. *Mexico: Tours Through the Egypt of the New World.* New York: C.G. Crawford, 1890.

Casa del Obrero Mundial. Tampico. "Informe de la sección local de la Casa del Obrero Mundial de Tampico sobre la huelga general del 3 de abril de 1916." *Historia Obrera.* Segunda época. Vol. 5. No. 19 (May 1980).

Castillo, Eduardo L. *Ramón Díaz vs. International Petroleum Company.* Mexico City: Talleres Tipográficos de "El Día Español," 1925.

Chambers, A. E. "Potrero No. 4." *Journal* of the Institution of Petroleum Technologists. Vol. 9. No. 37 (1923).

The Chapacao Oil Co. *La verdad de los acontecimientos que motivaron la escandalosa y atentatoria acusación que se hizo de nuestro gerente general, Sr. Don Ignacio Guijosa por el Sr. Edmundo Torreblanca Jus y socios.* Veracruz: Franco Impresor, 1924.

Chapman, Frank M. "A Naturalist's Journey around Veracruz and Tampico." *The National Geographic Magazine.* Vol. 25. No. 5 (May 1914).

Chávez Padrón, Martha. *Testimonio de una familia petrolera.* Mexico City: PEMEX, 1988.

Cleland, Robert G., ed. *The Mexican Yearbook 1920–1921.* Los Angeles: Mexican Year Book Publishing Co., 1922.

Cleland, Robert G., ed. *The Mexican Yearbook 1922–1924.* Los Angeles: Times-Mirror Press, 1925.

Clifford, Arthur B. "Extinguishing an Oil Well Fire in Mexico." *Transactions* of The Institution of Mining Engineers. Vol. 63. No. 3 (1921–1922).

The Commercial Petroleum Company. *First General Report of the Suit-at-law Against the Mexican Eagle Petroleum Company.* Mexico City: n/p, 1934.

Compañía Mexicana de Petróleo "El Aguila." *Directorio de Tampico.* Tampico: Compañía de Petróleo El Aguila, 1914.

Compañía Mexicana de Petróleo "El Aguila." *La huelga de los obreros de la Compañía Mexicana de Petróleo "El Aguila," S.A. en Minatitlán. Su origen y caracteres.* Mexico City: Talleres Gráficos, 1925.

Compañía Mexicana de Petróleo "El Aguila." *Frente a los ataques de que está siendo objeto por la explotación que hizo del lote 113 de Amatlán.* Mexico City: "El Aguila," 1930.

Confederación de Trabajadores de México. *CTM: 1936–1937: Informe del Comité Nacional.* Mexico City: CTM, 1938.

Confederación de Trabajadores de México. *CTM: 1936–1941.* Mexico City: CTM, 1942.

Connelly, W. L. *The Oil Business as I Saw It: Half a Century with Sinclair.* Norman: University of Oklahoma Press, 1954.

Daniels, Josephus. *Shirt-Sleeve Diplomat.* Chapel Hill: University of North Carolina Press, 1947.

"Doce trabajadores expropiadores: Nuestro petróleo, hacia las manos del 'gringo.'" *Proceso.* No. 134 (May 28, 1979).

Dunn, Gordon E., and Miller, Bauner J. *Atlantic Hurricanes.* Baton Rouge: Lousiana State University Press, 1964.

Esteves, José. "Testimonio: Entrevista con Miguel Ángel Velasco." *Historia Obrera.* Segunda época. Vol. 6. No. 22 (April 1981).

Fisher, Howard T., and Fisher, Marion Hall, eds. *Life in Mexico: The Letters of Fanny Calderón de la Barca.* Garden City, NY: Anchor Books, Doubleday & Company, 1970.

Formoso, Joaquín, de Sauville, Luis, Raynaud, Eugenio, Stubbe, Enrique, and Serralde, Francisco A. *Siguen los manejos tortuosos de la Mexican Petroleum Company.* Mexico City: Talleres Linotipográficos Carlos Rivadeneyra, 1925.

Furber, Percy Norman. *I Took Chances: From Windjammer to Jets.* Leicester: Edgar Backus, 1954.

Gadow, Hans. *Through Southern Mexico: Being an Account of the Travels of a Naturalist.* London: Witherby & Co., 1908.

Gallegos Martínez, Ariel, Díaz Rey, Alfonso, de la Torre Rivera, Manuel, and González Aguilar, Gabino. *Testimonios de la expropiación.* Mexico City: Editorial Nuestro Tiempo, 1990.

García Herrera, Apolo. *Memorias de un trabajador petrolero.* Mexico City: n/p, 1965.

Garner, Bess Adams. *Mexico: Notes in the Margin.* Boston: Houghton Mifflin Company, 1932.

Gibbs, Lois Marie. *Love Canal: My Story.* Albany: State University of New York Press, 1982.

Gordon, Wendell C. *The Expropriation of Foreign-Owned Property in Mexico.* Washington, DC: American Council on Public Affairs, 1941.

Government of Mexico. *Mexico's Oil. A Compilation of Official Documents in the Conflict of Economic Order in the Petroleum Industry, with an Introduction Summarizing Its Causes and Consequences.* Mexico City: n/p, 1940.

Hamilton, Charles W. *Early Day Oil Tales of Mexico.* Houston: Gulf Publishing Company, 1966.

Harper, Henry H. *A Journey in Southern Mexico: Narrative of Experiences, and Observations on Agricultural and Industrial Conditions.* Boston: The DeVinne Press, 1910.

Hastings Millward, Russell. "The Oil Treasure of Mexico." *The National Geographic Magazine.* Vol. 19. No. 11 (November 1908).

Haven, Gilbert. *Our Next Door Neighbor: A Winter in Mexico.* New York: Harper & Brothers Publishers, 1875.

Hayes, Miles O. *Black Tides.* Austin: University of Texas Press, 1999.

Holloway, Marguerite. "Soiled Shores." *Scientific American* (October 1991).

Huasteca Petroleum Co. *Mexico Labor Controversy: 1936–1938: Memoranda on the Controversy Arising Out of Mexico's Impositions on Foreign Oil Companies in Mexico Leading Up to the Expropriation Decree of March 18, 1938.* New York: Huasteca Petroleum Co., 1938.

Huasteca Petroleum Co. *Expropriation.* New York: Huasteca Petroleum Company and Standard Oil Company of California, 1938.

"In the Domain of Standard Oil." *The Industrial Pioneer.* Vol. 1. No. 6 (October, 1923).

International Petroleum Company. *Ramón Díaz vs International Petroleum Company: Historia de un complot.* Mexico City: International Petroleum Company, 1927.

Instituto Nacional Indigenista. *Memorias: densidad de la población de habla indígena en la República Mexicana.* Mexico City: Instituto Nacional Indigenista: 1950.

Instituto Nacional Indigenista. *Memorias: realidades y proyectos: 16 años de trabajo.* Vol. 10 (1964).

Jiménez, Ticiano. *Veracruz: ¡en las huelgas y en el hambre! 1920–1924.* Veracruz: n/p, n/d.

Kane, Joe. *Savages.* New York: Vintage Books, 1995.

Kellogg, Frederic R. *The Case of the American Oil Companies in the Controversy with Mexico.* New York: Association of Producers of Petroleum in Mexico, 1927.

Kellogg, Frederic R. *The World Petroleum Problem: Mexico.* New York: Association of Petroleum Producers in Mexico, 1921.

Knox, Thomas W. *The Boy Travellers in Mexico.* New York: Harper & Brothers, 1890.

Lambert, Paul F., and Franks, Kenny A. *Voices from the Oil Fields.* Norman: University of Oklahoma Press, 1984.

Lavín, José Domingo. *Maniobra (en le caso de la Compañía Petrolera Comercial vs. la Compañía Mexicana de Petróleo "El Aguila").* Pamphlet no. 9. Mexico City: n/p, March, 1934.

Lavín, José Domingo. *Memorandum (en el caso de la Compañía Petrolera Comercial vs. la Compañía Mexicana de Petróleo "El Aguila").* Pamphlet no. 10. Mexico City: n/p, April, 1934.

Lavín, José Domingo. *A los trabajadores y empleados de la Cía Mexicana (?) de Petróleo "El Aguila" y a los obreros mexicanos en general. Litigio sobre el lote 113 de Amatlán.* Mexico City: n/p, 1935.

London, Jack. "Our Adventurers in Tampico." *Collier's The National Weekly.* Vol. 53. No. 15 (June 27, 1914).

Lorenzama, Serapio D. *Un intérprete huasteco.* Mexico City: Oficina Tipográfica de la Secretaría de Fomento, 1896.

Lozano, Samuel. *El puerto del oro negro: o Tampico en un sueño.* Mexico City: Imprenta Guerrero, n/d.

Luna y Parra, Pascual, and Rodríguez, Blas. *Memorandum Súplica. R. Cortina vs The Texas Company of Mexico, S.A.* Mexico City: n/p, 1935.

Lynch, Gerald. *Roughnecks, Drillers, and Tool Pushers: Thirty-Three Years in the Oil Fields.* Austin: University of Texas Press, 1987.

Marett, R. H. K. *An Eye-Witness of Mexico.* London: Oxford University Press, 1939.

Marino. "Tampico: A Class War Skirmish." *The Industrial Pioneer.* Vol. 2. No. 21 (January 1925).

Martínez, Eduardo. *Informe al terminar su gestión como Presidente del H. Ayuntamiento de Tampico, Tamaulipas, el 31 de Diciembre de 1938.* Mexico City: Editorial Nuestra Patria, 1939.

McMahon, William E. *Mexico's Expropriation of American Oil Properties.* Dallas: Instutite of Public Affairs, Southern Methodist University, 1938.

McMahon, William E. *Two Strikes and Out.* Garden City, NY: Country Life Press Corporation, 1937.

Mendoza, Salvador. *La primera sentencia de la Suprema Corte en los asuntos del petróleo.* Mexico City: Imprenta Politécnica, 1921.

Mesa Andraca, Manuel. *Relatos autobiográficos: con las compañías petroleras; mi vinculación con la reforma agraria.* Mexico City: Editorial Nuestro Tiempo, 1981.

Mexican Eagle Company. *The Amatlán Suit: Commercial Petroleum Co. vs Mexican Eagle Oil Co: Texts and Statements.* Mexican Eagle Oil Company, 1934.

Mexican Petroleum Company of Delaware. *Cerro Azul No. 4: World's Greatest Oil Well.* New York: The DeVinne Press, n/d.

Mexican Petroleum Company of Delaware. *La Mexican Petroleum Company y la supuesta compraventa de acciones de la compañía "El Esfuerzo Nacional."* Mexico City: Mexican Petroleum Company of Delaware, 1924.

Mexico. *Ley Federal del Trabajo.* Annotated by Alfonso Teja Zabre. Mexico City: Ediciones Botas, 1936.

Mexico. *The True Facts about the Expropriation of the Oil Companies' Properties in Mexico.* Mexico City: Government of Mexico, 1940.

Mexico. Archivo General de la Nación. "La legislación petrolera en México, 1887–1927." *Boletín* of the Archivo General de la Nación. Tercera serie. Vols. 3–4. Nos. 24–25 (July–December 1983).

Mexico. Consejo Superior de Salubridad. *Instrucciones para precaverse de la fiebre amarilla y de las intermitentes o paludismo.* Mexico City: Consejo Superior de Salubridad, 1902.

Mexico. Departamento de Estadística Nacional. *Anuario de 1930.* Mexico City: Departamento de Estadísca Nacional, 1932.

Mexico. Departamento de Estadística Nacional. *Censo general de habitantes, 30 de noviembre de 1921: Estado de San Luis Potosí.* Mexico City: Departamento de Estadística Nacional, 1921.

Mexico. Departamento de Estadística Nacional. *Censo de población: Veracruz, 1930.*

Mexico. Departamento de Estadística Nacional. *Censo de Veracruz, 1921.*

Mexico. Dirección General de Estadística. *Censo general de la República Mexicana verificado el 20 de Octubre de 1895.* Mexico City: Oficina Tipográfica de la Secretaría de Fomento, 1899.

Mexico. Dirección General de Estadística. *Censo general de la República Mexicana verificado el 28 de Octubre de 1900.* Mexico City: Oficina Tipográfica de la Secretaría de Fomento, 1904.

Mexico. Dirección General de Estadística. *Tercer censo de población verificado el 27 de Octubre de 1910.* Mexico City: Oficina Impresora de la Secretaría de Hacienda, 1918.

Mexico. Ministerio de Fomento. Dirección General de Estadística. *Censo general de la República Mexicana: Tamaulipas.* Vol. 25. Mexico City: Oficina Tipográfica de la Secretaría de Fomento, 1897.

Mexico. Secretaría de Desarrollo Urbano y Ecología. *Informe sobre el estado del medio ambiente en México.* Mexico City: Secretaría de Desarrollo Urbano y Ecología, 1986.

Mexico. Secretaría de Fomento, Colonización e Industria. Dirección General de Estadística. *División territorial de los Estados Unidos Mexicanos; Estado de Tamaulipas.* Mexico City: Imprenta y Fototipia de la Secretaría de Fomento, 1913.

Mexico. Secretaría de Industria, Comercio y Trabajo. *Documentos relacionados con la legislación petrolera mexicana.* Vols. 1–2. Mexico City: Talleres Gráficos de la Nación, 1919–1922.

Mexico. Secretaría de Industria, Comercio y Trabajo. *La industria del petróleo en México.* Mexico City: Talleres Gráficos de la Nación, 1927.

Mexico. Secretaría de Industria, Comercio y Trabajo. *Reglamento de trabajos petroleros.* Mexico City: Talleres Gráficos de la Nación, 1927.

Mexico. Secretaría de Marina. *Estudio geográfico de la región de Veracruz, Veracruz.* Mexico City: Secretaría de Marina, 1980.

Mexico. Secretaría del Patrimonio Nacional. *Tampico/Madero: Plan directorio de desarrollo metropolitano.* Mexico City: Secretaría del Patrimonio Nacional, 1975.

Millan, Verna Carleton. *Mexico Reborn.* Cambridge, MA: The Riverside Press, 1939.

National Association for the Protection of American Rights in Mexico. *Plow with Petroleum.* New York: National Association for the Protection of American Rights in Mexico, 1915.

Norman, B. M. *Rambles by Land and Water, or Notes of Travel in Cuba and Mexico.* New York: Paine & Burgess, 1845.

Ober, Frederick A. *Mexican Resources and Guide to Mexico.* Boston: Estes and Lauriat, 1884.

Olsson-Seffer, Pehr. "Agricultural Possibilities in Tropical Mexico." *The National Geographic Magazine.* Vol. 21. No. 12 (December, 1910).

"The 'One-Man Fire Department of the Oil-Fields.'" *The Literary Digest* (December 27, 1930).

Palacios, Juan. "Memoria sobre el incendio del pozo de petróleo de 'Dos Bocas.'" *Boletín* of the Sociedad Mexicana de Geografía y Estadística. Quinta época. Vol. 3. No. 1 (1908).

Palma Alor, Augusto. *Las Choapas, ayer, hoy y siempre.* Mexico City: Federación Editorial Mexicana, 1975.

Palma Alor, Augusto. "Testimonio: Los trabajadores eventuales y la expropriación petrolera." *Anuario V* [1988].

PanAmerican Petroleum and Transport Company. *Mexican Petroleum.* New York: PanAmerican Petroleum and Transport Company, 1922.

Penn Mex Fuel Company. *Rocha-Nuñez vs Penn Mex Fuel Company: Memorandum.* Mexico City: Penn Mex Fuel Company, 1927.

La prensa metropolitana y el Artículo 27 Constitucional. Mexico City: Imprenta Azteca, 1926.

Prieto, Alejandro. *Discurso pronunciado en Tampico.* Victoria, Tamaulipas: Oficina Tipográfica del Gobierno, 1902.

"Prometeo." Pamphlet. Mexico City: n/p, 1918.

de Quevedo, Miguel Ángel. "A Six-year Forestry Plan for Mexico." *Journal of Forestry.* Vol. 33 (1935).

Ramos Aguirre, Francisco. *Corridos tamaulipecos.* Reynosa, Tamaulipas: Imprenta Valdéz y Estrada, 1987.

Reina, Leticia. *Las rebeliones campesinas en México (1819–1906).* Mexico City: Siglo XXI Editores, 1988.

Rodríguez, Abelardo R. *Laudo arbitral en la huelga del Istmo contra la Compañía Mexicana de Petróleo "El Aguila" S.A.* Mexico City: Royal Dutch Shell, 1934.

Rodríguez, Antonio. *El rescate del petróleo: Epopeya de un pueblo.* Mexico City: Ediciones "El Caballito," 1975.

Rothkugel, Max. "Brief Notes on Mexican Forests." *Forestry Quaterly.* Vol. 7 (1909).

Santos Santos, Pedro Antonio. *Memorias.* San Luis Potosí: Archivo Histórico del Estado de San Luis Potosí, 1990.

Santos Santos, Pedro Antonio. *Historia antigua de los tres partidos de la Huasteca potosina: Memorias de un criollo.* San Luis Potosí: Archivo Histórico del Estado de San Luis Potosí, 1991.

Serralde, Francisco L. *Refutación que ante la Suprema Corte de Justicia, hacen los accionistas de la Compañía Petrolera "El Esfuerzo Nacional."* Mexico City: Imprenta El Sobre Azul, 1924.

[Sindicato de Trabajadores Petroleros de la República Mexicana] *La cuestión petrolera: sus diversos aspectos.* Mexico City: STPRM, 1939.

[Sindicato de Trabajadores Petroleros de la República Mexicana] *Informe del Comité Ejecutivo General del STPRM, ante la Primera Gran Convención Extraordinaria.* Mexico City: STPRM, 1936.

Sindicato de Trabajadores Petroleros de la República Mexicana. "Snuffing out a Burning Oil-Well." *The Literary Digest.* (January 26, 1919).

Soto, Manuel Fernando. *El Nuevo Estado.* Mexico City: Imprenta de Igancio Cumplido, 1856.

Standard Oil Company of New Jersey. *Confiscation or Expropriation? Mexico's Seizure of the Foreign-Owned Oil Industry.* New York: Standard Oil, 1940.

Standard Oil Company of New Jersey. *Diplomatic Protection.* New York: Standard Oil, 1939.

Standard Oil Company of New Jersey. *Denials of Justice.* New York: Standard Oil, 1940.

Starr, Frederick. *In Indian Mexico: A Narrative of Travel and Labor.* Chicago: Forbes & Company, 1908.

Stevens, Guy. *Brief Statement of Facts Relating to the Mexican Oil Controversy.* Conference at the Institute of Politics, Watertown, Massachusetts, August 6, 1927. New York: Association of Producers of Petroleum in Mexico, 1927.

Storm, Marian. "Wells at the World's End: Life in the Pánuco Oil Region of Mexico." *The Atlantic Monthly.* April 1924.

Taibo, Paco Ignacio II. "Antología: La canción obrera mexicana de 1915 a 1937." *Historia Obrera 18.* Segunda época. Vol. 5 (January 1980).

Tamaulipas. *Colección de leyes, decretos y concesiones que se relacionan con los intereses petroleros y el puerto de Tampico.* Tampico: Imprenta Nueva, 1915.

Terry, T. Philip. *Terry's Guide to Mexico.* Boston: Houghton Miffin Company, 1923.

Terry, T. Philip. *Terry's Guide to Mexico.* Boston: Houghton Miffin Company, 1930.

Terry, T. Philip. *Terry's Guide to Mexico.* Hingham, MA: n/p, 1938.

Tweedie, Mrs. Alec. *Mexico as I Saw It.* New York: Macmillan, 1901.

U.S. Congress. Senate. Committee on Foreign Relations. *Investigation of Mexican Affairs.* 66th Congress. Vols. 1–2 (1919–1920). Washington, DC: Government Printing Office, 1920.

U.S. Congress. Senate. Sub-Committee of the Committee on Foreign Relations. *The Mexican Oil Controversy as Told in Diplomatic Correspondence Between the United States and Mexico, Excerpts From the Investigation of Mexican Affairs.* 66th Congress. 2nd Session. Part 21. 1920.

U.S. Department of State. *Papers Relating to the Foreign Relations of the United States, 1915–1922.* Washington, DC: United States Government Printing Office, 1924–1938.

U.S. Department of State. *Reprints of Correspondence Between the Governments of the United States and Mexico.* New York: Association of Producers of Petroleum in Mexico, November 1926.

U.S. Department of State. *Reprints of Correspondence Exchanged Between the Governments of the United States and Mexico Regarding the Two Laws Regulating Section 1 of Article 27 of the Mexican Constitution.* New York: Association of Producers of Petroleum in Mexico, 1926.

U.S. Fish and Wildlife Services. U.S. Department of the Interior. P. L. Fore, ed. *Proceedings of the 1977 Oil Spill Response Workshop.* New Orleans, Louisiana, 1977. Washington, DC: United States Government Printing Office, 1978.

U.S. National Climatic Center, in cooperation with the National Hurricane Center and National Hurricane Research Laboratory. *Tropical Cyclones of the North Atlantic Ocean, 1871–1980.* North Carolina: Asheville, July 1981.

Valadés, José C. *Memorias de un joven rebelde: Mis confesiones.* Vol. 2. Sonora: Universidad Autónoma de Sinaloa, 1985.

Valdés, Jacobo. *La Mexican Petroleum Company y su apoderado Jacobo Valdés.* Mexico City: n/p, 1925.

Valdivieso Castillo, Julio. *Historia del movimiento sindical petrolero en Minatitlán, Veracruz.* Mexico City: n/p, 1963.

Vargas, Elvira. *Lo que ví en la tierra del petróleo.* Mexico City: Ediciones de *El Nacional,* 1938.

Vázquez Schiaffino, José, Santaella, Joaquín, and Elorduy, Aquiles. *Informes sobre la cuestión petrolera.* Mexico City: Imprenta de la Cámara de Diputados, 1919.

Velázquez, Margarito. *La Mexican Petroleum Company: el Juez Sexto de lo penal y un acreedor de aquella.* Mexico City: n/p, 1924.

Veracruz. *Colección de leyes del Estado de Veracruz.* Veracruz: Gobierno del Estado de Veracruz, 1920.

Viesca, Francisco, and Cruz, Martín C. *Juicio reivindicatorio vs. Tamiahua Petroleum Company.* Mexico City: Imprenta Franco-Americana, 1921.

Villarello, Juan D. "El Pozo de Petróleo de Dos Bocas." *Parergones* of the Instituto Geológico de México. Vol. 3. No. 1 (1909).

The Wall Street Journal. "The Oil Settlement with Mexico." A series of articles reprinted. (September 1928).

Whitney, Caspar. *What's the Matter with Mexico?* New York: The MacMillan Company, 1916.

Whitney, Caspar. *Charles Adelbert Canfield.* New York: D. B. Updike, The Merrymount Press, 1930.

William of Sweden, H. R. H. Prince. *Between Two Continents: Notes from a Journey in Central America, 1920.* London: Eveliegh Nash and Grayson, Ltd, 1922.

Secondary Sources

Adamson, Joni, Evans, Mei Mei, and Stein, Rachel, eds. *The Environmental Justice Reader: Politics, Poetics, and Pedagogy.* Tucson: University of Arizona Press, 2002.

Adleson, S. Lief. "Coyuntura y conciencia: Factores convergentes en la fundación de los sindicatos petroleros de Tampico durante la década de 1920." In *El trabajo y los trabajadores en la historia de México.* Edited by Elsa Cecilia Frost, Michael C. Meyer, and Josefina Zoraida Vázquez. Mexico City: El Colegio de México, 1979.

Adleson, S. Lief. "La adolescencia del poder: La lucha de los obreros de Tampico para definir los derechos del trabajo, 1910–1920." *Historias.* No. 2 (October–December 1982).

Adleson, S. Lief. "Historia social de los obreros industriales de Tampico, 1906–1919." Ph.D. Dissertation. El Colegio de México, 1982.

Adleson, S. Lief. "Identidad comunitaria y transformación social: Estibadores y petroleros en Tampico (1900–1925)." *Historias.* No. 7 (October–December, 1984).

Adleson, S. Lief. "The Cultural Roots of the Oil Workers' Unions in Tampico, 1910–1925." In *The Mexican Petroleum Industry in the Twentieth Century.* Edited by Jonathan C. Brown and Alan Knight. Austin: University of Texas Press, 1992.

Aguilar-Robledo, Miguel. "Reses y poder: Notas introductorias a la historia de la ganadería en la Huasteca veracruzana." In *Huasteca I. Espacio y tiempo. Mujer y trabajo.* Edited by Jesús Ruvalcaba and Graciela Alcalá. Mexico City: Centro de Investigaciones y Estudios Superiores en Antropología Social, 1993.

Alafita Méndez, Leopoldo. "Trabajo y condición obrera en los campamentos petroleros de la Huasteca 1900–1935." *Anuario IV* [1986].

Alafita Méndez, Leopoldo. "La administración privada de las empresas petroleras, 1880–1937." *Anuario V* [1988].

Alafita Méndez, Leopoldo. "Perforación y perforadores: 1906–1938." *Anuario VII* [1990].

Alafita Méndez, Leopoldo, Benítez Juárez, Mirna, and Olvera Rivera, Alberto. *Historia gráfica de la industria petrolera y sus trabajadores (1900–1928).* Xalapa: Universidad Veracruzana, 1988.

Albers, Peter H. *Oil Spills and Living Organisms.* College Station, TX: Texas Agricultural Extension Service and U.S. Fish and Wildlife Service, 1992.

Alcorn, Janis B. *Huastec Mayan Ethnobotany.* Austin: University of Texas Press, 1978.

Alcorn, Janis B. "Development Policy, Forests, and Peasant Farms: Reflections on Huastec-Managed Forests' Contribution to Commercial Production and Resource Conservation." *Economic Botany.* Vol. 38. No. 4 (October–December, 1984).

Alcorn, Janis B. "An Economic Analysis of Huastec Mayan Forest Management." In *Fragile Lands of Latin America: Strategies for Sustainable Development.* Edited by John O. Browder. San Francisco: Westview Press, 1989.

Alejandre, Marcelo. "Noticia de lengua huasteca." *Boletín* of the Sociedad Mexicana de Geografía y Estadística. Segunda época. Vol. 2 (1870).

Almanza, Héctor Raúl. *Brecha en la roca.* Mexico City: Colección Ahuizote, Obregón S.A., 1955.

Álvarez Fragoso, Lourdes. "Álamo, Temapache: formación de una región." In *Huasteca I. Espacio y tiempo. Mujer y trabajo.* Edited by Jesús Ruvalcaba and Graciela Alcalá. Mexico City: Centro de Investigaciones y Estudios Superiores en Antropología Social and Secretaría de Educación Pública, 1993.

American Institute of Biological Sciences. *Conference on Assessment of Ecological Impacts of Oil Spills.* June 14–17, 1978, Keystone, Colorado.

Anderson, J. W., Neff, J. M., Cox, B. A., Tatem, H. E., and Hightower, G. M. "The Effects of Oil on Estuarine Animals: Toxicity, Uptake and Depuration,

Respiration." In *Pollution and Physiology of Marine Organisms*. Edited by F. John Vernberg and Winona B. Vernberg. New York: Academic Press, 1974.

Arenas, Rebeca. *Museo vivo o naturaleza muerta*. Xalapa: Editorial de la Universidad Veracruzana, 1989.

Ashby, Joe C. *Organized Labor and the Mexican Revolution under Lázaro Cárdenas*. Chapel Hill: University of North Carolina Press, 1967.

Bach, Federico, and de la Peña, Manuel. *México y su petróleo: Síntesis histórica*. Mexico City: Editorial "México Nuevo," 1938.

Baker, Dr. Jenifer M., Moeso Suryowinato, Prof. I, Brooks, Dr. Paul, and Rowland, Mr. Steve. "Tropical Marine Ecosystems and the Oil Industry; with a Description of a Post-Oil Spill Survey in Indonesian Mangroves." In *Petroleum and the Marine Environment*. Petromar 80 Eurocean Conference. London: Graham & Trotman, Ltd., 1981.

Barbosa Cano, Fabio. "La situación de la industria petrolera en 1938." *Anuario V* [1988].

Basauri, Carlos. *La población indígena de México: Etnografía*. Vol. 2. Mexico City: Secretaría de Educación Pública, 1940.

Basso, R. A. *En las garras del buitre*. Tampico: n/p, 1935.

Beals, Carleton. *Black River*. London: Victor Gallancz, 1935.

Bellingeri, Marcos, and Gil Sánchez, Isabel. "Las estructuras agrarias bajo el porfiriato." In *México en el siglo XIX, 1821–1910: Historia económica y de la estructura social*. Edited by Ciro Cardoso. Mexico City: Editorial Nueva Imagen, 1988.

Beltrán, Enrique, and Aguirre Pequeño, Eduardo. *Lecciones de paludogía*. Monterrey: Ediciones del Instituto de Investigaciones Científicas de la Universidad de Nuevo León, 1948.

Benítez Juárez, Mirna. "Organización y lucha sindical de los petroleros en Veracruz: 1918–1928." B.A. Thesis. Xalapa: Universidad Veracruzana, 1983.

Benítez Juárez, Mirna. "La lucha de los petroleros de la Huasteca Petroleum Company en el norte de Veracruz: 1926–1931." M.A. Thesis. Mexico City: Universidad Autónoma Metropolitana, Iztapalapa, 1987.

Benítez Juárez, Mirna. "La organización sindical de los trabajadores petroleros en la Huasteca veracruzana, 1917–1931." *Anuario V* [1988].

Benítez Juárez, Mirna, and Leopoldo Alafita Méndez. "La industria petrolera como frontera interior en el estado de Veracruz: 1900 to 1930." *Veracruz, un tiempo para contar... Memoria del primer seminario de historia regional*. Veracruz: Universidad Veracruzana, 1989.

Black, Brian. "Oil Creek as Industrial Apparatus: Re-creating the Industrial Process Through the Landscape of Pennsylvania's Oil Boom." *Environmental History*. Vol. 3. No. 2 (April 1998).

Black, Brian. *Petrolia: The Landscape of America's First Oil Boom*. Baltimore: John Hopkins University Press, 2000.

Blakey, Ellen Sue. *Oil on Their Shoes: Petroleum Geology to 1918*. Tulsa: American Association of Petroleum Geologists, 1985.

Blumer, Max, and Sass, Jeremy. "Oil Pollution: Persistence and Degradation of Spilled Fuel Oil." *Science*. Vol. 176 (June 1972).

Bonfil Batalla, Guillermo. "Notas etnográficas de la región Huasteca, México." *Anales de Antropología*. Vol. 6 (1969).

Bozada, Lorenzo, and Margarito Páez. *La fauna acuática del litoral.* Serie Medio Ambiente en Coatzacoalcos. Vol. 14. Mexico City: Centro de Ecodesarrollo, 1987.

Briseño, Juan, de Gortari, Ludka, Lartigue, Francois, Matías, Marcos, Pérez Zevallos, Juan Manuel, and Ruvalcaba Mercado, Jesús. "Tendencias históricas y procesos sociales en la Huasteca." In *Huasteca III: Movilizaciones campesinas.* Edited by Jesús Ruvalcaba and Graciela Alcalá. Mexico City: Centro de Investigaciones y Estudios Superiores en Antropología Social, 1993.

Brown, Jonathan C. "Jersey Standard and the Politics of Latin American Oil Production, 1911–1930." In *Latin American Oil Companies and the Politics of Energy.* Edited by John D. Wirth. Lincoln: University of Nebraska Press, 1985.

Brown, Jonathan C. "Why Foreign Oil Companies Shifted their Production from Mexico to Venezuela during the 1920s." *The American Historical Review.* Vol. 90. No. 2 (April 1985).

Brown, Jonathan C. "Foreign Oil Companies, Oil Workers, and the Mexican Revolutionary State in the 1920s." In *Multinational Enterprise in Historical Perspective.* Edited by Alice Teichova, Maurice Lery-Leboyer, and Helga Nussbaum. Cambridge: Cambridge University Press, 1986.

Brown, Jonathan C. *Domestic Politics and Foreign Investment: British Development of Mexican Petroleum.* Austin: University of Texas, 1987.

Brown, Jonathan C. *British Petroleum Pioneers in Mexico and South America.* Series Texas Papers on Latin America. Paper no. 89-17. Austin: Institute of Latin American Studies, University of Texas, 1989.

Brown, Jonathan C. *Oil and Revolution in Mexico.* Austin: University of Texas, 1993.

Bullard, Robert D. *Dumping in Dixie: Race, Class, and Environmental Quality.* Boulder, CO: Westview Press, 2000.

Burger, Joanna, ed. *Before and After an Oil Spill: The Arthur Kill.* New Brunswick, NJ: Rutgers University Press, 1994.

Carlberg, S. R. "Oil Pollution of the Marine Environment – with an Emphasis on Estuarine Studies." In *Chemistry and Biogeochemistry of Estuaries.* Edited by Eric Olausson and Ingemar Cato. New York: John Wiley & Sons, 1980.

Carmona Lara, María del Carmen. "La industria petrolera ante la regulación ecológica en México." In *La industria petrolera ante la regulación jurídico-ecológica en México.* Edited by Jorge Muñoz Barret Sylvia Vega Gleason, and María del Carmen Carmona Lara. Mexico City: PEMEX-Universidad Nacional Autónoma de México, 1992.

Carr, Barry. "The Casa del Obrero Mundial. Constitutionalism and the Pact of February 1915." In *El trabajo y los trabajadores en la historia de México.* Edited by Elsa Cecilia Frost, Michael C. Meyer, and Josefina Zoraida Vázquez. Mexico City: El Colegio de México, 1979.

Carr, Barry. "Marxism and Anarchism in the Formation of the Mexican Communist Party, 1910–1919." *Hispanic American Historical Review.* Vol. 63. No. 2 (May 1983).

Carr, Barry. *El movimiento obrero y la política en México, 1910–1929.* Mexico City: Ediciones Era, 1991.

Carr, Barry. *Marxism and Communism in Twentieth-Century Mexico.* Lincoln: University of Nebraska Press, 1992.

Carrillo, Alejandro. *The Mexican People and the Oil Companies.* Mexico City: n/p, 1938.

Carrillo, Atanasio. *Historia de la fiebre amarilla.* Monterrey: Tipografía del Gobierno, 1899.

Cato, I., Olsson, I., and Rosenberg, R. "Recovery and Decontamination of Estuaries." In *Chemistry and Biogreochemistry of Estuaries.* Edited by Eric Olausson and Ingemair Cato. New York: John Wiley & Sons, 1980.

Caufield, Norman E. "The Industrial Workers of the World and Mexican Labor, 1905–1925." M.A. Thesis. University of Houston, 1987.

Celis Salgado, Lourdes. *La industria petrolera en México: Una crónica. I: de los inicios a la expropiación.* Mexico City: PEMEX, 1988.

Chassen, Francie R. "La CTM y la expropiación petrolera." *Memoria del primer coloquio regional de historia obrera.* Mexico City: Centro de Estudios Históricos del Movimiento Obrero Mexicano, 1977.

Cházaro, Miguel. *La vegetación.* Serie Medio Ambiente en Coatzacoalcos. Vol. 6. Mexico City: Centro de Ecodesarrollo, Universidad Veracruzana, 1986.

Clagett, Helen L., and Valderrama, David M. *A Revised Guide to the Law and Legal Literature of Mexico.* Washington, DC: Library of Congress, 1973.

Clark, J. Stanley. *The Oil Century: From the Drake Well to the Conservation Era.* Norman: University of Oklahoma Press, 1958.

Clark, Marjorie Ruth. *Organized Labor in Mexico.* New York: Russell & Russell, 1934.

Cockcroft, James D. *Intellectual Precursors of the Mexican Revolution, 1900–1913.* Austin: University of Texas Press, 1976.

Collier, Ruth Berins, and Collier, David. *Shaping the Political Arena: Critical Junctures, the Labor Movement, and Regime Dynamics in Latin America.* Princeton: Princeton University Press, 1991.

Colmenares, Francisco. *Petróleo y lucha de clases en México, 1864–1982.* Mexico City: Ediciones "El Caballito," 1982.

Contreras, Francisco. *La riqueza del pantano.* Serie Medio Ambiente en Coatzacoalcos. Vol. 5. Mexico City: Centro de Ecodesarrollo, Universidad Veracruzana, 1986.

Coquet, Benito. *Ensayo histórico-político sobre los habitantes indígenas de Veracruz.* Xalapa, Veracruz: 1939.

Corzo Ramírez, Ricardo, González Sierra, José G., and Skerritt, David A . . . *nunca un desleal: Cándido Águilar 1889–1960.* Mexico City: El Colegio de México, 1986.

Cosío Silva, Luis. "La Ganadería." In *Historia Moderna de México.* Volume 7. Part 1. Edited by Daniel Cosío Villegas. Mexico City: Editorial Hermes, 1965.

Cosío Villegas, Daniel. *Historia Moderna de México.* Volumes 4–7. Mexico City: Editorial Hermes, 1957.

Covián Martínez, Vidal. *Cronología histórica de Tampico, Ciudad Madero y Altamira, Tamaulipas y de la expropriación petrolera.* Ciudad Victoria, Tamaulipas: Ediciones Siglo XX, 1969.

Cronon, William. *Changes in the Land: Indians, Colonists, and the Ecology of New England.* New York: Hill and Wang, 1983.

Cruz Bencomo, Miguel Ángel. "El proceso salud-enfermedad en los petroleros, 1938–1942 (notas)." *Anuario* V [1988].

Davis, Margaret Leslie. *Dark Side of Fortune: Triumph and Scandal in the Life of Oil Tycoon Edward L. Doheny.* Berkeley: University of California Press, 1998.

Dean, Warren. *With Broadax and Firebrand: The Destruction of the Brazilian Atlantic Forest.* Berkeley: University of California Press, 1995.

DeGolyer, Everett Lee. "Zacamixtle." *Bulletin* of the American Association of Petroleum Geologists. Vol. 5. No. 1 (January–February, 1921).

DeGolyer, Everett Lee. "Historical Notes on the Development of the Technique of Prospecting for Petroleum." *The Science of Petroleum.* Vol. 1 (1938).

DeGolyer, Everett Lee. "Memorial." *Bulletin* of the American Association of Petroleum Geologists. Vol. 34. No. 5 (May 1950).

DeGolyer, Everett Lee. "Historia de la exploración de petróleo en México antes de la expropriación, 1938." *Boletín* of the Asociación Mexicana de Geólogos Petroleros. Vol. 4. Nos. 7–8 (July–August, 1952).

Díaz, Lilia. "El liberalismo militante." In *Historia general de México.* Vol. 2 of 2. Edited by Daniel Cosío Villegas. Mexico City: El Colegio de México, 1976.

Dicks, B., and Westwood, S. S. C. "Oil and the Mangroves of the Northern Red Sea." In *Fate and Effects of Oil in Marine Ecosystems.* Edited by J. Kuiper and W. J. Van den Brink. Dordrecht, Netherlands: Martinus Nijhoff Publishers, 1987.

Dubofsky, Melvyn. *We Shall Be All: A History of the IWW, The Industrial Workers of the World.* New York: Quadrangle/The New York Times Book Co., 1969.

Ducey, Michael T. "From Village Riot to Regional Rebellion: Social Protest in the Huasteca, Mexico, 1760–1870." Ph.D. Dissertation. University of Chicago, 1992.

Ducey, Michael T. "Liberal Theory and Peasant Practice: Land and Power in Northern Veracruz, Mexico, 1826–1900." In *Liberals, the Church, and Indian Peasants: Corporate Lands and the Challenge of Reform in Nineteenth-Century Spanish America.* Edited by Robert H. Jackson. Albuquerque: University of New Mexico Press, 1997.

Durán, Esperanza. "PEMEX: The Trajectory of a National Oil Policy." In *Latin American Oil Companies and the Politics of Energy.* Edited by John D. Wirth. Lincoln: University of Nebraska Press, 1985.

Ekholm, Gordon F. "Excavations at Tampico and Panuco in the Huasteca, Mexico." *Anthropological Papers of the American Museum of Natural History.* Vol. 38. Part 5 (1944).

Escobar Ohmstede, Antonio. *Ciento cincuenta años de historia de la huasteca.* Veracruz: Instituto Veracruzano de Cultura, 1998.

Escobar Ohmstede, Antonio. *Historia de los pueblos indígenas de México: De la costa a la sierra: Las huastecas, 1750–1900.* Mexico City: Centro de Investigaciones y Estudios Superiores en Antropología Social, 1998.

Esteves Torres, José. "Las principales huelgas de los trabajadores petroleros en México en el año de 1924." B.A. Thesis. Universidad Nacional Autónoma de México, 1983.

Farran, A., Grimalt, J., Albarges, J., Botello, A. V., and Macko, S. A. "Assessment of Petroleum Pollution in a Mexican River by Molecular Markers and Carbon Isotopes Ratios." *Marine Pollution Bulletin.* Vol. 18. No. 6 (June 1987).

Faulhaber de Sáenz, J. "Los Huastecos y Mexicanos en relación con otras poblaciones de la faja costeña del Golfo de México." *Revista Mexicana de Antropología.* Vol. 13. Nos. 2–3 (1952–1953).

Fernández, Jorge, Jaber, Jorge, and Robles, Jorge A. "Alrededor de febrero de 1915: La COM, los Batallones Rojos, ATL y las huelgas." *Memoria del segundo coloquio regional de historia obrera.* Mexico City: Centro de Estudios Históricos sobre el Movimiento Obrero, 1979.

Ferrier, R. W. *The History of the British Petroleum Company: The Developing Years, 1901–1932.* Vol. 1 of 4. Cambridge: Cambridge University Press, 1982.

Fletcher, Thomas H. *From Love Canal to Environmental Justice: The Politics of Hazardous Waste on the Canada-U.S. Border.* Peterborough, Ontario: Broadview Press, 2003.

Fowler Salamini, Heather. *Agrarian Radicalism in Veracruz, 1920–1938.* Lincoln: University of Nebraska Press, 1978.

Fowler Salamini, Heather. "Revolutionary Caudillos in the 1920s: Francisco Múgica and Adalberto Tejeda." In *Caudillo and Peasant in the Mexican Revolution.* Edited by David A. Brading. Cambridge: Cambridge University Press, 1980.

Galinier, Jacques. *N'yuhu Les Indiens Otomìs: Hiérarchie Sociale et Tradition dans le Sud de la Huasteca.* Mexico City: Mission Archeologique et Ethnologique Francaise au Mexique, 1979.

Gallegos, Margarita. *Petróleo y manglar.* Serie Medio Ambiente en Coatzacoalcos. Vol. 3. Mexico City: Centro de Ecodesarrollo, Universidad Veracruzana, 1986.

García Granados, Jorge. *Los veneros del diablo.* Mexico City: Ediciones Liberación, 1941.

Garretson, F. C. *History of the Royal Dutch.* Vol. 4. The Hague: E.J. Brill, 1957.

Gatti, Luis María, and Chenaut, Victoria. *La costa totonaca: Cuestiones regionales II.* Cuadernos de la Casa Chata 158. Mexico City: Centro de Estudios Superiores en Antropología Social, 1980.

Gilly, Adolfo. *El cardenismo, una utopía mexicana.* Mexico City: Cal y Arena, 1994.

Golob, Richard S., and McShea, Daniel W. "Implications of the Ixtoc-1 Blow-out and Oil Spill." In *Petroleum and the Marine Environment.* Petromar 80 Eurocean Conference. London: Graham & Trotman, Ltd., 1981.

Gómez-Pompa, Arturo. *Ecología de la vegetación del estado de Veracruz.* Mexico City: Editorial Continental, 1977.

Gómez-Pompa, Arturo, and del Amo Rodríguez, Silvia. *Investigaciones sobre la regeneración de selvas altas en Veracruz, México.* Vol. 2 of 2. Mexico City: Instituto Nacional de Investigaciones sobre Recursos Bióticos and Editorial Alhambra Mexicana, 1985.

Gómez-Pompa, Arturo, del Amo Rodríguez, Silvia, Vázquez Yáñes, Carlos, and Butanda Cervera, Armando. *Investigaciones sobre la regeneración de selvas altas en Veracruz, México.* Mexico City: Editorial Continental, 1976.

Gómez-Pompa, Arturo, and Ludlow Wiechers, B. "Regeneración de los ecosistemas tropicales y subtropicales." In *Investigaciones sobre la regeneración de selvas altas en Veracruz, México.* Edited by Arturo Gómez-Pompa, Silvia del Amo Rodríguez, Carlos Vázquez Yáñes, and Armando Britanda Cervera. Mexico City: Editorial Continental, 1976.

González, Arturo. *Historia de Tamaulipas.* Ciudad Victoria: Librería El Lápiz Rojo, 1931.

González, Francisco Alonso. *Historia y petróleo.* Mexico City: El Caballito, 1979.

González, Luis. "El liberalismo triunfante." In *Historia general de México*. Vol. 2 of 2. Edited by Daniel Cosío Villegas. Mexico City: El Colegio de México, 1976.

González, Luis. *Los días del Presidente Cárdenas*. Series Historia de la revolución mexicana. Vol. 15 of 23. Mexico City: El Colegio de México, 1981.

González Bonilla, Luis Antonio. "Los Huastecos." *Revista Mexicana de Sociología*. Año 1. Vol. 1. No. 2 (May–June 1939).

González Salas, Carlos. *Tampico: Crónicas de una ciudad*. Mexico City: Ediciones Contraste, 1972.

González Salas, Carlos. *Los seis municipios conubados de la desembocadura del río Pánuco*. Ciudad Victoria: Universidad Autónoma de Tamaulipas, Instituto de Investigaciones Históricas, 1980.

González Salas, Carlos. *Tampico, mi ciudad*. Mexico City: Grupo Unido de Alijadores de Tampico and Ediciones Contraste, 1981.

González Salas, Carlos. *Del reloj en vela (Crónicas históricas de Tampico, Ciudad Altamirano y Ciudad Madero)*. Tampico: Grupo Unido de Alijadores de Tampico, 1983.

González Salas, Carlos. *Acercamiento a la historia del movimiento obrero en Tampico (1887–1983)*. Ciudad Victoria: Universidad Autónoma de Tamaulipas, 1987.

González Salas, Carlos. *Tampico es lo azul*. Mexico City: Miguel Ángel Porrúa and Universidad Autónoma de Tamaulipas, 1990.

González Salas, Carlos. *Breve historia de Tampico y Ciudad Madero*. Tampico: Ediciones Mar Adentro, 1993.

de Gortari, Rebeca. "Petróleo y clase obrera en Veracruz: 1920–1935." *Memoria del primer coloquio regional de historia obrera*. Mexico City: Centro de Estudios del Movimiento Obrero Mexicano, 1977.

de Gortari, Rebeca. "Petróleo y clase obrera en la zona del Golfo de México, 1920–1938." B.A. Thesis. Mexico City: Universidad Nacional Autónoma de México, 1978.

Grayson, George W. *The Politics of Mexican Oil*. Pittsburgh: University of Pittsburgh Press, 1980.

Grosser Lerner, Eva. *Los Teenek de San Luis Potosí: lengua y contexto*. Mexico City: Instituto Nacional de Antropología e Historia, 1991.

Guerrero Muller, Alma Yolanda. *Cuesta abajo: Declinación de tres caciques huastecos revolucionarios. Cedillo, Santos y Peláez*. Mexico City: Grupo Editorial Miguel Ángel Porrúa, 1991.

Gutiérrez Rivas, Ana María Graciela. "La familia Herrera, miembro del grupo de poder del norte de Veracruz, 1743–1890." M.A. Thesis. Centro de Investigaciones y Estudios Superiores en Antropología Social, 1998.

Hadley, Diana, Naylor, Thomas H., and Shutz-Miller, Mardith K., eds. *The Presidio and Militia on the Northern Frontier of New Spain*, Volume II, Part II: The Central Corridor and the Texas Corridor, 1700–1765. Tucson: University of Arizona Press, 1997.

Hale, Charles A. *The Transformation of Liberalism in Late Twentieth Century Mexico*. Princeton: Princeton University Press, 1989.

Hall, Linda. *Oil, Banks, and Politics: The United States and Postrevolutionary Mexico, 1917–1924*. Austin: University of Texas Press, 1995.

Hall, Linda, and Coerver, Don M. "Oil and the Mexican Revolution: The Southwestern Connection." *Americas*. Vol. 41. No. 2 (1984).

Hamilton, Nora. *The Limits of State Autonomy: Post-Revolutionary Mexico.* Princeton: Princeton University Press, 1982.

Hart, John M. *Anarchism and the Mexican Working Class, 1860–1931.* Austin: University of Texas Press, 1978.

Hermida Ruiz, Ángel J. *La industria petrolera mexicana: Los primeros 20 años de PEMEX.* Mexico City: PEMEX, 1959.

Hermida Ruiz, Ángel J. *Bermúdez y la batalla por el petróleo.* Mexico City: B. Costa-Amic, 1974.

Hertz, James R., Lewis, Lancelot, Chambers, Janice, and Yarbrough, James D. "The Acute Effects of Empire Mix Crude Oil in Enzymes in Oysters, Shrimp and Mullet." In *Pollution and Physiology of Marine Organisms.* Edited by F. John Vernberg and Winona B. Vernberg. New York: Academic Press, 1974.

Hoffman, Fritz L. "Edward L. Doheny and the Beginnings of Petroleum Development in Mexico." *Mid-America.* Vol. 24. New Series. Vol. 13. No. 2 (April 1942).

Huntley, L. G. "The Mexican Oil Fields." *Bulletin* of the American Institute of Mining Engineers. No. 105 (September, 1915).

Huntley, L. G., and Huntley, Stirling. "Mexican Oil Fields." *Mining and Metallurgy.* The American Institute of Mining and Metallurgical Engineers. No. 177 (September, 1921).

Hutchinson, T. C., and Hellesbust, J. A. *Oil Spills and Vegetation at Norman Wells, N.W.T.* Toronto: Department of Botany and Institute of Environment Sciences and Engineering, University of Toronto, 1974.

Joseph, Gilbert M., and Nugent, Daniel, eds. *Everyday Forms of State Formation: Revolution and the Negotiation of Rule in Modern Mexico.* Durham: Duke University Press, 1994.

Katz, Friedrich. *La servidumbre agraria en la época porfiriana.* Mexico City: Ediciones Era, 1991.

Katz, Friedrich. *Ensayos mexicanos.* Mexico City: Alianza Editorial, 1994.

Kimerling, Judith. *Amazon Crude.* Washington, DC: Natural Resources Defense Council, 1991.

Klein, Julius. *Mexican Petroleum*, reprinted from *The Military Historian and Economist.* Vol. 2. No. 4 (October 1917).

Knight, Alan. "The Working Class and the Mexican Revolution, c. 1900–1920." *Journal of Latin American Studies.* Vol. 16. Part 1 (May 1984).

Knight, Alan. "Mexican Peonage: What Was It and Why Was It?" *Journal of Latin American Studies.* Vol. 18. Part 1 (May 1986).

Knight, Alan. "Interpretaciones recientes de la Revolución Mexicana." *Secuencia.* No. 13 (January–April, 1989).

Knight, Alan. *The Mexican Revolution: Counter-revolution and Reconstruction.* Vol. 2 of 2. Cambridge: Cambridge University Press, 1990.

Knight, Alan. "Cardenismo: Juggernaut or Jalopy?" *Journal of Latin American Studies.* Vol. 26. Part 1 (February 1994).

Knight, Alan. "Peasants into Patriots: Thoughts on the Making of the Mexican Nation." *Mexican Studies/Estudios Mexicanos.* Vol. 10. No. 1 (Winter 1994).

Knight, Alan. "Popular Culture and the Revolutionary State in Mexico, 1910–1940." *Hispanic American Historical Review.* Vol. 74. No. 3 (August 1994).

Knowles, Ruth Sheldon. *The Greatest Gamblers: The Epic of American Oil Exploration.* New York: McGraw-Hill Book Co., Inc. 1959.

Konrad, Herman W. "Tropical Forest Policy and Practice During the Mexican Porfiriato, 1876–1910." In *Changing Tropical Forests: Historical Perspectives on Today's Challenges in Central and South America.* Edited by Harold K. Steen and Richard D. Tucker. Proceedings of a Conference Sponsored by the Forest History Society and IUFRO Forest History Group. Forest History Society, 1992.

Krauze, Enrique. *Lázaro Cárdenas. General Misionero.* Mexico City: Fondo de Cultura Económica, 1987.

Kuecker, Glen David. "A Desert in a Tropical Wilderness: Limits to the Porfirian Project in Northeastern Veracruz, 1876–1910." Ph.D. Dissertation. Rutgers, The State University of New Jersey, 1998.

LaBotz, Dan. *Edward L. Doheny: Petroleum, Power, and Politics in the United States and Mexico.* New York: Praeger, 1991.

Lankford, Robert R. "Coastal Lagoons of Mexico: Their Origin and Classification." In *Estuarine Processes.* Vol. 2. Edited by Martin Wiley. New York: Academic Press, 1976.

Lara Ceballos, María Cecilia. "La Sección 30 del STPRM (Poza Rica) y las compañías contratistas." In *Los sindicatos nacionales en el México contemporáneo: petroleros.* Edited by Javier Aguilar. Vol. 1. Mexico City: G.V. Editores, 1986.

Laughlin, Robert M. "The Huastec." *Handbook of Middle American Indians.* Vol. 7 of 16. *Ethnology.* Part 1. Edited by Evon Z. Vogt. Austin: University of Texas Press, 1971.

Lavín, José Domingo. *Petróleo: Pasado, presente y futuro de una industria mexicana.* Mexico City: EDIAPSA, 1950.

Lewis, R. R. "Impact of Oil Spills on Mangrove Forests." In *Biology and Ecology of Mangroves.* Edited by H. J. Teas. *Tasks for Vegetation Science Series* 8. Edited by Helmut Lieth. The Hague: Dr. W. Junk Publishers, 1983.

Lima Muñiz, Laura. "Dos haciendas veracruzanas en el siglo XIX." *Historia Moderna y Contemporánea de México.* Vol. V (1976).

López Portillo y Weber, José. *El petróleo de Veracruz.* Mexico City: Comisión Nacional Editorial, 1976.

Loyola Díaz, Rafael. "Los petroleros bajo la industria nacionalizada: 1938–1946." *Anuario* V [1988].

MacArthur, Robert H. *Geographical Ecology: Patterns in the Distribution of the Species.* New York: Harper & Row, Publishers, 1972.

Manrique Castañeda, Leonardo. "La posición de la lengua huasteca." *Actes du XLIIe Congrès International des Américanistes.* Vol. IX-B. Paris: n/p, 1979.

Martínez, Pedro. *Descripción de los pueblos de la provincia de Pánuco.* Mexico City: Editor Bargas Rea, 1952.

Martínez Hernández, Rosendo. "La explotación petrolera en la Huasteca veracruzana, el caso de Cerro Azul, Veracruz, 1884–1922." B.A. Thesis. Universidad Nacional Autónoma de México, 1990.

Martínez Hernández, Rosendo. "La Faja de Oro: una semblanza de las transformaciones estructurales en la Huasteca veracruzana." In *Huasteca I. Espacio y tiempo. Mujer y trabajo.* Edited by Jesús Ruvalacaba and Graciela Alacalá. Mexico

City: Centro de Investigaciones y Estudios Superiores en Antropología Social and Secretaria de Educación Pública, 1993.

Martínez Leal, Antonio. *Tampico.* Ciudad Victoria: Universidad Nacional Autónoma de Tamaulipas, 1985.

Meade, Joaquín. *La Huasteca veracruzana.* Vols. 1–2. Mexico City: Editorial Citlatépetl, 1962.

Meade, Joaquín. *La Huasteca tamaulipeca.* Vols. 1–2. Ciudad Victoria, Tamaulipas: Editorial Jus, 1978.

Meléndez de la Cruz, Juan. "Industria petrolera: El personal calificado ante la nacionalización." *Anuario* V [1988].

Melgarejo Vivanco, José Luis. *Tamiahua: una historia huaxteca.* Jalapa: Ediciones Punto y Aparte, 1981.

Melosi, Martin V. "Energy and Environment in the United States: The Era of Fossil Fuels." *Environmental Review.* Vol. 11. No. 3 (Fall 1987).

Mena, Ramón. *El libro del petróleo en México.* Mexico City: Porrúa Hermanos, 1915.

Menéndez, Gabriel Antonio. *Doheny el cruel: Valoración histórica de la sangrienta lucha por el petróleo mexicano.* Mexico City: Ediciones "Bolsa Mexicana del Libro," 1958.

Merchant, Carolyn. *The Death of Nature: Women, Ecology and the Scientific Revolution.* New York: HarperCollins Publishers, 1990.

Merchant, Carolyn. "Reinventing Eden: Western Culture as a Recovery Narrative." In *Uncommon Ground: Rethinking the Human Place in Nature.* Edited by William Cronon. New York: W.W. Norton and Company, 1996.

Merchant, Carolyn. *Reinventing Eden: The Fate of Nature in Western Culture.* New York: Routledge, 2003.

Mesa, Manuel A. "A propósito de la huelga petrolera." *Futuro.* (June, 1937).

Meyer, Jean. "Haciendas y ranchos, peones y campesinos en el porfiriato. Algunas falacias estadísticas." *Historia Mexicana.* Vol. XXXV. No. 3 (January–March 1986).

Meyer, Lorenzo. *México y los Estados Unidos en el conflicto petrolero: 1917–1942.* Mexico City: El Colegio de México, 1972.

Meyer, Lorenzo. *El conflicto social y los gobiernos del maximato.* Series Historia de la Revolución Mexicana. Vol. 13 of 23. Mexico City: El Colegio de México, 1980.

Montgomery, David. *Workers' Control in America: Studies in the History of Work, Technology, and Labor Struggles.* Cambridge: Cambridge University Press, 1981.

Morales, Isidro. "The Consolidation and Expansion of PEMEX, 1947–1958." In *The Mexican Petroleum Industry in the Twentieth Century.* Edited by Jonathan C. Brown and Alan Knight. Austin: University of Texas Press, 1992.

Muellerried, Friedrich K. G. "Algunas observaciones sobre los 'cues' en la Huasteca." *El Mexico Antiguo.* Vol. 2 (1924–1927).

Muellerried, Friedrich K. G. "Geología petrolera de las zonas sur del estado de Tamaulipas y el norte del estado de Veracruz." *Anales* of the Instituto Geológico de México. Vol. 3 (1929).

Muellerried, Friedrich K. G. "El mundo huasteco y totonaco." *México Desconocido.* Special Edition. No. 19 (1994).

Muñoz, Ignacio. *La tragedia del petróleo.* Mexico City: Ediciones Cicerón, 1938.

Murphy, Peter G., and Lugo, Ariel E. "Ecology of Tropical Dry Forest." *Annual Review of Ecology and Systematics.* Vol. 17 (1986).

The National Institute of Environmental Health Sciences, et al. "The Alaskan Oil Spill and Human Health Conference." July 28–30, 1989, Seattle, Washington.

Nelson-Smith, A. *Oil Pollution and Marine Ecology.* New York: Plenum Press, 1973.

Noriega, José S. *Bases para la política petrolera mexicana.* Mexico City: Imprenta Manuel León Sánchez, 1936.

Ocasio-Meléndez, Marcial E. "Mexican Urban History: The Case of Tampico, Tamaulipas." Ph.D. Dissertation. Michigan State University, 1988.

Ocasio-Meléndez, Marcial E. *Capitalism and Development: Tampico, Madero 1878–1924.* New York: Peter Lang, 1998.

Ochoa Salas, Lorenzo. "Atavío, costumbres, hechicería y religión de los huaxtecos." *Actes du XLIIe Congrès International des Américanistes.* Vol. IX-B. Paris: n/p, 1979.

Ochoa Salas, Lorenzo. "El origen de los huaxtecos según las fuentes históricas." In *Huaxtecos y Totonacos: Una antología histórico-cultural.* Edited by Lorenzo Ochoa. Mexico City: Consejo Nacional para la Cultura y las Artes, 1990.

Ochoa Villagómez, Ignacio. *Vegetación espontánea y repoblación de los médanos de la zona litoral de Veracruz.* Mexico City: Secretaría de Fomento, 1885.

O'Connor, Harvey. *The Empire of Oil.* New York: Monthly Review Press, 1955.

O'Connor, Richard. *The Oil Barons: Men of Greed and Grandeur.* Boston: Little, Brown and Company, 1971.

Odena, Lina. *Totonacos y Huastecos.* Mexico City: Museo Nacional de Antropología, 1968.

Olliff, Donathon C. *Reforma Mexico and the United States: A Search for Alternatives to Annexation, 1854–1861.* Alabama: University of Alabama Press, 1981.

Olvera Ribera, Alberto J. "Origen social, condiciones de vida y organización sindical de los trabajadores petroleros de Poza Rica, 1932–1935." *Anuario* IV [1986].

Olvera Ribera, Alberto J. "Acción obrera y nacionalización del petróleo: Poza Rica (1938–1939)." *Historias* 16 (January–March 1987).

Olvera Ribera, Alberto J. "Los trabajadores ante la nacionalización petrolera: el caso de Poza Rica." *Anuario* V [1988].

Olvera Ribera, Alberto J. "Los obreros del petróleo y la nacionalización de la industria petrolera: historia oral, historia oficial y sus límites." *Secuencia.* No. 13 (January–April, 1989).

Olvera Ribera, Alberto J. "La evolución de la conciencia obrera en Poza Rica, 1932–1959." *Veracruz, un tiempo para contar... Memoria del primer seminario de historia regional.* Veracruz: Universidad Veracruzana, 1989.

Olvera Ribera, Alberto J. "The Rise and Fall of Union Democracy at Poza Rica, 1932–1940." In *The Mexican Petroleum Industry in the Twentieth Century.* Edited by Jonathan C. Brown and Alan Knight. Austin: University of Texas Press, 1992.

Ordoñez, Ezequiel. "Occurrence and Prospects of Oil in Mexico." *The Engineering and Mining Journal.* Vol. 89 (May 14, 1910).

Ordoñez, Ezequiel. "The Oil Fields of Mexico." *Bulletin* of the American Institute of Mining Engineers. No. 94 (October 1914).

Ordoñez, Ezequiel. *El petróleo en México: Bosquejo histórico.* Mexico City: Empresa Editorial de Ingeniería y Arquitectura, 1932.

Ortega, Gustavo. *Los recursos petrolíferos mexicanos y su actual explotación.* Mexico City: Talleres Gráficos de la Nación, 1925.

Ortiz Wadgymar, Arturo. "Ensayo sobre la ganadería huasteca." In *Las Huastecas en el desarrollo regional de México.* Edited by Angel Bassols Batalla, Santiago Rentería Romero, Arturo Ortiz Wadgymar, Remedios Hernández A., Carlos Bustamante Lemus and Patricia Sosa F. Mexico City: Editorial Trillas, 1977.

Pasquel, Leonardo. *La revolución en el estado de Veracruz.* Vols. 1–2. Mexico City: Talleres Gráficos de la Nación, 1971.

Pérez Jr., Louis A. *Winds of Change: Hurricanes and the Transformation of Nineteenth-Century Cuba.* Chapel Hill: University of North Carolina Press, 2001.

Pérez-Osuna, F., Botello, A. V., and Villanueva, S. "Heavy Metals in Coatzacoalcos Estuary and Ostion Lagoon, Mexico." *Marine Pollution Bulletin.* Vol. 17. No. 11 (November 1986).

Petróleos Mexicanos. *El Petróleo.* Mexico City: PEMEX, 1980.

Piña Chan, Román. "El desarrollo de la tradición huasteca." In *Huaxtecos y Totonacos: Una antología histórico-cultural.* Edited by Lorenzo Ochoa. Mexico City: Consejo Nacional para la Cultura y las Artes, 1990.

Poggie, John J. Jr. *Coastal Pioneer Plants and Habitat in the Tampico Region, Mexico.* Coastal Studies Series No. 6. Baton Rouge: Louisiana State University Studies, 1963.

Portillo y Weber, José López. *El petróleo en Veracruz.* Mexico City: Editorial Libros de México, 1976.

Powell, J. Richard. *The Mexican Petroleum Industry 1938–1950.* Berkeley: University of California Press, 1956.

Prieto, Alenjandro. *Historia, Geografía y Estadística del Estado de Tamaulipas.* Mexico City: Tipografía Escalerillas, 1873.

Pulido, Laura. *Environmentalism and Economic Justice: Two Chicano Struggles in the Southwest.* Tucson: University of Arizona Press, 1998.

Quam-Wickham, Nancy Lynn. "Petroleocrats and Proletarians: Work, Class, and Politics in the California Oil Industry, 1917–1925." Ph.D. Dissertation. University of California, Berkeley, 1994.

Quam-Wickham, Nancy Lynn. "'Cities Sacrificed on the Altar of Oil': Popular Opposition to Oil Development in 1920s Los Angeles." *Environmental History.* Vol. 3. No. 2 (April 1998).

Quintal, Ella Fanny. "La Sección 30 del STPRM (Poza Rica)." In *Los sindicatos nacionales en el México contemporáneo: petroleros.* Vol. 1. Edited by Javier Aguilar. Mexico City: G.V. Editores, 1986.

Ramírez, José. *La vegetación de México.* Mexico City: Oficina Tipográfica de la Secretaría de Fomento, 1899.

Rivera Castro, José. "Periodización del sindicalismo petrolero." In *Los sindicatos nacionales en el México contemporáneo: Petroleros.* Vol. 1. Edited by Javier Aguilar. Mexico City: G.V. Editores, 1986.

Rivera Castro, José. "El conflicto obrero-patronal en la Huasteca Petroleum Company en 1936." *Anuario* V [1988].

Rodríguez, Blas E. *Tampico: Datos para la historia de la Huasteca.* Mexico City: Editorial Cultura, 1932.

Rodríguez, Blas E. *Culturas huaxteca y olmeca.* Mexico City: Editora Intercontinental, 1945.

Roediger, David. *Wages of Whiteness: Race and the Making of the American Working Class.* London: Verso, 1991.

Román del Valle, Mario, and Segura, Rosario. "La huelga de 57 días en Poza Rica." *Anuario* V [1988].

Romero, Matías. *Coffee and India-Rubber Culture in Mexico.* New York: G.P. Putnam's Sons, 1898.

Rosas, Irma, Báez, Armando, and Belmont, Raúl. "Oyster (*Crassostrea Virginica*) as Indicator of Heavy Metal Pollution in Some Lagoons of the Gulf of Mexico." *Water, Air, and Soil Pollution.* Vol. 20. No. 2 (August 1983).

Rosenweig, Roy. *Eight Hours for What We Will: Workers and Leisure in an Industrial City, 1870–1920.* New York: Cambridge University Press, 1983.

Roxborough, Ian. "The Mexican Charrazo of 1948: Latin American Labor from World War to Cold War." Working Paper #77. Kellogg Institute for International Studies. Notre Dame: University of Notre Dame, August 1986.

Ruvalcaba, Jesús. *Vigilia y dieta básica de los huastecos, complementos acuáticos.* Cuadernos de la Casa Chata. No. 113. Mexico City: Centro de Investigaciones y Estudios Superiores en Antropología Social, 1984.

Rzedowski, Jerzy. *Vegetación de México.* Mexico City: Editorial Limusa, 1986.

Sabin, Paul. "Searching for Middle Ground: Native Communities and Oil Extraction in the Northern and Central Ecuadorian Amazon, 1967–1993." *Environmental History.* Vol. 3. No. 2 (April 1998).

Sada, Jorge. *Los pescadores de la laguna de Tamiahua.* Cuadernos de la Casa Chata. No. 113. Mexico City: Centro de Investigaciones y Estudios Superiores en Antropología Social, 1984.

Salas, Guillermo P. "Geology and Development of Poza Rica Oil Field, Veracruz, Mexico." *Bulletin* of the American Association of Petroleum Geologists. Vol. 33. No. 8 (August 1949).

Sánchez R., María Elena. "Datos relativos a los manglares de México." *Anales of the Escuela Nacional de Ciencias Biológicas.* Vol. 12 (1967).

Sanders, William T. "Cultural Ecology and Settlement Patterns of the Gulf Coast." *Handbook of Middle American Indians.* Vol 11 of 16. *Archeology of Northern Mesoamerica.* Part 2. Edited by Gordon F. Ekholm and Ignacio Bernal. Austin: University of Texas Press, 1971.

Sanders, William T. *The Lowland Huasteca Archeological Survey and Excavation.* 1957 Field Season. University of Missouri Monographs in Anthropology. No. 4. Columbia: University of Missouri-Columbia, 1978.

Santos Llorente, Javier. *Episodios petroleros.* Mexico City: PEMEX, 1988.

Santos Llorente, Javier, Uribe Cruz, Manuel, Benítez Juárez, Mirna, Zavala, Rodolfo, and Olvera Rivera, Alberto J. *El petróleo en Veracruz.* Mexico City: PEMEX, 1988.

Saragoza, Alex M. *The Monterrey Elite and the Mexican State, 1880–1940.* Austin: University of Texas Press, 1988.

Schryer, Frans J. "Peasants and the Law: A History of Land Tenure and Conflict in the Huasteca." *Journal of Latin American Studies.* Vol. 18. Part 2 (November, 1986).

Schuller, Robert. "La posición etnológica y linguística de los Huaxteca." *El México Antiguo.* Vol. 2 (1924–1927).

Schuller, Rudolf. "Notes on the Huaxteca Indians of San Luis Potosí, Mexico." *El Mexico Antiguo.* Vol. 2 (1924–1927).

Schwartz, Peter, and Doug Randall. "An Abrupt Climate Change Scenario and Its Implications for United States National Security." Unpublished paper. Washington, DC October 2003.

Seed, Patricia. *Ceremonies of Possession in Europe's Conquest of the New World, 1492– 1640.* Cambridge: Cambridge University Press, 1995.

Serna, María Luisa. "Cronología: las luchas obreras en 1924." *Historia Obrera* 21. Segunda época. Vol. 6 (January, 1981).

Shaw, George P. "Review of the Petroleum Industry in the Tampico District." *Commerce Reports* (April 16, 1923).

Silva Herzog, Jesús. *Petróleo mexicano.* Mexico City: Fondo de Cultura Económica, 1941.

Simonian, Lane Peter. *Defending the Land of the Jaguar: A History of Conservation in Mexico.* Austin: University of Texas Press, 1995.

Sindicato de Trabajadores Petroleros de la República Mexicana. *Petróleo.* Mexico City: STPRM, 1939.

Slater, Candace. "Amazonia as Edenic Narrative." In *Uncommon Ground: Toward Reinventing Nature.* Edited by William Cronon. New York: W.W. Norton & Co., 1995.

Snodgrass, Michael. *Deference and Defiance in Monterrey: Workers, Paternalism, and Revolution in Mexico, 1890–1950.* New York: Cambridge University Press, 2003.

Spalding, Hobart A., Jr. *Organized Labor in Latin America: Historical Case Studies of Urban Workers in Dependent Societies.* New York: Harper Torchbooks, 1977.

Spender, J. A. *Weetman Pearson First Viscount Cowdray, 1856–1927.* London: Cassell and Company, Ltd., 1930.

Starr, Kevin. *Material Dreams: Southern California Through the 1920s.* Oxford: Oxford University Press, 1990.

Staub, Walter. "Some Data about the Pre-Hispanic and the Now Living Huastec Indians." *El México Antiguo.* Vol. 1. No. 3 (September, 1919).

Stresser-Pean, Guy. "Ancient Sources on the Huasteca." *Handbook of Middle American Indians.* Vol. 11 of 16. *Archeology of Northern Mesoamerica.* Part 2. Edited by Gordon F. Ekholm and Ignacio Bernal. Austin: University of Texas Press, 1971.

Stresser-Pean, Guy. "Los indios huastecos." In *Huaxtecos y Totonacos: Una antología histórico-cultural.* Edited by Lorenzo Ochoa. Mexico City: Consejo Nacional para la Cultura y las Artes, 1990.

Taibo, Paco Ignacio II. "Estadística: las huelgas en el interinato de Adolfo de la Huerta (1 junio–30 noviembre 1920)." *Historia Obrera 20.* Segunda época. Vol. 5 (September, 1980).

Taibo, Paco Ignacio II. *Bolshevikis: Historia narrativa de los orígenes del comunismo en México (1919–1925).* Mexico City: Editorial Joaquín Mortiz, 1986.

Taibo, Paco Ignacio II, and Vizcaíno, Rogelio. *Memoria roja: Luchas sindicales de los años 20.* Mexico City: Ediciones Leega/Jucar, 1984.

Tannehill, Ivan Ray. *Hurricanes, Their Nature and History.* Princeton: Princeton University Press, 1956.

Tenorio-Trillo, Mauricio. *Mexico at the World's Fairs: Crafting a Modern Nation.* Berkeley: University of California Press, 1996.

Taylor Frank J., and Welty, Earl M. *Black Bonanza.* New York: McGraw Hill Book Co., Inc., 1950.

Thorhaug, A., and Marcus, J. H. "Effects of Seven Dispersants on Growth of Three Subtropical/Tropical Atlantic Seagrasses." In *Fate and Effects of Oil in Marine Ecosystems.* Edited by J. Kuiper and W. J. Van den Brink. Dordrecht, Netherlands: Martinus Nijhoff Publishers, 1987.

Tinkle, Leon. *Mr. De: A Biography of Everette Lee DeGolyer.* Boston: Little, Brown, and Company, 1970.

Torrea, Juan Manuel, and Fuentes, Ignacio. *Tampico: Apuntes para su historia.* Mexico City: Editorial Nuestra Patria, 1942.

Toussant, Manuel. "Conquista de la huasteca por los mexicanos." In *Huaxtecos y Totonacos: Una antología histórico-cultural.* Edited by Lorenzo Ochoa. Mexico City: Consejo Nacional para la Cultura y las Artes, 1990.

Traven, B. *The Treasure of the Sierra Madre.* New York: Alfred A. Knopf, 1935.

Traven, B. *La Rosa Blanca.* Mexico City: Selector, 1994.

Trens, Manuel B. *Historia de Veracruz.* Tomo IV. Primer Volumen. Mexico City: n/p, 1950.

Trens, Manuel B. *Historia de Veracruz.* Tomo V. Primer Volumen. Mexico City: n/p, 1950.

Trens, Manuel B. *Historia de Veracruz.* Tomo VI. Mexico City: n/p, 1950.

Tutino, John. *From Insurrection to Revolution in Mexico: Social Bases of Agrarian Violence 1750–1940.* Princeton: Princeton University Press, 1988.

Universidad Obrera. *The Oil Conflict in Mexico 1937–1938.* Mexico City: Universidad Obrera Gabino Barreda, 1938.

Uribe Cruz, Manuel. "El movimiento obrero petrolero en Minatitlán, Veracruz, 1908–1924." B.A. Thesis. Universidad Veracruzana, 1980.

Uribe Cruz, Manuel. "Petróleo y clase obrera, orígines y conformación, 1908–1921." *La Palabra y el Hombre.* Nueva época. No. 56 (October–December 1985).

Van Young, Eric. *Mexico's Regions: Comparative History and Development.* San Diego: Center for U.S.-Mexican Studies, University of California San Diego, 1992.

Vanderwood, Paul J. "Mexico's Rurales: Image of a Society in Transition." *Hispanic American Historical Review.* Vol. 61. No. 1 (February 1981).

Vega Gleason, Sylvia. "Petróleo, medio ambiente y salud." In *La industria petrolera ante la regulación jurídico-ecológica en México.* Edited by Jorge Muñoz Barret, Sylvia Vega Gleason, and María del Carmen Carmona Lara. Mexico City: PEMEX and Universidad Nacional Autónoma de México, 1992.

Velasco, Miguel A. *del magonismo a la fundación de la CTM.* Serie la clase obrera en la historia de México. Mexico City: Ediciones de Cultura Popular, 1990.

Velasco Toro, José. "Indigenismo y rebelión totonaca de Papantla, 1885–1896." *América Indígena.* Vol. 39. No. 1 (1979).

Velasco Toro, José. "La política desamortizadora y sus efectos en la región de Papantla, Veracruz." *La Palabra y el Hombre.* No. 72 (October–December, 1989).

Velasco Toro, José. "Desamortización civil y resistencia india en México y Veracruz: de la independencia a la Reforma." *Anuario VIII* [1992].

Villegas Mora, Xavier. *Petróleo, sangre y justicia.* Mexico City: Editorial Relámpagos, 1939.

Walter, Jane. "Lázaro Cárdenas y la fuerza de trabajo: Tres huelgas en 1936." *Historias.* No. 5 (January–March, 1984).

Watkinson, R. J., and Griffiths, D. "Biodegradation and Photo-Oxidation of Crude Oils in a Tropical Marine Environment." In *Fate and Effects of Oil in Marine Ecosystems.* Edited by J. Kuiper and W. J. Van den Brink. Dordrecht, Netherlands: Martinus Nijhoff Publishers, 1987.

White, Richard. *The Organic Machine: The Remaking of the Columbia River.* New York: Hill and Wang, 1995.

Wilkerson, S. Jeffrey K. "Ethnogenesis of the Huastecs and Totonacs: Early Cultures of North-Central Veracruz at Santa Luisa, Mexico." Ph.D. Thesis. Tulane University, 1954.

Wilkerson, S. Jeffrey K. "Presencia huasteca y cronología cultural en el norte de Veracruz central, México." In *Huaxtecos y Totonacos: Una antología histórico-cultural.* Edited by Lorenzo Ochoa. Mexico City: Consejo Nacional para la Cultura y las Artes, 1990.

Williams, Roberto. *Introducción a las culturas del Golfo.* Mexico City: Instituto Nacional de Antropología e Historia and Secretaría de Educación Pública, 1961.

Wilson, Maureen Grace. "Mexico's Oil Workers: Incorporation and Insurgency." Ph.D. Dissertation. University of Toronto, 1986.

Yergin, Daniel. *The Prize: The Epic Quest for Oil, Money, and Power.* New York: Simon & Schuster, 1991.

Young, Desmond. *Member for Mexico, A Biography of Weetman Pearson, First Viscount Cowdray.* London: Cassell & Co., Ltd., 1966.

Zavala Montejo, Rodolfo. "Relaciones sociales y problemas regionales en una zona petrolera (El caso de Las Choapas, Veracruz, 1930–1940)." B.A. Thesis. Universidad Veracruzana, 1987.

INDEX

abandoned wells, 130
aboriginal groups. *See* indigenous peoples
accidents at oil facilities, 184, 184n143, 226, 263, 295, 360. *See also* Dos Bocas explosion; fires and explosions; Potrero del Llano
Ackerman, Carl W., 20
Agrarian Reform, Law of 1915, 274
agriculture
  banana industry, 53
  cattle industry, 2, 37, 39n73, 40, 43, 47, 71, 71n29, 277
  citrus industry, 2, 53
  Dos Bocas explosion, 141
  foreign ownership of land, 50
  indigenous farming practices, 9, 30–35, 36, 257
  labor shortages, 71
  large farming (haciendas), 9, 53
  logging in the rainforest, 24, 24n28, 50, 50n120, 50n121, 71
  restitution of indigenous lands, 274
  slash and burn/swidden farming, 30–35, 36
  tenant farming, 55
  wage work, 54
El Aguila. *See also* Royal Dutch Shell
  accident rate, 184
  "Book of Instructions" for labor, 172
  child labor, 154
  clearcutting, 105
  company store, 177
  company union, 293
  contract negotiations, 237, 293
  disciplinary practices, 200
  Dos Bocas explosion, 83, 133–134
  employment figures, 216
  environmental pollution, 125, 195

firings, 226, 238
forced labor practices, 155
health of workers, 189n158, 192, 200
housing of foreign workers, 165–166, 179
joint ventures with Mexican government, 288, 335
land acquisition, 67, 69n24, 74n40, 82, 99n118
land agents, 78n53
layoffs during the long depression, 311
number and density of wells, 105, 105n12, 106n14, 106n16
oil storage facilities, 107
oil terminals and refineries, 112
Poza Rica field, 283, 288
pumping stations, 111
sale to Royal Dutch Shell, 244, 267
Sindicato de Obreros, 293, 295n4, 298n19, 314
state attempts to expropriate, 264
strikes, 235, 243, 243n120, 293
Tamiahua Lagoon test wells, 131n129
in Tampico, 119, 119n69, 121n80
ties with Manuel Peláez Gorrochótegui, 91
union contract negotiations, 295n4, 298n19
union revolts of 1930s, 317
Veracruz federations, 319
white guards, 212
wildcat strikes of 1938, 337
Aguilar, Cándido, 215, 257, 259, 264, 265
El Agwi, 112
El Alamo, 105, 116n54, 188, 275, 318
Amatlán, 106n14, 112, 161
America, *See* United States
American Federation of Labor (AFL), 243

Constitution of 1917, 240
early development, 35–40
immigration, 44
land reforms, 37–40
large farming practices, 9
narrow sphere of responsibility, 201
oil bust of 1921, 7, 251
role of labor, 36, 54
welfare capitalism experiments, 296,
296n9, 299
Carbajal River, 138, 142
Cárdenas family, 70, 80n58
Cárdenas, Lázaro, 282
alliance with unions, 319, 323n106, 326,
352
closed-shop rules, 321
economic nationalist vision, 325, 329
election in 1934, 11
federation of unions, 326, 326n121,
353n19
Huasteca Petroleum strike, 306, 307
Huasteca Petroleum strikes, 306n42
joint ventures with oil companies, 286,
335
nationalization of the oil industry, 2, 8,
11, 292, 332n140, 337, 337n159, 347,
349n1
Petróleos Mexicanos, 350
regulation of the oil industry, 286
rift with Calles, 322, 328, 340, 347
union negotiations, 289, 291
Carpintero Lagoon, 20
Carrancistas, 215, 231
Carranza, Venustiano, 163, 215, 242
Agrarian Reform Law of 1915, 274
assassination, 250, 266
attacks on unions, 233, 236n91,
242
Constitucionalistas, 211
regulation of the oil industry, 258,
260n10, 264
union support, 217n39, 240n110
Carrillo, Anastasio, 303
Casa del Obrero Mundial (COM)
anarcho-syndicalist base, 217, 237
craft unions, 217, 218n42
defeats of 1919, 251, 302
Potrero del Llano strike, 231n79
support of Carrancistas, 217n39
Castillo, Antonio, 189
Catholic Church, 34, 43

cattle industry, 2
appropriation of indigenous lands,
37–40, 43, 47
Dos Bocas explosion, 141
environmental challenges, 71, 71n29
use of degraded lands, 277
Cedillo, Saturnino, 338n166
Cerro Azul, 1, 80, 80n58, 116n54
density of wells, 106
destajo and tarea work, 161
No, 4 well, 80, 146n194, 146n197,
185
oil spills and fires, 123
oil storage facilities, 123
pumping stations, 111n38
tenancy system, 55
CGT. *See* Confederación General de
Trabajadores
Chairel Lagoon, 20
Champayal Lagoon, 20
Chapman, Frank M., 18, 21, 36, 143
chapopote, 31, 71
Chávez Padrón, Martha, 22, 132
chicle, 33
children
child labor, 153, 154n25, 159n46
education, 154n25, 209
Chinampa, 106n14
Chinampa de Amatlán, 112
Chinese labor, 149, 152
Chinetti, Pablo, 192
los Científicos, 49, 63, 99
citrus industry, 2, 53
civil war. *See* Mexican Revolution
class structures. *See* social structures
class warfare of oil labor, 231–233, 351
Clifford, Arthur B., 157, 159n44
COM. *See* Casa del Obrero Mundial
Comisión Técnica del Petróleo, 258
communication lines, 109
Communist Party, 329
Compañia de Petróleo, S.A., 67. *See also* El
Aguila
Compañía Metropolitana de Oleoductos,
114n46
company stores, 177, 235
condueñazgos, 47, 51, 70, 80, 81n60, 82
Confederación de Trabajadores Mexicanos
(CTM), 299n24, 329, 333, 336, 353
Confederación General de Trabajadores
(CGT), 302, 303, 307, 310, 315n83

immigration, 6, 44, 344
  foreign colonizers, 53
  foreign workers, 149
  influx of European radicals, 152, 206,
    217n38, 220n48, 222n57
indigenous peoples, 4, 7, 344. *See also* labor
  abandonment of land, 98, 99n117,
    99n118
  agricultural practices, 9, 30–35, 36, 57
  Article 27 of the Constitution, 257
  communal land practices, 5, 10, 35
  condueñazgos, 47, 51, 70, 80, 81n60, 82
  disappearance, 53
  displaced communities, 98, 164, 164n67,
    252
  ecology of the rainforest, 30–35
  financial interactions with oil industry,
    74, 77, 82n65, 85, 86n79, 97
  forced labor, 162
  involvement in Peláez rebellion, 96
  labor for geologists, 74–78, 82n65, 85,
    154
  labor for hacendados, 50, 54
  labor for the oil industry, 6, 162
  language use, 28, 53
  literacy, 79, 81, 98
  loss of land to the oil industry, 80–88,
    90n85, 279
  participation in the market economy, 33
  rebellions against land reform, 19n14,
    40–47, 57, 74
  religion, 34
  repression in late twentiety century,
    48n111
  resistance to oil industry, 85–90, 155,
    345
  restitution of indigenous lands, 274
  standards of living, 56, 56n140
  stereotypes, 35, 36n62, 40, 46, 76, 85,
    161, 164, 192
International Workers of the World
    (IWW), 237, 238, 244, 248
Ixtoc I explosion, 142n179

Jacinto, Hilario, 82, 85, 86n79
Jacobsen, Alfred, 294, 297
Jácome, Apolonio, 80
Jara, Heriberto, 304
Jensen, A. E., 184
Juan Casiano, 109, 155
Juan de Dios, 225
Juan Felipe, 1, 99n117, 276

Juárez, Benito, 44, 47, 62

Kellogg, Frederic R., 145

La Atlántica
  Atlantica, 114n46
La Pez No, 1 well, 82n64
labor in the oil sector
  industry thuggery, 87n82, 88n83
  traditional female labor, 78n52
labor in the agricultural sector
  foreign ownership of land, 50
  shortages, 71
  tenant farming, 55
  wage work, 54, 54n129
labor in the oil sector, 3, 205, 344. *See also*
    health concerns; race and ethnicity;
    social structures; unions in the oil
    sector
  accident rate, 184, 184n142, 226
  anti-imperialist politics, 215
  capitalist analysis, 36, 200
  child labor, 153, 154n25, 159n46
  Chinese service workers, 149, 152
  contractors, 253
  destajo and tarea work, 161
  disciplinary practices, 171, 172n97,
    175n112, 200, 212, 226
  early organizing, 159, 175, 207n5
  early shortage, 104, 104n7, 148
  employment figures, 205, 206n2, 216,
    216n36
  el enganche/recruitment practices, 162,
    217, 225
  firings, 227, 245, 251, 271
  forced labor practices, 162
  foreign professionals, 149, 165, 165n71,
    179
  foreign workers, 151, 164, 165, 168n82,
    183, 206, 217
  housing, 1, 72, 81, 169n87, 171, 179, 193
  industry thuggery, 81n60, 86, 98, 176
  influx of radical politics, 152, 217n38,
    220n48
  oil bust of 1921, 7, 251, 271, 291
  politicization, 152, 216–224, 230
  professionals, 164
  protections under Article 123, 281, 295,
    332
  racial hierarchies, 6–7, 10, 148, 171, 173,
    199, 344
  resistance to oil industry, 85–90, 155

LaVergne, TN USA
01 August 2010
191560LV00004B/4/P